The Other Classical Musics
Fifteen Great Traditions

" Listen to the reed flute, how it does complain
And how it tells of separation's pain. "

> Jalaluddin Rumi on the Sufi yearning for divine union.
> Thirteenth-century Persia; translated by Annemarie Schimmel
> in *Rumi's World: The Life and Work of the Great Sufi Poet*

" There are the six *chhi* of heaven. Their incorporation produces the five flavours; their blossoming makes the five colours; they proclaim themselves in the five notes. "

> A fourth-century BCE Chinese text explaining the operation of
> the celestial emanations; translated by Joseph Needham in
> *Science and Civilisation in China*

" It was as though flowers and gods were coming out of my fingers. "

> Robert Schumann on improvising at the piano after playing
> four-hand Bach with Clara Wieck; Leipzig 1838

The Other Classical Musics
Fifteen Great Traditions

Edited by
Michael Church

AGA KHAN TRUST FOR CULTURE
Music Initiative

THE BOYDELL PRESS

© Contributors 2015

All Rights Reserved. Except as permitted under current legislation no part of this work may be photocopied, stored in a retrieval system, published, performed in public, adapted, broadcast, transmitted, recorded or reproduced in any form or by any means, without the prior permission of the copyright owner

First published 2015
The Boydell Press, Woodbridge

ISBN 978 1 84383 726 8

The Boydell Press is an imprint of Boydell & Brewer Ltd
PO Box 9, Woodbridge, Suffolk IP12 3DF, UK
and of Boydell & Brewer Inc.
668 Mount Hope Ave, Rochester, NY 14620–2731, USA
website: www.boydellandbrewer.com

A catalogue record for this book is available from the British Library

The publisher has no responsibility for the continued existence or accuracy of URLs for external or third-party internet websites referred to in this book, and does not guarantee that any content on such websites is, or will remain, accurate or appropriate

This publication is printed on acid-free paper

Designed and typeset in Scala and Scala Sans by
David Roberts, Pershore, Worcestershire

Printed and bound in the UK by Gomer Press

Boydell & Brewer acknowledge with gratitude the support of the Aga Khan Music Initiative, a programme of the Aga Khan Trust for Culture, in the publication and illustration of this book.

Contents

List of Illustrations viii
List of Contributors xvi
Preface and Acknowledgements xix

Introduction 1
Michael Church

1 Thailand, Laos, Cambodia, Vietnam 24
Terry E. Miller

2 Java 50
Neil Sorrell

3 Japan 74
David W. Hughes

4 China: The Guqin Zither 104
Frank Kouwenhoven

5 Chinese Opera 126
Terry E. Miller & Michael Church

6 North India 138
Richard Widdess

7 South India 160
Jonathan Katz

8 Mande Jaliyaa 178
Roderic Knight

9 North American Jazz   198
Scott DeVeaux

10 Europe   216
Ivan Hewett

11 North Africa and the Eastern Mediterranean: Andalusian Music   246
Dwight F. Reynolds

12 The Eastern Arab World   270
Scott Marcus

13 Turkey   294
Robert Labaree

14 Iran   320
Ameneh Youssefzadeh

15 Uzbekistan and Tajikistan   340
Will Sumits

Notes   361
Bibliographies   370
Index   387

▶ Illustrations

Béla Bartók collecting songs from Slovak peasants in 1907 (Photograph: G. D. Hackett)	xxii
Simha Arom, György Ligeti, and Pierre-Laurent Aimard with Pygmy musicians in Paris, 1999 (Photograph: Marie-Noëlle Robert)	4–5
Ca tru folk balladry in Hanoi (Photograph: Phong T. Nguyen)	7
The azan in a village outside Cairo (© Christine Osborne/ CORBIS)	11
China: jianpu (numeral) notation for the pipa lute (Liu Yizhi, ed., *Guoyue qianshuo* [*A General Introduction to Chinese Traditional Music*], Guoyue jinliang [Pillars of Chinese Traditional Music] (Taipei, Taiwan: Da Zhongguo tushu gongsi, 1966), 51)	13
Thailand: numeral and solfege notation together (*Son Thawng: Seminar Celebrating the Works of Luang Pradit Phairaw* (Bangkok [1982]), 68)	13
Japan: notation for the koto zither (Michio Miyagi, *Ikuta-Method Koto Music: 'Rokudan No Shirabe' and 'Kumoi Rokudan'* (Hougakusha: Hogaku Sha, 1996), 1)	14
Rhythmic notation for an excerpt of a Hindustani tablā composition. (Gert-Matthias Wegner, *Vintage Tablā Repertory: Drum Compositions of North Indian Classical Music* (New Delhi: Munshiram Manoharlal Publishers, 2004), 304)	14
Ethnomusicologists at the Cairo Conference, 1932 (Courtesy of the Librarian, University of Glasgow Library)	15
'Two demons', fifteenth-century Herat (Courtesy of the Freer Gallery of Art, Smithsonian Institution, Washington, DC: Purchase, F1937.25)	16
The Kyrgyz ensemble Tengir-Too (Photograph: Michael Church)	20
Rysbek Jumabaev recites Kyrgyzstan's Manas epic (Photograph: Michael Church)	20
The Kyrgyz komuz and the Kazakh dombra (Photograph: Cara Chanteau)	22
The Kazakh qyl qobyz (Photograph: Cara Chanteau)	22
MAP: Thailand, Laos, Cambodia and Vietnam in their wider geo-political context	24
Stone reliefs at Angkor Bayon (Photograph: Terry Miller)	27
Mural of a piphat ensemble, Bangkok (Photograph: Terry Miller)	31
A pinpeat ensemble plays at Ta Prohm temple (Photograph: Terry Miller)	31
Bangkok theatre group, 1900	38
Piphat ensemble honouring a teacher in Nonthaburi (Photograph: Terry Miller)	38
Mural of a piphat ensemble with shadow puppet performance (Photograph: Terry Miller)	43

ILLUSTRATIONS

Ca hue in a boat on the Perfume River (Photograph: Terry Miller)	45
Vietnamese chamber music on lute and zither (Photograph: Terry Miller)	45
Gamelan gongs in action (Photograph courtesy of Kathryn Emerson)	50
Set-up of a Javanese gamelan (Images courtesy of J. Bern Jordan)	53
Gamelan at Yogyakarta in 1888 (Photograph courtesy of Richard Pickvance)	54
Metallophones (Photograph courtesy of Kathryn Emerson)	58
Metallophone over trough resonator (Photograph: Eric Bajart)	58
Eighteenth-century representation of a gamelan ensemble (© The University of Manchester)	63
K. P. H. Notoprojo (Photograph by L. H. Muis, Tropenmuseum of the Royal Tropical Institute (KIT), http://www.tropenmuseum.nl)	63
Musicians of Uking Sukri and Ono Sukarna (Photograph: Jacques Brunet; courtesy of Ocora Radio France)	63
Mid-twentieth-century Wayang	69
Wayang at the Bentara Budaya institute, Jakarta (Photograph: Gunawan Kartapranata)	69
Woodblock print of the 1849 production of *Chūshingura*	74
Gagaku in the Imperial Palace, Tokyo (Courtesy of the Music Department, Imperial Household Agency)	78–9
The noh play *A Venerable Old Man* receives its formal dedication (Photograph: Matsuoka Akiyoshi)	81
Woodblock of kabuki at the Ichimura-za theatre in Edo, 1858	82–3
Shakuhachi	85
Komuso 'priests of nothingness' (© Michael Maslan Historic Photographs/CORBIS)	85
Shō mouth organ notation from 1303 (Lawrence Picken et al., eds., *Music from the Tang Court, Fascicle 1* (Oxford: Oxford University Press, 1981), plate 2, from the original score preserved in the Yōmei Bunko archive, Kyoto)	90
Modern day shō mouth organ notation (Kagawa Gaseikai, ed., *Gagaku hōshōfu* [Gagaku Shō Notation], 5th printing (Iiyama, Kagawa: Kagawa Gaseikai, 1985), 27)	90
Shō (Photograph: David Hughes)	90
Woodblock of two kabuki actors as musicians (Photograph: David Hughes)	93
Postcard of women playing the koto and shamisen (Image reproduced with permission from the Royal Academy of Music, London)	93
Sankyoku trio (Photograph: David Hughes)	101
MAP: China, showing the provinces mentioned in chapters 4 and 5	104
Scroll painting, 'Listening to the qin' (The Palace Museum, Beijing)	106
Tang-period qin (Courtesy of the Music Research Institute, Beijing)	110

THE OTHER CLASSICAL MUSICS

Tablature notation of *Jiu kuang* (*Qinqu jicheng* [*Anthology of Qin Pieces*] (Beijing: Zhonghua shuju, 1980–95))	112
Drawings from a Ming handbook of qin hand postures (*Qinqu jicheng* [*Anthology of Qin Pieces*] (Beijing: Zhonghua shuju, 1980–95))	117
Hand playing the qin (Photograph: Frank Kouwenhoven, CHIME)	117
Tang painting of a ladies' concert, anonymous, 10th century, 'Banquet and Concert' (Werner Forman Archive/National Palace Museum, Taipei)	119
Tang pottery tomb musicians (Michael Church Collection. Photograph: Irina Zolotareva)	119
Yu Shaozhe playing the qin (Photograph courtesy of Wang Di)	120
Han tomb figure of a qin player (Chongqing Museum)	120
Wu Man playing the pipa (Photograph: Ming-Shen Lee)	123
Sandstone carving of a qin player (Musée Cernuschi, Paris. Photograph: Guillaume Jacquet)	123
Actor making up for a performance, Taipei (Photograph: Terry Miller)	126
Performance at the Shandong Opera School (Photograph: Terry Miller)	129
Ensemble accompanying the Shandong performance (Photograph: Terry Miller)	129
Beijing Opera ensemble (Photograph: Terry Miller)	133
Mei Lan-Fang in costume	135
Mei Lan-Fang offstage	135
MAP: India's historic centres of musical activity mentioned in chapters 6 and 7	138
Ragamala miniature representing Raga Nat (Image courtesy of the Aga Khan Trust for Culture, AKM 176)	141
Miniature of Tansen receiving a lesson (National Museum – New Delhi Collection, Acc no: 48.14/61)	150
Sarangi bowed lute (Photograph: Jean-Pierre Dalbéra)	155
Fresco in Udaipur of Krishna playing his flute (Photograph: Pebble101)	155
Amjad Ali Khan playing the sarod (N. Scott Robinson)	156
Asad Ali Khan playing the rudra vina (Photograph: Vamsidhar Reddy)	156
Miniature of a tambura player (Fletcher Fund, 1996, Metropolitan Museum of Art, www.metmuseum.org)	156
Anoushka and Ravi Shankar playing sitars (Photograph: Michael Collopy)	156
Icon of Saraswati (© Victoria and Albert Museum, London)	160
Karnatak concert in Chennai, Tamil Nadu, 2005 (Photograph: N. Scott Robinson)	163
Tyagaraja concert in Cleveland State University (Photograph: N. Scott Robinson)	164

ILLUSTRATIONS

D. K. Pattammal postage stamp	167
M. S. Subbulakshmi poster	167
Karnatak concert at the Music Academy, Chennai, 2005 (Photograph: N. Scott Robinson)	172
Aruna Sairam in concert (Photograph courtesy of Aruna Sairam)	175
MAP: Mande music in Sub-Saharan West Africa	178
Mande jali ensemble in 1925 (Arthur St John Adcock, *The Prince of Wales' African Book* (London: Hodder & Stoughton, c. 1925))	182
Balo ensemble at a wedding (Photograph: Roderic Knight)	185
Mawdo Suso making a balo (Photograph: Roderic Knight)	185
Jali ensemble in Brikama (Photograph: Roderic Knight)	186
Jabele Kanuteh playing the ngoni (Photograph: Roderic Knight)	186
Detail of the kora (Photograph: Roderic Knight)	186
Sona Kuyateh playing the neo (Photograph: Roderic Knight)	189
Bassekou Kouyate and his family (Photograph © Jens Schwarz)	194
Ali Farka Toure (Photograph © 2000 Jack Vartoogian/FrontRowPhotos)	196
Salif Keita (Photograph: www.laurielewis.co.uk)	196
Toumani Diabate (Photograph: Dave Peabody)	196
Duke Ellington and his band in London in 1933 (SuperStock)	198
Cover of *The Mascot* (New Orleans) from 1890	205
The Original Dixieland Jazz Band	206
Jelly Roll Morton	206
Louis Armstrong and his Hot Five (Courtesy of Frank Driggs Collection)	208
Duke Ellington and his band in 1924 (Courtesy of Frank Driggs Collection)	208
Charlie Parker (Photograph: William P. Gottlieb/Ira and Leonore S. Gershwin Fund Collection, Music Division, Library of Congress)	210
Lester Young	212
Dizzy Gillespie	212
Ornette Coleman (Photograph: Tad Hershorn)	212
Thelonious Monk (William P. Gottlieb/Ira and Leonore S. Gershwin Fund Collection, Music Division, Library of Congress)	212
Miles Davis (Photograph: Tad Hershorn)	212
Mary Lou Williams	212
Fifteenth-century missal (Courtesy of the Royal College of Music, a gift from Sir George Donaldson)	216
Sixteenth-century drawing of the 'Guidonian hand' (University of California, Berkeley, Music Library MS 1087 recto)	219

Woodcut of Josquin des Prez from Petrus Opmeer's *Opvs chronographicvm orbis vniversi a mvndi exordio vsqve ad annvm M.DC.XI.* (Antwerp, 1611) — 223

Portrait of Giovanni Pierluigi da Palestrina (Oratorio dei Filippini, Rome, Italy/Bridgeman Images) — 223

Portrait of Claudio Monteverdi, c. 1597, by anonymous Cremonese artist (© Ashmolean Museum, University of Oxford) — 223

Engraving of Thomas Tallis by Niccolò Haym, after a portrait by Gerard van der Gucht — 223

Autograph manuscript of the Adagio of Johann Sebastian Bach's Sonata for solo violin in G minor (BWV 1001), 1720 (Bach digital, www.bach-digital.de) — 229

Drawing of an orchestra in 1770 by an unknown artist (© Internationale Stiftung Mozarteum (ISM)) — 230–1

Portrait of Niccolò Paganini (1782–1840) playing the violin (Image reproduced with permission from the Royal Academy of Music, London) — 235

The left hand of Yehudi Menuhin (1916–99); black and white photograph by Lotte Meitner-Graf (Image reproduced with permission from the Royal Academy of Music, London) — 235

Viktoria Mullova playing the violin (Photograph © Foto Puck) — 235

MAP: The geographical spread of the muwashshah song-form in the twelfth and thirteenth centuries — 246

Thirteenth-century painting of a musical gathering — 251

Four illuminations of musicians from the *Cantigas de Santa Maria* (Real Biblioteca del Monasterio de San Lorenzo de El Escorial. © Patrimonio Nacional) — 254

The Cofradia Al-Shushtari ensemble (Photograph: Eduardo Paniagua) — 260

The Briouel Ensemble (Photograph: Carl Davila) — 264

Rabbi Haim Louk (Photograph: Philip Murphy) — 264

Tar (Photograph: Carl Davila, 2013. Reproduced with permission of Ludwig Reichert Verlag) — 264

Violin played in the Andalusian style (Photograph: Philip Murphy) — 264

Rabab (Photograph: Carl Davila) — 264

Musicians' Capital, Cordoba (Courtesy of Archivo fotográfico, Museo Arqueológico y Etnológico de Córdoba) — 266

Performance at the Club Fils du Detroit No. 1, Tangier (Photograph of the Sons of Detroit © James Morris) — 268

Umm Kulthum mural in Cairo (Photograph: MARWAN NAAMANI/AFP/Getty Images) — 270

Henry George Farmer at the 1932 Cairo conference (Courtesy of the Librarian, University of Glasgow Library) — 273

ILLUSTRATIONS

Umm Kulthum ensemble figurines bought in Cairo (Photograph: Tony Mastres/UCSB Photo Services)	279
Umm Kulthum album cover (Photograph: Tony Mastres/UCSB Photo Services)	279
Umm Kulthum in performance (STAFF/AFP/Getty Images)	279
Three ouds (Photograph: Tony Mastres/UCSB Photo Services)	287
Poster of Farid al-Atrash (Photograph: Tony Mastres/UCSB Photo Services)	287
Qanun in playing position (Ariel Grippo)	288
Five riqqs or daffs (Photograph: Tony Mastres/UCSB Photo Services)	288
Nay flutes (Photograph: Tony Mastres/UCSB Photo Services)	289
Miniature of a musical gathering in Istanbul (Image courtesy of the Aga Khan Trust for Culture, AKM 218)	294
A Bektashi djem (Photograph: Jérôme Cler/Ocora Radio France)	297
Engraving of a band in Ottoman Aleppo in 1794	301
Ney (Photograph: Robert Labaree)	310
Oud (Photograph: Robert Labaree)	310
Kanun (Photograph: Robert Labaree)	310
Tanbur (Photograph: Robert Labaree)	310
Rebab (Photograph: Robert Labaree)	310
Bendir (Photograph: Robert Labaree)	310
Ottoman makam written in staff notation by Ali Ufki (1610–75) (Courtesy of Professor Dr Şükrü Elçin. Kültür Bakanlığı, 1976)	313
Engraving of Dimitrie Cantemir	313
Dimitrie Cantemir's instrumental notation using the Arabic alphabet	313
Evterpi (1830), Byzantine notation of Ottoman makam (Theodoros Fokaeus and Stavrakis Vyzantios, *Euterpi* (Istanbul, 1830))	313
Orchestral seating arrangement in Paris, 1810 (*Allgemeine Musikalische Zeitung*, August 1810; in Adam Carse, *The Orchestra from Beethoven to Berlioz* (New York: Broude, 1949), 46)	317
Sixteenth-century miniature of lute player (Image courtesy of the Aga Khan Trust for Culture, AKM 282)	320
Khosrow cliff relief and detail (Photograph © Paul Almasy/Corbis)	324
Private ensemble of King Nasir al-Din Shah; painting by Kamal al-Molk, 1893 (Golestan Palace, Tehran)	326
Nur 'Ali Borumand (Mahoor Institute of Culture and Art)	329
Barbad plays for Khosrow II Parviz (© The British Library Board, Or. 2265, fol. 77v)	332
Darvish Khan (Mahoor Institute of Culture and Art)	336
Dariush Tala'i (Photograph courtesy of Masih Azarakhsh)	336

Kayhan Kalhor (Photograph: Ali Boustan)	336
Miniature of kamancheh player (Image courtesy of the Aga Khan Trust for Culture, AKM 716)	336
Parisa in concert (Mahoor Institute of Culture and Art)	338
MAP: The Central Asian home of the *shashmaqom*	340
Registan square in Samarqand (© Gavin Hellier/Robert Harding World Imagery/Corbis)	342
Miniature of a ghijak player (Image courtesy of the Aga Khan Trust for Culture, AKM 205)	347
Nay player from c. 1870 (Library of Congress, Prints & Photographs Division [LC-DIG-ppmsca-14709])	348
Doira player from c. 1870 (Library of Congress, Prints & Photographs Division [LC-DIG-ppmsca-14719])	348
Ghijak player from c. 1870 (Library of Congress, Prints & Photographs Division [LC-DIG-ppmsca-12273])	348
Dutar player from c. 1870 (Library of Congress, Prints & Photographs Division [LC-DIG-ppmsca-14713])	348
Mohammed Alim Khan (Library of Congress, Prints & Photographs Division, Prokudin-Gorskii Collection [LC-DIG-prokc-21887])	350
Isfandiyar, last Khan of Khiva (Library of Congress, Prints & Photographs Division, Prokudin-Gorskii Collection [LC-DIG-prokc-20150])	350
Indigenous system of tablature for the tanbur, developed in the late nineteenth century for the Khorezm maqom (Image courtesy of Aleksandr Djumaev)	351
Turgun and Alisher Alimatov (Photograph: Theodore Levin)	353
Abduvali Abdurashidov and his ensemble (Photograph © Sebastian Schutyser/Aga Khan Music Initiative)	355
Munajat Yulchieva (Courtesy of Ocora Radio France)	355
Ash ceremony (Photograph: Will Sumits)	356
Ash ceremony (Photograph: Will Sumits)	356

■ Music Examples

Ex. 1.1	'Khaek Borathet' (Panya Roongruang (ed.), *Collected Works of the Thai Classical Repertoire* vol. 5, *Tab lao jaroensri, Khaek borathet thao* (Bangkok: Kasetsart University, 2001), 45)	33
Ex. 1.2	'Lao siang thian' (© Terry E. Miller)	35
Ex. 2.1	Ketawang Puspawarna laras sléndro pathet manyura	64
Ex. 2.2	Sléndro pitches (© Neil Sorrell)	65
Ex. 2.3	Ketawang Puspawarna (© Neil Sorrell)	66

ILLUSTRATIONS

Ex. 3.1	*Hagi no Tsuyu* (transcription © David W. Hughes, from *Abe Keiko no shigei 3*, Victor, 1997)	96
Ex. 4.1	*Xiao Xiang shui yun* (transcription © Frank Kouwenhoven)	121
Ex. 6.1	Basic moves in ragas Bihag and Kedar (© Richard Widdess)	143
Ex. 6.2	Alap in Bihag (transcription © Richard Widdess, from *The Raga Guide*, Nimbus, 1999)	144
Ex. 6.3	Gat in Bihag (transcription © Richard Widdess, from *The Raga Guide*, Nimbus, 1999)	145
Ex. 6.4	Improvisation in Bihag (transcription © Richard Widdess, from *The Raga Guide*, Nimbus, 1999)	146
Ex. 7.1	*Endu Dāginādo*, by Tyagaraja. Notation from a South Indian music primer	170
Ex. 7.2	Pallavi and anupallavi (Harold S. Powers, 'An Historical and Comparative Approach to the Classification of Ragas', *Selected Reports in Ethnomusicology* 1/3 (UCLA Institute of Ethnomusicology, 1970, © The Regents of the University of California), 25, ex. 9. Used by permission.)	171
Ex. 8.1	'Sherif Sidi' kumbengo (notation © Roderic Knight, from the traditional jaliyaa repertoire)	192
Ex. 8.2	'Allah l'a ke' kumbengo (notation © Roderic Knight, from the traditional jaliyaa repertoire)	193
Ex. 9.1	Charlie Parker's 'Now's the time' (transcription © Scott DeVeaux, from *Bird: The Complete Charlie Parker* on Verve, 1990)	210
Ex. 10.1	Alwynne Pritchard, *Nostos Ou Topos* II (© Verlag Neue Musik, Berlin)	243
Ex. 12.1	*Samāʿī Bayyātī al-Thaqīl* (transcription © Scott Marcus, after earlier transcription by A. J. Racy, UCLA)	276
Ex. 13.1	*Gel seninle yarın* (transcription © Yusuf Ömürlü, Kubbealtı Musiki Enstitüsü, 1975)	303
Ex. 14.1	Rumi's 'Masnavi' (transcription © Mohammad Taqi Mas'udiye, from Mohammad Taqi Mas'udiye, *The Vocal Radif of Traditional Iranian Music According to the Version of Mahmoud Karimi* (Tehran: Mahoor Institute of Culture and Art, 2003), 219)	335

The editor, contributors and publisher are grateful to all the institutions and persons listed for permission to reproduce the materials in which they hold copyright. Every effort has been made to trace the copyright holders; apologies are offered for any omission, and the publishers will be pleased to add any necessary acknowledgement in subsequent editions. The photographers named above reserve copyright in their work.

▶ Contributors

Michael Church has spent much of his career in newspapers as a literary and arts editor, and was one of the founding editors of the *Independent on Sunday*. He is a former television critic of *The Times*, and since 2010 he has been music and opera critic of *The Independent*. He has made BBC World Service programmes on folk music in many countries; his award-winning field-recordings of the music of Kazakhstan, Georgia and Chechnya were released on the Topic label.

Scott DeVeaux is Professor in the McIntire Department of Music at the University of Virginia. His book *The Birth of Bebop* (California UP, 1997) won several awards, including the Kinkeldey Prize for best book from the American Musicological Society, the ASCAP-Deems Taylor Award, and the American Book Award. With critic Gary Giddins he has co-authored *Jazz* (Norton, 2009), a comprehensive survey of the idiom.

Ivan Hewett has worked in music for thirty years as lecturer, promoter, broadcaster and journalist. In the late 1980s and early 1990s he programmed festivals and series at the South Bank Centre in London. He also worked as researcher and associate producer on TV music programmes, and from 1993 to 2002 presented the BBC Radio 3 magazine programme *Music Matters*. Since 2002 he has been a critic and writer for the Daily Telegraph, and he also lectures at the Royal College of Music. His book *Healing the Rift*, a meditation on the dilemmas of modern music, was published by Continuum in 2003.

David Hughes taught at the School of Oriental and African Studies, University of London, from 1987–2008, and is now a Research Associate there. He received the 2011 Japan Society Award for 'outstanding contributions to Anglo-Japanese relations and understanding' for bringing Japanese music to a wider public. His publications include *Traditional Folk Song in Modern Japan* (Global Oriental, 2008) and the co-edited *Ashgate Research Companion to Japanese Music* (2008).

Jonathan Katz is a Fellow of All Souls College, Oxford. Previously he was a Research Fellow at Wolfson College, and Master of the Queen's Scholars and Head of Classics at Westminster School. He has held visiting posts at Princeton and Oxford Universities. His interests combine Western and Indian music and literatures, and his publications include work on Indian musical theory and practice through Sanskrit and vernacular sources.

Roderic Knight taught ethnomusicology for thirty-two years at the Oberlin College Conservatory. Awakened to African music while teaching in Sierra Leone, he ultimately focused on Mande music, playing kora on Radio Gambia and directing the Oberlin Mandinka Ensemble. He later turned his attention to Central India while continuing to offer a full range of lecture and seminar courses in world musics. His publications may be found in *African Arts, African Music, Asian Music, Ethnomusicology, The Galpin Society Journal, The New Grove Dictionary, The World of Music,* and *Selected Reports in Ethnomusicology*. He has also made audio and video documentaries in Africa and India.

Frank Kouwenhoven is a music scholar from The Netherlands. He has published widely on Chinese music, mostly in cooperation with his partner Antoinet Schimmelpenninck (until her untimely death in 2012). Kouwenhoven is co-founder of the Chinese music platform CHIME. He is the main editor of the CHIME journal, a concert organizer and a producer of books, films and exhibitions on Chinese music. He teaches at Leiden University. His most recent book (edited jointly with Jim Kippen) is *Music, Dance and the Art of Seduction* (Eburon Delft, 2013).

Robert Labaree is an ethnomusicologist and performer specializing in Turkish music, with writings on improvisation, music and biology, and Ottoman-European musical interactions. Since 1984 he has been a member of the Musicology faculty at the New England Conservatory in Boston and is founder of the conservatory's Intercultural Institute. He co-founded and recorded with *The EurAsia Ensemble* from 1980–95 and in 2003 co-founded *Dünya*, an ensemble and non-profit educational institution that produces concerts, workshops and recordings exploring the shared traditions of the former Ottoman region.

Scott Marcus is Professor of Ethnomusicology at the University of California, Santa Barbara, specializing in the musics of the Arab world and northern India. His dissertation 'Arab Music Theory in the Modern Period' and numerous articles focus on the Arab system of melodic modes. He wrote *Music in Egypt* (Oxford, 2007), co-edited *The Garland Encyclopedia of World Music* vol. 6, *The Middle East* (Routledge, 2002), and founded and directs the UCSB Middle East Ensemble, whose performances have included a tour of Egypt in 2010 sponsored by the Egyptian government.

Terry E. Miller is Professor Emeritus of Ethnomusicology at Kent State University, Ohio, where he taught for thirty years. His research focus is Thailand and Laos, with added interest in the rest of SE Asia as well as China. In addition to his numerous books and articles, he was a primary editor and writer for the *Garland Encyclopedia of World Music* vol. 4, *Southeast Asia* (Routledge, 1998) and co-author of the textbook *World Music: A Global Journey* (Routledge). While at Kent State he founded both the Thai Ensemble and the Chinese Ensemble and performed with both for twenty-eight and eighteen years respectively. Currently he is researching the musical evidence found in Thailand's historic temple murals and preparing a book on a major classification of the Thai classical repertory.

Dwight F. Reynolds is Professor of Arabic Language and Literature at the University of California, Santa Barbara. His research areas include Arabic literature, oral poetry, music and folklore. He is the author of *Heroic Poets, Poetic Heroes: The Ethnography of Performance in an Egyptian Oral Epic Tradition* (Cornell, 1995) and *Arab Folklore: A Handbook* (Greenwood Press, 2007), as well as co-author and editor of *Interpreting the Self: Autobiography in the Arabic Literary Tradition* (California UP, 2001). He has published numerous articles on Andalusian music and is currently writing a book titled *The Musical Heritage of al-Andalus*.

Neil Sorrell teaches in the music department at the University of York (UK) and is the author of *A Guide to the Gamelan* (Faber, 1990; 2nd ed. Ithaca, NY: Cornell University Society for Asian Music, 2000). With his teacher, the *sarangi* master Pandit Ram Narayan, he is co-author of *Indian Music in Performance: A Practical Introduction* (Manchester UP, 1980). He began his study of gamelan performance at Wesleyan University (Connecticut) in 1969, making his first trip to Indonesia in 1971, and established Javanese gamelan music in the UK at the end of that decade.

Will Sumits is an ethnomusicologist working primarily in the cultural development sector for the Aga Khan Music Initiative. He was recently a research fellow at the University of Central Asia, Tajikistan, and has spent more than a decade in the field in Central Asia and the greater Middle East, exploring the performance and history of *maqam* traditions, and leading music education and performance programs.

Richard Widdess is Professor of Musicology in the Department of Music, School of Oriental and African Studies, University of London. He is the author of *The Ragas of Early Indian Music* (Oxford, 1995), *Dhrupad: Tradition and Performance in Indian Music* (with Ritwik Sanyal, Ashgate, 2004), and *Dapha: Sacred Singing in a South Asian City* (Ashgate, 2013).

Ameneh Youssefzadeh is currently a visiting scholar at the City University of New York Graduate Center and is Co-Consulting Editor for Musicology of the *Encyclopædia Iranica*. She has published articles, CDs, and a book, *Les bardes du Khorassan Iranien: le bakhshi et son répertoire* (Paris: Peeters, 2002; Persian edition, Tehran: Mahur, 2010).

Preface and Acknowledgements

THIS book is a team effort, driven by a shared desire to illuminate and celebrate the world's great classical traditions. Its ancestry as a piece of cross-cultural musical analysis goes back a thousand years, to the 'science of music' of the medieval Arab theorists. Its European precursors include the sixteenth-century Swiss theologian Jean de Léry, who notated antiphonal singing in Brazil, and the Moldavian polymath Prince Dimitrie Cantemir (1673–1723) who was enslaved by the Ottomans in Istanbul, became a de facto Turkish composer, and created the first notation for Turkish *makam*; also Captain James Cook, who made detailed descriptions of the music and dance of Pacific islanders in 1784. Meanwhile Chinese music was being admiringly analysed by French Jesuit missionaries – Chinese theorists had beaten their European counterparts in the race to solve the mathematics of equal temperament – and other Frenchmen were investigating the music of the Arab world. While serving on Napoleon Bonaparte's Egyptian campaign, Guillaume-André Villoteau made studies of Arab folk and art music, before going on to contrast those with the music of Greece and Armenia; his theories were then contested by the French composer Francesco Salvador-Daniel, who after a twelve-year musical sojourn in Algeria concluded, among other things, that Arab and Greek modes were one and the same. Long before 'ethnomusicology' was born in academe, the game was well established.

In recent years the ethnomusicologists' findings have been magisterially presented in two great publications: in the ten massive volumes of the *Garland Encyclopedia of World Music*, and scattered through the twenty-nine volumes of the *New Grove Dictionary of Music and Musicians*. But our book is, we believe, the first panoptic survey of the world's classical musics (I explain in the Introduction why we have settled on that somewhat contentious adjective). Although much of its information may also be found in *Grove* and *Garland* – many of its writers were contributors to, or editors on, those projects – its tight focus permits presentation in a single volume, rather than scattered through a six-foot shelf of tomes.

As editor I am deeply indebted to my writers, who have patiently put their chapters through numerous drafts in pursuit of non-academic accessibility, while in no way traducing their (often very complicated) subject-matter. I must particularly thank Terry Miller, whose resourceful problem-solving assistance has extended far beyond his own signed contributions; also his colleague Andrew Shahriari, for additional information on Persian classical music.

I am profoundly grateful to my partner Hisako Shiina, who suggested the basic strategy for this book; to Gilbert Pugh, who helped me define its structure; and to friends and colleagues who during its long gestation have provided many other forms of assistance. These include Pierre-Laurent Aimard, Sulamita Aronovsky, Debra Boraston, Radek Boschetty, Patricia Braun, Hilary Finch, Jonathan Freeman-Attwood, Mike Gavin, John Gilhooly, Rebecca Guillaume, Howard Hannah, Stephanie Hay, Colin Jacobson, J. Bern Jordan, Joseph Jordania,

Fariborz Kiani, Alison Latham, Ginny Macbeth, Lucy Maxwell-Stewart, Alison McKay, Charles Melville, Viktoria Mullova, Phong T. Nguyen, Xuanquynh Nguyen, Serge Noelranaivo, Laudan Nooshin, Mark Pappenheim, N. Scott Robinson, Jesus Ruiz Martinez, Anoushka Shankar, Martin Stokes, Charles Turner, Helen Wallace, Louis Wenger, and the staff of the London Library.

No editor could wish for stauncher support than that which I have received from my publishers Michael Middeke, Megan Milan and Mike Webb, nor for more meticulous editing than that which this book has received from Rohais Haughton and Emily Kilpatrick, nor for more beautiful designs than those which David Roberts has created. And that the project should have come so harmoniously to fruition is very much thanks to my dear friend Joyce Arnold who – immensely generous with her time – has been both picture editor with a magic touch, and overseer of the book's very complicated pre-production stages.

But the thinking behind it has evolved over many years, with input from many quarters. My travels in Central Asia with Yo-Yo Ma, Fairouz Nishanova, and the musicians of the Silk Road Project have been richly illuminating, as have my conversations with the SRP's musicological guru, Theodore Levin; he has been the guiding light for this project from the start. Meanwhile, by reading the full manuscript and suggesting detailed improvements, the composer and critic Bayan Northcott has significantly strengthened the argument. And I count myself blessed in having been able to draw, at every stage of the project, on the musicological expertise – and matchless editorial wisdom – of Cara Chanteau.

On a personal level this book is dedicated to two people. To my late father, Eric, who would have been pleased to see his son at last doing something a bit more durable than journalism. And with love and gratitude to my late wife Betty who, by her shining example as a painter and writer, taught me the value of pursuing a good idea to its logical conclusion, no matter how eccentric and outlandish it might initially seem.

Michael Church, London, 2015

▪ Note on spellings, fonts and diacritics

Ease of reading has dictated some streamlining in spellings, fonts and diacritical marks. Foreign terms are given in italics and in standardised local orthography on first use, and in roman font thereafter; diacritical marks are given only on first use.

Where the spelling of names of instruments is already standard in contemporary English dictionaries – 'sitar', 'tabla', 'oud' – these conventions are followed. Certain cognate words which sound almost the same in different languages – e.g. *makam, maqam, muqam, maqom, mugham* – may denote different regional traditions, and here the spelling reflects both those traditions and local conventions of transliteration. A distinction is observed between words with identical meaning differentiated only by orthography or transliteration, and words that are cognate but whose meanings and references are not the same. The spelling is not standardised, for example, between 'ney' and 'nay', since these not only represent different pronunciations, but also refer to different kinds of flute. The spelling of certain proper names varies slightly, reflecting local pronunciation and local orthographic convention.

'From the mouth of the people': Béla Bartók using a gramophone to collect songs from Slovak peasants in the village of Drazovce in 1907

Introduction

Michael Church

NEVER has the world of music been so open to exploration, nor so rich in paradox. Recording is abolishing history – the music of the past is being subsumed into a voracious and ever-expanding musical present. The shrinking of the globe to a digital village is abolishing geography: everyone can listen to everyone else's music, wherever they happen to be. But in a piquant irony, just as the short-lived 'world music' CD boom was whetting people's appetite for new sounds, so those sounds were becoming homogenised out of existence, in response to the demands of the global pop market.

The lament for lost musics is nothing new. The German song-collector Ludolf Parisius gave voice to it nearly two centuries ago: 'Whoever wishes to collect from the mouth of the people should hurry; folk songs are disappearing one after another.' It was this urge to preserve and celebrate, often intensified by patriotism, which drove ethnomusicology from the start. Writing in 1905, the Austrian comparative musicologist Erich von Hornbostel expressed a vaulting ambition for the quasi-science he had helped to found: 'We want to uncover the deepest recesses of the past, and to reveal the full and timeless sweep of the present ... We want to encounter everything there is to know about the historical and aesthetic foundations of music.'[1]

Today the existential threat to the world's musics is compared to the threat hanging over its spoken languages, which are dying out so fast that most of the existing six thousand will have gone by the end of this century. And there is indeed a parallel: a music may not be a language, but it will have a grammar, and like spoken languages – even like plants – it needs its own eco-system to thrive. Moreover, its loss is comparable to the loss of a biological species: as the expression of a particular society, and of a particular way of thinking and feeling, each music is a living organism which, if it withers, may not be capable of resuscitation. What tourist in present-day Ibiza would imagine that within living memory its villages echoed at Christmas with male-voice carols growled in a unique throat-trill style? Visitors to Malta before its culture became Europeanised would have been treated to *ghana* competitions in bars, with male falsettists vying to deliver impromptu rhymed verses with a killer punch. Local folklorists are now trying to revive this art-form, but the social impulse which motivated it has gone for ever. Two losses, from among thousands.

Yet music is also infinitely adaptable. It can fuse, absorb, and morph to a point where its original character is completely changed: self-transformation, not stasis, is its default mode. One of the classical traditions outlined in this book (the Tajik-Uzbek *shashmaqom*) has recently seemed to be on the verge of extinction, but most of the others are thriving, with two glaring exceptions. In Mali, musicians are enduring Taliban-style persecution by radical Islamists,[2] and the events currently unfolding in the eastern Arab world are threatening to obliterate all forms of traditional culture. It's hard to believe that the historic city of Aleppo, now bombed to rubble, had been for eight hundred years the celebrated centre for Andalusian music's *muwashshah* song form, in a tradition which had continued serenely unbroken until the Syrian Revolution erupted in 2011.

European music, meanwhile, is now transplanting itself so firmly to the East that 'Western' seems a misnomer; it is threatening to swamp all the other traditions, or at least to absorb them. One thinks of the musical responses of Debussy and Britten to gamelan as early evidence of this, and the responses of Stockhausen and Boulez to Japanese *gagaku*.[3] Or of the American Minimalists' discovery of the possibilities latent in repetition, which allowed them to plug directly into the aesthetics of Eastern styles. Borrowings of this kind are now standard practice in European music.

A comprehensive survey of the world's folk musics would stretch to many volumes, but this book has a more manageable compass. What its fifteen parallel narratives seek to present is a brief inventory of humanity's most sophisticated communal achievements in musical creation. With the same analytical model used in every case, each music is described in terms of its modes, scales, and theoretical framework; its instruments, forms, and aesthetic goals; and the social conventions governing its performance. Each chapter is prefaced by a snapshot of a typical event.

Sitting mid-way along a spectrum bounded at the academic end by the ethnographic *Garland Encyclopedia of World Music* and by the *Rough Guide to World Music* at the popular end, our book is designed for musically-literate readers. (Specialist terminology has been kept to a minimum, but people should not feel guilty if they feel impelled to skip the necessarily abstruse sections on modality in Turkey and the Arab world.) To obviate cultural bias, it operates on a strictly level playing field with no implied hierarchy of quality or importance. But if readers choose to regard those chapters on less familiar musics as beating the drum on their behalf, that is certainly part of its purpose. The 'other' in the title has no intended overtones of a threatening (or exciting) alien presence, nor does it imply breast-beating about the tragedy of North–South and West–East colonial encounters (though much music has been generated by those encounters). 'Other' simply refers to all the musics beyond each reader's native culture, be that in Beijing or Birmingham, Tehran or Tokyo. Thus is Western classical music brought level with the rest.

Our writers are almost all schooled in the European-American tradition of ethnomusicology, but some are accomplished performers of the music they have made their study. Their approach is essentially anthropological, based on the belief that music is best understood in the context of the culture which gave rise to it: music as a lens through which to view society, or as the distillation of a culture. The American ethnomusicologist Alan Merriam put the matter with provocative succinctness: 'Music *is* culture, and what musicians do *is* society.' His compatriot Anthony Seeger offers a more poetic metaphor in his comment on singing among the Suya people of the Brazilian rainforest: 'Suya society was an orchestra, its village was a concert hall, and its year a song.'[4] In other words, music as the means by which a society reproduces itself. As Bruce Chatwin has shown in his study of Australian Aboriginal culture, *The Songlines*, music can also be a way of marking territory; its therapeutic uses, often in tandem with dance, are legion.

■ Parallels

This is not a comparative study, but it does allow comparisons to be drawn. And even in technical terms, comparison of seemingly unrelated musics can produce striking parallels. In 1999 the French pianist Pierre-Laurent Aimard shared the stage of the Châtelet theatre in Paris with a group of Aka Pygmy drummers, and answered the polyrhythmic Aka pieces with studies by the Hungarian composer György Ligeti which deployed similar rhythms. Prompted by the researches of the French-Israeli ethnomusicologist Simha Arom, Ligeti's discovery that Congolese drummers followed metrical principles towards which he himself had been feeling his way led him to incorporate them into his own works. The message of this concert, which Aimard now acknowledges as a life-changing experience, was that the African rhythms were arguably even more sophisticated than those of Ligeti's famously convoluted music.

With several voices travelling simultaneously at different speeds, Steve Reich's *Music for mallet instruments, voices, and organ* marries African drumming rhythms with layering ideas drawn from gamelan. But layering devices of this kind have cropped up in many other places: in Sufi rituals in Baghdad (at least until the 1970s), in the *piphat* music of Thailand, in the Chopi xylophone orchestras of Mozambique, and even in Johann Sebastian Bach's chorale preludes in eighteenth-century Germany. Likewise the hocketing technique – a key weapon in the musical armoury of the medieval Christian church – can be traced across continents, linking Andean panpiping with drumming in Buganda and with the work of the British composer Harrison Birtwistle.[5] Across cultures, one finds many parallels in canonic forms: these include the variation, equivalents of the sonata, and instances of the fantasia at the start of a suite (which aligns European Baroque music with the classical music of the Arab world). Congruences and parallels were always meat and drink to ethnomusicologists, and this book reflects so many that one is tempted to speculate that, just as the world's treasury of folk tales can be reduced to a handful of archetypal plots, so the mechanics of music may be boiled down to a small number of strategies and forms.

■ Definitions

Mechanics are only one element in the formation of a classical music as it is defined here – and the word 'classical' must itself give pause. The term 'art music' is too broad because all music, even the simplest lullaby, is a form of art. 'Court music' would have worked for some traditions, but not for all; 'classical' is the adjective best capable of covering what every society regards as its own Great Tradition.

According to our rule-of-thumb, a classical music will have evolved in a

Cross-cultural influence: Pygmy musicians at the Châtelet Theatre (Paris), 1999, with *(back row, from left to right)* ethnomusicologist Simha Arom, composer György Ligeti and pianist Pierre-Laurent Aimard

political-economic environment with built-in continuity – in a theocracy or an aristocracy, or at the heart of an empire – where a wealthy class of connoisseurs has stimulated its creation by a quasi-priesthood of professionals; it will have enjoyed high social esteem. It will also have had the time and space to develop rules of composition and performance, and to allow the evolution of a canon of works, or forms; indeed, the concept of a canon, validated by a system of music theory, is a defining feature of all classical music. A canon's function extends beyond the time and place of its creation: it will speak to other generations, and other societies, when its original relevance has fallen away. Hence, for example, the perennial transplanting and re-contextualising of operas by Monteverdi and Mozart, Verdi and Wagner; hence the choice of Beethoven's Ninth as a vehicle for the Tehran Symphony Orchestra's triumphal rebirth during a political thaw in 2015.

It's important to dispel the notion that such music is 'elitist' in the negative and exclusive sense of the word, even though our definition does imply acceptance of a 'classical/folk-popular' divide. That distinction is made on the assumption that these categories simply occupy opposite ends of a spectrum, because almost all classical music has vernacular roots, and periodically renews itself from them; it makes no sense to ascribe superiority to one over the other. For example, few singing styles can match the restrained refinement of Vietnamese *ca tru*, a form of folk balladry delivered by a female soloist accompanying herself by beating a wooden board with two sticks while being shadowed by the sound of a lute. And no polyphony could be more finely calibrated than that of the village choirs in the Albanian province of Laberia. Densely dissonant, tightly structured, and liberatingly wild, this form allots very specific functions to each of its four voices, creating a form of music which its champions claim has been performed at weddings and funerals since the days of Homer. We might consider a truth neatly put by the American musicologist Harold S. Powers: 'One of the great humanising values in a "classical" music is that, with application and talent, anyone can learn it. To a "folk" music one can only be born.'[6]

We should also remember that the Western definition of 'classical' is just that – a Western notion. In one of the earliest known definitions, *classique* is translated as 'classical, formall, orderlie, in due or fit ranke; also, approved, authenticall, chiefe, principall'.[7] The implication there was: authority, formal discipline, models of excellence. A century later 'classical' came to stand also for a canon of works in performance.[8]

Yet almost every non-Western culture has its own concept of 'classical' and many employ criteria similar to the European ones, though usually with the additional function of symbolising national culture, as in 1960s Tehran: concerned about the increasing influence of Western culture, the Iranian government of the day decreed that Persian classical music should be standardised and celebrated as a unifying symbol for the nation. In India, as the chapters by Richard Widdess and Jonathan Katz demonstrate, similar ideas are thought to have played a role in the crystallisation of both the classical Hindustani tradition and its South Indian counterpart: some scholars claim that

Ca tru folk balladry in Hanoi: Nguyen Van Mui (drum), Nguyen Thuy Hoa (voice and *phách*) and Nguyen Manh Tien (dàn dáy lute)

these musics' standardised forms only date from their espousal by the nationalist movement at the start of the twentieth century.

The Twelve Muqam is a series of suites blending Sufi poetry with ecstatic ritual which has become accepted as the indigenous classical music of Uyghur Xinjiang in north-west China, and its story is particularly instructive. Local myth dates it from the sixteenth century, when a talented village singer named Amanissa Khan was discovered by Sultan Rashid Khan while out hunting. She was taken to live in his court, where she devoted herself to the collection and ordering of the songs which eventually crystallised as this repertoire. But some Uyghur enthusiasts hold the Twelve Muqam to have originated in fourth-century China, thus predating Islam and the Middle-Eastern modal forms with which this music has much in common. Pulling the rug out from under both these claims, the British ethnomusicologist Rachel Harris has argued persuasively that until the twentieth century the Twelve Muqam was a fluid, oral tradition, and that the concept of a fixed repertoire is a modern, nationalist invention, with politics being the spur for its official enshrinement.[9] When the People's Republic of China was consolidating control of its 'autonomous regions' in the 1950s, Uyghur music – as the 'national' music of Xinjiang, and possessing a high degree of sophistication – became one of the minority art-forms selected for preservation. Recently China has vigorously promoted the Twelve Muqam as a UNESCO 'masterpiece of the oral and intangible heritage of humanity', thus conveniently strengthening its political claim that Xinjiang is an inalienable part of China. Such are the minefields which the term 'classical' may conceal.

Our selection

The musics focused on here have an uneven geographical spread, but they do reflect the course of history. By definition, the conditions required for the evolution of a classical music don't exist in newly-formed societies: hence the absence of a representative tradition from South America. Little is known about the music of the Aztec empire, which might otherwise have qualified. Latin-American Baroque, meanwhile, is the product of a happy fusion created when the Jesuit missionaries of the seventeenth century – armed with music as their chief ideological weapon – blended their European instruments and styles with those of the Indians they hoped to convert in what is now Peru, Brazil, Bolivia, and Argentina.

It may seem arbitrary to single out just one of Africa's many ancient styles, but Mande music, which extends through six West African countries, makes a revealing contrast to the other musics in this book. Its early history can only be intuited – with help from travellers' accounts like that of Mungo Park in 1796 – but with its small number of practices cultivated to a high degree of aesthetic sophistication, it offers a strikingly distinctive pattern.

As a newish nation whose dominant culture is essentially European, America has – like Australasia – imported Europe's classical music, but in jazz it has its own indigenous classical form. Those in doubt as to whether jazz belongs in this book should bear in mind that its controlled-improvisatory nature aligns it with almost all other classical musics. Doubters might also consider how closely jazz's historical trajectory mirrors that of European music, if telescoped into a much shorter time. It too has vernacular roots, and was raised by a series of master-musicians to the status of an art-music; it too has evolved via a 'classical' period through a succession of modernist phases, and has become every bit as esoteric as European classical modernism. Since the 1950s jazz has had its own early-music revivalists (from trad bands to Wynton Marsalis) and, again like Western classical music, it too seems unsure where to go next. And now that it's gone native on every continent, jazz is as global as Beethoven.

The absence of a Slavonic chapter prompts other questions. While European music was escaping the bonds of organised religion during the fifteenth and sixteenth centuries, and embarking on its still-continuing journey of exploration, the dominant music of the Slavonic world, which was based on Byzantine chant, remained ecclesiastical and largely unchanged. Russian music was the exception: with the aid of harmony, staff notation, and an influx of Italian musicians, church music there gave way to the brightly-coloured, folk-influenced strand of the European tradition epitomised by Musorgsky, Borodin, Rimsky-Korsakov, and Stravinsky. However, some musics based on Byzantine chant have remained freestanding, and could in many respects count as 'classical'. The most prominent of these is the music of the Greek Orthodox Church, which has preserved its character intact for eight hundred years. Byzantine Greek chant implicitly looks east, not west, in that its governing principle is closer to that underpinning Arabic modal music: its building-blocks are fragmentary melodic motifs combined and ornamented by the singer, with a formal equilibrium being the goal. The flamboyant achievements of singer-composers like the thirteenth-century master Ioannes Koukouzeles have been justly compared to the achievements of medieval icon-painters, who worked in similarly circumscribed forms.[10]

Then there is the music of Georgia. While Greek chant is characterised by an undulating fluidity, Georgian liturgical polyphony feels as though it has been carved out of granite, and it has survived pristine for a similar period. Church congregations in Tbilisi today sing music which is thought to be very similar to that which was taught in the academies of twelfth-century Georgia. Their 'Alilo' songs are derived from Jewish alleluias, and their drone-accompanied chants are muscular variants on the Greek *ison* style, but the vibrantly dissonant modal polyphony of their hymns is unique. Moreover, this music is still an integral part of Georgian daily life.[11] Both these traditions might have merited a chapter, as might the *mugam* of Azerbaijan which, though it follows the same basic system as Persian classical music, is much more than a mere offshoot of that.[12]

■ *Contrast and congruence*

This book's fifteen traditions may seem diverse, but they coalesce into a handful of stylistic families. Gong-chime music links Thailand, Laos, and Cambodia with Indonesia, while the music of China's Tang dynasty became the foundation for the court music of Japan. And it's a vertiginous thought that European classical music and the music of the Muslim Middle East have a common root in classical Greek theory, which itself derived from ancient Babylon.[13] Translated by Arab theorists in the eighth and ninth centuries, the writings of the Pythagoreans became the underpinning for *ilm-i musiki*, the Arabic 'science of music', which laid down rules for the structure of scales and the mathematical tuning of intervals; versions of this were absorbed by the medieval church.

An even more arresting congruence is to be found along a line extending eastwards from Morocco via Algeria, Egypt, Turkey, Iraq, Azerbaijan, and Iran, to Uzbekistan, Tajikistan, and Xinjiang. Each of these nations has its own classical tradition deriving from Arabic and Persian medieval court music, and each has its own theoretical system. All weave their vocal and instrumental pieces into suites, and all deploy a richly-ornamented melodic style; all stipulate that creative licence should be founded on rigorous training.

But what unites these musics most crucially is the modal principle. A mode differs from a scale in that it implies a specific melodic pattern in which some notes have more importance, more pulling-power, than others. In Middle-Eastern modal music, known generically as *maqam*, each mode has its own mood and sound-world. Maqam embraces a multitude of styles, ranging from austere lute-accompanied Tajik *maqom* songs to the convivial maqam of a Syrian *takht* ensemble; from Azerbaijan's barnstorming religious *mugam* to the intricate grandeur of Iraqi oud suites as performed by the great Munir Bashir.[14] And although Muslims strenuously deny that the a*zan* – the intricate and melodically beautiful Islamic call to prayer – is 'music', that too is a manifestation of maqam. The scales used in maqam differ from one region to another, but they all depend on microtonal refinement. While Western music conventionally divides a whole-step interval into two semitones – Harry Partch's 43-step octave being very much the exception – Turkish makam divides it into nine infinitesimally fine pitch-differences which its musicians fastidiously observe. One of the messages of this book is that there is no such thing as a 'natural' scale. 'Natural' simply means what the ear is used to.

The word 'maqam' is itself so rich in connotation that it's hard to define (and in Central Asia it has a secondary meaning, as a suite). Its primary meaning indicates a melodic mode with specific intervals, note-patterns, and modulations; as Robert Labaree observes of Turkish *makam*, it's part scale, part melodic template, and part aesthetic rule-book. It amounts, in fact, to a kind of philosophy, with extra-musical associations embedding it in cultural life. In the *radif*, which is Iran's version of maqam, poetry is pervasive, and each of the radif's twelve modes has a colour, mood, and time of day for performance; each of its 250-odd pieces has its own melodic character. And if all this sounds reminiscent of Hindustani raga, that is appropriate, because north Indian music bears strong Persian influences; raga is in many ways analogous to the Arabic modal forms.

Further east, in Javanese gamelan, one finds a modality seemingly unrelated to Arabic forms, but which is again similar in principle. As Neil Sorrell observes, even the Javanese have difficulty in explaining their word *pathet*, despite their intuitive grasp of it. It translates as 'constraint' or 'limitation', but by dramatic shifts in perspective on a small number of basic pitches, and by incorporating symbolism relating to everything from mood and colour to points in the life-cycle, it opens the door to worlds of thought and feeling.

Since the emergence of tonality, European music has barred itself from drawing on the modal well of wisdom. Yet its own beginnings were modal, and its composers continued to capitalise on modal music's expressive possibilities, as in the Baroque fashion for relating specific keys to specific emotions: one thinks of Mozart's predilection for G minor as a vehicle for melancholy, or Beethoven's for the heroic potential in C minor. But the arrival of diatonic scales and tonal harmony ironed out such associations, with the result that for two centuries European musicians largely lost touch with the modal aesthetic (though Beethoven did, towards the end of his life, begin composing in the old church modes). At the start of the twentieth century certain composers began re-absorbing modality from folk music while, from another angle, Schoenberg attempted to reconnect with it through his concept of a motif-centred musical 'idea', with its associated colour, mood, and expressive charge. But when the pianist András Schiff tries to highlight what he sees as the individual colours of Bach's Preludes and Fugues – when he aims, in other words, to create modal effects – the tuning of his equal-tempered instrument works against him.

Further divisions are pointed up by the maqam world's prevailing monophony, as opposed to Europe's harmony-based polyphony, and by Europe's dependence on notation: this sets it apart – both in terms of how music is created, and how it is taught and transmitted – from most other classical musics. While a Western

> The azan in Cairo, Egypt. Most Muslims deny that the call to prayer by the muezzin is 'music', but it is nonetheless a perfect manifestation of maqam modality.

composer can devise labyrinthine complexities with the aid of pen and paper (or computer software), in other cultures composition and performance happen simultaneously in real-time, through controlled improvisation. Thailand's densely polyphonic music sits midway between these polarities: each piece is pre-composed but without notation, and is dictated by the composer to his musicians.

But we need to qualify the concept of 'improvisation'. For Western musicians this has come to mean not only impulsive composition-on-the-spot, but also everything in a performance which cannot be fixed in advance by notation. In musics ranging from jazz to the Persian radif, on the other hand, improvisation means the acceptance of strict conventions, yet it also implies an unfettered creativity: it has nothing to do with an unquestioning adherence to formulas. Persian musicians are instructed to become like the *bolbol* – nightingale – the bird which is supposed never to repeat itself. Bruno Nettl makes this point another way in his peerless primer *The Study of Ethnomusicology*: 'My teacher in Iran told me that he taught the radif [his particular performance version of a suite], and that it itself would teach a student to improvise.'[15] Speaking of Azeri mugam, the Russian-American ethnomusicologist Izaly Zemtsovsky says that, in order to appreciate what he calls the 'creative correlation' between canon and improvisation, it's essential that the listener knows who the teacher was of any given player.

Notation takes hundreds of different forms, with its symbols ranging from physical gestures and spoken syllables to graphic signs and pictures. Its usefulness has been widely acknowledged, even among professional musicians in pre-Meiji Japan for whom it was a jealously guarded secret (rather than a practice to be shared) because they didn't want to give up their monopoly. In India and Indonesia notation is not integral to performance – no notation could adequately reflect the way south Indian ornamentation is integral to the melody – but it is widely used there as a teaching aid.

Western staff notation is in many respects a case apart. It grew out of a nifty little invention a thousand years ago by a Benedictine monk: by creating a system of pitch notation, Guido of Arezzo made it possible, for the first time in history, for a man to sing a melody he had never heard – to *read* music, thus liberating it from the vagaries of memory, and thus laying the foundations for European music's architectural triumphs. Present-day staff notation has its own limitations – it can't reflect sound texture, and its concept of a 'note' is a mere abstraction (eliminating overtones, it's only a rough approximation to sonic reality) – but it has become accepted across most of the world as the most efficient means of transcription, and thus of preservation.

But there's a potential downside with notation of any sort. In the Eastern Arab world, as Scott Marcus shows, it almost sounded the death-knell for the old improvised forms. In Tajikistan-Uzbekistan it helped turn the *shashmaqom* – the local classical repertoire – into what the American ethnomusicologist Theodore Levin has described as frozen music, with students made to reproduce officially-approved performances with slavish fidelity down to the smallest ornamental detail.[16]

■ *Varieties of notation*

Above: China: jianpu (numeral) notation for the pipa lute. There are four beats per measure. Numbers indicate degrees of the scale (C diao, or C major). A plain number is one beat, a single line beneath subdivides by two, two lines subdivides by four. Plain numbers are the middle octave, a dot above being the higher octave and a dot below being the lower octave. The characters above are the title and those in the notation are the song text. This is read like Western notation, top to bottom, left to right.

Terry Miller

Below: Thailand: numeral and solfège notation together, read top to bottom and left to right. Each unit represents four beats, each usually transcribed as eighth notes. The downbeat is the fourth in each measure, because Thai music is end-accented. The letters represent solfège; numbers indicate degree of the particular mode; in this case *do* is 4, because when transcribed into staff notation, 4 is F for the pentatonic mode F–G–A–C–D. Dashes indicate held beats. The title is at the top, and the figure in the upper left indicates 'section one'.

TM

Above: Japan: notation for the koto zither. The notation is read right to left and top to bottom, each box indicating a time unit. Following the title *(upper right)*, bold figures indicate which string or strings must be plucked (sometimes simultaneously). Certain figures indicate a 'pull' or 'press' or 'repeat'. The tiny characters to the left are called *shoga* or *kuchi-shoga*, onomatopoeic syllables dating from before the development of notation and used to teach and remember the piece. Two figures in a box indicate subdivision of the beat.

TM

Below: Rhythmic notation for an excerpt of a Hindustani tablā composition. Each grid in this system (designed by Nikhil Gosh and Gert-Matthias Wegner) represents one cycle of the tala, in this example sixteen beats. Each pair of upper (high drum) and lower (low drum) boxes represents a single beat. When one grid is connected to an additional grid, it indicates that the rhythmic phrase is longer than one cycle (in this case two and one beat including the bracketed repetition). The brackets indicate a section repeated with total number of repetitions shown by the number following the bracket. The arrows indicate glissandi of the lower drum (bayan). The circles with a dash are rests for that drum. The solfège syllables represent timbres and rhythmic phrases. The symbols outside the grid (3, 4) represent fingering, while 'k' indicates the edge of the drum and 'o' an un-damped stroke.

N. Scott Robinson

INTRODUCTION

Rethinking the musical relationship between East and West at the Cairo Conference, 1932, with the Austrian musicologist Erich von Hornbostel *(far left)*, composer Paul Hindemith *(third from left)* and the eminent British Arabist Henry George Farmer *(seventh from left)*. Bartók also attended.

A related malaise has afflicted music across a swathe of the globe, from the Middle East and Central Asia to China and Japan: the belief that traditional styles must be 'modernised' to compete on the international stage, and that Western classical music holds the key to success. In mid-twentieth-century Central Asia this meant the replacement of small maqom ensembles with 'folk orchestras' delivering Western harmonies in equal-tempered scales; thus did the finely-calibrated microtonal sound-world of Uzbek maqom become smudged and blurred. In Turkey the German composer Paul Hindemith was brought in to advise the modernising Mustafa Kemal Atatürk on music education; he told him that Turkish makam was unsuited to polyphonic treatment, and that polyphony was essential if Turkish music was to develop. Melody was backward stuff, and harmony was the future.

But Hindemith was also a guest – along with a distinguished group of European ethnomusicologists including Béla Bartók – at an extraordinary conference held by Egypt's King Fu'ad in 1932 at Cairo's Academy of Oriental Music. Its official aim was to make Egyptian music more 'civilised', and to 'rebuild it on acknowledged scientific principles'. From that self-hating colonial perspective, Egyptian music's 'primitive' microtones and oral methods of transmission were to be replaced by European scales and notation; one compromise result was a commercially-produced piano with a keyboard

Spike-fiddlers of the spirit world, found in the Afghan city of Herat. This pen-and-wash drawing by the mysterious fifteenth-century artist known as Muhammad of the Black Pen testifies to the religious significance of music in Central Asian culture.

converted to play quarter-tones. The debates themselves were more nuanced, with Bartók turning the conference's premise on its head by extolling the spontaneity and expressiveness of Arab peasant music. However, most of the conservatories set up in the Middle East during the early decades of the twentieth-century were heavily biased toward European music, and although they now also teach maqam they still retain that bias.

But underlying all these divisions and distinctions is one great truth: classical music, however defined, is intimately connected with religion. The image of music coming down from the gods, and being sent back up to them with professional performers as bearers of the sacred flame, is to be found in every civilisation. As is the belief that musicians are the equivalent of Shelley's poets, those 'unacknowledged legislators' of the human race. And so is the idea of fulfilment implicit in the Zen Buddhist injunction 'in one sound, become the Buddha', and in the Sufi yearning for divine union, as expressed in the poet Jalaluddin Rumi's lovely image of severance from the primal reed-bed: 'Listen to the reed flute, how it does complain / And how it tells of separation's pain.' The Chinese guqin sounds the cosmos; the ancient Greeks, for whom music was the dominant metaphysical principle of the universe, heard the music of the spheres. Even the contentious Islamic notion of music being *haram*, forbidden, is a back-handed testimony to the power which music possesses in the moral realm: several chapters of this book deal with that matter, and with the problems it can present for musicians in Muslim societies. Yet Plato himself would have understood the prohibition, as would those Christian sects throughout the ages which have forbidden the playing of instruments in church. With classical music, we enter the spirit world.

■ Erosion and conservation

It may be a truism, but it still needs to be stated that with the exception of European music – which has become a lingua franca – most classical musics are now being eroded. Technology is a two-edged sword: it can liberate musicians in isolated and impoverished communities, but at the same time it is continuing to intensify what the American song-collector Alan Lomax fifty years ago termed 'cultural grey-out'. Recording has had profound effects on the way music is created and performed: in parts of India and the Middle East it stopped musical evolution in its tracks. In the early twentieth century, pieces which had once been free to find their own length became routinely standardised at three minutes for marketing on shellac discs; present-day commercial recordings of Eastern music for Western consumption often rob it of its microtonal soul. The amplification which is now a regular component of musical performance in Africa, the Middle East and Central Asia has offered new scope for virtuoso playing on quieter instruments, but in terms of sheer decibels it has had a coarsening effect – and it's significant that some African superstars are now voluntarily renouncing it. But the most serious erosions derive from the political and economic shifts which are destroying the social frameworks which have given classical music its meaning; mass-entertainment, meanwhile, is obliterating diversity with its homogenising tide.

Yet countervailing forces are also at work. Governments are realising anew the propaganda value of traditional music as a way of bolstering national identity, and are enshrining its teaching in schools. Diaspora communities are making traditional music their rallying-point: both the Persian radif and raga on the Afghan *rubab* are thriving in California, while Uzbek maqom is alive and well in

Queens, New York, and Israel pullulates with the musics brought in by successive waves of immigrants. If you want to hear Iraqi maqam, London is the place, while for the music of expatriate Lusophone Africa, you need to go to Lisbon. Moreover, UNESCO is playing a constructive – if at times also blatantly political – role, with its ever-growing 'intangible cultural heritage' list. On this, music joins a variegated range of activities covering everything from weaving and pottery to rituals and festivals (even if it also includes such exotica as Croatian gingerbread-craft and Kirkpinar oil-wrestling). Many of the traditions described in this Introduction – including the polyphonies of Georgia, the Aka Pygmies, and Albanian villagers – have received the UNESCO seal of approval, and it's heartening to see Vietnamese *ca tru* on a special list requiring 'urgent safeguarding', which that art-form – too refined for its own good – undoubtedly does.

And it is to UNESCO's credit that it has moved beyond the museum-culture approach: leading practitioners are now being encouraged to pass on their skills, and to experiment with new forms. This policy underpins a visionary initiative by the Aga Khan Trust for Culture (AKTC), whereby Uzbek shashmaqom (also on UNESCO's list) has become one of a number of Central Asian musics being actively revived. A shashmaqom academy has been set up, with a network of schools throughout Central Asia in which instrumental and vocal masters teach their art to students. Twenty years ago shashmaqom was on the musical equivalent of life-support, but thanks to these initiatives – plus the fact that Uzbekistan and Tajikistan are both brandishing it as part of their national heritage – this music now looks fit enough to emerge from intensive care and make its way unaided.

Recording is another weapon in the conservationists' armoury. The AKTC has co-produced a series of CDs on the Smithsonian Folkways label reflecting many varieties of traditional music in Central Asia, with the dual aim of spreading the word in the West, and of giving back to local people the music they have largely lost. Archive recordings (plus film and video) are seen as of growing importance, with 'cylinder projects' – which transfer old recordings to new technology – allowing the music of the past to be repatriated to the people whose heritage it is.[17] Aaron A. Fox's story of the Inupiat (Eskimo) song recordings which he repatriated from his Columbia University archive to the musicians' descendants three generations later is typically inspiring: these became the core repertory of a successful new Inupiat song-and-dance group. 'Giving it away again', he says, 'is a traditionally Inupiat way of thinking about what it means to own something, be it a harpoon, a cellar full of meat, or a song/dance. It is not yours, unless you share it without reservation.'[18]

Currently, Italian folk singers are reviving the all-but-lost melodies recorded by Alan Lomax on his Italian travels in the 1950s; musicians in the Arab world are re-learning forgotten styles from records made in the early twentieth century by European companies hopefully staking out new markets in the Middle East. There's now intense interest in the contents of the great sound archives in Berlin, London, Indiana, and Washington, which allow a perspective stretching back to the invention of the phonograph; new national sound archives are being set up in emergent states.

The new kaleidoscope

'Timeless' is a word ethnomusicologists fight shy of, because no music is unchanging. Not even the ultra-conservative traditions of Thailand and Cambodia; not even Japanese gagaku, which is the most-cited example of alleged musical stasis. The usual paradigm – found pre-eminently in the music of the Islamic Orient, in European music between 1600 and 1900, and in jazz – has evolution taking place while staying true to a fixed set of principles.

Music, moreover, does not stand still. When people migrate, it migrates with them as it has always done along trade routes, most famously that of the Silk Road. And by inducing musicians from points along that road to create fusions in his Silk Road Project, the Chinese-American cellist Yo-Yo Ma has highlighted one of the key processes by which music perennially renews itself.

The word 'fusion' covers a multitude of things. Some of the most productive fusions have been triggered by politics, as with the introduction of Latin music to the countries of West Africa when they were on the brink of independence. Countless fusions have been generated by the 'world-music' boom, sometimes between musicians from very disparate cultures, and from opposite ends of the earth. Occasionally something durable may emerge from these, though not often: fusions which are arbitrarily willed rather than the result of deep cultural pressures have little life beyond the moment of their creation. The American Kronos Quartet, however, has shown, through four decades of cross-cultural collaboration, what exhilarating fusions can emerge through a dedicated immersion in alien musical styles.[19] Even a record producer's whim can result in something illuminating, as with a CD on which classical musicians from many different cultures were invited to rework Bob Dylan standards in their own style.[20] The ostensible aim was to celebrate Dylan, but the disc is in effect a celebration of musical diversity. The melody of 'Every Grain of Sand' becomes the occasion for a virtuoso performance on the Persian lute, and is then harnessed to a poem by Rumi and turned into an ecstatic Sufi chant; Dylan's depiction of a poet-prophet in 'Jokerman' unlocks the heady magic of a Rajasthani desert ensemble.

Indeed, musical oaks can grow out of the most unpromising acorns. The 'prepared piano' emerged as a recognised instrument when John Cage, invited to create a score for a dance work in 1938, transformed a grand piano into a percussion orchestra with the aid of nails, screws, and pieces of rubber. And who could have predicted that a visiting German artist to Bali in the 1930s would encourage a dancer to turn the accompaniment for an ancient trance-dance into the *kecak*, an exuberant chant to the Hindu god Hanuman which is now a prized element in the island's musical heritage?[21] This may seem a frivolous example, but by such unpredictable steps does music evolve.

So what can be said about the future evolution of classical music, or musics? This book is essentially retrospective: all its traditions, including jazz with its African origins, have their roots deep in the past; all embody a sense of unfolding history. Will we see the emergence of new traditions conforming to our definition of 'classical'? Or is this simply the wrong question? Each of the

Above: The Kyrgyz ensemble Tengir-Too, here performing in a sylvan setting near Lake Issyk-Kul, have dedicated themselves to resurrecting half-forgotten instruments and styles, and function as both archaeologists and innovators in Central Asian music.

Below: By the sacred rock of Kochkor-Ata, Rysbek Jumabaev – in a shamanic trance – recites Kyrgyzstan's celebrated Manas epic. He and Tengir-Too have joined forces to create a composite new art-form.

musics focused on here is the result of a grand historical accident, of a specific set of conditions coinciding in a particular way. In what new contexts might such a combination of conditions occur? And if they do not, does it matter?

Globalisation and the commodification of taste – with search engines working on the principle 'if you liked that, you'll love this' – point in other directions, as does the 'world music' which has been talked into existence over the past thirty years. But that phrase has many meanings. When and how does a given music qualify as 'world music'? The London record producers who hit on this as a marketing category at a meeting in an Islington pub in 1987 offered a profitable commercial answer to the question, and world-music radio programmes in London, Berlin, and New York have reinforced the message that the term can cover everything which doesn't fit neatly into a rack marked jazz, blues, rock, pop – or Western classical music.

At an academic level it's significant that, defeated by the multiplicity of possible interpretations, the contributors to the *Cambridge History of World Music* should tie themselves in knots trying to agree on what it is they are talking about. Insofar as they reach a (shaky) consensus, it's that 'world music' denotes not music itself so much as the angle from which it is viewed, with the history of colonialism as the primary perspective (with the vogue-word 'alterity' enthusiastically brandished, and with 'other' employed as a finger-wagging transitive verb). But in a chapter entitled 'Western music as world music' the British musicologist Nicholas Cook proposes a fruitfully paradoxical way to consider the matter. Adducing examples including Toru Takemitsu's discovery of traditional Japanese aesthetics via the ideas of John Cage, Cook shows how Western musical styles can be used to construct non-Western identities. Western classical music, he argues, transcends time and place, 'and can therefore act as world music in a way that "world music" cannot'.[22]

It is likely that the future development of music will be determined, as it often has been in the past, by new technology, although digital technology, despite the claims of its cheerleaders, may inhibit creativity as much as liberate it. But since music will still be grounded in place and social milieu, one may ask whence the new impulses will come. Globetrotting musicians from the Middle East, some displaced by war and persecution, are now among the stars of the international festival circuit: Germany's Morgenland Festival, which in 2013 put out an offshoot in the Kurdish-Iraqi city of Irbil, annually plays host to players and singers from Iran, Turkey, Syria, and Iraq, and reflects the extent to which music from those countries is finding a receptive response in Europe. And as our chapter by Dwight Reynolds suggests, history can play its own part in such jamborees: Arabo-Andalusian and Sephardic-Jewish musics are now increasingly being performed together, in an attempted recreation of the multicultural harmony of medieval Spain. Meanwhile the Fez Festival of Sacred Music, now in its third decade, testifies to an enduring desire among classical musicians from the Middle East, Africa, and Europe to use their art to break down political polarisations. As Edward Said and Daniel Barenboim have shown with their West-Eastern Divan Orchestra, Western classical music can offer a 'practical Utopia' where Levantine strife can be neutralised, even if that process is only

Left: Two folk lutes of the Central Asian steppes: the Kyrgyz komuz *(left)* and the Kazakh dombra

Right: The Kazakh qyl qobyz, a bowed fiddle traditionally used for shamanic purposes. It is carved from a single block of wood and has a hide resonator; the mirror set into the back of the bowl is to ward off evil spirits.

temporary and symbolic. It's worth noting that past alumni of this orchestra are now spreading its ethos further afield.

Over the past two decades the European and American airwaves have been benignly suffused with music from three regions: Cuba, Mali/Senegal, and the Balkans – all purveying popular traditions, and all having a wide impact. I would like to think that Central Asia, whose musical riches are still a well-kept secret, might rival the Middle East as one of tomorrow's sources of inspiration. The shashmaqom emerged from Central Asian soil like an outgrowth of exotic vegetation, but the region's vast tracts of nomad-territory have given rise to an extraordinary profusion of Turkic and Mongolian-influenced styles. The most ubiquitous Central Asian instrument is the jaw (Jew's) harp, which can call forth remarkable virtuosity when players accompany themselves by throat-singing; and the most expressive instrument is the shamanic two-string *qyl qobyz* fiddle, whose cello-like timbre has inspired twentieth-century Kazakh compositions of a Baroque complexity. No less impressive are the tone-poems played on the Kazakh *dombra* and the Kyrgyz *komuz* lutes, as are the folk-instrument settings of Kyrgyz trance-recitations.[23] But the supreme glory of this nomad culture lies in self-accompanied singing by bards. Some of these singers purvey love songs and homespun moralities, others deliver epic tales; Kazakhstan's tradition of sung-poetry contests is so deep-rooted that the Soviets were impelled to harness rather than expunge it, by substituting collective-farm champions for village stars. The vocal timbres range from florid bel canto, to black-toned earthy contralto, to a ballad idiom whose vibrato-free purity goes straight to the heart.[24] Central Asia's musicians have fought off the challenge of global pop by replacing it with their own form of club music, but their traditional musics have yet to penetrate the wider world.

All this is to dream a little. More to the point is our sudden and unprecedented freedom, thanks to the internet, to summon up with a couple of clicks every form of music described in this book. This can have its downside: musicians can feel stifled by the weight of the musical past, and by its discouraging message that everything conceivable has already been done, and better than could be done now. For readers of this book, however, the internet represents a gigantic archive where they can encounter every tradition's keys to form and musicianship. They can explore the Japanese concept of *ma*, that all-important 'space between sounds'; they can pursue the concepts of 'flavour' and 'journey' which govern the performance of Turkish makam; they can investigate the elusive Javanese concept of *irama*, a system of tempo-relationships best likened to the gear-box of a car. Musical wisdom of this sort has developed and matured over centuries. If the past has become the present, and as the future is unknown, we should celebrate the riches we have.

Thailand, Laos, Cambodia and Vietnam in their wider geo-political context

1 Thailand, Laos, Cambodia, Vietnam
Terry E. Miller

The door is surrounded by a sea of shoes: even the audience must remove them and sit cross-legged on the floor. And this is no ordinary concert. At the front is a spectacular altar consisting of musical instruments arranged in multiple layers; even more striking is the central platform filled with masks, flowers, bowls of food and sundry mysterious objects. A group of young students come in and sit together, some giggling, others looking confused; the elderly ritualist enters and begins a monotone chant. When he has finished he announces the title of a composition to be played by the musicians arranged behind xylophones, gong-circles, drums, percussion and a thick wooden wind instrument: 'Sathukan!' ('greeting the teacher'). Initially the music is a sweep of seemingly unrelated pitches, an outpouring of activity by each individual musician that is hard to grasp: despite the percussion, it's difficult to perceive anything resembling a measure or a phrase. Finally, after many more such pieces, each student comes forward to receive a ritual 'first lesson' either on the large gong-circle or the flute, in which the teacher holds the student's hands to simulate the playing of the piece. Each then receives a soot-mark on the forehead, and over one ear a piece of banana leaf with a flower. Having greeted the teacher (*khru*, guru in Thai) whose lineage extends to the gods themselves – since all knowledge derives from them – each student is now eligible to be instructed in music.

■ History

To address the question of whether any music in mainland Southeast Asia can be called 'classical', we must first consider the term. 'Classical' is an English word that not only denotes a vast corpus of European and American music but carries connotations of hierarchy, value and sophistication. Applied to music in Thailand, Laos, Cambodia or Vietnam, it risks creating inappropriate associations, especially in the case of Vietnam, yet commentators from both Southeast Asia and elsewhere have long used 'classical' to describe this music. Just as the European elite were the patrons of Western classical music, in Southeast Asia the aristocracy, and especially the extended royal family, performed this function too. Add to that local perceptions of this music in those same terms of hierarchy, value and sophistication, and you may conclude that 'Thai classical' and 'Lao classical' are indeed appropriate.

Discussing the classical traditions of Thailand, Laos and Cambodia together makes sense. Not only do they have much in common, but their intertwined histories have created a more homogeneous style than most nationalistically-inclined commentators may be willing to admit. However, unlike these three cultures – all deeply Indianised through the influences of religion, language, literature, art and dance – Vietnam's must be addressed separately because there Chinese influence was paramount. The Indianisation typical of the other countries only penetrated Vietnam through Chinese Buddhism, or as acquired from a conquered people – specifically the Cham – who now represent a minority culture in southern Vietnam. To understand all this requires some history.

To paraphrase an old saying, when they gave a war in Southeast Asia, everyone came. Over the two last millennia of the region's history there have been many conflicts among the kingdoms and other political entities which have risen and fallen. It became customary that upon conquering your enemy, you not only destroyed his palaces and capital city, but you also carried off as much of his population as you could. Back home you forcibly resettled these people in under-populated provinces, to farm the land and provide labour for digging canals and moats, building walls, and even for fighting wars. It was also customary to bring the conquered court's musicians, dancers, instrument makers, painters, poets and artists to the victorious capital, where the local culture would undergo a transformation, especially when the conquered culture was viewed as superior.

The first millennium CE saw the Khmer rise to prominence. When they were building their court and temple centres around Angkor in what is now western Cambodia, between the ninth and fifteenth centuries, the Viet were still divided, with many living far to the north in what is now China, while neither the Lao nor the Siamese (as the Thai formerly called themselves) had coalesced into political entities larger than villages. It was the Khmer empire, centred at Angkor, which became Southeast Asia's first great kingdom, extending from southern Vietnam in the east to the Thai-Burmese border in the west, and to the northern reaches of the Central Thai Plain and part-way down the Malay Peninsula.

The rise of the first historical Siamese kingdom in the late thirteenth century, centred in Sukhothai, well north of modern Bangkok, coincided with a weakening of Angkor, and over the next three centuries there was near-constant conflict between the two. Siamese victories over the Khmer led in 1431 to the near-extinction of Angkor, after which this once-great kingdom sank into poverty and despair. Following custom, when the Siamese conquered the Khmer, they carried off much of the population, including most of their musicians, to be resettled in what is now Thailand. There is no way to know to what extent or in what ways the old Khmer musical culture transformed that of Siam, or whether the Thai preserve a repertory that was originally Khmer: our only evidence of Angkor's musical past is seen in the stone bas reliefs of Angkor Thom and Angkor Vat, and few of these resemble anything found in today's Thai music.

The first historical Lao kingdom, Lan Xang ('Million Elephants'), blossomed only in the mid-sixteenth century. In 1767 the Burmese conquered the Siamese kingdom of Ayuthaya and forced much of the population, including musicians and dancers, into exile in Burma. Following this disaster the Siamese kingdom regrouped in Thonburi, across the river from present-day Bangkok. The Siamese king Taksin marched an army north to the Lao capital, Vientiane, in 1774, and

Angkor's Bayon, part of Angkor Thom and constructed around 1200 CE, has numerous stone reliefs showing musical activity. *From left to right:* small cymbals with handles, a drum, a gong suspended from a pole and played by a disproportionately small figure, and a horn.

laid waste to the city, forcibly bringing much of the population back to Thonburi, including the Lao royal family plus their entire music and dance establishment. Tensions between Bangkok and Vientiane continued. Rama III (1824–51), feeling threatened by an advancing Lao army, marched to Vientiane, levelled the city, and carried off virtually all of the population, resettling the majority in the provinces surrounding Bangkok, and others in the north-eastern provinces. At that point Lao court music ceased to exist, except for that practiced by the artists who remained in Bangkok. Thai music then resumed its development, continuing uninterrupted to the present day. During this long period of peace, Thai music, dance and theatre have achieved both depth and variety.

During this same period the court musics of Laos and Cambodia struggled to survive. Most Lao court musicians and dancers had been kidnapped and brought to Bangkok, and the Cambodian court, barely restored after the fall of Angkor, remained weak and modest since the French were colonizing 'French Indochina' (Vietnam, Laos and Cambodia). In 1930 a contingent of Thai court musicians, the most prominent being composer-performer Luang Phradit Phairoh, were sent to Phnom Penh to help restore Khmer court music. As a result, Khmer 'classical' music became a regional variation of Thai music – modestly distinct thanks to subtle differences in playing style and instrumental idiom – with

Cambodia having no known independent tradition of composition. Lao court music was also re-established with Thai help, and many Lao musicians studied in Bangkok. Similarly, then, Lao music shows few distinctions from Thai.

Later both Lao and Khmer classical musics underwent second extinctions. When the Khmer Rouge overthrew the Cambodian King Silhanouk in 1970 and began a reign of terror during which some two million people died, around eighty per cent of the court musicians were wiped out, with only a few surviving and some fleeing to the West. A second restoration began in the late 1980s and has continued to the present, with the re-establishment of the Royal University of Fine Arts. Meanwhile in Laos, when the Pathet Lao overthrew the royalists and forced King Sisavang Vong to abdicate in 1975, the Lao court tradition was again dispersed, with the performers ending up variously in France, the United States and elsewhere, and unable to regroup effectively. For some years the communist government pursued a policy of condemning classical music, but during the 1980s a partial restoration began. Consequently performance standards in Laos have not yet returned to those of even the recent past.

It is important to understand that the above narrative is that of an outsider, and that some nationalist observers in Laos and Cambodia might disagree with parts of it, claiming either independence or an unbroken history for their respective musical traditions. Many Lao still resent the Thai invasions from the early Bangkok period, and many Khmer, seeking to restore their well-deserved national pride, have asserted cultural independence from Bangkok. Whether or not one accepts these nationalist interpretations, it remains possible – as well as desirable – to unify this discussion, using Thai music as the primary focus because of its long and uninterrupted history, its vast repertory, and its high level of sophistication.

■ (Mis)understanding the music

The first time I heard Thai classical music, as a graduate music student on a visit to Bangkok in 1970, I could make little sense of it. I found some of the ensemble music 'melodic', but I could not understand the forms or the performance process, and the timbres were not immediately appealing. Much later I discovered a pamphlet written in 1884 by Frederick Verney, Secretary to the Siamese Legation in London during the visit by Siamese musicians to the International Inventions Exhibition. Verney noted that a great 'stumbling-block' for many Westerners in their attempts to appreciate non-Western music was education, which 'precludes the possibility of a full appreciation of music of a foreign and distinct school … In order justly to appreciate the music of the East it would be necessary to forget all that one has experienced in the West.'[1] This is wise advice in the case of Thai classical music, especially for its most advanced forms and genres, which even the most open-minded of listeners may find cacophonous at first.

Indeed Thai, Lao and Khmer classical music can be an acquired taste even for citizens of those countries: because most people listen to local popular music of some type on a daily basis, their norm is equal temperament, tonal harmony and the timbres of Western instruments such as guitar, saxophone or keyboard. But Thai also grow up routinely encountering their own classical music, usually in 'serious' or ritual situations such as the teacher-greeting ceremony. And whether they understand it or not, they associate it with important life-events, and with the soul of the nation and its culture. It stirs deep feelings in them; they feel proud when television programmes on national or royal matters use classical background music, and are profoundly moved by it at funerals. Though Thai studying abroad may not listen to classical music privately, most choose it to represent their culture to outsiders, sensing its inherent Thai-ness.

Alas, not everyone who encountered Southeast Asian classical music during the early centuries of contact (sixteenth–nineteenth centuries) found it either charming or meaningful. Giovanni-Filippo de Marini, an Italian Jesuit who visited the Lao court in 1666, wrote:

> Different types of music preceded this pompous march coming out of the Palace of the King, but with so much confusion on their part, and from instruments so badly played, and from voices so rude and so discordant without observing bar lines, that there is heard absolutely nothing but noise and a confusing sound more capable of irking and deafening the people, than of being pleasant to the ear.[2]

Yet a French Jesuit who visited Ayuthaya, capital of old Siam, wrote in 1688: 'There was nothing extraordinary, neither in the Musick nor Voices; yet the novelty and diversity of them, made them pleasant enough not to prove tedious the first time.'[3] Some of the most vitriolic statements came later, from English-speaking diplomats and missionaries, such as the American Frederick Arthur Neale, who wrote in 1852: 'I consider the Siamese music execrable; nor, indeed, is there any nation in the East that can be said to possess even the first rudiments of music.'[4]

■ Creating the music

Although mainland Southeast Asia reflects profound influences from India in terms of language, literature, religion, dance and art, its music is fundamentally different from anything known in India today. Where Indian music emphasises individual artists, Thai emphasises ensembles. Where Indian music is generated through a complex modal system – embodied in the word *raga* – which provides the basis for composition and performance to happen simultaneously (what Westerners call improvisation), Thai music consists of fixed compositions by known composers, albeit with flexible instrumental idioms. Where Indian music emphasises individual virtuosity, Thai music emphasises cooperation, balance and restraint. Where raga creates dramatically-varied levels of tension and relaxation, Thai music strives for emotional evenness.

Thai classical music's fundamental ensemble, the *piphat* (Lao, *sep nyai*, Khmer *pinpeat*), consists of tuned percussion, a single wind instrument playing melody, drums and a pair of small cymbals to articulate the metrical/rhythmic foundation. Minimally there are five instruments: (1) a xylophone (*ranat ek*) with twenty-one wooden or bamboo keys suspended on two cord lines over a boat-shaped wooden resonator; (2) a circular rattan frame supporting seventeen or eighteen horizontally-mounted bronze gongs (*khawng wong yai*); (3) a bulbous wooden wind instrument (*pi*) (in Western terms, an oboe) with a quadruple reed mounted on a short metal bocal at the upper end; (4) a horizontally-mounted drum with two heads played with the hands (*taphon*); and (5) a pair of small bronze cymbals (*ching*) which articulate the strong and weak beats of a closed metrical cycle of beats. For expanded ensembles, one adds a second (and lower-pitched) xylophone (*ranat thum*) and a second (higher-pitched) gong circle (*khawng wong lek*). Musicians normally use hard mallets (*mai khaeng*) because, historically, the ensemble played outdoors for ritual and theatrical events and needed to be loud. There is also a variant piphat ensemble using soft mallets for indoor performance (*piphat mai nuam*), but in this case there is a bamboo vertical fipple flute (*khlui*) and a coconut-body two-stringed fiddle (*saw u*) instead of the oboe. The soft mallet ensemble, however, is little known to the Lao and Khmer. The following table shows the equivalent names for the instruments.

Type	Thai piphat	Lao sep nyai	Khmer pinpeat
higher xylophone	ranat ek	lanat ek mai	roneat ek
lower xylophone	ranat thum	lanat thum mai	roneat thom
lower gong circle	khawng wong yai	khong vong nyai	kong vong thom
higher gong circle	khawng wong lek	khong vong noi	kong tauch
oboe	pi	pi	sralai
drum	taphon	kong taphone	sampho
cymbals	ching	sing	ching

Thailand has two other major ensembles, one paralleled in Laos and Cambodia, one not. The *mahori* ensemble consists of both xylophones and gong circles but is led (in its most proper form) by a distinctive three-stringed fiddle (*saw sam sai*) whose body is the bottom part of a coconut shell with three bulges pierced by a long spike neck. The bow is separate, but in moving from string to string the player rotates the fiddle slightly on its spike, rather than changing the bow angle. Because this instrument is probably the most challenging of all Thai instruments, many mahori ensembles omit it. Otherwise a mahori includes two two-stringed fiddles, the higher-pitched *saw duang* with a cylindrical body and the

Above: In a mural illustrating the Thai version of the Indian Ramayana, a piphat ensemble performs at a noble house in Bangkok. While the murals at Wat Phra Kheo (Temple of the Emerald Buddha) are sometimes dated back to the eighteenth century, they have been continually repainted – and even re-imagined – up to the present day. *From left to right: (lower row)* klawng tat drums, khawng wong yai gong circle, khawng wong lek gong circle, khawng mong gong, ching small cymbals; *(upper row)* ranat ek upper xylophone, pi reed, ranat thum lower xylophone, drum.

Below: At Ta Prohm temple, an ancient Khmer ruin south of Phnom Penh near Tonle Bati lake, a pinpeat ensemble plays for visitors on a Sunday in 1989. *From left to right: (left front row)* sampho drum, skor thom drum pair; *(middle row)* roneat dek upper metallophone, roneat ek upper xylophone; *(right)* khong vong thom lower gong circle.

THAILAND, LAOS, CAMBODIA, VIETNAM

lower pitched *saw u* with a coconut body, both having the bow hairs pass between the strings. The wind instrument is always the *khlui* bamboo flute. The Lao equivalent, though without the *saw sam sai*, is called *maholi* or *sep noi*, and the Khmer equivalent is called *mohori*. The Thai ensemble without equivalent is the *khrueang sai*, a term meaning literally 'stringed instruments'. Developed more recently – probably late in the nineteenth century – this ensemble combines the two-stringed fiddles and flute with several other possible instruments, including a crocodile-shaped zither (*jakhe*) and a hammered dulcimer originally borrowed from southern China (*khim*). All ensembles also include one or two drums plus the small cymbals.

Regardless of whether listeners find the music meaningful, they cannot but be impressed by the appearance of the instruments. The two xylophones hang suspended over wooden resonator boxes, the higher xylophone's box being boat-shaped on a pedestal while the lower one's sits directly on the floor. Cases may be finished natural wood, but many are painted red or blue, with gold highlighting the patterned carvings; sometimes the circular rattan frames of the gong circles are also painted. The finest instruments, especially in the past, included parts made of elephant ivory; royal instruments could add extensive carving and even embedded stones along with the gold highlighting. The decoration of the instruments echoes the ornamentation of the music.

■ *Forms*

All classical music in Thailand, Cambodia and Laos consists of fixed compositions, with most from the nineteenth century onward having known composers. In this respect, classical music in mainland Southeast Asia resembles that of Europe in principle, but not in process. Whereas a Western composer notates the work on paper in a more or less fixed form (the degree of detail varying from skeletal scores in the Baroque that allow for improvisation to the most detailed scores of the mid twentieth century), Thai classical composers notate nothing: their compositions are created in their minds and then committed to memory. Consequently knowledge regarding date, provenance and composer remains confined to oral tradition. Further, there being little sense of ownership and virtually no copyright law, composers have freely added new sections or variations to existing pieces, including by other composers, over the years. The key word is flexibility, a concept which permeates Thai life.

Because composers are also performers, most dictate their compositions to their musicians by first playing the fundamental form of the piece on the large gong circle (*khawng wong yai*). This version, *luk khawng*, is the least dense in terms of notes, but it is not the 'original' melody; it is simply the composition played 'in the idiom' (*thang*) of the gong circle, primarily expressed in single notes, octaves and pairs of fifths or fourths. On hearing this version, each musician then 'realises' that structure in the idiom of his/her particular instrument (e.g. into *thang ranat ek* – the higher xylophone). The work is only completed when the ensemble plays this 'composition' structure as a series of simultaneous variants, the differences deriving from each instrument's idiom

EX. 1.1 The first phrase of 'Khaek Borathet' transcribed into staff notation and showing the polyphonic stratification (or heterophony) and the instruments, each playing its own idiomatic version of the melody

and the level of the musician's skill. A given composition, then, could be 'realised' into an extremely complex form by advanced musicians, or into a simple form by beginners. Instrumental idioms are flexible, and could be described as a highly controlled process of improvisation on a fixed structure, somewhat analogous to jazz. Although this texture is a form of heterophony, scholars prefer the more precise term 'stratified polyphony' when discussing Southeast Asian music.

Though composers trust musicians to complete a work through this process of idiomatic realisation, they maintain control of an astounding variety of forms and compositional techniques, many being of a complexity that requires detailed study in transcription in order to understand. Groups of compositions can be organised into suites (*tap*), some related musically and others organised for a specific situation, such as the teacher-greeting ceremony (*wai khru*) or a specific Buddhist ceremony for chanting in the morning (*homrong chao*) or evening (*homrong yen*). The highest class are ritual suites consisting of 'action tunes' (*phleng naphat*), so named because they are also used to accompany dance or action in classical theatre, including masked dance, large shadow theatre and some forms of dance drama. Most phleng naphat are highly motivic, with little clear phrasing and rarely anything resembling a 'tune'; they unfold like a late European Baroque work, with an endless melody created through *Fortspinnung*. But there are also many suites – and independent pieces – consisting of shorter, tuneful compositions with clear phrasing, less differentiated instrumental idioms and colourful titles.

While some compositions have titles that indicate compositional techniques (for example, 'Tayoi', a complex pattern manipulating phrases into sub-phrases and motives) or formal patterns (for example, 'Thao', indicating that the basic melodic structure is presented in three 'tempo levels' – the original, expanded and diminished), most titles suggest a programmatic connection to something non-musical, such as nature, literature, Buddhism, love or history. Further, many composition titles are preceded with a word indicating ethnicity: *khamen* (Khmer), *jin* (Chinese), *phama* (Burmese), *lao*, *mon* or *khaek* (Muslim or Malay). These terms denote a complex of traits that may or may not have anything to do with the original, since all are by Thai composers and all are in Thai style. Nonetheless, each has its own scale or mode, its own metrical/drum pattern, its own melodic style, and often the use of a particular drum associated with its ethnicity. Perhaps the best known composition in the classical repertory is 'Khamen sai yok'. 'Khamen' indicates its 'ethnic' characteristics ('Khmer style'), and 'Sai Yok' alludes to a beautiful waterfall in Kanchanaburi province in western Thailand. The composition's lyrics describe the scenery, the birds, the trees, the plants, and allude to the observer's feelings, but not directly to Cambodia. 'Lao siang thian' is in the 'Lao' mode, while 'siang thian' ('oracle of light') alludes to a Buddhist festival in northern Thailand during which worshippers carry candles three times around a temple.

Most compositions also have a vocal version, typically sung with accompaniment by drum and small cymbals, before the instrumental version is played. Because Thai is a tonal language – where syllables must be inflected (high, low, rising, falling) – singers must correctly express the lexical tones while conforming to the skeletal structure of the composition. The vocal idiom, however, can differ so markedly from the instrumental version that it is not recognisable as the same composition. These discrepancies result from the added pitch inflections that clarify the lexical tones, along with the custom of adding textless melismas between words, especially in the 'third tempo level' where structural tones are spaced further apart in time. These melismas, called *uean*, are subtle flourishes similar to those played by the fiddles and the flute, sometimes almost under the breath: here resides the real art of Thai singing, not in the main tones. (The same is true of Lao singing, since Lao is also tonal; Khmer singing tends to be plainer, as Khmer is not a tonal language.)

Students learn to sing through imitation, and can start very young. One famous female singer, Suntharawathin, began learning from her father. She wrote:

> When my speaking was clear enough, he started teaching me to sing 'Ton phleng ching', as it had to be the first song every beginner learnt. The first line was 'kaki pongpat salat kawn', but on the first day I learnt how to sing just the word 'kaki': 'ka' followed by uean and then 'ki'. The sound of the *uean* must be the same as the trilling sound of the fiddle. I had to practise every morning and evening. Once I could sing that word, he taught me the next one, and so on until the song was complete.[5]

Vocal timbres, because they lack vibrato and are nasal and seemingly 'pinched', differ greatly from the ideals of Western singing.

Among the most creative Thai musical forms is a tripartite structure called *phleng thao*, 'thao' alluding to a set of nesting objects, similar to sets of Russian dolls or mixing bowls. The composition consists of three versions of the same melodic pitch structure played continuously, using three 'proportional tempo levels' (*chan*). First the composer creates the 'second tempo level' (*sawng chan*) and plays it on the large gong circle (*khawng wong yai*), because that is the simplest idiom of all the ensemble instruments. He then *expands* the structure to twice its length by adding notes between the main ones (this section is called *sam chan* or 'third tempo level'), and *reduces* the structure to half its length by simplifying the idioms of the other instruments (*chan dio* or 'first tempo level'). Other members of the ensemble "realise" both the original and the expanded/reduced versions in the idioms of their own instruments. Although the compositional process begins with the middle level, in performance the expanded or augmented form is presented first, followed by the original form and finally the diminished form, the whole often completed with a stock 'coda' (*luk mot*). The individual instrumental sections (or levels, *chan*) consist of more, fewer or no extra embellishing notes between the main structural pitches, making each 'level' sound like a different melody, though fundamentally each is the same. Thao compositions are therefore lengthy: the shortest of them requires at least ten minutes, but a long composition played fully in all three tempo levels including vocal parts could last more than thirty minutes. Phleng thao are free-standing compositions more often played by mahori and khruang sai ensembles than by piphat, and are among the most popular of Thai compositions.

EX. 1.2 A comparison of the melodic structure of a phleng thao composition entitled 'Lao siang thian', the respective versions coinciding on two structural pitches, G and D (circled). A circle above the staff indicates the undamped 'ching' stroke of the ching cymbals; a + indicates the damped 'chap' stroke; + in a circle indicates the 'chap' stroke on a structural pitch ending a cycle.

Thai compositions, while fixed in structure, allow each musician great idiomatic flexibility. Most instrumental sections require 'repeats', but skilled musicians rarely play a repetition as they did the first time: this is where improvisation is permitted. But there are limitations to this. The more melodic a composition, the fewer changes can be made. Ritual compositions, although highly motivic, cannot be varied at all, for this would threaten their spiritual integrity. Not all compositions are uniform in pattern, however. Within pieces, composers also alter texture, mood and tension by using a variety of named techniques. Many works include passages of antiphonal playing, where the higher instruments lead and the lower instruments follow: this may sometimes produce passages of contrapuntal polyphony. In *luk law luk tam* the answering instruments repeat antiphonally what the leading instruments play; in *luk nam luk taw* the following instruments complete a phrase begun by the leading group; in *luk khat* the groups play short passages – musical motives – in quick alternation while in *luk luam* they do the same, but overlapping. These give the music added excitement and forward drive. That all these procedures should be created orally, without the aid of notation, and memorised by thousands of musicians, is remarkable.

■ Tunings, scales, modes

Like the music itself, Thai music theory remains unsystematic and largely unwritten. Beyond the descriptions of a few scholars – some Thai, some foreign – a comprehensive, logical explanation of Thai theory remains to be set down. Terminology exists, but terms such as *thang* have multiple meanings (idiom, school of a master, mode) both generally and musically. Ever since A. J. Ellis wrote his pioneering study of 'the scales of various nations' based on instruments housed in British museums in the early 1880s, the conventional wisdom has been that the Thai tuning system consists of seven equidistant tones. Using his 'cents' system, with 1200 cents in an octave, each Thai degree is therefore 171.4 cents, smaller than a Western equal-tempered whole tone (200 cents) and greater than a semitone (100 cents). While it is true that Thai instruments of fixed pitch are tuned to be functionally equidistant, allowing compositions to be played starting on any of the seven pitches, equidistant tuning is not encountered with the voice, winds or stringed instruments, except when they must conform with keyed percussion. Thus it is correct to say that the tuning of Thai music (and by extension that of Laos and Cambodia) is 'in tune' with itself, but sounds 'out of tune' to listeners conditioned to twelve-tone equidistant tuning.

Each degree of the seven-tone tuning system can be the starting pitch for a scale or mode, and each has a name. But a tuning system is not necessarily the same as a scale, and most Thai compositions are composed to pentatonic scales (pitches 1 2 3 5 6), though one class uses six. Some compositions, however, especially the ritual *naphat* 'action tunes' (because they are also associated with the masked drama), modulate freely, and thus the apparent use of all seven pitches does not indicate a seven-tone scale. Like the language, Thai melodies tend to flow in conjunct undulating motion and avoid large intervals. Each player embellishes the basic structure according to the conventions of his instrument. The lead xylophone (*ranat ek*) plays a continuous stream of notes, usually in octaves, in a density that doubles or quadruples the rate of notes on the large gong circle. The lower xylophone (*ranat thum*) plays a highly syncopated idiom involving many fourths and fifths, pitch displacements and rapid note-runs. The higher gong circle (*khawng wong lek*) plays an active idiom involving many rapid note-runs, fourths and fifths, and can often be heard above the fray because its high metallic notes penetrate well. The resulting polyphonic stratification can sound chaotic to inexperienced listeners, because each idiom is so different, and there is no regard for pitch congruence except at certain points, where these congruencies maintain the coherence of the rhythmic/metrical structure.

This is significant for several reasons. First, certain instruments clearly and audibly articulate the metrical/rhythmic structure, which is organised in closed cycles of beats, analogous to the cycle of time on a clock face. Virtually all Thai classical music is in duple metre, and when transcribed into notation appears to be merely continuous measures of two or four beats, conceived in cycles of two, four or eight measures. The final beat of each cycle, *siang dok* or 'falling pitch', is the strongest. The small bronze cymbals, onomatopoetically named *ching* after their ringing tone when struck together, articulate the metre, the undamped 'ching' stroke being the weak beat and the damped 'chap' stroke being the strong beat. Because the 'chap' stroke falls on the last beat of the cycle, Thai classical music is end-accented, unlike traditionally front-accented Western music.

Each cycle normally consists of four strokes: ching, chap, ching, chap. Melodic pitches sounded on 'chap' strokes are the most fundamental to the compositional structure, while those on the 'ching' strokes are of secondary importance. Thus, a composition consists of a skeletal structure of pitches sounded simultaneously with strokes on the ching cymbals, and this structure is played with little embellishment by the large gong circle. The other instruments play the same structure but, following their individual idioms, embellish it with a greater or lesser number of pitches. The idiomatic embellishments flesh out the more tuneful compositions and allow for a degree of flexibility that some might call improvisation. In the most tuneful pieces, that flexibility is limited by the melody, but in ritual naphat works, players are expected to play exactly the version/idiom taught them by their teachers.

Although there are no concerts of purely instrumental music analogous to the West's symphony concert, listeners sometimes encounter a competition among ensembles whose leaders choose the most virtuosic pieces possible. Such competitions trace their roots at least to the early twentieth century when members of the extended royal family lived in great houses that included, besides the usual gardens, furniture and art objects, a resident classical ensemble. It was customary for these ensembles to compete in a more or less friendly manner, a custom that figures prominently in Ittisoontorn Vichailak's 2004 film, *Homrong* (*The Overture*), one of the few Thai films to have been distributed outside Thailand with English subtitles.

■ Preserving tradition

A comprehensive history of the classical musics of Thailand, Laos and Cambodia does not exist, and probably never will, because the documents necessary for such a history either do not exist or exist in distorted form. This is especially evident in the many descriptions of early Siamese music written by foreign visitors from the sixteenth century onwards. These documents shed an uncertain light, because the writers were rarely musicians themselves and often wrote negative and ethnocentric assessments of the music they heard (as seen earlier in this chapter). Less biased writers did at least describe instruments and performances they encountered. The most valuable early record is that of French ambassador Simon de La Loubère, whose 1691 report *Du Royaume de Siam* included illustrations of instruments and an attempt at transcription of a classical song with a phonetically written text that continues to puzzle Thai scholars, because the transcriber did not know Thai and could only guess at the sounds. Further, he had difficulty notating pitches because, first, Thai music is tuned equidistantly, and second, singers often slide among pitches. Even taken together these documents cannot support a reliable, chronological history of the development of music in Siam.

Moreover, scarcely any written documents of Siamese origin exist, partly because anything written before printed books would have been incised on palm leaf, and neither insects nor the climate permit such fragile documents to last long. The present author is currently exploring whether there is reliable historical evidence in the colourful murals painted on the inside walls of many temples, but because these were painted on dry plaster, few early ones survive: the oldest originated during the late Ayuthaya period, around 1675. While many survive from the Bangkok period starting in the early nineteenth century, it is often impossible to know whether restorations have taken place, or whether the artist was depicting musical activity accurately or in generalised form. For Laos and Cambodia, few such documents survive, and no one has yet explored them.

The limited evidence suggests that classical music flourished and continued developing during the nineteenth century, in spite of the efforts to Westernise Thailand initiated by Kings Rama IV (Mongkut) and Rama V (Chulalongkorn), who reigned in sequence from 1851 to 1910. Where Rama V's long reign saw Thailand develop modern government and consequently escape the colonial designs of both Britain and France, the reign of Rama VI (1910–25) saw perhaps the greatest flowering of the classical arts, in both music and theatre, in the country's history. This golden age resulted largely because Rama VI, far less interested in government than in the arts, not only patronised the arts but

Above: A theatre group from Bangkok in 1900, in a photograph probably taken in Thailand prior to the ensemble's departure for Germany, where they performed in the Zoological Garden in Berlin, and allowed the ethnomusicologist Carl Stumpf to make the recordings now preserved in the Berlin Phonogramm-Archiv.

Below: A Thai piphat ensemble performs at a festival honouring a great teacher in Nonthaburi. The two drummers playing klawng khaek are seated in front because the piece showcases them. Behind are the gong circle players and in front the xylophones, with the double-reed stage-right.

himself composed music and wrote theatre pieces; as the many princes and princesses of the extended royal family copied him, this led to the rise of new composers, the development of instrumental virtuosity, and the making of fine instruments. This was the period of Luang Phradit Phairoh, now considered Thailand's leading classical composer and one of the greatest virtuosos in memory; his life also figured in the film *Homrong*. This 'high Baroque' of classical music, however, was not to last.

Following the Revolution of 1932, when the absolute monarchy of King Rama VII (1925–35) was abolished and replaced with a constitutional one, the vast court music establishment was transferred to a new government bureaucracy later called the Department of Fine Arts, where it continues to this day. After Rama VII abdicated in 1935, although the crown passed to a young Rama VIII, the monarchy ceased to be either powerful or relevant until the present king, Rama IX, Bhumibol (1946–) rebuilt the kingship, but without any special support for classical music. Democracy in Thailand has long been plagued with military meddling, if not direct military rule, and during the regimes of Field Marshall Plaek Phibun-songkhram, who governed between 1938–44 and 1948–57, Thailand underwent a forced Westernisation that included the near-banning of Thai classical music from public performance. For the country's musicians and composers, this was a modern Dark Age. By the time I arrived in 1972, Thai classical music had been released from its prison but remained obscure, housed in the Fine Arts Department, or offered piecemeal like finger-food in restaurants to tourists. Music was not considered a fit academic subject, and only one college, Ban Somdet Chao Phraya, offered a degree in music education. Elsewhere, classical music could only be enjoyed by students as a music-club activity.

Yet classical music, dance and theatre flourish throughout Thailand today, and the past forty years have seen radical changes in their fortunes. By the late 1980s music had become accepted in academia, and most institutions of higher education now have music departments, often offering both Thai and Western specialisms, thus allowing the graduation of skilled players who have become teachers at all levels. Thai classical music is now known to virtually all the population, and tens of thousands of elementary and secondary students have participated in ensembles and dance. In addition there are many private ensembles playing at a remarkably high level: these operate in private homes, in conjunction with the police and army, or with support from temples.

The situation in Laos reflects a radically different history. As noted earlier, the monarchy was extinguished in 1975 by the communist Pathet Lao regime, during whose time the economy collapsed, relations with the Western world (the Soviet Union excepted) soured, and Laos was mostly closed to all but 'Eastern Bloc' visitors. The court was eradicated and what remained of 'classical' music was considered tainted by association; it became confined to private homes and a few temples, with neither visibility nor status. When I returned to Laos in 1991 the Fine Arts school in Vientiane was again operating, but at a low level, and the only musical activities in Luang Phabang, the former royal capital, took place in private homes. Over the next ten years, however, realising that international audiences would respond positively to Lao classical music and theatre, the Lao government began a modest restoration which continues today. The influence Bangkok once had on the Lao and their repertory has not disappeared: there is no known independent tradition in Laos. While the Fine Arts College in Vientiane is now operating vigorously, the restored music and theatre at the former palace in Luang Phabang, primarily staged for tourists visiting this UNESCO World Heritage City, is basic in comparison to that of Thailand or even Cambodia.

Cambodia's recent history has been marked by more savage extremes. When the Khmer Rouge swept into Phnom Penh in 1975 and emptied the city of its population – much of which was murdered or died of starvation and disease – a few of the artists, musicians, dancers and instrument-makers fled to camps in Thailand, where they immediately began to recreate their music because they felt it represented the soul of their culture. Eventually most of these artists resettled in the West, with some managing to re-establish their art in exile. In 1979 Vietnam, allied with Khmer Rouge defector Hun Sen, invaded Cambodia and drove the Khmer Rouge into exile on the fringes of the country. When I visited Phnom Penh in 1988, well before tourists were allowed back in, I found classical music at the former palace to be slowly recovering, thanks largely to a small number of survivors, plus Australian aid and the work of the Australian ethnomusicologist Bill Lobban. We documented classical dance in the former dance pavilion of the ruined palace, and we heard about performances for the few tourists then able to visit Angkor, whose great temples reflected the glories of the long lost Khmer Empire. Since then, with the restoration of the monarchy in 1993 under King Norodom Silhanouk, and now under his son King Norodom Sihamoni (2004–), the University of Fine Arts has been reconstituted as the Royal University of Fine Arts. Much that was lost has been restored, including the classical ensembles, dance and masked drama.

The social status of classical musicians in Southeast Asia depends on a variety of factors. In Thailand it differs between musicians who only perform, and those who teach as well. The former, especially those employed by the Fine Arts Department, willingly endure social prejudice – that they may be unreliable, drunkards, rebellious, poor marriage risks – but those who teach are universally respected, enjoying higher status than musicians who play commercially. In Laos and Cambodia, where so many musicians fled or were killed, the senior players who survived are venerated as carriers of a vital tradition.

Moreover, the classical traditions of Thailand, Laos and Cambodia are exceptionally conservative. In contrast to the Chinese musicians induced by progressive movements to 'improve' and 'develop' both their music and their instruments, Thai musicians, despite extensive modernisation and Westernisation, have chosen to change nothing. Tuning technologies, one of the first indicators of 'improvement', remain what they have been for centuries. For example, players tune the xylophones and gong circles by adding or removing a mixture of lead and wax applied beneath the keys or gongs. A few composers have offered works that combine Western instruments with Thai, but neither the works nor the clash of tuning systems have become popular. Today's composers – and they are relatively few – continue to create works that are indistinguishable from the works of the past. Innovation is a non-issue in Cambodia and Laos, where simple restoration of the traditional music has been the goal.

■ Performance contexts

In Thailand there are plenty of opportunities to hear classical music, though performances are rarely publicised. Tourists are most likely to encounter it as part of a cultural show at one of the major tourist attractions such as The Rose Garden, the Ancient City, or one of the many restaurants that offer foreigners a 'spicy' (but actually mild) Thai dinner followed by a show that includes de-contextualised snippets of masked theatre, dance drama, sword fighting and folk dance. Astute travellers may discover performances at the National Theatre, or find their way to a new theatre in Bangkok's Chinatown where masked drama is performed throughout the year.

But one is more likely to encounter classical music as accompaniment to dance and theatre than as solo performance. These forms include the masked theatre (Thai *khon*, Lao *Pha Lak Pha Lam* [after the main characters], Khmer *lkhaon khaol*), the large shadow theatre (Thai *nang yai*, Khmer *sbek thom*), and rarely (mostly in the past) other forms of puppet theatre. Dance drama (Thai *lakawn*, Lao *lakhon*, Khmer *lkhaon*) also requires classical accompaniment, and – although considered debased – two other Thai genres use classical music: the popular *likay* theatre, and a kind of dance-drama (*lakawn jatri*) seen at a few temple shrines, especially the 'city pillar shrine' (*lak muang*) in Bangkok, the Erawan Shrine in Bangkok, and at Wat (temple) Mahathat in Phetchaburi.

Many schools have student ensembles which give concerts and participate in competitions, but the crucial event in education is the teacher-greeting ceremony held annually in all schools where classical music is taught. These ceremonies reflect the belief that the 'gods' – a vaguely defined pantheon from Hinduism, animism and folk Buddhism – are the source of all knowledge. And because teachers transmit this sacred knowledge to students, they must also be revered: traditionally students must keep their heads lower than that of the teacher, and because instruments are integral to this process, all must treat them with respect, never stepping over them, pointing one's foot at them, or treating them roughly. Classical music and those who transmit it are held as quasi-sacred.

■ Vietnam

Describing the traditional ensemble and theatrical music of Thailand, Laos and Cambodia as 'classical' may make sense, but there is little music in Vietnam so clearly analogous to the Western notion of 'classical'. Unlike the countries discussed above, Vietnam was profoundly influenced by China rather than India, and, because of its status as a Chinese vassal state for much of its earlier existence, followed by French colonization, its dynasties and courts tended to follow Chinese examples first and the European conservatory model later. In addition, China had nothing comparable to the classical music discussed above, and does not form part of the Southeast Asian gong-chime world. One could

In a mural illustrating the Thai version of the Indian Ramayana, a piphat ensemble accompanies a performance of nang yai (large shadow puppets) for the funeral of Piphek, in Bangkok's Wat Phra Kheo (Temple of the Emerald Buddha). *From left to right:* klawng tat drums, pi reed, khawng wong yai gong circle, ranat ek upper xylophone and taphon drum.

argue that the court music of the Nguyen dynasty centred in imperial Hue's 'forbidden city' from 1802 to 1945 constituted Vietnam's classical music, but this was found only at the court, was reserved for court functions, and was not diffused to the broader population, nor even to the aristocracy. What music and dance survived the end of the Nguyen dynasty in 1945, when Emperor Bao Dai abdicated, was at least maintained as a cultural institution until 1968, when the disastrous 'Tet offensive' saw the near-total destruction of Hue, the death of most of the court musicians, and the silencing of this music until its restoration began in 1993; it continues today with UNESCO help.

Identifying other Vietnamese musical genres that might qualify for designation as 'classical' is still possible, because Vietnamese musicians have evolved a subtle and complex method of generating music, along with genres that require sophisticated musicianship. But it is also true that both aspects can be practiced by musicians ranging from master artists and 'professors' to merchants and farmers. This is because much of Vietnam's most developed music is regional chamber music, created and performed by non-professionals whose training may not have gone beyond informal lessons from family members or local practitioners. These chamber genres are also echoed in theatrical genres, with at least those in the central region (*tuong* theatre) and the north (*cheo*) having a level of artistic development that would justify inclusion as 'classical'.

While it is true that Vietnam was long under Chinese influence or control, and that many Vietnamese instruments have Chinese equivalents, several factors differentiate Vietnam's music from that of China and suggest India as a possible source. These are the highly developed modal system for generating music, and the presence of extensive improvisation, neither factor being a part of the Chinese musical world. Elsewhere in Southeast Asia, although there are simple modal systems (e.g. Java's *pathet* system), free improvisation is either non-existent or restricted to instrumental idiomatic variation. The only exception is the *khaen* free-reed mouth organ of northeast Thailand and Laos, which has a moderately developed modal system (*lai*) to support improvisation, but it is still far simpler than that of Vietnam.

Vietnam's modal system, denoted by the term *dieu*, is a complex of all the elements needed to generate music, both in composition and improvisation (the latter actually being composition simultaneous with performance). These include tonal material (pitches organised into scales), typical melodic motives, required ornamentation, a generalised mood, cadential formulas and other subtleties appreciated by connoisseurs. The modal system has been extensively theorised in writing, though different scholars offer varying rationalisations and orders. Each modal scale has a name and each is fundamentally pentatonic, but the only degrees that are fixed and consistent are 1 and 4, the others being variously above or below Western tempered pitches, which results in Vietnamese music sounding somewhat out of tune to ears accustomed to Western tuning. However, these very particular pitch levels are necessary, both for the realisation of the mode and to satisfy the demands of the art.

As for instruments, the Chinese-derived fretted ones preserve the more rigid tuning of Chinese scales, but, to accommodate the Vietnamese modes, instrument-makers use exceptionally high frets and loose stringing that allows for the string-pulling necessary to realise flexible pitches. Musician and scholar Nguyen Thuyet Phong explains this matter in reference to the *dan nguyet* (moon lute with long neck), a two-stringed instrument with these high frets: 'Because the *dan nguyet* is fretted, there are fixed pitches. The Vietnamese modal system, however, is exceptionally complex, requiring a great number of pitches beyond those produced by the frets. These are not merely ornamental or passing pitches, but ones absolutely basic to a given scale.'[6] This is also true of the Vietnamese version of the Spanish guitar, where makers scoop out the wood between frets to give players the space for string-pressing. With unfretted stringed instruments and aerophones (flutes and oboes), players can stop strings where they wish, or 'lip' pitches to create the tuning.

Vietnamese musicians who specialise in the sixteen-string zither (*dan tranh*), the monochord (*dan bao*), the moon-shaped long-neck lute (*dan nguyet*), the

THAILAND, LAOS, CAMBODIA, VIETNAM

Above: Ca hue, the traditional chamber song of Vietnam's central region, is usually performed on a covered boat while floating down the Perfume River west of Hue. The singers are accompanied by a chamber ensemble including a lute, zither, flute and monochord. Pairs of teacups are played like castanets by a female singer.

Below: Vietnamese chamber music played on the dan nguyet lute and dan tranh zither

Vietnamised guitar (*luc huyen cam*), the two stringed fiddle (*dan nhi/dan co*) and the horizontal flute (*sao*) are often capable of playing solo modal improvisations. Normally begun unaccompanied and non-metred, the metred sections, including the playing of relatively fixed named compositions, are organised within metrical cycles articulated by a clapper. Usually the *song lang* (a wooden slit gong with a beater attached to a springy piece of buffalo horn) is used but the *sinh tien*, consisting of three long flat pieces of wood, two of which are hinged, can also be employed. In the case of the latter, the lower piece has teeth cut into its lower side and a separate piece of wood is used to scrape along these teeth, causing several coins mounted on a nail on the upper piece to rattle. The *song lang* clapper plays infrequently, only on certain fixed beats according to the particular cycle.

■ Chamber music

Vietnam is considered to have three regional cultures, the south, central and north, based around Ho Chi Minh City, Hue and Hanoi respectively, each with its own distinctive forms of theatre and chamber music. Though chamber music best exemplifies the idea of 'classical' in Vietnam, none of these are professional activities, with most performers being amateurs who join clubs where the purpose is to sing sophisticated poetry with instrumental accompaniment. In the north, *ca tru* is rarely heard outside club meetings or competitions: the accompaniment is provided by an exceptionally long-necked lute with a trapezoid body called *dan day*, while the singer plays the *phach*, a wooden base struck with two beaters; during the performance a 'critic' responds by beating a small drum and calling out stock praises or criticisms. In the central region, *ca hue* songs are customarily sung on small boats floating on the Perfume River west of Hue, the former imperial city: accompanying musicians, typically five, play the zither, fiddle, various lutes and perhaps a flute and monochord. In addition someone, even a singer, plays a small pair of wooden clappers or a pair of ceramic tea cups. Thanks to tourism in Hue, now a UNESCO World Heritage City, there are public opportunities for hearing *ca hue*, and some performers earn a living playing for tourists. In the south, especially in the Delta of the Nine Dragons (*Cu Long*, or in English the 'Mekong Delta'), the chamber genre is *nhac tai tu* ('music and songs of talented persons'), which is normally encountered in club settings; accompaniment is provided by a small ensemble which may include fiddle, lute, guitar, zither, flute or some other melodic instrument.

Refined though these genres are, both in terms of poetry and music, they are performed by non-professionals including housewives and farmers. As a result, they are viewed by the general public as recreation rather than art, though each genre has its connoisseurs. Outsiders can argue that Vietnam's chamber music meets many of the criteria for classification as a 'classical' music, but perhaps because Vietnam was a colony of France and received the tradition of European music conservatories that taught only Western classical music, few Vietnamese would see the equivalence, or agree to apply the term *classique* to this music.

Guide to pronunciation

Thai. To avoid complication, we do not indicate tone. Words sound according to standard pronunciation except for the following: t, k and p indicate unaspirated sounds, which sound slightly percussive. Th, kh and ph are aspirated and sound as in 'tango', 'can' and 'Paris'. Final consonants are not clearly articulated but spoken *sotto voce*. Thus *piphat* sounds approximately 'bee-pa(t)'. The letter 'u' is sounded as in 'you'. The combination 'ue' approximates the sound of a German *umlaut* as in 'ü'.

Lao. The 'V' in Lao (e.g. in Vientiane) sounds halfway between a 'v' and a 'w'. The 'X' (e.g. in Xieng Khouang) sounds 's'. The combination 'ou' is sounded as in 'you'. Because Lao has no 'r', equivalent words in Thai that have 'r' change to either 'h' or 'l' in Lao; for example, *mahori* (Thai) becomes *maholi* (Lao).

Vietnamese. Although first written in Chinese characters, Vietnamese came to be Romanised in Latin script in the seventeenth century following the work of French Jesuit Alexandre de Rhodes. This system, called *quốc ngữ* or 'national script', is standard today. A complex system, showing both tones and exact pronunciation of consonants and vowels, it still requires readers to know regional pronunciation differences. A 'd' without a horizontal line is 'y' in the south and 'z' in the north, while the 'đ' sounds 'd'. A 't' sounds as an unaspirated 'd'. A 'tr' (as in *dan tranh*) sounds closer to 'ch', while 's' (as in *sao*) sounds 'sh'. A 'ph' (as in *phach*) sounds 'f'.

Further reading

For a variety of reasons – extended wars involving Vietnam, Cambodia and Laos being one of them – there is little scholarship on the court/classical music of mainland Southeast Asia. Vietnam, however, has a long tradition of local scholars (the pioneer being Tran van Khe), which has now expanded to include Western and expatriate scholars as well. Thailand's music was most thoroughly covered, based on the work of David Morton beginning around 1960, although his focus was on analysis rather than the broader musical culture. No one seems to have specialized in the classical music of Laos, while that of Cambodia has been written about primarily by one scholar, Sam-ang Sam, a native of Cambodia. Classical Cambodian dance has attracted far more attention than has the music. The best comprehensive studies are found in the *New Grove Dictionary of Music and Musicians* and *Garland Encyclopedia of World Music* vol. 4 (*Southeast Asia*). Patricia Shehan Campbell has contributed three studies (Thailand, Cambodia and Vietnam) for the classroom, each co-written with a local scholar. Thanks to the old tradition of French scholarship within its 'Indochinese' colonies, numerous studies of dance and music were published during the first half of the twentieth century. Since Morton's retirement, the present author has been the leading scholar writing about Thailand's classical music, and to lesser extents, those of Cambodia and Laos as well.

Recommended listening

▶ *Cambodia*

Cambodge: Musiques du Palais Royal (Années soixante), Ocora C 560034, 1994. Recorded at the palace in 1966 and 1970.

Cambodia/Cambodge: Royal Music/Musique royale, Auvidis D 8011, 1989. Originally recorded in 1971 by Jacques Brunet before the Cambodian holocaust.

Les musiques du Ramayana vol. 2, *Cambodge*, Ocora C 560015, 1990. From the masked dance drama *Reamker* performed in France in 1964.

The Music of Cambodia, vol. 1, *9 Gong Gamelan: Royal Court Music/Solo Instrumental Music*; vol. 2, *Royal Court Music*; vol. 3, *Solo Instrumental Music*, Celestial Harmonies #13074/5/6-2, 1993.

▶ *Laos*

The Music of Laos, Rounder CD 5119, 1999. Reissue of a 1960s vinyl album from Baerenreiter.

Traditional Music of Luang Prabang (2 CDs), Bangkok: College of Music, Mahidol University, 2000.

Laos: Musique de l'ancienne cour de Luang Prabang/Music of the Ancient Royal Court of Luang Prabang/Tiao Phün Muang, VDE–Gallo CD-1213, 2008. The restored music of the former court in Luang Prabang, but the musicianship is modest.

▶ *Thailand*

Thai Classical Music Performed by the Prasit Thawon Ensemble, Nimbus NI 5412, 1994. The *piphat mai kaeng* (hard mallet) ensemble is led by national artist Prasit Thawon.

Royal Court Music of Thailand, Smithsonian-Folkways #40413, 1994.

Siamese Classical Music, vol. 1, *The Piphat Ensemble before 1400 AD*; vol. 2, *The Piphat Ensemble 1351–1767 AD*; vol. 3, *The String Ensemble*; vol. 4, *The Piphat Sepha*; vol. 5, *The Mahori Orchestra*, Marco Polo 8.223197–8.223200 and 8.223493, 1991–2 and 1994.

▶ *Vietnam*

Eternal Voices: Traditional Vietnamese Music in the United States (2 CDs), New Alliance NAR CD 053, 1993. Recordings of Vietnamese musicians in the United States with extensive notes by Phong Nguyen and Terry Miller.

Viêt-Nam: Le dàn tranh: Musiques d'hier et d'aujourd'hui, Ocora C 560055, 1994.

The Perfume River Traditional Ensemble, *Music from the Lost Kingdom: Hue, Vietnam*, Lyrichord LYRCD 7440, 1998.

Vietnam: Mother Mountain and Father Sea: An Introduction to the Traditional Music of Vietnam (6 CDs), White Cliffs Media, 2003. Covering all regions of Vietnam including the Central Highlands, with a 48-page booklet by Phong Nguyen and Terry Miller.

Gamelan gongs are made from an alloy of ten parts copper to three parts tin, and are filed to a golden colour. The exception is the biggest gong *(left)* which is left in its black state, with the marks from the hammer blows still visible.

2 Java

Neil Sorrell

A crowd of men, women and children are gathered in a courtyard, and more are in the street, squeezing into the gateway and sitting on the walls, or in rickshaws which have stopped for the show. An array of instruments – large and small gongs, xylophones, keyed metallophones, a bowed instrument, a bamboo flute – is spread out on the raised stone floor of a pavilion where a woman sings; players not absorbed in the music smoke and chat on the fringes. The only real light on this hot dark night is projected onto a white sheet stretched on a carved wooden frame at which a man sits, moving flat leather puppets of fantastical shapes while speaking their parts and singing songs; he also directs the gamelan, as this collection of instruments is known. At times one single instrument creates a shimmering background; at others the group produces loud snatches of repetitively-twirling melody. The musicians don't use notation but watch the screen, laughing uproariously with the audience at the comic bits. Shows like this traditionally last all night without a break, with the puppeteer being the only one never to leave his place. The spectators come and go freely, knowing the story and format so well that they can decide which parts to watch, and when to go somewhere to doze, lulled by the background music which fuses magically with the buzzing and humming of insects.

On a visit to Java in 1971 I stayed with a cultured and musical family. The father listened for hours to gamelan music on the radio, and extolled its subtlety and power. Among the many beautiful ways he found to describe it, the most memorable was 'like raindrops falling from leaves after a shower'. Writing in 1937, the Dutch author Leonhard Huizinga gave a similarly poetic description: 'There are only two things one can compare it with: moonlight, and running water. It is pure and mysterious like moonlight; it is always the same and yet always changing, like running water.'[1] The aquatic metaphor common to both descriptions is not far-fetched, as at least one sound in the gamelan actually has an aquatic origin. One of the drums derives its name, and many of the sounds it produces, from *ciblon*,[2] a game in which children slap the surface of water. Despite being a percussion orchestra, the gamelan produces sounds that are essentially fluid, with legato holding sway over staccato.

The documented history of the modern gamelan begins in the eighteenth century, but its history is commonly held to stretch back to mythological times, when the god Sang Hyang Guru allegedly made a gong to summon the other gods. To permit further messages, two more gongs were added, and this three-note ensemble formed the nucleus of the first gamelan (*Lokananta*). The word 'gong' may have originated in Java, but the instrument almost certainly did not, although its origins are uncertain: locations as far apart as China and Greece have been proposed. What is beyond doubt is that gongs have reached an unsurpassed state of refinement in Java, with the gamelan including gongs of all shapes and sizes, and the largest being the most revered. What sound could be more grave, majestic and portentous than that of a large gong?

But 'gamelan' refers to many different kinds of ensemble in Java, Bali and other parts of Indonesia and Malaysia. And within Java there are significant differences between the ensemble from Central Java[3] discussed in this chapter, and the smaller Gamelan *Degung* of Sunda (the region of West Java around the city of Bandung). Meanwhile Bali, the much smaller island to the east, vibrates to the shimmering sounds of its own huge variety of gamelans including the *Gong Kebyar*, *Semar Pegulingan* and *Angklung* ensembles. Despite a shared Hindu-Javanese culture until the sixteenth century (when Muslim rule in Java led many nobles to resettle in Bali) the Javanese and Balinese styles have evolved to be immediately distinctive, with enormous changes over the past hundred years. Balinese gamelan music tends to be loud and fast, and it relies on rapid interlocking rhythmic patterns that require great skill and accuracy. The Central Javanese gamelan, variously referred to as Gamelan *Jawa*, Gamelan *Ageng*, and sometimes even Gamelan *Klasik*, is the best-known in the world, with a core repertoire of 'classical' pieces plus a variety of recent popular compositions.

The gamelan exists in royal courts and the poorest villages; it is played by amateurs and professionals, children and adults; it is used for the most refined and spiritual of ceremonies, and for the bawdiest of parties. In its full form it is probably the world's largest instrumental ensemble after the symphony orchestra, but there is a crucial distinction between the two. As is often observed, the orchestra is an ensemble of players, but the gamelan is an ensemble of instruments. When a symphony concert has ended, the stage is bare, but the gamelan remains in its place after the players have departed. Moreover, the same gamelan will be played by different musicians over several generations, but it retains its sound, appearance and character. This helps explain why it functions as a cultural emblem, telling us much about Javanese concepts of ownership and communal artistic activity. The performance described at the start of this chapter is called a *wayang*, and it brings Javanese people together in a way which transcends all barriers of social class.

The foundations of Javanese culture were laid down 1,700 years ago, with a thousand years of Hindu and Buddhist kingdoms establishing much of today's language, mythology and religion. The ancient Hindu-Buddhist civilisation is still proudly visible: the Buddhist stupa of Borobudur and the Hindu temple complex at Prambanan – both well over a thousand years old – are in their general shape and detailed carvings almost indistinguishable from their Indian models. Moreover, Javanese wayang and dance draw on the Mahabharata and Ramayana, the great Hindu epics which are as well known in Java as they are in India. Some of the terminology of Javanese gamelan music (for example *nada* or note, *rasa* or feeling) as well as the names of some pieces (for example,

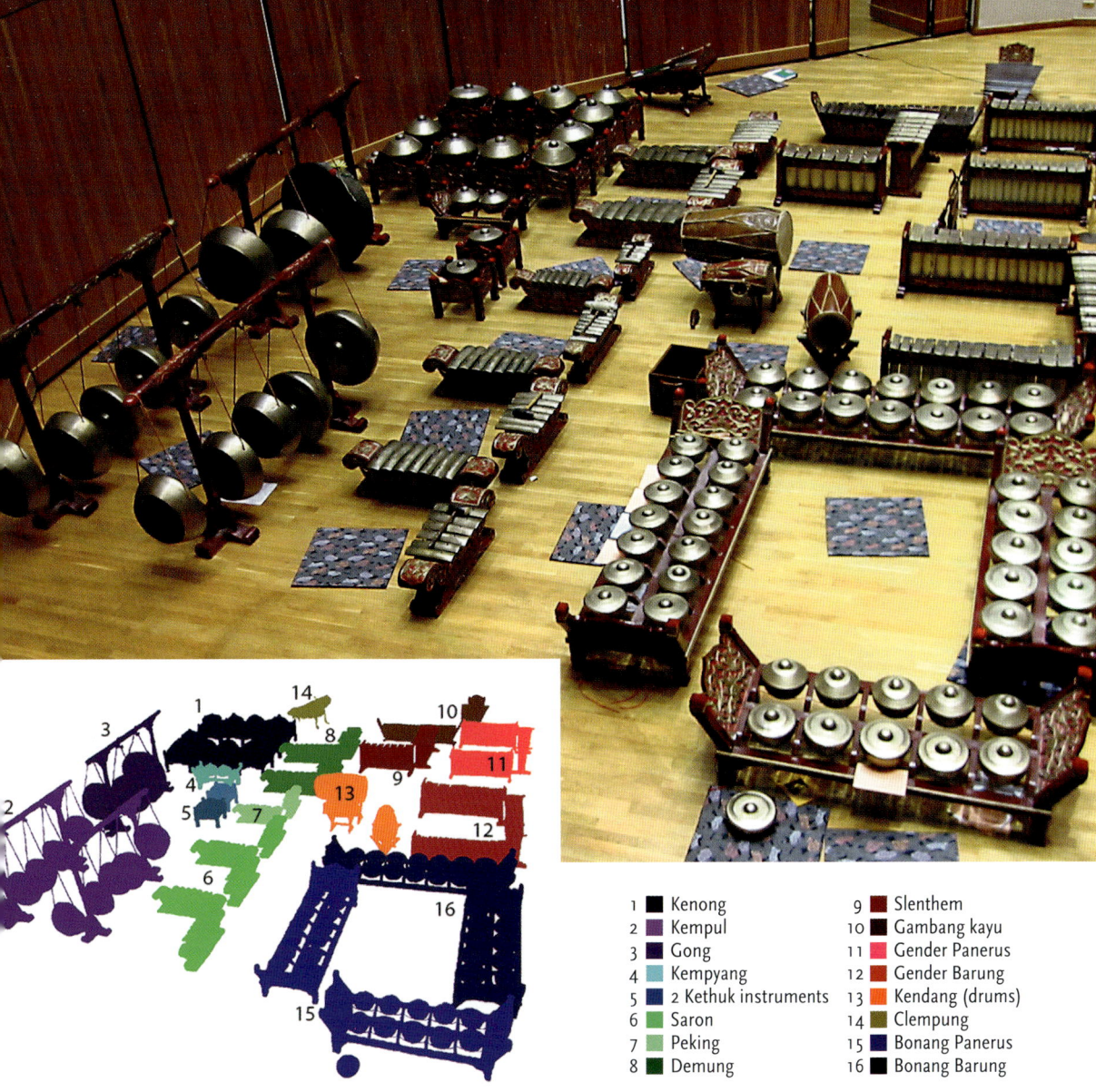

1 ■ Kenong	9 ■ Slenthem
2 ■ Kempul	10 ■ Gambang kayu
3 ■ Gong	11 ■ Gender Panerus
4 ■ Kempyang	12 ■ Gender Barung
5 ■ 2 Kethuk instruments	13 ■ Kendang (drums)
6 ■ Saron	14 ■ Clempung
7 ■ Peking	15 ■ Bonang Panerus
8 ■ Demung	16 ■ Bonang Barung

The Javanese gamelan 'Kyai Telaga Rukmi' at the University of Wisconsin-Madison, with a key to the instruments

Puspawarna, meaning kinds of flowers) is derived from Sanskrit, which influenced both the modern Javanese language and also the archaic form used in a wayang.

The arrival of Islam in the fifteenth century, and the subsequent European trading contacts – Portuguese, then the Dutch colonialists attracted by the spice trade – caused significant power shifts in Java, from whence the migration of nobles mentioned earlier helped ensure that to this day Bali remains a predominantly Hindu island. Even in modern Indonesia, home to the largest Muslim population in the world, the Hindu-Javanese legacy and the indigenous

This photograph, taken by Kassian Cephas at Yogyakarta in 1888, shows a traditional gamelan set up for a shadow-puppet performance at the annual Sekaten festival.

animist religions pre-dating the advent of Hinduism still permeate the arts. And this applies to Java, with its Muslim majority and sizeable Christian minority as well. Some of the surviving ceremonial gamelans in Javanese palaces are used only for specific rituals and ceremonies, or dates in the religious calendar, with the best example being the Gamelan *Sekatèn*, which is reserved for commemorations of the Prophet Muhammad's birth and death. These gamelans comprise far fewer instruments than the typical Central Javanese kind, but the instruments (larger gong chimes and keys of the metallophone group) are bigger, supporting the theory that the gamelan evolved from a small ensemble of large instruments to a large ensemble of relatively smaller ones. Wayangs accompanied by the modern gamelan are often closely connected with birthdays, weddings and inaugurations of important enterprises, but they also celebrate Java's distant past, going back beyond the Hindu period to animist worship of spirits and ancestors; in villages they mark key stages of the agricultural cycle.

In 1755 the Dutch instigated the partition of the Mataram kingdom, last of the great independent Javanese empires, which took its name from the region around present-day Yogyakarta. With partition came the establishment of the Javanese *kratons* (courts) of Surakarta (Solo) and Yogyakarta (Jogja), just thirty-five miles apart. Later two additional minor courts were created, one in each city (the *Mangkunegaran* in Solo and the *Pakualaman* in Jogja) and all four survive to the present day. As military and political power passed to the Dutch, the Javanese courts devoted their attention to the arts, and much of what is performed to this day derives from these centres of patronage. The rivalries between them served as catalysts of artistic excellence and prevented standardisation, the avoidance of which is still a key feature of gamelan music. Although the political influence of the courts never recovered after Dutch rule, the remarkable fact is that all four courts have survived under the modern Republic of Indonesia. They now thrive both as tourist attractions and as centres of performance, and remain significant centres of patronage for gamelan players, whose other sources of income are independent performances, radio work and teaching. There are noticeable differences of instrumentation and performance practice even within the typical Central Javanese gamelan, and the expert eye and ear will immediately tell the difference between a set from Solo and one from Jogja: the instrumentation may be different, as may the shapes of the wooden troughs of the metallophones (raised at the ends in Jogja, but flat in Solo), though the sound will remain roughly the same.

■ Form, shape, function

The gamelan is mostly comprised of knobbed gongs of two main shapes, plus families of keyed metallophones, which is how instruments that are more like xylophones are usually described. These are sets of thin plates or thicker bars, suspended respectively over tube or trough resonators. Those of the thick bar and trough resonator family are played with a single, uncovered *tabuh* or wooden mallet, whereas all other mallets in the gamelan (used for thin plates over individual tube-resonators, as well as all gongs) are padded, mostly with cloth rings or string, but with thicker padding for the large hanging gongs.

The preferred gamelan metal is a special bronze alloy called *gangsa* which is usually ten parts copper to three parts tin, and the craft of manufacturing instruments, especially the gongs, is as steeped in Javanese tradition as the music itself. Cheaper metals like iron are often used, though these do not require the unique skills essential to bronze-working. Unlike bells, the gongs cannot be cast, but must be hammered into shape from a disc hardly wider than a dinner plate. Nowhere else are these instruments produced with such precise mixtures of copper and tin, and with such carefully calibrated heating in a furnace, hammering for hours, and finally tuning by further hammering and filing; the protracted filing process transforms the black bronze, pock-marked from the hammer-blows, into its beautiful golden colour. In many gamelans the largest gong is left in its black state, with the marks from the hammer blows clearly visible, except for the central knob which is filed to a smooth finish. Fine tuning is mostly achieved by cold-hammering, a highly skilled process, plus further filing.

The craftsmen making gamelans and the players of the finished instruments have much in common, with the same men sometimes fulfilling both functions; both skills depend on teamwork, and craftsmen and gamelan players routinely exchange jobs. Some craftsmen take names according to their particular job, or use ones from Javanese mythology (a notable example being Panji, a legendary

Javanese prince, for the man who has the very important job of turning gongs in the fire), so the work may take on the aura of a ceremony. 'Gamelan' can literally mean hammering, or handling,[4] a fact which further connects manufacturing process and musical product.

The instrumental groups of a gamelan perform specific functions, and their dense polyphony is created from just one melodic strand, drawing from a repertoire of patterns peculiar to each instrument. (An example of how this occurs will be provided later.) The whole gamelan can be divided in various ways. Two binary divisions are made according to tuning (to be examined later) and dynamics ('loud' and 'soft' instruments), but these criteria give little sense of how the music works, or of the function of each instrument. For that purpose a division into three broad functions is usually proposed: a central group of around five metallophones, which plays a simplified outline of the core melody – the *balungan,* or skeleton – on which the entire piece is based; a group of horizontally and vertically suspended tuned gongs at the rear, which mark the phrase structure of the melody; and a diverse group of instruments at the front, collectively referred to as the *panerusan,* which elaborate the melody by performing faster patterns around it, each pattern derived from the repertoire of the individual instruments, and dictated by the structure and motion of the main melody. The *bonang*s (double rows of small gongs supported in bed-like racks) perform the main elaborations in loud music, and also play in soft styles. Elaborating instruments tend to anticipate the balungan, rather than follow it: the destination of a phrase is in the minds and music of the players long before the balungan reaches it. The principal elaborating instruments (panerusan), which give the music its subtle polyphonic density, are nearly all soft instruments (incapable of playing loud), and are thus placed at the front of the gamelan to enhance their audibility. As the loud instruments may also be played softly, the full gamelan texture will include them regardless of dynamic, while soft panerusan instruments will drop out of loud music. Within this group are the bronze *gendèr barung,* or simply gender, with its smaller version gender *panerus,* metallophones that delicately trace intricate parts using two padded mallets. The soft group also includes some important instruments which are neither metal – such as the *gambang* (wooden xylophone) – nor classified as percussion (i.e. instruments struck with mallets), such as the *suling* (end-blown bamboo flute), *celempung* and smaller *siter* (both plucked stringed instruments). The set of hand-beaten drums (*kendhang*) which directs the tempo and cues transitions is not part of the panerusan, and plays in all gamelan music, whether loud or soft. Prominent within the panerusan is the two-stringed bowed *rebab,* which often functions as melodic leader of the ensemble: despite its importance in the modern gamelan, this is a relatively recent addition, and – retaining its Arabic name to this day – probably arrived from the Middle East in the sixteenth century, as Islam gained ascendancy in Java. The subsequent combination of soft and loud instruments created the modern full gamelan, with the rebab centre-stage.

Another reason for the rebab's special status is the centrality of vocal lines, for which it is the ideal companion. The typical line-up of singers consists of three or four men singing a pre-composed chorus (*gérongan*) with which the gamelan players may join in, plus a female singer (*pesindhèn*) who weaves quasi-improvisatory lines. The voice gained steadily in importance alongside the rebab: the pesindhen is now the nearest thing to a soloist, and is usually the only performer to be named. Not only does her solo line stand out (often with the aid of amplification), but she is also the only woman in a traditionally male environment. These days women increasingly play gamelan, and a small team of pesindhèn often take it in turns to sing, so the lone female is a less common sight.

All instruments played with mallets require damping, except for the largest gongs. This is easily achieved if only one mallet is used, with the free hand damping the key by pinching it between the forefinger and thumb as the next one is struck, or holding the gong steady while gently pressing the mallet against the central knob that has just been struck. The gambang requires no damping as the sound from the wooden keys decays rapidly. In the case of the genders, the thumbs, little fingers and the side of the hand (whatever is not used to hold the mallets) must control the damping, so that four things happen simultaneously: the two mallets produce two lines of music while the rest of the hands damp each line. While the gamelan is usually thought of as an egalitarian ensemble, where all contribute to the sound and none should dominate or even be considered more important, some instruments make greater demands on the player's technique and musical knowledge than others. But this enhances the gamelan's attractiveness as a mixed-ability ensemble: novices can join in and, when ready to face greater challenges, can graduate to other instruments. The formalised sonic architecture of the full gamelan gives acoustic cohesion to the music, and the fixed relationship between instrument and function helps memorisation of an entire repertoire. It also gives the sound and texture of gamelan music a particular stability: once the piece begins, it maintains its texture with very limited dynamic changes; there are almost no silences in gamelan music.

■ *Performance*

Palaces and wealthy households have *pendhapa*, special pavilions designed to house gamelans. With their concave roofs and hard marble floors these create the ideal acoustics, in which the sounds blend well and with no instrument or voice predominating; it is sometimes said that a gamelan is one instrument played by many, and that is how it should sound. But now gamelans are mostly played in more modest, less reverberant surroundings, from village halls to little more than shacks. Gamelan concerts do take place – though these tend to be more of an informal playing session, *klenèngan*, than a Western concert – but the main function of this music is to accompany a ceremony or theatrical performance involving dance or puppetry.

The combination of the gamelan's mythological origin – as a signalling system invented by the gods – with residual animist beliefs in which objects may have spirits, helps explain why gamelans may be revered, and why some, especially in the royal courts, are regarded as *pusaka*, or sacred heirlooms. This

The metallophone *(right, in its Balinese form)* is at the heart of the gamelan: sets of thin plates or thicker bars, suspended over tube or trough resonators.

sacred element should not be over-emphasised – lest the gamelan be falsely regarded as symbiotically tied to a specific religion – but respect for it must also be shown by non-Javanese players, who are instructed to remove their shoes and never step over instruments (which would imply an uncouth individual dominion over a communal object). And in Java such considerate behaviour is not reserved for the gamelan: it is expected in everyday comportment. The word *alus* (smooth) lies at the heart of Javanese ideas of culture, education and self-control: it denotes refinement, calm, restraint, subtle allusion and understatement rather than brazen directness. It can be seen in Javanese dances and wayang shadow plays, where the alus hero will remain calm, engage in periods of meditation and preserve his inner strength by avoiding excessive outbursts or losing control. This principle governs most of the gamelan repertoire, although it also includes more raucous and catchy items. The general term for gamelan music is *karawitan*, which is closely related in meaning to alus. Another ideal, linked to the importance attached by the Javanese to meditation, is *iklas*, a kind of detachment and mental repose. These qualities are reflected in the music, where abrupt contrasts and harsh noise are usually avoided, and they make ideal criteria for 'classical' in the Javanese sense, as does another Javanese term, *adi luhung* (beautiful and glorious).[5] Yet since the dramas have their clowns, ogres and villains, the music must sometimes erupt into raucousness.

■ Tuning Systems

Each gamelan has its own spirit and personality, and many sets are given names. Some of these are enigmatic, like the famous old Gamelan *Kyai Kanyut Mèsem* ('Revered and moved to smile') in the Mangkunegaran palace in Solo; others are more explicit, like Gamelan *Sekar Petak* ('White flower'), made in 1981 to reside in the English city of York. The age, appearance and quality of the carving of the metal and wood – and even the colours or oils applied to the wooden frames – can vary considerably, but what gives a gamelan its acoustic personality is its tuning. The two unique tuning systems of Java (*laras sléndro* and *laras pélog*) are consensual rather than standardised, thus no two gamelans are tuned identically. These tunings define karawitan (gamelan music) even more than the instruments themselves. Laras sléndro is a pentatonic tuning in which the intervals are more or less equidistant (between a whole tone and minor third), thus distancing it quite radically from the pentatonic scale produced on the black notes of the Western keyboard. Laras pélog is also conceived as pentatonic but has seven available notes, from which three pentatonic sets can be extracted.[6] The intervals of the pélog heptatonic set vary quite widely, from ones little bigger than a semitone to others close to a minor third. A gamelan in just one laras (tuning) is perfectly viable, though what is commonly described as a complete gamelan is generally assumed to have both, necessitating a set of instruments for each laras. To work as an integrated set, the two tunings must coincide on one pitch, which can serve as a pivotal note (*tumbuk*) when changing from one tuning to the other.

Within each tuning are three sub-tonalities or *pathet*, a word suggesting constraint or limitation, and the constituent notes of the two tunings are organised into three pathets per tuning: pathet *nem*, pathet *sanga* and pathet *manyura* in sléndro and pathet *lima*, pathet *nem* and pathet *barang* in pélog. Pathet is one of the glories of karawitan, focusing the available pitches of the gamelan and giving them nuance, depth and subtlety, but its complexities make it the hardest aspect to define and describe. Even the Javanese have difficulty in explaining it, if not in grasping it intuitively: it must be absorbed over time, so that it becomes more instinctive than intellectual, but it is based on the principle of hierarchy. If the tonic can shift from one note to another (and with it the dominant) the whole character of the pentatonic set will change. Javanese theory does have a concept equivalent to tonic and dominant, and the Javanese ear is finely tuned to these different ways of organising the notes so that their relative strength changes. We should therefore talk of *a* pentatonic mode (varied according to pathet) rather than *the* pentatonic scale.

The tonal shift just described, affecting the hierarchy of pitches, impinges on extra-musical features such as mood and time of performance. The pathets reflect the passage of time through the day or night, and even the life cycle. First comes sléndro pathet nem, with its corresponding pélog pathet lima, representing youth; then sléndro pathet sanga, with its corresponding pélog pathet nem, reflecting the transition to adulthood; and finally sléndro pathet manyura, with its corresponding pélog pathet barang, for the wisdom of old age. The attendant moods, however, do not progress in the same way – in fact they seem to reverse what one might expect: sléndro pathet nem/pélog pathet lima have a low tessitura and fairly sombre mood; sléndro pathet sanga/pélog pathet nem have a higher tessitura and brighter mood; sléndro pathet manyura/ pélog pathet barang have the highest tessitura and brightest mood. In short, while pathet may seem to behave like tonality it is actually much closer to a modal system, in which note hierarchies, moods and times of performance are significant. Different keys (Western tonalities) depend on emphasising different notes from within the twelve semitones; sléndro uses exactly the same five pitches but, as it were, alters the viewing angles and perspective. A similar notion applies to the pathets of pélog, though the process of taking different pentatonic sets from the available seven notes makes the task of distinguishing between the pathets much easier. In fact, the five-note set within sléndro can be expanded by adding 'chromatic' notes to certain pieces; such notes, absent from the basic pentatonic set to which most instruments are pre-tuned, can only be produced vocally or on the rebab. This practice, known as barang *miring* (oblique), is restricted to a few pieces, and its effect is to change the mood from happy to sad.

■ The canon

Just as terms like 'symphony' and 'concerto' automatically suggest classical music to Europeans, in Java the word *gendhing* fulfils a similar role. It can be a generic word for a gamelan piece, but it is also used to describe the largest and noblest compositions, as opposed to the shorter forms in the traditional canon and the catchy, popular pieces that have come to occupy an important position in the repertoire. The large gendhing are also closely associated with court music, as they mostly originated in the palaces; they are nearly always in two main sections, each repeated several times. A common practice is to attach shorter pieces to the initial large gendhing to make a kind of continuous suite which can last from twenty minutes to over an hour. The most important determinant of duration is tempo, and what in Javanese gamelan music is known as *irama*, which is not quite the same thing as tempo but rather a system of tempo relationships.

The simplest way to understand this is to consider simply the core melody (balungan). As its tempo slows down, the time-gaps between its notes lengthen, allowing the elaborating instruments to fill in the gaps with more notes. Thus in the faster irama (where the balungan is moving most quickly) an elaborating instrument may only have time to play two notes per one of the balungan. When the music slows down to the next irama, the same elaborating instrument will play four notes per one of the balungan; in the next irama eight, and so on. There are essentially five irama, working in this system of ratios. Each can move within a wide range of tempi; it is only when the ratios change that the irama changes. A useful analogy can be made with the gears of a car: a range of speeds is tolerated in one gear, but at a certain point in slowing down or accelerating a change of gear – hence ratios within the mechanism – becomes necessary. Moreover, while some gamelan instruments may be playing four notes per one of balungan, others may be doubling that to eight, yet the whole ensemble is still playing in the same irama, since two or more are not recognised as occurring simultaneously.

How the musicians respond to irama, but also to pathet and everything else that is fundamental to the organisation of gamelan music, is a key aspect of performance. In the absence of scores and parts, the musicians must know not only the balungan but also how to create their parts and relate them to it. This practice of realisation is known as *garapan,* or 'process of working'. While admitting a certain amount of freedom, this is not quite improvisation, as the player of each elaborating instrument must choose an appropriate pattern according to the pathet and irama from the available repertoire for that particular instrument.

Another feature of gendhing is sung poetry. (A small but important group of gendhing, using relatively few instruments, have no singing, but the bulk of classical pieces feature parts for the solo female singer and male chorus.) Vocal music has influenced the composition of many instrumental gendhing, and Javanese gamelan music has come to feature singing more and more, with the female soloist emerging as a star. Song texts are based on the old Javanese poetic metres and deal with noble and elevated topics. Perhaps the most famous of all begins with the line 'Parabé Sang Marabangun' ('The name of the noble king Marabangun'). Another frequently sung text begins 'Nalikanira ing dalu wong agung mangsah semedi' ('In the night a great man meditated'). Around midnight, at a crucial point in the wayang shadow play, the dhalang (puppeteer) sings a chant containing the words roughly translated as 'the prayers of the wise priests grace the witching hour'. The status of many texts and melodies is further enhanced by their ascription to the rulers of the Javanese courts. For example, the well-known *Puspawarna* (mentioned earlier for its Sanskrit-derived title, with a notated extract given later in this chapter) is attributed to Mangkunegara IV (reigned 1853–81), and is still used in the Mangkunegaran palace to announce the ruler's entrance. The modern, popular style of gamelan music, characterised by shorter pieces with catchy tunes, by contrast uses humorous texts or ones that deal with everyday life, and may even carry government propaganda. Such pieces are great favourites in wayang performances, especially in clowning episodes.

Notation

Gamelan has always been an oral tradition. Although notation systems emerged in the nineteenth century, with a more recent one found throughout the global gamelan diaspora, notation is never used in performance by experienced Javanese musicians, who rely on their memory and spontaneous creativity. They will have learnt the art in childhood by observation and imitation. One often sees children taking over a gamelan when the adults have left, and trying to reproduce what has just been played. Notation is used to teach beginners in schools and music colleges, and also to preserve a canon of melodic outlines and complex patterns, but it is never used for anything like a full score.[7] Even with unfamiliar modern compositions that disrupt the traditional functions of the instruments and other stabilising forces such as pathet, musicians will either learn the work orally or, if they must use notation, dispense with it at the first opportunity. The more competent they are, the more they will memorise everything they need, including the balungan. This ability enhances the process of mutual listening, which in turn ensures cohesion and a refined sense of ensemble.

The peripheral status of notation is also reflected in the fact that the cipher system ubiquitously encountered for gamelan is only one hundred years old. Its name, *kepatihan*, comes from the compound in Solo serving as residence for the equivalent of prime minister to the court. The musician and theorist R. L. Martopangrawit (1914–86) said that before notation was invented, musicians would learn gendhing through humming.[8] In fact they still do, and it is common to hear a musician hum the main melody (or a kind of composite line that brings as much of the ensemble together as humming can achieve) while playing another part against it.[9] The greatest virtue of the kepatihan system is simplicity, and it can be mastered in minutes. By assigning a number to each pitch, the music can be speedily notated without further need to specify precise intonation (which would not work in a musical culture that prides itself on pitch variability from one gamelan to another). But complex rhythms are harder to capture, and dynamics and tempo are not usually indicated. Above all, the notation is confined to what can most easily be notated: it acts as a reference point from which to construct a whole piece.

Earlier a 'core melody' was mentioned, on which the entire piece is based: this corresponds to the European *cantus firmus* or 'nuclear melody'. The Javanese term balungan has found almost universal acceptance, partly because its literal meaning (skeleton) captures the essence so well. But debate has focused on the nature and role of this melody, and the mistakenness of assuming it to be the main melody. In some contexts, especially very slow music, it is barely recognisable as a melody at all, and is better described as points along the path of more complex melodic strands. But because it outlines the melodic flux, and gives musicians a basis on which to construct their parts – and is the only line

Gamelan tradition has shown remarkable continuity, as evidenced by this eighteenth-century manuscript *(above left)* and by photographs of K. P. H. Notoprojo, a renowned Javanese performer *(above right)*, and the Sunda gamelan led by Uking Sukri and Ono Sukarna in 1972 *(below)*.

played by more than one instrument – it is the part that is notated and preserved to represent the piece.

In the kepatihan system, each note is given a number. In the examples below, the numbers refer to the notes in the sléndro tuning. The pélog heptatonic set is simply numbered from 1 to 7; the five sléndro notes are numbered from 1 to 6 (low to high), omitting note 4. (The reason is that the notes also have names which predate the cipher notation system: for example note 2 is called *gulu*, note 3 *dhadha* and note 5 *lima* in both sléndro and pélog. Thus the numbering and nomenclature correspond, and note 4 is treated as a feature of pélog alone.) The balungan melody can thus be shown as a sequence of numbers. Dots between notes can be rests, but usually double the duration of the previous note; dots below notes indicate the lower octave; those above indicate the higher octave; those without dots, the middle octave. This information is necessary for the elaborating instruments, though not for the ones actually playing the balungan, as they must fit it within their one-octave range. Thus no one actually plays the balungan exactly as notated below.

The simplicity of the kepatihan system and the minimal nature of what is chosen for notation mean that several hundred pieces can be preserved in as many pages or less. Housed in the music academies from which they emanated, and also online or on the shelves of gamelan enthusiasts around the world, this body of pieces has assumed the status of a canon.

▪ Notation and theory in practice: a case study

To demonstrate briefly the workings of melody, formal organisation, and other theoretical concepts discussed, as well as the kepatihan notation, the following examples give a snapshot from a well-known traditional gamelan piece, *Ketawang Puspawarna* (mentioned earlier in this chapter).[10] The title gives the formal organisation (ketawang) found in several pieces, and also the Javanese name of this composition, which is from Sanskrit: *pushpa* (flower); *varna* (variety or colour). It is a kind of love-song to the harem of the ruler (Mangkunegara IV), as the different flowers listed in the nine verses of the complete text celebrate feminine virtues and attributes, though this can be extended to human ideals in general, and even to the nine rasas (sentiments) of ancient Indian aesthetics. Example 2.1 shows the extract in the kepatihan notation, as it might appear in collections of gamelan pieces: normally this would be just an outline, showing the balungan (by numbers) and main phrase-marking instruments (by symbols).

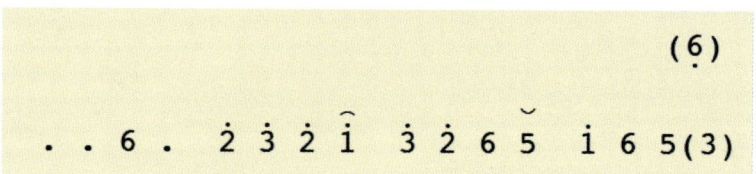

EX. 2.1 *Ketawang Puspawarna laras sléndro pathet manyura*: the opening of the second section (*ngelik*) in kepatihan notation

While simple and instantly intelligible to gamelan players, this pared-down example requires further explanation for the lay reader, which is given below in the fleshed-out version. In kepatihan notation, the balungan melody is set apart in four-beat units (which flow on in the same tempo). Each unit, or *gatra*, forms a crucial structural element in the music, enabling musicians to work out their parts from its shape and its final, cadential note. For that reason, the gaps between gatras assist reading and analysis.

The representation by numbers has only one disadvantage (apart from its unfamiliarity to those outside the gamelan community) compared with staff notation: a series of numbers cannot convey the shape and contours of melodies graphically. Thus an adapted staff notation has been devised to show the same extract from *Ketawang Puspawarna* (Example 2.3 overleaf), with the addition of some of the main elaborating instruments and voices. As the piece is in the sléndro tuning, its five notes fit conveniently on to the five lines of the staff, and even their (approximate) equidistance is maintained. The principle also applies to ledger lines, preserving the equidistant pattern, though without the octave equivalents of a normal staff. No clef is given, however, in order to avoid an association with precise pitches of the European system, and drawing attention to the anomaly just mentioned. Example 2.2 shows the pitches required for this extract.

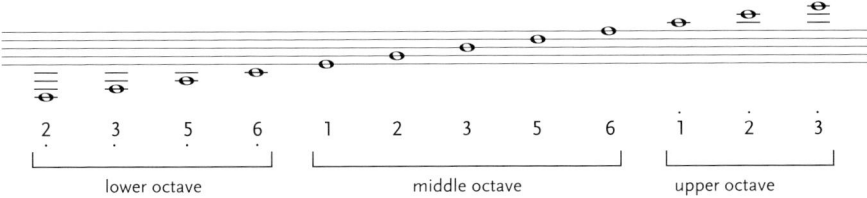

EX. 2.2 Sléndro pitches on a staff

To save space and excessive detail, this extract is presented as it might be performed by the chamber gamelan known as *gadhon*, comprising one balungan instrument (*slenthem*) and the main soft elaborating instruments: the rebab; the gendèr barung (a metallophone played with both hands); the gambang (a xylophone, also played with both hands). While greatly reduced, the ensemble preserves the main layers of the music (the central balungan with its supporting phrase-marking structure, and overlay of different elaborations, plus a simple vocal line) and adequately conveys the essence of the music. Note that the balungan is written as it would be played (on the one-octave slenthem) rather than in its true register as shown in Example 2.1 above. The phrase-marking instruments would probably be restricted to just the large gong *ageng* but in this example the others – *kenong, kethuk-kempyang* and *kempul* – have been added as they require so little space in the notation. They are indicated above or below the balungan by the following symbols:

      ( )   gong ageng (largest hanging gong)
      ^   kenong (gongs supported from beneath)

THE OTHER CLASSICAL MUSICS

EX. 2.3 *Ketawang Puspawarna laras sléndro pathet manyura*: the opening of the second section (*ngelik*) in modified staff notation

v   kempul (smaller hanging gongs)
+   kethuk (smaller gongs supported from beneath)
o   kempyang (paired with the kethuk)

The gong ageng (with the kenong) marks the end of each cycle or main section (comprising sixteen beats in the ketawang form); the kenong also marks the halfway point, which the kempul subdivides in the second half of the cycle; the kethuk sounds on the second beat of each gatra, sandwiched by strokes on its higher-pitched companion, the kempyang; the male chorus (gérongan) is also included. The words of this extract translate as 'Flower of the *kencur* [possibly to suggest a young girl or virgin] always spoken of with enchantment'.

The irama of this extract is irama *dados*, in which the balungan moves quite slowly (about one beat every two seconds), allowing the gendèr barung to fit four notes per one of balungan and the nimbler gambang twice that number. This shows the complexity of gamelan polyphony, which is often described simplistically as heterophony, meaning different versions of the same melody occurring simultaneously at different speeds. The lines of the rebab, gendèr barung and gambang show how much more it is than that; at the same time the relationship between the rebab and gérongan shows the occasional heterophonic imitation. Otherwise what happens is a series of lines which converge with the balungan at important structural points, but otherwise diverge in varying degrees from it. The extract starts and ends with a stroke on the gong ageng, marking the principal section endings, and all parts meet on the gong notes 6 at the beginning and 3 at the end. These notes of special emphasis are also most prominent in the hierarchy of the pathet (manyura) of this piece. All parts again converge on note 1 at the kenong (∧) which marks the halfway point, and also on note 5 when the next most significant phrase-marking gong, the kempul (v) sounds.

A pair of kendhang (drums) would normally be included, but since they are not melodic and their part is notated as a series of symbols unfamiliar to the non-player, they have not been included in Example 2.3.

■ Music theory

Despite its long and rich literary tradition, Java has no comparable legacy of musical studies, and those texts that do enjoy quasi-classical status do not delve deeply into music theory, and are mainly of recent origin (since the early nineteenth century). Music theory gathered momentum in the early twentieth century, when Javanese intellectuals formulated an equivalent to the European music theory of the Dutch colonialists. In the independent Republic of Indonesia (proclaimed in 1945) the establishment of music schools and academies created an even more fertile ground for the theoretical study of music as well as its practice.

The process of garapan – creating a piece from just the balungan (a line that at times becomes so sparse that one may wonder how it can be used as the basis for such rich polyphony) – points to the existence of accepted conventions, which can be described as a kind of music theory. The performers are thus not only players and singers but also analysts and theorists in action, and vice versa: analysts and theorists are expected to perform. This gives rise to an interesting issue in gamelan music. At the beginning of my studies I was taught that the monumental *Music in Java* (first published in 1934 as *De toonkunst van Java*) by the Dutch scholar Jaap Kunst (1891–1960) was marred only by the fact that the author did not play the gamelan and was thus basing his information on the written and spoken words of others. His student the American ethnomusicologist Mantle Hood (1918–2005), who coined the term 'bi-musicality', placed learning through playing at the heart of his gamelan program at UCLA, and his ideology has become the norm. The criticism of Kunst did not take into account the fact that he was a fine musician; what prevented him from playing was the attitude prevalent in that colonial era – a Dutch official could not sit down with the Javanese and play their music. This kind of criticism also ignored the contribution of Javanese 'non-playing captains' who, around the same time as Kunst, spearheaded a nationalist music theory. In their work, the noun 'classicisation' (a conscious, active process, motivated by national assertiveness as well as intellectual curiosity) is perhaps of greater significance than the familiar and relatively inert adjective 'classical'. Furthermore, theory and notation can empower those who formulate and use them, as they imply a literate elite, and even intellect over intuition.[11]

■ Today

Javanese gamelan music has achieved a longevity comparable to that of the classical music of Europe or the Indian subcontinent, and the tradition is being sustained by the growth of music academies and the worldwide gamelan community. The ancient craft of gamelan manufacture is also being supported by the demand for new sets, often for export. But the process of transplanting music from a royal location to an urban milieu and public concert hall, as happened with other classical musics, only applies in limited ways to Javanese gamelan music. The Javanese courts remain important cultural centres, maintaining high standards in music and the other arts and cross-fertilising with more modern institutions such as the radio stations and music academies.

And gamelan still flourishes at village level: it is scarcely more an urban tradition than it was in the heyday of the royal courts in the century leading up to independence, though the growth of teaching institutions in large cities such as Solo and Jogja has drawn young players from the villages to study in an urban environment. This limited migration has had some effect on the selection and training of musicians. Some come from families of hereditary musicians, and some small towns are known as artistic centres: for example, Klaten, midway between Solo and Jogja, is famous for its families of puppeteers. From this head-start of childhood training, many students move on to the urban academies and

Above: Wayang (shadow puppets) from central Java, in a scene from 'Irawan's Wedding' in the mid-twentieth century

Below: A shadow puppet performance of the story 'Gathutkaca Winisuda' by the celebrated master Ki Manteb Sudharsono at the Bentara Budaya Institute, Jakarta

continue their training in more formal surroundings. What is now the largest academy of the arts in Indonesia started in an annexe of the main court in Solo in 1965, shifting to its own greatly enlarged campus in the 1980s, and has drawn students from all over Indonesia and the world.

Experience of gamelan in the West has drawn on its value as an ideal mixed ability ensemble, with great educational benefits. These have long been understood in Java, where the gamelan is open to a wide spectrum of ages and abilities and has also acquired a new social dynamic thanks to the growth of women's groups which play for pleasure. Other clubs existing for social reasons are drawn from the ranks of bankers, doctors, army officers and Chinese merchants. Expert players routinely rub shoulders with novices, and competitions between amateur groups are common. Radio Republik Indonesia has become a major patron of professional groups, while the schools and academies offer teaching employment to expert players, and extra income can be earned through performances at weddings and wayangs.

■ Influences

There are two main reasons for the gamelan's global fame. One is that ethnomusicologists spearheaded the incorporation of gamelans, along with Indonesian teachers, into American universities, with their example being followed thirty years later in Britain; meanwhile the Netherlands already had a significant home-grown gamelan tradition from its colonial past. Many other European countries, as well as Australia, New Zealand and Japan, have also adopted the gamelan. The other reason lies in the interest shown by leading composers: from Debussy to the present we can trace a continuum, starting with limited understanding and involvement, and moving towards total immersion. Debussy's encounter with the gamelan (and dance) of Java at the 1889 Paris universal exhibition is well known, but whether he imitated the gamelan, even in a stylised and indirect way, is debatable. There is a big difference between his hyperbolic written remarks about Javanese music, on the one hand, and his compositions, especially the piano piece 'Pagodes' (the work most cited as his response to the gamelan), on the other. 'Pagodes' is certainly an example of musical Orientalism and is largely pentatonic, with deep – some would insist gong-like – resonances and filigree patterns. But to relate such vague resemblances specifically to Javanese gamelan music, without any evidence beyond Debussy's admiration for it, is stretching the point.[12]

Leading figures from the next generation of French composers made matters clearer by acknowledging their use of gamelan elements. Olivier Messiaen (1908–1992) did so in his *Turangalîla-Symphonie* of 1948, and Francis Poulenc (1899–1963) imitated the Balinese music he heard at the 1931 Paris exhibition so closely that it approaches transcription, notably in his *Concerto in D minor for two pianos and orchestra* of 1932. Benjamin Britten (1913–76) achieved a similar effect in his ballet *The Prince of the Pagodas* (1957), but there the relationship to the Balinese source was even clearer, as the composer had visited the island during his tour of Asia (1955–56) and had made transcriptions of some of the music he heard. But neither he nor Poulenc learnt to play gamelan instruments, and Britten's first encounters with Balinese music were through playing transcriptions by the Canadian composer Colin McPhee (1900–64) at the beginning of the 1940s during his stay in the United States. McPhee is better known as a pioneering ethnomusicologist than as a composer; his studies of Balinese music and culture from the 1930s remain among the most extensive and penetrating available in English. Moreover, these composers imitated the gamelan by using Western instruments rather than gamelan ones (making Britten's orchestral imitation of a Balinese gamelan in his ballet a challenge extraordinarily well met). As field trips to Indonesia became common among ethnomusicologists, performers and composers, attempts at total immersion were made, leading to compositions for the real gamelan following traditional principles. Not surprisingly, a rift developed between performing groups dedicated to the pursuit of traditional gamelan music, and those who sought to use the gamelan as a stimulus to a new kind of composition. Yet some managed to combine the two harmoniously, most notably the American Lou Harrison (1917–2003), who combined field trips, playing experience and composing for the gamelan (of his own construction). He followed traditional Javanese models, earning criticism from some Javanese musicians and praise from others. The British composer Michael Nyman (b. 1944) has epitomised a diametrically-opposed approach. He was commissioned to write a piece for the 1983 UK tour of the English Gamelan Orchestra (which existed from 1980 to 1983 under my direction), though he had not studied gamelan as Lou Harrison had. The resulting piece, *Time's Up*, had nothing to do with balungan, pathet, garapan and Javanese phrase-structure, but was instead 'echt-Nyman'. The Javanese musicians involved in its performances, clearly baffled by a work that followed none of the methods to which they were accustomed, nevertheless committed it all to memory between the first rehearsal and the next a few days later.

Everyone seems to love the sound of a gamelan, but what draws people from all over the world to attempt to play it? The answers include the beauty of the instruments, the gentle ordering of sounds, the refinement of the music and the conduct of the players: it is all a lesson in restraint, and a check on inflated egos. One of the attractions lies in there being no pressure of expectation: one does not have to be trained in music, nor does one have to be able to read it. Moreover, the gamelan's openness to new influences and its sheer versatility (even to the extent of mixing different tunings and extraneous instruments) protect it from accusations of being a 'museum culture', or even an elitist art. The Indonesian word klasik – neither the exact equivalent of 'classical' nor used anything like as frequently – can be used to distance gamelan music from pop, but tends to be used more to distinguish between strands within gamelan music, for example between the traditional models (klasik) and various modern types (*kontemporer*) which admit influences from pop music and even from the Western classical avant-garde.[13] But what may appear simple on the surface conceals a wealth of subtle detail. The variety of non-Javanese responses to gamelan may be dazzling, but they have often tended towards a standardisation that is contrary to the whole spirit of the gamelan, and of Javanese creativity.

Further reading

An excellent and concise way into Javanese gamelan music is Benjamin Brinner's *Music in Central Java*, which has the considerable advantage of a CD and guides for listening to its many tracks. Intended also as a compact guide, with some contextual information and a notation and analysis of a gamelan piece, is Sorrell's *A Guide to the Gamelan*. Following in its footsteps but greatly extending its technical information, and aimed at players and readers who want to get beyond the basics, is Richard Pickvance's *A Gamelan Manual*. Sorrell's book was designed to fill the enormous gap between Jaap Kunst's monumental 1973 study of Javanese music (*Music in Java*) and Jennifer Lindsay's brief introduction *Javanese Gamelan*. The former gives an unsurpassed depth relating to the music as it existed in the 1930s but is not always easy to relate to what one sees and hears today, while the latter gives an excellent overview of the culture, but does not concern itself as much with the nuts and bolts of the music. The remaining books suggested tend to be more for a specialist readership and have the advantage of recent scholarship by many of the biggest names in gamelan studies. A special place must be given to Sumarsam's *Gamelan*, as it not only has the authority of a Javanese musician and scholar but also provides the best history of the music, with some fascinating insights into how and why gamelan music evolved in the way it did. Judith Becker and Alan Feinstein's *Karawitan* is a collection of writings by other Javanese musicians and scholars (including Sumarsam) which delve mostly into music theory, while Marc Perlman's *Unplayed Melodies* gives the theory a fascinating new interpretation and relates it to Western music theory. Although relating to the decades immediately after Indonesian independence, Judith Becker's *Traditional Music in Modern Java* is an excellent study of the modern popular repertoire. The questions of who the actual musicians are, how they think about music, how they interact and other issues that give the essential social context to the music are skilfully addressed by Brinner's *Knowing Music, Making Music*. Finally, as *wayang kulit* is so central to Javanese culture, a concise, informative and illustrated introduction is Edward Van Ness and Shita Prawirohardjo's *Javanese Wayang Kulit*.

Recommended listening

Indonesia, Java – Court Gamelan (3 vols), Nonesuch Explorer Series, 972044, 2003. These excellent recordings from the 1970s were made in three of the four major palaces in Solo and Jogja, one CD per palace, and the piece studied in this chapter (*Ketawang Puspawarna*) is featured in the first two volumes.

Indonésie, Java Centre, Gamelan de Solo, le Jeu des Sentiments (*Indonesia, Central Java, Solonese Gamelan, A Garland of Moods*), Inédit, Maison des Cultures du Monde, W 260125, 2006. A 4-CD set from 2006 providing fine examples of *klenèngan* (gamelan music for its own sake) and also many excerpts from the *wayang* repertoire.

Gamelan of Central Java (15 vols), Dunya-Felmay records, FY8041-2, 8073-5, 8103-4, 8119-20, 8144-5, 8166-8, 8181.

Gamelan of Java (5 vols), Lyrichord, LYRCD 7456-60. A varied collection of 20 CDs curated by the Italian composer and record producer known as John Noise Manis.

3 Japan

David W. Hughes

The accelerating rhythm of two hardwood clappers signals the opening of the curtain: an audience of several thousand watches as the immense stage is revealed. At its rear are eight singers, eight players of three-string, banjo-like instruments, five drummers and a flautist, all male and wearing matching kimono with broad-shouldered waistcoats and skirt-like trousers. A flute melody in free rhythm – a slow sliding stream of intervals, which may strike Western ears as otherworldly – accompanies the entrance of a samurai character, to enthusiastic yells from the audience. In stylised speech he introduces himself, and sets the scene. The lead singer launches into a slow chant-like song, accompanied by two hand-drums. Between drum-strokes, the drummers shout like martial arts competitors: *yooo! ho! ya! ha!*

Soon the banjos join in in unison, and the music becomes more rhythmic and melodic, the vocalists seeming to chase the string tune, a split-second behind the strongly-plucked beats. Actors enter along a runway passing through the audience, who shout further cries of encouragement. The flute re-enters, its melody seemingly unrelated to the voices and strings. At a dramatic climax the hero – a powerful warrior-priest – strikes an exaggerated pose, arms akimbo, eyes crossed. Accenting his pose, a deep-voiced stick-drum sounds from behind a screen offstage to the left, while – barely visible to the far right – a man in black pounds on a wooden board with two hardwood bars.

This is how a performance of a kabuki play might begin and develop. Sounds come at you from every direction: music from onstage and offstage musicians, heightened speech from the actors, shouts from the drummers and the audience, sound effects depicting insects or symbolising natural phenomena. Such a soundscape, however, would be unthinkable in the other genres of Japanese classical music covered in this chapter: each is specific to its social, physical and historical environment.

Ask a Japanese about classical music in Japan, and the names likely to pop up are those of Bach, Beethoven and Tchaikovsky. Or maybe the pianist Uchida Mitsuko, who studied in Vienna from the age of twelve and is now a British citizen. Or two recent figures of worldwide fame: composer Takemitsu Tōru and conductor Ozawa Seiji.[1] But that's if you are conversing in English. In Japanese, you would have had to choose between two words for 'classical'. One is the

◀ A woodblock print by Unita Kunisada (1786–1865) of a figure from the 1849 production of the kabuki drama *Chūshingura*, one of Japan's best-loved tales of samurai honour. All-male but with flamboyantly erotic simulations of femininity, kabuki spawned a huge trade in fan magazines and woodblock prints.

Japanese pronunciation of 'classic' *kurashikku*, which refers only to what is called 'Western art/classical music' by those who realise that there are also *non*-Western art/classical musics. The other is *koten*, a native word mostly referring to the world's 'other' classical musics, especially those of Japan.[2]

Japan's many classical genres are historically related but highly diverse. Each has its own moods, social contexts and musical forms. This chapter focuses on those *koten* genres which foreigners most often encounter: *gagaku* 'court' music, the theatre genres noh and kabuki, the solo shakuhachi flute tradition and non-court music for the koto zither.

■ Gagaku, noh and kabuki

Gagaku (literally 'elegant music') is generally perceived and translated as 'court music'. But it is also performed in Buddhist temples and Shinto shrines, and since the modernisation of the late nineteenth century numerous other professional, amateur and religious groups have been allowed to get in on the act. Many Japanese proudly proclaim gagaku to be the world's oldest continuously transmitted orchestral tradition. Though this claim is fanciful – there have been several interruptions in transmission, and a myriad changes to the music and performance practice – gagaku's existence is indeed well documented by the eighth century, with both instruments and examples of notation surviving from more than a millennium ago.

The term 'gagaku' embraces several sub-genres; space permits dealing only with the best-known, *tōgaku*, specifically its purely instrumental style known as *kangen*, 'pipes and strings' (when accompanying dance – *bugaku* – the same pieces are today performed without strings and with some alterations in percussion, rhythm and articulation). As its name suggests, togaku ('Tang music') reached Japan primarily from Tang-dynasty China (618–907) during the seventh to ninth centuries. Japan's imperial court, based in Nara and then in Kyoto in west-central Japan, hoped to bolster its status by persuading the Chinese to allow it to adopt the ritual music of that great empire. Eighteen different types of instrument from the period, many imported from Tang, survive to this day in the Shōsōin treasure-house in Nara; some of these types, including the ancestor of the shakuhachi, were soon dropped from the togaku orchestra, yielding the present-day ensemble of eight instruments described below.[3]

The repertoire received was actually Chinese banquet music, and it became expanded and Japanised over the centuries, becoming the ritual music of the Japanese palace, and of nearby religious institutions. Court nobles, including the emperor, pursued togaku performance as an artistic accomplishment, in part reflecting Confucian beliefs in the importance of music for sustaining social order. Early examples of court notations were compiled by high-ranking nobles, and professional musicians (*gakunin*) supplemented their performances when necessary. Such employees have always been of high importance – being deemed essential to a good ritual or concert – though occupying less lofty status. As hereditary professional families were established, the art came to be passed from father to son, and to some degree this practice continues today.

The civil wars of the fifteenth and sixteenth centuries disrupted the imperial court so badly that many gakunin fled the palace and the capital, Kyoto. Gagaku then continued mainly in temples and shrines in the region, which did allow the eventual revival of palace performance. Gagaku was also established in Edo (modern-day Tokyo) when the shogunate moved there at the start of the seventeenth century, thus launching the Edo Period (1603–1868).

Like other genres, gagaku was profoundly affected by the Meiji Restoration of 1868, when imperial rule replaced the military shogunate. After more than two hundred years of a closed-door policy, the Meiji Period (1868–1912) saw those doors flung wide open as Japan strove to catch up with the West in every way – militarily, economically, politically and culturally. Thus began a period of modernisation and westernisation affecting all aspects of Japanese culture. With the Restoration, the imperial capital relocated from Kyoto to Tokyo, and court gagaku was now handed over entirely to professionals selected from the Kyoto palace as well as from various temples and shrines. Significantly – due in part to an awareness of the importance of notation in Western classical music – the repertoire was captured in detailed part-scores published in 1876 and 1888: the *Meiji sentei-fu* is still the standard for virtually all togaku performances today. Moreover, as with other genres, the modernising government eliminated restrictions as to who could perform togaku, thus leading to the eventual establishment of skilled groups outside the court and religious institutions. With foreign dignitaries beginning to visit the palace, musicians were required to provide Western music as well: a *ryūteki* flute player had also to perform Bach (or some national anthem) on a Western flute to honour and entertain these visitors.

Notation collections from various eras help us detect changes to performance practice over time, alterations due only in part to the disruptions of war and relocation. Over the centuries the tempo of togaku was greatly slowed down, as befitting its increasingly dignified purposes. Originally the melody of a piece was played on *ryūteki* transverse flute (seven fingerholes), *hichiriki* double-reed pipe (seven fingerholes, two thumbholes), *shō* mouth organ (with seventeen bamboo pipes of which fifteen contain metal free reeds), *biwa* four-string fretted lute and *koto* thirteen-string zither, plus other instruments no longer used. But each instrument's version of the melody would vary somewhat from the others in idiomatic ways, resulting in heterophony. As a result, perception and audibility of this core melody has over time become obscured by horizontal and vertical elaboration, yet those ancient tunes are still there, hidden away in today's practice (there is a parallel here with the development of European motets from sloweddown Gregorian chants).[4] A sparse but effective rhythmic structure is provided by the large *taiko* and smaller *kakko* stick-drums, and by the small *shōko* gong. Typically there are three performers of each wind instrument, two for koto and biwa and one for each percussion instrument.

Japan's three most prominent music-theatre genres – noh (*nō*), kabuki and bunraku – have all been designated by UNESCO as Masterpieces of the Oral and Intangible Heritage of Humanity. Historically the three are closely linked, with kabuki drawing on both noh and bunraku.

Gagaku in the Imperial Palace, Tokyo, where it is performed at state events and occasional public recitals. Derived from Tang-dynasty China, and documented as far back as the eighth century, this art-form's instruments have stayed substantially the same.

Noh is a *Gesamtkunstwerk,* or all-embracing art work – a music-dance-drama which is also valued as literature and for the beauty of its costumes and masks; the word itself means 'accomplishment' or 'ability'. Today it is so dignified and austere that one can hardly believe its roots lay in some vigorous folk performances seven centuries ago. The popularity of these performances led to troupes being invited to perform in aristocratic mansions, and even in

Front row: shoko, taiko (gakudaiko), kakko; *middle:* koto, biwa; *back:* ryuteki, hichiriki, sho; *far back, at each side:* two very large taiko (dadaiko) which replace the gakudaiko for dance pieces

the shogunal headquarters in Kyoto. The modern form of noh had its roots in the late fourteenth century, and is principally credited to Zeami (c. 1363–1444), the son of a respected actor, who was adopted into the shogun's court in 1374. From that time until the liberalisations of the 1870s, noh flourished under the patronage of the military aristocracy, while still being performed for the masses as well; many amateurs from the military and merchant classes took lessons in it.

Zeami entered the military court at a time when Zen Buddhism was influential within samurai culture; thus did the influence of Buddhist chant on noh vocal style grow even stronger. Zeami strove to raise the status and dignity of noh: a serious intellectual, he produced several treatises on aesthetics and performance which are still frequently quoted (and are mostly available in English translation). He adopted terms and concepts from gagaku, though not always in ways easily understood: passages specifically relating to musical elements are often vague, and hard to relate to current practice, given the thorough-going changes to performance over the centuries. Yet Zeami's words are often evocative: 'Forget the voice, and understand the shading of the melody. Forget the melody, and understand the pitch. Forget the pitch, and understand the rhythm.'[5]

Like gagaku, noh has slowed considerably since its founding, reaching its current tempo and style by the mid-nineteenth century. Bodily and vocal expression are today remarkably austere and restrained: this suits the nature of many noh plays, whose action often takes place in dreams and/or involves spirits from the afterlife. The plays are traditionally assigned to one of five types, often translated as god, warrior, woman, miscellaneous and 'concluding noh'. A full day's performance may include one of each.

Another major change since Zeami's day is the tuning of the noh flute (*nōkan*), the only melodic instrument employed. An inserted bamboo tube, lacquered over, constricts the flute's bore between mouth-hole and nearest finger-hole, creating an irregular scale whose intervals shrink as the pitch rises. This insertion may originally have been an attempted repair of a cracked instrument, but the result evokes an otherworldly mood. The melodic elements of noh consist of the vocals of the main actors and a chorus usually of eight unison voices, plus the flute. One curiosity is that the flute's intervals are today intentionally quite unlike those of the vocals, so that when flute and voice overlap there is no musical connection between the two.

Three drums provide a rhythmic underpinning: the *kotsuzumi* and *ōtsuzumi* hand-drums, which work together, and the taiko laced stick-drum. The most notable feature of their use is less the drum sounds themselves than the drummers' dynamic cries (*kakegoe*), which often seem to overpower the vocalists. These swooping, powerful *yo*'s and *ho*'s, not unlike the cries of martial artists, add a layer of musical texture crucial in establishing both mood and timing, and further support the dreamlike atmosphere. A professional drummer once told me that seventy per cent of noh drumming is in the voice.

One thing has not changed: all roles in professional noh are played by men (with the exception of one or two women's troupes whose status is still under debate). Even the voice of a young female character would be intentionally in a deep register. Moreover, the masks worn by the lead actors (*shite*, pronounced

> Like gagaku, noh enjoys UNESCO's Intangible Cultural Heritage status, and over the seven centuries of its existence it has become progressively more inward and austere. An integration of music, dance and drama, it is also valued as literature and for the beauty of its costumes and masks. In this picture, the play *Okina – A Venerable Old Man* receives its formal dedication; kotsuzumi drums and noh flute are seen.

sh'tay) further muffle the wavering voice. The resultant vocal colours enhance the eerie mood.

Eventually five different schools of noh emerged, and continue today, with the Kanze school, descended from Zeami, being the largest. These share most of the repertoire of more than two hundred plays, and their musical style and dance movements are very similar, though the differences are enough to prevent, say, singers from the Kanze and Kita schools from performing together.

Kabuki emerged in the early seventeenth century in the burgeoning urban areas of the Edo Period, as audiences gradually lost interest in the restrained expressiveness of post-Zeami noh. Kabuki drew on noh but aimed successfully to cater for the growing merchant and middle classes: it reversed the inwardness of noh and went for flashy large-scale productions. Though it was created by female performers kabuki soon became an all-male preserve too, after the government banned women from the stage in 1629 for excessive eroticism. Huge noisy audiences gathered, their fanatical interest spawning endless fan magazines and woodblock prints of famous actors. The samurai class were attracted too – it was still erotic – despite being officially forbidden to attend performances.

Noh's austerity was reflected in its small stage without curtain or scenery, and with very limited props. Kabuki came to be performed on a huge stage, with complex scenery which might appear suddenly from behind a curtain at the

rear of the stage, or be wheeled into position on a rotating central platform, or emerge (with actors aboard) via trap doors from beneath the floor. Noh generally featured only two or three main characters, with the facial expressions of the lead actor usually hidden behind a mask, while even the naked faces of the other actors showed no emotion. Kabuki eschewed masks in favour of painted faces and over-the-top facial expressions, and many more actors appeared. Whereas the young women of noh may be played by deep-voiced double-chinned men, kabuki developed the celebrated *onnagata* acting style in which male actors strove to be the epitome of femininity, and indeed were worshipped as such.

Kabuki adopted the flute and three drums of noh, but soon added many more instruments. The most striking is the 'banjo' of our introductory vignette: the *shamisen*, a three-stringed long-necked lute whose four-sided resonating chamber was faced and backed with catskin, and whose silk strings were plucked with a large heavy plectrum to produce a wide range of timbres and volumes. The

JAPAN

Kabuki theatre was always a convivial social event, as seen in this woodblock print by Utagawa Toyokuni III. It depicts the 1858 production of *Shibaraku* at the Ichimura-za theatre in Edo with, to the left, the *hanamichi* walkway via which actors may enter and exit, and from which they may make key speeches.

shamisen developed in the late 1500s from the snakeskin-covered Okinawan *sanshin*, which in turn had reached those southern islands from China (as the *sanxian*) in the fourteenth century. Like the modern guitar, the shamisen developed different forms to suit new genres; it would vary in absolute and relative thickness of strings, height and weight of bridge, size and sharpness of plectrum, thickness of neck and membrane, and in playing technique. Such fairly subtle differences match the distinct vocal timbres of each shamisen-accompanied genre; one of these, the lyrical *nagauta* ('long song'), considered the heart of kabuki music, is discussed in detail later in the chapter.[6] In kabuki the nokan (noh flute) alternates with a second transverse flute, the lyrical bamboo *shinobue*, which, unlike the nokan, plays heterophonically in tune with shamisen and vocalists.

Offstage to the kabuki audience's left is a room (*kuromisu, geza*) with musicians playing some of the above instruments plus other forms of percussion and countless devices to evoke birds, waves, temple bells, and so forth. In

83

noh, much is left to the imagination; in kabuki, far less so. Yet it still takes an aficionado to recognise the offstage drum pattern symbolising snow – a regular but slow-pulsed sequence of gentle muffled beats on a large taiko drum: this language of symbolism must be learnt. In most kabuki plays, there are no on-stage musicians: all sounds and music apart from the voices of the actors (who speak but do not sing) come from offstage.

Kabuki absorbed and interacted with many other art forms. Some plays derived from noh; these would often begin with a close imitation of noh style (as in this chapter's introductory vignette), then yield quickly to kabuki flashiness, suddenly bringing in perhaps eight shamisen and changing to a higher-pitched and sharper vocal style. Others were based on bunraku plays; these would invariably include bunraku's *gidayū* music, with its rough-voiced chanter (and matching shamisen) supplementing the actors' voices. Actors might even imitate the movement style of puppets from the original play. Kabuki hand-drummers, while still using the patterns and vocal yells of noh, also developed a distinctive style known as *chirikara* (from the oral mnemonics used to transmit the often breathtakingly rapid interlocking parts). In the passage of lexically meaningless mnemonic syllables *chirikara chiripopo tsu pon tsutatsuta tsu pon*, the syllables with vowels *i* and *u* represent a loud sharp stroke on the otsuzumi, while the vowels *a* and *o* represent two contrasting sounds from the deeper-voiced kotsuzumi.

Some kabuki 'plays' are in fact dance pieces lasting between fifteen and forty minutes accompanied onstage by up to three types of shamisen music, with nagauta being the most common. Many of these dance plays are performed outside a formal kabuki context, as 'Japanese [classical] dance' (*nihon buyō*). In this latter context, most teachers and dancers are women.

▪ The shakuhachi and its music

Times change. During his US tour in 1973, the renowned shakuhachi master Aoki Reibo II (b. 1935) was adamant that I should tell the audience that he was not a Buddhist priest but a musician, and that he was playing a musical instrument (*gakki*), not a religious tool (*hōki*). He had found that shakuhachi aficionados in the West tended to have a romantic view of the instrument, as a tool for Zen spiritual experiences. This was hardly surprising: many Japanese themselves saw it that way until the late nineteenth century, and indeed many still do.

The shakuhachi is an end-blown bamboo notch-flute. Its ancestor came from China with the togaku ensemble by the eighth century, but had virtually disappeared from that ensemble by the twelfth century. The Tang dynasty examples in the Shōsōin storehouse had five fingerholes plus one thumbhole, yielding a diatonic scale suitable for togaku. All subsequent Japanese descendants, however, have only four fingerholes plus a thumbhole, most naturally yielding an anhemitonic ('no semitones') pentatonic scale (i.e. five intervals approximating to major seconds and minor thirds).[7] A treatise from 1233 links the shakuhachi to blind itinerant monk-priests, and thus to Buddhism.

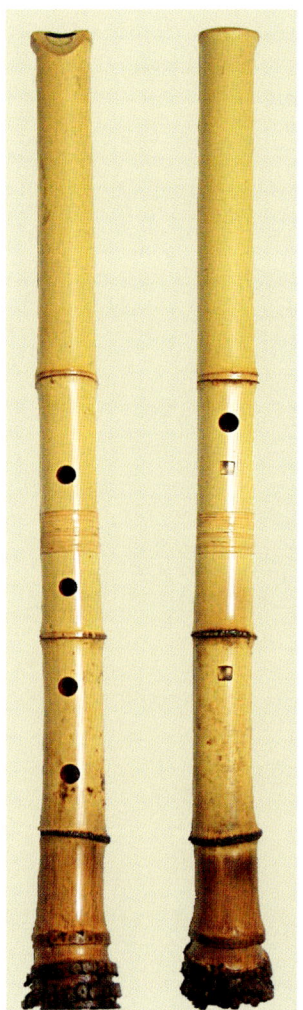

The shakuhachi *(left)* was associated with Buddhism and blind itinerant monks from the thirteenth century onwards, and still has religious connotations. *Right:* Komuso 'priests of nothingness' with straw baskets over their heads to obscure the face and erase the self, photographed in the 1950s.

Blind men often became monks, at least informally, and made a living as musicians and/or masseurs. Such men would have played what was later called the *hitoyogiri*, a short, narrow shakuhachi incapable of producing the volume of the modern instrument; this is well documented from the seventeenth century as accompanying popular songs, or playing in a trio with koto and shamisen.

The form of the instrument that we know today seems to have arisen in the early seventeenth century. It takes its generic name from its current standard length: one *shaku* (about one foot) plus eight (*hachi*) tenths of another – about 55 cm, though soloists today may play shakuhachi ranging from about 1.4 to more than 3 feet. The modern shakuhachi is much heavier and thicker than its predecessors, occasionally appearing as a weapon of self-defence in kabuki plays. The bore is lacquered inside, though the earlier non-lacquered (*jinashi*) type, with its less powerful tone, is increasingly being revived among those who see it as ancient, and thus linked more closely to Zen.

To distinguish it from predecessors, the modern form is now called the Fuke shakuhachi – reminding us of the instrument's historical links with Zen. By the late fifteenth century the itinerant priest-monks mentioned above were often called *komusō*, 'straw-mat monks', after the sleeping mats they carried. By the mid seventeenth century this term had evolved to mean 'priests of nothingness', to stress links with Zen philosophy. Around that time the Fuke sect of Zen was established and spread rapidly throughout the land, its members being masterless samurai seeking an alternative living in times of peace. They did indeed use the shakuhachi as a 'religious tool', in services or while playing on the street to receive alms. These komuso wore baskets of woven straw or bamboo over their heads, obscuring the face and thus the 'self' – another Zen concept. In the later seventeenth century the Tokugawa shogunate granted the Fuke sect a monopoly on playing shakuhachi for profit (though others, including some geisha, managed to subvert that). Such priests were guaranteed the freedom to travel round the country, apparently in exchange for serving as the government's eyes and ears in the regions.

Many pieces generated by Fuke practitioners form the core repertoire of what is now called the Kinko school, which arose from the activities of Kurosawa Kinko (1710–71), a priest who visited Fuke temples to collect local tunes. Today's Kinko school (a loose agglomeration of sub-schools) generally recognises thirty-six tunes, all solos except for the duet 'Shika no tōne' ('Distant calling of deer'), in their *honkyoku* ('main/true/original melodies') repertoire. The titles of these tunes are often redolent of spirituality and nature: 'Kokū' ('Emptiness'); 'Tsuru no sugomori' ('Cranes tending their nestlings'). Almost all are in free rhythm, with long drawn-out and highly (but generally slowly) ornamented notes suitable for a meditative mood. Players used to speak of 'attaining Buddha-hood [achieving enlightenment] with a single sound' (*ichion-jōbutsu*). Hence we should not evaluate this music solely on the interest of its melodies, but rather on shifting timbres, subtle pitch inflections and dynamic changes on the level of the single tone or short phrase.

The government's dissolution of the Fuke sect and its quasi-monopoly in 1871 led to two major developments. First, the shakuhachi now found a role in a secular ensemble with shamisen and one or two koto – a genre called *sankyoku*, described further below. There it plays a subsidiary role, heterophonically supporting the original melodies created for those string instruments. Then, at the start of the twentieth century, a new school of shakuhachi emerged to rival Kinko: the Tozan school, named after its founder Nakao Tozan (1876–1956). A former komuso, Tozan began to compose his own honkyoku. Produced in an era of Western musical influence, Tozan's twenty-eight tunes differ strikingly from Kinko/Fuke honkyoku. Only three are entirely solos; free rhythm plays less of a role, yielding to a metric ensemble style; microtonal pitches are far less common; and some pieces have sections in an organum-like parallel homophony, though maintaining traditional Japanese modal style to avoid mere imitation of Western harmonies. Though several other schools exist today, Kinko and Tozan have by far the most members.

Western influence in the early twentieth century saw the creation of seven- and nine-hole instruments as well, facilitating the playing of Western-style chromatic pieces. But using these instruments for traditional pieces would potentially ruin what is possibly the most distinctive feature of honkyoku style, a technique known as *meri*: dropping the chin to change the blowing angle, resulting in a lower, often non-chromatic pitch from the same fingering. (Part-holing may also be employed.) That lowered pitch will have a somewhat different timbre, usually breathier and quieter – a crucial part of shakuhachi aesthetics. The twentieth-century instruments, which could execute those lowered pitches through simple fingering with no change in timbre, are thus avoided for honkyoku.

■ *The koto and its music*

The koto is a thirteen-string zither, around six feet long, with a moveable tuning bridge under each string. Picks of ivory or plastic are worn on the thumb, index and middle finger of the right hand. While the koto remains a mainstay of togaku, most people know it as a non-court instrument. Arriving from Tang China, it was originally called by its Chinese name. In modern standard Chinese, this name (written 箏) is pronounced *zheng*; in Japan, the word lost its final nasal and became *sō*, as in the words *gakusō* ('gagaku koto'), *zokusō* ('popular koto') and *sōkyoku* ('koto music/melodies'). But *koto* is a Japanese word which previously designated a six-string zither known since the second century BCE; now called *wagon* ('Japanese zither'), it still features in pre-Chinese court genres.

Even a millennium ago, the koto was enjoyed as a solo instrument, often for private pleasure. In *The Tale of Genji*, a novel from around the year 1000, the hero Prince Genji urges one girlfriend after another to take up the instrument, judging their attractiveness in part by their musical skill, and by their grace in performance: '[Genji] thought her delightful as she leaned forward to press a string with her left hand.'[8]

The koto spread to various parts of Japan in the hands of nobles and warriors, sometimes as they fled the capital after finding themselves on the losing side in a war. By the late sixteenth century, a non-togaku koto tradition had developed in the Tsukushi region of Kyushu, southern Japan. Its repertoire included instrumental solos and accompanied songs, some deriving their melody from the best-known togaku piece, 'Etenraku'. The elitist Tsukushi school specifically instructed adherents not to pass its teachings to blind musicians, who at this time were most prominently performing ancient battle stories or Buddhist chants, accompanied by the four-string *biwa* lute (descendant of the Chinese *pipa*), and gradually also adopting the shamisen which had only recently arrived in Japan. They were considered little more than beggars, though since the 1340s many blind musicians belonged to a government-supported organisation called the Tōdō-za, a welfare system with its own ranks and emoluments.

Ironically, then, this elitist koto tradition was transmitted by a Tsukushi performer visiting Edo in the 1630s to a blind shamisen master now generally seen as the founder of 'popular koto' (*zokusō*). This was the man later known as Yatsuhashi Kengyō (1614–85). *Kengyō* was the highest rank in the guild of the blind, and subsequently 'popular koto' became the official prerogative of members of this guild until 1871 and the Meiji modernisation. *Zoku*, 'popular', can also be translated as 'vulgar' and 'inelegant' – doubtless what the sophisticates back in Tsukushi would have been thinking. But there was nothing inelegant about Yatsuhashi's music. He adapted some of the koto-accompanied songs from Tsukushi while adding new compositions, and is also thought to have introduced to koto music the *in* mode, with its evocative semitones (see 'Scale and mode' below). The koto's moveable tuning bridges made it easy to change some of the intervals of court-derived tunings to introduce these semitones while maintaining a pentatonic scale. Pitches between the basic five are obtained – for melodic or ornamental purposes – by pressing a string to the left of the tuning bridge with fingers of the left hand.

In Yatsuhashi's day, aside from various short song-centred pieces, there was a small repertoire of instrumental tunes known as *danmono*, each consisting of several sections (*dan*) of equal length, 52 bars of simple duple metre. One of these, 'Rokudan' ('Six sections'), is the best-known koto piece today. But the vast majority of compositions from the late seventeenth century until Meiji include vocals. There are two main 'schools' (*ryū*) of zokusō, both named after their founders, who like Yatsuhashi were kengyō: the Ikuta school was formed in the late seventeenth century, and the Yamada school at the end of the eighteenth. Both encouraged the combining of koto and shamisen; the Yamada school drew influence not only from shamisen narrative genres but even from noh, giving Yamada vocal stylings a different flavour from Ikuta. While continuing to flourish as a solo instrument, the koto is often heard in the sankyoku ('three melodies') format: one or two koto, one shamisen and one shakuhachi. Vocals are provided by one of the string players.

In the Edo Period, many sighted people studied with blind koto masters. The Meiji Period saw the koto being made available to all, and now blind teachers are rare. Playing koto soon became a badge of culture and grace for marriageable upper- and middle-class women; today the piano has largely replaced the koto in this respect.

In musical terms, the first significant effects of Western influence surfaced with the launching of the New Japanese Music (*shin nihon ongaku*) movement in 1920. A central figure was Miyagi Michio of the Ikuta school (1894–1956), a blind koto and shamisen master. His compositions for koto, shamisen and/or shakuhachi, while generally avoiding Western harmonic language, nonetheless departed from tradition in some respects. His most famous piece, 'Haru no umi' ('Spring sea', 1929), gives the melody to the shakuhachi, with the koto providing the accompaniment almost as if on a piano, with no Western triads but arpeggios and chordal accompaniment nonetheless (though his chords drew on pitches from traditional modes). Miyagi's solo koto composition 'Eihei no kōtai' ('Changing of the guards', 1954), by contrast, does use Western triads, because he was imitating the sound of the brass instruments at Buckingham Palace he heard on his sole visit to England; it also features slapping the strings to evoke the drums. Miyagi's compositions are hugely popular today in the koto world. More recent contemporary and avant-garde koto pieces by Western-style composers are less commonly performed.

Miyagi also created the seventeen-string bass koto to supply a somewhat Western bass part, and commissioned a single eighty-string koto; the latter languishes unplayed in the Miyagi Michio Museum in Tokyo, as he and others quickly recognised its irrelevance. As in twentieth-century China and Korea, some Japanese have also expanded the number of strings: koto with twenty-one to thirty strings are often exploited for contemporary composition.

Musical aspects of Japanese classical genres

Notation and transmission

Notation for the instruments of togaku survives from as early as the eighth century, with abundant examples by the late twelfth century; today's notation looks remarkably similar, though it is interpreted very differently (see illustration overleaf). Buddhist chant was also being notated a thousand years ago.

However, there is no unified notation system equivalent to Western staff notation, as each instrument and vocal genre has its own system: there is, for example, no 'full score' for togaku. Moreover, each instrumental school tends to use notation incompatible with others. Written notation was rarely used at all until Meiji, for a variety of reasons. First, professional performance and teaching of some genres were restricted by law to the blind. Second, genres such as gagaku and noh were transmitted, often from father to son, through immersion from early childhood. Third, the availability of detailed notation could have threatened the professionals' monopoly on musical knowledge and thus reduced their income. Since the Edo Period the guild-like, quasi-familial *iemoto* ('househead') teaching system has allowed the autocratic head of each school to keep firm control of the musical product.

Since the Meiji loosening of restrictions on transmission and the encouragement of Western influence, ever more detailed notations have appeared. For example, a century ago a tablature notation called *bunka-fu*, 'culture notation', was devised, and can theoretically be used for any shamisen. ('Tablature' here means a notation that shows where to place one's fingers, rather than what pitch to play. Most notations currently in use for Japanese melodic instruments are tablature in that sense.) But many types of notation are in use for nagauta shamisen, and yet others for *jiuta* shamisen, which is the style generally heard in sankyoku.

Until the twentieth century, such notation as existed was generally for reference – to help recall what had already been learned aurally – rather than for use in instruction or performance. Teaching has usually involved one-to-one rote imitation: many instruments were and are taught with the aid of sophisticated

THE OTHER CLASSICAL MUSICS

systems of oral mnemonics.9 Thus a beginning noh flute student might first – before being allowed to touch the flute – learn to sing a melody using mnemonics such as *ohyarai houhouhi* ...; or, as noted above, a student of the hand-drums of kabuki dance music will learn the interlocking patterns for these two drums orally: *tsu ta pon tsutatsu popopon* ... Many written notations include these mnemonics, and indeed may consist of little else. The fact that much Japanese music is constructed from recurring rhythmic or melodic units (often named) facilitates memorisation.

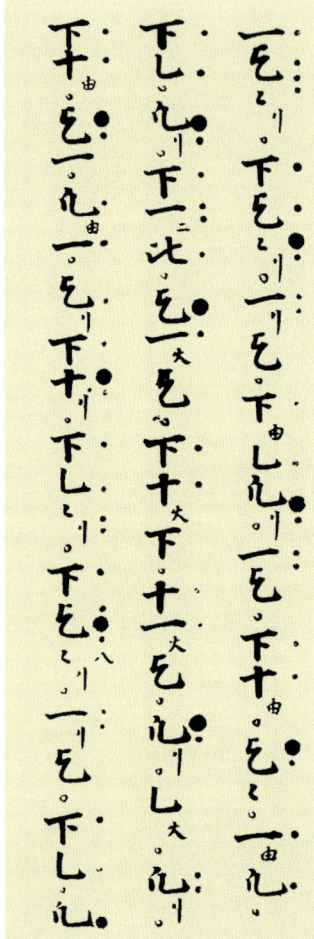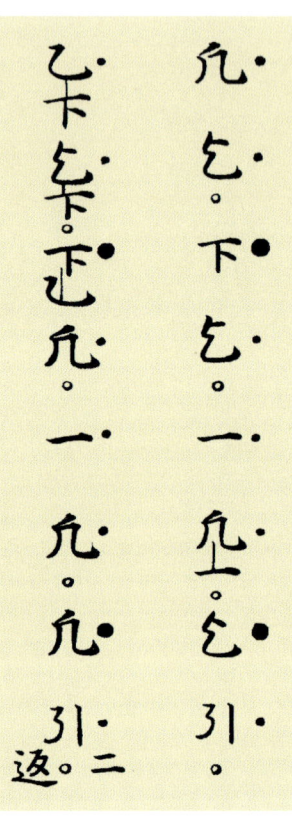

Two examples of shō notation, seven centuries apart, together with a shō *(right)*. The three-line example dates from 1303, the two-line one from the present. They read from top to bottom and from right to left. Black dots represent beats and small circles bar lines; the main symbols indicate specific pipes, but today also demand the playing of standard chords based on the pitch of each pipe. The most significant difference is that the 1303 notation has a symbol 由 representing a melodic ornament, supporting Laurence Picken's claim that no chords were played then, but rather a brisk single line.

Ryuteki flute master Shiba Sukeyasu (b. 1935) is the son of a hereditary palace performer and later taught gagaku at Tokyo University of the Arts. He told me that his experiences were similar to other sons of court musicians: from around the age of five he began learning the repertoire by singing the mnemonics, but was not allowed to try playing the flute for several years. Court musician Ohno Tadaaki (b. 1959) confirmed that he learned the sho only via mnemonics for eight years. One wonders whether he and Shiba had tried out their instruments in secret at some point – but I never asked that potentially embarrassing question. With a smallish repertoire of a couple of hundred short pieces, and with many standardised phrases and techniques, any court instrumentalist should be able to memorise down to the smallest ornament.

It is still uncommon for professional players in traditional genres to use notation in performance – and unthinkable in the palace, or for noh. Singers in shamisen or koto genres are more likely to have notation, though primarily in order to remember the lyrics. For contemporary compositions, notation is more commonly used. Intentional alteration or variation of what one has learned is rare in the classical genres. Although only the head of a school is thought to have the right to make changes, an advanced student may be able to set up his or her own school, and pass on variant versions of traditional pieces.

▶ Scale and mode

Japanese music is primarily pentatonic, using five different principal pitches per octave. However, the scale systems are different for gagaku, Buddhist chant, noh, folk song and the various Edo-period urban musics. Moreover, one or two notes often differ in ascending and descending passages, as with the European melodic minor, effectively creating heptatonic (seven-tone) scales. For this reason, I encourage the replacement of 'pentatonic' with the invented term 'pentacentric': centred on five tones, but with other notes substituted at times. Modulations within a piece do not affect modal theory *per se*.

It is important to keep in mind the distinction between scale (the collection of pitches used in a particular genre or composition) and mode (the way that these pitches function). Koizumi Fumio showed how most Japanese scales can be analysed as built from one or more of four types of tetrachord (see 'Koizumi's modal types' overleaf).[10] In ancient Greek theory, this term indicated two notes a fourth apart with two other notes in between. Applied to Japan, the term designates a framework of two 'nuclear tones' a perfect fourth apart, with a single note – an 'infix' – positioned between them. The nuclear tones serve as competing centres and goals of tonal movement (hence we cannot speak of a single 'tonic' as in Western music). Combining two identical tetrachords to make an octave yields four pentatonic modes. The names of these are used by scholars, but rarely – except in gagaku – by musicians, although Koizumi's system is now familiar to many performers.

> **Koizumi's modal types**
>
> *Underlined pitches indicate nuclear tones.*
>
> miyako-bushi ('city melody'; a.k.a. *in*)
> common in urban genres of Edo-period origin:
>
> $\underline{c}-d\flat-\underline{f} + \underline{g}-a\flat-\underline{c'}$
>
> ritsu (common in gagaku and some folk music):
>
> $\underline{c}-d-\underline{f} + \underline{g}-a-\underline{c'}$
>
> inaka-bushi ('countryside melody'; a.k.a. *yō*) mostly in folk song, thus also called the 'folk song scale', min'yō onkai:
>
> $\underline{c}-e\flat-\underline{f} + \underline{g}-b\flat-\underline{c'}$
>
> Ryūkyū (only in music of the Ryukyu islands, including Okinawa):
>
> $\underline{c}-e-\underline{f} + \underline{g}-b-\underline{c'}$
>
> NOTE *The miyako-bushi and ritsu modes often use inaka-bushi tetrachords in ascent, while the Ryūkyū mode may use ritsu tetrachords in descent.*

To revisit the analogy with the melodic minor: in miyako-bushi, one might encounter a rising and then falling passage like $g–b\flat–c'–a\flat–g–f–d\flat–c$. Though $a\flat$ is the default infix for this mode, in rising passages the gravitational pull of the high nuclear tone c' can encourage substituting $b\flat$ for $a\flat$.

But the pitches shown above are only relative. Song-centred genres dominate Japanese music, and instrumentalists need to accommodate the singer's range, so compositions are not written in a specific key (except in gagaku). In noh, the chorus takes its pitch from its leader, who may choose a pitch totally unrelated to that of the main actor's most recent song. String instruments are easily retuned; shinobue flutes, as used in kabuki nagauta and to accompany folk songs, are made in multiple keys to suit the singer. Unlike the Western orchestral flute, it is very rare to play in multiple keys on one shinobue, except for temporary mid-tune modulations of a fourth or fifth.

In terms of precision of pitch, while the fourths and fifths separating nuclear tones hold firm, the infixed, non-nuclear pitches may be flexible, yielding non-Western intervals; this is most noticeable in folk music, noh, gagaku, bunraku and shakuhachi. In Western music, the upward-leading seventh degree may be raised slightly by singers or violinists, producing an interval less than a semitone; the same occurs in reverse with the downward-leading semitones of miyako-bushi. Once such flexibility of intonation is acknowledged, Koizumi's model works well enough, but it cannot quite accommodate the *ryo* modes of togaku or the *tsuyogin* vocal style of noh (explained below).

Left: An eighteenth-century woodblock print by Ishikawa Toyonobu (1711–85) showing two kabuki actors in the role of street musicians playing for donations on a shamisen and kokyu fiddle

Below: A colour postcard from the early twentieth century showing two young women playing the koto and shamisen

▶ *Togaku*

Togaku uses six basic modes (*chōshi*). Each is pentatonic, with two exchange tones (*hennon*) replacing the infixes in certain melodic contexts (see the note to the list of Koizumi's modal types above). These six are divided into two groups of three called *ritsu* and *ryo* which feature different intervallic structures. The three modes within each group differ in pitch level; thus the three ritsu modes have their fundamental pitch (*kyū*) – the closest to the concept of a tonic – at different levels: E for *hyōjō*, A for *ōshikichō*, B for *banshikichō*. A given composition may often be played in all three modes from the same group, but this is not a matter of simple modulation: each instrument's part will change somewhat due to limitations in the range of the instrument, and to different tunings for different modes. Ryo modes differ from ritsu in that the basic five pitches are *do re mi sol la* rather than *do re fa sol la*.

Today, the main melody of togaku is felt to be shared between ryuteki flute and hichiriki double-reed pipe, which have greatly elaborated their melodies of a millennium ago; the sho usually provides ethereal chords (selected from a small fixed corpus), while the koto and biwa supply standardised arpeggios. The lowest pitch of the sho chord and the highest pitch of the koto and biwa arpeggios generally correspond to the now almost indiscernible ancient melody. There are some divergences, however, due to historical disruptions in transmission, as well as for other reasons. For example, the hichiriki, with its narrow range (g'–a''), cannot preserve the melodic contour as well as the ryuteki with its two-octave range (e''–d''''); it has idiomatic ways of solving this problem. The koto, meanwhile, is always tuned pentatonically: its open strings can only play five of the seven main pitches of each mode. As our quotation above from *The Tale of Genji* confirms, historically the player could press a string to the left of the tuning bridge to play the missing pitches, as in today's popular koto music. But as this technique was lost in transmission in togaku, the koto is often a semitone or so away from the winds.[11]

Togaku also features a set of short modal preludes (*netori*), one for each of the six modes. These are standardised free-rhythm pieces in which one player of each instrument enters successively, with overlap. Like the *pathetan* of central Javanese gamelan, these allow the musicians and audience to prepare their ears for what follows. Theoretically these netori allow for checking the tuning, but I have never seen a performance where any retuning occurred – that would be an unthinkable embarrassment for the musician. Pieces also end with a brief modal coda.

▶ *Noh*

Noh vocals (collectively called *utai*, 'singing') include *kotoba*, a non-metric heightened speech style used for most dialogue sections, and *fushi*, 'melody'. Melodic singing centres around three nuclear pitches called *jō* (upper), *chū* (middle) and *ge* (lower). How these are realised, however, depends on which of two singing styles is used. In 'soft singing' (*yowagin*), these three pitches are separated by fourths, and other pitches gravitate around them; vocal range may just exceed an octave. In 'strong singing' (*tsuyogin*), these pitches are collapsed into the total range of about a major third; a strong vibrato obscures precise pitches, and the pitch level often slides up perceptibly during a passage. These two styles suit different plot situations: yowagin for a young maiden, tsuyogin for a battle with a vengeful warrior's spirit, and so forth.

▶ Nagauta (and most other shamisen genres), shakuhachi, koto

All of these are dominated by the miyako-bushi mode with its downward-resolving semitones, and it is quite common to modulate in mid-flow to another 'key' a fourth or fifth away. In nagauta, some other shamisen genres, and the koto repertoire where a piece may run for twenty minutes or more, interest may be added by retuning in mid-piece, effectively shifting the preferred tonal centre though usually retaining the basic mode. For shamisen, the three standard tunings are a fifth over a fourth, a fourth over a fifth, or two fourths. On the koto, tuning bridges will need to be moved under several strings.

▶ Melody and polyphony

Japanese melody lines are generally highly ornamented, and appreciation centres on this horizontal dimension of musical complexity. The vertical combination of tones – polyphony – is less exploited, and there is no system of functional, chordal harmony. But several types of polyphony do exist. Most common, as throughout Asia, is heterophony, in which each instrument, including the vocal part, performs its own idiomatic variant of a single melody. This is perhaps clearest in sankyoku and least obvious, though still true, in togaku. Example 3.1 shows a passage of a jiuta piece, featuring voice, koto, shamisen and shakuhachi in heterophonic variation. The koto and shamisen, with their sharp plucked attacks, keep the pulse; voice and shakuhachi often lag just behind. This is common to many genres: plucked instruments keep a beat while voices and flutes play around the plucked melody. Japan's only bowed instrument, the upright three-string fiddle *kokyū*, rarely heard now, would also be able to elaborate the plucked melodic lines.

Koto and shamisen genres occasionally feature a highly independent second melodic line (*kaede*), in the same metre and key but otherwise vertically unrelated; two such parts converge in unison at cadential points. (See above for the unique interaction of flute and vocals in noh.)

▶ Rhythm and metre

Many traditional pieces have no beat or pulse, and thus no metre. Such 'free metre/rhythm' is most common in shakuhachi solos and folk song, where durations are at the performer's discretion, within reason. Scholars and performers take great pride in a concept they consider uniquely Japanese: that of *ma*, the 'space' between sounds. This often refers to a correct execution of

EX. 3.1 An excerpt from the sankyoku piece *Hagi no Tsuyu*, composed by Ikuyama Kengyo in the 1870s, and transcribed from the CD *Abe Keiko no shigei 3* (Victor VZCG-128, 1997). A diagonal line between two tied notes indicates portamento; the note-head *x* denotes non-fixed pitch.

difficult free rhythms, but it can also refer to the (impossible to quantify) perfect amount of silence inserted in a metric passage, and also in general to a good sense of rhythm. The native view is that only Japan has *ma*, though the Western term rubato covers many similar phenomena. Japanese jazz musicians, seeking credence in the West as more than mere imitators, have sometimes cited *ma* as a unique feature of their performances.[12]

Metrical music is overwhelmingly in duple metres corresponding to Western 2/4 or 6/8, the latter being common only in folk songs and dances. (Triple metre, dominant in nearby Korea, is largely absent from Japan.) The beat, however, can be elastic. In many shamisen pieces the first of a pair of eighth-notes may give a small but noticeable portion of its length to the second; in *nagauta* this may be called *tsume-ma*, 'compressed duration' – that magic word *ma* again. Scholarly staff notations of togaku pieces can capture the pitches and inter-part relations fairly well, but they cannot show the gradual extending of durational values near the end of each four-bar phrase. There is no conductor in togaku (nor in any Japanese genre): performers 'feel' the beat – a challenge, given the extremely slow tempo. Different instruments help convey the beat at different points: for example, the sho player, whose instrument sounds continuously as he inhales and exhales, begins to move his fingers individually to play the chord for the next bar. Perhaps one to three pitches out of the six or so in the chord will thus be shifted just before the next strong beat.

Concepts of metre and rhythm differ among genres. Let us consider – greatly simplified – the most complex example, noh. Though most metrical passages are in eight-beat units called *kusari*, their execution is less simply described. First, sometimes the drums keep a beat but the vocal is in free rhythm. Second, there are several different ways to set texts: twelve syllables per kusari in slower passages (with perhaps four kusari per minute), up to sixteen in more urgent sections, and eight syllables in the rapid final section (often fifteen or sixteen kusari per minute). Third, in those twelve-syllable kusari the drums sometimes keep a steady (though often rubato) metre; at other times the vocal part dominates and the drums must omit some half-beats. Each of these features relates to specific places and moods in a play; even a first-time listener will feel some of the effects.

▸ *Tone colour and timbral preferences*

Contrasting with Western classical music's traditional emphasis on relatively 'pure' sounds, the Japanese musical aesthetic – as in much of the world, and in contemporary Western music – embraces various types of pitchless sounds. Some listeners might consider these mere 'noise', but they result from conscious musical choice.

The shamisen and biwa lute feature a buzzing sound called *sawari*, whose quality and amount is crucial in evaluating a given instrument. A distant historical relation is hypothesised with India, where a similar effect is called *jawari* or *jiwari*. The percussive striking of the large plectrum against the instrument's face is another such feature of Japanese lute genres. Koto and shamisen players often scrape a string lengthwise to create a swishing sound. Solo shakuhachi pieces may employ *muraiki*, a dramatic pitchless blast of air. Sometimes such effects imitate the sounds of insects, wind or an arrow striking its target. At other times the symbolism is abstract: conventionalised drum patterns of off-stage kabuki musicians can represent a river, the seashore, rain, snow or even a thief, though only an aficionado will recognise the connection.[13] Japanese vocal tone is also generally less 'pure' (though no more artificial) than Western bel canto. Preference varies by genre, and both loudness and clarity must be matched to the venue and audience. Puppet-theatre chanters, for example, once strove to develop powerful yet raspy voices by trying to 'out-sing' waterfalls.

■ Musical forms

Do Japanese classical genres have structural forms on a par with sonata allegro, symphonic form and the like? To some degree yes, though such formal tendencies are less clearly named or theorised than in the West, as we will see with some significant forms.

▶ Togaku

We can look at togaku pieces at two structural levels. First, a typical piece will have a structure similar to an Irish reel or jig – though the moods and tempi could not be farther apart. The best-known piece, 'Etenraku', consists of three sections, each of which is repeated before moving to the next (AA BB CC); the entire structure is then repeated, though generally ending after the repeated B section. In togaku the first phrase is performed by a solo flute, with the other instruments gradually joining in.

'Etenraku' is a complete piece on its own (though preceded by an appropriate modal prelude). But some pieces are in effect one movement of a tripartite structure called *jo-ha-kyū*, a concept imported from Tang China, whose court-music connections caused Zeami to seek relevance for it in noh as well. Such prestigious ancestry has encouraged its attempted application by theorists and performers in many genres ever since, even when of doubtful relevance. In general, it implies a slow beginning (*jo*), followed by a more forceful and rapid middle section (*ha*) and finally a rush to the end (*kyu*). The typical progress of a noh play is seen in this way. More surprising for me, yet useful, was being told by kabuki hand-drummer Mochizuki Tasaku III that hitting the drum was a matter of jo-ha-kyu: slowly move the arm back in preparation; begin a steady movement towards the drumskin; finish with an accelerating flick of the wrist.

▶ Noh

There is no overall standard structure of a noh play, but the jo-ha-kyu concept works well: things move more slowly at the beginning and eventually rush to a vibrant climax. Plays last from sixty to eighty minutes; most are in two acts, with no interval but instead a transitional scene preparing the way for the second act. During this transition, the main actor (*shite*) leaves the stage to change costume and identity: the local peasant of the first half may be revealed as the ghost of someone renowned who died there in tragic circumstances long ago. These changes can have musical implications, as in the play *Funa-Benkei*: in the first act, the shite is the beautiful young woman Shizuka, parting tearfully from her lover, the warrior hero Yoshitsune; all the songs in Act I are in the soft, melodic yowagin style suited to such sadness. In Act II, the shite returns as the ghost of the slain warrior Tomomori, seeking revenge on Yoshitsune; now the singing is in the powerful tsuyogin style.

Noh employs hundreds of named, stereotyped elements, ranging from roughly two hundred brief recurring patterns of each drum part, to long dance sections, to standard opening pieces suitable for different characters (priest, courtier and so on). A single dance and its music, for example 'Chū no mai', can recur in several plays with minor differences.

▶ Nagauta

Detailed analyses of nagauta structure are available, but the most common outline is a six-part form whose application varies (as does symphonic form).[14] Nagauta is through-composed. The introduction (*oki*), generally in free rhythm, has one singer and one shamisen setting the scene, and draws on a large number of standard named patterns. The vocal may be partly in heightened speech. The rhythmic *michiyuki* then accompanies the entrance of the dancer(s); though varying with the nature of the plot and characters, it generally begins with the full instrumental ensemble. Next comes the *kudoki*, a softer, lyrical vocal passage usually without drums. A lively dance section (*odoriji*) then brings the taiko stick-drum to vigorous prominence. The final two sections are shorter and generally accelerating: *chirashi* and *dangire*. In the chirashi, the taiko and noh flute often play as a unit, but out of phase with the other instruments, thus providing a fascinating tension. Listening to such a piece, you will be able to follow these changes of mood, and perhaps imagine the dance style that might match each of them.

▶ Shakuhachi honkyoku

In Kinko and other pre-Meiji pieces, the basic formal unit is the single breath-phrase, lasting eight to twelve seconds; many of these phrases recur as melodic units in different pieces, with a few being named ornaments (similar to Western terms such as mordent). Thus a *nayashi* is a phrase beginning as a *meri* (lowered pitch, discussed above) of the preceding pitch, then slowly resolving up to that preceding pitch, and perhaps ending with an almost inaudible wispy return to the meri. Nayashi occur in most tunes.

As for the overall form of a piece, many patterns exist, none standard: these include arch form, A–B–C–B', and others eluding simple description.

Japan's classical musics today

All of these genres underwent important changes from the 1870s onward, due both to Meiji modernisation and the impact of the introduction of Western music. The single most crucial step, still affecting musical tastes today, was the decision in the 1870s to prioritise Western style in school music education. Sadly, for well over a century afterwards, no schoolchild in Japan was ever required by the national music curriculum to perform on a traditional instrument: the musical language, and the instruments they encountered, were Western, with the new songs written for school use being heavily influenced by Western scales and harmonies. In recent decades, Japanese traditional musics have been introduced, but only via recordings and brief written descriptions. Music teachers were not required to learn anything about traditional music, nor were they generally interested or competent enough to excite the interest of their pupils. Not surprising, then, that students of piano or violin far outstrip those of koto or shamisen; the sho is left in the dust by its descendant, the accordion.

A glimmer of change occurred in the 1960s. Japan had recovered from the damage to its national pride and its economy by the Second World War, and was becoming an economic superpower. Western-style 'classical' composers such as Takemitsu and Miki Minoru began producing pieces for Japanese instruments, often combined with Western ones. Performers have continued to produce new works for Japanese instruments alone, some neo-traditional, some strikingly modern; among the more renowned are koto master Sawai Tadao (1938–97) and shakuhachi master Yamamoto Hōzan (1937–2014). Then there is Tōgi Hideki (b. 1959), descendant of a togaku lineage, who has taken his decade of hichiriki playing in the imperial ensemble in the direction of New Age compositions. The young listeners he attracts have a very different perception from that of court lady Sei Shōnagon (c. 966–1017) who, a thousand years ago, found this instrument 'very hard on the ear'.[15]

Since 2003, efforts have been made to include traditional music teaching in the national curriculum: first, middle school students were required to experience hands-on a traditional instrument of some kind; and today students at all levels are to learn to sing local folk songs (considered more accessible than, say, noh). Moreover, all music teachers must now have studied a traditional instrument during their training. Alas, class time devoted to traditional genres is still only a desultory few hours per year in some schools, as teachers focus on preparing their students for the national choral competition and other Western-inclined events.

Meanwhile the training of future professionals still depends largely on the traditional artistic schools (*ryū(ha)*). To succeed in noh, you need to study with a (male) master from one of the five schools. But desperation for successors in kabuki led to the creation in 1972 of a training school for actors at Tokyo's National Theatre; from there, graduates still need to apprentice themselves to a successful professional. Tokyo University of the Arts and NHK (the national broadcasting company) have for decades trained and examined performers in

A sankyoku trio with koto (Ginevra House), shamisen (Shino Arisawa) and shakuhachi (Matt Gillan) performing at the School of Oriental and African Studies in London in 2003

many genres. The high importance but low status often accorded to traditional musicians in the past has, ironically, been somewhat reversed. Some musicians who in the past would have been excluded from – or relegated to the fringes of – polite society are now Living National Treasures (*ningen kokuhō*) under the government's scheme that laid the foundations for Intangible Cultural Heritage policy worldwide, as enshrined in UNESCO's scheme. But this lofty official status rarely translates into interest from the general public, and these initiatives surely come too late to have a major positive impact on the future of traditional music after a century of neglect. Yet there are still millions of committed adherents, which means that the major classical genres are indeed 'living' and can be enjoyed in today's Japan – with a bit of searching.

Hope may also lie beyond the borders of Japan. Composers worldwide have been stimulated by Japanese music, and many have written for Japanese instruments: Stockhausen's *Jahreslauf* was commissioned by the court togaku ensemble, and two years later (1979) was arranged for Western instruments as well; Henry Cowell's 1940 composition for shakuhachi was endearingly titled *The Universal Flute*; and John Kaizan Neptune continues to produce an amazing diversity of shakuhachi solo and ensemble pieces, crossing cultural boundaries. Many others have written for Western instruments under influence from Japan: Benjamin Britten's 'church parable' *Curlew River* (1964) was based on the noh play *Sumidagawa*, which he saw in Japan in 1956; he intentionally avoided seeing noh again until the work was completed, to prevent producing a mere imitation of its musical language (though in fact there is arguably as much influence in it from gagaku as from noh).

Moreover, all these genres are being performed abroad, and not just by Japanese expatriates. Skilled koto players abound; a gagaku group practices in Cologne under a Japanese teacher; there is a thriving European Shakuhachi Society, and a World Shakuhachi Festival has been held in Boulder, Colorado and in Sydney, Australia. A noh troupe merging Japanese and US performers presented a new play in English (to a libretto by a British-born Chinese) in London in 2009, then in Japan and China in 2011.

What does the future hold for the classical musics of Japan? Only time will tell if later generations will prefer the New Age musings of Togi Hideki to 'real' togaku, or J. S. Bach as played on a twenty-one-string koto in preference to Yatsuhashi Kengyo (d. 1685) played on thirteen strings.

Further reading

Five easily-found sources give valuable overviews of Japanese traditional music, including the genres above. Each has extensive transcriptions as well as a useful bibliography leading to numerous other sources. Malm's *Traditional Japanese Music and Musical Instruments* (including a CD) is user-friendly and well-illustrated. Tokita and Hughes's *The Ashgate Research Companion to Japanese Music* (with CD) is much more detailed. Wade's *Music in Japan* is shorter but accessible, though confusingly inconsistent in its romanisation (thus *shakuhachi* is given as *syakuhati*, using the Kunreishiki system, even though most other terms are in the more common Hepburn system). The *New Grove Dictionary of Music and Musicians* is now also online via Grove Music Online. Finally, the East Asia volume of *Garland Encyclopedia of World Music* (vol. 7, with CD) has extensive coverage of Japan, though it too uses the less common Kunreishiki romanisation. See also Malm's *Six Hidden Views of Japanese Music* for, among other things, a direct comparison of noh and kabuki music, and a comparison of Britten's *Curlew River* with the noh play *Sumidagawa* on which it was based.

Recommended listening

These CDs were chosen for their musical quality, English-language liner-notes and relatively easy availability outside Japan. To order items from Japan when abroad, start with the website of Far Side Music (www.farsidemusic.com), which also handles DVDs of noh, kabuki and other genres. The CDs with books listed in the Bibliography have a range of excerpts. To find performances on YouTube, search by instrument name, genre, composition title or for contemporary pieces perhaps by composer's name.

Tokyo Gakuso (Tadaaki Ohno): Gagaku and beyond, Celestial Harmonies 13179-2, 2000. A good cross-section of court music genres, with extensive English notes by Steven Nelson.

Musique du nô: Shakkyô, Ocora C 559005, 1987. The music of this noh play is analysed in Malm's *Hidden Views of Japanese Music*.

Kineya Ensemble, *Japan: Nagauta*, Ocora C 560144, 2000. Four nagauta pieces, one in somewhat modern style from 1933. Offstage *geza* music is not recorded.

Katsuya Yokoyama, *Zen: Katsuya Yokoyama Plays Classical Shakuhachi Masterworks* (2 CDs), Wergo SM1033-34, 1988. A variety of Kinko-school pieces by a Living National Treasure performer.

Ensemble Yonin no Kai, *Japon: Jiuta*, Ocora C 580069, 1998. Koto, shamisen, shakuhachi, voice; includes a sankyoku piece, a Tozan-school shakuhachi piece and two others.

Japan: Koto Music, Nonesuch 451836-2, 2008. Koto, shamisen, shakuhachi, voice, sankyoku.

China, showing the provinces mentioned in this and the following chapter

4 China: The Guqin Zither

Frank Kouwenhoven

A scholar – and owner of a zither – pauses in his climb up a mountain; as a rich man he can afford a servant or pupil to carry his heavy instrument to the top. After a while he sits down cross-legged under a pine tree, places his instrument on his lap and begins to play for the gods – or for himself. The wind touches his strings furtively, and he might sing a poem or two, plucking the strings randomly to produce soft sounds: some evasive and questioning slide tones, and a sonorous buzz on the lowest string, reminiscent of the sound of a distant bell; or perhaps some clear and pure harmonics in the highest register, brought forth by touching the strings very lightly. All this is interspersed with contemplative pauses; the music merges delicately with the surrounding silence. The mist on the mountain serves as a reminder of the world's deep emptiness: vast crags and abysses mock the futility of human strife and ambition.

Is this a real performance? It might be, but more likely it's just a scene from our imagination, or from an old painting or ink-drawing portraying an age-old ideal of *qin* performance. Back in the Tang dynasty (618–907 CE), playing the qin, China's seven-stringed classical zither, was one of the four 'gentlemanly skills', along with chess, calligraphy and painting; one of the pastimes of Chinese intellectuals. Sage-like figures playing the instrument are a popular topic in classical lore; Confucius himself (551–479 BCE) was reputed to be a fine player. Steeped in both Confucian and Daoist philosophy, the qin is strongly associated with the natural world, and with its assumed ability to 'sound the cosmos'. A performer playing on top of a mountain or in a bamboo grove remains a potent fantasy of what qin players try to achieve: they foster a dream of spiritual communion with nature, even to the extent of themselves vanishing at the end of their music. For thousands of years qin players have aspired to attain wisdom and redemption with their art, and through it to live in blissful harmony with their environment. These ideals are still cherished by some in China today.

The Chinese visual arts abound in pictures of outdoor zither performers – mostly men, but sometimes also women – playing their instrument in garden pavilions, or amid impressive scenery. A vast body of poems, myths and tales portray the qin as mystically connected with nature, though genuine outdoor playing must always have been rare: the soft sound is easily lost in the wind, and the instrument can be damaged through exposure to moist air and outdoor conditions. In overcrowded twenty-first-century China, qin enthusiasts are usually confined to playing in small apartments in skyscrapers, amid the constant din of traffic, or in teahouses. This does not prevent their appreciating the instrument's associated imagery and philosophical connotations. For many, the seven-stringed zither is a way of life.

CHINA: THE GUQIN ZITHER

With a history of nearly three millennia, the qin, or guqin ('gu' means 'old', 'qin' simply means 'instrument') is at once one of the most humble and haughty of instruments. One thirteenth-century source praises it as an emblem of spirituality and moral virtue, and warns players not to perform in 'the presence of a vulgar man, a courtesan, an actor' or in 'a drunken and noisy atmosphere'. More than ten centuries earlier, another text claimed that 'of all those things the Superior Man always has around him, he loves the qin best, and he does not suffer it to be separated from him'. Scholars have produced a vast store of notations: some three thousand tablatures, amounting to an estimated 650 individual pieces plus many variants, contained in some 150 handbooks; most date from the fifteenth to nineteenth centuries, but one piece survives from the seventh century. Notations exist for a number of China's musical traditions, from medieval Tang court music to eighteenth-century *pipa* music, and from 'silk and bamboo' music to operatic tunes, but there is nothing to match in size or scope the vast body of qin scores, which provide unique insights into the music of the past.

Today it is no longer only 'superior men' who play the instrument. A renewed interest in China's native cultural roots has led to a widespread boom in qin playing, which is now taught in conservatories and art institutes, and privately in teahouses and homes, and it can often be heard on television. From the 1980s onwards, composers such as Tan Dun started to write new pieces for the qin, and some players have taken pride in improvising on it, and in collaborating with jazz and rock musicians. A recording of the piece *Gaoshan liushui* ('High Mountains and Flowing Streams') as played by Guan Pinghu, one of the guqin masters of the twentieth century, was sent into space on the Voyager spacecraft in 1977 as one of the samples of the Earth's music.

Some purists regret the qin's modern transformation into an 'ordinary' instrument, arguing that ties with the classical tradition have been lost. Qin players of the past often took pupils into their own homes, offering them lodging and a full education into the bargain: the qin did indeed become a way of life. For modern conservatory students the main challenge of the instrument may lie in its technical difficulties, not in the associated metaphysical or moral aspirations, but many view this as a liberation. And although the qin cannot match the popularity of the piano or the Chinese 21-stringed *zheng* zither among the urban middle classes, more young people than ever before are now learning to pluck a few tones. They may know little of its history, but they understand its importance as an emblem of traditional high culture.

A qin performance speaks both to the ear and the eye. The melancholy sliding tones and the trance-like state of the performers may at times be almost reminiscent of American guitar blues, but the grace of the hand and finger movements, the characteristic timbres, the architecture of the pieces and the poetry, imagery and philosophy which frame the tradition represent an art which is 'classical' in every sense of the word.

◄ 'Listening to the qin'. Part of a scroll kept at the Palace Museum in the Forbidden City in Beijing, this painting is thought to be by Zhao Ji, court painter to the Song dynasty Emperor Huizong (1082–1135). It shows the emperor playing the qin under a fir tree, while two men listen in pensive mood. Their simple attire and the peacefulness of the setting suggest an intimacy far removed from the business of state.

Qin and concepts of classical music in China

The term *gudian yinyue* ('classical music') was coined in China in the 1950s to denote Western classical music. It was a translation of the Western term, a contraction of *gudai jingdian yinyue*, which can be rendered as 'old' (*gudai*) 'classic'/'essential' (*jingdian*) 'music' (*yinyue*). In recent years it has begun to gain alternative currency as an umbrella term for prestigious native genres, from qin to Buddhist music and beyond. This signals not only increasing sympathy in China for qin and other traditions, but a growing cultural pride, as well as changing attitudes towards foreign music. Before exploring the 'historical' qin we must consider the tremendous impact which Western music and culture had on twentieth-century China, and how deeply it changed ideas about native music.

Virtually unknown in China around 1900, Western piano, choral and symphonic music rose to great popularity after the 1940s – despite Maoist criticisms of its 'decadence' – and became unstoppable by the 1980s. Today, many urban Chinese would rate Western music – be it classical or pop – higher than any of their own traditions. Western aesthetics, teaching methods, musical structures and concepts quickly found acceptance in the urban China of the 1950s, as music history and musicology were established on the Western model, which was deemed superior. The ideal of educational reformers like Xiao Youmei (who co-founded the Shanghai Conservatory) was not so much to develop Chinese traditional music alongside Western music, as to 'upgrade' it by making it conform to Western conventions.

Founded mostly in the 1950s, the conservatories – and the music departments established later in hundreds of universities – dealt primarily with Western music. Most had departments focusing on Chinese traditional music, but the teaching of native instruments came to rely increasingly on Western methods. The qin, being less adaptable to this than many other Chinese instruments, found a foothold in such institutions only with difficulty, if at all. The China Conservatory in Beijing, founded in 1964, was the one exception in that it specialised primarily in native instruments. Even here, however, students of *pipa*, *zheng* or *erhu* soon spent much of their time racing through scales and etudes in major and minor keys, exploring staccato, ritardando, functional harmony and other foreign inventions. Playing techniques, repertoire and even the designs of native instruments were modified to match assumed Western ideals: the composer He Luting criticised them for their 'unstable pitch' and for not having a bass register, and he and many others supported innovations such as equal-tempered tuning, enlarged resonance chambers and steel strings to enhance loudness. What began as spontaneous reforms took on the aspect of official directives, even government regulations. In 1958, most mainland Chinese qin players switched from silk to steel strings, and some began to incorporate Western classical ideas of phrasing, rhythm and structuring. But the changes in qin music were still subtle compared to the way in which the erhu two-stringed fiddle was turned into a Chinese bravura equivalent of the Western violin.

The government of the People's Republic encouraged modernisation of Chinese traditions, and propagated the development of 'patriotic' elite music.

A new class of professionally-trained urban musicians was expected to raise Chinese traditions to new standards of excellence; this reflected a dream of replaying the glories of the Confucian court music of imperial times. Large ballet and opera troupes and 'Chinese orchestras' (*minzu yuetuan*, modelled after Western symphony orchestras with mostly native instruments) would help foster a new and stronger China, and invigorate native culture. But many rural genres and regional forms did not fit the bill: they were too rough, too religious, and too embedded in village rituals and other 'backward' practices which – so the government felt – China should abandon. Folk music was therefore largely ignored, at least in urban music education and in the government's cultural support policies. And the qin seemed a particularly bad fit with the new policies: its players thought of themselves as sophisticated amateurs rather than modern music professionals, and the idea of becoming concert virtuosos (let alone political propagandists) appealed to few, as did the dream of a new 'national' music for the masses. Moreover, many had been landowners before 1949, and preferred to keep a low profile in communist China. Consequently, the voice of the ancient zither was not much heard until the 1980s and '90s, when China embarked on its boom, opened up once more (and more liberally) to influences from outside, and began to take a fresh look at its own traditions. The qin was still slow to gain wide attention, but the number of commercial recordings increased tenfold. It certainly became more visible, but the question remained: could it be called 'classical'? A minority of urban intellectual Chinese would say yes, but there was – and still is – no broad consensus.

Gudian yinyue – initially adopted for Western classical music – is now applied differently by different users to a wide variety of native genres, including qin but also rural shawm bands, teahouse ensembles and Tibetan opera (though for some the term still merely points towards Haydn or Beethoven). A shorter term, *jingdian yinyue,* ('the very best music') came into use in the 1990s, mainly in commercial contexts like CD advertisements and names of CD shops, and it signalled a similar broadening of view, with shops selling Western classical as well as Chinese pop and traditional music including qin. This more liberal application of the term *jingdian yinyue* sits well with history. Antiquity had its own criteria for 'high' and 'low', but the Confucian elite of ancient imperial times liked all kinds of music, from *bangzi* (rural opera) to large ceremonial court orchestras, from the rough-and-ready sound of shawm bands, which they employed for their life-cycle rituals, to the ethereal qin, with its role as a vessel through which divine revelation flowed.

■ A static tradition?

The form of this instrument has barely changed through two millennia, with the oldest surviving examples equivalent in size and shape to the modern qin dating from the Tang dynasty. But as stone reliefs and tomb figurines from the Han dynasty (206 BCE–220 CE) show, the model goes back much further in time. It was during the Western Han (206 BCE–24 CE) that the instrument attained its current size, its familiar trapezoidal form and its seven strings.

This qin is arguably the most famous of all Chinese zithers surviving from antiquity. Believed to be from the Tang (618–907 CE), it is kept at the Forbidden City Museum in Beijing. Its name, Jiu xiao huanpei ('Heavenly jade jewel'), is inscribed on the instrument's reverse, above the two soundholes. Poetic lines on the back, probably added later, state that this qin sounds 'bright and melodious as in former times' and evoke (in words by the Tang poets Ting Jian and Su Dongpo) scenes from nature. The framed seal carries the characters bao han ('all-encompassing'), which may have Daoist connotations. The patterns of cracks in the lacquer are known by special names, shifu duan ('snake stomach') and xi niumao ('cow skin').

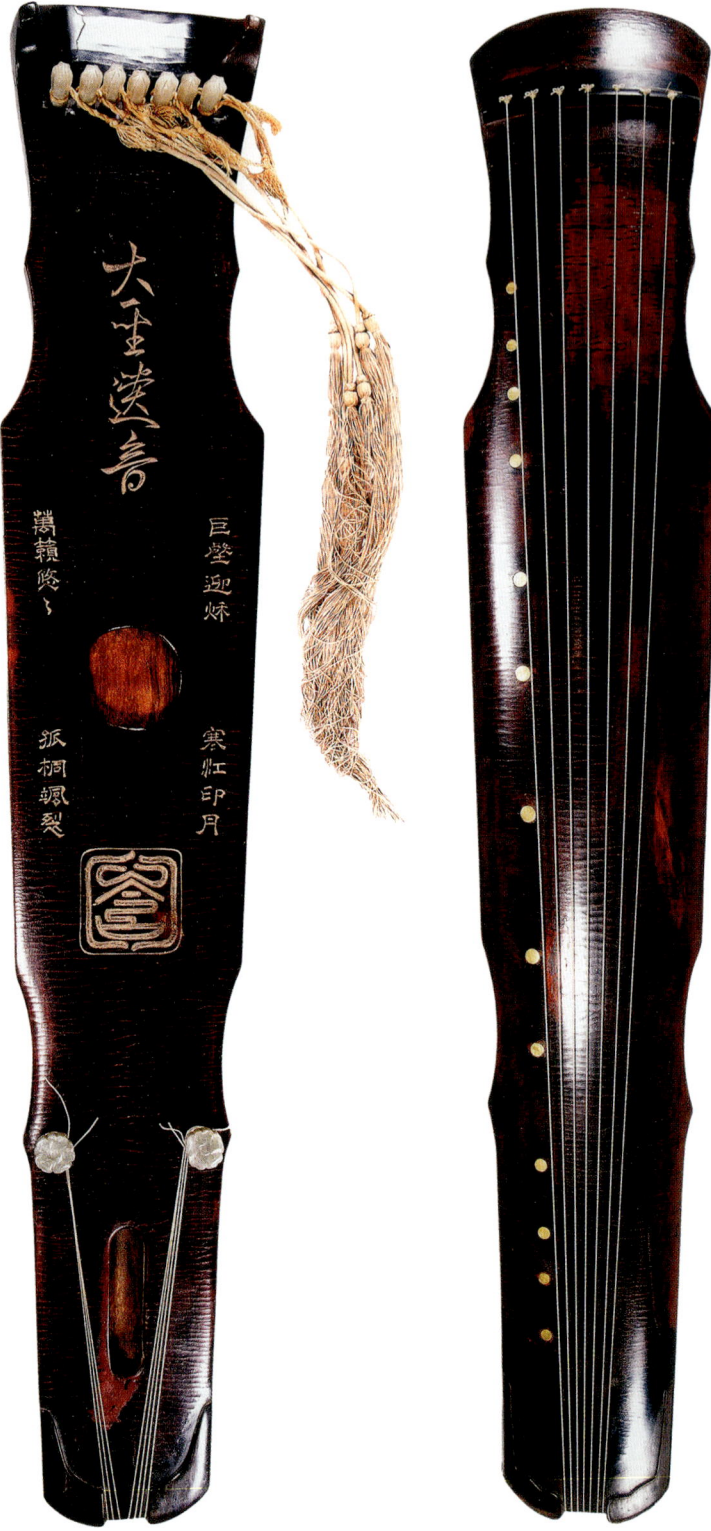

A 'standard' qin has a body approximately 120 cm long, 20 cm wide at one end and 15 cm at the other, and is made of two pieces of wood joined to make a sound chamber with two holes underneath. The upper board, slightly domed, is made of softer wood, traditionally *wutong* (*firmiana simplex*), while the flat lower board is made from hard *zi* wood (Chinese *catalpa*). The dome's top is traditionally said to symbolise heaven and the flat base earth, with the player forming the third point in this triangle. The entire instrument is coated with layer upon layer of hard red or black lacquer whose thickness and quality to a large extent determines the sound quality. The seven strings are fastened to two wooden knobs driven into the bottom board. On the top side the strings fan out between a bridge at the left end and a longer one on the right, where they are spaced out enough for the right hand to pluck them. In between, the strings are freely suspended, and are stopped by being pushed onto the lacquer surface with the left hand. Thirteen mother-of-pearl markers (*hui*) are inset into the body to indicate harmonic nodes showing where to stop the strings. The left bridge of the qin is poetically known as the 'harmony pond', the right is described as the 'mountain', and the strings then pass through holes through the instrument to seven 'precious pegs' for tuning.

Most of these elements have been in place for many centuries. The earliest known references to the hui stem from a third-century qin essay by Ji Kang; the earliest known picture of them is a fourth- or fifth-century tomb brick relief from Nanjing. This shows a group of Daoist scholars known as the Seven Sages of the Bamboo Grove relaxing outdoors; two sit cross-legged with qin on their laps; one can clearly see the hui on the surface of their instruments.

Some surviving prototypes for the 'modern' qin predate the Han period by several centuries, but these are very different in appearance. Their bodies are much smaller (67–82 cm), their shape is different (a broad box with a narrow neck), their playing surface so uneven that probably only open strings were plucked, with the number of strings varying from five to ten. How exactly we got from these instruments to the later versions is unclear, but there is little doubt that these early zithers are qin, too. Their black-lacquered bodies carved from a single piece of wood, their very thick soundboards (up to 48 mm), and the string-count and the use of tuning pegs for fine-tuning all point towards the later instrument.

Following the Han standardisation, individual qin could still vary in contours and size. Modern scholarship identifies fourteen different basic models, ranging from fairly straight and rectangular qin to more curved instruments such as the oval type *Jiaoye* ('banana leaf') or the wavy-lined *Luoxia* ('evening cloud').[1] The qin's colours are subject to variation too, with instruments painted purple, red, vermilion, yellow, brown or a combination of colours, or – in the last few centuries – mainly black. After hundreds of years cracks emerge spontaneously in the lacquer and form distinctive patterns of considerable beauty. No less evocative are the engravings on the underside of many instruments: dates, names of owners, seal impressions, bequests, lines of poetry or laudatory prose, all carved in gracious Chinese characters, often in deliberately ancient pictorial forms to increase the impression of antiquity. Proud owners gave names to

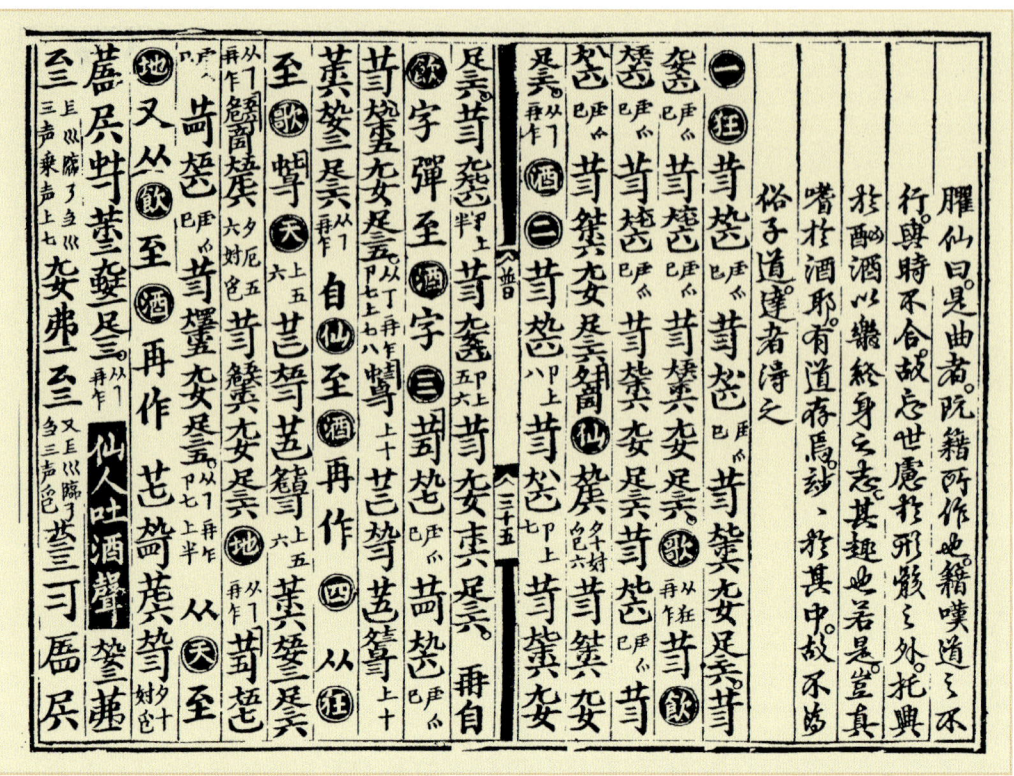

Tablature notation of *Jiu kuang* (*Drunken madness*), a piece from the 1425 qin music anthology *Shenqi mipu* (*Handbook of Spiritual and Marvellous Mysteries*). The score is read from top to bottom and from right to left. The compound symbols indicate fingering, plucking and stopping modes and string positions.

their instruments like 'Celestial Jade Jewel', 'Spring Thunder', 'Singing bell' or 'Dragon's Thunder'. Traditions of name-giving and calligraphic writing on the bottom of the instrument continue today.

Except for the engravings most instruments are not decorated, but one surviving qin from the Tang period, now kept at the Shoshoin, the Imperial Treasury at Nara in Japan, is lavishly ornamented, a magnificent artefact with inlaid gold and silver decorations, plant and bird patterns and line drawings of men playing music and drinking wine outdoors. There were also lavishly decorated qin in Han times, but none seem to have survived. After the Tang, instruments became plainer, but they remained collector's items, semi-sacred objects ideal for decorating a wall. Forgeries of 'ancient' qin were probably of all ages, too.

At all events, antiquity matters: qin players are proud of their tradition's long lines of transmission. This has led some music historians to speak of a 'static' or 'rigid' tradition, but that may be misleading: two performers in an imagined encounter across time might not really have much in common except for a handful of tunes. What do we truly know about the past of the qin? There are many gaps in our knowledge, the interpretation of data can be problematic, and we constantly run the risk of interpreting China's musical past too exclusively through the eyes of the country's ruling elite, whose legacy monopolises our sources. Any attempt to sketch the instrument's history must be tentative.

■ *The seven-stringed zither in earliest times*

In antiquity the qin was played both as a solo instrument and in ceremonial court ensembles in groups of six or twelve qin together with other instruments. Initially, perhaps only the open strings were plucked. Qin was used to accompany dance, presumably in music that was measured and in folk style; some evidence suggests that the qin may have served as a percussion instrument. The oldest surviving literary references to it – in the *Shujing* (Book of History) and the *Shijing* (Book of Odes), dating from 1000–600 BCE – state that the qin could be 'swept or gently touched' or even 'drummed'; clay figures of musicians from the Han dynasty, unearthed in Sichuan, show the performance combination of qin and hand drum.[2] The qin was also used to accompany songs.

From the Han period onward, the instrument became increasingly the preserve of connoisseurs, but there is no evidence that commoners were ever barred from playing it. Tomb reliefs from the fourth century BCE to the second century CE show large ceremonial court orchestras with bells, stone chimes, drums, pipes, mouth organs, various types of zithers (qin and *se*) and dancers. Grand 'heaven and earth' rituals were held at fixed calendrical dates as sacrificial ceremonies for the gods. The Book of History refers to chimes and zithers being 'struck loudly or gently' to summon the spirits of imperial ancestors, but the qin also featured in more intimate contexts of entertainment and courtship. A tomb relief from the fifth century CE shows five ladies strolling at leisure with qin, panpipes, a mouth organ and a moon lute, amid outdoor scenery. The Book of Odes contains references to gallant courtship and family happiness: 'loving harmony with wives and children is like the union of qin and *se*'. The *se* was a larger and more unwieldy type of zither with about twenty-five strings supported by movable bridges; after the Han it went into decline and was replaced by a lighter successor, the fourteen-stringed *zheng*, but until that time the se was widespread, and probably – with its wider compass and louder sound – a more popular type of zither than the qin.

The qin had risen to new prominence during the Han era, when it became bigger and standardised, and saw its ideology and aesthetics firmly established. Han sources hint at a fixed repertoire and the existence of different styles of playing. The *Qincao*, a well-known qin treatise attributed to mathematician, astronomer and composer Cai Yong (132–92 CE), lists the titles of forty-seven qin songs, plus in many cases the names of their presumed composers, including Confucius and various dukes and kings as well as 'an anonymous woman of Wei state'. As in later times, music in Chinese antiquity was customarily transmitted in oral form; if qin notations existed during the Han era, they have not survived.

That era was a period of territorial expansion, political unification and economic and cultural prosperity. China's money economy expanded, warring kingdoms were united under a single government, and the foundations were laid for the Silk Road trade network. Court and literati traditions (from written language to philosophy, from literature to music) spread, and were infused in turn with ideas from regional and tribal cultures. This was a formative era for the qin, as reflected in writing and art. Noble families in Sichuan – one of Han China's richest and most fertile regions – owned large plots of land, presided over hundreds of servants and had the leisure time to host lavish entertainments. Clay figurines and reliefs of players and dancers found in the Han tombs of Sichuan attest to the richness of elite cultural life during this epoch. There was room for sports, hunting, chamber music with bells, drums, flutes, mouth organs and stringed instruments, and also for rowdy dance spectacles and extravaganzas, as the tomb statues of disfigured drumming and singing dwarfs show; among the figurines are smiling musicians playing the qin.

The mix of 'high' and 'low' culture was nothing new. Excavated in 1978, the fifth-century BCE tomb of Marquis Zeng of Yi in Suizhou, Hubei Province, had already harboured an intriguing contrast in the form of two of the oldest musical ensembles surviving from any culture: one was a sizeable orchestra intended for state ceremonies with large sets of bronze bells, chime stones, twenty-five se zithers and eight wind instruments; the other was an intimate group of eight instruments, presumably for the nobleman's private entertainment. The marquis was buried in a side-room of his tomb, together with eight young female attendants and the chamber instruments, which included a prototype qin with ten strings. His private music may well have been more appealing to the Marquis than the solemn hymns played on bells during state banquets or sacrificial rites.

Intimate string and wind ensembles continued to flourish in China in later centuries, right down to the 'silk and bamboo' orchestras of teahouses in China today. Many types of ceremonial music too have persisted in one form or other since antiquity. Bells and chime stones eventually went out of fashion (except in fanciful 'reconstructions'), but native ancient instruments like mouth organs, end-blown and transverse flutes, vessel flutes (ocarinas), panpipes and zheng zithers still feature in several regional cultures. Wind and percussion ensembles continue to play a role in ritual processions, funerals and other formal or festive occasions.

In all these genres there has always been a sharp divide between the world of amateurs and that of professionals. The traditional amateur ideal in Chinese music, which prevailed until the 1950s, is the very opposite of its counterpart in Western music. Westerners tend to think of amateurs as 'lesser' players, and of professionals as high-level performers. But in Chinese traditional music, amateurs were always high-level musicians, people rich enough to have the time to indulge in art; professionals had lower status because they made money with music, and frequently came from the poorest social strata. Status was further determined by the origin of genres and instruments.

Throughout the centuries China witnessed a substantial import of foreign drums, shawms, plucked lutes and fiddles, as well as musical ideas, especially from Central Asia. 'Barbarian' instruments tended to be looked down upon, at least until they were Sinified – a process which could take centuries. The pipa (of which the prototypes were originally imported from abroad after the Han era) had a hard time surviving during the Ming, which was a xenophobic period. The qin never had such a problem, unless Bo Lawergren is right that the qin was also a Central Asian import,[3] but he gets little support for his views in China.

Today we tend to think of the qin so much as a solo instrument that we may overlook a long history in which it featured in ensemble contexts, starting from its ancient partnership with se (or with *yueqin* moon-lute) right down to the first half of the twentieth century, when players like Guan Pinghu and Pu Xuezhai sometimes played it in combination with bamboo flutes, pipas, mouth organs and other instruments. Some of the oldest citations explicitly connect the instrument with pleasure – indeed, the very character for music is an ancient ideograph which can be pronounced either *yue* (music) or *le* (joy), emphasising the link between them. Interpretations of the meaning of qin music started to change in the Han era, when many scholars began to view the instrument as a tool for intellectual introspection, and as a vehicle for sadness – a shift in perception which influenced all subsequent qin ideology.

■ The birth of modern qin ideology

In the early part of the second century CE, Emperor Wu founded a large music bureau, the *Yuefu*, which he ordered to document the nation's music, including regional folk songs and 'barbarian' tunes. It had to supervise imperial music-making and provide new songs; it organised court spectacles and arranged cavalry music for the army, bringing in tribal drummers and wind players performing on horseback. Such music reflected a growing cosmopolitan spirit.

In this same period, the qin was increasingly played as a solo instrument, and it had to find a new niche. Han intellectuals were fascinated by 'sadness' (*bei*) and by grave sentiments in music, which they associated with exalted emotional states. Under the influence of Confucian and Daoist ideas, qin proponents like Cai Yong and a century later Ji Kang began to promote the instrument, with its delicate sound, as a sacrosanct realm, a kind of cosmic 'hearing-aid'[4] which epitomised the assumed mystical relationship between music and nature. The mystery of qin performance was neatly captured in poetic lines accompanying the Song dynasty (960–1279 CE) score *Liezi yu feng*, 'Liezi riding on the wind':

> I do not know whether the wind is riding on me
> Or whether it's me riding on the wind

But this metaphysical musical quest was very much limited to a small number of intellectuals, and the qin gradually became regarded as a 'lonely' or even 'forgotten' instrument, as the Tang poet Liu Changqing lamented on hearing a qin being played:

> Your seven strings resemble the voice
> Of a cold wind in the fir-trees,
> Singing an old and once beloved song
> Which no one loves any longer

Thus were nostalgia and the idea of neglect integrated into qin lore. This may be easier to understand if we realise that the true historical backdrop of the qin tradition was not some festive court gathering of wealthy literati, but an ancient country of rural poverty, corruption, wars, power struggles and social inequality: qin pieces were full of references to this troubled past, and often emerged in direct response to social tragedies. In this respect, the qin belongs to the same intellectual realm as many Chinese poems and paintings created in exile by dissidents banished to remote areas and barred from official posts. Such people poured their sadness into art.

Ji Kang's claim that 'music has neither sorrow nor joy' has been interpreted as an early reaction against the overriding vogue for sadness; but he did not deny that qin music could evoke emotion. His main polemic was directed against crude escapism and the theatrical exhibition of feelings.[5] For him and for most later qin aficionados, the qin was a symbol of sophistication and intellectual restraint: in the mind of 'superior' man, music would transcend trivial everyday concerns, and sadness and joy would merge in one united experience. This view finds echoes in writings on music from many other cultures.

■ From mountains and rivers to birds and trees

It was thanks to thinkers like Ji Kang, and notably to their mystification of nature, that the qin came to be regarded as an 'instrument of nature'. The nature symbolism of the qin is echoed in paintings, poetry and titles of musical pieces, as well as in qin organology: parts of the instrument have been named 'immortal's shoulders', 'dragon's toothgums', 'phoenix' eye', 'goose feet' and 'dragon's pond'. This even applies to the patterns of cracks appearing in its lacquer coating: 'serpent belly cracks', 'cow's hair', 'turtle back', 'cracked ice'.

Sometimes qin music directly imitates natural sounds such as the flowing of water, the singing of birds, or the dropping of a woman's tears. Hand and finger postures frequently correlate with the shapes of animals or trees, as in the *Taigu yiyin* of 1413, where one finds drawings and descriptions of 'the leopard catching its prey', 'a crane calling in the shade' and 'the lonely duck looking for the flock'. Such drawings – much copied and re-used – have served as practical aids for hand positions, and also as metaphorical extensions of ideas from qin philosophy. The basic task for any traditional player is to capture and faithfully reproduce the spiritual essence or 'mood' (*yijing*) of a piece, an enterprise which invariably leads through mountains and involves encounters with animals, narrative characters and events as reflected in titles, prefaces, poems and illustrations.[6] Not all players experience qin music as mystical evocations of nature, however. The twentieth-century master Zhang Ziqian never spoke to his students about high mountains, great rivers or spiritual aims: he simply instructed them to reproduce the finger techniques he demonstrated and to practice in front of a mirror – and things were probably no different in antiquity. There was always room for more than one approach to the instrument.

Playing the qin 'in nature' as a spiritual exercise probably did occur, though few performers can have wanted to expose their instrument to severe cold or

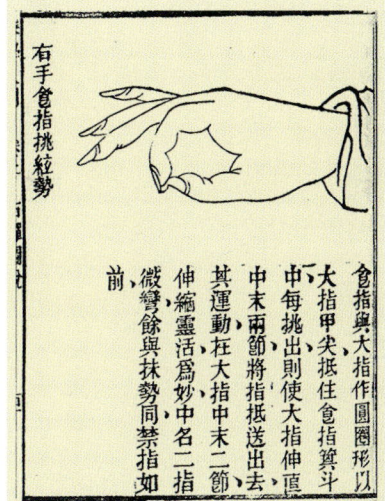

Qin hand postures, as reflected in the Ming dynasty handbook Qinshu daquan (1590). Every posture is compared to an image from nature – a crane, crab, monkey and so on.

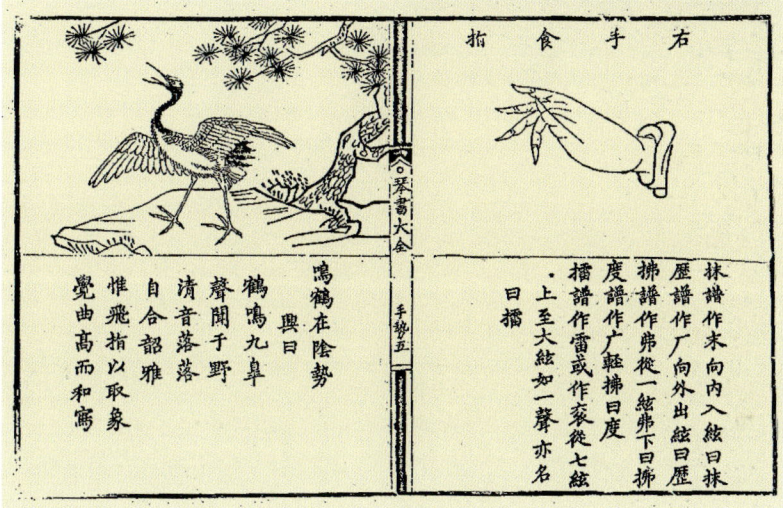

dangerous mountain climbs. Documents from the Song (960–1279) and Ming (1368–1644) list – among ideal situations for playing the qin – 'sitting on a stone', 'having climbed a mountain', 'resting in a valley' or 'resting in a forest', but also advise against playing the qin 'when there is wind and thunder, or in rainy weather'. These rules were presumably made by Daoist monks living in temples and secluded spots who felt an overriding need to live by strict regulations. Some modern qin players like Zheng Chengwei and Lin Youren have confessed an interest in occasionally playing the qin outdoors, on solitary mountain walks. Zheng Chengwei, on one CD cover, honours ancient tradition by sitting in front of a bamboo bush, but also by holding his instrument on his lap in the classical pose, rather than playing it on a table, as became the habit after the Tang and Song.

Qin music from Tang to modern times

We do not know what qin music sounded like before the Tang period. In the third century, Ji Kang urged players to carefully observe the rhythms of pieces, to move their fingers with dexterity and to play slides quickly; he also claimed to distinguish forty-two different types of vibrato, including a fast 'flying vibrato' known as *fei yin*. This may hint at a preference for fast tempi, but without notations we really cannot say much about it. It was only during the Tang that the first surviving notations emerged, and that regional styles of playing proliferated, foreshadowing famous schools such as those of Zhejiang and Jiangsu.

Tang imperial patronage brought an unprecedented synthesis of the arts and blending of cultures, with the great imperial court at Chang'an maintaining thousands of foreign and native musicians and dancers who participated in lavish spectacles. Qin music was now less fashionable at the court, but was still respected in the homes of literati. Detailed musical notations for court ensemble music, as well as for solo qin pieces, began to appear. Some survive in manuscript copies of later dynasties, but one qin piece, *Youlan* ('Solitary Orchid') is extant in the original seventh century manuscript currently kept in Japan (which at that time maintained extensive cultural contacts with China).

The Tang was also an era of great poets, whose lyrics, sung to music, could become instantly popular. But the downfall of the Tang saw a decline of interest in the instrument, with much notated music lost in the ensuing political upheaval, and with a revival documented only from the twelfth century onwards. During the Ming, the first extant full anthologies of notated qin music appeared, starting with the *Shenqi mipu* (Handbook of Spiritual and Marvellous Mysteries), sixty-four pieces printed in 1425 under the auspices of a Ming prince.

Traditional qin notations are mostly in shorthand tablature form (see the illustration on p. 112 above), and indicate fingerings and playing techniques for executing individual pitches or groups of pitches; the beginnings and endings of melodic phrases and of separate sections in the music are marked, but there are few indications of rhythm or metre, and few pieces are attributed to specific composers. Players in the seventeenth century began to record their fingerings in more sophisticated ways, but rhythm – with the exception of a few formulae – was still not indicated.

The first surviving piece to be notated, *Youlan*, is different from all later notations in the sense that it is a descriptive text, explaining sentence by sentence (without abbreviating symbols) the fingering of both hands. One of the oldest surviving pieces of any written melodic music in the Far East, this five- to ten-minute work has been variously attributed to a sixth-century qin player (Qiu Ming) and to Confucius. The score is damaged in places and contains many ambiguities; its interpretation has been subject to debate, and when *Youlan* was revived in the mid-twentieth century, it came as a shock that the piece did not sound nearly as pentatonic as many had expected. Pentatonicism plays a substantial role throughout Chinese music history, but most surviving traditional Chinese tunes are heptatonic, and the melodies of early Chinese music may

CHINA: THE GUQIN ZITHER

Music enjoyed high prestige during the Tang dynasty.

Above: Ladies at an informal court concert with players on the sheng, se, pipa and xiao

Left: Pottery tomb musicians from the Tang period

still be more varied, as the example of *Youlan* shows. The American qin player John Thompson has shown analytically that the predominant (relative) scale of *Youlan* is C–D–E–F♯–G–A–B–C, with F as an occasional alternate to F♯, and C as the tonal centre. There are also incidental occurrences of C♯ (three times) and B♭ (once), resulting in a ten-tone scale, and the piece has an ascending slur of five microtones at the end of each of its four sections.

Most later qin melodies are built on a pentatonic or heptatonic structure, though chromatic features continue to play a role.[7] Ultimately, much of the expressiveness of qin relies on special types of vibrato, slides and a lingering on tones, which turns the landscape between finite pitches into an essential part of the music.

Above: Yu Shaozhe (1903–88) was a celebrated qin master in the Sichuan style. Here he performs during a qin meeting, probably in his native town Chengdu in the early 1980s.

Right: This ecstatically laughing musician, from an Eastern Han period tomb in Sichuan, belies the stereotype image of zither players as being solemn, stern and contemplative. It was excavated in 1951 in Ziyangxian and is kept in the Chongqing Museum.

Qin pieces usually come with specific tunings, with by far the most common one (starting from the lowest string) being C–D–F–G–A–C–D. This is known as *zheng diao*, 'correct scale'. Many variants are known, in which one or more strings are lowered or raised by a semitone or a whole tone. The famous *Xiao Xiang shui yun* (*Mist and Clouds over Xiao and Xiang Rivers*, a ten-minute piece which Liang Ming-yueh once compared in dramatic fervour to Richard Strauss's *Alpensinfonie*)[8] is played with the fifth string raised by a semitone (see Example 4.1). Other familiar tunings include *mangong diao* ('lowered first tone scale'), in which the first, third and sixth strings are lowered by a whole tone, and *qingshang diao* ('bright upward scale') in which the first, fifth and seventh strings are raised a semitone.[9] There is no fixed pitch for tuning a qin, one's choice depending on the length of the instrument, the quality of the strings, regional traditions and personal preference. Chinese conservatories usually recommend tuning the fifth string to an A at 110 Hz.[10]

■ Narration, musical structure, vocal aspects and freedom of rhythm

Qin handbooks contain poems, stories and programmatic explanations which are as dynamic and changeable as the music: the same story may find its way into different qin pieces, or the same piece may be explained in very different ways.[11] Programmatic ideas, particularly those of Ming dynasty handbooks, are often marvellously suggestive. Longer pieces frequently consist of individually-titled sections, and the divisions can be a practical help in determining the music's architecture. Song-like or rondo-like structures with the repeated occurrence of themes, motives or gestures occur, but much qin music is rhapsodic, and the emphasis on timbral and ornamental detail can become dominant to the point where music is experienced on a note-by-note or gesture-by-gesture basis.[12] Silences also play a major role; the enormous variety of ways in which the strings of the qin can be approached includes the option of not touching them at all – just making silent hand movements in the air over the soundboard.

EX. 4.1 The slow and spacious beginning of *Xiao Xiang shui yun* (*Water and Clouds of the Xiao and Xiang Rivers*) in a version played by Wu Jinglüe. The first section up to the double bar line is played entirely in harmonics. Sounds indicated with 'x' refer to a pitchless slow vibrato, produced by rubbing a string with fingers of the left hand.

Rhythmic freedom is another major asset of qin playing: no repeated performance of a qin piece will ever sound exactly the same.[13] The process of translating the unmeasured and free qin notations into performance versions with more definite rhythmical contours is known as *dapu*. Some scholars interpret the freedom of rhythm as a musical reflection of players' aspirations towards spirituality, but perhaps too much has been made of this: players still work within an established framework of rhythmic formulae and convention, and do not reinvent tradition every time they touch the instrument.[14] In deciphering old notations, they face a challenge comparable to that of Western instrumentalists faced with trying to perform French harpsichord preludes from the times of Louis Couperin – pieces written in whole note sequences, which leave the players free, without metrical constraint, to invent their own pace and rhythmic divisions.[15] Usually after a few playings recognisable melodic sequences begin to emerge, and the same happens in qin pieces revived via the *dapu* process. The parlando-rubato nature of many qin melodies may suggest vocal origins, with some styles – such as the Qinling style of Nanjing – reportedly being influenced by the ornamentations and vocal techniques of specific singing styles.[16]

Many pieces in the handbooks are qin songs, with lyrics; lauded by poets as a 'singing' instrument, the qin has probably always been one of the most 'vocal' of Chinese instruments, and players often teach their pupils by simultaneously singing and playing to them. The instrument's flexible rhythmical properties and spiritual connotations might seem to turn its music into a Chinese equivalent of the *stile fantastico* of the Western Renaissance and Baroque, with its connotations of rhetorical speech and theatrical content, of the human (or superhuman) voice 'speaking' in mysterious ways, but the sound of the qin is unique, and its repertoire is too varied to merit such comparisons wholesale. Epic and dramatic pieces like *Xiao Xiang shui yun* form a surprising contrast to the plain lyricism and song-like simplicity of tunes like *Jiu kuang* (*Drunken madness*; see the illustration on p. 112 above), or *Meihua san nong* (*Plum blossom melody*) – shorter pieces dismissed by some qin players as 'superficial', but praised as gems by others.

■ Playing and players in modern times

Following the Ming, regional ensemble and opera styles flourished, and Western culture began to make an impact in China, perhaps at the expense of qin music which again went into decline. But it experienced another (modest) comeback during the early Republican period, and was allowed to develop further under Maoism, in spite of its elitist past. Players had to hide their instruments and remain silent during the Cultural Revolution of 1966–76, and some were persecuted, but the tradition continued with renewed enthusiasm from the early 1980s onwards.

In recent decades, an ideological battle has emerged between players in Hong Kong who promote the qin strictly as a gateway to self-cultivation, and mainland players who prefer to regard it as a 'mere' musical instrument. Behind this

Left: The Chinese pipa player Wu Man has earned her instrument world-wide recognition.

Above: A sandstone carving in the Musée Cernuschi, Paris, showing how the pipa was held at the time of the Northern Wei dynasty (386–534 CE)

looms a debate about who can claim to represent genuine tradition. In reality, however, there have always been many traditions; no single model from the past can claim to be prescriptive, nor can any players from the past be excluded, not even the 'old gentlemen with very long fingernails' whom Laurence Picken and Robert van Gulik met at Xu Yuanbai's home in Sichuan during the early 1940s, 'who couldn't use their nails to pluck the strings, so they played with continuous glissando, moving their nails on the qin surface all the time; it sounded like giant cockroaches seeking hiding'.[17]

The transition from silk to metal strings in the 1950s resulted in greater volume and longer resonance, but also in a loss of clarity and timbral richness; some also say that the traditional aura of qin suffered from its transfer to the concert hall,[18] but at all events playing styles changed dramatically. Recordings from the 1940s and 1950s show that qin players then tended to follow a much more steady pulse than they do today; the free-floating melodies we may hear in recent performances – with abrupt shifts in tempo and frequent ritardandos and accelerations – are a development of the last fifty years, in part under the influence of Western music. Moreover, many traditional pieces were abbreviated to fit contemporary tastes. The newly dramatic approach to qin music has created a different musical landscape, and has won new audiences.[19]

Whatever approach one prefers, its current success does not derive, as has been suggested, from amplification or from 'mass ideology'.[20] It is the legacy of an eclectic group of artists who, in many different ways, gave new impetus to the tradition: men like the mild and soft-spoken gentleman-scholar Pu Xuezhai (1893–1966), kin to China's last emperor Pu Yi, who made the instrument politically acceptable to communist leaders Zhou Enlai and Mao Zedong. And like Guan Pinghu (1897–1967), who became China's most influential interpreter of old qin scores, or like Zha Fuxi (1895–1976), co-founder of the influential Jinyu Qin Society (1936), who became the country's leading qin researcher and (with Wang Di and Xu Jian) carried out major fieldwork in the spring of 1954, travelling across China and recording and documenting the music of eighty-six local players. Zha Fuxi also published important collections of scores which became the basis for the monumental multi-volume anthology *Qinqu jicheng* (from 1981 onwards). Wu Jinglüe (1907–87) and Wei Zhongle (1908–88) promoted a modern concert and conservatory career for the instrument, and introduced folk elements in their playing, partly borrowed from the *pipa* (which they both played). Wu Jinglüe became the most ardent proponent of steel strings, helping to make them fashionable in China. There were important women, too, not least Tsar Teh-yun (Cai Deyun) (1905–2007) who almost singlehandedly raised a whole new generation of *qin* players in Hong Kong. Other artists, like Wu Zhonghai (1908–95), Sun Yuqin (1915–90) and Hu Guangjing (d. 1973), launched the instrument in Taiwan. John Thompson revived complete collections of ancient qin scores in historically-informed performances. Many others could have deserved inclusion in this list.

The qin lives on, in oversized concert halls, on the internet and in commercial recordings, as well as in intimate surroundings. And, as in the past, the crucial element may be its sound: the qin's great strength may lie in its *fragility*, in the evanescent quality of its music, and not – as in the romanticised, imaginary past – in its magical powers and cosmic connotations. It enchants as much by what it keeps silent about, as by what it says.

Further reading

Van Gulik's landmark book *The Lore of the Lute* (1940, reissued 1969) is still the best in-depth monography on qin, and is eminently readable, though a formidable modern competitor is Cecilia Lindqvist's *Qin* (2006), which includes a wealth of illustrations, fine personal reminiscences of how she came to study the qin in China in the 1950s, and informative chapters on almost every aspect of the instrument including its manufacture. Sadly, Lindqvist's book is so far only available in Swedish and in Chinese. The best one-volume general introduction to Chinese music is Liang Mingyue's *Music of the Billion* (1985). A classic on Chinese music philosophy which puts qin lore in historical perspective is DeWoskin's *A Song for One or Two*.

Connections with Asian art are explored in Stephen Addiss's *The Resonance of the Qin in East Asian Art* (1999). Ji Kang's classic essay on the qin is still worth reading, translated and commented by Van Gulik (*Hsi K'ang and his Poetical Essay on the Lute*, 1941/1969), or in French by Goormaghtigh (*L'Art du Qin*, 1990). A Chinese teaching manual, translated and with instructive commentary, is Lieberman's *Zither Tutor* (1983). A substantial website on qin is John Thompson's *www.silkqin.com*

Readers with access to Chinese should explore Zha Fuxi's landmark essays on qin (*Zha Fuxi Qinxue wencui*, 1995). A concise general survey of qin history is Xu Jian's *Qinshi chubian* (1982); a fine introduction to twentieth-century qin history is Lin Chen's *Chumo qinshi* (2011).

Recommended listening

Favourite Qin Pieces of Guan Pinghu, Roi Productions RB-951005-2C, 1995. Double album by the 'father' of twentieth-century qin playing. Recordings from the 1950s, played on silk strings, yet with amazing resonance and clarity of sound.

An Anthology of Chinese Traditional and Folk Music: A Collection of Music Played on the Guqin (8 vols), China Record company, Shanghai, CCD-94/342-349, 1994. Rough sound editing, but a landmark historical anthology, featuring Zha Fuxi's pioneer recordings. Includes many great masters of the past: Guan Pinghu, Pu Xuezhai, Yao Bingyan, Gu Meigeng, Shen Caonong etc.

Hugo Records in Hong Kong has produced over 30 qin solo CDs since 1989, many dedicated to important senior and regional masters, including some, such as Wang Hua-De, Yu Shaoze and Liu Shaochun, who have been little recorded elsewhere.

Wu Wenguang, *Music of the Qin*, JVC World Sounds VICG-5213, 1992. Features one of the finest performances ever of the oldest known qin piece, *Youlan*.

Dai Xiaolian, *China: The Art of the Qin Zither*, Auvidis B 6765, 1992. A vigorous player of a younger generation, recorded in Paris.

Tsar Teh-yun, *The Art of Qin Music*, ROI Productions RB-001006-2C, 2000. Fine classical performances by Hong Kong's first lady of the qin.

John Thompson, *Music Beyond Sound: Qin solos from the Zheyin shizi qinpu (1491)*, Toadal Sound TDS 10001, 1997. Beginning of an unprecedented project to revive and record little-known early qin music.

With her assistant, a hua dan — female character — prepares for a performance, Taipei, 1978

5 Chinese Opera

Terry E. Miller & Michael Church

The curtain opens to reveal a table flanked by two wooden chairs in front of a dark red backcloth. With two strident oboes and a mighty roar of percussion, the instrumental ensemble – out of view stage-left – announces the start of the play. A general with a long beard, high wooden shoes, brilliantly-patterned painted face and a strikingly-coloured costume that makes him look like a giant, arrives by 'chariot', attended by six young soldiers plus a staff of military officers. The fiddle begins a nasal riff garnished with swoops and slides which is punctuated by drum, cymbals and gongs; the general begins to sing in a declamatory manner, with broad gestures and contorted expressions to suggest anger. The brilliant clashes of the unblended instrumental sounds combined with the intensity of the singing – much of it in the upper register, to contrast with the hoarse outbursts of the rougher characters – create an exhilarating effect, as do the events of the story, which concerns two rival generals, the rougher of them fighting for a pretender to the emperor's throne. None of the actors or musicians at this opera school is over twenty, yet all are highly accomplished.

IN technologically-advanced modern urban China, why would a young teenager wish to join the archaic world of Beijing Opera? For most Chinese it is a difficult art to accept, but for some it remains irresistibly fascinating, and both in the People's Republic and among expatriate Chinese it has a small but fiercely loyal following. While neophytes may respond to its visual exoticism, connoisseurs, like Western opera buffs, will already be familiar with their favourite operas and performers, savouring every gesture and eye movement, every syllable whether spoken or sung, and every twist and turn in the stories.

English lacks a good translation for what the Chinese call *xiju*. Customarily we translate this as 'opera', but that term carries inappropriate baggage from European tradition. Calling it 'theatre' suggests spoken drama, and calling it 'musical theatre' evokes images from Gilbert and Sullivan or the Broadway musical. None conveys the essence, because Chinese *xiju* is an amalgam of acting, singing, acrobatics, the visual arts and theatre. Lacking an alternative, we will follow convention in calling it 'opera'.

Including Chinese opera in a work devoted to 'classical' musics might seem to contradict the original nature of the art, for most forms of it are intended for farmers, merchants, factory workers and housewives. However, two forms do justify the classical label. *Kunqu*, which evolved in the fourteenth century, is 'classical' by virtue of its high literary quality and its original appeal to the Confucian scholars who constituted the Imperial bureaucracy. *Jingju* or *jingxi* – usually translated as 'Beijing opera' – evolved from a wide diversity of traditions into a distinct genre in the late eighteenth century, when it won favour with the Qing court and was brought to perfection by a series of great actors and actresses in the first half of the twentieth century; it still maintains its status as China's 'national opera'. Both these genres have much in common with Chinese opera's multifarious regional operatic forms, which reflect localism in everything from language to food, lifestyles and architecture. There are some 350 individually-named forms of opera in Han China, in addition to many forms of puppet theatre including string, marionette, glove and shadow varieties.

The normal venue for an operatic performance – in both human and puppet form – is a temple. Temples in China are not easily distinguished as Buddhist or Taoist, for in Mahayana Buddhism temples have altars for multiple deities, many local in origin. Taoist temples are similar, but without altars to the Buddha or a related figure like Kuan Yin. Even today it is customary to offer the chief deity of the temple a theatre performance on his birthday, on a stage that faces (or at least can be seen by) his image; humans are also welcome to watch. Local troupes, sometimes amateur, give these performances accompanied by musicians seated on either side of the stage. Even Beijing opera had this origin, but it, like a number of other forms (for example Cantonese opera) migrated to formal indoor theatres in the twentieth century.

Local operas are differentiated by music, singing style and language. Although all Chinese can communicate with a common writing system, the spoken languages vary dramatically, with some being mutually unintelligible. Though each local opera may have its own repertory of plays, musical styles are more uniform over wider areas. As 'national' styles with formal indoor performances, jingju and kunqu are a case apart.

■ History

Chinese opera probably developed from narrative-singing genres (*shuochang* – speaking-singing), some of which survive today. Narrative singing by one or two singers – either accompanying themselves or accompanied by others – transmitted age-old tales, both local and epic, through speech, song and gesture, with a single singer sometimes taking the roles of several characters plus a narrator. During the Yuan dynasty (1279–1368) two basic forms of opera emerged from the same body of tales, *zaju* in the north and *nanxi* in the south. Because the plays were written by and for the literati, many scripts have survived, but apart from the names of the tunes, no music has done so.

Over time and a wide area, two basic creative approaches developed. One was the *qupai* system, where the librettist wrote lyrics to go with standard named tunes called *qupai*. To put it in Western terms, the librettist might specify, 'sing to the tune (*qupai*) Yankee Doodle'. This form of operatic construction is also described as 'stringing tunes together', and here periods of speech alternate with songs (arias). Kunqu opera is predominantly *qupai* opera.

The second way of generating operatic music requires the actors to create their heightened speech and arias through a controlled process of modal

CHINESE OPERA

Above: A xiao sheng (young male) is flanked by two military jing (painted face) with a lao sheng (old man) in the left background. Teenage students at the Shandong Opera School in Jinan, 1996.

Below: The large ensemble accompanying the performance

improvisation called *shengqiang*; the melodies must additionally be governed by the words. This is because Chinese languages are tonal: as well as having consonants and vowels, each word has its own tonal inflection. Singing a rising-tone word to a descending melodic pattern contradicts pronunciation, and may lead to confusion when the falling-tone word also exists. *Shengqiang* embodies comprehensive systems for both composing fixed melodies, and generating improvised singing and playing.

■ Visual elements

Performed on their temple stages, local operas deploy hand-painted scenery-cloths hung from bamboo poles and operated by ropes and pulleys. Stage props are simple, with the trademark table and chairs (and sometimes a screen) representing a fortress. Kunqu and jingju don't even use scenery cloths, and are much more stylised and symbolic, requiring the audience to use its imagination. Soldiers crossing over the table flanked by the chairs indicate they are crossing a mountain; a figure lying on the table is sleeping in a bed; a warrior carrying a stick with a 'mane' is riding a horse, while soldiers flanking a general with two flags and painted wheels indicate that he's travelling in a chariot. Actors enter imaginary buildings, stepping high over the imaginary threshold. And the characters conform to one of four archetypes, each with its sub-categories. *Dan* are females, subdivided into young, 'flowery', old and military; *sheng* are males, subdivided into young, old and military; the painted-face *jing* sport designs and colours representing their character (a white face indicates an evil person, a blue face is trustworthy); *chou* are comedians and supernumeraries, including servants and soldiers, the more important ones distinguished by a round white facial patch.

Though today women routinely perform in opera, in the past they were sometimes banned, for acting was considered little better than prostitution. Consequently males had to play female roles, with the homosexual ones expecting sensual gratification from their apprentices – a practice loudly condemned by the Communists when they took power in 1949. Genuine females and the older or military men, along with painted-face characters, sing in chest voice, but female impersonators and 'young men' (*xiao sheng*) sing in falsetto.

■ Kunqu

Kunqu originated in the Suzhou-Kunshan area of Jiangsu province, west of Shanghai, and to this day Suzhou symbolises all that is elegant about China, with its temples and water gardens laced with paths and bridges. Opera reached a peak of refinement there during the sixteenth century, thanks to support from the literati and patronage by wealthy families. In comparison with local operas and jingju, kunqu is notably restrained. Since large, flashy military scenes and acrobatics are less prominent than scenes of romantic love, its accompaniment is less raucous and its instruments are smaller, with the main melodic one being the *dizi* (transverse bamboo flute), customarily doubled by a small *sheng* mouth organ. Ensembles may also include plucked stringed instruments, in contrast to the bowed instruments which lead the melody in other genres. Percussion includes a wooden clapper, small drum, cymbals, gong, a larger drum for specific movements, and occasionally a long trumpet. Singing in kunqu became highly developed, with extensive and subtle ornamentation and a variety of vocal techniques tailored to the requirement for melody-word tone coordination. Because kunqu used pre-existing melodies, duets and trios could flower.

By the end of the eighteenth century kunqu's popularity had peaked, with some critics regarding it as over-sophisticated, even decadent: challenged by the rise of new popular genres, it went into decline, largely disappearing until the twentieth century when successive revivals – first in the 1920s and then in the 1980s – were attempted. The Lincoln Center's 1988 commissioning of a new and spectacular production, *The Peony Pavilion*, might have brought kunqu renewed attention, but at the last minute the Chinese government objected to the nature of this new-style work and refused to let the Shanghai Kunqu Company go to New York. In 1999 director Peter Sellars reconfigured the work as a modern theatre piece.

▪ Jingju, or Beijing Opera

Jingju, which literally means 'capital city opera', implicitly refers to Beijing (China having had several capitals over the centuries). The genre reflected a coalescence following the Chinese pattern where, as older genres declined, their elements blended with those of other fading genres to give rise to new and more vigorous forms. Thus did jingju evolve from the combined effects of the near-death of kunqu and the arrival in Beijing, at the end of the eighteenth century, of four major troupes from Anhui province, where opera had flourished under Qing patronage. Emperor Renzong tried unsuccessfully to suppress jingju because he thought it encouraged decadence in the ruling class, but with enthusiastic support from the Empress Dowager Cixi (1835–1908) the art-form flourished, with a special split-level stage being built for it at her Summer Palace. Jingju may have had popular roots, but court patronage – plus the influence of individual artists – led to its enjoying a highly sophisticated golden age between the end of the Qing dynasty in 1911 and the Japanese invasion of China in 1937.

A typical evening of jingju consists of three or four excerpts from longer stories, normally beginning with a fairly static play, followed by a short but raucous and dramatic military play and completed by the main billing, whose plot is probably more complex and may involve subjects as varied as court intrigue and love relationships. Many scenes are from the great novels of China, including *Romance of the Three Kingdoms*, *Journey to the West*, *All Men are Brothers* (also called *The Water Margin*) and *The Emperor's Farewell to his Concubine*. Others feature the imagined exploits of China's greatest judge, Judge Pao, who, like Agatha Christie's Poirot, forces the truth to come out and administers swift and fair justice. Thus an evening will encompass a variety of dramatic terrains, often laced with acrobatics.

Musically, jingju combines elements not only of kunqu but also *bangzi* ('clapper opera') and two forms of modally-constructed 'system opera'. As in kunqu, actors specialise in role types, and indeed those types are the same, though with many variations, especially in the *ching* painted-face actors. Jingju's domestic and romantic plots emphasise singing, but its biggest attraction lies in the scenes of individual combat, massed battles and acrobatics. Little of this complexity emerges when jingju groups tour, as their producers seem to think Western audiences cannot tolerate much of the stylised speech or the falsetto singing, and therefore tend to eliminate everything except the acrobatics. But jingju's soundscape is admittedly challenging, especially the timbre of the *jinghu* lead fiddle. And since naturalism is not a goal of Chinese theatre, jingju is replete with symbolism, mannered speech and a tense, nasal, high-tessitura vocal style; some roles, like that of the 'young man', are sung in falsetto, though the apparent gender-conflict is not without parallels elsewhere in the world, most notably in the castrato roles in Handel opera.

Seated mostly out of sight, the accompanying ensemble normally divides into two sections, the *wuchang* (military) group and the *wenchang* (civil) group. The leader (*sigu*) marks time with a wooden clapper (*ban*) in his left hand while beating a single-headed drum with a stick (*ban gu*) with his right. He must closely follow the singers, and the instrumentalists must follow his beat. The leader of the 'civil' group plays the jinghu, which is the genre's most distinctive instrument, being a short-necked two-stringed fiddle with cylindrical body and snakeskin resonator whose nasal timbre can penetrate virtually any degree of percussive din. The other strings include the *jing erhu*, similar to a normal Chinese two-stringed *erhu*, a short-necked lute called the *yueqin*, a three-stringed *sanxian* lute, plus other plucked strings. For certain scenes, wind instruments may be used, including the horizontal flute (*dizi*), the *sheng* mouth organ and one or two *suona* double-reeds with flared bells. The 'military' group includes the clapper (*ban*)/drum (*gu*) pair, a small metal gong with a raised square centre struck with a flat stick and producing a rising pitch called the *xiao luo*, a large flat gong struck with a padded beater and producing a falling sound called the *da luo*, a pair of *naobo* cymbals and sometimes the *tanggu* 'military' drum played with sticks.

The ensemble does more than just accompany singing: it plays introductions, interludes and codas to arias, while for military scenes the double-reeds play martial music. The percussion players called the 'gong-drum' group (*luogu*) also have separate functions: they accompany actors' movements and specific stage actions, they punctuate singing and speech and provide sound effects. The jingju has an extensive repertory of fixed patterns (*luogujing*) for specific actions such as letter writing, drinking, ascending stairs or expressing a variety of emotions; these patterns also signal structural changes in the play, such as scene changes or the closing of an act. Some sound effects have specific connotations: rubbing the cymbals together in different ways may indicate the creaking of a boat or even a change of temperature.

Jingju is also a linguistic challenge for many in the audience, for both dialogue and singing are in a formal stage language so arcane that some theatres

A small Beijing Opera ensemble in 1972. Jing hu *(left)*, yue qin *(centre)*, percussion *(back)*, jing hu *(right)*

project the Chinese characters; only the comic characters speak in the vernacular. Unlike some forms of local theatre, jingju has no normal spoken dialogue, 'speaking' being a highly mannered form of recitation that exaggerates the lexical tones; indeed, there is a range of speech types which follows a continuum from speech to song. But singing (*chang*) is generated differently from speech (*shuo*), and to understand how that is done, it is necessary to understand something of the *pihuangqiang* system on which jingju is based.

Pihuang combines the names of the two modal systems – or 'tune families' – that govern how jingju singing is generated, through a process of simultaneous composition and performance. *Xipi*, considered appropriate for happy, energetic or forceful situations, consists of pitches 6 123 5/A CDE G while *erhuang*, considered dark, serious and heroic, consists of pitches 56 123/GA CDE. These, like other Chinese musical modes, have no pitch acting as a tonic; instead two pitches anchor the melody in a polarity that is usually at the interval of a fifth but sometimes a fourth. *Xipi* emphasises pitches 6 and 3 while *erhuang* emphasises pitches 5 and 2, each a fifth apart. The *jinghu* player leading the 'civil' ensemble keeps as many individual fiddles as is necessary for each mode and its sub-modal transpositions, since retuning during performance is impractical.

In generating melody, singers must coordinate a number of variables that together give rise to distinctive idioms peculiar to each role type. The elements that must be coordinated include the singer's 'school', the mode, the couplet line, the melodic centre, the metrical structure and the general modal character. While numbingly complex from an analytical point of view, for the singers, juggling them into a coherent whole becomes intuitive.

The metrical patterns open up another range of variables. Underlying each 'aria' is a beat pattern consisting of a tempo and a beat/metrical structure articulated by the combination of clapper and drum played by the leader. Each pattern has a name, many being associated with specific situations (narrative, agitated, declamatory) and specific role types. For connoisseurs these subtleties constitute the whole art; for those less familiar, the differences may be too arcane.

All this is every bit as complex as it sounds. But while the resulting melodies are consistent with the rules, the system is not quite as rigid as it appears, since it leaves singers the latitude to develop a personal style. And it is this that separates run-of-the-mill singers from master artists, some of whom have achieved great fame and left their stamp on the genre as a whole. The most celebrated was Mei Lan (1894–1961), a male singer who specialised in the 'flowery female' role (*qingyi*) and later changed his name to Mei Lan-Fang (Lanfang being a girl's name meaning 'perfumed flower'). It's in part to the spirit of this great actor-writer that Beijing Opera owes its character today.

Mei was born into a family of jingju and kunqu artists and began performing in both genres at ten. After attaining master status at a time when Chinese opera was allowed to flourish, he made several world tours in the 1930s. He was feted by Stanislavsky and Meyerhold in Moscow, mobbed in San Francisco, and received American doctorates galore, while Charlie Chaplin and Mary Pickford queued up to be photographed with him. One of his unlikelier admirers was the soprano Amelita Galli-Curci; another was Bertolt Brecht, who wrote rapturously of his style: 'This way of acting is healthier and worthier of rational beings.'

A wealth of extant photographs – plus a few pieces of film – reflect his singular art, with him looking martial in sword dances, heroic in tragedies, bereft in romances and wild in comedies as he stars in 'A Strand of Flax', 'Beauty Defies Tyranny' and 'Chin Xiang Upsets the Study'. But it's the gender-ambiguity of his stance in operas like 'The King's Parting with his Favourite' and 'The Disguised Warrior Maiden' where we really scent his genius: a pose at once sweet, vulnerable and threatening, and a mesmerising gaze. No stage art was more finely calculated and calibrated than Mei's. Photos show him in his 'ten standard postures' – 'Posture of dozing', 'Posture of shyness', 'Posture of considering' – and his hands in dozens of different modes, including 'Expression of shock', 'Expressing surprise lightly', 'Brushing off tears' and gnomically 'Pointing the void'.

A devoted paterfamilias, he was also a staunch patriot: during the Japanese occupation (1937–45) he wrote a series of inspirational dramas, with 'The Disguised Warrior Maiden' designed to stiffen his compatriots' resolve; he also grew a moustache so that he couldn't impersonate women as the Japanese oppressors wanted. When Mao's revolution was accomplished, Mei Lan-Fang was invited to be founding director of the newly-formed National Beijing Opera Theatre, whose current incarnation is thriving. In 2009 Mei's life was celebrated in a film by Chen Kaige, entitled *Forever Enthralled*.

CHINESE OPERA

Mei Lan-Fang, the most celebrated Beijing opera actor-writer of all time, in costume and off stage

During the Cultural Revolution (1966–76) traditional jingju was prohibited. Chairman Mao appointed his wife Chiang Ching (later condemned as one of the Gang of Four and executed) to head cultural transformation, and she decided to revolutionise opera by requiring troupes to write new (or rewrite old) librettos that championed the peasants, workers and soldiers over their enemies – Chiang Kai-shek's nationalists, the Japanese, the Americans and the bourgeoisie. To this end she designated five as 'revolutionary model operas' (*yangbanxi*) along with two model ballets and one model symphony. Some versions of the model operas used a modified traditional ensemble, some mixed Chinese and Western instruments, and some were entirely Western, all with fully-written scores using harmony. The stories were realistically portrayed, with the brightly lit Communist characters presented as dignified and strong, while their enemies were portrayed as rascals, often bent over and dimly lit; good versus evil was clearly differentiated. Although China has morphed into a government-dominated market economy, the revolutionary operas have regained a certain nostalgic popularity, being re-released in many formats including karaoke VCD.

After the Cultural Revolution ended Beijing Opera made a gradual reappearance and, like Mei Lan-Fang, some senior artists re-established their careers. New schools opened for performers and former schools re-opened. Both the genre and China's new but hesitant freedom in the arts came to world attention when Chen Kaige's film *Farewell, My Concubine* won a *Palme d'Or* at the 1993 Cannes Film Festival; this portrays turmoil in a jingju troupe during the chaos of the 1920s and 1930s, and deals with love-intrigue on a vast political and cultural canvas.

Jingju survives today, less because it is popular with the public than because it has become seen as China's representative opera. Governments at various levels continue to support training schools and troupes, some of which perform within China and others which perform throughout the world. Meanwhile it flourishes in many ways beyond the country's borders. It receives government support in Taiwan and Hong Kong; in Singapore, Thailand, Malaysia, Indonesia and the Philippines, so-called local operas are popular. The fact that jingju also thrives in private clubs in the West indicates the enduring appeal of its exuberant flamboyance. What is indisputable is that jingju has become firmly implanted in the public mind as an ideal representation of Chinese 'tradition', creating an exotic and riveting spectacle that can be appreciated on numerous levels.

Further reading

Beijing opera has been extensively written about, but most writers focus on history, practice and visual aspects. Relatively little has been written about its music, the three main sources being Gerd Schönfelder's study (published in German), Elizabeth Wichmann's *Listening to Theatre*, based on her first-hand experience as a performer, and Rulan Chao Pian's article in *The Garland Encyclopedia* and other articles in scholarly journals. Where William Dolby (*A History of Chinese Drama*) treats the history of Beijing opera within a much longer history of Chinese theatre, Colin Mackerras, in addition to writing similarly broad histories, has focused on Beijing opera in two books and numerous articles. Several editors have provided collections of plays, either fully written out (such as Dolby's *Eight Chinese Plays from the 13th Century to the Present*) or summarized. Otherwise, there are extensive publications on the genre written and published in Chinese only.

Recommended listening

Hou Yu-tzung Percussion for Peking Opera (1), Chinese Traditional Music Series 1 Taipei, Council for Cultural Planning, 1992. Two compact discs and a 196-page book in English and Chinese detailing the *luogu jing* (standard patterns) for Beijing opera, with each performed on the disc.

Mei Lan-Fang: Beauty Defies Tyranny (Historical Recording), HK 8-880056, 1991. Extended excerpt of opera performed c. 1950s by China's most famous female impersonator, Mei Lan-Fang.

Fang Rongxiang, *Peking Opera Rhyme Schemes*, Beijing: China Record Co., 1991. Eight opera excerpts by a senior artist. Minimal notes in English and Chinese.

The World of Peking Opera, CD Ethnic Sound Series 6, JVC VID-25016, 1986. Excellent recording of excerpts, with notes in Japanese only.

Highlights from Beijing Opera, Taipei: Linfair Magnetic Sound, 1987. Nine excerpts of Beijing opera recorded in Beijing in late 1987, with notes in English and Chinese.

Opéra de Pékin: La forêt en feu, La princesse cent-fleurs/The Peking Opera: The Forest on Fire, The Princess Hundred Flowers, Musique du Monde/Music from the World. Buda 92618-2, 1994. Six excerpts from two plays recorded in Dalian, Liaoning, with extensive notes in English and French.

A Treasure of Peking Opera Recordings vol. 1, *A Complete Play of 'In the Shade of Willows'*, Beijing: Central People's Broadcasting Station of China/China Broadcasting A&V Publishing House, 1992. A 1961 recording with minimal notes in English and Chinese.

The Chinese Opera: Arias from Eight Peking Operas, Lyrichord LLST 7212. Originally released on vinyl and available on demand, this collection of eight excerpts is annotated in detail by a specialist in opera.

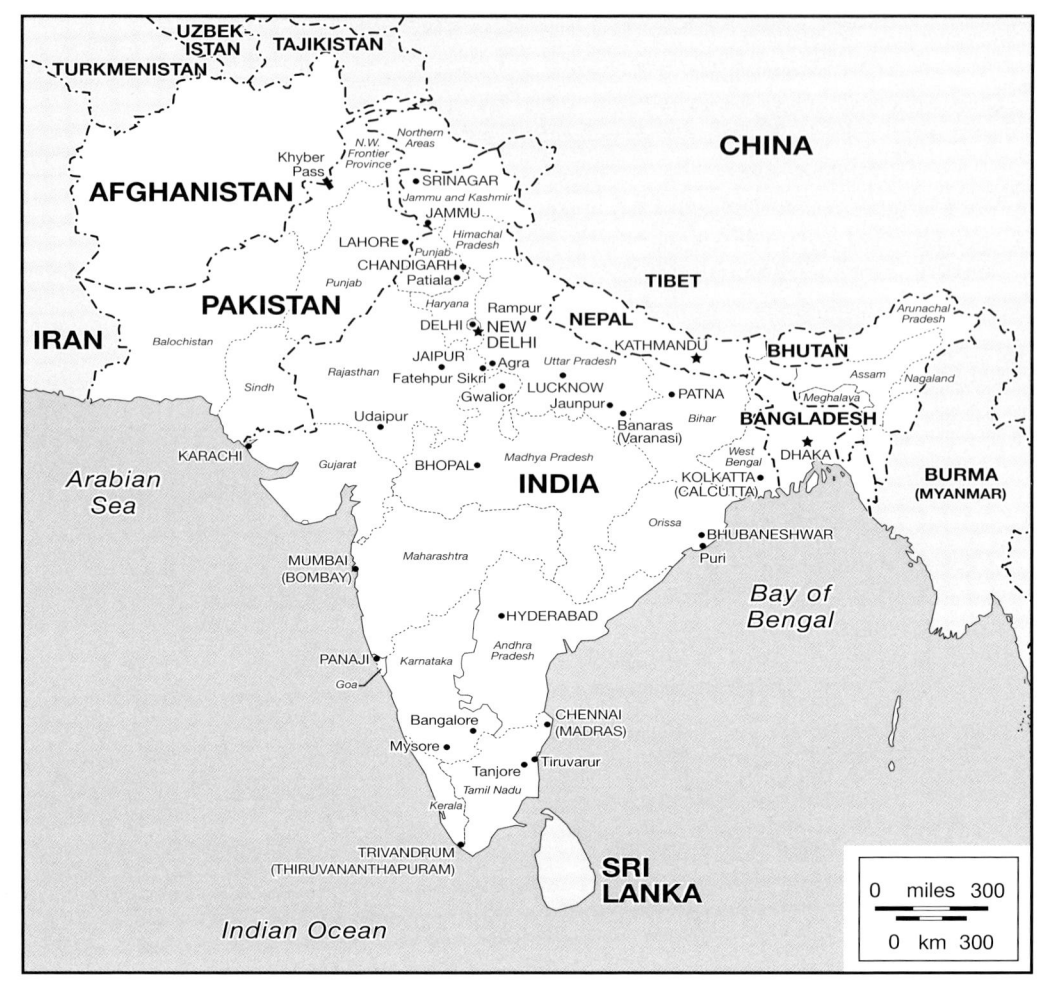

India's historic centres of musical activity

6 North India

Richard Widdess

The man in the silk shirt raises his outstretched hand towards the younger of the two sitarists seated before the small audience, and says 'Wah!' The musician pauses momentarily to acknowledge the compliment by touching his forehead, before repeating the admired phrase. This time it's extended with a new twist, and continues seemingly unstoppable, rising, falling and unexpectedly rising again to reach new heights before eventually subsiding towards the tonic note. Foreseeing this conclusion, the audience bursts out with a chorus of 'Wah! Wah! Shabash! [very good] Kya bat! [wonderful]' which almost drowns the final notes.

The tabla accompanist, waiting his turn to play during the free-tempo introduction, shakes his head in approval. The elder sitarist says nothing, but his eyes gleam with pleasure at his son's improvisation, which his own fingers soundlessly follow on own fret-board. Now he throws the young man a new challenge: a phrase that, instead of starting low, rising to a peak, and falling to its starting point, does the opposite. In reply, his son repeats his father's rising conclusion, but brings it to a low ending.

The audience is again delighted. The man in the silk shirt, without whose presence in the front row no house concert in this part of town is considered complete, turns to his neighbour and mutters: 'Such mastery! And he is so young!'

'INDIAN classical music' is a familiar concept. While it is necessary to distinguish the music of North India and its neighbours – principally Pakistan, Nepal and Bangladesh – from that of South India, both have become seen as parallel traditions of 'Indian classical music'. This is a result partly of international tours by Indian concert musicians, and partly of the settlement of diasporic South Asian communities in many areas of the West. This chapter concerns North Indian, or Hindustani, music.

In India, 'classical' music is sharply distinguished from other types of music including folk music and popular music (such as the music of Bollywood movies), though it overlaps with dance, certain forms of which are also called 'classical', and with some types of religious singing, which are not. Our opening vignette illustrates several aspects of what is considered 'classical' about Hindustani music. It is music played (or sung) for the delectation of an attentive audience, typically drawn from an educated, wealthy, urban social elite. Such listeners ideally display sophisticated connoisseurship, based on extensive listening to the best artists, and sometimes on first-hand experience of learning to sing or play. They admire the musical knowledge, artistry and skill of individual soloists and accompanists, many of whom are professionals. The music is governed by a system of melodic and rhythmic modes (*rāga*,[1] *tāla*) and a choice of traditional styles and forms, which allow shared understanding of what is expected, acceptable and exceptional. This system is largely independent of writing; although notation is used for some pedagogical or theoretical purposes, performance depends entirely on memory and creativity.

Music is created in real time by the performers; it is not the 'work' of a separate composer, and any pre-composed item such as a traditional song will constitute only a small part of the performance. 'Improvised' elaboration (*upaj*), within the constraints of raga and tala and the appropriate style, predominates, leading to the kind of inspired interaction between performers described above. Musicians and audiences alike stress the importance of oral tradition as the only means of transmitting Hindustani music that leads to outstanding performance; the key to this process is the close relationship over many years between teacher (if Hindu, called *guru*; if Muslim, *ustād*) and student (*shishya* or *shāgird* respectively), a relationship that is often likened to the transmission of religious knowledge and practice. Sometimes the teacher is also the father – less often, the mother – of the student.

Indian classical music is believed to be a form of knowledge and practice that has been continuously maintained and refined by successive generations of teachers and pupils, transmitted from time immemorial. One of the earliest literary accounts of musical performance, the *Guttila Jātaka* from around the third century BCE, sounds uncannily familiar, for it already embodies enduring characteristics of Indian classical music. In this Buddhist story, Guttila is a highly respected court musician to the king of Banaras, then as now one of the principal centres of musical art in North India. The instrument he played, the *vīnā*, would have been an arched harp similar to the *saung-gauk* of Burmese music, though this has long since been replaced in India by other instrument types. Musila is a no-hope student from Ujjain whose playing initially sounds like rats scratching a mat. But Guttila is a generous and conscientious guru and teaches Musila everything he knows. Eventually he finds himself challenged by the ungrateful Musila in open competition for supremacy at court. Feeling old and vulnerable, and fearing to be outshone by his own pupil, Guttila shrinks from the contest. But the gods intervene, and instruct Guttila to break the strings of his vina one by one, continuing to play on those that remain. To the astonishment of the listeners, Musila is able to replicate this feat, until finally Guttila breaks the last string. Ethereal music continues to pour out of his instrument, but Musila's is mute, and the audience drives him out of town for his presumption.

This tale embodies the conception of music, still current today, as a form of unwritten, non-verbal knowledge. Such knowledge can only be acquired from a guru, not through the efforts of the student alone. The guru should transmit his knowledge to disciples who in return must show commitment, respect and loyalty to him. Competition for patronage between bearers of such knowledge is endemic among musicians today, in the politics of self-presentation and manipulation of audiences, agents and media. Competition also occurs on stage: in a friendly form, almost any performance can involve competitive exchanges

'Ragamala' means 'a garland of melodies'. Designed as adjuncts to musical performance, these miniatures evoked the music's mood and often provided stories to accompany it. (Nata Raga, folio from a dispersed Ragamala series, Deccan, India, about 1690. Paper, opaque watercolour, gold. 35.2 × 23.7 cm.)

between performers. Audiences are easily impressed by the precocity of young prodigies, but they deeply respect the knowledge and artistry of senior musicians, even those no longer at the top of their technical form. And musical sound is widely believed to have a spiritual or god-given aspect, as a result of which musical knowledge is typically treated as a form of sacred knowledge akin to religious scripture or philosophy. The moral dimension of musicianship which Musila singularly lacked is essential to conveying music's deeper spiritual meaning.

That meaning can be interpreted in a variety of ways, according to individual preference. In ancient philosophy the sound of music shares with that of ritual mantras the power to control the material universe; even today ragas should still be performed at the appropriate time of day (which may be any hour from early morning to late night) or season of the year to be in tune with the natural world, and are sometimes credited with supernatural powers, such as causing rain to fall or trees to flower. At a religious level music is a channel of communication between the devotee and his chosen deity, whether Krishna or Ram, Shiva or the Goddess. The aesthetic of classical music is explained in terms of *rasa*, the 'juice' or 'essence' of an emotion (such as love, mirth or compassion) that the listener tastes; this aesthetic experience is believed by Hindus to lead to spiritual liberation (*moksha*), or in the Sufi (devotional Islamic) tradition to an ecstatic yearning for union with God (*sama*). The assumption that music evokes emotion is suggested by the choice of the Sanskrit term *rāga* (pronounced *rāg* in Hindi), meaning 'passion', for the central melodic concept. The performer's self-immersion in a single raga for an extended period of time is sometimes seen as a quasi-meditative state that the listener can only partly share; in his improvisation, the raga, conceived as a semi-divine being existing outside the performer, takes control of the musician, rather than the reverse, and flows through him to the listener. It is above all the concept, system, practice and experience of raga that makes Hindustani music 'classical'.

▪ Raga and tala, composition and improvisation

A raga is what musicians announce they are playing, and what connoisseurs enjoy recognising even if it is not announced. A raga is a map of that melodic terrain that lies between scale and tune. It is not a scale: there can be many ragas in the same scale. Nor is it one specific tune: there can be many tunes in one raga. The essence of a raga can be heard in any of its tunes; but a full-length performance of the raga will include not only one or two composed pieces, but also extensive improvised passages, all of which will conform to and explore the features of the raga 'map'. Such improvisation often includes an opening prelude, the *ālāp*, in which the performers gradually unfold the melodic features of the raga and which can last anything between a minute and an hour.

Bihāg is a famous raga traditionally performed in the evening. Its scalar material resembles the Western major scale, plus a sharp fourth in some phrases. In Example 6.1, the tonic is represented as C, though this pitch is not fixed but is chosen by the soloist. This note, together with the fifth, in this case G, would normally be sustained throughout the performance on a drone instrument, and also sounded repeatedly on the drone strings of the sitar. This drone, which one hardly notices once the performance is under way, anchors the raga to a constant reference point, and enables the musicians to judge the tuning of each note with pinpoint accuracy.

Example 6.1 shows typical ways of moving in raga Bihag, from tonic to fifth and back, and from fifth to upper tonic and back. It also shows, for comparison, corresponding melodic moves for raga *Kedār*, another evening raga, in which almost the same scalar material is used, but different pitches are emphasised, and different ways of moving from one point to another are employed. It is these typical phrases of the raga that the connoisseur listens for, and a phrase that perfectly brings out the unique melodic character of the raga will elicit an appreciative 'Wah!' So here we see that the ascent from tonic to fifth in Bihag goes (typically starting from the seventh degree rather than the tonic itself) B–C–E–F–E–G, with particular emphasis on E, the strongest note of the raga; whereas in Kedar one starts with a bold leap from C to F (which is a strong note in this raga), and proceeds via the merest suggestion of E direct to G. In both ragas, the second degree (D) is omitted from this ascending movement; but it appears in the corresponding descent, as a weak note in Bihag, and a strong one

EX. 6.1 Basic moves in ragas Bihag and Kedar

in Kedar. Both ragas include F♯ as a weak note, but the way of combining this note with the adjacent notes is slightly different.

Example 6.2 represents the opening two phrases of a short alap in raga Bihag, as played on the *sarod* by Buddhadev Dasgupta.[2] It illustrates how the raw materials of a raga (here corresponding to the second line of Example 6.1) can be used to develop a musical argument: the second phrase is an 'expansion' (*vistār*) of the first. In particular, the note E is highlighted: it is the focal pitch of the raga, sometimes known as 'the note that speaks' (*vādī*). On hearing these phrases alone, even with no announcement of the raga, connoisseurs might say to themselves: 'Ah – Bihag!'

Alap is not in principle pre-composed (alap in the same raga can be played longer or shorter, depending on the time available). In these two short phrases one can see how Buddhadev Dasgupta interprets the well-known raga. A different musician might play the same underlying phrases with a different rhythm and different ornamentations. No one 'composed' raga Bihag, and there is no definitive written representation of it; it seems to have originated in the seventeenth century, and is still evolving – the prominence of F♯ has gradually increased over the past fifty years. Bihag is part of a canonical repertoire, but it is a canon of orally-transmitted, evolving practice rather than of written 'works'.

Hindustani musicians commit to memory large numbers of vocal or instrumental compositions. Most of them could be performed, in the form in which they have been memorised, in under two minutes. Each one will be 'in' a particular raga: there can be any number of compositions in the same raga, and they will all exhibit the features of the raga, in different ways. Example 6.3 is the instrumental composition or *gat* that Buddhadev Dasgupta plays after the alap in Example 6.2 (with slight rhythmic variations on the repeats). The same melodic phrases that we heard in the alap recur here in a different rhythmic style, and within *Tīntāl*, the most common tala – or cyclic metrical framework – in Hindustani music. This comprises measures or cycles of sixteen beats, each cycle

⌣ = glissando by sliding left-hand finger on string

EX. 6.2 The beginning of an alap in raga Bihag, played by Buddhadev Dasgupta (sarod)

divided into four groups of four-beat segments (shown by the dotted bar-lines in Example 6.3). The first beat of the cycle (marked *x*) is the most emphasised. Once it has begun, the tala can gradually increase in speed, but it cannot otherwise change in structure. The gat is accompanied by tabla.

The term *gat* implies rhythmic movement or gait, and this one has a lively, almost jerky rhythm, with a note on almost every beat, frequent subdivisions of the beat and syncopations: these are typical of fast compositions. But the first phrase, which comes back as a refrain after the other phrases, leads to an unexpected long held note at beat nine – the *vādī*, E – followed by a quietly played F before the rhythm picks up again at beat fifteen; the performers momentarily seem to stop playing, though of course the tala continues in their minds throughout. This charming rhythmic surprise is typical of the subtle idiosyncrasies for which compositions are treasured by musicians and connoisseurs.

A composition of this kind is just the starting-point for improvisation using the melodic phrases of the raga and the rhythmic framework of the tala. Example 6.4 shows part of Buddhadev Dasgupta's performance. A novice would have to learn passages like this, but a master would be able to invent them spontaneously. Notice how the improvised rhythm cuts across the framework of the tala, until the return to the composition at the end. The melody follows the phrases of the raga with some slight variations, and repeatedly hints at the beginning of the composition. The essence of this style of improvisation is the combination of changing rhythmic groupings and unexpected twists and turns of the melody, all at a fast speed that keeps the listener from guessing what will happen next.

Although each raga is said to have its own unique mood, this is hard to characterise because the mood can be varied by the performer, either by emphasising different notes and phrases at different times, or by changing the rhythm and tempo (always in the direction from slow to fast). In Example 6.2,

EX. 6.3 A gat composition in raga Bihag, Tintal, played by Buddhadev Dasgupta

the slow tempo and free-floating rhythm enable Dasgupta to bring out a feeling of profound calm while dwelling on the major third, and sliding slowly between it and the similarly peaceful fifth and tonic. Curvaceous movements bringing in other notes more fleetingly introduce a sensuous element, suggesting perhaps a mood of intense love enjoyed or recollected in tranquillity. Later in this short alap, however, as the pitch and intensity rise, the seventh (B) takes on a yearning quality as it seemingly strives to reach the upper tonic (C), yet only touches it momentarily before subsiding poignantly into the more tranquil regions below (compare the fifth line of Example 6.1). This combination of moods changes abruptly, with the introduction of the fast tempo composition (Example 6.3) and ensuing improvisation (Example 6.4), to one of confidence, energy and exuberance, with occasional touches of tenderness (Example 6.3, line 1, semibreve E and minim F) almost jokingly thrown in for surprise effect. The whole performance is a miniature, barely four minutes altogether, yet in terms of Indian aesthetics it seems to elicit flavours (*rasa*) of love, tranquillity and compassion in the alap, and manly vigour, surprise and humour in the gat; of the traditional nine aesthetic flavours, only fear, anger and disgust are avoided here (and would indeed be out of place in this raga). One is reminded

EX. 6.4 Improvisation in raga Bihag by Buddhadev Dasgupta, and reprise of the gat melody

of the philosopher Abhinavagupta's comparison (c. 1000 CE) of a work of art with a dish in which various different spices combine to impart a unique flavour; but the music theorist Nanyadeva (c. 1100) observed that the flavours of different ragas, like food, cannot be adequately described in words, and must be experienced for oneself.

■ Invasions, empires, Independence

It is assumed by most musicians and listeners that Indian classical music has been transmitted from generation to generation of performers for hundreds, indeed thousands of years. The antiquity of the 'classical' Hindustani tradition, however, is currently in dispute. Cultural historians point out that the term 'classical' has no indigenous equivalent (the commonly heard *shāstriya sangīt* is a translation into Hindi of the English 'classical music'). The idea of Indian classical music, they claim, arose in a colonial context as a response to the threat of Western cultural dominance; it was systematised, standardised and promulgated as a public art-form by musical theorists, reformers and educators of the early twentieth century, and was embraced by the nationalist political movement. Before the twentieth century, these historians claim, there was no 'classical music' in either North or South India; merely a variety of musical traditions performed in different places by different social groups with little cultural or social prestige, and no uniformity. On the basis of these miscellaneous materials, Indian classical music was 'invented' in modern times.

This 'invention hypothesis' is a salutary reminder that many musical changes did occur in the twentieth century, as South Asia emerged from its colonial experience into the modern world, and it captures important changes in the way Hindustani music has been perceived and represented. But the documented historical record shows that change in music is nothing new, although there have also been significant continuities over very long periods of time. Change is most obvious in the musical instruments, most of which have acquired their present forms since the eighteenth century (see **Voices and instruments** below), but it can also be seen in vocal styles and in the social background of musicians, as we shall see in this section and the next. But twentieth-century theorists were not the first to attempt to systematise Indian music in written texts. Systems of raga and tala have been repeatedly re-codified in Sanskrit theoretical treatises (*shāstra*) beginning with the *Nātyashāstra* (c. third or fourth century) and the *Brihaddeshī* (c. eighth or ninth century), attributed to the mythical sages Bharata and Matanga respectively. Such early texts relate to modern practice in the general sense of establishing the nature of the concepts and some basic technical vocabulary: for example, the *Brihaddeshī* is the first text to discuss the raga concept in terms that are still valid today. Repertoire and performance practice, on the other hand, continue to change from generation to generation.

Despite this common tradition of theory in writing, until the fifteenth century or even later there was no twofold division of Indian music into North and South, but rather a diversity of *deshī sangīta*, 'local music', differing from region to region and from one level of society to another, rather as the 'invention hypothesis' would predict. Two particular factors caused these performance traditions to coalesce into Hindustani (North Indian) and Karnatak (South Indian) traditions. One is language: the linguistic families of Dravidian languages in the South and Indo-Aryan in the North underlie the corresponding grouping together of vernacular song repertoires and their associated music. The other is the arrival of successive waves of invaders from Central Asia, beginning with the conquest of large parts of north-west India by Turkish generals in 1192–98, and culminating in the establishment of the Mughal Empire, by rulers of Mongol origin, in the sixteenth century. These invaders brought with them not only the Islamic religion, but also – despite the problematic status of music within orthodox Islam – new musical instruments, scales and modes, poetic and musical genres, languages and musicians. Their impact was felt mainly, though not exclusively, in the North.

The infusion of the indigenous musical culture (which was highly regarded by the new political elite) with these foreign elements was a gradual process. By the fifteenth century the court singers of Man Singh Tomar, Hindu ruler of Gwalior, were composing songs in a partly new, partly traditional form called *dhrupad*, in the local Hindi dialect, to praise the ruler, the beloved and the gods; but at the contemporaneous court of the Muslim ruler Hussein Shah Sharqi of Jaunpur, some 300 miles to the East, they were singing Sufi poetry in a locally developed style that later came to be known as *khayāl*. These and other musical strands met at the courts of the Mughal Emperors, from Akbar (ruled 1556–1605) to Mohammed Shah Rangile (1719–1748), who unified the whole of northern India under their rule, and achieved much the same for Hindustani music.

The court of Akbar, in Agra and nearby Fatehpur Sikri, boasted an extensive musical establishment, including Muslim instrumentalists from Central Asia and Hindu singers from Gwalior. The former played instruments including the long-necked, fretted lutes that would later be transformed into the modern sitar and tambura. The singers, reputed to be the finest of the age, and headed by the incomparable Tansen (c. 1531–c. 1620), sang *dhrupad* songs set in ragas and talas; these were performed in semi-choral style by two or more male singers, with accompaniment of the indigenous barrel-shaped drum *pakhāvaj*. The poetry was largely secular, and the style of performance was majestic and impressive, perhaps expressing the grandeur and power of the Mughal regime. Each song would be prefaced by *ālāp*, a wordless, free-tempo, solo improvisation on the raga of the song. *Dhrupad* thus became the basic model for the performance of a raga in Hindustani music.

In 1648 Akbar's grandson, the emperor Shahjahan, moved the Mughal capital from Agra to Delhi, where local musicians introduced to his court the songs of Amir Khusrau (a local Sufi poet of the thirteenth century) and Hussein Shah Sharqi of Jaunpur. Known as *khayāl* ('fantasy, imagination'), and devoid of the abstract raga-development of alap, this style of singing was noted for its emotional intensity (*dard*). Dhrupad and khayal continued to develop and influence each other under the emperor Aurangzeb (1658–1707), who, contrary to popular myth, was a generous patron of music (in later life he refrained from listening to music out of religious piety, but he did not prevent others from doing so). It is perhaps not too fanciful to compare dhrupad with the massive grandeur of a Hindu temple colonnade, and khayal with the florid delicacy of a Mughal cusped arch; at all events, these two vocal styles, as developed at the Mughal court, are the key to understanding the musical idiom and performance structures of Hindustani music today. Thus in the performance by Buddhadev Dasgupta discussed above (Examples 6.2–4), the sequence of alap and composition follows the dhrupad model, but the convolutions of the improvisation (Example 6.4) reflect the khayal style.

By the time of the last great Mughal, Mohammad Shah Rangile, the wealthy elite of Delhi had developed an insatiable appetite for khayal, which has remained the more popular style to this day. Dhrupad and alap, and indigenous accompanying instruments, continued to be preserved by a few descendants of Tansen (a contemporary account describes how their loud voices 'overpowered the thunder and seemed to pierce the ceiling'); but by this time the sitar and tabla were starting to replace the *bīn* (described below) and *pakhāvaj* as more suitable instruments for the khayal style. Of the female khayal singer Kamal Bai it was said: 'Her melancholic voice is so melodious that it enraptures the hearts of the people ... She can sing like a nightingale all night long and still retain the freshness of her voice'.[3]

A devastating attack by the Persian emperor Nadir Shah in 1739 inflicted a blow on Delhi's musical culture from which it would never fully recover, and the later eighteenth and nineteenth centuries saw the consequent rise of provincial centres of music, including Lucknow, Gwalior, Agra, Banaras, Patiala, Rampur and the Rajasthani courts of Jaipur and Udaipur. As the Mughal Empire contracted to the region of Delhi itself, British colonial rule (based in Calcutta) correspondingly expanded, and by relieving local rulers of their political independence and responsibilities, enabled the more cultured rulers to maintain expansive musical establishments in the declining decades of their influence. These provided the leading musicians and dancers of the day (many of them from the waning Delhi court) with the opportunity to develop vocal and instrumental styles to unprecedented heights of virtuosity and sophistication. Typical of this period is the emergence of *tappā*, an exceptionally florid style of song, originating in the Panjab and developed into an art form by Miyan Shori of Lucknow; and *thumrī*, a delicate and sentimental song-style associated with Lucknow's courtesan singer-dancers. These styles are considered 'semi-classical', because they do not present ragas in a systematic manner. By contrast, khayal singers, sitarists and sarodists developed their own styles of alap, thereby ensuring the 'classical' status of their art; the alap of dhrupad singers thus became an essential model for the development of other vocal and instrumental styles.

The later nineteenth and early twentieth centuries were a period of major disruptions and changes in Hindustani music. The tragic events of the 1857–58 'Mutiny', in which Indian and British communities attacked each other with unprecedented violence, spelled the end of the Mughal Empire and the establishment of the British; during this time many musicians were displaced from court to court in search of secure patronage. But the subsequent growth of

The legendary sixteenth-century composer and singer Tansen dominated music at the court of Akbar. He is depicted in this eighteenth-century Rajasthani miniature receiving a lesson from the composer Swami Haridas, while the emperor looks on.

the railways gave musicians the opportunity to establish reputations beyond the confines of their patrons' palaces.

Meanwhile, in the colonial cities of Calcutta and Bombay, the educated middle classes took up the cause of music with reforming zeal. As part of the ancient cultural heritage of India, music was too precious to be left to the increasingly discredited and impoverished princes and their court musicians: it had to be brought into the public life of a rejuvenated, modern and ultimately independent India. The efforts of Vishnu Narayan Bhatkhande, Vishnu Digambar Paluskar and other reformers transformed the status and perception of Hindustani music, by reforming theoretical systems, establishing public teaching institutions, creating textbooks and promoting public concerts. Every city of northern India now has at least one music college at which members of the public – especially, for social reasons, young women – enrol in sitar or singing classes. Such colleges use printed textbooks explaining the theory of Indian music with exercises and compositions in music notation; early experiments with staff notation having been abandoned, the notation system used is an adaptation of traditional Indian solfège (*sargam*). The college teaching system does not produce professional performing artists, who invariably train with a guru or ustad, but it educates a significant popular audience for Hindustani music, who can hear public concerts by local artists or visiting stars for a modest ticket price (Paluskar had inaugurated this practice when he gave one of the first public, ticketed concerts in Gwalior in 1897). Such public events are held today in concert halls and theatres, or in large festival marquees set up near a temple or on the banks of a sacred river. Smaller concerts in private homes remain the quintessential context for music listening, however, and are usually by invitation.

Those musicians fortunate enough to have inherited court positions were initially reluctant to participate in the reform movement, which was largely aimed at taking music out of their control. But as their princely employers lost their budgets, or expended them on lavish lifestyles in Paris or New York, musicians needed to find new patrons. Gradually they embraced the new technology of gramophone recording, introduced in 1902, which allowed those wealthy enough to own a record player to hear the greatest musicians in their own homes. Broadcasting, which began in India in 1927, also became an important source of income for musicians; a system of graded artists was established, with 'staff artists' permanently on station to accompany the A-grade soloists for their live broadcasts. For many years, classical music was protected by All India Radio from competition from popular film music, but it is now increasingly a niche market for radio and television. Until the 1970s EMI/HMV India held a virtual monopoly of the record industry in India, and published a limited selection of 78 and 33.3 rpm records of classical artists, many of which are still treasured as classic recordings by connoisseurs today. The arrival of cassettes in the 1970s and CDs in the 1990s, however, opened the market to many other companies and allowed a wider diversity of genres and artists to be heard. This diversification has also allowed a 'grey market' in previously unpublished archive recordings to develop, bringing back to older listeners their favourite performers of the 1950s and 1960s (such as Amir Khan or Bade Ghulam Ali Khan), who, though fêted as innovators in their day, now seem to evoke the musical values of pre-modern India.

Outside India, a post-colonial world has embraced the idea of Indian classical music with considerable enthusiasm. Starting with the tours abroad of Ravi Shankar and Vilayat Khan in the 1950s, a variety of instrumentalists, and a few vocalists, have achieved fame and fortune in Europe, North America, Australia, Japan, Israel and elsewhere. This helped to enhance their status in India too, as representatives of Indian culture and of the newly modern Indian nation, to the outside world. This role has been largely supplanted by film music, which is now heard almost everywhere, and is seen more readily as a musical emblem of modern India; but there are still frequent tours by classical musicians, festivals of Indian classical music, and courses of instruction in many parts of the world. Indian musicians resident and teaching abroad (for example, the late Ali Akbar Khan in California) have helped non-Indian musicians to learn the art themselves, and thereby have established a global community of performers and connoisseurs.

■ Voices and instruments

It would be hard to overstate the importance of the voice in Indian culture. In Hinduism, the chanting of Vedic scriptures in ritual was believed in ancient times to sustain the universe; this belief led to the development of the science of phonetics, which also influenced music theory. In Islam, rhythmic chanting of the name of Allah, *zikr*, is prized by Sufi devotees as an ecstatic form of communion with the Divine, and this too has echoes in classical music. Most popular religious traditions in India use sung poetry in various regional languages as an expression of devotion to the chosen deity, and songs of this kind are also found in the classical music repertoire, alongside more secular ones.

Theory books have much to say about the virtues and faults of singers, but there is no one method of voice training for classical music; each teacher will have his or her own methods, tailored to the individual pupil. Voice production not only varies between the three principal vocal styles described below, but has also changed across the stylistic spectrum during the twentieth century. A beautiful natural tone is not especially prized, and older singers prioritised loudness over tone quality, both to express intensity of feeling, and in order to be heard in the larger spaces of the palace or temple over the sound of loud accompaniment (especially the drum *pakhāvaj*); singers often sang in small groups to achieve even greater resonance for the pre-composed parts of a performance, as still happens in temple music. The advent of the microphone, essential for performances in marquees and now used everywhere, has enabled classical singers to sing more quietly and with more subtlety of tone and ornamentation; quiet instruments need no longer struggle to be heard and more subtle effects can be exploited (provided the sound system is adequate).

The main requirements of the classical singer include:

> *mīnd*: the flexibility to glide smoothly from one pitch to the next
>
> *ās*: resonance – a strong tone throughout the range (usually three octaves)
>
> *shruti*: precise intonation
>
> *gamak*: ornamentation

These and other criteria combine to form the 'vocal style' (*gāyakī*) of the singer, which is partly unique to him or her, and partly inherited from the 'household' (*gharānā*) or lineage of teachers and disciples he/she belongs to.

Vocal style also correlates to some extent with historical genres, repertoires and social communities of performers. Three distinct vocal genres are recognised, dhrupad, khayal and thumri, whose historical origins are traced above. Hereditary male solo singers who can trace their ancestry to the Mughal court are called *kalāvants* and their special preserve is dhrupad; few such families now survive, but many musicians claim to have inherited the tradition of Tansen's descendants through their teachers. Hereditary female singers sing thumri and trace their origins to the courtesan communities that graced the courts of Lucknow, Banaras (Varanasi) and Delhi in the nineteenth century. Again, few such lineages survive, because of the rejection of the courtesan profession by the 'respectable' urban middle classes in the early twentieth century. Khayal singers have probably always included a mixture of professional and non-professional, hereditary and non-hereditary, male and female, Muslim and Hindu musicians. Today they include singers originally from the Mirasi community, a Muslim caste of hereditary folk musicians from the Panjab, who moved into the urban centres as accompanists of courtesans in the nineteenth century, playing tabla and the bowed lute *sārangī*; by re-training as khayal singers they came to dominate classical music in the twentieth century. All these social categories of musician have been largely supplanted in the later twentieth century by non-hereditary Hindu musicians from high caste, urban, educated middle-class backgrounds. While these include both male and female musicians, women still avoid playing tabla and *sārangī* because of their former association with the courtesans and their male accompanists.

Instruments and instrumental music can be discussed alongside the three vocal genres because they have evolved to emulate vocal style; melody instruments, at least, are effectively surrogate voices. Instrumentalists often take training from a vocalist and it is a compliment to an instrumentalist to say that one can hear the voice in their instrument.

The dhrupad vocal style is considered to be very plain, almost unornamented apart from smooth glissandos and slow oscillations. Performance begins with a long, slow alap, followed by a song which can be slow or fast. Performers usually bring their performance to a vigorous climax by improvising on the words of the song in lively rhythmic competition with their accompanist, who plays the majestic barrel-shaped drum *pakhāvaj* rather than the lighter-toned tabla. Although it was a secular art-form at the Mughal court, performed in praise of the monarch, dhrupad is now considered a religious or spiritual act of devotion, with words in praise of Hindu deities or Allah, or on philosophical subjects including music theory. Dhrupad singers are considered to be experts in raga, tala and intonation (*shruti*).

The instrument traditionally played in dhrupad style is the *bīn* or *rudra vīnā*. It comprises a hollow tube of wood onto which are mounted four melody strings, frets, bridge and three drone strings. Behind the tube, which is held vertically or horizontally in front of the player, hang two very large gourd resonators; nevertheless the sound of the instrument is very quiet. The size of the instrument and its exceptionally deep pitch make it unsuitable for rapid playing, but it is ideal for alap in the dhrupad style. Two features of the instrument are especially important for cultivating a vocal style: the bridge is carefully shaped to induce a slight buzz, which gives the sound resonance and duration; and the strings can be pulled at the fret to produce a smooth glissando or oscillation. Unfortunately today there are no more than a handful of players of this instrument, which used to be cultivated especially by the kalavant descendants of Tansen's daughter Sarasvati (the last of whom, Ustad Dabir Khan, died in the 1960s).

In contrast to dhrupad, khayal style is very florid, employing a wide range of ornamental and virtuoso techniques, most of which are strictly forbidden in dhrupad. Accompaniment is on the tabla. Performance usually begins with a composed song rather than the long alap of dhrupad, and ends with bravura *tāns* – rapid and convoluted arabesques sung to the vowel *ā* – which are unique to the khayal style. Between the song and the tans the singer may develop the raga in a leisurely 'expansion' (*vistār, barhat*); this is similar to alap but is accompanied by the tabla throughout, and periodically the singer will remind us of the song by repeating its first phrase. If the speed of the tala is slow (tempi of five seconds per beat or slower became common in the later twentieth century), the performance usually ends with a second, fast-tempo composition in the same raga, ending with further tans. Slow-tempo expansion of the raga is believed to have been introduced to khayal in the mid-twentieth century in emulation of the slow alap of dhrupad.

Khayal singers, male and female, usually also sing the thumri style – often for the last item of a concert – though there are also specialist thumri singers. The emphasis here is on the delicate interpretation of the words, which are flirtatiously or poignantly addressed by a female to her lover, typically imagined as being either absent and longed for, or present and mischievous. If the lover is addressed as Krishna, it is to evoke well-known stories of his youthful amorous frolics with the milkmaids of Braj (the Indian Arcadia) rather than his religious status as an *avatār* of the great god Vishnu. Only the 'light' ragas are used – those that have a playful or melancholy mood, and folksong-like charm – and in place of the abstract melodic development of alap or the bravura flourishes of khayal, the singer improvises around the words, with delicate ornamentation, extracting every ounce of emotional meaning, even if that means occasionally going beyond the melodic boundaries of the raga.

Most melodic instruments today are played in khayal style, often blended with elements of dhrupad and/or thumri; it is the flourishes of khayal that give most scope for the astonishing instrumental virtuosity that has been perhaps the most remarkable development of Hindustani music in the post-colonial age. The best known of all Indian instruments, the sitar, only reached its pre-eminence in the mid-twentieth century, in the hands of internationally famous players such as Vilayat Khan and Ravi Shankar; it is played today by musicians of both genders and almost any social background, including a number of non-Indian players. Its development began with much smaller, delicate, long-necked lutes played at the Mughal court, similar to the *setār* of Persian music. Its transformation over three centuries into the modern instrument involved making the neck broader to allow more pulling of the string at the fret, transferring to it the buzzing bridge, gourd resonators and high frets of the bin, and cultivation of a lyrical, vocal style that combines elements of dhrupad alap and khayal ornamentation. Even closer in sound to the bin is the bass sitar or *surbahār*, invented in the nineteenth century, which is used mainly for alap. Both the sitar and the surbahar normally have a bank of sympathetic strings that add lustre to the sound by resonating in sympathy with the notes played on the melody strings. Originating from the same Central Asian lutes, the *tambūrā* or *tānpurā* has evolved into a large, fretless instrument of exceptional resonance, the open strings of which provide

Left: A sarangi bowed lute   *Right:* When the infant Krishna played his flute, the cow-girls flocked to his side: a fresco on an interior wall of City Palace, Udaipur.

the ethereal background drone to a vocal or instrumental performance. Playing tambura is a traditional role for disciples or female relatives of the soloist.

The nineteenth century was an era of rapid development in the design of classical instruments, and Indian museums are stocked with innumerable, sometimes bizarre, experiments in enlarging traditional instruments or combining Indian and Western instruments. Apart from the surbahar most of these failed to catch on, but an important success story is that of the *sarod*. In the early nineteenth century, Pathan settlers in the area of Rohilkhand were playing the Afghan *rabob*, a short-necked lute with a narrow-waisted resonator that is deeper than it is wide, four gut melody strings and many steel sympathetic strings. Despite the latter, the sound of the melody notes was of short duration, and the four gut frets on the neck made it difficult to emulate the smooth glides of dhrupad or the rapid ornaments of khayal. By removing the frets, bolting a polished steel plate to the fingerboard and enlarging the bowl of the resonator, Indian musicians, including several from Tansen's family, transformed the rabob into a more resonant instrument, on which glissandos could be played by sliding the stopping finger along the string. On this new instrument, the *sarod*,

THE OTHER CLASSICAL MUSICS

Descended from the Afghan rabob lute, the sarod has been so effectively championed by players including Amjad Ali Khan *(top left)* that as a solo instrument it now rivals the sitar, played here by Anoushka and Ravi Shankar *(bottom right)*, and seen *(bottom left)* in an eighteenth century Rajasthani miniature. Mastery of the rudra vina, or bin, played here by Asad Ali Khan *(top right)*, is these days confined to a small handful of musicians – despite its being ideally suited to the dhrupad style.

they could reproduce aspects of thumri, khayal and even dhrupad styles; today the sarod rivals the sitar as one of the main vehicles for Hindustani instrumental music. Musicians of Afghan descent such as Amjad Ali Khan, or of Tansen's discipular lineage such as the late Ali Akbar Khan and Buddhadev Dasgupta, have been prominent among players of the modern *sarod*.

Like the sitar and the sarod, the *sārangī* has Central Asian ancestry and can be traced to the Mughal period or even earlier. It is a bowed lute, box-shaped with incurved sides, carved from a single block of wood; like the rabob and sarod, it has a skin table and many sympathetic strings. Because the bowing technique and sympathetic strings give resonance, while the fingers can slide freely along the string, it is not only played in vocal style, but is regarded as the ideal accompaniment to the voice; its melancholy solo sound is also associated with funeral occasions and replaces other music on the radio when a national leader dies. It is largely played by male hereditary musicians of Mirasi or similar background. Because of its former association with courtesan culture the instrument and its players are marginalised in India, and there are concerns for its survival. In the twentieth century, however, the virtuoso player Ram Narayan, and recently his daughter Aruna, have earned greater respect for the sarangi as a solo instrument.

Though not a melodic instrument, and traditionally an accompanying rather than solo instrument, the tabla has achieved enormous popularity within and outside India, owing to the virtuosity of its players and the remarkable range of sonorities and rhythmic effects they can produce. It is a pair of small drums, played with the hands; one drum is tuned to the tonic pitch of the raga chosen by the soloist, the other to a deeper pitch which can be modulated by varying the pressure of the hand while striking. This modulation gives a vocal character to the sound, and in fact all the sounds of the instrument are encoded in a syllabic 'notation'; vocal recitation of the syllables (*bol*) at high speed is an essential skill for tabla players. The players are almost invariably male, like sarangi players, and traditionally came from the same families; now players come from a wide range of backgrounds and a small number of women players are emerging.

While the above instruments constitute the most 'traditional' instruments of Hindustani music, instruments from outside the classical tradition can also be used, provided their technique and construction allow the Hindustani vocal styles to be rendered on them. The oboe *shahnāī* ('royal flute') is played mainly in outdoor settings for temples and weddings, but was brought into concert music by the late Bismillah Khan. The bamboo flute *bānsurī*, traditionally played by the same families of temple musicians as the shahnai, was revived by the late Pannalal Ghosh in an enlarged, deeper form on which alap and khayal could be played, as they are today by Hariprasad Chaurasia and others. Instruments of Western origin include the harmonium, a small portable reed organ that since the nineteenth century has increasingly replaced the sarangi as an accompaniment to the voice; the violin, used mainly as a solo instrument; and the guitar, modified for playing in Hindustani style by Vishwamohan Bhatt and others. The *santūr*, a box zither with steel strings played with delicate finger-held beaters, is of ancient Middle Eastern origin, but was introduced to Hindustani film and classical music by its supreme exponent today, Shivkumar Sharma. Although the sound is attractive to many listeners, it is impossible to produce a true glissando on the santur. As if to compensate for this limitation, some proponents of the santur make exaggerated claims for its antiquity in India. The re-invention of Indian classical music, and of its history, continues as it has always done.

Further reading

Perhaps the best starting point for an exploration of Hindustani music is Joep Bor's *The Raga Guide*, which helpfully combines discussion, notated examples and audio tracks on CD, not to mention examples of *rāgamālā* paintings with their inscriptions translated, and a glossary. More analytical approaches to the subject of rāga can be found in Nazir Jairazbhoy's *The Rāgs of North Indian Music* (1971), and in the articles 'India, subcontinent of' and 'Mode' in the *New Grove Dictionary of Music and Musicians*. James Kippen's chapter in *The Garland Encyclopedia of World Music* vol. 5, *South Asia*, is an excellent introduction to the Hindustani *tala* system, and more detail is to be found in Martin Clayton's *Time in Indian Music*. Neil Sorrell and Ram Narayan's *Indian Music in Performance* and George Ruckert's *Music in North India* combine discussion of performance and structure in Hindustani music with aspects of the cultural context and the performers themselves; more detail on the latter will be found in Daniel Neuman's anthropological study *The Life of Music in North India* (1980). The musical characteristics, cultural contexts and historical evolution of the vocal styles dhrupad, khayal and thumri are traced in Ritwik Sanyal and Richard Widdess's *Dhrupad*, Bonnie Wade's *Khyāl* and Peter Manuel's *Thumri in Historical and Stylistic Perspective* respectively; for instrumental music, studies by Allyn Miner (*Sitar and Sarod in the 18th and 19th Centuries*), Adrian McNeil (*Inventing the Sarod*) and James Kippen (*The Tabla of Lucknow*) have illuminated the development and social history of the sitar, sarod and tabla respectively. The history of Hindustani music in its formative centuries (thirteenth to twentieth) is spectacularly illustrated in Joep Bor and Philippe Bruguière's *Gloire des princes, louange des dieux*, and authoritatively surveyed in Bor, Françoise Delvoye, Jane Harvey and Emmie te Nijenhuis's *Hindustani Music*. Musical systems and speculations of the preceding era are lucidly documented in Lewis Rowell's *Music and Musical Thought in Early India*, while the history of the West's encounter with Hindustani music is traced in Gerry Farrell's *Indian Music and the West*. Donna Marie Wulff's chapter 'On practicing music religiously' in Joyce Irwin's book *Sacred Sound* is a judicious assessment of the relationship between classical music and the spiritual traditions of North India.

Recommended listening

Numerous 78 rpm and LP recordings of great twentieth-century Hindustani vocalists and instrumentalists are considered classics by Indian musicians and music-lovers, and are now available through online services such as iTunes, or in dedicated Indian music websites such as the ITC Sangeet Research Academy (http://www.itcsra.org/). The following is a small sample of historic and contemporary recordings.

The Raga Guide (4 CDs with book), Nimbus NI 5536/9, 1999. Each of seventy-four ragas, including all the most important ones, is illustrated on CD by a five-minute miniature vocal or instrumental (flute or sarod) performance, in which a composition and improvised raga-development are both briefly encompassed. Examples 6.2–4 in this chapter are based on a track from this collection. The accompanying book includes commentary, transcribed excerpts and song texts and translations.

Uday Bhawalkar, *A dhrupad recital*, Navras Records NRCD 0058, 1996. A contemporary rendering of the dhrupad vocal style, but very true to tradition.

Zia Mohiuddin Dagar, *Rag Yaman and Suddh Todi* (2 CDs), Nimbus Records NI 7047/8, 1991) Perfection of dhrupad-style alap performance on the rudra vina (bin).

Amir Khan, HMV EALP 1253 (LP). Available from Saregama through iTunes as *Amir Khan – Marwa and Darbari*. Two definitive raga performances in khayal style, by the singer that many Hindustani musicians most admire.

Living Music from the Past: Kesarbai Kerkar, Underscore Records 04AM011, 2004. Available in iTunes. A compilation of 78 rpm recordings from 1935–8 by one of the first female khayal singers to win popular acclaim in North India. One of her tracks (not in this compilation) was included in a sampler CD carried on the Voyager 1 and 2 spacecraft. Here the final track is an example of thumri style.

Pandit Rajan and Sajan Mishra, Navras Records NRCD 0057, 1996. A characteristic performance by two of the most popular khayal singers today.

Ustad Vilayat Khan, *Raga Yaman*, HMV ASD 2425 (LP), 1968. Available from Saregama through iTunes as *Evergreen Yaman*. Extended rendition of this major raga in khayal style by the most admired sitarist of the twentieth century.

Ravi Shankar, *Sound of the Sitar*, World Pacific (LP), 1965. Available from Angel Records through iTunes as *The Ravi Shankar Collection: Sound of the Sitar*. The world-renowned sitarist at his peak, in an extended alap (raga Malkauns) showing the influence of dhrupad style on sitar.

Amjad Ali Khan, *Atma*, Audiorec Classics ACCD 1004, 1990. Illustrates contemporary sarod style as played by a leading exponent of Afghan descent, and includes a full-length performance of raga Bihag (cf Examples 6.2–4 in this chapter).

7 South India

Jonathan Katz

Clad in traditional Hindu dress, a boy removes his shoes, approaches the shrine at the side of the stage and pays homage to a deity sitting garlanded under its canopy. Walking centre stage, making a bow with hands joined in salutation, he then takes his place in a little group seated cross-legged facing the audience, in the front of which are his family and teachers. The other musicians have been tuning their instruments: to his right the percussionist with the double-ended drum laid horizontally before him; to his left a violinist, instrument wedged between chest and foot so as to allow the left hand freedom of movement; behind him a woman gently strumming with one hand the four open strings of the long-necked drone lute. Now the young singer intones the first words of a prayer-song to the elephant-headed Lord Ganesa, the text composed by a sixteenth-century South Indian saint-poet. Against the background drone of upper and lower tonic and perfect fifth, the vocal line of the hymn is inflected and ornamented with little slides and oscillations: an affirmation of religious faith and poetic beauty. People in the audience call out their appreciation during the performance, and with hand-gestures mark the metre of the works the boy sings in his improvisation.

THIS is a South Indian *arangētram*, or 'coming to the stage': a debut performance for family, teachers and friends. The young artist's programme will have been prepared through years of study, and whether staged in India or abroad, this ceremony and its music are strongly redolent of the atmosphere of a Hindu temple. In stark contrast to the Muslim and Central Asian influences pervading Hindustani music, South Indian music's religious underpinning is everywhere apparent. In a famous scriptural passage, an ancient sage asks the God Vishnu how people may best come to know Him, and the God replies: 'I dwell not in heaven, nor in the hearts of the Yogīs, nor in the sun. Where my devotees are singing, O Nārada, that is where I stand.'

In addition to its primary purpose as an artistic rite of passage for a boy or girl, in expatriate Indian communities the arangetram also makes a statement of cultural identity, and can be supported by musicians and teachers invited from India to take part. It may last two or three hours and will follow the form of a professional performance – a sequence of compositions designed to show how the young musician has absorbed technical expertise and aesthetic understanding, and can thus represent the continuity of the classical tradition. But the story of this tradition, and of the evolution of its definition as 'classical', is far from straightforward.

◂ Saraswati, the Hindu goddess of wisdom, knowledge and the arts, is traditionally represented holding the vina lute, as in this nineteenth-century Bengali watercolour.

History

The classical musics of North and South India differ greatly in both sound and system, with contrasts more striking than those between the subcontinent's numerous folk traditions. In regional folk music, if we were to listen to melody and rhythm alone, and were able to disregard the language of the texts and the distinctive sounds of instruments from different regions, we might not so easily realise which part of India we were in. But the classical traditions have developed more immediately distinguishable styles, and even a very brief passage will normally identify itself as Northern or Southern.

The South Indian musical style known as Karnatak (anglicised as Carnatic) employs a repertoire of compositional forms based on melodic and rhythmic principles derived both from a long and continuous oral tradition and from an interpretation of ancient and medieval theory. There are clear contrasts between this music and 'Hindustani' music. Many would describe Hindustani music as more fluid, and Karnatak as more angular, but other differences involve instruments, melodic and rhythmic organisation, compositional structures and above all the characteristic melodic inflections that give each music so distinctive a sound. Yet many underlying principles are common to both. A widely held but simplistic view is that the systems resulted from a 'bifurcation' within one single tradition, which took place sometime after the thirteenth century. It is more likely that within a general musical culture, encompassing many regional dialects, certain styles have prospered under patronage.

Imagine a line running from the west coast of India a little south of Goa to the east coast a little south of the Orissan temple town of Puri. Karnatak music is the dominant classical culture south of this line, where the major Dravidian languages – Kannada, Malayalam, Telugu and Tamil – are spoken. Tamils from Sri Lanka have helped the South Asian diaspora introduce Karnatak music and dance to the rest of the world, but it is less well-known in the West than the heavily-promoted music of the North. Though there are musicians trained in both Hindustani and Karnatak performance, and though there have been experiments at combining the two, musical 'bilingualism' is rare, and an upbringing in one tradition does not automatically bring with it an understanding of the other. To cross the artistic border, a new musical language must be learned.

Southern classical music is instantly recognisable by the sound of its characteristic instruments, by the singer's method of voice production, and above all by the highly ornamented style of its melody. The *vīnā* (plucked lute) has a rounder timbre, nearer to the human voice, than the north Indian sitar; the Karnatak flute is deeper than the Hindustani, and the normal percussion accompaniment played on the double-ended *mrdangam* drum creates a mellower background than the northern tabla. Vocal and instrumental techniques have been developed in ways that enable particularly rapid shakes, appoggiaturas and oscillations, understood by Karnatak musicians as essential characteristics of melodic notes. A song-notation does not normally attempt to indicate this feature of melody, simply recording the main note as a degree in a scale. The

SOUTH INDIA

A Karnatak concert in Chennai, Tamil Nadu, 2005: Raja Rao (mridangam), B. Shreesundarkumar (tala and kanjira drum), N. Ramani (venu flute) and R. K. Sriramkumar (violin)

ornamentation is learnt through oral tradition, the pupil imitating the teacher, and the note itself often seems to be the centre of an enveloping cluster, an 'idea' beautifully attired.

When South Indian musicians describe music as 'Karnatak' or 'South Indian Classical', they are referring to an art characterised by seriousness, complexity and a need for rigorous training and cultural conditioning. Associated with this is a 'great tradition' of music theory understood by scholars who are not necessarily performers themselves. It is generally agreed that the origins of present-day Karnatak music can be traced as far back as the seventeenth century, with some survivals from earlier centuries. But many principles of Karnatak theory and practice have more distant origins, and may be linked to ancient and medieval technical musical treatises in classical Sanskrit as well as vernacular Indian languages. Moreover, Karnatak music is both an independent art form and a 'supporting' art central to dance and drama. Patronage is crucial to its status; in the past this meant a ruling elite who, while not necessarily practitioners, regarded themselves as connoisseurs.

Indian musical history is not a history of 'works' or even 'pieces'; there are composed songs, but these act only as starting points in performance. Nor is it possible to know much about what this music sounded like before the recording era. Old treatises tell us about general concepts, and from these sources and other branches of literature – plus representations of musicians in painting and sculpture – we know something about players and performance, instruments and notations. There are notated compositions using solfège note-names, but in India musical notation has always been mnemonic – a simple 'aide-memoire' used as an adjunct to an essentially oral tradition; it does not suffice as a method

A concert in honour of Tyagaraja in Cleveland State University, Ohio, with an image of the composer as a backdrop: A. S. Murali (ghatam), Jayanthi Kumaresh (vina), Pramath Kiran (morsing) and Arjun Kumar (mridangam)

of prescribing or determining performance. You have to hear what is being notated, and what is notated is never more than a small, abstracted part of a performance.

The Kannada poet-singer Purandaradāsa (d. 1564) is popularly seen as the grandfather of Karnatak music on the strength of his poems, but it is impossible to know how he intended them to be sung. Yet many are sung in both Northern and Southern Indian traditions, to melodies of much more recent origin. It is the same with other famous South Indian names from the early seventeenth century; the Telugu poet Ksetrayya, for instance, has left poetic texts highly esteemed in the Karnatak repertoire, but there is little authority for the musical detail of their original performance.

Clearer foundations for what we now know as the classical Karnatak tradition are to be seen in the rich musical culture at the eighteenth-century Hindu Maratha court of Tanjore (Tanjavur) in present-day Tamil Nadu. Here were born the three towering figures commonly known as the Karnatak 'Trinity': Tyāgarāja, Syāma Shāstrī and Muttusvāmi Dīkshitar. These musicians were all born around the same time in the same town of Tiruvarur in the Tanjore district: theirs are the poetic texts, and the origins of the melodies, that have become the basis of the concert repertoire. In a full-length public performance today, one may often hear song compositions mainly, or even solely, by these composers.

What, then, is meant by the word 'composer'? The great masters of the Karnatak tradition often carry the title *vāggeyakāra*, a Sanskrit word inherited from medieval Indian theoretical treatises and meaning a 'maker of words and music'. Many of the texts and song compositions which are now sung, or played by instrumentalists, as melodies, are presented as authentic both in verbal text and in melody and metre, but many new melodies may have been introduced much later by subsequent singers. Even when a performing tradition has kept some form of a melody in the repertoire, changes are inevitable; we can observe such changes in recordings, as compositions are performed by different artists at different times.

Both the thirteenth-century treatise *Saṅgītaratnākara* ('Mine of Jewels of Music'), and later sources which were inspired by it, define the characteristics of the good vaggeyakara. He needed to be a versatile talent, learned in linguistic, musical and other subjects, conversant with local traditions as well as orthodox theory and doctrine, intellectually gifted, unprejudiced, able to create quickly as well as powerfully, and steeped in the details of musical style and its appropriate melodic embellishments. Since Karnatak music theory has kept the term alive, the required attributes of song-composers have remained unchanged.

Tyagaraja (1767–1847), who came from a Telugu-speaking Brahmin family in what is now Andhra Pradesh, was venerated as more than a composer; out of respect for his authority his disciples avoided referring to him as a vaggeyakara, and saw him as a leading religious *Svāmī*, spiritual master and devotee, in his case of the Lord Rāma. Since it is his compositions, together with those of the other two members of the 'Trinity', Syama Shastri (1762–1827) and Muttusvami Dikshitar (1775–1835), that have dominated Karnatak music, the inseparable association between the South Indian religious devotional tradition (*bhakti*) and its philosophy and poetry has framed the whole musical culture. South Indian regional music is hugely diverse, and all communities and religions are part of its mosaic, but Karnatak concert music is pervasively Hindu.

Though royal patronage of the arts at Tanjore ensured a flourishing musical tradition, it is thought that the Trinity rarely performed for the Maratha court as such. But Tyagaraja helped enshrine the *kriti* – a hymn-like song-form – as a staple in the courtly repertoire. This drew on temple singing, and also the less formal devotional prayer- and praise-singing known as *kīrtanam*; his compositions, which were copied down by disciples, form part of the nucleus of vocal and instrumental Karnatak classical music. The kirtanam and the more elaborate kriti forms were also cultivated by Syama Shastri in Telugu, and by Muttusvami Dikshitar, who composed Sanskrit texts though his inherited vernacular language was Tamil. The use of a vernacular for religious poetry suggests popular accessibility, and Sanskrit is the more 'canonical' medium, the language of the early scriptures and of religious temple ritual, but in many Hindu religious traditions the two coexist comfortably. There are extensive literary repertoires of both religious devotional works and secular lyric and narrative forms in all of the major vernacular languages.

These three great composers were followed by a succession of disciples – both singers and vina players – in a tradition known by the Sanskrit term *guru-shishya-paramparā* (teacher-pupil-succession); thus the Karnatak song repertoire and its associated musical lore were kept alive and passed to other religious and political centres. The courts of Travancore (in present-day Kerala) and Mysore were particularly important. In Travancore the young Raja Svāti Tirunal (1813–46) was himself a respected composer and connoisseur of both South and North Indian styles; several hundred kritis and other compositions, many of great poetic merit, are attributed to him, and many are now regularly performed; during his rule the court also received musicians from Tanjore. Mysore was ruled by the Wodeyar dynasty, active patrons who employed many musicians from Tanjore, and provided the focus for a special tradition of vina-playing. The survival of this 'classical' tradition, carrying many Western connotations of the term – prestige, connoisseurship, cultural sophistication and so on – owes much to its dissemination from Tanjore, and even more to the growth in importance of Madras (now Chennai) as a fertile field for urban culture, for new and more diverse patronage, and for the cultivation of the practice of music by a wider public. Meanwhile other courts and princely states in South India became centres of music and dance, with schools being set up to train amateurs as well as professionals. Alongside these forms of patronage were the temple traditions, in which music formed a vital part of worship.

■ *The classical and canonical*

It has often been observed that in India, compared with other parts of the world colonised by the West, indigenous music remained relatively secure in its practice and patronage, and unthreatened by the diffusion of Western music. There was, however, a different pressure, as music became part of a nationalist agenda accompanying the drive towards independence and the establishment of new elites. While princely patronage weakened – as the courts came under British colonial control towards the end of the nineteenth century – a growing clerical and professional middle class was encouraging the pursuit of authentically Indian traditional arts, music and dance, as emblems of cultural identity. Knowledge and connoisseurship, it was felt, could go hand in hand with excellence in musical practice, and could bolster the new elite's self-respect. This contributed to the 'classicisation' of music: it has even been argued that classical South Indian music and dance were 'invented' in the twentieth century by Brahmin elites in Madras, and that in the process great damage was done to the traditional musical culture, since the old-style hereditary artists did not fit the new middle-class mould. At all events, the notion of an underlying 'great tradition' inevitably involved not only standardisation, but also the marginalisation of local variations, particularly those associated with social classes outside the new elite.

This is not to say that no music in the earlier nineteenth century could be regarded as properly 'classical Karnatak', but rather that through new teaching systems and institutions there came a new understanding of what the 'classical

SOUTH INDIA

Only in the twentieth century did women performers achieve the same professional status as men, thanks in large measure to two great singers, D. K. Pattammal (here celebrated with a postage stamp issued in 2014) and M. S. Subbulakshmi (in a poster for the 1945 film *Meera*)

tradition' actually meant. Institutions like the Madras branch of the Gayan Samaj (founded in 1883 to encourage interest in Karnatak music) and the Madras Music Academy (founded in 1928) sponsored research and the publication of notated compositions, and promoted music tuition in schools. But the publication of song notations and scholarly music theory led to an exaggerated sense of standard (or 'correct') versions of songs, marginalising aesthetically powerful variants; the shape and timing of performances also became more standardised.

Since Indian Independence in 1947, All India Radio and a vast recording industry have been the prime sources of patronage. As one of the largest broadcasting networks in the world, All India Radio has employed its own staff musicians, run numerous programmes of classical and regional music, documented music festivals and archived broadcasts. Meanwhile recordings on disc, cassette and CD have wrought their own changes to musical culture. Musicians now have greater access to each other's performances than ever before. There have been developments in technical proficiency, but some more adventurous departures in performance styles have at the same time been weakened.

It took longer for women to be able to appear on the concert platform on the same professional basis as men. This development came in the twentieth century thanks to the inspirational work of singers such as the superstar M. S. Subbulakshmi, born in 1916, whose mother was from a *Devadāsī* (temple dancer) background and was herself a good musician, and D. K. Pattammal, born in 1919, who came from an orthodox Brahmin community, and whose brilliant singing career set an example for gifted middle-class and upper-caste Hindus to become professional musicians rather than confining their gifts to family and private functions.

■ Concerts and programmes

Today Karnatak music is performed in many contexts, from devotional singing and playing in the temple, to small domestic concerts, to large festivals like the annual Tyagaraja commemorative celebrations held in Tamil Nadu and in other places with resident South Indian communities. But it is the public concert that now enjoys the greatest prestige. Such events, often called *kachēri*, are another legacy of the shift in patronage in the late nineteenth century, when musicians could no longer depend exclusively on support from their former court employers. They began to travel more, and new music societies sponsored performances for a widening public audience. Amplification is now almost de rigueur in all but the smallest venues, and has offered musicians new acoustic possibilities.

The young aspirant described at the start of this chapter, with his mix of composed and improvised material, would follow a format which has been standard since the 1930s. After an initial salutation and prayer the first item is normally a tripartite song form called a *varnam*, preceded by a brief *ālāpana* ('discourse') which is an improvised introduction to the raga (being the underlying melodic and modal structure of the piece). As the varnam is designed to show technical virtuosity and mastery of the musical material, it makes a good opening item.

Then follow some kritis, texts mostly composed by one or more members of the Trinity, set to melodies also ascribed to them, and in metrical cycles (tala) prescribed by them. One kriti may be particularly elaborate, the others shorter, but each will be preceded by an unmetred melodic introduction without drum, and each will feature some improvisation reflecting the soloist's inventiveness and command of melodic and rhythmic patterns.

Like the varnam, the kriti has three parts – *pallavi, anupallavi* and *charanam*. The kriti (Sanskrit for 'creation') is essentially an elaboration or distillation of the devotional kirtana composition, and the two terms are often used interchangeably; the text of the anupallavi responds to that of the pallavi. The Telugu song by Tyagaraja (*Endu dāginādo* – 'Where has He hidden?'), illustrated in both Tamil and Western notation in Examples 7.1 and 7.2 below, reflects the devotee's anguished longing for reunion with the absent deity:

Pallavi: 'Where has he hidden? When will he have mercy on me and come to me? Oh, my [troubled] Mind!'
Anupallavi: 'Why worry? Assuredly, as often before, the Lord must have hidden only to protect his devotees.'

There follow several verses of charanam which illustrate and extend the theme of the *anupallavi*, giving examples of how the Lord has indeed previously hidden himself from a devotee out of compassion, and concluding that he has done so once again. In the musical rendering of the poem, the pallavi is returned to between sections, like a refrain (as with a European rondo form). Pallavi, a Sanskrit loan, means 'sprout', and may indicate the evolution of the nuclear idea of the poem, to which the anupallavi ('following the pallavi') responds.

The many ways in which this poetic scheme can convey argument and meaning are heightened by the music. The melody of the anupallavi not only responds to that of the pallavi but builds on it by rising to a higher pitch, and the singer has freedom to repeat and emphasise this greater tension. Commonly the charanam melody relaxes a little in intensity before rising again to the anupallavi. Text and melody each have their independent power and beauty, but the artist may also present a counterpoint of the two, for instance by taking portions of the melody and extending them through additional cycles of the tala, departing for a time from the full sense of the text, and then returning to a crucial phrase at a moment of rhythmic emphasis.

Pride of place in a full concert goes to a large-scale structure called the *rāgam-tānam-pallavi*, a form thought to have originated in nineteenth-century contests of musical ingenuity and virtuosity. Here the first section is an extensive alapana exposition of the raga, the most thorough of the evening. The principle is similar to that of the Hindustani *ālāp*, though the procedure differs, since a conspectus of the whole raga structure is typically offered before returning to finer details of each part of the lower, then upper pitch ranges. In a second section this exposition continues in a rhythmic, but as yet unmetred form, normally still without drum, using non-verbal but articulated syllables ('*nam*', '*tham*'), much like the *nom-tom ālāp* of Hindustani music. The third section, the pallavi, is a pre-composed, texted, metred and drum-accompanied song, shorter than the kriti and elaborated in a different style. The soloist takes adventurous paths in improvisation, with tempo augmentations and diminutions and increasingly complex extensions of melodic phrases. In this item the mrdangam player

THE OTHER CLASSICAL MUSICS

EX. 7.1 The beginning of the composition (kriti) *Endu Dāginādo* by Tyāgarāja. Text and notation are in Tamil script, set out in a conventional metrical (tāla) scheme. See Example 7.2 opposite for a transcription into staff notation.

routinely has a prominent part, not only as accompanist and partner but in a lengthy solo cadenza towards the end.

This concert centrepiece is normally followed by some shorter and lighter items, many of which are used elsewhere as an accompaniment to classical dance: *padams* (devotional love-songs), secular love-songs called *jāvalis*, and the *tillāna* – a form, much like the Hindustani *tarānā*, using non-verbal phonetic syllables as a text in a fast-moving composition exploited to surprise and beguile the audience with unexpected turns and rhythmical 'events'. A concert will normally end on a religious note with a musical address to the deity.

■ Melody and rāga

As in North Indian music, there is no fixed standard pitch corresponding to one of the Western 'concert pitches'; pitch is set to the convenience and tessitura of a voice or instrument. The pitch repertoire is a twelve-semitone set conceived as a scale of seven notes (*svaras*), of which the tonic first degree and the fifth are fixed and unmodifiable, while the remaining five are differently variable through flattening or sharpening. Performances are accompanied by at least one drone instrument, normally the four-stringed *tambūrā* (or *tānpūrā*), which continuously sounds the tonic and the fifth, or the natural fourth if the raga being performed does not feature the fifth note.

Most Indian music is 'modal' in the sense that a performance starts and ends with reference to a single unchanging tonic and an essential melodic

SOUTH INDIA

EX. 7.2 Parts of the pallavi and anupallavi of the composition in Example 7.1, transcribed into Western staff notation by Harold S. Powers, with some indication of the various kinds of ornamentation (gamaka)

A concert at the Music Academy, Chennai, 2005: Kumbakonam Ramakrishna (mridangam), Tirukakkara S. Shantaram (kanjira), singer T. V. Ramprasadh, and Avanbeeshwaram S. R. Vinu (violin)

substructure. The monodic, single-voice and richly embellished melodic line of Karnatak music is based on the raga system, and is closely related historically to Hindustani and other regional South Asian musics. In the Karnatak tradition too there was always recognition of the distinctive aesthetic and emotional power of individual ragas; there is, for example, still a common observance of the appropriate ritual performance hours for particular ragas in the instrumental music of the temple *nāgasvaram* (large shawm) tradition. But South Indian theory and teaching place greater emphasis on the scale-types of the ragas and on their characteristic melodic 'direction', rather than on the extra-musical associations found in the earlier tradition of musical lore still current in the discourse of Hindustani musicians.

This understanding of raga goes back to a classificatory scheme called the *mēlakartā* system of seventy-two scales, thought to have been first devised and developed by scholar-musicians at the Tanjore court in the seventeenth century. The patterns in this system form a comprehensive set of the possible scalar combinations of the seven notes. Only a few of these were, or are now, actually used as ragas, but from these scales all the ragas that are found or may be newly invented can be theoretically derived. For a raga is more than a scale, containing within its definition stronger and weaker notes, characteristic patterns in ascent and descent (including zigzags), and characteristic ornamentation of particular notes. Indeed the concept of an 'ornamented note' may be a misapplication of a Western idea of pitch-identification, for in Indian classical music the ornamentation is often a part of the essential identity of the note within its raga context. Exactly how the notes are thus rendered is learned by the student from the teacher. There is a recognised set, and nomenclature, of 'ornaments', collectively known as *gamakas*, including various kinds of oscillation, shake, approach from another pitch and deflection from the primary pitch.

The songs we have referred to, their introductory alapana and the variations and expansions they undergo in performance, are set in individually prescribed ragas. Some musicians and listeners would indeed mentally identify a raga not only through its theoretical 'abstraction' – its ascending and descending scalar pattern and other characteristic features – but by association with one or more known compositions which 'represent' it. Each raga is individual, distinct, named and recognised by musically trained members of the audience.

■ Rhythm and tāla

Rhythm can be unmeasured in Indian music, as is commonly the case when a pulse is established but not metrically organised, for example in the *tānam* section of the alapana in the ragam-tanam-pallavi form. Organised musical time, as used in the song compositions and in solo percussion playing is, as in Hindustani music, realised through metrical cycles called *tālas*. These are normally sounded by a drum – in the kacheri context normally the double-ended mrdangam – sometimes with other percussion instruments stressing the more important beats. Each tala has a fixed number of regular beats grouped into smaller units. But the Karnatak system has preserved features of an older understanding of tala than that of Hindustani music. This system of seven different talas (known as the *sūlādi tālas*) is traditionally said to have been established by Purandaradasa in the sixteenth century. Interestingly a similar system is used, and attested in theoretical texts, for the devotional kirtana music of Orissa in Eastern India, not normally classified as Karnatak: it seems that a wider regional tradition was already in existence, and was eventually treated as the Karnatak standard. The discipline and beauty of Karnatak rhythms are often admired, and sometimes even envied, by Hindustani musicians.

The kriti described and illustrated in Examples 7.1–2 above uses the seven-beat tala known as *Mishra Chāpu*, which is grouped 3 + 2 + 2. Perhaps the commonest tala is the eight-beat *Ādi*, grouped 4 + 2 + 2. We saw in our opening arangetram performance how musically trained members of the audience keep time by using hand and finger gestures to mark the beats, especially those at the beginning of each group. The percussion instruments also give varying emphasis to the constituent parts of the cycle, and the drummer's practice includes also a system of articulated syllables (solmisation) known as *solkattu*, phonetic imitations (e.g. ta-ka-di-mi-ta-ka-ta-ki-ta) of drum strokes whose patterns can be 'spoken'. These are an essential part of the training of percussionists, but are also routinely used by the dance teacher as a feature of the musical accompaniment to dance performances, and they are even sometimes incorporated in the text of a kriti.

The melodic line of the song is thus measured, and audibly marked, by the beats of the tala, but there can also be considerable independence of melody and rhythm. The opening note of the melody does not necessarily coincide with the first beat of the tala, or even with its first group of beats, though the notes that do coincide with the strong beats of the tala will be particularly prominent; most easily recognised will be that word in the text that falls on the beginning (i.e. the first strong beat) of the tala. And in the rondo-like returns to the pallavi this can inspire in the audience a sense of resolution or relief at the end of a section in which the melody has been improvised and extended over many tala cycles, before coming back to the familiar grounding of the first phrase. In concert performances the main percussionist is not a mere accompanist but a true partner to the singer or instrumentalist, and the essential metrical character of a tala has sometimes to be taken for granted under a sophisticated overlay of rhythmic improvisation; this can produce an exhilarating tension, in which the listener marvels at the rhythmic complexity and technical detail, while at the same time keeping a mental grip on the basic tala structure underlying the virtuosity.

■ Voices and instruments

Our young singer will have learned to build a vocal range up to around two octaves, practising gradually more complex note patterns after mastering a system of exercises which combine svara and tala – a system traditionally attributed to Purandaradasa himself. In Indian classical music, and indeed from ancient times, the voice has traditionally been viewed as the primary instrument; all melodic instruments are expected to emulate the voice in some way, and many teachers insist that in instrumental playing there must be constant mental reference to the verbal text. In Karnatak music the instrument enjoying the highest prestige is the Southern vina (or *sarasvatī-vīnā*), a fretted plucked lute with four main playing strings and three extra strings strummed to punctuate rhythm, a wooden resonating chamber and a supplementary gourd resonator; its present form derives from seventeenth-century Tanjore. Despite the predetermined position of the frets, notes can be 'stretched' in ornamentation and glissando by pulling the plucked (and still resonating) string to the side of the finger board with the fingers of the left hand. Another kind of lute that has been popularised as a solo instrument in recent decades is the *gottuvādyam*, unfretted and of the same basic shape as the sarasvati-vina, but stopped not by the fingers but by a rod of smooth wood or some other material held in the left hand.

The violin is both a solo instrument and the commonest accompaniment to the voice. It acoustically strengthens the vocal line by echoing the melody, but also sometimes by unison playing with the voice in pre-composed sections such as the main statement of the kriti. This instrument was introduced into Karnatak music in the early years of the nineteenth century by Muttusvami Dikshitar's younger brother Balusvami, and adapted through retuning (the strings are set to the tonic and fifth) and through the changed playing position which, as we

The singer Aruna Sairam in concert, accompanied by *(from left to right)* J. Vaidyanathan (mridangam), Karthick (ghatam), Girija (tanpura) and Vittal Ramamurthy (violin)

saw at the young singer's arangetram, allows freer sliding and oscillation on the finger board. But Balusvami and other early players were not merely transferring Karnatak melody to a new instrument; they were also influenced by European musical idioms and playing techniques associated with the violin in dance and band music. The violin is also historically associated with Svati Tirunal's Travancore court, where one of a prominent group of musicians known as the Tanjore Quartet, employed at Travancore in the 1830s, was a famous violinist named Vadivelu Pillai.

Among wind instruments, the most important since the 1950s has been the transverse wooden flute, an instrument with a long history in Indian devotional and theatrical music. The eight (previously seven) holes can be wholly or partially stopped so as to produce the same subtleties of intonation and embellishment as can be achieved by 'stretching' notes on the vina. Another wind instrument strongly associated with South Indian music is the double-reed *nāgasvaram*, which is a type of shawm resembling the Hindustani *shahnāī* but larger, deeper-pitched and stronger-toned. It is primarily an outdoor instrument, particularly used in temple and processional religious music. Associated with it is a special, and probably ancient, tradition of ensemble practice and repertoire.

This is the *periya mēlam*, 'great ensemble', in which groups of nagasvarams are accompanied by the *tavil*, a double-headed drum (rather than the more discreet mrdangam of the kacheri ensemble).

Rhythmic and metrical accompaniment in the kacheri is often supported by a small hand-held *kanjira* frame-drum, or by the *ghatam*, a large open-topped earthenware pot played with the fingers and capable of an astonishing range of sounds with crisply piercing articulation, thus supplementing the role of the *mrdangam*; there may also be a small pair of metal cymbals (*tālam*) and sometimes a mouth-harp (*morsing*) stressing the beats which mark the major divisions of the tala.

Further reading

An accessible introduction to the culture and repertoire of Karnatak music, setting the *kacheri* concert tradition in a more general musical and social context, is Tanjore Viswanathan and Matthew Harp Allen's *Music in South India*. For technical detail of both musical practice and musicological theory and history there are good chapters by Catlin, Nelson and Kassebaum in *The Garland Encyclopedia of World Music* vol. 5, *South Asia: The Indian Subcontinent*. South Asian Music is the subject of a major multiple-author article in the *New Grove Dictionary of Music and Musicians*, covering history, theory and practice with many illustrations and analysed musical examples and extensive bibliographies of works published before 2000. A wealth of technical, sociological and pleasantly anecdotal information about Karnatak music, containing accounts of some subjects not very fully accounted for elsewhere, may be found in Ludwig Pesch's *The Oxford Illustrated Companion to South Indian Classical Music*. There is of course a rapidly growing field of internet sites featuring South Indian music in performance and in history and theory. The musicological and historical detail must be read with caution, as much is unedited and unauthenticated, but much will be found to illustrate performance conditions, including some of the foremost artists of recent years. A helpful guide to internet sites available at the time of publication is given by Viswanathan and Allen (*Music in South India*) as an appendix to their useful bibliography and list of other sources.

Recommended listening

In addition to the sound and video recordings and websites recommended by Viswanathan and Allen (*Music in South India*), a useful range of performances will be found in *An Anthology of South Indian Classical Music* (4 CDs), Ocora B000027HXV, 1991. This set, compiled by L. Subramaniam, offers an excellent range of vocal and instrumental forms by highly reputable artists. CDs and DVDs of the Chennai (Madras) 'December Music Seasons' are released each year by Charsur Digital Workstation, Chennai. On the internet listeners may search under 'Carnatic', as well as the names of Tyagaraja (also spelt Thyagaraja) and other famous South Indian composers, and under the names of instruments and the popular concert forms such as kriti. Many excellent performances may be heard and watched by searching under 'Madras Music Academy' and 'Chennai Music Academy'.

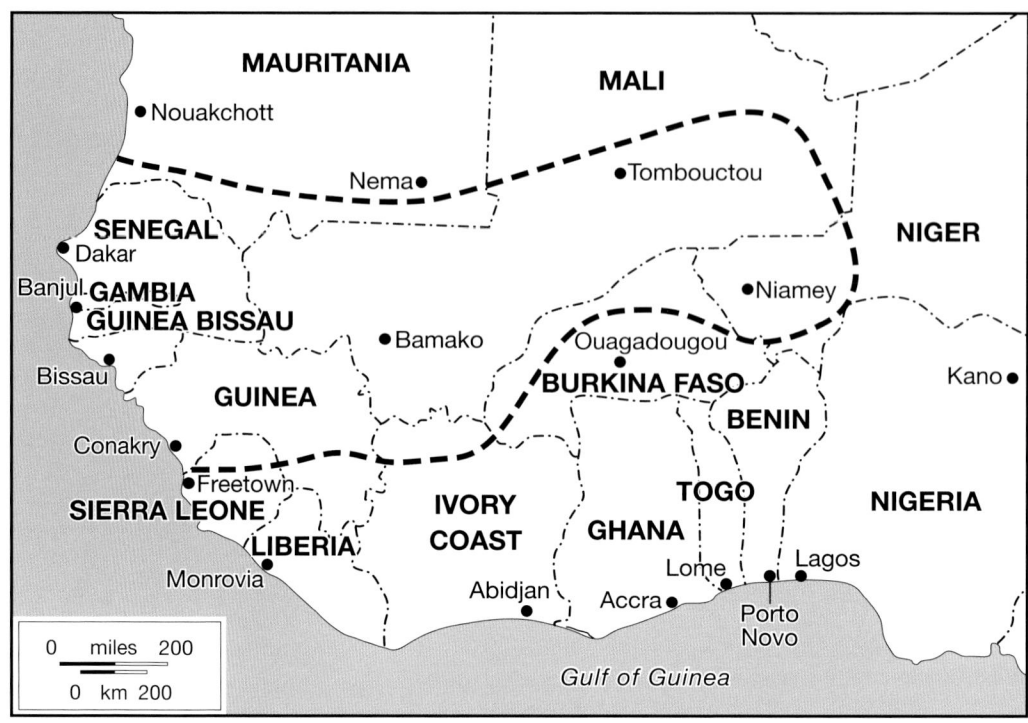

Mande culture is spread across a wide swathe of West Africa today, dominant in some areas, secondary in others. The capital cities are the cultural centres: Bamako in southern Mali, and along the coast Dakar, Banjul, Bissau, and Conakry, capitals of Senegal, Gambia, Guinea-Bissau, and Guinea.

8 Mande Jaliyaa
Roderic Knight

Ranged over the State House lawn are perhaps fifty musicians. Some are acrobats doing hand-stands, others are women's groups singing to the melodic thump of gourds. Two flautists, one playing left-handed, accompany a singer, his head tilted high. This is a naming ceremony, held for the president's new-born. The largest contingent is a mixed vocal and instrumental ensemble; one man plays a guitar while others pluck lutes. At the centre sit several women forming a chorus. Some gently strike a tubular bell, while in front of them are three xylophonists and a dozen men positioned behind tall harps: this combination of instruments marks out Mande professionals. There is no conductor, and there was no rehearsal, but the lead singers are clearly in command. One man, starting high in his range, sings a cascading and undulating solo line which the women's chorus finishes in unison. Now a celebrated female singer takes over, her strong voice needing no microphone. With their majestic sound and heroic content, the melodic lines float in free rhythm over an instrumental ground: this is performed in unison and yet not in unison, as each player mingles his variant, with some adding a virtuoso flourish. At the close, with one of the musicians announcing on his behalf, the president appears and presents money for distribution to all.

F ew people, if asked to identify the classical musics of the world, would readily point to Africa. However, the scene described above – if imagined in the setting of Africa's pre-colonial kingdoms and empires – does take on the courtly sheen of a classical tradition, and gives a hint of its existence. The reason most African classical-music traditions have escaped our attention is that they lack many of the usual markers. For example, African musicians have no use for notation – but then neither do classical musicians in many other cultures, except as a pedagogical aid. And should not a classical tradition be supported by a body of theoretical writing? In Africa, not only is the music transmitted aurally, the languages are too, so there is no written theory. Western listeners to African music typically notice constructs of melody, rhythm and metre that seem familiar, yet the musicians say nothing of these. In fact, an oft-repeated observation is that African musicians don't even count (as in identifying a downbeat), let alone think in terms of metre. But spend some time performing with African musicians, and a theoretical system becomes evident. It is based in practical matters of performance and embedded in aesthetic observations, and it underpins what the musicians do just as well as a written system. It is similar to the practical knowledge that Indian performers regard as more important to their art than the revered theoretical heritage that has grown up around what they do.

Other features we associate with 'classical' music are rehearsal and practice. In India these are givens, but in Africa, they are uncommon. An African instrumentalist might take time alone now and then to do some 'woodshedding', but it is not the goal-oriented event associated with many classical traditions. Instead, practice in Africa is more like on-the-job training, where one hones skills by performing with others. Then there is the question of dance. Drum ensembles play for dancers, and in Africa, dancing, even if only a few steps, is a typical way to show one's appreciation of almost any performance. Can dance music be classical? If so, must it be dignified, like the ballroom dances of eighteenth-century Europe, or choreographed as in ballet? Perhaps victory dancing qualifies. An African tradition that springs to mind in this context is the huge Chopi xylophone orchestra of Mozambique. The ensemble consists of xylophones, called *timbila*, built in graded sizes. They join with rattle players and singers to produce an elaborately stratified sound, with fast-moving high parts, medium-speed middle parts and plodding bass-register parts played on xylophones with huge oil-drum resonators. The singers celebrate heroic deeds with impassioned choral refrains, and strapping young men in warrior regalia strut in choreographed dances out front.[1]

Another African tradition that one might imagine with a 'classical' mantle is the music of the former kingdom of Buganda, outlawed in the formation of the independent nation of Uganda in 1966. The king, or *kabaka*, hosted musicians from different regions, with each musician having a residency at the court. The Kiganda sound was an intense, rapid, patter style of singing, with even more rapid instrumental decoration. It was typified by a singer accompanying himself on a small arched harp called *innanga*, or by an ensemble of tuned drums called *entenga*, in which the harp parts are divided among four players. Other strings, flutes, horns and xylophones were also part of the succession of royal sounds;[2] some of these traditions are being revived today.

Searching for other candidates, what about the jubilant a cappella singing of the Ba-aka people of Central African Republic, or the Shona music of Zimbabwe? The list of African musics that might vie for the label 'classical' could grow long. We need an additional criterion: for whom is the music performed? Hindustani and European classical musics, for example, have traditionally been defined by the social class of their audience. Applying this criterion to Africa, the Chopi warrior dance of Mozambique and the pointedly royal nature of the music of Buganda would both qualify. Both Ba-aka singing and the plucked-metal sound of the *mbira* with massed chorus might qualify in one sense: Tony Perman, Shona music scholar, notes that they are much like the sacred choral music we call 'classical'.[3] But the widely participatory nature of these genres, in which there is essentially no audience, sets them apart from the criterion here: performers in front of a select and passive audience.

The hierarchical societies of Africa are perhaps less prominent in the popular imagination than the egalitarian ones, but they formed the great kingdoms and empires of the past. Buganda was one, Ashanti another; Old Mali (after which the present country is named) is perhaps the best known today. Identify the top ranks of these societies – the warriors and royalty of the past, or the political, business and religious leaders of the present – and you will find a music performed specifically for them. This chapter will turn the spotlight on the last of these – today's descendants of the thirteenth-century empire of Mali, spread across West Africa and known collectively as the Mande.

■ Mande music and its history

Today's Mande people, known better by their local names – the Mandinka of Gambia, Senegal and Guinea-Bissau, the Malinke or Maninka of Guinea, the Bambara of Mali and the Dyula of Burkina Faso, to name just a few – trace their ancestry to Old Mali. (Gambian Mandinka spellings are used in this chapter.) The empire was founded by Sundiata (Sunjata, Son-jara), who surmounted a crippled childhood to unify warring communities in present-day southern Mali.[4] After only a century the empire was overrun by Songhay, and the Mande diaspora began.

Mali was not a literate state, so we are reliant upon outside observers for our knowledge. Of particular interest for music history is the account of Ibn Battúta, an Arab geographer who ranged across the Muslim world in the fourteenth century, ultimately visiting Mali in 1353. There he witnessed both Muslim feast days, the 'id al-fitr and 'id al-adha, and described the pageantry surrounding the presence of the *mansa*, whom he referred to as the sultan:

> The sultan is preceded by his musicians, who carry gold and silver guimbris [lutes] ... On reaching the pempi he stops and looks round the assembly, then ascends it in the sedate manner of a preacher ascending a mosque pulpit. As he takes his seat the drums, trumpets and bugles are sounded.[5]

At these events, Battúta took particular notice of a person called Dugha, who was clearly the master of ceremonies and served as go-between when someone wished to speak. He also played an instrument which Battúta described in a now-famous passage: 'A chair is placed for Dugha to sit on. He plays on an instrument made of reeds, with some small calabashes at its lower end, and chants a poem in praise of the sultan, recalling his battles and deeds of valour.'[6] This was the first description of the xylophone in Africa. To read Battúta is to verify that today, when a *balafola* (xylophone player) relates the oral tradition of Sundiata and his great xylophone-playing adversary Susu Sumanguru, the player is not inserting his instrument into the story – it was there.

We may begin to form a picture of the royal music of Mali by focusing on the man named Dugha. It seems certain he was a *jali* [*jeli, dieli*], or music professional, although Battúta did not use the term for him. (He did actually use the term, but in reference to poets in bird costumes.) He functioned as solo performer, announcer and go-between, aspects that remain part of the profession today. The art of *jaliyaa* (literally 'what the jali does') is a very individualised practice. Even though all the countries where the Mande live have national troupes, before their development an ensemble such as that described in the opening scene was (and still is) a pick-up affair: musicians flocked to an event where music was called for, a de facto ensemble formed, then disbanded again.

The first known photograph of a Mande jali ensemble, in Gambia. There are seven kora players, five bolon players and several singers. It was published in *The Prince of Wales' African Book* by Arthur St John Adcock (London: Hodder & Stoughton, c. 1925).

It was the individuals who carried their traditions forward from the time of Sundiata to the present. When Mali collapsed, the lesser kingdoms remained; the trade networks were intact, and Mande culture continued to spread along them. Wherever a Mande leader went, whether warrior, politician or wealthy merchant, his 'own' jali, or a group of *jalolu*, would follow. Mande music scholar Lucy Duran has observed that in the nineteenth century jalolu actually travelled quite a lot, building up a network of patrons, but they aspired to anchor themselves to one of them.[7]

In much of the literature on West African culture, the term *griot* is used to refer to the jali. This term emerged in seventeenth-century French writings and has become the generic term for the hereditary professional musician common to several West African societies. Eric Charry, author of the most comprehensive book on the music of the Mande, did extensive research on the etymology of the term; he notes that it is neither French nor African, but could have been drawn from any of the regional terms for such people: *gaulo, gewel, iggio, jeli, jaare*. He also posits that these terms themselves may derive from the Arabic word *qawal* (word, speak, sound).[8]

From kingdoms to colonies

The hierarchy of Mande society is legendary, with surnames identifying people as belonging to one social group or another. The most basic distinction is between *foro* (in Bambara, *horo*), meaning freeborn, versus *jongo*, or slave. Slaves were either war captives or domestic, the latter typically a result of destitution severe enough to make a person or family put themselves at the mercy of someone else. Today slavery is gone, with the only vestige being the occasional whispered reference to someone's ancestry.

Among the freeborn are certain families who have become leaders, typically through military and political prowess. Sundiata's surname was Keita. Today, having the surname Keita is a marker of the ruling class, even if only symbolically. Other names grant a similar distinction because of family history – Toure (Turay), Traore (Tarawally), Kurubally, Darbo, Jammeh, Janneh, Sonko, Sanyang. Another subset of surnames identifies a group of freeborn as the *nyamakala*. On the surface, the *nyamakalolu* are people who manipulate the natural world – the tradespeople, such as blacksmiths, leatherworkers, woodcarvers – but among them are also the musicians, whose craft is the spoken word. On a deeper level, nyamakalolu are regarded as privileged by their knowledge and specialised skills: they are felt to be in close contact with the spirit world and with life forces, and as a result are held in awe. To guard their trade secrets, nyamakalolu typically practiced endogamy, or marriage within their own group, with each of these endogamous groups adding their level to the hierarchy. Thus, a blacksmith, although freeborn, would not be called *foro*, but *numo*, and even though he made the spears essential for battle or the hoes needed by farmers, his status was a rung below. The jalolu, with the strongest power (the spoken word), were near the bottom of this hierarchy (but above slaves). But subordinate status was no bar to achievement: because of the essential nature of their work, the nyamakalolu could expect to be paid and supported by the patron families of Mande. The musicians had an added benefit: since they always appeared in public with their patrons acting as their publicists, it was only fitting that they be dressed in finery of equal elegance.

Sundiata had his own jali, Bala Faseke Kouyate, who played the *bala*, or xylophone. Bala Faseke was valuable enough for Susu Sumanguru, Sundiata's main adversary, to capture him: he wanted this Kouyate to be *his* bala player, to sing his praises. Primarily because of this affiliation with the two greats of Mande history, people with the surname Kouyate (Kuyateh, Koite) are regarded today as being of the original jali line. Together with Kouyate, two other names – Suso (Sissoko, Cissoko) and Jebateh (Jobarteh, Diabate) – account for perhaps ninety per cent of today's jali families, each with a narrative of how their ancestors took up the profession.

As the nineteenth century progressed and contact with the West became a significant factor in people's lives, the traditional role of leading families as patrons began to break down. The changes of the colonial era eventually resulted in the picture we see today: some musicians might enjoy a permanent association with the president or a government minister, but most would be more aptly described as freelancers, working independently, alert to events that call for music and making a point to be there for them.

European visitors to Mande in the eighteenth and nineteenth centuries might have seen a leader with his *jali ke* (male jali) at his side; but they might also have seen a jali buttonholing a man with a noble surname, singing an impromptu praise and expecting a tribute. Somewhere during this time the English word 'beg' came to be used to describe what the jali was doing, and the term has stuck, with even the jalolu themselves using it when speaking English. This gives an erroneous impression. If a jali shouts praise spontaneously to a recognised nobleman in the street, he or she is not begging; it is because he knows this person to be someone of note in Mande culture, and it is the duty of a jali to publicise this. By the same token the person so recognised should acknowledge the gesture with a gift, typically money. It is easy to see how a cash-poor nobleman could be put on the spot by this cultural requirement, but the dark side of the situation has been grossly exaggerated. In general, jalolu and their patrons enjoy a wonderful camaraderie.[9]

The jali must know not only what music to perform at which events, but also family histories, the genealogy of potential leaders and a large repertoire of proverbs and sayings. The enduring importance of this role is reflected in the diasporic Mande communities of any big city today. It has never been common to see blacksmiths, leatherworkers or woodcarvers plying their trades in these communities, but the jalolu are there in force, because all dignitaries need the services of the jali.[10]

The term 'folk' is not typically applied to African music, but by identifying a classical tradition one implies that a non-classical one exists alongside it. In Mande, this means dance drumming and singing. Drum troupes, usually all male, play for a large variety of village events, where the primary participants are women. They themselves are the subject of their songs.[11]

■ The instruments of jaliyaa

The *bala* (*balo, balafon*) described by Battúta in 1353 is a frame xylophone, and the name balafon is now applied to virtually any West African xylophone. (The etymology is *bala fo*, which means 'play the bala', or more literally 'bala speak', in Mande languages). It has sixteen to twenty keys of African rosewood, tuned seven notes to the octave. Underneath each key is a resonating gourd, in the side wall of which a hole is cut and covered with a thin membrane. Formerly this was made from the egg-case cover of a certain spider, but today it is usually replaced by cigarette paper. The purpose of this membrane is to add a buzz to the sound, as in a kazoo. On the bala this adds high frequencies to the plain wooden tone of the keys and imparts a more metallic quality. The keys are struck with mallets wound with natural rubber. The normal playing position is sitting cross-legged in front of the instrument, but the instrument is tightly built, allowing the player to sling it on his shoulder and play standing as well. The bala is the signature instrument of the Susu people of northern Guinea (remember Susu Sumanguru and his bala-playing jali), but it has become a generic Mande instrument.

MANDE JALIYAA

Above: A balo ensemble led by Modulai Syllah at a wedding in Conakry, Guinea. The drummers play the kunang kettle-drum with one hand and the nenge iron bell with the other.

Right: Mawdo Suso of Sabiji, Gambia, making a balo

Above: A jali ensemble at a political rally in Brikama, Gambia, with koras and *(right)* the bolon

Left: Jabele Kanuteh, of Tambasansang, Gambia, playing the ngoni or kontingo

Below: Detail of the kora, showing the nyenyemo attached to the bridge

The *ngoni* (*konni, konting,* in Wolof, *xalam*) is a plucked lute, also noted by Battúta in his narrative (as the *guimbri*). The body is canoe-shaped, covered in cowhide. The neck, a slender dowel, runs part-way beneath the face. Where it ends, a hole is cut in the hide and a fan-shaped chip of calabash (gourd) is attached to protrude and form the bridge (see the illustration opposite, bottom left). This construction, sometimes called a half-spike lute because the neck does not span the entire length of the body, is not unique to West Africa, but rather derives from ancient Egypt. Its trip across North Africa is undocumented, but the renowned Arabic music scholar Henry George Farmer surmises that it came via pre-Islamic Arab migrations.[12] The ngoni typically has five strings, two of which are full length, the others shorter. Monofilament nylon is standard today, replacing the twisted hide once used. The long strings are stopped with the left hand, while the shorter strings provide a strummed three-tone cluster. The ngoni exists in numerous sizes and variants, and in Mali dominates the sound of jaliyaa.

The *kora* was the last jali instrument to come to the attention of the West: Mungo Park, a Scottish physician and explorer intent on mapping the course of the Niger River, described it at the end of the eighteenth century.[13] The kora is a harp, of a type unique to the Mande. Harps, in distinction to lutes, lyres and zithers, whose strings lie parallel to the face or sound table of the instrument, have their strings aligned in a perpendicular plane. There are several Mande harps, all called spike harps, meaning that a single piece of wood 'spikes' the body, which typically consists of a large half calabash covered in cowhide, to form both neck and tailpiece. The kora is distinguished from its cousins (or rather, ancestors) by its straight neck, resembling a lute. To make a harp of this lute-like body, a tall bridge is mounted on the face, giving the instrument its own sub-category: bridge harp. The twenty-one strings are attached to braided rawhide collars on the neck and pass over the tall bridge in notches down the sides, forming two rows both perpendicular to the face. The performer sits (ideally on the floor for added resonance) with the instrument upright in front of him. The strings are plucked with only the thumbs and forefingers. The fingers are near the high strings and play the melody, while the thumbs play a bass line. The arrangement lends itself to virtuoso speed and a chordal sound, since the strings on each side of the bridge ascend in thirds. Today's recordings of the kora are missing a sound that was important in the past: a sizzle produced by a metal leaf with wire loops in holes around the edge called the *nyenyemo*. Since it was fitted atop the bridge and thus too close to a studio microphone, recording engineers eliminated it early on. Today it has disappeared, but it once was the kora's amplifier, carrying farther in the open air than the sound of the strings alone.

To this list must be added one more instrument, even though it is not played by the jali. This is the *bolon*, a large spike harp made from a more-than-half gourd covered in goatskin with the hair left on. It has four thick rawhide strings tied directly to the neck and knotted in holes in a bridge-like string holder braced upright on the face. The player cradles the bolon between his knees and catches the strings with his thumbs as he hammers the calabash with his fists. Bolon players have a different repertoire and patrons from those of the jalolu: it is said that the bolon was carried into battle with the warriors, while the other instruments were primarily played in courtly settings. Today most jali ensembles include a bolon player, to add a lively bass line.

Until recently, tradition dictated that a *jali muso* (woman jali) did not play a melodic instrument, but today the picture is changing, spearheaded by a few Western women who travelled to Gambia to continue their kora studies after taking the ground-breaking classes given by Jali Nyama Suso at the University of Washington in 1971. But the jali muso has her own instrument too, the *karinya* or *neo* (the latter meaning simply 'iron'). Made by a blacksmith, this is a tube with a serrated slot. In Mande hunters' villages, musicians scrape the serrations to accompany their *donso konni* (hunter's harp). But in the hands of the jali muso it becomes a bell. Every singer has one and can pull it out at a moment's notice to attach across her palm and clang with a slender iron rod, in a graceful wrist-twisting action; the sound is loud and festive.

■ Tonal material of Mande music

Mande jaliyaa is easy to identify: plucked strings or a xylophone play a 'groove', and a solo voice, in tenor or alto range, soars over it. The sounds of the bala, ngoni and kora have captured the world's attention, but the voice is still primary. Western-trained singers describe the sound as a tight-throated chest voice; more exactly it is a sound produced with the larynx high. It is too rich in high partials for the conventional Western ear, but it is a sound shared by many cultures where the ideal is a loud, well-projected voice, good for outdoors, for being heard over crowds and for expressing heroism.

Vocal lines in Mande jaliyaa, especially those that are sung extempore by a soloist, typically start high and cascade down. This feature grows from the language itself. Mande languages are tonal, with some words spoken at a high pitch, others low. This is not merely inflection for emphasis as in English, but phonemic tone, in which not only pronunciation but also tone determines the meaning. The tones are not fixed however, but relative. Linguists describe a typical utterance as 'downstepped': a low tone in a sentence draws down the next high-tone word, resulting in a stair-stepped profile. And this profile is critical, since it contains meaning. Thus, when a singer extemporises, typically with proverbs, standardised praise lyrics or actual sentences sung about someone present in the audience, the first note is typically high, then cascades down, much as it would if merely spoken. A second phrase might start halfway up again, and cascade again; sometimes the singing trails off into speech on the last word or two. The instrumental part forms a backdrop for the voice, with a short ostinato that marks off time in a metred way as the voice moves more in speech rhythm. A solo singer achieves renown if he or she infuses the vocal line with varieties of vibrato and ornamental turns and slides. Women are regarded as the best singers, and are emulated by men.

The fluid and malleable vocal line of jaliyaa is supported by instruments with fixed pitches. Early researchers in Africa noted that in some areas pentatonic melodies were the norm, while in others instruments were tuned to seven-tone, or heptatonic, scales. The Mande area actually includes both: the Bambara

Sona Kuyateh, a jali muso from Serekunda, Gambia, playing the neo, a tubular iron bell

xylophone is pentatonic, but the more widespread Susu bala is heptatonic. Many scholars, beginning with the pioneer Gilbert Rouget, have studied the tuning of the seven-tone instrument, which has been dubbed equi-heptatonic. Laboratory results now confirm what balafon players know: a builder tunes the keys with the intention of making each ascending step the same size. When playing, this translates into the ability to start a tune on any note and it will sound the same.[14]

String tunings are best studied with the open strings of the kora. But the picture now becomes more complicated: the kora is also tuned heptatonically, but not to the balafon scale. Some players recognise four tunings, others only three, and all bear a resemblance to Western scales in that they consist of intervals of different sizes. The most common is called *Tomorabaa* (Big Tomora) or *Silabaa* (Main Road). This 'main road' tuning resembles the Western major scale, but with the third and seventh slightly flat (to our ears), the second and seventh slightly sharp. From this tuning one moves to *Tomora mesengo* (Little Tomora) by fully flattening the third and seventh. The result is a sound resembling the Dorian mode, or a D scale on the white keys only. The third tuning, *Hardino*, also resembles the Western major scale, but with the third and seventh ever so slightly sharp. For some kora players, this replaces Tomorabaa as their principal tuning. From Hardino one tunes to the last, *Sauta*, by raising the fourth degree a semitone. The result is the sound of the Lydian mode, or F on the white keys only. Many songs in the repertoire are in Sauta; singers love to dwell on its raised fourth.[15]

The question of microtones now arises. The tunings are microtonally different from each other and kora players are careful to tune to the 'right' one for a given song, but at the same time there are often several ways to play a piece, with different tunings. Thus, even though microtones are part of the picture, they are not quantified or assigned aesthetic value as they are in the Middle East; their application is more casual. Further evidence of this may be seen when the kora and balo play together. Here microtonal clashes are inevitable, since one tuning is equi-heptatonic, while the other is diatonic. To play with a balo, the kora player does not try to tune to the balo's tuning. Rather, he adjusts his overall pitch level, if necessary, to match the balo key that is closest (since the balo can play a tune starting on any pitch), and the performance can proceed. If the piece calls for Sauta tuning on the kora, for example, the tritone fourth will clash with the balo's equi-heptatonic one, which is close to the Western perfect fourth, but the difference will be ignored. The lesson is that tuning matters greatly, but it is flexibly applied. Kora tunings also have modal applications. Without retuning, a kora player can play a given song on a different tonic, so to speak, much as we might play one tune in C on the piano, and another on A, still on the white keys only. The ngoni has a similar set of tunings and modes. Their use might be compared to banjo tunings, one more suited to a given piece than another. A feature unique to the ngoni is that when two players play together, they tune to two different tunings to differentiate their high and low parts.[16]

Because of the individualised nature of jaliyaa, there is no standard pitch, but there is an approximate de facto standard, since xylophones are built to play with each other and the stringed instruments must tune to them (or to each other) when playing together.

■ Structure of jaliyaa

The dominant style in jaliyaa is a solo voice cascading in speech-rhythm, as described above. This is termed *sataro*, or reciting. It is much like *recitativo* in opera, except that it is never used for dialogue. But to begin a song, one typically employs another style, called *donkilo*, which literally means 'call the dance'. A donkilo melody is metred and usually spans one or two repetitions of the ostinato. If there is a chorus, they sing the donkilo. Some songs could be deemed strophic, in the sense that many lines of text may be sung to this melody. In overview, a performance might start with donkilo, proceed to solo sataro passages, return at any point to the donkilo, then continue again with sataro. Although not required, the donkilo is often regarded as a fitting way to end a song.

The instrumental part contains additional structural details. The ostinato, which kora players call the *kumbengo* (a term that also means 'tuning'), underpins all of the singing. Some pieces have a segmented kumbengo with several sections that can be introduced at different times. Even beginning players unconsciously include variations as they play the kumbengo (thus making it quite different from the unchanging ostinato of the West), but the mark of a master is how he incorporates another style, called *birimintingo*. This term means 'rolling' or 'busy', and refers to rapid flights of melody in the high register of an instrument, often sequential in nature. Some birimintingo passages fit inside the kumbengo, but especially if playing solo, a player is free to break from the kumbengo at any time to play an extended birimintingo, which might not even keep to the metre. When Gilbert Rouget heard this style in his 1950 recordings from Guinea, long before mass media reached Africa, he was convinced he was witnessing one of the roots of jazz.[17]

In a solo performance (singer and instrumentalist one and the same), or in a typical unrehearsed ensemble, it is impossible to say in advance what the structure of a given song will be. One of the skills of jaliyaa is the ability to string together the basic elements to form an aesthetic whole. Each piece will consist of kumbengo and birimintingo, donkilo and sataro, balanced into a structure created on the spot as the performance proceeds.

Singing is the root of jaliyaa, but increasingly today one hears more and more instrumental solos. This trend is largely a product of the media – radio, television and the recording industry – all of which bring jaliyaa to new settings where words take second place. But it also grows from the interests of improvisers across the globe eager to play together. Probably the best known purveyor of this new style is Malian kora player Toumani Diabate. He never sings, but has made it his mission to pair up with musicians of any other improvising tradition to produce kumbengo/birimintingo-like musics of great variety.

■ Aesthetics of Mande music

We have identified kora tunings, noted their approximate Western equivalents and talked about the 'tonic', a concept not expressed by Mande performers. But what do the performers say about their music? Among kora players, tuning, with its inherent individualism, is much discussed. Some are fussy about perfect octaves and fifths; others carefully prepare a tuning with a certain amount of acoustic beating built in, with the octaves not perfect, and other intervals more individualised. Kora and bala players might comment on how this or that jali integrates a birimintingo passage, or how an elder player might not 'finish' a birimintingo as well as a younger player. But the most important judgments focus on singing. Vocal quality is not the overriding criterion: a beautiful voice is appreciated, but it is regarded as God-given. What matters more is the power, courage and confidence that a singer projects. The late Nyulo Jebateh, a celebrated Gambian jali muso thus described what it takes to be a *ngara*, or accomplished singer:

> A *ngara* is a woman who is not afraid of crowds, not afraid of anything, except God. She can stand before a crowd with all eyes upon her and not become confused [*kijo fara*]. She can shout [*feteng*], literally 'split the air' with her voice, but do it with feeling [*wasu*] and sentiment [*balafa*], so that people will sympathise

with her. She sticks to her forte [*taburango*] in performing, never jumbling the words together [*faranfansandi*] so that they are unintelligible, but choosing words that contain the essence of her message [*sigirango*], words that all listeners will agree are true [*sahata*].[18]

■ Metre and rhythm in jaliyaa

If jaliyaa is rooted in singing, its foundation is still the kumbengo. The word translates as 'a meeting of heads' (*kung* = head, *bengo* = meeting). The kumbengo is metred and usually consists of a pair of short phrases, the second only slightly different from the first. 'Sherif Sidi' and 'Tabara' have a kumbengo of six counts or beats (3 + 3); the majority have eight (4 + 4); 'Kura' is unusual, with ten (5 + 5). The 'grand-daddy' is 'Janjon', with a kumbengo spanning 32 (8 + 8 + 8 + 8). The length of a kumbengo is not important to a performer, but is readily discerned. There are a few songs in the kora repertoire that have no kumbengo, so to speak, since the player merely doubles the donkilo line, but such melodies are treated to the usual variations and birimintingo when played. Rhythms in jaliyaa tend to be duple-pulsed (that is, fast notes moving in twos and fours), but the triple-pulsed feel of the Western 6/8 or 12/8 metre is also common. Hemiola – the simultaneous use of duple and triple rhythms – is exploited wherever possible. 'Sherif Sidi' provides a clear example. In the kumbengo variation shown in Example 8.1, the player adds a left-finger chord after each bass note for a steady count of six, while playing four evenly-spaced notes with the right finger.

Just as Mande musicians do not talk about beats or pulses, neither do they bother with the concept of the downbeat. Although a Western listener looking for the first beat can usually find it by noting how dancers step to a beat, or where a donkilo line begins, it can in fact be ambiguous. One reason is another temporal feature of Mande instrumental music: offset parts. This is absolutely basic to balafon playing: give a straight four-note melody to a bala player and he will convert it into two parts, playing the four given notes in the low register with his left hand, while playing the same four notes ahead of time with the right hand, creating a 'pick-up' effect. Offset parts are found in kora music as well. In the kumbengo for 'Allah l'a ke' (Example 8.2), note how the high-register finger melody consistently anticipates the low register thumb part.

EX. 8.1 'Sherif Sidi' kumbengo with hemiola variant

MANDE JALIYAA

EX. 8.2 'Allah l'a ke' kumbengo showing consistent offset parts

■ Learning jaliyaa

How are the skills of jaliyaa acquired? It differs for boys and girls. A boy will most likely inherit his family's instrument, whether kora, balo or ngoni. In earlier days he would have been apprenticed to his father or an uncle, a bit like the *guru-shishya* relationship in India, but less formal. Today an apprenticeship is likely to be even less formal, with peers teaching each other. Either way, the approach is to impart basic knowledge, without detailed instruction in birimintingo or etudes that might lead to smoother or faster playing – these are acquired by imitation alongside accomplished performers. The final steps involve learning to build and tune one's own instrument. In the case of the kora, one might imagine that during an apprenticeship the student would have internalised the details of tuning: quite so, but the *pro forma* tuning lesson is a formal key to independence. Although schooling and the economic necessities of today have transformed the landscape, a traditional apprenticeship remains the ideal.

For the girl *jali ndingo* ('small jali'), becoming a jali muso is more just a part of living. She hears her mother and aunts performing as soloists or as chorus members, and as a teenager she will join this chorus herself. She will not have any voice lessons per se, nor will she be required to memorise a repertoire: she will acquire it through imitation and participation. With the right aptitude and encouragement from her elders and peers, she may move from the chorus to standing in front as a soloist. In traditional times, a career as a soloist would have been secured by becoming the wife of a promising instrumentalist, thus forming an ideal duo for jaliyaa. But the careers of famous Mande 'divas' such as Kandia Kouyate, Oumou Sangare, Ami Koita and Rokia Traore reflect the importance today of being noticed by arts organisations, radio and television stations, national troupe leaders and the recording industry. The most recent development in the role of the jali muso involves playing a melodic instrument such as the kora. The prime example is Sonah Jobarteh, Anglo-African granddaughter of the celebrated Gambian player Amadu Bansang Jobarteh: she sings but also plays the kora with the verve of her late grandfather.

Poised by their profession to be in the spotlight in traditional settings, jalolu adapt easily to the international spotlight, but they do not reject their roots. The late guitarist Ali Farka Toure, world famous for his unassuming style that resonated strongly with a blues-loving audience, was always – despite his fame – most happy when he got back to his farm in Mali.

THE OTHER CLASSICAL MUSICS

■ *Jaliyaa today*

If you lived in an African colony, whether English or French, you could learn music, whoever you were, and you might have played foxtrots, waltzes and marches in the small orchestras that formed in the capital cities. Or, presaging independence, you might have formed an ensemble of your own to promote traditional music, as did the Guinean Fodeba Keita, who, while living in Paris in the 1950s, organised Les Ballets Africains. The primary thrust, clearly implied in the name, was drumming and dancing, but their first recording also featured guitarist Facelli Kante; in their 1959 New York debut, a kora player was also in the line-up.[19] By this time Guinea had become the first West African nation to achieve independence from France (1958), and Keita's ensemble had become the national ensemble. Today every nation where the Mande live has such an ensemble. But note the names of these musicians: Keita, Kante. To any Mande person, these names immediately conjure Sunjata Keita, the noble first emperor of Mali, and his rival, the greatly feared blacksmith Sumanguru Kante. Nyama Suso, the pioneering kora teacher mentioned earlier, had an expression for this: *kiriba-karaba* – mixed up. The ensembles were mixed, and you did not have to be a jali to do jaliyaa. Salif Keita, today one of Africa's pre-eminent singers, is the first to acknowledge that he is actually an imposter, coming from a noble family but doing jaliyaa. Ali Farka Toure was another, but the term 'imposter' can no longer apply, because this is today's reality: jaliyaa is becoming more democratic, but it remains the core value for Mande music. Whether ensembles are large or small, jaliyaa and the related griot traditions of the Wolof and FulBe

Bassekou Kouyate, his first son Madu Kouyate with ngoniba, his wife and lead singer Amy Sacko, and his second son Moustapha

dominate the sound. Mali's Ensemble Instrumental is perhaps the best known example. Founded in 1961 by Mali's first president, Modibo Keita, the intent was to celebrate the country's many melodic traditions. All the jali instruments are included, plus FulBe flute players and fiddlers, Wolof xalam players and a large female chorus. And though the ensemble rehearses under the direction of a person trained in stage presentation, the process remains aural. Beyond the national ensembles, Mande musicians have circled the globe, performing either as individuals or more typically in small ensembles. Mande communities in London, Paris and New York have their own troupes.

The dominant trend today is for collaboration between improvisers from different cultures to create new sounds. The Gambian kora player Foday Musa Suso was one of the first to do this: teaming up with a 1976 Oberlin College graduate named Adam Rudolf (now head of the renowned jazz ensemble Moving Pictures), whom he met in Ghana, the two formed the Mandingo Griots Society. This was basically a rock band, with the kora out front; Suso later worked with the avant-garde Kronos string quartet and with Herbie Hancock. The list of innovative performers is long, with kora players dominating: another Malian, Mamadou Diabate, now based in North Carolina, heads an ensemble with balafon, string bass and drums: he has an ear for taking a traditional Mande song and creating his own popular sound with it. These trends continue on the African continent also, with different ethnic groups collaborating. In the present day a downside has emerged in the form of Islamic extremism. Just as the Taliban crushed music in Afghanistan at the end of the twentieth century, in recent years extremist groups with a similar bent have terrorised musicians in Mali. The good news is that historically, in many different settings, strong communities of musicians and their supporters have ultimately triumphed over their detractors.

■ Conclusion

For those watching the kora or balo on YouTube, or twitching to the beat of Bassekou Kouyate's group Ngoni Ba in the concert hall, the question might still arise: is this classical music, or is it maybe jazz? Today's jazz educators will be quick to point out that jazz *is* America's classical music. Improvisation is serious business, requiring extensive knowledge and practice. It also involves composing, arranging, voicing and formal planning. Jaliyaa went through a dark period in the eighteenth and nineteenth centuries, when it seemed every mention of the 'singing man' by travellers was derogatory. But with the advent of recordings, radio, television and the attention of scholars, the world is finally able to hear this music and appreciate it for what it is; it needs no special advocacy. Today's Mande musicians can spin endless and fascinating solos from kumbengo and birimintingo, the singers can string together long memorised praise lyrics with extempore sung commentary on notables in the audience (to such powerful effect that the person comes up and hands them money), and any pick-up group can quickly put on a spectacular performance, constructed on the spot. Listeners from the non-Mande world can now join the 'class' that this music is intended for. It is indeed one of the world's classical musics.

The flexibility of jaliyaa has enabled it to adapt to changing times, rather than fade into the past. The late Ali Farka Toure *(top left)* still remains a looming presence, and a pointer to the Mande kinship with the bluesmen of the Mississippi; Salif Keita *(above right)* and Toumani Diabate *(bottom left)* are the best-known of today's innovators.

(Photo credit: Salif Keita www.laurielewis.co.uk)

Further reading

The author's 1973 dissertation characterized Mande *jaliyaa* as 'professional', but Lucy Duran first described it as 'classical' in a short article in the British journal *Country Life* (1985). Duran has become the authority on women's roles in *jaliyaa*, as exemplified in her 2007 article 'Ngaraya: Women and Musical Mastery in Mali'. Thomas Hale is also an excellent source for the traditional social roles of both men and women in *jaliyaa*, in his 1998 book *Griots and griottes*. Two DVDs by the author, from films made in 1970 and 1987, include booklets with extensive documentation of social contexts and song translations: *Mande Music and Dance* (2005) and *Music of West Africa: The Mandinka and Their Neighbors* (2010). An excellent feel for the contemporary life of *jaliyaa* is provided by Banning Eyre (documenting his time as a student of guitar in Mali) in his 2000 book *In Griot Time: An American Guitarist in Mali*, and by Lisa Feder in her 2007 PhD dissertation on the practice of *jaliyaa* in New York, 'Learning Culture through a Musical Practice with Manding Jalis'. To delve more deeply into the early history of the Mande people and *jaliyaa*, scholarly editions of the writings of Ibn Battúta and the Sundiata epic have appeared since the classic sources cited in the body of the chapter. The best edition of Ibn Battúta's African writings is that of Nehemia Levtzion and J. F. P. Hopkins, *Corpus of Early Arabic Sources for West African History* (2000). The best scholarly editions of the Sundiata epic are by John William Johnson (*The Epic of Son-jara: A West African Tradition*, 1986) and David C. Conrad (*Sunjata: A West African Epic of the Mande People*, 2004). Finally, even in the digital age, one should not forget the book *Africa: Its Peoples and their Culture History* (1959) by George Peter Murdock, which is still an invaluable resource for ethnic group names, their relationships, geography (including a large outline map) and basic cultural ways.

Recommended listening

Ali Farka Touré and Toumani Diabaté, *Ali and Toumani*, Nonesuch 522937-2, 2010. The two most world-famous Mande instrumentalists.

Bajourou: Big String Theory, Green Linnet GLCD 4008, 1984. Ensembles with ngoni and guitar, notes by Lucy Duran.

Jali Nyama Suso, Gambie: l'art de la kora, OCORA C580027, 1996. The first solo kora album, recorded at the University of Washington and first released on LP in 1972. Notes by Roderic Knight.

Guinée: kora et chant du N'Gabou, Buda Records 92629-2, 1996. Guinea's best kora player M'Bady Kouyaté and his wife Diaryatou Kouyaté, recorded by Stéphane Larrat.

Guinée: musique des Malinké (Paris: Le Chant du Monde CNR 272 1112, 1999). The classic pioneer high fidelity recordings from 1950 by Gilbert Rouget.

Jali Kunda: Griots of West Africa & Beyond, Ellipsis Arts 3511,1997. Compiled by *kora jali* Foday Musa Suso, including rare recordings from Guinea-Bissau and some Western/Mande fusion numbers.

Mamadou Diabate, *Behmanka*, World Village 468039, 2005. Kora solos by a leading player of both traditional and innovative *jaliyaa*, now living in the US, with notes by Banning Eyre.

Morikeba Kouyate, *Music of Senegal*, Traditional Crossroads 4285, 1997. Kora solos and vocals by another leading player living in the US, with notes by David Novak.

The Divas from Mali: Kandia Kouyaté, Mah Damba, Sali Sidibé, Oumou Sangaré, World Network 28.301, 1997. The four best-known *jali musolu* from Mali, notes by Barbara Wrenger.

The Rough Guide to the Music of Mali, World Music Network RGNET1208CD, 2008. Eighteen famous singers and performers on all *jali* instruments.

9 North American Jazz

Scott DeVeaux

It's jazz night at a local restaurant. There's no permanent stage: musicians squeeze into a small nook at the front. The drummer and bass are in the rear, their backs against the neon sign in the plate-glass window. The leader of the group, a silver-haired trumpet player, brings in the band with brief grunts on the backbeat before launching into a complicated unison line with his saxophonist. His improvisations are melodically inventive and rhythmically brisk, pulling the band into sharper focus. When he finishes playing, he strolls away from the stand to chat with a friend, while keeping an eye on the band.

The atmosphere is casual: many in the audience simply drink and chat. Yet there's an atmosphere of seriousness and expectation. People are deeply attentive, leaning forward and cheering the end of each solo. The musicians don't seem to notice either the audience or the music on their stands; their concentration and satisfaction is evident. The saxophonist leans against the wall, his eyes closed, while the guitarist rocks back and forth, a smile warming his face. The music is wild and chaotic, but always under control, and it ends on a crisply-timed syncopation.

JAZZ does not have a long history. Indeed, compared to many of the musics covered in this book, which often span centuries, it barely has a tradition at all.

It emerged about a hundred years ago in rough, working-class neighbourhoods of New Orleans with a jaunty, polyphonic style that bears little relation to the intricate chamber music that is played today. 'Modern jazz' – the kind currently heard in nightclubs, concert halls and other venues across the country – did not take shape until the 1940s and 1950s, well within living memory. As an improvised music, it gives little sense in live performance that it cares terribly much about its past.

Beneath this surface, though, are layers of cultural meaning – especially for African Americans, who are disproportionately represented among its creators. Although musicians of every race play jazz, there is general agreement that its origins lie in black culture. Indeed, it is the most highly developed musical tradition created by African Americans over a period that encompasses their most stringent trials for citizenship. Some would argue that this music should be understood today as a kind of alternative classical music, firmly ensconced in academia and in such official venues as New York's Lincoln Center.

◀ Duke Ellington and his band in London in 1933, framed by a set reflecting the influence of Picasso's designs for the Ballets Russes

■ Forms

Despite the brevity of its history, the ancestry of jazz is murky. Like most African-American musics, it is a hybrid. In certain ways it is an offshoot of European classical music, using that tradition's fixed intonation of twelve equal steps within the octave, borrowing much of its instrumentation (piano, bass, trumpet, clarinet, etc.), and displaying a firm command of chromatic tonal harmony. But this does not begin to describe jazz. Much of what makes it distinctive, clearly separate from classical music, lies in its African roots.

Tracing these roots is not easy. Languages disappeared: because slaves were captured from diverse regions of Africa, they dropped their native tongues in favour of English. Entire village traditions would have quickly faded from memory. Not even the drum traditions from the coastal portions of West Africa most plagued by slavery could be easily transplanted: drums were routinely banned in the colonies out of fear that their sounds could be used to incite slave rebellions. Africans came to the New World with only their bodies and their minds, with few resources and little freedom. The harshness of their labour encouraged them to focus on the present and forget their past.

Yet a kind of syncretic African music-making did survive. It could be heard on rare occasions of holiday gatherings, or 'jubilees', in eighteenth-century cities such as Philadelphia and New York. More detailed accounts come from Albany, New York in the early 1800s: on 'Pinkster Sunday' (the Colonial term for Whitsunday), slaves from across the countryside gathered for a three-day celebration; white observers noted a communal singing and dancing accompanied by a drum made from an eel-pot covered with sheepskin.[1] More famous gatherings in New Orleans attracted onlookers to Congo Square, where the tradition of dancing on Sundays continued into the 1840s. 'They indulged in dancing with music made by thumping on the head of a barrel with a skin stretched over it', recalled one African-American visitor from Tennessee. 'The dancers used to wear tin or some substitute on their legs to make a sort of jingle. I judged it was African music'.[2]

Yet this music had little to do with jazz. The blending of African with European music came when these former Africans decided to become popular dance musicians. As early as the seventeenth century, slaves learned that playing the fiddle or the banjo (which originated in West Africa) for local dances could release them from labour, offer them social mobility and earn them real income. Even before Emancipation, a number of free blacks in the North became professional musicians, plying their trade on European instruments. Some, like Frank Johnson of Philadelphia, were internationally recognised as leaders of legitimate dance orchestras. But a glimpse of the lower life in the slums of New York City suggests a more ordinary reality for black musicians. Indeed, according to one observer the music they played in the 1840s might have uncanny resemblances to jazz: 'That red-faced trumpeter ... looks precisely as if he were blowing glass, which needles penetrating the tympanum, pierce through and through your brain without remorse ... the bass-drummer ... sweats and deals his blows on every side, in all violation of the laws of rhythm'.[3] These mannerisms, as well as a rough copy of blacks' physical appearance, were soon adopted by whites in the 'minstrel show', where under a mask of burnt cork performers claimed to offer music direct 'from the plantation'. Current research, however, suggests that they may have heard it on the waterfront of New York, where free blacks sang and danced for spare change.[4]

What, then, could early jazz musicians have derived from their African heritage? Jazz scholar Gunther Schuller offered one answer by directly comparing a New Orleans band with a West African drumming group.[5] Another was provided by the African-American composer Olly Wilson: in attempting to pin down the essential elements of black music, Wilson listed what he called 'conceptual approaches to music-making' linking African-American music to Africa.[6] These principles form a deep, underlying grammar that has served as the DNA for all manifestations of black American music, jazz among them. To align this list more directly with jazz, here is my own version of Wilson's list:

- The musical form in Africa is the *cycle* – a short, repeated rhythmic framework whose end simultaneously begins a new repetition. In jazz, the cycle is known as the *chorus*. A chorus can be a brief two-bar chord vamp, but more commonly it runs from twelve to thirty-two bars. It can be repeated indefinitely, allowing jazz musicians to stretch a performance for as long as they see fit.

- African music also depends on *rhythmic contrast*: the constructive disparity of two categories of rhythmic layers. The first is the *foundation layer*: a stable, repetitive pattern such as the time-line pattern heard throughout West Africa (commonly played on a piercing percussion instrument such as the bell). In jazz, this foundation can be the string bass's four-beats-to-the-bar 'walking bass' line and the drummer's insistent ostinato ('ding dit-d'-ding') on the ride cymbal. Such instruments are said to be 'keeping time'. The second layer is the *variable layer*, more mercurial in temperament and often improvised. To understand jazz, you need to hear and understand both layers: the steady, head-nodding repetition of the foundation instruments, and the continuous flood of improvisation from the soloist and the rest of the ensemble.

- Another crucial principle is *call-and-response* – for which an alternative name might be the 'principle of interaction' or 'principle of dialogue'. Much of traditional West African music is built up from back-and-forth exchanges, such as between a variable part (the 'call') and a fixed part (the 'response'), between two fixed parts, or through the spontaneous interaction of different musical parts. To be sure, call-and-response is not simply African – it is a basic principle in many kinds of music around the world. In jazz, this kind of interaction can be formal (as in the convention of 'trading fours' in small group jazz, where two soloists exchange four-bar solos), but it can also be as spontaneous as casual conversation. Competence in jazz means having 'big ears' – slang for

- the keen aural attentiveness that makes jazz musicians ready to respond in a split second to what they've just heard.

- In jazz, as in the blues, the fixed intonation of European classical music is abandoned for a more flexible method of stretching, or 'bending', pitches. These are called *blue notes*; their genesis in West Africa has been recently confirmed by the ethnomusicologist Gerhard Kubik.[7] Unlike Indian classical music, where subtle microtonal fluctuations are pervasive throughout the scale, blue notes are usually restricted to the third, fifth and seventh degrees.

- *Timbre variation* is another principle. Rather than aiming for a single pure tone, as in classical music, jazz musicians use a wide variety of timbres for expressive purposes. This encouraged jazz musicians, from the outset, to devise new ways of playing otherwise familiar instruments like the trumpet, and a bewildering variety of growls and snarls from the newer saxophone.

- In general, whenever there is empty 'space' in the music (pauses in melodies, thin texture), African musicians *fill it up* with spontaneous contributions. Much of the sonic density of jazz arises from this principle.

- While classical ensembles aim to blend sound within a section, jazz relishes *contrasts in timbre*. It's easy to distinguish the sizzle of a crash cymbal from a plucked string bass, or to define the sharply varying timbres of trumpet, clarinet and trombone in a New Orleans jazz *front line*.

- Finally, there is the interconnection of *music and dance*. In African music, these two terms are often indistinguishable: a particular piece is simultaneously a set of dance movements and the music that accompanies the dance. Jazz may no longer be dance music, but it began in dance halls, and even in a concert auditorium its rhythmic drive forces everyone – audience, musicians – to move.

The music we know as jazz results from these effects. Jazz is structured by repeating cycles (or choruses), which are defined not just by their rhythmic length but also through their harmonic contour. Each chord fits into a precise position in the rhythmic cycle. To choose a simple but crucial example: in a traditional twelve-bar blues, the harmony *must* move to a IV chord (i.e. a chord built on the fourth degree of the major scale) on the downbeat of the fifth bar. Everyone knows and respects these conventions. Indeed, the harmonic basis for jazz must be understood rhythmically. Within this framework, of course, all kinds of trickery are possible: musicians may substitute one chord for another (as in the 'tritone substitution' discussed later in the chapter), or fill in harmonically static places with complex progressions. And this is expected. One further consequence of these 'conceptual approaches' is that they empower individual musicians to participate fully in all levels of musical decisions, including many thought to primarily involve composition. Unlike their classical counterparts, jazz musicians forge their own roles, creating new music as they do so.

All of this leads, then, to improvisation, jazz's most celebrated and most misunderstood feature. European concert artists have – at least over the last two centuries – been bound to the printed page. Jazz musicians seem to simply pull their notes out of thin air. As their competitors in New Orleans complained in the early twentieth-century, they were 'faking it' – a term that still survives in the term 'fake book' (the highly condensed sheet music often used on a jazz gig). And the fact that most performers were black only seemed to heighten this misperception. If black people couldn't read, the reasoning went, they certainly couldn't decipher music notation; ergo they must be fakers. Black musicians took this in as part of the baggage of racial segregation: some bands even hid their music to confirm the impression that the music came from nowhere. Even today, musicians parry inquiries with mystification: 'If you've got to ask, you'll never know.'

Yet the notion of jazz as an 'illiterate' music is a myth. Improvisation is not a magical process, but resourcefulness honed by years of practice. Non-musicians should compare it with daily conversation, where everyone 'improvises' their speech. Creating sentences involves inserting words (vocabulary) into systems of speech (grammar). For the language of music, this is more difficult, but hardly impossible. Much as no individual sentence is made up of utterly original material, jazz too uses phrases (known as 'licks') that are widely shared among jazz players. Originality in jazz improvisation comes from speed, wit, variety and responsiveness. To finish the comparison with speech, we may think of it as eloquence.

Many of the immediate choices made by jazz improvisers are rhythmic – responding to, or reacting against, other members of the ensemble. Indeed, one might say that their aim is to make their music *swing*: that famous, indefinable word that sums up all the drive, lightness and exhilaration of jazz polyrhythms.

The choices of pitch are somewhat harder to explain. Musicians create melodies in relationship to harmony – the chords that sound, in sequence, during each chorus. They know which pitches will work against that harmonic background, taking advantage of subtle dissonances in their improvised line to propel the line forward. Their solos use short, melodic ideas that are common to many musicians; yet each solo is unique. Jazz soloists listen carefully to their creations, building their improvisations through what drummer Max Roach has called 'a conversation with myself'.[8] 'It's like you've got this third ear that oversees the whole business – the craft part – and that's what tells you what to do', observes pianist Fred Hersch. 'If you're going to repeat a phrase, repeat it in a different way, change it a little bit; make it say something; make it speak differently.'[9]

History

The formal history of jazz begins at the dawn of the twentieth century in New Orleans. A polyglot port, New Orleans was added to the United States through Thomas Jefferson's Louisiana Purchase of 1803. As a complex city, it was an anomaly – indeed, the only city of any size in the South at the time. Because of its French (and also Spanish) heritage, it was (and still is) a lively place, more given to rowdy public celebrations like Mardi Gras than its staid counterparts in Protestant America. Its musical life was extraordinary: throughout the year, the humid night air was pierced by the sounds of parade bands, string bands and dance orchestras.

New Orleans was also distinguished by an unusual system of racial classification. While the United States was shoring up its racial lines by insisting that any trace of Negro ancestry classified one as 'colored' – the so-called 'one drop of blood' rule – New Orleans harboured an intermediate class of mulattos. Known as the Creoles of color (*gens de couleur libre*), these French-speaking Catholics saw themselves as socially superior to the more recent black migrants from the countryside. Creoles dominated many of the skilled trades, such as carpentry, masonry and cigar-making, which were largely closed to blacks. One such trade was music, a profession that required years of training and a highly specialised form of literacy. Secure in their musical pre-eminence, Creoles sneered at poorly educated black musicians ('yard and field Negroes', as one remembered them)[10] and guarded their most prominent and lucrative gigs.

By the end of the nineteenth century, however, the shadow of segregation spread across New Orleans. The passing by Louisiana of Legislative Code 111 in 1894 brought New Orleans under the 'one drop of blood' rule, deeply eroding, if not ending, the special status of the Creoles. In 1896, the Supreme Court decision *Plessy v. Ferguson* (Plessy was a Creole activist protesting laws segregating railway cars) made it clear that the 'separate but equal' policy of racial separation was fully constitutional. Now openly in competition with their darker-skinned colleagues, Creole musicians learned, however reluctantly, how to satisfy the tastes of their new audience. 'A fiddler is *not* a violinist, but a violinist can be a fiddler', reflected Paul Dominguez. 'If I wanted to make a living, I had to be rowdy like the other group. I had to jazz it or rag it or any other damn thing.'[11]

The pre-eminent embodiment of this change was Charles 'Buddy' Bolden, a black musician often hailed as the first pioneer of jazz. Lower-class and proud of it, Bolden staked his reputation on translating black folkways to his cornet. 'He played nothing but blues and all that stink music', one musician remembered, 'and he played it very loud'.[12] Jazz folklore remembers his peak years, from 1900 to 1905, as the time of triumph, the moment when New Orleans turned toward this dangerous and exciting new musical phenomenon. Yet an illustration from a New Orleans newspaper in 1890 (see opposite page) suggests the tide may have turned a decade or more earlier: a group of black musicians, sitting on an outdoor balcony, brings white passers-by to their knees with raucous, presumably improvised music.

NORTH AMERICAN JAZZ

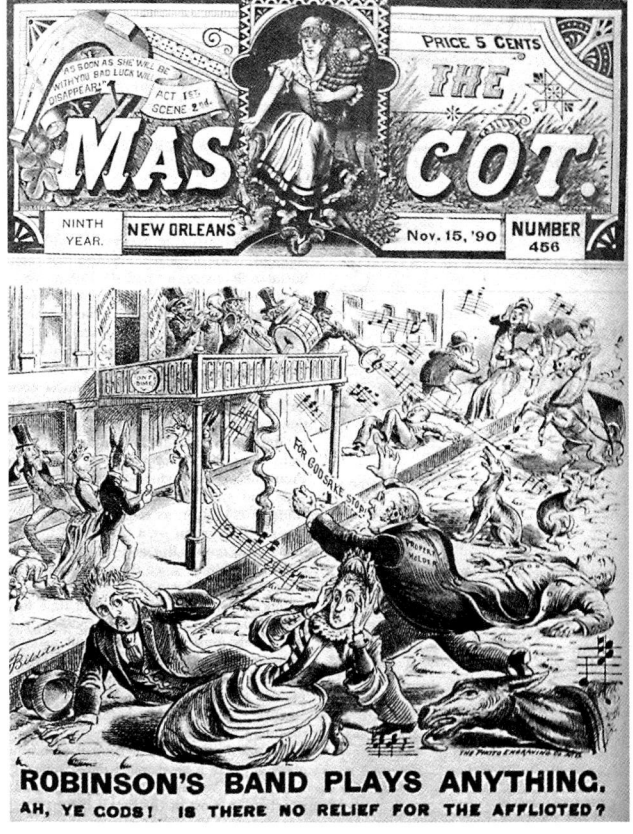

This cover of *The Mascot* (New Orleans) from 1890 is one of the earliest known depictions of a jazz band. The Afro-American musicians on the balcony are advertising a dime museum, but the white citizens (and their animals) can't handle the din.

Had this music remained in New Orleans, it might have remained a provincial novelty. But the more ambitious jazz musicians were on the road. They found lucrative work on nationwide vaudeville tours, where jazz was marketed as a racially-tinged form of entertainment. Indeed, the very term 'jazz' came not from New Orleans (the locals preferred 'ragtime') but from the theatrical circuit. (The etymology of the term is obscure. Its origins are often assumed to be sexual in nature, but the first occurrence of the word 'jazz' in print, in 1912, referred neither to music or to sex, but to professional baseball.)[13] The first jazz musicians to record were vaudevillians: the Original Dixieland Jazz Band, a group of well-travelled white New Orleans musicians who came off the road to preserve their untidy polyphony on records for Victor in 1917. This music so strongly affected the dance music of rebellious youth that the coming decade of the 1920s took on the nickname 'The Jazz Age'.

By this time, black Americans were also on the move. The Great Migration, probably the biggest demographic shift in American history, pulled them away from the South toward ghettos in Northern cities. In nightclubs on Chicago's South Side, New Orleans jazz found a new audience. It took recording companies a few years to discover the newly urban black specialty market, but after 1923 black bands recorded frequently. Among the bandleaders was Jelly Roll

The Original Dixieland Jazz Band *(left)* were the first jazz musicians to record.

Jelly Roll Morton *(below)* brought a new order to the chaos of collective improvisation.

Morton (the stage name of Ferdinand LaMothe), a Creole pianist and composer who brought a fastidious order to the chaos of collective improvisation. Another master was Joe Oliver, known in Chicago as 'King', whose recordings with the Creole Jazz Band have often been taken as the best representation of the New Orleans style.

New Orleans style was distinguished by its rhythmic energy and its polyphonic texture. The *front line* – cornet, clarinet and trombone – improvised simultaneously, each instrument adding its distinctive rhythmic layer in a raucous but balanced mix. The bands played ragtime pieces, in elaborate multi-strain form, or the new twelve-bar blues. Although this form of jazz faded during the Great Depression, it was eventually revived by enthusiasts. Today, many groups (mostly white) still enjoy 'Dixieland' jazz, a style well suited for rough, amateur playing.

Yet even as the collective sound of New Orleans jazz reached a mass audience, it was changing into a more modern form. Polyphonic texture was displaced by a homophonic texture. One of these new soloists was Sidney Bechet, a virtuoso on clarinet and soprano saxophone who spent much of the 1920s overseas, spreading the music as far away as Russia, inevitably diluting his influence at home. Instead, Louis Armstrong emerged as the indisputable genius of solo improvisation. A protégé of King Oliver on cornet (and later trumpet), he had made his way from New Orleans to Chicago to play with the Creole Jazz Band, and his hard-swinging rhythm and penchant for clear, soaring melodies concentrated all the energy of collective improvisation into a single line. His recordings with the Hot Five simultaneously exemplified the beauty of the older polyphonic New Orleans style while demolishing it with powerful solos, and the effect was immediate. 'There were thousands of dancers, all yelling and clapping', remembered tenor saxophonist Coleman Hawkins. 'I stood silent, feeling almost bashful, asking myself if I would ever attain a small part of Louis Armstrong's greatness.'[14] From that point, Hawkins and virtually every other jazz musician since have pursued the goal of becoming a soloist.

A different kind of jazz, an orchestral sound, also emerged at this time. As early as 1920, Paul Whiteman, a former violist who led a large dance band, sold two million copies of 'Whispering'. This recording featured the saxophone, an instrument largely absent from New Orleans groups: originally intended for the symphony orchestra, the saxophone family (soprano, alto, tenor, baritone), invented by the Belgian Adolphe Sax in the mid-nineteenth century, had found a new home in dance bands, where its rich timbre and flexibility helped it to displace strings. New dance bands sprang up almost immediately, including black bands led by Fletcher Henderson and Duke Ellington, which emulated the Whiteman band's 'symphonic jazz'.

The big bands took over the jazz world during the 'Swing Era' (1935–45), launched by the surprising success of the Benny Goodman Orchestra in the summer of 1935. Large, successful orchestras of fifteen or more musicians with uniforms, conductors and elegantly matching stands zigzagged across the country, saturated radio airspace and sold millions of copies of recordings. Their repertory was partly commercial (current popular songs from New York's

Above: Louis Armstrong and his Hot Five – formed in 1925, and including his wife Lil Hardin Armstrong on piano – combined the beauty of the older polyphonic New Orleans style while demolishing it with Armstrong's brilliant solos.

Below: Duke Ellington and his band in 1924 with *(from left to right)* Sonny Greer, Charlie Irvis, Otto Hardwick, Elmer Snowden and Bubber Miley

Tin Pan Alley) and partly original: either way, each band needed arrangers to compose and orchestrate the tunes. Room was left in each arrangement for solo improvisation, now constrained to short bursts within an otherwise composed piece. The new name for the music, *swing*, was drawn from jazz musicians' slang to describe its lively, danceable qualities. Its steady, four-beat rhythmic foundation, worked out in ballrooms like the Savoy in Harlem, suited the 'Lindy hop', a loose, athletic dance that offered a jazz-like improvisatory freedom for its practitioners.

Swing was defiantly commercial. The big bands of the 1930s were lucrative vehicles for entertainment, enmeshed in twentieth-century mass-market capitalism. Yet the orchestral qualities of swing also attracted serious composers, and none more than Edward 'Duke' Ellington. Beginning with his stint at the Cotton Club in Harlem in 1927, Ellington wrote over a thousand works for his orchestra: not only three-minute masterpieces for the 78 rpm records that filled the juke box, but also large-scale pieces, often written in collaboration with his partner Billy Strayhorn. Ellington listened carefully to the spontaneous contributions in his band, from the plangent wailing of alto saxophonist Johnny Hodges to Cootie Williams's trumpet growls, fully incorporating them into his scores – yet it is only recently that his compositional skills have been fully recognised. In 1943 Aaron Copland urged composers to move beyond the 'legitimate' audiences 'of the concert hall, the school, the elite', and seek the 'vastly enlarged audience music commands over the air or through records'.[15] Surprisingly, he failed to mention Ellington, who had just premiered his *Black, Brown and Beige,* a 48-minute survey of African-American history, at Carnegie Hall.

Yet even during the Swing Era, small-group jazz improvisation continued behind the scenes. In 'jam sessions', small groups of musicians gathered late at night, after clubs and ballrooms had closed, to focus on solo improvisation without regard for time or commercial format. This was music for professionals, meant to be heard in places that only musicians and fellow entertainers would frequent: there they performed without pay (their salaries, of course, came from the swing bands). Gradually, this music developed a small audience of jazz enthusiasts, closely monitored by the musicians' union which insisted that its members should not play for nothing: the result was small-group jazz housed in nightclubs in places like New York's 52nd Street.

By the mid-1940s, a new style had emerged out of this setting. Known as *bebop* – from scat syllables denoting a distinctive two-note phrase at the end of phrases – it quickly became the default format for jazz. Bebop was inventive, challenging modernist music. Its harmonies were chromatic and dissonant, relying on a harmonic twist known as the 'tritone substitution', where a dominant seventh chord could be sounded with a different root a tritone away. European art composers, such as Stravinsky and Bartók, were admired and imitated for their level of dissonance. Virtuosity arose from competition, reinforced by jam sessions (where second-raters would be weeded out by the more proficient). Musicians could play in any key, at any tempo and through any chord progression. Rhythms became doubled up – improvisers shifting without

THE OTHER CLASSICAL MUSICS

Charlie Parker (1920–55) used his Houdini-like subtlety of invention to turn bebop into jazz's most esoteric form. What he could do with a simple melody still fascinates his many imitators today.

EX. 9.1 Opening chorus from Charlie Parker's 'Now's the Time', 1953

warning to alarming double-time passages, interspersed with blues fragments. It was complex and demanding, both for musicians and audiences. Bebop could not compete with the immediate audience-appeal of swing and sank quickly from public view by the end of the 1950s. But within the musical community, it became the foundation for jazz. This led to jazz becoming known as an elite music, appealing to smaller, specialised, educated audiences.

From this point, we can identify three subsequent movements in jazz.

The jazz **avant-garde** took the modernist implications of bebop and pushed them to their logical conclusion. It can be traced to the quirky experiments of 'cool jazz' in the 1950s, which systematically questioned the basic convention of jazz: instrumentation (adding horns from the orchestra, or subtracting drums and piano), metre (adopting additive metres such as 5/4 or 7/4) and repertory (taking on techniques from classical music, like the polyphonic fugue). By 1960, with the daunting music of Ornette Coleman, Cecil Taylor and John Coltrane, it had established itself as 'free jazz' or 'the new thing', moving fearlessly into atonality. The avant-garde assumes that the artists, seconded by their champions in the press, are in charge of the music's development: audiences are continually confronted with new and disruptive twists. Not surprisingly, this is a marginal art music, its followers few but dedicated.

By contrast, **fusion** insists on a dialogue between jazz and popular fashion. Although the term derives from the jazz/rock mixture of the 1970s, it can be used to describe musicians who regretted the gulf that bebop had placed between them and the mass audience since the 1940s. It responds immediately to new dance grooves and readily absorbs technical innovations (such as electrical instruments, amplification and editing). One can hear fusion in Latin jazz, 'soul jazz' and the varied ways jazz has approached rock and soul. Like the swing of the 1930s, it trades complexity for mass appeal. Today it is known as 'smooth jazz' – a slickly packaged amalgam of jazz and R&B aimed at young audiences who have 'outgrown' rock. It's easy for hard-core jazz fans to despise, but smooth jazz remains a powerful force in the marketplace.

Finally, there is a **historicist** approach to jazz. This situates contemporary jazz against the backdrop of the music's past. Some historicist work is presented by 'repertory ensembles' – groups that aim to keep alive music that time has passed by, or by musicians no longer living. It has gained prominence with Wynton Marsalis's Lincoln Center Jazz Orchestra, a highly skilled band of conservatory-trained musicians capable of playing fluently in diverse historical idioms. Stylistically, it is conservative; but in practical terms it has been relentlessly effective. Building on the music's history, it has claimed recognition from arts organisations (public and private) as 'America's classical music'. In education, it has discreetly become an alternative art music.

The musicians who play jazz today are thorough professionals. Originally, jazz was a lucrative occupation that drew from a wide range of social backgrounds from the urban underclass (Louis Armstrong, Billie Holiday, Benny Goodman) to the upper crust (Teddy Wilson, Charlie Barnet). Most of them would have received a basic training on their instrument through a conventional classical music program, such as those offered in the public schools, but the more serious

education came on the job, where neophytes observed (and were observed by) seasoned players. 'I began to learn a new method of sight reading', remembered clarinettist Artie Shaw:

> I found out about new methods of tone production, and the various kinds of tone that could be used in different types of ensemble playing. In short, I had to learn so many technical and non-technical aspects of the seemingly simple procedure of blowing a horn in a dance band, that after a few weeks of it my head buzzed.[16]

These days, such subtleties of performance are typically learned in higher education. College-level jazz programs began in the wake of World War II (fuelled by the GI Rights Bill, which gave returning veterans the means to attend college) and rapidly accelerated during the 1970s. Although critics routinely express their distrust of the academic approach to training, the majority of current jazz stars have now passed through this system.[17] Indeed, jazz is becoming increasingly comfortable in the conservatory, where it provides an alternative method of training to the long-standing classical music tradition.

Jazz has also moved well beyond its place of origin. Indeed, as early as the 1920s, when it was inseparable from popular culture, it was a symbol of globalisation, travelling as a commodity (the 78 rpm recording) throughout Europe and into Asia.[18] Among the places that many black American musicians found themselves (including Buck Clayton, later a soloist for Count Basie) was Shanghai, a hotbed of up-to-date dance music for its expatriate community. By the Second World War, jazz was no longer a casual popular music, but seeds of interest in it as a form of alternative art music had sprouted around the world. There are now separate, individual strains of jazz in virtually all corners of Europe, to say nothing of such diverse countries as Brazil, Japan, South Africa and Israel.

■ Performance

While jazz was once dance music, it is rarely that any more. Instead, the prototypical venue for jazz is the nightclub, where patrons can relax in an intimate club setting, complete with food and alcohol. An evening in a nightclub can be expensive: as a thoroughly commercial venue, it draws its income from steep prices for admission fees and drink. Conversation is permitted, and in some places, inescapable; but loud talking is discouraged and, in some places known as 'listening rooms', proscribed. Until recently, smoking was *de rigueur* (and still is in many European clubs), but anti-smoking laws in the United States have cleared the air. Musicians play for hour-long sets, after which the room is emptied and restocked with new paying customers.

In the early days it was rare for jazz to be enjoyed in concert auditoria, as when Benny Goodman made his celebrated 1938 appearance in Carnegie Hall. But it is now a routine component of the programmes in major concert venues, where audience behaviour is not much different from that for classical concerts, though there musicians expect applause at the end of each solo as they do in the clubs.

> Leading lights *(clockwise from top left)*: Lester Young (1909–59), Dizzy Gillespie (1917–93), Thelonious Monk (1917–82), Mary Lou Williams (1910–81), Miles Davis (1926–91), Ornette Coleman (b. 1930)

Has jazz become an art music – or, in the phrase coined by pianist Billy Taylor, 'America's classical music'? This, perhaps, is the question for which jazz has long been waiting for an answer. Many of its advocates have felt that it has been an art music from its beginning. But it has only recently begun to acquire the trappings of official support that such traditions normally expect in the United States. And it's about time: although its African-derived beat is much closer to commercial pop than European art music, jazz is no longer a 'popular' music, or a 'mass' music, and it needs support to survive. Yet the music's looseness, its willingness to try almost anything, suggests that jazz will never become what many have feared – a second-rate classical music clinging to its achievements of yesteryear. Its semi-marginal status allows it to remain what it has been since mid-century: a virtuosic music, made by musicians for musicians. With one foot in the academy, and the other in the street, jazz is in a position to surprise everybody for decades to come.

Further reading

Jazz writing has a tradition dating back to the 1930s. Although the literature has become increasingly scholarly, the earliest histories were anecdotal. Perhaps the most famous collection of stories came with Shapiro and Hentoff's *Hear me Talkin' to Ya* (1955): a colourful anthology of first-person testimonies, drawn from numerous interviews in the jazz trade press and arranged into a loose, ongoing conversation. It offers a glimpse into musicians' lives, and is still the place many people go for insights into jazz and its early history.

Scholars often came to the music sideways. One of these was the Marxist historian Eric Hobsbawm, who in his youth took a liking to this rough, rowdy music. Becoming a professor, he supplemented his income by writing reviews of jazz records, but to protect his career, he chose the pen name Frances Newton – an inside reference to the trumpet player Frankie Newton, who among other things was a member of the Communist party. Under Newton's name, Hobsbawm published *The Jazz Scene* (1959), a beautifully written survey that adds a subversive political slant to jazz history. Decades later he updated the book, which now appears under his own name. The latest edition (1993) adds lengthy reviews by him from the *New York Review of Books* plus some retrospective essays.

Another jazz scholar came from the world of classical performance. Gunther Schuller was an orchestral horn virtuoso, conductor and composer, with remarkably broad and inclusive tastes. As a performer, his playing can be heard on Miles Davis's famous *Birth of the Cool* recordings from 1949–50. As an author, his work is concentrated into two magisterial volumes: *Early Jazz* and *The Swing Era*. His writing focuses heavily on recordings – indeed, to read his treatises on Ellington and Armstrong requires access to virtually everything those artists ever put on shellac. Each chapter is densely illustrated with music examples, drawn from Schuller's own transcriptions.

Not everyone will agree with his critical judgments, but everyone will admire his wit, tenacity and keen ear.

In 2001, jazz invaded the television screen with Ken Burns's 10-part series, *Jazz: A History of America's Music*. The series itself had many flaws, including a lopsided emphasis on early jazz, but the visual images were stunning and the writing was excellent, thanks to the participation of Geoffrey Ward. Ward's companion volume ploughs the same furrow as the television series, but with incredible grace. *Jazz*, which I co-wrote with the former *Village Voice* jazz critic Gary Giddins, is a textbook-cum-historical survey. Giddins's own sparkling essays are collected in two large anthologies, *Rhythm-a-Ning* and *Weather Bird*.

Recommended listening

Miles Davis, *Kind of Blue*, Columbia 40579, 1959. Perhaps the most famous, and best-distributed, single album in the history of jazz.

Louis Armstrong, *The Complete Hot Five and Hot Seven Recordings*, Columbia/Legacy 63527, 2000. A recent anthology gathering Armstrong's early revolutionary recordings from the 1920s.

Charlie Parker, *Bird: The Complete Charlie Parker on Verve*, Verve 837-142-2 to 837-154-2, 1988. An excellent anthology of Parker's later work for Norman Granz's Verve label.

John Coltrane, *A Love Supreme*, MCA Records MCAD-5660, 1964. The most accessible of Coltrane's experimental recordings from the 1960s.

Duke Ellington, *The Blanton-Webster Band*, Bluebird 5659-2-RB, 1986. Ellington's superb recordings from the early 1940s.

Charles Mingus, *The Complete Columbia and RCA Albums Collection*, Sony Legacy CD107898, 2012. A wide variety of Mingus's albums from the 1950s and '60s, including *Ah-Um, Tijuana Moods* and *Mingus Dynasty*.

Thelonious Monk, *Brilliant Corners*, Riverside 30501, 1956. A superb collection of Monk originals, with a band featuring tenor saxophonist Sonny Rollins.

Bill Evans, *The Complete Riverside Recordings*, Riverside RCD-018-2, 1987. A 12-disc set, documenting Evans's recreation of modern jazz piano from 1957 to 1963.

Benny Goodman, *Live at Carnegie Hall: 1938 Complete*, Definitive DRCD 11378, 1999. The single appearance of the top swing band at Carnegie Hall, presented here with painstaking completeness.

Sonny Rollins, *The Complete Prestige Recordings*, Prestige 7PCD-4407-2, 1992. The finest 1950s recordings (including *Saxophone Colossus*) of an artist whose career stretches from the late 1940s into the twenty-first century.

10 Europe
Ivan Hewett

We are in one of those large buildings peculiar to the Western classical tradition known as concert halls. Around us are 1,500 or so people, and on stage is an army of musicians, around thirty of whom are playing a miscellany of instruments – woodwind, bowed strings, gleaming brass. With them is a choir of about the same number, four solo singers and – facing all these – the conductor. The music begins in a severely martial tone, the serious rat-a-tat of the kettledrum answered by a similar rhythm in the trumpets. The large body of strings play angry minor chords on strong beats, creating an atmosphere of implacable judgement and terror. Eventually the choir bursts in with the word 'Kyrie'. This tells us that we are listening to a musical setting of that part of the Roman Catholic Mass which remains unchanged from day to day, the Ordinary. This one is by Joseph Haydn, from 1798, and is called the Nelson Mass.

On one level this scenario offers something straightforwardly comprehensible. The music rouses emotions in a way that seems familiar for anyone with even a minimal acquaintance with tonal harmony, that unique invention of the West. We feel with ease the stern darkness of the prevailing key of D minor, the martial sound of drums and trumpets, and the joy created by the eventual move to the major key, as if these things were the voice of nature.

On the other hand there are things about the experience that do not seem natural at all. Some of these are institutional and social, such as the way audience feels obliged to sit in stillness and silence, even when moved. The performers' nineteenth-century formal dress is equally striking. And the music, despite its familiar tonal grammar, is in many ways remote. The neatly balanced articulated phrases and the clean-edged sound-world with no Romantic or impressionistic haze – all this lends the music a period flavour. The music is rooted in a very specific style, the 'Classical', which flourished in Europe from around 1770 to around 1810.

This last fact raises a problem. The Classical style reflects a mere half-century in a tradition that has so far lasted more than a millennium. Within that millennium are innumerable other styles. Which of them is typical of classical music in the broader sense of the word? None. Perhaps the single most striking fact about Western classical music is the colossal disparity of sound and language and style across its history. A survey of a musical tradition usually begins by

◀ A page from a late fifteenth-century missal, probably Florentine, showing two chants. By this date, pitch was specified exactly by a four-line staff provided with a clef – in this case a C (or Doh) clef – which here 'migrates' between the second and third line down; rhythm was indicated by symbols such as the triangular 'torculus' at the beginning of the third group of lines, which bundles together three one-beat notes sung to a single syllable.

laying out its fundamental materials – its instruments, genres, modes and melodic and rhythmic features. The enormous historical dynamism of Western music rules this out. Any attempt to lay the major styles of classical music side by side – Medieval, Renaissance, Baroque, Romantic, Modern – and tease out what they have in common cannot work, because the disparities are just too great. The musical elements would be couched in such vague generalities that we'd end up sweeping Bluegrass and Bulgarian folk music into the same net.

So is Western classical music just a sociological category, no more than the music that gets played in concert halls, taught in schools and conservatories and is liked by the middle classes? Not at all. Institutional and ideological factors certainly play a big role, particularly from the eighteenth century onwards when the idea of 'classical music' took root. But there are also elements in the music itself which mark it out. These elements themselves change, so we can't hope to boil them down to an essence. What we have to do is describe the narrative that links them together. To understand classical music, we have to tell its story.

■ From sound to symbol

Where to begin? The ninth century seems apt, as this was when the form of music that is classical music's distant ancestor – namely 'chant', the unaccompanied song that adorned the liturgy of the Western church – was first notated in sketchy form. If we want a date, Christmas Day 800 is as good as any. That was when Charlemagne was crowned Emperor of the Romans, laying the foundations for the Holy Roman Empire, a supra-national entity stretching from the Pyrenees to the Baltic and down to Northern Italy. Charlemagne continued the work of his father, King Pippin III of the Franks, who had agreed with Pope Stephen II to suppress local chant repertories, and impose the Roman repertoire in its place. The result was a hybrid of Roman and Frankish chant which became known as 'Gregorian' (referring to Pope Gregory 'The Great', who presided between 590 and 604, for complex reasons having nothing to do with music).

This constitutes the beginnings of Western classical music, for several reasons. These chants did not belong to the 'folk': they belonged to the elite, the numerically tiny but politically powerful network of clerics and monks associated with the Papacy, major monastic establishments and courts, particularly that of the Holy Roman Emperor. In addition these chants were sacred objects in their own right, as each was linked with a sacred, often liturgical text, and with a particular day in the church calendar.

The sheer importance of these chants, in both the sacred and secular spheres, was a powerful incentive to controlling them. But the emergence of notated music from the womb of a purely aural transmission – which was how church music began – was slow and patchy. The earliest chant books with musical notation, which date from the ninth century, show only the rise and fall of the melody, without exact pitches.

To modern Western ears chant may seem monotonous, but the use of such things as recurring melodic formulas shows that we are dealing with something pre-meditated and artful, rather than just a notated version of something

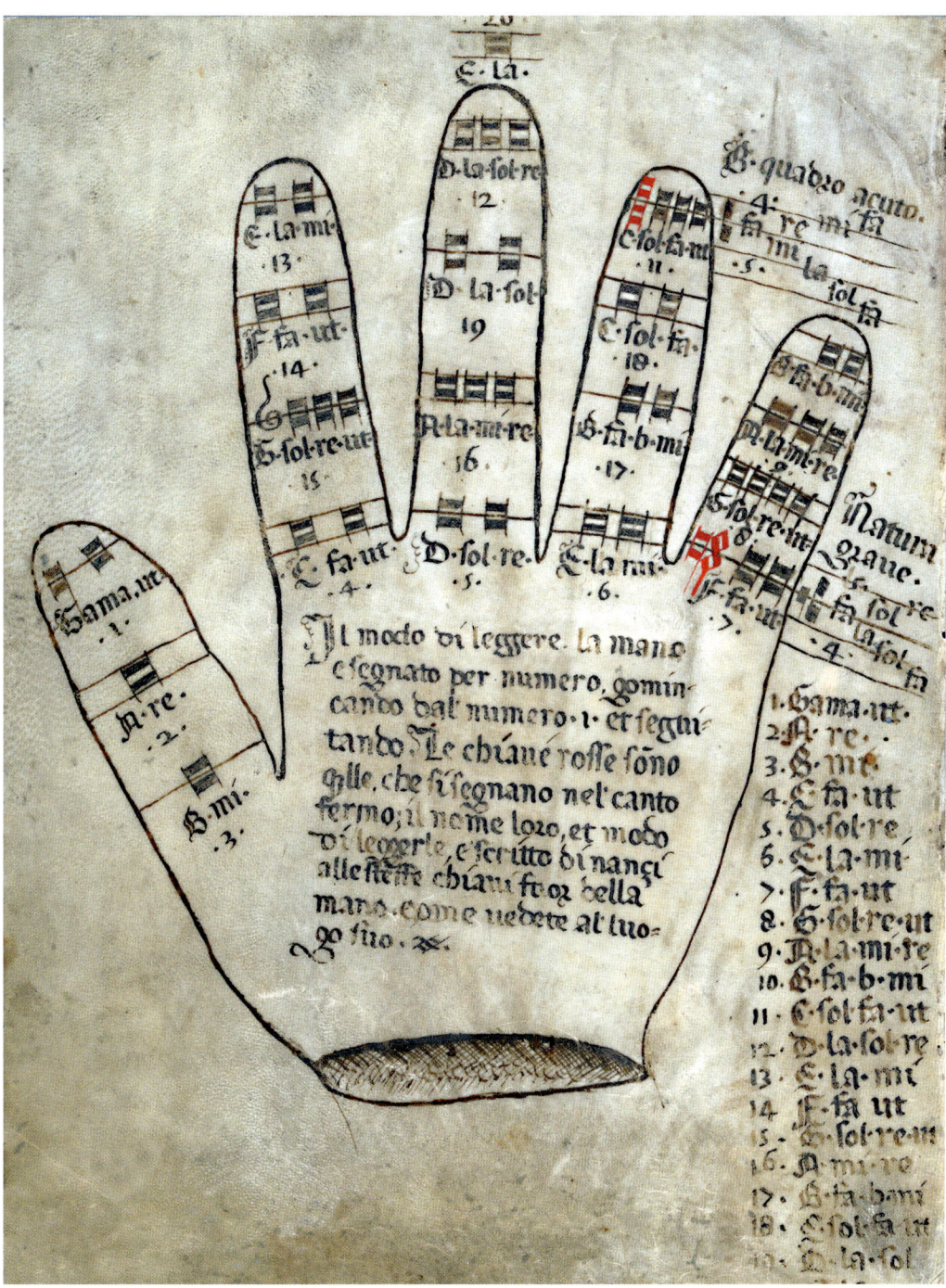

A sixteenth-century drawing of the 'Guidonian hand', showing pitch-intervals related to the joints of the fingers. From a manuscript in the Berkeley Music Library, University of California.

improvised. Another sign of artifice is the way a given chant is restricted to the notes of a particular scale or mode, as they were known. These modes were codified in a system loosely derived from the ancient Greek modal system: by the ninth century there were eight of these, rising eventually to twelve. What distinguishes each mode is its own individual pattern of whole and half-steps, which differ from the now-familiar major and minor scales (apart from the Ionian, which corresponds to C major). The modal system would dominate Western classical music until well into the sixteenth century, and it is what gives music of this early period its floating, antique quality.

The story of classical music takes a leap forward in 1030, when a monk named Guido d'Arezzo completed a treatise describing a new way to notate music. He devised a staff where lines and spaces represent exact pitches, together with a way of associating patterns of intervallic step with joints of a hand (the so-called Guidonian hand), and with a set of syllables, known as solmisation syllables (which we know as do-re-mi, or solfège). The sequence of pitches traced by Guido's line as it wanders back and forth over the joints of the hand maps out the entire range of notes available to musicians at that time. The surprising thing is how narrow it is – another sign of the influence of the Greeks, for whom the available spectrum of pitches, or gamut as it was known, was correspondingly narrow. As Guido declared proudly in a letter written in 1032, his invention meant that for the first time in history, a singer could sing a melody he'd never heard.

This was a giant step towards a conception of music as a set of fixed, determinate 'pieces', reproducible in all their detail, rather than as evanescent performances done from memory, which by their nature were unrepeatable except in broad outline. And it allowed the modern conception of composing to emerge, as the putting together of independently conceived parts to make a sounding whole. The combining of independently conceived lines – polyphony – is indeed a defining characteristic of Western classical music.

An early form of polyphony was created when a second (and sometimes also a third) voice-part mimicked the up-and-down movement of a chant or newly composed melody, at a fixed distance: this was one of a number of early polyphonic practices known collectively as 'organum'. Moving from this to genuinely independent melodic lines moving in opposite directions was another momentous development. In its earliest form this was known as 'discant'. Two masters of these styles arose out of the flourishing musical establishment at the cathedral of Notre Dame in Paris: Léonin (c. 1130–1201), known as 'optimus organista', and Pérotin (dates unknown, but active from c. 1185–1205), known as 'optimus discantor'. Perotin's two immense pieces of four-part polyphony (*Viderunt omnes* and *Sederunt principes*) are genuine 'pieces of music', with a complication of texture and long-range architecture that is sophisticated by any standard; they also have an irresistible triple-time rhythmic swing. Much medieval music shows a bias towards triple time, because of its associations with the Holy Trinity. In the complex system of medieval rhythmic modes, the various rhythmic layers could be cast either in 'perfect' (meaning triple-time) or 'imperfect' (meaning duple) time, in various combinations. When this system was refined at the beginning of the fifteenth century it encouraged extraordinary flights of rhythmic fancy. In the followers of the great French poet-composer Guillaume de Machaut (c. 1300–77) we find a rhythmic complexity not seen again until the 1950s.

In the earlier centuries of the Middle Ages, sacred music and 'elite music' (it is too soon to speak of 'classical music') might seem to be one and the same. For a long time the church was the centre of literate culture in general. Look down a list of the great medieval philosophers, doctors, poets, musicians and you find they are either clerics themselves or in the employ of the church. And the music the composers created was strictly functional – to adorn the liturgy. However, the idea that music could be beautiful and pleasing as well as useful already existed. Theorists thought that only those vertical combinations that answered to a concept of Divine perfection could be pleasing – an infusion of the ethical into the aesthetic which can be traced back through the Church Fathers such as Augustine, and late Antique thinkers such as Boethius, all the way to Plato. John of Salisbury taught at the University of Paris in the late twelfth century, and was fascinated by this new polyphony. He warned that if taken to excess 'it is more fitted to excite lust than devotion; but if it is kept in the limits of moderation, it drives away care from the soul ... confers joy and peace and exultation in God, and transports the soul to the society of angels.'[1]

However, the secular world also had its elites – emperors, kings, feudal lords – and they too cultivated an elite music. This also initially consisted of monophonic song, though it later evolved into such polyphonic (many-voiced) secular forms as the *rondeau* and *ballade*. As with sacred music, the secular form existed to serve the word, secular poetry; the fundamental difference is that whereas in church instruments were forbidden (apart from the organ), courtly songs were sometimes accompanied, perhaps by a stringed instrument such as the bowed fiddle, or plucked instruments such as the harp or psaltery. The performers were usually professional scholar-poets or minstrels, though there is evidence that noblemen themselves wrote and performed. The first European poet in the vernacular whose work has survived was Guillaume, Seventh Count of Poitiers and Ninth Duke of Aquitaine (1071–c. 1127). The chief topic of this repertoire is the ideal of 'courtly love', the idealisation of the eternally unreachable beloved, expressed in verse of astounding technical sophistication.

These songs were cast in the same modes that obtained in church music, though with more liberal use of chromatic notes foreign to the mode. They were notated centuries after they were written, using the same notation as sacred music. This dependence of the secular on the sacred realm was manifested at every level, from the training of musicians in church choirs to employment (there were many more sacred jobs than secular ones), right down to the basic polyphonic fabric of the music itself.

The one area of secular music that owed nothing to the church was dance music, for the simple reason that the church considered dancing to be sinful. Round dances such as the carol were popular all over Europe, and this period also saw the emergence of instrumental music, in genres such as the *estampie*, performed on such medieval precursors of modern instruments as the medieval fiddle, the harp, and drone instruments such as the hurdy-gurdy; both these forms are often found with texts. The old saying about music, that 'it's either a song or a dance', is not always true about medieval secular music, which was often both at once.

■ Music as divine euphony

The word 'euphony' denotes a state of perfect harmoniousness, without tension. Clerics and theorists exalted it as the mirror of Divine perfection, but – to modern ears at least – medieval music only fitfully suggests it. Much of the sacred music composed during the Renaissance seems as close to perfect euphony as music has ever come in the West.

There were many continuities between the medieval and Renaissance periods, above all the continuing importance of chants and church modes. Nevertheless, there were significant changes. Polyphonic music became more rhythmically supple as the system of the rhythmic modes faded in the thirteenth and fourteenth centuries. Chants retained their importance as raw material, but they were now increasingly elaborated in ingenious ways. Alternatively a composer might focus on a particular fragment of chant, making it the foundation for a towering polyphonic edifice. In the many-voiced settings of Latin texts known as the motet – the dominant form of polyphonic music from the twelfth century onwards – the *cantus firmus* (as these altered chants were known) is in many cases easy to spot amongst the freely composed voices, as it is laid out in relatively long notes in the tenor (whose name derives from the Latin verb meaning 'to hold').

This abstract view of chant as musical shape rather than sacred object opened the door to *canti fermi* based on secular sources such as folk songs and street cries. And it created the conditions for an explosion of exuberant abstract constructivism unparalleled until the post-war modernists. Composers vied with each other in the invention of abstruse linkages between melody, rhythmic pattern and symbolic meaning, which lay buried until uncovered by the patient detective work of twentieth-century scholars. The bigger the canvas the more abstruse the transformations could be, which is why composers increasingly cultivated the cyclic Mass. This term refers to the use of the same piece of plainchant in a polyphonic setting of the complete Ordinary of the Mass (typically this consists of the Kyrie, Gloria, Credo, Sanctus, Benedictus and Agnus Dei), and over the following two centuries and more a vast repertoire of cyclic masses was created. This is one of the glories of the Western tradition, worthy to stand beside the symphony and the sonata.

Despite the continuities there was a profound change in the sound of the music. Put simply, a Mass written in 1550 by Thomas Tallis makes more musical sense to us than Machaut's fourteenth-century Mass, and this change in sound went hand-in-hand with shifts in the political and cultural landscape. The monastic foundations faded in importance, and cathedrals and universities associated with cities – now becoming increasingly prosperous – took the lead, along with centres of secular power. During the later medieval and early

EUROPE

Creating harmony and polyphony out of raw chant

Above: Josquin des Prez (c. 1450–1521), Giovanni Pierluigi da Palestrina (c. 1525–94)
Below: Claudio Monteverdi (1567–1643), Thomas Tallis (c. 1505–85)

Renaissance periods the centre of musical gravity shifted to the Flemish-speaking northern regions of the Duchy of Burgundy. In the late fourteenth century the Burgundian court became the centre of musical patronage, and in the early fifteenth century, under the influence of English composers – above all John Dunstable (1390–1453) – a new generation of Flemish composers began to create a more fluid and aurally pleasing style. The bright sound of the major triad – that key component of what would later become 'tonality' – starts to appear. Beginning with Guillaume Dufay (1397–1474), these Flemish composers created a euphonious vocal polyphonic style which soon spread across Europe.

The dominant figure of the period was Josquin des Prez (c. 1450–1521), in whose work we see the perfection of the so-called imitative style, a key technical device in classical music. This would dominate all forms of music – sacred, secular, vocal and instrumental – from 1450 to 1600, and it has remained hugely important ever since. It describes a musical texture made up of independent lines or voices, in which each voice, as it enters, imitates the melodic shape of the previous one. In a mass or motet by Josquin each new line of text is introduced through a new musical figure, which is imitated in turn in an unceasing flow. The *cantus firmus* is still threaded through the texture, sometimes in long notes, sometimes in more subtle ways which make it hard to spot.

Josquin became a legend in his own lifetime. Martin Luther praised the way his pieces 'flow freely, gently and cheerfully, are not forced and cramped by rules, and are like the song of the finch'.[2] The idea of the wayward 'genius', whose services even the greatest princes had to vie for, had finally appeared in music. Many Flemish composers had plum jobs in the courts and city-states of Italy, which were now on the rise. Fuelled by their mercantile pre-eminence, Venice, Florence, Mantua and Milan – plus the Vatican, which had its own kind of pre-eminence – would in the later sixteenth century displace Flanders as the motor of elite musical culture. As if to symbolise this shift of musical power, Italy produced the composer who became the epitome of the High Renaissance vocal idiom, Giovanni Perluigi da Palestrina (1525–94).

Palestrina is one of the key figures of Western classical music. The sound of his music (and also of his great contemporaries such as Orlande de Lassus, William Byrd and Tomás Luis de Victoria) is beautifully euphonious, in a way that 'makes sense' to modern ears. The *cantus firmus* has now declined in importance, giving way to a multi-voice texture of perfect equality. Palestrina's music has become a touchstone of technical and aesthetic perfection, shown by the fact that learning to compose 'Palestrinian counterpoint' is still an essential component of university and conservatory curricula. Technically speaking, we are now approaching classical music's heartland.

Another key feature of classical music that appears in the Renaissance is what might be called portability. This is the notion that a piece of music can retain its identity even when it undergoes a drastic change of sound. This allowed pieces of vocal music to be transferred wholesale to another medium, such as a keyboard, or string or recorder consort (a transfer facilitated by the fact that instruments at that time were conceived in families from high to low, in a similar manner to voice-ranges). This portability was also shown in music's social function. A bit of finely woven vocal polyphony might be refitted with secular words, to be sung in an aristocratic household: the ability to sing music was part of a nobleman or woman's education, as Baldassare Castiglione's famous manual of aristocratic manners *Book of the Courtier* (1528) makes clear.

We are now on the threshold of the era of what has become known as the Common Practice, a set of rules and procedures that governed – albeit with increasing strain – the unfolding of harmony and counterpoint between 1600 and 1900. But we are not quite there yet. Many people who profess a deep love of Western music have no interest in sacred polyphony, for the simple reason that the music is actually too euphonious. It lacks drama, sudden changes of direction, thrilling climaxes – and naturally so, as to admit those into a piece of sacred music would be a serious lapse of taste. But in any case, musical discourse as it existed in 1550 lacked the means to create those effects.

■ Spectacle, drama, dance

All this was to change. Only half a century later, in 1607, a scene presented in a sung drama contained a truly shocking change of direction. The occasion was a performance of a new *dramma per musica* in a large chamber in the palace of the Gonzagas in Mantua, a thriving city in Northern Italy. The music was by a composer then on the Duke's payroll, Claudio Monteverdi (1567–1643). In the acting area (there was no stage as such) a wedding scene was being performed. As with all music-theatre spectacles at that time, the personages were mythical – nymphs, Gods, the Muse of Music and at the centre the god Orpheus, waiting for his bride Eurydice. But then a messenger arrives. Eurydice has been bitten by a snake, and has now been claimed by the Underworld.

The moment of reversal is marked by a startling change of harmony, against which the messenger's vocal line on 'Ah casi acerbo!' ('Ah, bitter misfortune!') pushes in angular, anguished dissonance. Dissonance is an agent of dissolution and anarchy, which in Renaissance music is governed by strict rules. In Monteverdi's *Orfeo* we see the unruly power of dissonance, once those rules are relaxed. It was not the first attempt at opera – there were several precursors created by writers and poets in the circle around the Florentine Count Bardi, including *La Dafne* of 1598 – but it is the first masterpiece, and still holds the stage today. The news of Monteverdi's epoch-making event travelled like wildfire, and it prompted many attempts to match or even surpass it, including several from Monteverdi himself: as Richard Taruskin points out, musical progress up to and beyond this date proceeded as much by emulation as by imitation, with composers striving to outdo each other in intellectual ingenuity or straightforward aural splendour.[3]

These early operas were different from nineteenth-century ones in many ways. The focus on mythological personages or figures from ancient history was one (not until comic opera arose in the eighteenth century would 'ordinary people' enter the operatic arena). Another was the orchestra. With its families of lutes, recorders, strings, wooden trumpets or 'cornets' and trombones, the early seventeenth-century orchestra was less numerous and less loud than the one pictured at the beginning of this chapter. But it was no less colourful, and the sound had a connotation of splendour and luxury that ours lacks. This is a reminder that the connection between cost and value was indissoluble at this time: only those things which were rare and costly could be beautiful, and in music, as in cultured life generally, any useful object – such as a book of notated music – had to be a thing of beauty in its own right.

The rise of opera went hand in hand with the emergence of a new kind of expressive song. One manifestation of this was a desire to emulate the powerful expressivity of ancient Greek music – or rather, what theorists imagined was the powerful expressivity of Greek music, because no-one had a clue what it had really sounded like. This was part of the more general trend in the rich and self-confident Italian city-states to try to outdo the achievements of classical civilisation. It threw down a challenge to the many-voiced polyphonic style, which still reigned supreme in the key secular vocal form the madrigal, as well as in sacred music.

By the time we reach the later madrigal-books of Monteverdi, the smoothly many-voiced madrigal had been definitively ousted by the new so-called 'monodic' sort, where an impassioned vocal line is pitted against a chordally-conceived accompaniment, often for lutes. Just as important as the new vocal style was the emergence of instrumental music from under vocal music's shadow. We see this already emerging in keyboard music in the sixteenth century. The toccatas of Frescobaldi (1583–1643), one of the first great keyboard composers, show a simple relish for the fact that fingers can move so much faster than the vocal tract, over a much bigger range. The emergence of distinct instrumental idioms is a feature of Baroque music, but even more characteristic of the era is the notion that these idioms could be shared. We see violin music imitating the sobbing ornamentation of vocal music, we see voices imitating trumpets, and in Bach's music we see organ pedal-patterns being transferred to bass stringed instruments.

It is this sharing of idioms between instruments, as much as the idioms themselves, that facilitated a key aspect of Baroque music: this is the so-called 'concertato' principle, whereby contrasting groups of voices and instruments are pitted against each other in dialogue. This feeling of movement is often bolstered by dynamic contrast (echo effects were much used) and sharp contrasts of instrumental colour. In a large-scale sacred piece by Giovanni Gabrieli – organist at St Mark's Cathedral in Venice from 1585 until his death in 1612 – a group of recorders over here might be answered by cornets over there, and a faster-moving pair of violins somewhere else. This style soon spread all over Europe, appearing in South Germany in the music of Heinrich Schütz (Gabrieli's favourite pupil) and in English composers of the late seventeenth century such as John Blow and Henry Purcell.

It is no accident that this spectacular 'concertato' principle arose in the era when supra-national entities like the church and the Holy Roman Empire were ceding authority to newly confident secular powers – the city-states of Italy, the ducal courts of Germany and monarchies such as those of France and England.

These new powers asserted their legitimacy partly through spectacle, which is why the period from 1600 to 1750 was the era of spectacle *par excellence*. Spectacle on its own is dramatically inert, as is shown by the numerous courtly pageants of the pre-operatic era. But when combined with expressive song a marvellous hybrid was created, potent enough to create a new audience prepared to pay handsomely for it. Monteverdi's first opera was written for an invited aristocratic audience; his last, *The Coronation of Poppea* of 1643, was written for a commercial theatre in Venice. Here we have an example of a profound change wrought on Western music by the needs of musical drama. (Other examples are the rise of comic opera in the eighteenth century and Wagner's new conception of 'music drama' in the nineteenth.)

Another striking new feature of Western art music at this time is the emergence of distinct national schools. Italy's was pre-eminent, thanks to its numerous courtly and clerical musical establishments, its bustling cities and its dominance in opera. This explains why many musical scores to this day have directions for tempi, dynamics and expression in Italian, and why from the mid-sixteenth to the early nineteenth century Italy was an essential destination of any ambitious young musician, either to learn the trade or to ply it. Handel had his first big success in Italy in 1706–7, and sixty-three years later the boy Mozart made his obligatory trip to Italy (where he submitted his scores for approval to the legendary musical cleric Padre Martini, to whose authority everyone had to defer).

Opera and sacred music were two sources of Italy's dominance, but it was equally strong in the new emerging secular forms such as the trio sonata (for small spaces) and the concerto (for larger ones). In the concertos of Arcangelo Corelli (1653–1713) and Antonio Vivaldi (1678–1741) the delicious lute- and viol-based sound of the opera orchestra gave way to a more homogeneous sound based on the new violin family (violin, viola and cello, with the double-bass as a hangover from the now out-dated viol family). This ensemble was perfect for the 'motoric' concerto style of the Concerto Grosso, the principal genre of large-scale music from the 1680s onwards. The formal principle was still that of the 'concertato', an energetic dialogue of solo instruments against the massed ensemble, but driven by motoric rhythms and cast in a much more regular phrase structure.

From around 1700 to 1760 this formidable culture swept over the whole of Europe, though it didn't drive out all native traditions, meeting stout resistance particularly in France. The French style was the cultural expression of a highly centralised absolute monarchy, and so was bound to be different. Song, of a heavily ornamented kind specially suited to French diction, was one source of this musical culture; the other was the highly formalised dance idioms cultivated at the royal court. These found their apotheosis in the ballets and operas of Jean-Baptiste Lully (1632–87) – as all-powerful in French music as the Sun King Louis XIV was in France as a whole – and later of Jean-Philippe Rameau (1683–1764). French declamation could not be exported, but French dance certainly was. Instrumental and orchestral suites based on French dances forms were composed all over Europe.

In German-speaking lands the old Flemish polyphonic tradition persisted longer than anywhere else, though its musical and devotional bedrock had by now been replaced by sturdy vernacular hymns, created a century and half previously during the Protestant Reformation. Beginning with Heinrich Schütz, this old tradition entered into a fascinating alliance with new Italian idioms, and (from the late seventeenth century) with French traditions of highly ornamented melody and of dance. These three elements could be artfully juxtaposed (as in the music of Telemann), but the idea that they could be fused into a profound synthesis seems on the face of it impossible. It is a large part of the genius of Johann Sebastian Bach (1685–1750) – by common consent the greatest figure in Western classical music before the Classical era – that he achieved it. In his church cantata 'Wachet Auf', written to accompany the German protestant form of Sunday Eucharist (one of several hundred such cantatas), the stately formality of the French overture, a German hymn tune (or chorale) and a busy Italianate concerto texture are all woven together.

We are now more than a century into the era of the Common Practice, and so well within the familiar territory of 'Western classical music'. Corelli, Vivaldi, Handel and Bach are all staples of Western concert life, and part of the reason is that in their music tonal harmony, that peculiarly Western invention, finally shines forth in perfect lucidity.

A full description of tonal harmony is beyond the scope of this chapter, but a metaphor can point to its essence. If you had to picture a piece of Renaissance counterpoint, it would be as a procession of lines. As they unfold these lines inevitably create simultaneous sounds – chords, in common parlance. The range of permitted chords was small, consisting mostly of euphonious (consonant) intervals. Dissonances between the parts were allowed only in strictly controlled circumstances. The new harmonic conception of music which emerged from 1600 onwards is best pictured as a series of pillars between which garlands of melody are strung. Rather than being a by-product of linear movement, these pillars – the chords – are now the governing factor. Take the famous Bach slow movement known as the 'Air on a G String', from his Orchestral Suite in D major. The long note with which the first phrase of the famous melody begins makes no sense without the procession of five different harmonies beneath. These chords are not simply a series of euphonious vertical combinations. They form a dynamic progression over a descending bass line, which carries us irresistibly onwards from the 'home chord' (the so-called tonic chord of the movement's key), towards a new but related chord, then another and another, before the phrase comes temporarily to rest over a chord several steps away from the first.

Compared to this essentially dynamic harmonic movement, Renaissance polyphony seems to move in circles, and it is this more than anything that makes it seem antique to modern ears. This change marked the ending of the old modal system, in favour of just two sorts of scale, the diatonic major and minor. The reason these scales emerged triumphant is that they embody within themselves

An autograph manuscript of the Adagio of Johann Sebastian Bach's 1720 Sonata in G minor for solo violin (BWV 1001), showing the composer's characteristically undulating calligraphy

Debate will probably go on for ever as to whether the boy standing at the keyboard is Mozart, but much else can be gleaned from this pen-and-ink depiction of an orchestra by an unknown artist around 1770. It reflects the number of musicians who shared the same music stand, how the bass was scored, how the bow was held, how many types of instrument were used, and in what groupings. It is now owned by the Salzburg Mozarteum Foundation.

the dynamism and hierarchies of this new tonal universe. Play any major scale from the first note (the tonic) and you can feel how the fifth note has a sense of being an opposite pole of attraction and stability, the moon to the tonic's sun. This mirrors the fact that in tonal harmony, the basic movement is from a chord based on the tonic to the chord based on the fifth, or dominant (it is this movement that is traced out, via a brief visit to the fourth, by the long opening arch of 'Air on a G String'). Note also how the seventh note leads irresistibly to the eighth or 'top note' (which is the tonic again), a tendency reflected in its name: leading-note.

■ Music in the market-place

As the eighteenth century progressed, the social framework of music-making began to take on a more familiar cast. The secular sphere had burgeoned enormously, to the extent that church music was now ceding pride of place. And within the secular sphere, 'elite' music – that is to say, cultivated or 'art' music, as distinct from vernacular music – was no longer the province of the top layer of society. It was open to anyone with money and the requisite 'cultural competence'. A genuine market for music had emerged, and spaces for music where the aristocracy and the rising middle classes could mingle. The first commercial opera house had opened in Venice in 1637. Concerts began to take place in London in the late seventeenth century, but these were small affairs in taverns. In the eighteenth century we see the beginnings of large-scale concerts on something like a modern pattern, involving advertisements in newspapers and subscription schemes. Georg Telemann, the composer and friend of Bach, created the first subscription series in Germany, in 1723, with Paris following two years later. In go-ahead mercantile London, George Frideric Handel (1685–1759), a German emigré who arrived in England via Italy, became the earliest great composer to live largely as an entrepreneur, risking his own money on seasons of Italian opera and English oratorio. The church's monopoly on the teaching of music through its choir schools was challenged from the mid-sixteenth century by the famous orphanages, convents and other charitable institutions of Italian cities. These *conservatorios* offered musical training for free to the children in their charge, but started to admit fee-paying students as their musical standards rose.

Last, but hardly least, elite music was starting to acquire a keen awareness of its own past. Until the mid-eighteenth century, the 'latest thing' was the only kind of music anyone was interested in. But the spread of the Classical style in architecture, combined with Enlightenment ideas of a universal, rational human nature, gave rise to the idea that music could itself take on the virtues of 'classicism', thus making it immune to fashion. The Austrian Baron von Swieten had a taste for Bach's music long after it had dropped out of fashion, and passed on his enthusiasm to Wolfgang Amadeus Mozart (1756–91). Another symptom of this classicising trend was the founding in London in 1726 of a concert-promoting body known as the Academy of Ancient Music, where the rule was that no work less than twenty years old could be played.

The liberation of elite music from its traditional social function was one essential emancipation. Another was its liberation from the guiding presence of the word. No less an authority than Plato had deemed that words were a constituent part of any music that deserved the name. This ancient prejudice had been massively reinforced both in the church – where music existed only to glorify the liturgy – and by the huge dominance of opera. The contempt for purely instrumental music ran deep in Western culture, as the scorn directed towards 'fiddlers' attests. Lord Chesterfield, in a 1749 letter to his son advising on the behaviour appropriate to a gentleman, wrote, 'If you love music, hear it ... but I insist upon your neither piping nor fiddling yourself. It puts a gentleman in a very frivolous, contemptible light; brings him into a great deal of bad company; and takes up a great deal of time, which might be much better employed.'[4]

In the late eighteenth century an extraordinary change occurred, which elevated instrumental music to a level not just equal to vocal music, but actually above it. Previously, the difficulty of specifying what instrumental music 'meant' had been a stumbling block to its acceptance. Now that became its glory. Unburdened by words, music could penetrate into areas of the spiritual realm where mere words stumble and fail. As Mendelssohn later remarked, the problem wasn't that the feelings in music were too vague to be described in words; they were too precise.

As if in response to this new ideology, a new form of instrumental music arose in the last quarter of the eighteenth century. Instead of the smooth *moto perpetuo* continuities of the Baroque concerto, this new sort was nervously articulated. The first great master of this style – indeed the inventor of it – was Joseph Haydn (1732–1809). His string quartet Op. 33 no. 1 of 1781 begins with a quiet two-bar phrase which seems to outline D major, but which tips at the last minute towards B minor. The tension this creates is screwed higher by an answering phrase, which seems to insist on B minor but at the last minute swerves away on a weak beat to an unexpected harmony. Then comes a silence, followed by what we think may be a 'rounding-off' phrase. But no; it leads back to that strangely tense answering phrase, which we now realise is no 'answer' at all. Only in bar 11 is the key of B minor firmly established, but soon the silences and hesitations return.

This quartet is a striking early example of what would become labelled as the Classical style, which arose out of the dying embers of the Baroque in the 1760s and eventually gave way to new Romantic forms in the 1820s. Its hallmarks are directional momentum, dramatic contrast – even discontinuity – and textural variety. Horizontally, the music is made of different kinds of activity all happening at once. Listen to the slow introduction to Mozart's great E♭ major Symphony (no. 39, K543), at the point where the long bass B♭ begins. While that persists the middle parts sustain long lines, the flute has a countermelody moving relatively fast, and the violins exchange little phrases in very rapid notes. This layering of activity is visible on the page, even to someone who does not read music. The parts of a Baroque piece tend to be much more similar to each other. Vertically the music is also discontinuous, as we saw in the Haydn quartet. It stops and starts, and is full of unexpected loud outbursts (as in Haydn's famous 'Surprise' symphony) or indeed sudden soft moments, which can be just as startling.

This new dynamic had a profound effect on musical form. Until now, form had either been parasitic on something else such as the form of a text, whether sacred or secular, or the patterned steps of dance, or on something architectural, as in the stately repetitions and symmetries of the Baroque concerto. Now musical form became psychological, something best described in terms of a drama or narrative. The best known of these musical dramas was 'sonata form'. Here the narrative begins with an assertion of identities: the principal theme or themes, and the home key. The themes suffer all kinds of dramatic vicissitudes, in the process leaving the home key far behind, and return in the home key towards the end of the movement, triumphantly unscathed yet mysteriously enriched. Notice that a symmetrical conception (basically ABA) survives in this scenario – a reminder that musical evolution is a matter of grafting new things onto old, rather than wholesale revolution.

The effect of all this is to mobilise the listener's mental powers in a new way. The reigning aesthetic dogma of Bach's time said 'only one emotion within a given movement', which ties in nicely with the music's continuous texture. But the new era of 'sentiment' and 'feeling' that emerged in the late eighteenth century – symbolised by the immense popularity of novels like Sterne's *Sentimental Journey Through France and Italy* (1768) – needed something more exciting and changeable. Music of the Classical era is dramatic in its essence, and it's no surprise to discover that one of the sources of the new style was comic opera, which began in Italy in the late seventeenth century and reached its peak in the 1780s with the works which Mozart created with the writer Lorenzo da Ponte. Surprise and quick nervous movements of thought and emotion could not be allowed into serious opera, as it would compromise the dignity of the heroic and mythological characters that peopled it. But in the *opere buffe* of Mozart we have servants getting the better of their masters, and women outwitting their husbands. These situations lead to all kinds of shocking revelations, artful fibbing and absurd pratfalls, on which the music gleefully seizes.

All these subversive happenings on the operatic stage were symptoms of upheavals in the world at large. Mozart's *Così fan tutte* was premiered in Vienna in 1790, the year after the French Revolution erupted, when the streets of the city were swarming with informers and secret police, determined to make sure the bacillus of revolution did not spread to Vienna (their efforts to keep history at bay were not successful for long – in 1805 Napoleon's troops invaded the city). The threat to the power of the established order did not just come from the angry mob; it came also from the rising middle class, whose growing economic power would soon oust the aristocracy as the main source of patronage for composers.

The change can be seen in the lives of the three great Classical composers, most strikingly in the one who lived longest, Joseph Haydn. Most of his career was spent as a liveried servant to a great Hungarian aristocrat, in modest quarters above the stables. By the 1790s he had become a freelance musician, playing publishers off against one another, and making two extended visits to

Above: Niccolò Paganini (1782–1840) playing the violin, in a portrait monogrammed 'JG', 'JC', or 'TC'; pencil on cream paper with a little ink

Above right: The left hand of Yehudi Menuhin (1916–99); black and white photograph by Lotte Meitner-Graf, London

Right: The Russian violinist Viktoria Mullova (b. 1959)

London, where he was lionised by smart society. Mozart too became a freelancer, but struggled in the commercially less advanced city of Vienna. With Ludwig van Beethoven (1770–1827), the growing economic independence of the creative artist was allied to something new, which Haydn and Mozart would have found incomprehensible. This was the idea of the artist as Romantic seer, someone who scorned proprieties, refused to bend the knee to established power and lived a life entirely according to the dictates of his genius. Beethoven, with his determination to 'take fate by the throat,' fits the image perfectly – indeed he to a large extent created it. Even his deafness seems the perfect Romantic attribute, as it symbolises his remoteness from ordinary life.

However in many ways Beethoven was an Enlightenment figure more than a Romantic one. His sole opera *Fidelio* celebrates the triumph of liberty and light over darkness and despotic power, in a manner not so different to the numerous 'rescue' operas inspired by the French Revolution. He liked to quote the sources for Kant's sense of the sublime in the universe: 'the starry heavens above me, the moral law within me'.[5] As for his music, it embodies a sense of ethical striving unmatched before or since. The blazing C major of the finale of the Fifth Symphony is like a purely instrumental version of the ending of *Fidelio*. And yet the musical language Beethoven employed was in its essentials the same as that of Haydn and Mozart. It relied on the same tonal dynamics, in which sharply articulated phrases dramatised and made real an underlying tonal tension. The difference was that Beethoven enormously expanded the range and power of these tensions, without shattering the structure on which they depended.

Take the Appassionata Sonata, composed in 1804–5, when Beethoven was in his mid-30s. We hear a phrase full of dark foreboding, which moves – just as a Mozart opening phrase would – from the tonic chord of F minor to the so-called 'dominant', C major. The huge arch of the phrase, and the articulating silence that follows it, have already charged the air with electricity. Then we hear the same phrase in the startlingly remote tonal centre of G♭. Mystery and awe are now added to drama, in a move that neither Mozart nor Haydn would have attempted. It will take the rest of the movement, in all its stormy grandeur, to resolve that tension.

■ Music as inner life

The creation and resolution of huge tonal tensions is a defining feature of the Classical style. Having risen to a peak in Beethoven, it vanished quite quickly in the Romantic era. Already in the music of the following generation – Weber, Chopin, Schumann – we find a different, much looser conception of tonality. The ethical fervour of Beethoven ebbs away, and in its place we find a quite different world of feeling, more picturesque, more wayward, more inclined to give way to dreams and digressions. Poised on the cusp between the two eras was the tragically short-lived Franz Schubert (1797–1828). In Schubert's later works, Beethoven's sonata procedures are relaxed to release a haunting new sense of tonal and emotional ambiguity.

These changes were in part a result of the change in the composer's status we've already observed, from being the humble servant of established political order to the proudly independent freelancer. This change was bound to be slow. The Polish pianist-composer Fryderyk Chopin (1810–49), who settled permanently in Paris after the Warsaw uprising of 1830, still relied hugely on the generous patronage of aristocrats. Franz Liszt (1811–86) married an aristocrat, and in 1848 became director of music at the Ducal Court in Weimar, a curiously old-fashioned move for this paragon of fiery Romantic individualism. But the appearance of continuity with old forms of aristocratic patronage is deceptive. Chopin was the honoured guest of the Parisian aristocrats, not their servant, and he was liable to simply leave the salon, or refuse to play the piano, if the mood took him. Liszt sorely tried the patience of the Duke of Weimar by spending vast amounts of his money on productions of operas by Richard

Wagner (1813–83), whose music the Duke couldn't bear. And Wagner, in turn, annoyed his long-tern patron King Ludwig of Bavaria by his arrogance and extravagance.

In earlier times these transgressions would have led to instant dismissal. But now composers were regarded as possessors of a special life-enhancing quality known as genius, which shed a bright light on a society that was growing increasingly mundane. During the nineteenth century life in Europe and America was increasingly subject to what the sociologist Max Weber called 'the iron cage of rationality'.[6] As the grip of custom and the Church weakened, and the cities swelled under the pressure of mass migration from the countryside, so governments had to resort to more rational, bureaucratic methods of control. At the same time industry was transformed by new technologies and a rational division of labour.

The process of rationalisation and standardisation was seen in music too, in such things as the standardisation of tuning and pitch, and the mass production of pianos for domestic music-making. The orchestra, which had settled into something like its modern form by the mid-nineteenth century, was a perfect example of the new, modern 'division of labour'. The players were defined purely by a single specialist function such as 'violinist' or 'bassoonist', as opposed to the all-round musicianship required of court musicians in earlier centuries. They were controlled by a conductor whose increasing eminence mirrored the rise in importance of the literary critic. No mere time-keeper, he was a creator in his own right, offering a personal interpretation of the music he directed.

This new notion of the performer as 'interpreter' reflected the fact that music was now a haven where subjectivity and 'feelings' could flourish. Sometimes these feelings were purely subjective, focused on the swirling inner life of an imaginary protagonist. In the *Symphonie fantastique* by Hector Berlioz (1803–69), which was premiered in 1830, just three years after the death of Beethoven, the music portrays a tormented soul who pursues his beloved (or to put it better, is pursued by the thought of his beloved) through a series of picturesque scenes – a ballroom, a field on a mountainside, at an execution and a witches' Sabbath. These feelings could be expressed on an intimate scale too. In the songs and piano pieces of Robert Schumann (1810–56) the scene is more often the domestic hearth, but the feelings are no less powerful. In *Frauenliebe und -leben* of 1840 the music portrays a love-affair through a woman's eyes. The fluttering excitement of love's beginnings, the contented bliss of motherhood, the anger and bleak sorrow of bereavement are all portrayed with heart-stopping power.

Clearly a different world of feeling was emerging, one suited to the notion of listeners sitting in silence in order to be 'lost' in a private world. To create it music had to call on the other arts, particularly literature and painting. Berlioz was a trailblazer in this regard. He was a friend of the French Romantic artist Delacroix, and he was fond of declaring that his two great inspirations were Shakespeare and Virgil. Franz Liszt read avidly in French Romantic poetry, and many of his piano works were inspired by writers such as Senancourt. The ballades of Chopin were not inspired by a particular writer, but it's impossible to understand these works without hearing them as disguised narratives in music. Take the second Ballade, of 1839. It begins with a gentle nostalgic introduction, which suggests 'Once upon a time, long ago'. This is roughly torn aside by furiously agitated music, in a way that suggests we are now being plunged into a dramatic story. As with these other arts, music now felt emboldened to explore worlds of feeling which had previously been thought of as repellent, dangerous or simply beneath the dignity of art. The most striking one is the diabolical. Liszt was fond of it, as well-known pieces such as the *Mephisto Waltzes* show; Berlioz evoked it in his *Symphonie fantastique*, and it's a recurrent presence in Romantic opera from Weber to Verdi and Wagner.

All this suggests a kind of music designed to carry the listener away to an imaginary realm. To do this, music required new technical means. Painting vivid scenes requires a large palette, and it's no accident that during the mid- and late nineteenth century the orchestra expanded enormously. Beethoven had already added piccolo and trombones in his later symphonies, but his orchestra seems modest compared to the vast orchestras required by Wagner, Mahler and Richard Strauss. The increased size is not primarily a matter of adding new colours, though there were plenty of these (chromatic harp, tuba, bass clarinet and cor anglais are among the most prominent). It's more to do with giving the composer the means to create artful transitions from one kind of sound to another. This was especially important to Wagner, who said that it was the discovery of 'the beautiful necessity of transition' which opened the door to the mature style of his music-dramas.

The increased size of the nineteenth-century orchestra went hand in hand with the vastly increased harmonic palette of Romantic music (though it should be said that not all nineteenth-century music was gargantuan; the suggestive piano miniature was equally typical). Music of the preceding Classical era was animated by the dramatic tension between the home key and one or two closely related key centres. Romantic music dissolved these tensions, along with the articulated, balanced phrase structure that animated them. In their place we find a more continuous texture, where the melodies, instead of falling into neat phrases, burgeon in waves towards a high point of expressivity (the so-called *idée fixe* from Berlioz's *Symphonie fantastique* is the classic example). The harmony that underpins this new sort of melody tends to move quickly away from the home key, usually towards a remote key. These moves produce an expressive effect which is profoundly different from the tense, dynamic, goal-directed music of the Classical era, being marked by intense inwardness, nostalgia and a sense of indefinable yearning.

This talk of yearning and rising to climaxes points to the erotic quality of Romantic harmony, a quality pushed to its extreme in Wagner's opera *Tristan und Isolde*, premiered in 1865. The subject here is the all-consuming quality of erotic passion which can only find release in death, and Wagner's language mirrors that quality precisely in its refusal ever to come to a harmonic full-stop. All Romantic composers were keen to weaken the power of the cadence, that familiar harmonic movement which marks the end of a phrase or paragraph, which had been a defining characteristic of music since Baroque times. But no one before Wagner had succeeded in creating a texture in which cadences are avoided for minutes at a stretch.

All this suggests that Western classical music in the Romantic era derived its meaning entirely as an assertion of personal feeling in the face of society – which is tantamount to saying it was a huge exercise in escapism. But Wagner's *Tristan* is hardly typical of all nineteenth-century music. One vast social force with which classical music engaged fully was the effort of many nineteenth-century societies to forge a new, specifically national identity, and Wagner himself was caught up in this. His *Die Meistersinger von Nürnberg* formed part of the wave of German nationalism that led to the creation of the German Reich in 1871. All over Europe a burgeoning national awareness was reflected and given focus by composers, from Dvořák in Bohemia to Sibelius in Finland.

Notice that whatever theme in nineteenth-century culture one turns to, Wagner's name appears. Wagner is the great incommensurable figure of Western music, because his influence went so far beyond music. He is one of those giant nineteenth-century figures like Marx or Darwin who dominated the cultural and intellectual climate, not just in their own time but for decades afterwards. Only Johannes Brahms (1833–97) had the imaginative power to frame a completely opposing view of music. While Wagner dreamed of 'The Art-Work of the Future' Brahms looked back, forging a mighty yet deeply nostalgic synthesis of Baroque, Classical and even Renaissance procedures. Brahms and a few other conservatives aside, the entire musical world fell under Wagner's spell, and those later figures that fought him off – like Debussy, Sibelius and Stravinsky – acknowledged his power by the force of their rejection. Although almost all Wagner's output was for the operatic stage – whose practices he revolutionised – his concept of musical theatre necessitated a profound transformation of music's expressive means. A history of Western classical music that leaves aside such a giant figure as Giuseppe Verdi (1813–1901) – the great master of Italian Romantic opera and Wagner's great antipode – is justified on the grounds that he made no great transformation of the musical language as such. But a history of Western music without Wagner is inconceivable.

■ *Things fall apart*

The surge of national consciousness in the nineteenth century naturally brought in its wake new musical colours. We speak of the Russian strain in Musorgsky, the Bohemian colour in Dvořák. This inevitably weakened the sense that classical music had to obey norms of excellence defined at the 'centre' – the centre being the German speaking lands that nurtured the great canonical composers of classical music, from Bach to Brahms. This sense that 'the centre cannot hold', to quote Yeats's famous line, was mirrored in the fabric of music itself. The governing power of tonality was weakened both by the wayward, wandering chromaticism of Romantic music epitomised by Wagner, and by the exotic and folklore elements brought in by the nationalists.

This tendency to fragmentation accelerated enormously as the nineteenth century gave way to the twentieth. The settled, orderly language of classical music, handed down in conservatories, fixed in textbooks of harmony and counterpoint, was now assailed on all sides. One of these disintegrating factors was the lure of the exotic, which was now brought to people's doorstep thanks to improved travel and communications and the spread of European empires (the same vast historical forces carried Western classical music overseas, to the Americas, India and to Japan, where it was enthusiastically embraced). Spain is hardly seen as exotic now, but it certainly was in the nineteenth century, and French composers in particular strove to capture the intoxicating vitality of its indigenous song and dance music. Bizet's opera *Carmen* (1875) was the trailblazer, followed by Chabrier's *España* and later still by Ravel's *Rapsodie espagnole*. By the early twentieth century composers were looking further afield. Claude Debussy (1862–1918) attended the Paris Exposition Universelle in 1889 and was astounded by the subtlety of the Javanese gamelan orchestra. 'Javanese music is based on a kind of counterpoint by comparison with which that of Palestrina is child's play', he later wrote.[7] In Debussy's piano piece 'Pagodes', published in 1903 as part of the set known as *Estampes*, one hears unusual effects of rhythmic layering and tempo fluctuations, wrapped within an exotic-sounding harmonic stasis and gong-like resonances. As the pianist and French music scholar Roy Howat says, these 'make little sense by Western norms but fall into place when treated as gamelan gestures'.[8]

Mingled with the lure of the exotic was a fascination with the ancient and the primitive, which reflected a general sense that European civilisation was tired and needed to be put back in touch with the *élan vital* (the vital force, to use the phrase of the most fashionable philosopher of the time, Henri Bergson). In Russia this took the form of a search for the ancient pre-Christian Slavic soul. The young Igor Stravinsky (1882–1971) briefly fell under the spell of this movement, and the result was his ballet *The Rite of Spring*, premiered by the Ballets Russes in Paris in 1913.

The ballet caused one of the most famous scandals in the history of the arts, though it's now acknowledged that the dance rather than the music was the principle cause of offence. Although it begins with a sinuous melody borrowed from a Lithuanian source, the music on the whole eschews melody. Instead there are brusque little melodic fragments, repeated with tiny variations like the musical equivalent of shamanic incantation. Instead of artful transitions and modulations, the music simply leaps from one tempo and texture to another, without warning. Most offensive of all is the sheer brute energy of the piece, hurling grindingly dissonant harmonies at the listener in propulsively irregular rhythms.

Perceptive observers at that premiere noted that the music's primitivism was rooted in its mechanistic, unfeeling quality. Primitivism and 'machine music' were indeed not so far apart, as the numerous twentieth-century pieces evoking sounds of urban life eloquently demonstrate. Urban sounds began to appear everywhere in music. Usually these were metaphorically evoked by the orchestra, but the French composer Edgard Varèse (1883–1965) – inspired by the trains and river-boats and factories of New York – actually incorporated sirens and whistles in his trail-blazing scores from 1920s such as *Intégrales* (this was a first step in the 'emancipation of noise' that would eventually lead to electronic music). In 1918 came another invasion of something primitive, but also excitingly modern: jazz. That was the year James Reese Europe's big band visited Europe, followed a year later by the Original Dixieland Jazz Band. Ragtime and jazz left its mark on many composers, from Stravinsky and Milhaud in Paris to Kurt Weill in Berlin.

Many composers, particularly in Austro-German lands, rejected primitivism entirely. But in the music of these composers one hears something equally disturbing, namely an irruption into 'civilised' musical discourse of disturbed mental states. The expressionist works of Arnold Schoenberg (1874–1951) deal in states of obsession, nightmare and hallucination, and therefore the musical fabric has to mirror the irrationality of these states. His monodrama *Erwartung* ('Expectation'), which describes the distressed state of mind of a woman searching for the body of her lover in a forest, is famously resistant to musical analysis. The music pours forth in a flittering phantasmagoria of fragmentary motifs, nervous tics and sudden shrieks. The apparent lack of continuity and the tendency to dream-like states was also characteristic of the new art-form which would become the dominant art-form of the century: cinema.

All this meant that the orderly tonal system that had governed Western classical music for around three centuries was seriously weakened. Some say that the Common Practice era was already over by 1900. Others point to the continuing loyalty of many composers to tonal ways of thinking up to the Second World War and beyond. Richard Strauss (1864–1949) is the exemplar of these latter-day Romantics, and his *Metamorphosen* for solo strings, composed in 1946, is an obsequy both for a Germany ruined by Nazism and for the collapse of the old musical certainties.

Wherever the arguments about the date, most agree that the Common Practice era did indeed come to an end. But this doesn't mean that Western classical music came to an end. The accumulated body of works composed within the practice still existed, from Bach to Strauss and Elgar, and people continued to enjoy them, as they do to this day (and an increasing number enjoy Renaissance and medieval music too). It is a striking fact about the tradition that many of its devotees are sustained entirely by this inherited treasure: they feel no need to inquire into what living composers are doing. Indeed, within the public at large there is a perception that classical music came to a dead stop decades or even a century ago. Nonetheless new works aspiring to the status of classical music continue to appear, created by people who call themselves composers and feel a kinship with the great composers of the past. How can this be, when the rules underpinning the great tradition of classical music seem to have dissolved away?

The answer is that classical music now defines itself not by a sophisticated syntax that binds its notes together, nor by the use of inherited forms like the symphony, nor by inherited media like the orchestra. These days the defining feature is much more nebulous, and is best described as an alliance of a subjective attitude and an institutional framework. This subjective attitude is one of willed seriousness. A classical composer now does not necessarily want to entertain; he or she is more likely to want to create something that poses a challenge and an adventure to the listener. This aim requires the existence of an institutional framework that is at least partially free of the marketplace, and because the governing elites of Western societies accept (with varying degrees of enthusiasm) that art is a good thing, this framework does exist. In the USA the state's role in providing it is vastly outweighed by private patronage, while in Europe the reverse is true. This framework takes the form of subsidised concert venues, performing ensembles and public-service broadcasting companies, plus specialist educational institutions such as conservatories.

The new 'classical music' created within this framework is of many kinds. It may be knottily intellectual, as in the case of those many composers, beginning with Schoenberg, who created rigorous new methods for composing to replace the now-defunct rules of the old Common Practice. It may erect anarchy and chance into ruling principles, as in the music (or perhaps one should call it 'anti-music') of John Cage (1912–92) and his followers. It may return to the expressive tonal vocabulary of the past, sometimes in conjunction with the repetitive patterning of so-called minimalist composers such as Philip Glass and Steve Reich. It may make use of pop or world music idioms or use digital technology, or even all these things at once. The musical works that result are termed classical because they turn their back on popular acclaim and make a self-conscious appeal to a small select public.

This small select public is now defined by education, rather than privilege and power as it was in previous times. Nonetheless, the idea that classical music might be exclusive in any way is an embarrassment for some people. They want to stress classical music's increasingly democratic character in recent times, pointing to such things as the populist music of the French composers of the 1920s, the social-realist Soviet symphonists of the 1930s, and Aaron Copland's engagement with American folk music in his ballets. Nowadays some classical composers go even further in their desire to appear egalitarian, mingling drum and bass beats into their own idiom with knowing sophistication. But these examples only highlight classical music's inherent loftiness. It stoops down to the demotic, in order to raise it up. In that sense, classical music is now what it always has been; music of, and usually for, an elite.

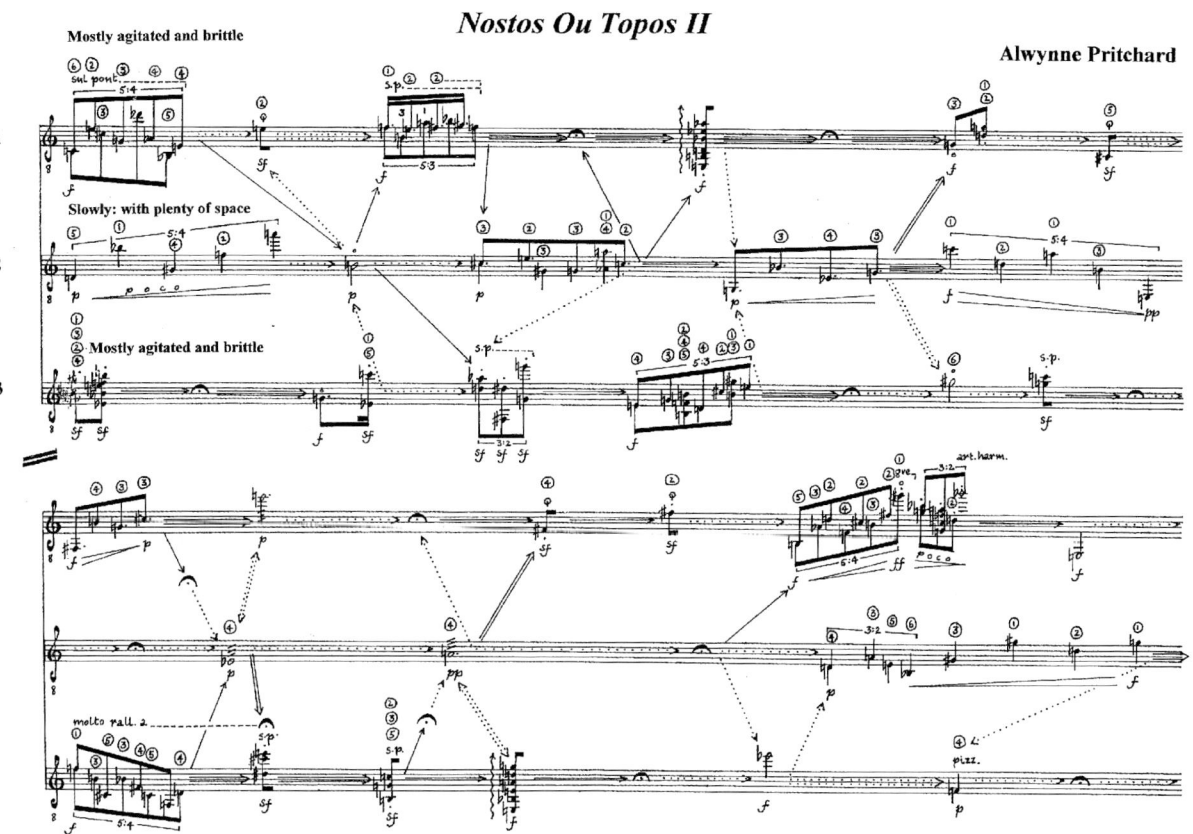

EX. 10.1 An excerpt from *Nostos ou Topos* II, composed for solo guitar in 1999 by the British composer Alwynne Pritchard, © by Verlag Neue Musik, Berlin. The piece is an example of a 'mobile' form, an invention of post-Second World War modernism. This gives the performer some freedom to determine the order of events. The piece is in three movements which are printed concurrently, one above the other. Pritchard encourages the player to make 'frequent but brief excursions' into adjacent movements, with the arrows indicating the direction and speed of these excursions. The impression should be of three movements of distinct character, each with fleeting memories or anticipations of its neighbour.

Further reading

The bibliography of Western classical music is vast. The music has been a field of scholarly research and intellectual speculation for centuries, as well as an art form with wide appeal, so the books that describe it range from amusing pot-boilers to abstruse scholarly tomes. In between are the books which readers of this one might actually find useful, and a few are listed in the Bibliography. Some, like those by Howard Goodall (*The Story of Music*) and John Powell (*How Music Works*), are entry-level books, breezy in tone, but still offering basic historical and technical guidelines. At the other end of the scale are classics of intellectual history, which situate music within culture as a whole (Max Weber's *The Rational and Social Foundations of Music*). Some books offer close readings of individual works (Donald Tovey's *Essays in Musical Analysis*) or descriptions of music's technical apparatus (Powell's *How Music Works*).

In terms of historical surveys, the most impressive is Richard Taruskin's *Oxford History of Western Music*, in five magisterial volumes – though its later volumes have been criticised as pushing an anti-modernist agenda of his own. This is now available in an abbreviated 'College Edition' in one volume, co-authored by Taruskin and Christopher Gibbs. Of the numerous one-volume dictionary-format guides to Western classical music, the *Oxford Companion to Music* and *Harvard Dictionary of Music* are the most authoritative.

There are also innumerable critical appraisals of individual composers. The traditional format is a 'life and works', that is, a discussion of the music interwoven with a biography; two from a field of thousands are detailed below.

Another sub-genre is the survey of a style or genre. Cambridge University Press has a long-running series examining a single topic, under the generic title of The Cambridge Companions to Music. There are now sixty-four titles, ranging from genres like the Symphony to individuals from Bach to the Beatles (see www.cambridge.org/aus/series). Turning to individual publications, Tess Knighton and David Fallows's *Companion to Medieval and Renaissance Music* is the best survey of its eras. Manfred Bukofzer's survey of Baroque music (*Music in the Baroque Era*) is dated in some ways, but still hugely authoritative. No introduction to the Classical era beats Charles Rosen's *The Classical Style*, while Carl Dahlhaus's survey of nineteenth-century music is intellectually acute and wide-ranging. Among surveys of modern music, Paul Griffiths's *Modern Music and After* has a modernist focus on the intricate workings of contemporary music. Alex Ross's *The Rest is Noise* takes the opposite perspective, showing how the strange idioms of new music make most sense when seen in their cultural and historical context.

Recommended listening

Josquin des Prez, *Missa Pange Lingua, Missa La sol fa re mi*, The Tallis Scholars, dir. Peter Phillips, Gimmell CDGIM009, 1987. Two mass settings showing the late fifteenth-century Flemish contrapuntal style at its absolute peak.

Claudio Monteverdi, *Lamento d'Arianna, Madrigals Book 7–8*, Soloists & Concerto Vocale, dir. René Jacobs, HMA1951129, 2007. A key moment in the emergence of the new, operatically expressive Baroque style.

Johann Sebastian Bach, *Brandenburg Concertos*, Concerto Italiano, dir. Rinaldo Alessandrini, Naïve NC 40030, 2005. The greatest of all Baroque *concerti grossi*.

Joseph Haydn, *String Quartets Op. 33*, Quatuor Mosaïques, Naïve E8801, 2000. Terse drama, wit and lyricism meet in these masterpieces of the classical style.

Ludwig van Beethoven, *Symphony No. 9*, Soloists, London Philharmonic Orchestra & LPO Chorus, cond. Klaus Tennstedt, LPO Live 0026, 2007. The symphony that broke the mould and inspired numerous later symphonists, from Berlioz to Mahler.

Robert Schumann, *Dichterliebe, Belsatzar* (etc.), Christopher Maltman, baritone and Graham Johnson, piano, Hyperion CDJ33105, 2001. Schumann's song-cycle catches the essence of the romantic spirit in music.

Claude Debussy *Prélude à l'après-midi d'un faune, La Mer* (etc.), Berlin Philharmonic Orchestra, cond. Sir Simon Rattle, EMI 558045-2, 2005. Debussy's *L'Après-midi d'un faune* threw open the door to modern music.

Igor Stravinsky, *The Rite of Spring, Firebird Suite*, Orchestre du Capitole du Toulouse, cond. Tugan Sokhiev, Naïve V5192, 2013. To some *The Rite of Spring* was a brutal assault on music, to others a liberation.

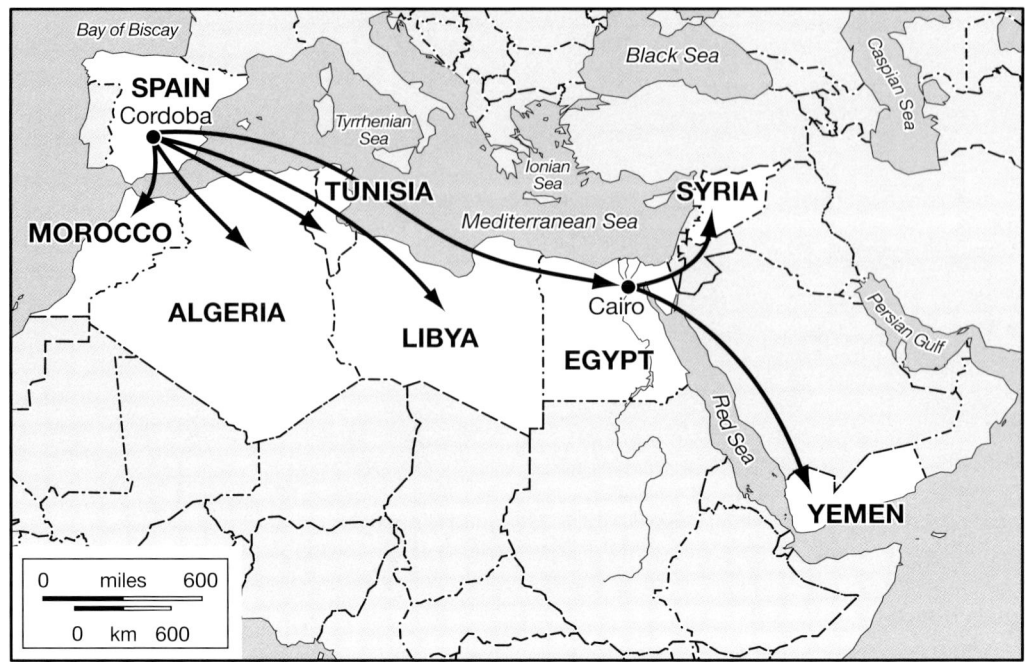

The emergence of the Arabic muwashshah song-form, with its elaborate rhyme-schemes but easy-to-memorise melodies, marked the beginning of a distinctively Andalusian tradition. This map shows its geographical spread in the twelfth and thirteenth centuries.

11 North Africa and the Eastern Mediterranean: Andalusian Music

Dwight F. Reynolds

A dozen men are seated in a semicircle, identically dressed in long-sleeved, loose-fitting white robes, red fez hats with black tassels and pointed, open-heeled slippers of yellow leather. Some have violins or violas balanced vertically on their knees, others have lutes; one plays a goblet drum resting on his left thigh, another a tambourine; the lead singer has no instrument. They begin with an instrumental prelude with no discernible rhythm, seeming to feel their way forward through the melody. When the drum enters, the orchestra seizes the steady beat and launches into a substantial overture. The musicians are all playing the same melody, but ornamenting it in slightly different ways, giving a rich, complex texture. After this introduction they become a chorus as well as an orchestra, with the players singing in unison; the leader sings along and occasionally leaps up an octave or a fifth so that his voice pierces through the choral and instrumental background. They perform a sequence of songs, each with a similar structure, all in the same rhythm and melodic mode so that they fit together almost seamlessly. Suddenly there is a break for a solo improvisation on different instruments, after which the leader sings a highly ornamented solo, climbing so high that his voice seems in danger of cracking with the strain. The group then launches into another series of songs, the rhythm getting gradually faster, with the final one ending amid applause and ululations from the audience.

THE scene described would be typical of a performance in Morocco, but similar music can be heard in many other parts of the Arab world: from Sufi Brotherhoods where musicians and listeners sit cross-legged on the floor, to the Cairo Opera House where male musicians wear black-tie and tuxedos and the women floor-length, brightly coloured gowns, to gatherings of Sephardic Jews in Israel where the same melodies are sung to Hebrew lyrics. In modern times this tradition is most often referred to as 'Andalusian Music' – that is, the music that originated in medieval Muslim (or 'Moorish') Spain, known as *al-Andalus* in Arabic. Outsiders sometimes assume that this music has been passed down unchanged from medieval Muslim Spain to the present, but that is not true; it has for many centuries been a living, changing musical repertory, with most of the pieces now performed having been composed in later periods and in other places, but always in the Andalusian style.

In Arabic, the term 'Andalusian music' – *al-mūsīqā al-andalusiyya* – is understood to mean not that all of it comes from medieval al-Andalus, but rather that it is composed within the genres, themes and style first established there. Indeed, composers and poets who have added to the repertory over the centuries have cleaved so closely to these models that we cannot today easily distinguish a piece of Andalusian music that is only a few decades old from one that dates back centuries. But though this tradition does not possess clear historical periods, it does have different regional performance traditions. Composers through the centuries have always striven to add to the repertory while retaining the basic style; for those wanting to compose something new and distinctive, there were many other genres they could turn to. 'Andalusian music' is therefore a useful term to denote a distinctive repertory and style of Arab music, one that has its origins a thousand years ago in medieval Iberia, but which continues to be learned, performed and enjoyed in many parts of the modern Arab world. In some Middle Eastern countries today it forms a vital component of regional and national identity.

■ History

With the rise of Islam in the seventh century and the spread of the Islamic Empire, the culture of the Arabian Peninsula was rapidly transformed into a cosmopolitan, multi-ethnic and multi-lingual entity. Within a few short decades the new Empire had expanded as far as Morocco in the West and China in the East, and although the Arabs were the social elite – in charge of both the military and the government – they originally constituted only a small percentage of the population of this vast new territory. Indeed, one of the most remarkable aspects of the early Islamic conquests is that Arab culture and the Arabic language were not swallowed up and absorbed by the older and more established civilisations that were being incorporated into this new society. Instead, new elements from other cultures were fused into that of the expanding Islamic polity, and subordinated to certain key features of Arab culture. Two of these features were the Arabic language (which soon replaced Aramaic, Coptic Egyptian, Greek, Latin and, for a while, Persian as well) and Arabic poetry, which was utterly distinct from that of all neighbouring civilisations in its use of mandatory end-rhyme (other poetic traditions had metre, but did not use rhyme except as an occasional embellishment).

In 711, almost exactly a hundred years after Muhammad first began preaching the new religion of Islam in Mecca, Muslim forces crossed the straits separating North Africa and the Iberian Peninsula and waged a campaign of conquest against the Germanic Visigoths who then ruled what is now Spain and Portugal. But this Muslim invasion was only the third of three great invasions that shaped Iberian history and culture. First the Romans had conquered Iberia, bringing with them the Latin language and Roman culture, to a great extent supplanting the indigenous cultures by colonisation campaigns that brought tens of thousands of settlers from Italy, and later Christianity as well. Following the collapse of Rome, the Peninsula was conquered and ruled by Germanic tribes. Finally Muslim forces defeated the Visigoths, bringing with them the Arabic language and the religion of Islam. Once the Muslim conquest was complete and a semblance of order had been brought to the new province, the cosmopolitan tastes of the eastern Islamic Empire soon flowed westwards, including new forms of architecture and landscaping, new varieties of plants and crops, food, clothing, etiquette, customs, poetry, music and musical instruments.

In the eastern heartland of the new empire, the first Islamic dynasty, the Umayyads, ruled from Damascus until 750 when they were abruptly overthrown by the 'Abbasid dynasty. All but one member of the Umayyad royal family were killed, but that lone surviving prince, 'Abd al-Raḥmān, fled first to Morocco (his mother was a Moroccan Berber) and then crossed over to the Peninsula and was subsequently recognised as the Emir of al-Andalus. His descendants went on to rule al-Andalus for another two and a half centuries. 'Abd al-Rahman's accession to power set in motion a cultural rivalry between the Umayyads of al-Andalus (with their capital in Cordoba) and the 'Abbasid dynasty of the eastern Islamic Empire (in their newly founded capital of Baghdad). By the ninth century there was a flourishing musical scene in Cordoba and other urban centres of al-Andalus which attracted singers from the eastern Mediterranean, the most famous of whom was the black singer from Baghdad 'Alī ibn Nāfi', nicknamed Ziryāb (blackbird).

Over the centuries Ziryab's fame has growth to mythic proportions and, for those who know only the glorified image of him that was created centuries after his death, it is a surprise to read the early accounts of his life. The oldest biographical text states that he was a black slave who travelled from Baghdad to the royal court of Tunisia, where he angered his patron and was publicly humiliated and expelled from that country. He then travelled to al-Andalus where he found favour with the Emir 'Abd al-Rahman II. The author of this account, Ibn 'Abd Rabbihi (860–940), was born in Cordoba and wrote while there were still many people alive who had actually known Ziryab and had heard him sing: his account is therefore probably the most historically accurate. An account written a generation later portrays him as a spoiled favourite; only in the eleventh century, two hundred years after his death, did a more positive version emerge, with writers giving intriguing descriptions of his music, including the claim that he added a fifth string to the lute. Oddly, he is said to have added this string in the middle of the instrument, between the second and third strings and without changing the tuning of the others, so it does not seem that it added to the instrument's range.

Whatever the historical truth, Ziryab has for centuries been considered the apogee of medieval Muslim musicianship and an icon of the golden age of Muslim Spain (ninth to twelfth centuries). His status is reflected in the following anecdote about the writer Ibn 'Abd Rabbihi:

> Ibn 'Abd Rabbihi stopped beneath the balcony of one of the notables of Cordoba where he heard beautiful singing. The women in the house sprinkled water on him to make him go away, not knowing who he was. So he went to a nearby mosque and asked to borrow a slate from the one of boys there, and wrote the following poem:

> O you who hoard the voice of the singing bird,
>   I would never have believed anyone to be capable of such avarice!
> Since even if all the ears of the world were listening,
>   Her voice would not thereby be diminished or augmented.
> Don't be mean in preventing me hearing her, shutting up a voice
>   so beautiful that it occupies the place of the soul in the body.
> If Ziryab were alive, after hearing her,
>   He would die of envy and shame!
> As for wine, I have not drunk any,
>   I come to you with but nothing but this poem in my hand.[1]

The greatest praise he could offer was that her voice surpassed that of Ziryab. When the singing-girl's owner read these verses, he invited Ibn 'Abd Rabbihi into his salon and allowed him to hear her sing.

In the era of Ziryab, the Emir and his nobles vied as patrons of a sophisticated musical tradition performed by professional singers like the one in this story. Most of the female singers were *jawārī* or *qiyān*, singing slave-girls. These were indeed slaves, in that they could be bought or sold, but they were also highly-trained performers, sometimes fetching extraordinary prices, and many living a life of luxury. The male singers, on the other hand, were mostly freemen, though their lives were frequently controlled by the whim of their patrons; both male and female singers were often of mixed, or non-Arab, background. One famous female singer in Cordoba in the early ninth century was taken prisoner as a girl during a battle between the Muslims and the Basques in northern Spain, and eventually acquired the stage-name of Qalam, which in Arabic means 'reed pen'. Here is a brief seventeenth-century account of her life:

> She was of Andalusian origin, a Christian, from among the Basque captives. As a young girl she was taken East and ended up in Medina, the city of the Prophet – Peace and God's Blessings upon him! – and there she learned the art of singing and mastered it. She was refined, clever, possessed a beautiful hand in calligraphy, was a reciter of poetry, a memoriser of historical accounts, and was knowledgeable in all genres of literature and etiquette.[2]

At that time Medina, in the Arabian Peninsula, was the most important centre for the training of musicians and singers in the Islamic world. The best performers had all been educated there, by teachers who were often themselves retired court singers.

Historical documentation tells us a lot about this courtly style, but none of the melodies have survived since notation was not commonly used: music was transmitted orally, and good singers would memorise thousands of songs. On the other hand, many of the lyrics have come down to us; they were easy to record because they were usually very short extracts (often only two to four verses) from well-known poems. Musically, the songs usually consisted of two separate sections: the first of these was relatively improvised, and the second was pre-composed and sung to a set rhythm. The vocal technique often involved a great deal of ornamentation, which only the most skilled singers could master;

NORTH AFRICA AND THE EASTERN MEDITERRANEAN

The most famous singer in Muslim Spain was 'Alī ibn Nāfi'. Nicknamed Ziryāb ('Blackbird'), he is thought to have been a dark-skinned slave who arrived in Cordoba from Baghdad, and became chief court musician to the Emir 'Abd al-Rahman II. This thirteenth-century painting, now in the Vatican library, is from a Maghrebi manuscript of *The Story of Bayâd und Riyâd*, and depicts the kind of scene at which Ziryab – whose talents embraced astronomy, botany, poetry, cuisine and even sartorial fashion – would have officiated.

the voice was the most highly prized element in this tradition. Although instruments were used for accompaniment and improvised solos, there were very few pre-composed instrumental pieces.

This may have been a refined courtly tradition, but it was still essentially imported from the East, and was not yet something that could truly be called 'Andalusian'. Medieval sources note that the earlier eastern-style repertory of the Cordoban court was at first supplemented, and eventually supplanted, by a completely new type of poetry and song, one that was truly Andalusian in origin. It is that music which continues to be performed today.

THE OTHER CLASSICAL MUSICS

■ Forms

During the tenth century two new and closely-related song forms – the *muwashshaḥ* and the *zajal* – emerged in al-Andalus. These were unlike previous forms of Arab music and poetry, and appear to have been forged in the cultural interaction among Arabs, Berbers, Jews and Iberian Christians. The emergence of these new forms marks the beginning of a tradition that was distinctively Andalusian. In order to understand this tradition, it is crucial to understand the song forms that lie at its heart, for 95 per cent of the repertory is vocal, with only a handful of instrumental overtures and preludes. Instead of using a few lines from older, well-known poems, these songs featured newly-written and lengthy texts, with exuberantly complex rhyme-schemes, using many different rhymes in fanciful patterns. The new songs were also strophic or stanzaic in form, meaning that a set pattern was repeated many times: this made them easier to learn than the courtly repertory, and consequently more popular. Writing in the fourteenth century, the historian Ibn Khaldūn (d. 1406), himself of Andalusian origin, noted that these new songs 'were appreciated by all the people, both elite and masses, due to the ease of understanding them and the familiarity of their style'.[3] This was still a high musical tradition, but one that could be enjoyed by a much broader audience. It is this tradition that has survived as 'Andalusian music'.

Classical Arabic poetry had until that point been composed in the same basic structure: each verse (or line) was the same length, was broken in the middle by a pause (medial caesura) and ended in the same final syllable (end-rhyme), here shown as X:

```
_____        _____X
_____        _____X
_____        _____X
_____        _____X
                (etc.)
```

The new Andalusian song forms broke with this tradition, first by having two separate alternating sections in which the verses were of different length. In one section the rhyme stayed the same at each reprise (although the words were different, so it was not a refrain), and in the alternating section the rhyme was different at each reprise. A song could begin with either the changing or unchanging rhyme section, and the two alternating sections each consisted of from two to six lines, but had to contain the same number of lines each time. One sequence of these two parts, for example, of AA BBB, is called a stanza or strophe; the next stanza or strophe would be AA CCC, then AA DDD, and so on.

```
_____        _____A
_____        _____A
_____        _____B
_____        _____B
_____        _____B
_____        _____A
_____        _____A
```

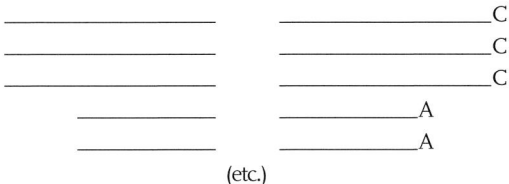

(etc.)

But poets soon began to experiment with flamboyantly complex rhyme schemes, such as the following:⁴

```
_____C_____G          _____E_____A
_____C_____G          _____E_____A
_____F_____G          _____H_____B
_____F_____G          _____H_____B
_____F_____G          _____H_____B
```
(etc.)

This new song-form was called *muwashshah* if the text was in classical Arabic, and *zajal* if it employed colloquial Andalusian dialect. One of the theories about the origin of the word muwashshah is that it derives from the word *wishāh*, a medieval embroidered belt or sash worn by women, and that the shape of the alternating long and short verses suggested the form of a woman wearing one; the term is therefore sometimes translated into English as a 'girdle-poem'. Other scholars believe that it was the embellishment of the poems with multiple rhymes that caused them to be likened to intricately embroidered sashes. The word zajal derives from a verb 'to shout' or 'cry out', and may be a reference to the coarser, more colloquial language used.

But the new songs also represented a musical revolution, for they consisted of two alternating melodies that changed whenever the rhyme changed. Thus both melodies in each song would be repeated many times, which made both melody and text easier to learn, even when the lyrics were twenty-five lines or more in length.

One of the intriguing aspects of the emergence of these new forms is that some of the oldest examples end in a couplet or a triplet of final verses (called the *kharja* or 'exit'), which are in a mixture of Arabic and early Romance (the vernacular form of medieval Latin that later developed into present-day Spanish, Catalan and Portuguese). It was only in the mid-twentieth century that Oxford scholar Samuel Miklos Stern realised that what had appeared to be jumbled, senseless clusters of Arabic letters in some of the medieval manuscripts were in fact transcriptions of Romance words in Arabic script. That discovery unleashed a flood of academic speculation about whether the origins of these new song forms were Arabic, Romance or a product of cultural hybridisation.

Meanwhile, Jewish poets in al-Andalus, who were bilingual in Arabic and Hebrew, soon picked up the new song forms and began composing Hebrew versions which included kharjas in various combinations of Hebrew, Arabic and Romance. Some of the oldest Hebrew muwashshahs were modelled on Arabic poems, following the same rhyme scheme and sometimes incorporating the

The thirteenth-century Galician-Portuguese *Cantigas de Santa Maria*, one of the largest collections of solo songs from the Middle Ages, have come to us complete with notation and illuminations, and are frequently performed by early-music groups. The significance of the illustration at top left is that a Muslim and a Christian are playing side by side; the instrument at bottom right is the albogon.

same themes and motifs. Later, however, a full-blown Hebrew muwashshah tradition emerged and flourished for several centuries, which is one of the reasons that this period is regarded as a golden age for Hebrew poetry. Many of these poems contain biblical imagery and even phrases from the Bible itself.

The themes of the new muwashshah poetry combined older elements from classical Arabic poetry with new ideas and motifs. A typical muwashshah would be set in a drinking party in a garden, where companions were passing around cups of wine served by a graceful young cup-bearer. There are intricate descriptions of the colour of the wine, the shape of the cup, the beauty of the cup-bearer, the sights of the garden, the songs of the birds, all organised around the central theme of love. These songs do not usually tell of reciprocal love relationships, but rather of the intense yearning of the Lover for his Beloved (male or female). The Beloved is at times unattainable because distant, at other times because there are social obstacles, and at times because the Beloved spurns the Lover's advances. The Lover sings of the pain caused by separation from his Beloved and how he lives for but a glance or sign that his feelings are reciprocated. He bemoans the Beloved's cruelty in not acceding to his desire to meet, and recalls the sweetness of a few furtive moments alone with the Beloved and a stolen kiss. He pines, loses his appetite, withers away from lack of sleep, drowns his sorrows in wine, is visited at night by the spirit of the Beloved, and notes ironically that he, the Lover (usually a high-ranking figure), has been transformed into the humble servant of the Beloved (often portrayed as a servant boy or girl), whom he therefore refers to as his Master or Lord, admitting that his own power and wealth are useless in the face of Love.

It is often claimed that this poetry may have influenced the poetry and music of the Provençal Troubadours. Troubadour poetry emerged sometime after the sudden spread of the Andalusian muwashshah, and possessed similar characteristics – a corresponding fascination with complex patterns of end-rhyme, stanzaic structure, a final set of verses similar to the kharja known as the *tornado* – as well as some shared themes and motifs such as the cruelty of love, distance from the Beloved, love as sickness, the lover's near madness, hallucinating visions and portrayal of the Lover as the vassal or servant of the Beloved. Whether these similarities represent influence, parallel development, or evolution from a shared source such as Romance folk poetry, or pan-Mediterranean oral culture, remains a cause for debate today. Musically, however, the structure of those Troubadour songs for which transcribed melodies have survived does not closely resemble the bipartite melodic structure of the muwashshah.

But both the Arabic and Hebrew muwashshah were often understood to have a second, spiritual, meaning. In the Sufi interpretation of their texts, images of love are understood ultimately as references to love of the Divine, the desire for the human soul to know, grow close to and even unite with its Creator. The imagery of the garden signifies the beauty of Paradise and proximity to God; the drunkenness caused by the wine is but a symbol of the ecstasy the soul experiences in the love of the Divine; the beauty of the cup-bearer is a pale reflection of the glory of the Godhead; and the complaints of distance, separation and pining away all reflect the soul's suffering during separation from God in this earthly life. Building on this mystical interpretation of the Andalusian muwashshahs, some of the most famous Sufi poets of the medieval period went on to devote themselves to composing songs that were overtly religious in nature. The following example is by the great Sufi composer of muwashshahs, al-Shushtarī (1212–65), rhymed in alternating couplets and triplets, that includes a garden setting, singing birds and many references to love and wine, which he declares has nothing to do with wine made from grapes:

> My dearest one visited me, how sweet those moments! The Beloved heeded me
> Generously he forgave all my lapses, infuriating the Watchman.
>
> My heart's desire visited me, darkness fell away, in that union he was generous
> He attended my gathering, the wine glass went round, and my hopes were attained
> In good cheer we drank of that wine which is not forbidden.
>
> Fill up my glass, in it is my joy, let us drink, dear one!
> My Beloved is my intimate confidant and my lamp, present, so close
> What drink! What wine! What a vintner! What music! What song!
> In a garden blooming with flowers that fill us with light
> From their pulpits in the trees the birds speak among us
>
> My bottles are full, yet in my cup there is no grape or raisin
> O you who listen, understand my allusions, truly my time is wondrous.
>
> How fine is that wine, how excellent that drink, in a place of joy
> Let me drink and love my Beloved, each day anew
> Foolish is the one who bids me repent, for I am wisely guided
>
> (trans. Lourdes María Alvarez)[5]

In short, the tenth to twelfth centuries in al-Andalus saw the emergence of new song forms that were truly Andalusian in origin and style; were a radical break from the poetry and music of the older Arab tradition; rapidly developed both a more classical-toned and more colloquial form; flourished in Hebrew as well as Arabic; and had become both a secular and a religious tradition. By the mid-twelfth century this new music began to sweep across North Africa and into the Eastern Mediterranean, such that by the beginning of the thirteenth century the genre was known from Morocco in the west to Iraq in the east, from Syria in the north to Yemen in the south. At first performers in other parts of the Middle East sang and played the repertory that had actually been composed in, and transmitted from, al-Andalus, but soon composers and poets in other regions began to try their hand at this new style. Sometimes they borrowed the melody of an Andalusian song and put new words to it, at times even copying the rhyme scheme of the original. Eventually composers and poets began to write completely new muwashshahs, retaining the flavour and form of the Andalusian style, but incorporating more local elements. Over the centuries, each city or region where the Andalusian tradition had taken root came to have its own distinctive repertory.

Although the music was never notated – musicians have always learned this repertory aurally – by the sixteenth century songbooks had begun to circulate.

These included the lyrics along with musical indications of the melodic modes and rhythms. By the seventeenth century these collections show that widespread cross-fertilisation was occurring, for song lyrics are sometimes transcribed with the comment that these same words are also sung to other melodies, or that the melody to a particular song is also performed with other lyrics: words and tunes often travelled separately. As a result of centuries of oral transmission, the spread of songbooks, and the fact that composers and poets sought to imitate the original Andalusian style rather than transform it, it is almost impossible to determine the age of individual songs or instrumental pieces simply from listening to them. Connoisseurs of this tradition, however, can easily pick out distinctive features signalling that a performance or recording was from Fez, Tlemcen or Aleppo.

■ Performance

As described above, the courtly music of Muslim Spain before the invention of the muwashshah and zajal forms had been an elite musical tradition performed and composed primarily by professionals. The single most common form of performance was a singer accompanying him- or herself on the lute, or being accompanied by a lute-player and sometimes also a percussionist; these were intimate performances given before a patron plus guests. In the central court in Cordoba, concerts were at times more elaborate because the Emir often had many singers to choose from. When he wished to have his singing slave-girls perform but not be seen by his male guests, he would have them sing behind a curtain (Ar. *sitāra*: this term came to mean a private ensemble or orchestra of female musicians maintained by a wealthy nobleman).

Another common venue was the garden that is the setting of so many of the songs, which could make the performance a virtual enactment of the lyrics. Here is an account of one such performance from the eleventh century:

> I was in Malaga in 1015 and at one point I fell ill and was confined to my bed. I spent the entire night awake because of the pains from which I was suffering and I heard the sound of lutes and *ṭunbūr*s from every direction, mixed with voices singing. At first this increased my pain and my soul loathed hearing those rhythms. But then I heard something that eased my soul and soothed it, such that I imagined that the floor of the house rose up with me and its walls began to spin round me. I was not able to regain control of myself until I rose and headed towards the source of that voice, which was in the centre of a garden in which there were about twenty men ... They had wine and fruit and singing-girls with lutes and *ṭunbūr*s and other musical instruments, as well as *mizmār*s ... and one singing-girl was sitting apart with her lute in her lap, while everyone gazed at her and listened intently while she sang.[6]

The author was so moved by this scene that he memorised the songs the girl had sung and finally declared: 'It is as if I had never before known pain!'

Aḥmad al-Tīfāshī, the thirteenth-century Tunisian author, wrote that in his day there were four main genres or forms, known as *nashīd*, *sawṭ*, *muwashshaḥ* and *zajal*. The first two forms are from the older non-strophic repertory; the main point of interest here is that the muwashshah and zajal had by al-Tīfāshī's time become fully recognised parts of the elite musical tradition. He described one performance in which a female singer owned by a noble household in Morocco had improvised for two hours on a single verse of poetry, and one in Tunisia in which a male singer of Andalusian origin embellished a single verse with seventy-four *hazza* (shakes, or trills); he also notes that there were both 'light' and 'heavy' songs in the Andalusian repertory, and that the 'heavy' songs could only be performed by the most highly-skilled singers.[7] He seems to have been indicating that the older courtly repertory could only be sung by professionals, whereas the muwashshah and zajal forms were easier.

One of his passages contains remarkable information about the training of female singers, their sale, and the performance of Andalusian music in his day:

> Among the cities of al-Andalus, this music is primarily located in Seville where older professional women singers teach singing to *jawārī* whom they own, as well as to hired, mixed-race female servants. These girls are sold from Seville to the various rulers in North Africa from Morocco to Tunisia. One is sold for a thousand Maghribi dinars, sometimes more, sometimes less, according to her singing, not her face, and she must be sold with a document that lists what she has memorised ... Some of these are light songs that are good for the beginning of a performance, and others are heavy songs which a skilled performer only sings at the end, such as 'al-Kumayt Complained'[8] and 'The Palm Tree and the Palace',[9] for these songs and others like them are only sung by experts, and for that reason they are considered obligatory for the sale, and the lack of such songs would necessarily lower the price. Among the Andalusians a singing slave girl must also be skilled in calligraphy, and must submit the document listing what she has memorised to someone who corrects it for her in terms of the Arabic language. Her buyer reads what is in her document, indicates what he wishes to hear, and she sings it for him on the instrument specified in her bill of sale. She might also be skilled on all of the different instruments, as well as all forms of dance and shadow-puppetry,[10] and possess her own instrument and her own servant-girls who accompany her with percussion and wind instruments, in which case she is known as 'complete' and is sold for several thousand Maghribi dinars.[11]

One of the most interesting details here is that a 'complete' singing-girl came with her own accompanists who played percussion instruments like drum or tambourine, and wind instruments like the reed flute and various forms of oboe and clarinet. Thus the purchase of a single singing-girl could mean the acquisition of an entire professional ensemble.

Descriptions of non-elite performances are rare, but here is a brief account of a wedding performance in the streets of Cordoba in the late tenth century:

> I found myself at a wedding in the streets of Cordoba and al-Nakūrī, the woodwind player was seated in the middle of the crowd wearing a brocade cap and a suit of raw silk in the *'ubaydī* style. His horse was richly decorated and was held by his servant. He performed on the *būq* verses by Ahmad ibn Kulayb about Aslam, his beloved, and an excellent singer sang while he played:

> Aslam, that young gazelle, delivered [Ar. *aslama*] me to passion,
> An antelope with an eye that obtains whatever he desires.
> An envier slandered us and questions will be asked of that slander,
> If he desires a bribe for our union, my very soul shall be that bribe.[12]

This is one of the very few accounts in which the instrumentalist is the star, and the singer is not even named; the reverse is far more common.

In subsequent centuries, a significant thread of transmission for the Andalusian repertory opened up in Sufi brotherhoods. Here there was naturally a focus on spiritual songs, or those which lent themselves to mystical interpretation, but there was also a major difference in performance style. In religious contexts, there has often been a debate within Islam surrounding the use of melodic instruments, particularly woodwind and strings, whereas simple percussion (such as drums, tambourines and cymbals) has been much more widely accepted in the performance of religious texts. Different brotherhoods have arrived at different decisions about which instruments are or are not acceptable: though some Sufi orders fully embrace instrumental music, others sing entirely a cappella and some sing with percussion instruments, while others allow a small number of melodic instruments such as a reed flute. This type of performance is sometimes referred to as 'raw', and is often found in the same locales as more secular performances that incorporate many melodic instruments. Many musicians perform both styles, each in its appropriate venue – without melodic instruments in Sufi performances, and with melodic ones at weddings or concerts for rich patrons.

The perennial debate among Muslim religious scholars about the licitness of instrumental music (particularly its use in religious venues) echoes similar discussions in medieval Christianity and Judaism. The prohibition of instruments, however, was rarely enforced, and even then only under the most fervently religious regimes; it appears never to have fully suppressed musical performance, even temporarily. It is more accurate to say that in conservative Muslim communities there is a strong preference for not using melodic instruments in overtly religious contexts; some very conservative Muslims reject secular music entirely, as have some Calvinists, Methodists, and other strict Protestant sects.

Interestingly, a similar distinction was also made in Jewish communities of North Africa, between secular performances with musical instruments and religious performances without them. However, Andalusian music was so powerful and so popular a tradition in these Jewish communities that Jewish poets continued to write new Hebrew lyrics to the familiar Andalusian tunes, even centuries after the expulsion of the Jews from Spain in 1492. Because musical instruments were not allowed inside the synagogue these were often performed a cappella, much as the neighbouring Sufi orders were performing the same Andalusian music with Islamic religious lyrics, at times only a short distance away.

THE OTHER CLASSICAL MUSICS

Sufi brotherhoods were an important conduit for the transmission of the Andalusian repertory in the thirteenth and fourteenth centuries. Here the Cofradia Al-Shushtari ensemble are seen in devotional mode.

■ Modes, rhythms and the nūba

Many of the classical musical traditions of the Middle East possess compound or 'suite forms' in which a series of different genres of instrumental and vocal pieces are combined into a larger whole (as in the Ottoman *fāṣil*, the Eastern Mediterranean *waṣla* and Central Asian *shashmaqām*). Although these suite-forms are distinct from region to region, they share a similar structure: a series of instrumental and vocal pieces is performed in different sections (or movements) with the sections sometimes being defined by a distinctive rhythm, sometimes by a distinct poetic genre or musical form, and with pre-composed pieces alternating with improvised vocal or instrumental solos. In North Africa this suite-form is called a *nūba* (from the classical Arabic term *nawba*) and is used only for the performance of Andalusian music: each nuba is dominated by a particular melodic mode and the sequence of the movements is dictated by their respective rhythms, with an overall progression from slow to fast.

The modal system of modern North Africa is distinct from that of the modern Eastern Arab world, but both are historically related to the modes of the courtly music of the eighth to twelfth centuries. In the time of Ziryab, for example, the melodic modes in use in Cordoba and Baghdad are presumed to have been the same, since singers regularly moved back and forth between East and West and there is no historical evidence that suggests they had to learn new modes. Although notation was rare, scholars have been able to reconstruct from treatises on music theory the notes of the melodic modes in use in this period.[13] The difficulty, however, is that a mode differs from a scale precisely in that one needs to know more than just the notes, for the notes in a mode have specific relationships to each other and are combined in a variety of ways. To borrow examples from modern Arab musical practice, some modes have an 'arch-structure', meaning that compositions in that mode usually begin in the lower tetrachord (such as D–E–F–G–A) and work their way up to a high point before returning again, while other modes have a 'descending' structure, in which compositions start at in the upper octave and progressively move downward. In some modes, as in the Western melodic minor, one or more tones may be higher when the melody is ascending (for example, F♯ or B♮), but lowered when the melody descends (to F♮ or B♭). In many modes the notes of the central octave are not the same as those used in the notes below or above that range, so that one must know the notes of two octaves (the central octave plus several notes above and below) to fully understand the basic structure of the mode.

Another way modes differ from scales is in the hierarchy of the notes – that is, the weight or importance given to each note. Two modes might have exactly the same notes in their lower tetrachord, but in one mode the most important notes may be the tonic D and then G (as in the modern mode *bayyātī* in the Eastern Mediterranean) while a contrasting mode with the same notes (such as the modern mode *ḥusaynī*, in the same region) might instead emphasise D and then A. In addition, many modes possess characteristic melodic motifs that serve to distinguish them. In ḥusayni, for example, a very common sequence at the juncture between the lower and upper tetrachords is A–C–B♭–C–A (B♭ being a 'half-flat' located between B♭ and B♮), whereas bayyati is immediately recognisable from its characteristic three-fold cascading pattern of B♭–A–G–F, A–G–F–E♭, G–F–E♭–D. So although we can reconstruct from medieval treatises on music theory which tones and intervals were used in the early medieval Arab modes, we do not have the characteristics that give a mode its character and hence its feel. In the Eastern Mediterranean, treatises from the last few centuries attempt to describe the path or flow of individual modes in prose descriptions (see Chapter 12), but no such text concerning medieval or modern North African Andalusian music is known.

It is often stated that pre-modern Andalusian music used twenty-four melodic modes, though in fact this number may be an artificial creation by theorists wishing to have a symbolic or 'complete' number of modes (for example, to match the twenty-four hours of the day), which are categorised as primary and secondary (or 'branch') modes. In modern North Africa, however, there are only about half this number of nubas, which has given rise to the idea that the others have been 'lost' through faulty transmission within the oral tradition. But it is very likely that there never were twenty-four nubas (i.e. one for every mode) and that there never existed full suites in the less common secondary modes. For a full understanding of the modes of Andalusian music, we must therefore rely on analyses of recordings and notation from the past century.

The few treatises on music theory from the medieval Andalusian period that have been found tend to follow the music theory being written in the Eastern Mediterranean during the same period, except in the matter of intervals. In modern North Africa, Andalusian music is performed almost entirely with intervals of semi-tones, tones and augmented seconds; it is popularly believed that this practice stems from medieval al-Andalus, although this is a matter of debate. In the Eastern Mediterranean, on the other hand, the Andalusian repertory is performed within a system that uses tones, semi-tones, augmented seconds and a variety of 'three-quarter' tones that lie in between the half- and whole-tone.[14]

In modern Morocco, Algeria and Tunisia, there is a shared idea that the Andalusian nuba consists of instrumental and vocal 'preludes' and an 'overture' which are followed by five vocal 'movements', each performed to a distinct rhythm. But there are different ways of realising this in performance. In Morocco, for example, the entire Andalusian repertory has been codified and ordered, and modern performances consist of set sequences from this formidably large repertory. The order of the songs does not change, and an ensemble typically plays a sequence from only one of the five movements. Following this sequence there may be an intermission, after which another sequence will be performed, but it will often be from a different nuba in a different melodic mode.

A typical Moroccan performance might be structured as follows: first come the preludes (*mshāliya*, *inshād* and *tawshiya*) and then the main 'movement' (*mīzān* – literally 'rhythm') with its four constituent parts (*muwassa'*, *mahzūz*, *inshād* or *mawwāl* and *inṣirāf*) all of which are played to the same rhythm:

preludes	*mshāliya*	instrumental – unmeasured
	inshād	solo vocal – unmeasured
	tawshiya	instrumental – rhythmic 'overture'
mīzān	*muwassa'*	'broad' – stately tempo (vocal with instrumental accompaniment)
	mahzūz	'moving' – slightly faster tempo (vocal with instrumental accompaniment)
	inshād or *mawwāl*	vocal solo with instrumental solo interludes
	inṣirāf	'exit' – even faster tempo (vocal with instrumental accompaniment)

In this example, two unmeasured 'preludes' lead into a rhythmic instrumental 'overture' which then leads into the performance of one of the five *mīzāns* (movements) of the nuba. Only one of the five movements is performed, and the entire movement employs one basic rhythm, but in three distinct sections that grow progressively faster, with a break for vocal and instrumental solos between the second and third sections.[15]

Next door in Algeria, there is no accepted ordering to the songs, only to the five vocal movements, and when performing a nuba it is common practice to perform one or two songs in each of the five movements, such that the performance moves rapidly through five different rhythms and five different speeds, from slow and stately to fast and lively at the end. Thus while the two regions share the idea of a nuba and the idea of five vocal movements each with a separate rhythm, an Algerian performance contains more rapid changes in rhythm and speed than a typical Moroccan performance, where the idea is to maintain a sense of unity by not varying the rhythm or speed in any dramatic way. In Algeria the leader selects which songs are to be sung, so listeners never know what they will hear next; in Morocco, a connoisseur always knows what comes next, because the order is set.

Further east, in Egypt and Syria, there was historically an even more diverse suite-form known as the *waṣla* which consisted of a variety of different song genres, only one of which is the Andalusian muwashshah. This form continues to be performed in Syria, but has all but disappeared in the last two decades or so in Egypt. Here one can speak about individual 'Andalusian muwashshahs', which have been a part of the repertory for centuries, but the larger suite form itself is not Andalusian. In this region it is more common to have a few Andalusian-style muwashshahs included in a suite that includes many other song types.

Andalusian music, as with almost all other forms of music in the Arab world, has not traditionally been characterised by polyphony, homophony or even strict monophony, but rather by heterophony. Instrumentalists and vocalists sing essentially the same melody, but each embellishes it in his or her own way, which results in an intricate and ever-changing texture. As with jazz there is always an element of improvisation, and no two performances, or even iterations of the same melody, are identical. This aesthetic is closely connected to small traditional ensembles where there was often only one representative of each instrument. The growth of ensembles to orchestral size in the late nineteenth and twentieth centuries has resulted in the curtailing of this practice, but it is still very much present in traditional performances.

■ Instruments

The primary musical instruments used in medieval performances of Andalusian music were the lute (Ar. *al-'ūd*), the reed flute, a type of clarinet called *al-būq*, the bowed *rabāb* (Spanish 'rabel', French 'rebec'), as well as drums and tambourines. The buq is of particular interest because medieval writers saw it as being iconic of Andalusian music due to its popularity there. Aḥmad al-Tīfāshī, for example, wrote:

> The noblest instrument among the Andalusians, and that which gives them the most perfect pleasure in dancing and singing, is al-buq ... It is shaped like an oboe, is as large as trumpet, and inserted into its head is an animal horn, then into the horn is inserted a reed-cane, then into the reed-cane is inserted a small tube, and

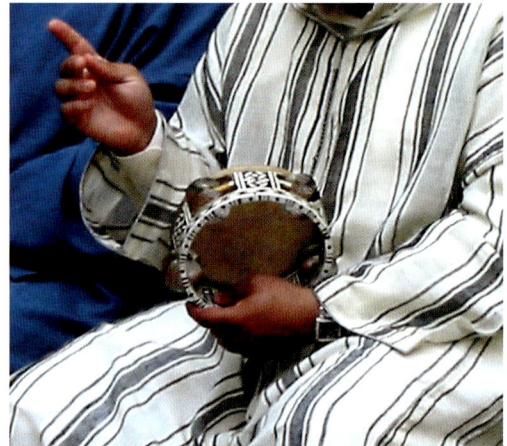

it continues thus in sections until it ends in a straw at the very end – that is where it is played, and the real art lies therein. It produces strange and beautiful sounds of the most wondrous and ecstasy-inducing kind. Among the Andalusians it is the most festive of instruments for singing and dancing in their drinking parties.[16]

The term *al-būq* has survived in Spanish as *albogue* and its derivative *albogón* (the big *albogue*). Not only are there a number of medieval images of this family of instruments in Spanish texts, but forms of the instrument have survived in Iberian folk music until the present, particularly among the Basques of the North of Spain, where it is called the *alboka*.

One instrument that has remained almost unchanged from medieval times to the present in Andalusian music in Morocco and Algeria is the rabab, a short, boat-shaped two-stringed viol, which has become an icon of this musical tradition. Since bowed string instruments are now found the world over, it can be surprising to learn how recently the technique was invented: it appears to have emerged from Central Asia in about the eighth century, then spread rapidly east and west; before that time, string instruments were plucked or strummed, but not bowed. Various forms of bowed string instruments followed the flow of Islamic civilisation westwards and into Muslim Spain, where they then passed into Northern Christian Spain. The oldest European images of bowed-string instruments are found in Mozarabic manuscripts from Christian northern Spain from the last quarter of the tenth century; a possibly slightly older carving of the same instrument is found on the famed 'Musicians' Capital', which portrays four musicians, one on each face of the capital of a column from a tenth-century Cordoban palace.[17] Nearly all later bowed string instruments in Europe derive from the introduction of this technique via Muslim Spain. One medieval Andalusian author writing of Seville (the musical capital of Iberia in the later Middle Ages) and Cordoba (the seat of learning), wrote: 'When a scientist dies in Seville, they send his books to Cordoba to be sold, and when a musician dies in Cordoba, they send his instruments to Seville to be sold.'

◂ *Top:* Members of the Briouel Ensemble performing in the Fez medina in 2002 at a celebration of Eid al-Fitr, the feast which marks the end of Ramadan

Middle: Rabbi Haim Louk in performance *(left)*; the tar, Andalusian music's version of the tambourine *(right)*

Bottom: The same bowing techniques are used for both the rabab *(right)* and the violin *(left)*.

The Musicians' Capital, from a tenth-century Cordoban palace, reflects the importance of string instruments in Andalusian music at that time.

■ Today

Andalusian music is known and performed throughout the modern Arab world and in Israel, but in each region it occupies a different social niche, plays a different role in local and national identity, and is regarded very differently. In Morocco, for example, this music is closely associated with the royal family and with certain social elites in the north, particularly those who claim historical descent from families that fled the Christian *Reconquista* of Iberia in the Middle Ages. Andalusian music is regularly featured at official government functions, and a conservatory system was established in the twentieth century to help transmit and preserve it, but the repertory is considered closed; no new pieces of Andalusian music are now composed. Because of this many young people – and people of all ages in the south of Morocco, where the connection to medieval al-Andalus is weaker – feel little connection to this music.

In Algeria, due to the French occupation of the country from 1830 to 1962, the situation is different: the country underwent a brutal campaign of colonisation by the French who 'annexed' it and declared it an inseparable part of France. Public education during the colonial period was conducted entirely in French, and schoolchildren were taught only French history and literature, not the history and literature of their own country. In this context, Andalusian music became a symbol of Arab culture that people in many urban centres clung to, not only out of love for the music, but also as an act of cultural defiance. Voluntary associations were formed, some of which are now nearly a century old, in which young people were and still are taught this music, and in the past half-century a series of festivals and competitions have provided further impetus for young people to learn it. The repertory is less rigid than in Morocco: there is no 'canonical' order to the songs and the style of performance allows for more diversity in mood, rhythm and tempo than the Moroccan style. Andalusian music still has a strong presence in cities such as Tlemcen, Algiers and Constantine.

Cairo, by contrast, has for centuries been a cosmopolitan centre where the musical scene has been characterised by innovation and the emergence of new genres and styles. As the capital of the Arab world's most populous country, it has also until very recently dominated the recording industry, as well as the production of film and television. Although Andalusian muwashshahs, usually referred to here as 'the old muwashshahs', still occupy a respected place in the repertory among musicians and connoisseurs, they are rivalled in terms of prestige by other genres including the nineteenth-century *dōr* and *ṭaqṭūqa*, both of which are of Egyptian origin. Andalusian muwashshahs are now performed only rarely, at the Cairo Opera house and in a few other venues; even there they are almost never performed alone, but rather as one element in a concert that may include other genres as well.

Aleppo, in Syria, has been a centre for Andalusian music since the twelfth century, and this plays a strong role in both local and national identity – indeed, one might say that there is nothing more Syrian than Andalusian music. The most popular singer of recent decades, Sabah Fakhry, sings muwashshahs in every concert (along with other genres), and his reputation was to a great extent built on his interpretations of that repertory. This music is now taught in a series of government-supported conservatories and has a strong presence on government-owned television and radio stations. The most popular singer of the past half century in Lebanon, the female singer Fayrouz, is also closely associated with Andalusian-style muwashshahs: one of her best-selling albums, the songs of which are still popular today, was titled *Andalusiyyāt* ('Songs of al-Andalus') which combined traditional songs with new compositions. In addition, during the late 1960s, '70s and '80s she created popular concert versions featuring medieval costumes and pageantry. Both the Syrian and the Lebanese traditions of Andalusian music admit new compositions, as well as re-workings of traditional songs.

In Israel there has been an official national orchestra since the founding of the state, but that orchestra has always performed Western classical music which has appealed primarily to Ashkenazi Jews (of European origin). In recent decades, however, with the growing political and cultural presence of Sephardic Jews (who trace their cultural heritage to medieval Spain) and of Mizrachi Jews (Eastern Jews from Arab, Iranian and Central Asian origins), a second national orchestra has been officially recognised by the government: the Israeli Andalusian Orchestra. This group performs a diverse repertory, but pride of place is given to Andalusian music sung in both Arabic and Hebrew.

In modern Spain, Andalusian music has in recent decades achieved a growing presence, thus returning the repertoire to its geographical origins. A number

Players on two ouds and a rabab support the singers in this ensemble performing at the Club Fils du Detroit (Sons of the Straits of Gibraltar) No. 1, in Tangier, Morocco, in 1987.

of ensembles now specialise in Andalusian music, most often borrowed from neighbouring Morocco. For some musicians this is a purely aesthetic choice; for some it reflects a decision to embrace a tradition that originated in their homeland and was performed there for centuries. For others it represents a political decision to perform Arabo-Andalusian music – sometimes alongside Sephardic Jewish music – in order to promulgate the image of a medieval Spain of *las Tres Culturas* (the Three Cultures) in which Jews, Christians and Muslims lived together in relative mutual tolerance. The hope is that a similar degree of cultural understanding can be achieved once more.

Further reading

The only full-length works devoted to the history of Andalusian music are in French, such as Mahmoud Guettat's *La musique arabo-andalouse*, or in Arabic; an historical summary in English can be found in Dwight F. Reynolds's chapter 'Music' (*The Cambridge History of Arabic Literature*). Studies of several modern regional traditions are available in Jonathon Shannon's *Among the Jasmine Trees* (Syria), Ruth Davis's *Ma'lūf* (Tunisia) and Mark Wagner's *Like Joseph in Beauty* (Yemen), though the latter focuses more on poetry than music. A general account of medieval Arab music which deals briefly with Andalusian music is found in Henry George

Farmer's *A History of Arabian Music*. Benjamin Liu and James Monroe's *Ten Hispano-Arabic Songs in the Modern Oral Tradition* traces the history of ten Andalusian muwashshahs from medieval to modern times, though their findings have been challenged by some scholars. Reynolds's 'Music in Medieval Iberia' offers a survey of medieval cultural interactions in the formation of Andalusian music; his 'The Re-creation of Medieval Arabo-Andalusian Music in Modern Performance' provides an evaluation of recordings of groups that attempt to 'recreate' medieval Andalusian music in modern performances, and 'Al-Maqqarī's Ziryāb' re-examines the legendary figure of Ziryab. Finally, the single best resource for the study of Middle Eastern music is *The Garland Encyclopedia of World Music* vol. 6, *The Middle East*, which contains several articles relevant to the study of Andalusian music by Guettat, Habib Hassan Touma and L. JaFran Jones.

Recommended listening

The Music of Islam vol. 7, *Al-Andalus, Andalusian Music, Tetouan, Morocco*. Celestial Harmonies B0000007Z2, 1998. The regional tradition of Tetuan, Northern Morocco; ensemble led by El Kacimi Mohamed.

Andalusian Music From Tangier, Institut du Monde Arabe B000E6UZBO, 2006. From Tangiers, Northern Morocco; ensemble led by Cheik Ahmed Zaitouni, selections from the Nuba of Hijaz Kabir.

Andalusian Music From Morocco, BMG Harmonia Mundi B000026N17, 1991. Selections from Rasd and Maya, led by Abd al-Karim Rais from Fez.

Ustad Massano Tazi: Musique classique andalouse de Fès, Ocora France B0000271D8, 1988. Selections from Hijaz Kabir and Istihlal, led by Massano Tazi of Fez.

Algérie: Anthologie de la musique arabo-andalouse vols 4–5 (2 CDs), Ocora France C560044/45, 1994. Selections from Sika performed by the Essoundoussia orchestra of Algiers, and selections from Zidane by the ensemble Ahbab Cheikh Larbi Bensari of Tlemcen.

Algeria: Andalusian Music From Algiers / Musique Andalouse d'Alger al-Djazairiya al-Mossiliya, Institut du Monde Arabe B000004VTDO, 2001.

Tunisie: Anthologie du Malouf, Musique Arabo-Andalouse, Inédit W260044, 1992. Selections from al-Dhil, led by Abdelhamid Bel Eljia.

Songs From Aleppo, Institut du Monde Arabe B00004R7PY, 2000. Selections from the Andalusian tradition of Aleppo, northern Syria, featuring soloist Sabri Moudallal.

Ahavat Olamim Andalusian Hebrew Song from the Maghreb to Jerusalem (2 CDs), Jewish Music Research Centre, The Hebrew University of Jerusalem B00815MN10, 2011. Featuring Rabbi Haim Louk.

12 The Eastern Arab World

Scott Marcus

As the orchestra and chorus take the stage – the men in tuxedos, the women in traditional gowns – people in the audience call out to their favourites, particularly the tambourine player who is the sole percussionist; the maestro emerges to applause. After an initial instrumental piece, songs dominate, presented by the male and female choruses standing behind the orchestra, or by vocal duets or trios at the front of the stage; after a while there is an extended solo improvisation. The audience listens quietly, having been schooled in the Western way to save applause until the end of each piece; with a ritual wave of their programmes, people demand repeats of their favourite songs. Western string instruments – violins, cellos and double bass – predominate, though their long-time presence in this culture gives the orchestra a traditional feel. Indigenous instruments – reed flute, lute, zither and tambourine – fill out the ensemble, adding textures that keep the overall sound decidedly local. This sense is intensified by the use of more than twelve notes per octave: the 'extra' non-Western notes help build an atmosphere of enchantment.

THE art music of the eastern Arab world has a long and dynamic history: with roots going back two millennia, it has evolved greatly over time and continues to evolve today. Concentrated in Cairo, Beirut, Damascus and Aleppo, it has many shared features across the region; we may think of it as a single tradition, but there are local variations. The shared features include scales and rhythms, instruments, types of ensemble, repertoire and performance contexts. As such, the above description – of a 1980s performance by the Arabic Music Ensemble in Cairo – could represent similar concerts in many parts of the eastern Arab world. Yet compositions by the Egyptian Sayyid Darwīsh and Muḥammad 'Abd al-Wahhāb, for example, are regarded as distinctly Egyptian; performances by the singer Fayrouz are felt to exhibit a uniquely Lebanese character; and traditional songs performed by the Aleppan singer Ṣabāḥ Fakhrī are regarded as reflecting a quintessentially Syrian tradition. Thus do styles differ within this shared music.

◀ Although Umm Kulthum died forty years ago, this great singer's recordings still top the charts throughout the Arab world: she created an art music which also became the region's popular music. Photographed in 2002, this mural in a Cairo suburb reflects the ubiquity of her fame.

Early history

The history of Arab music predates the birth of Islam. Early vocal and poetic traditions from nomadic tribes and flourishing urban centres like Mecca were further developed in opulent court settings from the seventh century, first in Damascus, the capital of the Umayyad dynasty (661–750), and then in the Abbasid-dynasty capital, Baghdad (750–1258). The courts became virtual conservatories of music, populated by the greatest performers and scholars of the day, with the caliphs serving as enthusiastic patrons. Many treatises were written during this period, by such famed philosophers and music theorists as al-Kindī (c. 801–73), al-Fārābī (872–950), Ibn Sīnā (980–1037) and Ṣafī al-Dīn al-Urmawī (c. 1216–94). The twenty-volume *Book of Songs* (*Kitāb al-Aghānī*) by Abū l-Faraj al-Iṣbahānī (897–967) contains stories of musicians, patrons and songs (including tales of singers who also composed hundreds of songs), as well as descriptions of performances from pre-Islamic times to the tenth century. We also learn of separate classes of instrumentalists and singing slave-girls (*qaina*; pl. *qaināt* or *qiyān*), these being part of the pre-Islamic culture. The British scholar Henry George Farmer, who was the first to introduce the wonders of the medieval Arab world to modern readers, described a situation where caliphs, nobility and rich merchants kept musical establishments in which singing-girls were part of the household; these girls were trained in special schools and fetched fabulous sums.[1] Al-Isbahani tells us much about the lives of qaina women, including Sallāma al-Qass, who sang in caliphs' courts in the eighth century. This knowledge was spread anew in the mid twentieth century when the Egyptian singer Umm Kulthūm starred as Sallama in the 1945 musical film of the same name: we follow Sallama as she is sold and re-sold to different wealthy men, being finally bought by a prince who became the caliph Yazīd II (720–4).[2]

But the music scene was multicultural, with many imports from Persian culture: the oud, a new type of lute, which in time became the dominant instrument of Arab culture; the Persian terms that came to permeate Arab music theory; and new styles of song. Of the latter, Farmer wrote that by the mid-seventh century, Persian melodies had become so popular that Arab musicians found it necessary to become better acquainted with this Iranian art in order to satisfy their clients.[3]

This variety of influences led to conflicts over style and aesthetics, most notably in the ninth century between those who sought rigorously to maintain the old music traditions (a central figure in this camp being Isḥāq al-Mawṣilī, d. 850) and others who felt free to cultivate a lighter and freer style (led by Ibrāhīm ibn al-Mahdī, d. 839).[4] Such competing forces of tradition and innovation were a constant feature throughout the history of Arab music, and continue to be today.

Early writings also reflect a perennial conflict concerning the very admissibility of music in Islamic society. From the beginning of Islam to the present day, many have held that music itself is *ḥarām*, unlawful according to the tenets of the religion, and a distraction from the proper focus of a religious life. The Qur'ān offers no explicit guidance on this point: the words and acts of the

THE EASTERN ARAB WORLD

The celebrated British Arabist Henry George Farmer *(right)* with other delegates at the 1932 Cairo conference, a unique musical meeting of East and West.

prophet Muhammad can be adduced in support of both views. The second ruler of the Umayyad dynasty, Yazīd I (d. 683), was not immune to this conflict: in response to his patronage of musicians, the pious responded with horror.[5] Even musicians in present-day Cairo acknowledge that they have long been confronted by people who regard music as haram. Nevertheless it has continued to thrive in eastern Arab culture, performed and widely patronised despite occasionally vehement disapproval.

The early treatises reflect dramatic developments in music theory. One by Ibn al-Munajjim (d. 912) details the Arab scale as it was conceived in the eighth and ninth centuries and performed by Ishaq al-Mawsili and his followers. Al-Munajjim describes eight melodic modes in terms of finger positions on the lute: each mode was composed of a series of whole-step and half-step intervals, and thus did not have the extra notes (half flats and half sharps) that are a characteristic feature of the modern Arab scale.

A profound shift began in the middle of the ninth century when scholars, assembled in a caliphal institute called the House of Wisdom (Bayt al-Ḥikma) in Baghdad, translated Greek treatises by Aristotle, Aristoxenes, Euclid and Ptolemy. One of the results of this huge project was the work of the philosopher, mathematician, physician and music theorist al-Kindi. Following Greek influence, he presents music as a mathematical science, with individual notes in a scale identified in terms of numerical relationships: for example, the first note of a given scale is labelled 1/1, while the note an octave higher is indicated by the ratio 2/1. The Arab scale came to be perceived as stretching over a two-octave span (the Greek Greater Perfect System), and tetrachordal theory – a method for naming and analysing four-note scalar segments – was adopted.

Beginning with al-Farabi, we finally find theorists who tell us that, despite al-Mawsili's determined touting of a scale of only whole and half steps, there was in fact a long-standing practice of using additional notes. Some of these notes were called 'Persian', after their origins in Persian practice; others were called 'Zalzalian' after the celebrated court musician, Manṣūr Zalzal (d. after 842), who is said to have introduced a third scalar degree very close to the equal-tempered half-flat third of present-day theory. Another stage in the development of medieval music theory occurred with the writings of Safi al-Din al-Urmawi, who posited a scale of seventeen tones per octave. While twelve of these notes correspond to the notes of the Western scale, the scale also includes five of the 'extra notes' that are characteristic of Middle Eastern scales. Interestingly, Safi al-Din used Pythagorean mathematics to assign these notes to significantly higher pitches than heretofore: while the Western-corresponding twelve notes had standard positions, the placement of the 'extra' notes was a subject of controversy. The controversy suggests competing forces, the Persian and Zalzalian thirds coming from the realm of practice, Safi al-Din's third coming from the realm of theory. These worlds continue to clash in Arab music today.

■ Recent history

Such developments laid Arab music's foundations, but its modern form has much more recent roots: the oldest pieces of today's repertoire, it seems, don't go back beyond about one hundred and fifty years. The earliest performers and composers cited today date from the late nineteenth century, such as the Egyptian singers/composers, 'Abduh al-Ḥamūlī (1841–1901), Muḥammad 'Uthmān (1855–1900) and Salāma Ḥigāzī (1852–1917), as well as the Egyptian female singer Almaẓ (1860–96) and the Syrian composer Aḥmad Abū Khalīl il-Qabbānī (1836?–1903?). While there surely is repertoire that pre-dates this period, the histories of specific compositions are unknown: they are reverently labeled 'min it-turāth', 'from the [distant] heritage'.

Throughout the nineteenth and early twentieth centuries, eastern Arab art music was performed by a small chamber ensemble called a *takht*. At full size, a takht had one each of five traditional instruments: a short-necked lute (oud), a plucked zither (*qānūn*), an end-blown flute (*nāy*), a two-string bowed fiddle (*kamānja*, replaced by the end of the nineteenth century with the Western violin) and a single percussion instrument, the tambourine (*riqq*). Smaller versions of the ensemble were common; excellent archival takht recordings remain which feature only two or three musicians. And while a takht could give instrumental performances, the group was most commonly fronted by, and named after, a solo singer who would stand before the seated musicians. A two- or three-member chorus, standing behind the group, completed the ensemble.

Takhts performed at gatherings in upper-class parlours and royal palaces: the most famous singers caught the attention of Ottoman rulers in Istanbul, and were summoned there from Cairo. An evening's performance consisted of pieces arranged in two or three suites (sing. *waṣla*), the pieces of each suite sharing a similar aesthetic quality by virtue of employing the same scale or melodic mode (*maqām*). From a songbook written c. 1840 we learn of the contents of a typical early nineteenth-century wasla. Dominated by a song genre called *muwashshaḥ* (pl. *muwashshaḥāt*, with roots in medieval Andalusian Spain; see Chapter 11), an individual suite would progress through twelve or more such songs, beginning with examples in slow and heavy rhythms and then moving towards lighter rhythms. Improvisations (the vocal *layālī* and *mawwāl*, and the instrumental *taqāsīm*) were undoubtedly interspersed among the pre-composed songs, while instrumental compositions might have been limited to the short prelude-like *dūlāb*.

By the late nineteenth century, the wasla had evolved with the addition of new vocal and instrumental genres. The most prominent of the new vocal genres was the *dawr*, a lengthy song with lyrics in colloquial Egyptian Arabic, which came to assume the climactic point in the wasla. The greatest musicians of the day – notably the renowned Muhammad 'Uthman – composed many dozens of new songs in this genre. A dawr typically included a section in which the solo singer and chorus would alternate extended passages on the syllable 'āh', bringing new levels of excitement just prior to the song's concluding lines.[6]

One of the new instrumental genres added to the wasla was the *samā'ī*, introduced from Ottoman Turkish music. The Ottoman Empire had conquered the eastern Arab world in 1516–17, and the sama'i is but one example of the many layers of influence that the imperial power exerted on eastern Arab traditions. Further examples are the many melodic modes (*makam* in modern Turkish) that eastern Arab musicians adopted from Ottoman practice.

While eastern Arab musicians absorbed many Ottoman sama'i compositions into active repertoire, they also began to create their own, many of which became popular throughout the region. Let us now look at a sama'i thought to be one of the earliest examples of an Arab composition in the genre (Example 12.1). As its exact origin is unknown, it is labelled 'min it-turath'. A sama'i is based in a specific maqam, after which it is named. Our example is set in maqam *Bayyātī* and is thus known as *samā'ī Bayyātī* (or *samā'ī Bayyātī al-Thaqīl*, the last word referencing its 10/8 rhythmic mode).

Compositions in the sama'i genre all share the same basic structure: four instrumental 'verses' (sing.: *khāna*) each followed by a single recurring refrain (*taslīm*). The first two sections (the first khana and following taslim) are given the task of evoking characteristic features of the base maqam, here maqam Bayyati. By contrast, the remaining sections (the second, third and fourth khanas) are given the task of presenting other *maqāmāt* (pl. of maqam). The process of changing from one maqam to another is called modulation, which is a highly-valued aspect of maqam performance. Sama'is are thus considered ideal pieces from which musicians can learn about specific maqams and also modulatory practices common to them. As such, they gained a prominent place as pedagogical pieces in the music institutes that appeared throughout the region later in the twentieth century. All institution-based instrumentalists learn sama'i Bayyati al-Thaqil as part of their early training.

In Example 12.1 we see a transcription of sama'i Bayyati al-Thaqil. The initial khana and taslim are set in maqam Bayyati, a D-based mode in which the second scalar degree is half flat (positioned between E♮ and E♭): the slash over the E♭ sign in the key signature is used to indicate that the Es are half flat. The remaining sections of the composition present three other maqams: the second khana features maqam *Rāst* based on G (with its B♭ – B half flat, positioned between B♮ and B♭); the third khana presents maqam *Ḥijāz* based on D (with its E♭ and F♯); and the fourth khana features maqam *Ṣabā* on D (with its G♭). From sama'i Bayyati al-Thaqil, then, we learn about four maqams, Bayyati, Hijaz and Saba, all based on D, and maqam Rast based on G. Sama'is had become a common feature in waslas by the beginning of the twentieth century.

EX. 12.1 A transcription of *Samā'ī Bayyātī al-Thaqīl*

There was one last addition to the wasla. During the eighteenth and nineteenth centuries women musicians commonly performed in separate groups apart from the men. Termed 'awālim (literally, learned women), the women sang and played both melodic and percussion instruments in private settings for female audiences. Beginning in the late nineteenth century, male composers and performers began to include the ṭaqṭūqa, a short strophic song in colloquial Arabic which had been the preserve of female performers, into their wasla performances; in the twentieth century the taqtuqa evolved into a lengthy multi-sectional song.

From the last decades of the nineteenth century, a number of changes brought art music into new contexts. One was the development of musical theatre, which was centred initially in Syria. This created a sensation throughout the region, and induced Egyptian musicians to study with the Syrian musicians leading the new genre, notably with the composer Ahmad Abu Khalil al-Qabbani. By the early twentieth century musical theatre was enthusiastically adopted in Cairo and taking place in new public halls, where musical entr'actes were as important as the theatrical productions, showcasing the talents of old and new generations of performers.

Meanwhile the new record industry was bringing more change. European companies including Odeon (Germany) and Gramophone (Britain) led the way, their agents seeking renowned singers who were propelled to fresh levels of fame as the new medium reached people in the countryside. The industry brought an emphasis on new compositions: while in the wasla tradition of the early nineteenth century singers performed sequences of traditional songs, often disseminated in songbooks for all to sing, now singers were asked to record original compositions, as record companies maximised profits through their ownership of copyrights. At the same time, the three-minute format of the earliest recordings had its own effect on the performance tradition, favouring snapshot presentations of what were in many cases expansive compositional genres.

When silent films were superseded by 'talkies', music found yet another medium. Musicals became the dominant form of cinema, with Cairo becoming the region's Hollywood, and singers topping the record charts starring in the medium. The Egyptian diva Umm Kulthum (c. 1900–75) and the singer/composer Muhammad 'Abd al-Wahhab (c. 1900–91) thus rocketed to even greater levels of fame. Talent flocked to Cairo from the surrounding countries, including the brother and sister team of Farīd al-Aṭrash (1905–74) and Asmahān (1918?–44) from Syria. Films also encouraged the expansion of the takht ensemble, a process that had begun in musical theatre, with additional violins plus the cello and double bass. Choral accompaniment became rare, leaving the lead singer as the sole vocal performer.

Since music comprised a large part of its programming, radio also became an importance force and as the signals became more powerful, concerts – especially those of Umm Kulthum – were broadcast throughout the entire region. Starting in 1937, Kulthum was given the unique honour of live-concert broadcasts on the first Thursday of each month throughout the winter-spring concert season.

People still speak of streets becoming deserted from Morocco to Lebanon and Syria as everyone crowded round radios to listen; her concerts were now held in large halls and Cairo's most glamorous cinemas, while television later offered yet another outlet. Throughout this period, the size of the ensemble accompanying the solo singer continued to grow, peaking in the 1960s and 1970s with an ensemble called a *firqa* with sixteen violins, three cellos and, with increasing regularity, an accordion, electric guitar, saxophone and/or electric keyboard. The takht now came to symbolise older practices.

Ever since the Khedive Ismail decided to celebrate the 1869 opening of the Suez Canal by building an Italian opera house in the centre of Cairo, indigenous musicians had had to fight their corner. The first opera production was a staging of Verdi's *Rigoletto*, followed in 1871 by the world premiere of his *Aïda*. Such events reflected the mind-set of many of the intelligentsia, who came to view their corner of the Middle East as essentially part of Europe: they sought to adopt aspects of European culture ranging from dress and the arts to architecture and street-design, and parts of downtown Cairo were renovated to give a Parisian feel. This was the climate in which performers of indigenous art forms have had to fight ever since, to win patronage on a level with that given to Western forms. For example, between 1959 and 1967 the Egyptian government founded the Cairo Symphony Orchestra and the National Conservatory for the study of Western classical music, but it made no new initiatives during that period in support of Arab art music. Umm Kulthum and Muhammad 'Abd al-Wahhab led protests against this bias, resulting in the creation of two new government ensembles: the Arabic Music Ensemble, the focus of this chapter's introduction, was founded in 1967, and an Arab music ensemble based at the Higher Institute for Arabic Music was created in 1969.[7]

Meanwhile, as the twentieth century progressed, nationalist pressures brought other changes to the art-music tradition. In 1932 a Congress of Arab Music was held in Cairo – hosting music scholars from Europe, America and countries throughout the Middle East – with the aim of devising programmes to introduce music to a newly-conceived national audience. Music education became a mandatory component of the school curriculum, and conservatories were established with the dual goal of creating new generations of musicians, and teachers for the nation's schools.

With Arab art music now institutionally enshrined from Beirut and Damascus to Cairo, a new pedagogy was also needed. Concepts and understandings that had been implicit now had to be systematically presented in written form, requiring new layers of theory. Understandings of scale and melodic intervals, freshly configured in the eighteenth century but still not widely disseminated even in the early years of the twentieth, were now codified in books on Arab music theory. Students were taught that while Western music recognises twelve notes per octave, Arab music acknowledges twenty-four, with the intervals between adjacent notes conceptualised as quarter steps (not the half steps of Western music). The modes (maqams) of Arab music came to be analysed in terms of single-octave scales and a newly-adopted system of tetrachordal analysis: tetrachordal theory – present in medieval Arab music theory – had been lost in

THE EASTERN ARAB WORLD

Umm Kulthum's name was transliterated in many different ways – another of which can be seen on this 1960s album cover *(bottom left)* – and here she is represented with her band in some folk-art figurines bought in Cairo in 2010 *(top)*. Her musicians are playing *(from left to right)*, the accordion, violin, qanun, oud, nay, cello, tabla and riqq. She is depicted holding her signature scarf and wearing the dark glasses she needed for an eye ailment, but which she never wore while performing, as pictured *(right)* in 1967.

the intervening centuries, and had to be re-introduced. To aid in both musical analysis and in teaching repertoire to school students, educators adopted Western staff notation, applying newly-created symbols (for example, the slashed-flat sign) to accommodate the 'extra' notes of Arab music. This had profound effects on musical culture: an aurally-transmitted tradition now became a written one, with the ability to read staff notation becoming a basic requirement. Since this ability could only be acquired through formal tuition, institution-based education came to be seen as a fundamental component of a musician's training.

Moreover, the new reliance on notation changed the music which that notation was meant to preserve and disseminate. When a given piece had existed in the aural realm musicians routinely varied its melodic lines, but once written down, the melody was regarded as fixed. According to an age-old performance aesthetic, musicians had been encouraged to render a given melody according to their own creative impulses and the idiosyncratic capabilities of their instruments; this quality was often lost with staff notation, where a melody would be performed uniformly, and without variation. An additional result was erosion of the importance of the vocal layali and mawwal, and of the instrumental taqasim, all of which – as improvised forms – virtually disappeared from Egyptian art-music performances. Taqasim were still a regular feature of concerts by the Arabic Music Ensemble in the early 1980s, but are not any more.

The rise of the composer was another factor contributing to the decline of improvisation. By the 1940s, songs had grown in length, particularly in genres such as the expanded taqtuqa, which came to be known as *ughniya*. A composer would now create a single long composition that contained most of the elements that would have occurred in the older suite form: the suite of songs was replaced by a single song with many verses, each of which had its own music. Instrumental pieces that might have occurred between songs in the old suite-form were replaced by unique instrumental introductions to a song's various verses, all conceived as a single composition. Muhammad 'Abd al-Wahhab, who retired from singing in the 1960s but continued composing for the most prominent singers of the day, became the most renowned eastern Arab composer, and led the trend away from the improvisatory genres towards lengthy ughniya compositions and the uniform performance of melodic lines. The ughniya genre had its golden age between the 1940s and the 1970s, as represented by the songs of Umm Kulthum, Farid al-Atrash and 'Abd al-Ḥalīm Ḥāfiẓ.

There are four necessary caveats to this account of the disappearance of improvisation in eastern Arab art music. First, taqasims, although often brief, do remain in performances of a few celebrated Syrian and Lebanese singers, especially those who seek to retain the older wasla performance structure (see below). Second, the taqasim genre retains a vibrant place in other musics, for example, in certain folk traditions and the music accompanying cabaret or belly dance. Third, the most virtuosic musicians retain the ability to improvise melodic variations, even when reading what may seem like the definitive staff-notated version of a melody. And fourth, among musicians and aficionados, taqasim remains an important marker of musical competence, and is thus often featured in private gatherings.

Yet art music's twentieth-century changes have also had a contrary effect: by taking on many of the features so characteristic of Western classical music – institutionalised pedagogy, staff notation, a written music theory, performances in concert halls, large orchestras led by a conductor and featuring a chorus – Arab music acquired a 'classical' hue. While this adjective is still not commonly applied – it's generally referred to as 'Arabic music' (*al-mūsīqā al-'arabiyya*) – the new attributes legitimised it for Western-influenced Arabs, and enhanced its prestige.

▪ Melodic and rhythmic modes: Maqām and Īqā'

Eastern Arab music is based on distinct systems of melodic and rhythmic modes. This is the case whether the music be high art music (setting aside music composed in Western idioms), folk, religious or even modern popular music. Melodies are built from melodic modes called maqamat, and any given maqam dictates a wealth of melodic features. These include the notes used (conceived today as a specific scale with a tonic); ideas about the intonation of the notes and which notes should be emphasized; a specific tetrachordal structure with the possibility of alternative tetrachords; a sense of tessitura (how high and how low a melody extends); the idiomatic use of specific accidentals; common melodic motives and modulations to other maqams; a characteristic general progression (a kind of road map for moving through a mode's various features); and for some maqams, extra-musical associations.

There is no definitive statement of a given maqam's features, either in terms of a single authoritative sound recording, or a theoretical writing. Indeed, it is felt that no one piece of music could possibly exhibit all the features of a given maqam. Thus, a comprehensive definition would only appear if we were (hypothetically) to analyse all the ways that the maqam has been used in practice, both in compositions and improvisations. Additionally, while composers and improvisers generally stay within tradition (not trying to be 'out there', in the manner of some jazz musicians), there is always the possibility that an insightful musician might present a maqam in a new way. Depending on the reception of that novelty, it might over time be adopted into the mainstream understanding of the mode, or it might be rejected and continued only in that musician's performances. There is no definitive list of existing maqams: conservatory students may be required to know over fifty for their exams, but many musicians recognise far fewer, labelling lesser-used ones simply as variations within the most prominent modes.

Sometime in the eighteenth century the eastern Arab melodic system was reconceptualised as using a general scale of quarter-step intervals. The main theoretical scheme prior to this was the scale by al-Urmawi that recognised seventeen notes per octave; the new scale recognised twenty-four per octave, occurring at 50-cent intervals. The earliest known reference to this scale is in a French-language encyclopaedia of 1780,[8] while the first available Arabic-language presentation is found in a treatise by the Lebanese Mīkhā'īl Mashāqa from c. 1840.

Among the maqams, primary place is given to maqam Rast. Based on C, Rast has the following basic scale: C–D–E♭–F–G–A–B♭–C. Interestingly, the conceptualisation of the modern-day maqams in terms of simple scales is a practice that dates only from around 1900. Prior to this, theorists like Mashaqa described the individual maqams by giving short characteristic melodies for each: this was done by listing the consecutive notes of each melody, using the Arabic/Persian name for each note. Present-day theory books usually present some version of the following diagram, comparing the scale of maqam Rast with the Western major scale. This is part of an overarching orientation in twentieth- to twenty-first-century Arab theory presentations that first offer detailed instruction in Western scalar theory (whole-step and half-step intervals, major and minor scales, and step-by-step introduction to staff notation) before beginning to present the specifics of Arab music theory, always starting with maqam Rast.

The Western major scale in terms of half-step intervals:

C | D | E F | G | A | B C'

Maqam Rast in terms of quarter-step intervals:

C | | | D | | E♭ | | F | | | G | | | A | | B♭ | | C'

From this we may summarise that, while the whole step is conceived as containing two half-steps in Western theory, the same interval is understood to contain four quarter-steps in eastern Arab music; the E and B of maqam Rast are positioned a quarter-step lower than their corresponding notes in the major scale; and in the twentieth century these non-Western notes came to be called 'half flats' (*niṣf bīmūl*). Using solfège syllables rather than the letter symbols that are commonly used in the West, Arab musicians label E♭ and B♭ 'mī niṣf bīmūl' and 'sī niṣf bīmūl' respectively. Prior to this, the two notes were designated with their traditional Arabic/Persian note names, respectively *Sīkāh* and *Awj*. (Half-sharps are similarly notated with an altered version of the sharp sign, ⧣.)

With the new quarter-tone scale, modern Arab music theory commonly recognises four sizes of intervals between adjacent pitches in a scale: two quarter-steps, four quarter-steps and six quarter-steps (equivalent to the Western half step, whole step and augmented second, respectively), and a three-quarter-step interval (for example, from D to E♭).

Rast is not only the primary maqam in presentations of Arab music theory, it is also one of the most prominent maqams in performance, occurring in countless songs and instrumental pieces in every genre.[9] It occurs most conspicuously in the Islamic call to prayer, recited five times a day: most traditions of recitation use one or another of the maqams to render an improvised presentation of the call's five lines of text, and in much of the Arab world Rast is the maqam of choice. (You can hear such a call by the renowned 'Abd al-Bāsiṭ 'Abd al-Ṣamad on numerous YouTube videos.) Since for many Muslims music falls within the secular realm – with some regarding it as haram – when maqam melodies are used to render the call to prayer, or the holy Qur'an, these practices are not considered as 'music' per se. This understanding is reflected in the vocabulary used to describe these forms: the individual who renders the call, or the Qur'an, is not a 'singer' but a 'reciter'; a 'caller' may be said to 'say' or 'give' the call to prayer.

In order to glimpse some of the many layers implicit in each maqam, we will consider maqam *Nahāwand* which, on a basic level, may be considered the equivalent of the Western minor scale. As we learn progressive layers of detail, however, we will see that we have gone far beyond the definition of the minor scale and are, instead, coming to understand aspects of an eastern Arab mode.

Readers with little background in detailed music-theory discussion should go through the following section of this chapter without getting bogged down by specific points, seeking instead to come away with a general sense of the issues and features that characterise the eastern Arab maqam system.

■ Maqām Nahāwand

The basic scale of *maqām Nahāwand* is: C–D–E♭–F–G–A♭–B♭–(or B)–C. In the twentieth century, tetrachordal theory became the dominant method of analysing a maqam's scalar structure. The first four notes of a given maqam constitute a mode's lower tetrachord; the upper part of the scale constitutes the mode's upper tetrachord, thus giving a quick shorthand for analysing and naming the two halves of any scale. In maqam Nahawand, the lower tetrachord, with an intervallic structure of 4–2–4 (in terms of quarter-steps) is called a Nahawand tetrachord. The upper tetrachord is either a Kurd tetrachord when there is B♭ (with a 2–4–4 intervallic structure) or a Hijaz tetrachord when there is a B♮ (2–6–2). (The tetrachords are named according to the prominent maqam in which they occur as the lower tetrachord.)

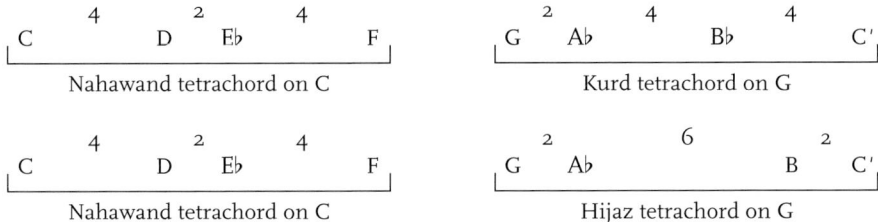

When maqam theory became enshrined in the new institutional curriculum in the mid-twentieth century, it was commonly limited to the three elements already discussed: each maqam was defined in terms of a single-octave scale, and further analysed in terms of intervallic and tetrachordal structures. But musicians also learn about additional elements by listening to, and learning to perform, compositions and improvisations. For example, musicians are generally quick to point out that, in terms of intonation, the E♭ of maqam Nahawand is especially low. The tuning of this note is contrasted with the E♭ in another maqam, Hijaz, where it is 'a little higher.' As the standard music theory recognises only a single E♭, the presence of two differently pitched E♭s in performance highlights the often conflicting realms of theory versus practice. Since the staff notation that is used for Arab music also recognises only a single E♭, a student must learn about examples of variant intonation aurally, by listening to music and in music lessons. Since many maqam scales do not simply duplicate at the octave, students must also learn what happens below the tonic and above the octave note. Maqam Nahawand uses B♮ below the tonic C, even though it may use both B♭ and B♮ in the central octave.

Additionally, most maqams have characteristic accidentals that occur in specific ways and contexts. Nahawand commonly uses an occasional E♮ accidental, which functions as a lower neighbouring tone to F, temporarily replacing the E♭. This accidental may occur when the note F is given emphasis. A common and somewhat dramatic way of removing the E♮ and bringing back the E♭ is in the phrase F E F–, E F G–F E♭—D C, where the return of the E♭ is accented and the note is held momentarily. Other accidentals include A♮ as a leading tone to B♭ (paralleling the E♮ accidental leading to F), A♯ as a leading tone to B♮ when the maqam has a Hijaz tetrachord on G, and F♯ as a leading tone to G. In addition, G♭ might temporarily occur as an upper neighbouring tone above F. While the G♭ might well be understood as a single-note accidental, theorists commonly interpret this as a brief modulation to a closely related maqam called *Nahāwand Muraṣṣaʿ* (whose full scale is C–D–E♭–F–G♭–A–B♭–C). Most musicians will, however, understand this as simply a characteristic movement within maqam Nahawand. It must be emphasised that none of these accidentals are obligatory: a composer or improviser chooses what to include.

But the most complex body of knowledge that a musician or composer must learn about a given maqam is the general manner of passing through a mode's many features, including where and how to start, what notes to focus on and when to insert alternative tetrachords. This knowledge is perhaps best preserved in the taqasim genre. For maqam Nahawand, a taqasim will commonly begin by focusing on the third degree of the scale, E♭, using the notes C, D and the B♮ leading tone to do so. Thus an initial phrase might be C B C D E♭ D E♭ D E♭—, followed by a fall to the leading tone (E♭ D C B—) and a cadence on the tonic (B C D E♭ D, C D C, B C—). The subsequent progression is commonly divided into a series of individual paragraphs, each ascending slightly higher and focusing on a new note or tetrachordal region, and each concluding with a return to the tonic note and a short cadential phrase (called a *qafla*): each qafla is followed by a few moments of silence before the next paragraph is begun. In maqam Nahawand, a second paragraph might focus on the note F, possibly with its E♮ accidental. After a cascading return to the tonic, qafla and brief silence, the next paragraph would commonly rise to and focus on the note G. Subsequent paragraphs might focus first on the Kurd tetrachord on G (with its B♭), then on the Hijaz tetrachord on G (with its B♮), and finally on the octave region by presenting a Nahawand tetrachord on the upper octave C. Modulations to related maqams might occur at this point, or possibly while the focus was on the G-based tetrachords.

In time, the improviser would return the melodic focus back to the tonic and perform a final, usually grandiose qafla, one that quickly ascends a full octave and just as quickly returns and closes on the tonic. The G♭ accidental might be inserted right before the final qafla as a dramatic pre-cadential accidental. Interestingly, this body of knowledge is not generally taught; a student picks it up by listening to senior musicians, and by learning compositions. Although I have described the progression in terms of a series of ascending paragraphs, it is not common that musicians explicitly conceptualise the progression in this manner. One of my own teachers in Cairo simply advised, 'Play a little of the scale here, and a little of the scale there', and 'Play from your heart.' If there is any more explicit verbalising, it might be a naming of the sequence of tetrachords: a Nahawand tetrachord on C, then the two upper tetrachords, Kurd and Hijaz on G, then a Nahawand tetrachord on the upper octave C, returning, perhaps with the Kurd tetrachord on G and finally closing on the tonic.

When creating a new composition, a composer might seek to give a condensed version of the complex progression just described. Alternatively, he or she might choose to focus on a specific moment in the larger progression. A given piece of music might contain only the maqam's most basic elements (no accidentals, alternative tetrachords or modulations) or the composer might choose to add a series of insightful points, making the piece a complex portrait of many of the maqam's unique features. From the former type of composition, a student learns how to move around in the maqam's basic scale. From the latter type of composition, a student learns about the maqam's complexities. When listening to and analysing a sophisticated composition during one of my lessons in Cairo, one of my teachers would excitedly exclaim, 'It is a school [*madrasa*]! There is so much to learn from this one composition!'

■ *Īqā'*

In eastern Arab music, the rhythms (singular *īqā'*; plural *īqā'āt*) are cyclical. Numbering in the dozens, individual iqa'at are created by the consistent recurrence of two primary sounds, a low resonant sound called *dumm* and a contrasting high pitch sound called *takk*. The dumm (D) is heard when the percussionist activates the sound of the entire drumhead, while the takk (T) is commonly produced by striking the rim of the drum or tambourine. Common rhythms for art music are *waḥda*, usually written in staff notation as filling a 4/4 measure with the pattern D--T--T- (where the dashes represent rests and each D, T or - indicates an eighth-note (quaver) duration), and *maqṣūm*, also filling a 4/4 measure, with the pattern DT-TD-T-. While I have given the basic skeletal patterns for these two rhythms, a drummer or tambourine player has great freedom to embellish the rhythms with additional strokes (usually additional takks) in response to the energy level of the given moment. Thus wahda might be presented as D-MT-KT- (pronounced dum-ma tak-ka takk, where the ma and ka represent additional takks) or, perhaps DtktkTtktkTT (pronounced dumm takka takka takk, takka takka takk takk, where the strokes in large capital letters are eighth notes (quavers), and the strokes in small capitals are sixteenth notes (semiquavers)). The art music vocal genre muwashshah is especially renowned for its use of a great variety of iqa's, including *mudawwar* (12/4), *muḥajjar* (14/4), *mukhammas* (16/4), *murabba'* (13/4), *nawakht* (7/4), *samā'ī thaqīl* (10/8) and *samā'ī dārij* (6/8). Each maqam and iqa' is understood to have its own aesthetic feel; changes in either thus commonly represent dramatic moments in a composition.

Instruments

The traditional takht ensemble consisted of four melodic instruments. The oud is a short-necked unfretted lute, with a thin spruce or cedar face and a rounded back made of strips of a variety of woods. It is common for musicians to approach an oud maker and specifically request the type or types or wood for the back and also the levels of ornamentation on the instrument as a whole. Some request a single wood, perhaps mahogany with thin stripes of white celluloid separating the strips; others ask for an alternation of different coloured woods, perhaps different shades of brown, or brown, white and red; some like highly ornamented faces while others favour a simple look.

The shape of the oud has changed over time. At the beginning of the twentieth century, Cairo ouds were largely unornamented and had a single rosette, but by mid-century a larger, highly ornamented version with three rosettes became popular. At the beginning of the twentieth century, ouds commonly had five double courses of strings, tuned to a low G followed by series of ascending fourths, starting a step higher with A, then D, G and C. By the end of the century a sixth course had become normal; this was added either at the high or low end of the instrument at an interval of a fourth: thus, either a high F above the C or a low D below the low G. Variation in the tuning of the lowest two strings is common: many tune these two strings down a step, to low C and F. The strings are plucked with a plectrum that was traditionally made from an eagle feather, but today is commonly made of thin strips of plastic.

The oud traditionally held a primary place in the takht: it was considered ideal for evoking the state of deep aesthetic involvement called *ṭarab* (often translated as ecstasy) that would, ideally, pervade musicians and audience alike.[10] The old-style wasla often began with a solo oud improvisation.

The nay reed flute comes in seven different sizes. Each is able to play all of the maqams, but in only one root position: if you want to play a given maqam at a higher or lower position, you simply pick up a different nay. The instrument has six finger holes on the upper side and one thumb-hole below; the player rests his lips on one end of the reed and blows across the rim to produce the sound, a technique that gives the nay its characteristically breathy timbre. Extending downward from the player's mouth, the instrument is held obliquely on the right side of the body.

The qanun trapezoidal zither is played across the performer's lap or placed on a special table in front of the seated performer. Stretched from right to left across the face of the instrument are twenty-five to twenty-seven sets of strings, mostly triple-coursed; the highest and lowest may be single- or double-coursed. Plucked with two short plectra attached to the index finger of each hand, the strings are tuned to consecutive seven-note scales, giving a range of over three octaves. From the early decades of the twentieth century a set of tiny metal levers (*'urab*) were placed under each course of strings (by the player's left hand) in order to allow the player to change their length and thus the tuning: this facilitates the use of accidentals and the execution of modulations from one maqam to another. Before the introduction of these levers, performers would press their

THE EASTERN ARAB WORLD

Above: Three ouds: *(left)* a 1919 instrument with a single rosette; *(middle)* the back of an oud showing the multiple strips of wood separated by thin ornamental bands; *(right)* a 1970s instrument with three highly ornamented rosettes

Left: The most famous oud-player of the twentieth century, Farid al-Atrash (1910–74), was born in Syria but moved to Cairo, where he had a glorious career as a singer, composer and film star. Note his highly ornamented oud in this publicity poster.

287

THE OTHER CLASSICAL MUSICS

Above: A qanun in playing position. The rings on the index fingers serve to hold small plectra in place. This instrument is triple-coursed: each group of three strings is tuned to the same note and attached to the tuning pegs on the right. The long bridge on the left (half of it extending under the player's right hand) sits on five rectangular pieces of white fish skin; the tiny metal levers under each course of strings by the player's left hand allows the player to change the tuning.

Below: The Arab tambourine, known as the riqq or daff. The two examples on the left represent the traditional inlay-ornamented animal-skin (here, fish-skin) instruments that were used until the 1970s. A succession of plastic-headed types have since appeared, with screw mechanisms for tightening the head. Note that all have five sets of cymbals.

left thumbnail (and occasionally one of the left-hand fingernails) on a set of strings to achieve temporary changes in tuning. The instrument's natural levels of amplification are greatly increased by five taut rectangular pieces of fish skin that are set under the five legs of the qanun's long bridge resting near the player's right hand.

The European violin was adopted into Arab music in the latter part of the nineteenth century, replacing the indigenous two-string coconut-gourd spike-fiddle in art-music performances and even usurping this instrument's name, kamanja or *kamān*. For Arab music, the violin is tuned to g–d'–g'–d", rather than the European tuning g–d'–a'–e". In art-music ensembles, the number of violins increased throughout the first half of the twentieth century, beginning with a single violin and ending with a violin section of twelve or more, in imitation of Western orchestras.

The traditional takht had only a single percussion instrument, the riqq tambourine. With five sets of cymbals distributed around the frame, it is valued for its great variety of sounds: these are created by an assortment of different strokes on the head (customarily made of fish or goat skin, but now commonly of plastic) with all cymbals dampened, by striking only a single set a cymbals, or by activating all the cymbals together. When

Nay flutes of four sizes, made of reed. Note the six finger-holes on the top and the thumb-hole on the bottom.

the takht expanded to orchestral size, a single-headed goblet-shaped hand drum called *ṭabla* or *darbukka* was added. With a body traditionally made of fired clay and a sounding head of goat, calf or fish skin, a plastic-headed, aluminum-bodied version became the instrument of choice from the mid-1980s. The instrument rests across the seated musician's upper left thigh, and is held in place with the left elbow, with the right hand creating the dumms and either hand the takks that make up the rhythms.

Additional instruments were added in the second half of the twentieth century. The accordion and keyboard had to be modified so that they could produce non-Western quarter-tones; guitars were occasionally given two extra frets for this purpose, while saxophone players learned to modify their embouchure or fingering to produce these extra notes.

Regionality highlighted in two portraits

In order to highlight distinct traditions within the larger eastern Arab framework, here are two brief portraits of renowned singers. Based in the northern Syrian city of Aleppo, Sabah Fakhri (b. 1933) is a star throughout the Arab world and beyond, his music featured on television, cassettes, CDs, DVDs, and now countless YouTube videos. He has performed prolifically throughout the world, and maintains the old style of performing waslas, the suite-form that faded in Egypt in the early twentieth century. With an expanded takht ensemble – including four or more violins, cello, darbukka and a small male chorus – Fakhri regales his audiences with an array of traditional genres including the instrumental sama'i and taqasim, an occasional dawr and numerous muwashshahs. (Aleppo has been celebrated as one of the great centres of the muwashshah ever since the form's importation from Andalusia nearly a millennium ago.) Highlighting the lack of clear boundaries between classical, folk and popular, Fakhri includes the local Aleppan genre of *qudūd* songs in his performances. These are short strophic songs known to all, and Fakhri often concludes a wasla with a series of them, and with the audience singing along the energy of the performance builds to ecstatic levels.

The Lebanese superstar Fayrouz (b. 1935) is one of the most famous Arab singers, having developed a unique style and sound working with a composer/poet duo, the Raḥbānī Brothers 'Aṣṣī (whom she married) and Manṣūr. Set in maqams and iqa's, but also including strong elements of Western orchestration, Fayrouz's repertoire has a modern feel with both Middle Eastern and European components, matching the sense that Lebanon, as a country, stands as a bridge between Europe and the Middle East. Like Fakhri, she has performed throughout the world, but accompanied by a large orchestra (divided on stage into Western and Arabic sections) and large male and female choruses. Her repertoire is wide and varied: she has recorded albums featuring muwashshahs (many in new arrangements) and played the lead role in some two dozen theatrical productions (musicals) between the late 1950s and the 1970s, many of these staged at the ancient Roman temples at Ba'albek in eastern Lebanon and including Lebanese folk music and dance. Throughout her career, Fayrouz has maintained a close connection with her country's political life, responding to current events in song texts and with specific concerts: her historic 1994 performance in Martyrs' Square in Beirut, for example, marked the revitalisation of the reunited city after fifteen years of civil war.[11]

THE EASTERN ARAB WORLD

■ *Today*

The passing of a generation of superstar singers in the 1970s (Farid al-Atrash, d. 1974; Umm Kulthum, d. 1975; 'Abd al-Halim Hafiz, d. 1977) was a turning point for eastern Arab art music. Working with the greatest poets and composers of their day in recordings, film, radio, television and live performance, these singers had created an art music that was also the region's popular music. Musicians and the intelligentsia considered the repertoire to be high art music; the common folk knew and loved thousands of these songs. By the 1970s, however, a new wave of popular music began featuring shorter dance-oriented songs with lighter lyrics and simpler, more catchy melodies. Performed with an ensemble that commonly included two keyboard players, electric bass and trap drums, two new styles emerged: *sha'bī* and *shabābī*. A break had occurred: this was no longer the art music of the past. The new pop music grew exponentially over the next decades, progressively taking over the new media, cassettes and CDs, VCDs and DVDs, then satellite television channels and websites.

It became common for people to mourn the loss of the old art music, but that has nonetheless survived in a variety of ways. First, some of the oldest singers have continued to perform – Sabah Fakhri through 2014 and Fayrouz until 2011. Second, the songs of the mid-twentieth century (sung by Umm Kulthum et al.) are still found on all media. Meanwhile national governments have stepped in and created national ensembles dedicated to reviving, preserving and celebrating the older music (Egypt's Arabic Music Ensemble is an early example). Performing both nationally and internationally, these ensembles serve as markers of national identity, though they have introduced many changes to the music they seek to preserve. Concerts using staff transcriptions are not open to 'in the moment' decisions that were such an integral part of the original music; choral renditions of solo vocal repertoire are now common; and because a number of government-supported ensembles are based in conservatories, young musicians are being harnessed for the propagation of this music. The new generation of musicians have nevertheless created their own connections with the older music: contestants on the American-style Arab Idol competition sometimes choose to sing an Umm Kulthum song, while young composers sample and add beats to the songs of the mid-century stars.

Over the past decade individuals and non-governmental organisations have emerged, devoted to the support of traditional Arab culture. In Cairo some have borne interesting fruit: The House of Oud (*Bayt al-'Ūd*), run by the Iraqi oud player Naseer Shamma, has seen the graduation of several classes of oud players since its foundation in 1998, with its most successful students being given leadership positions in parallel institutions in neighbouring countries. El Sawy Culturewheel, a multi-hall complex founded in 2003, offers a great variety of concerts and classes in music and other arts.

Moreover, the traditional practice of musicians gathering in living rooms continues to flourish, with some celebrated musicians attracting large groups of followers and even forming their own ensembles to play both traditional art music and their own compositions, as the violinists 'Abduh Dāghir (b. 1936) and Alfred Gamīl (b. 1957) are doing in Cairo. Some groups emphasise their determination to go beyond preservation by creating and performing new repertoire. The Iraqi-born singer Kāẓim al-Sāhir (b. 1957), whose initial fame was as a pop star, is another example of a musician who is determined to go beyond preservation by creating and performing new repertoire: his songs with lyrics by the Syrian poet Nizār Qabbānī (d. 1998) have brought him the mantle of a respected classical singer.

But Arab art music has also put down roots beyond the Middle East. Some musicians have established careers in America, leading their own ensembles and teaching the music to new generations of Americans, including Arab-Americans. Most famous is Simon Shaheen who, in 1982, founded (and still directs) the New York-based Near Eastern Music Ensemble and the week-long Annual Arab Music Retreat; held in New England, this brings together top Arab musicians to teach and perform. Performer and ethnomusicologist Ali Jihad Racy is eastern Arab music's leading American musician-scholar: based at UCLA since 1978, he has published extensively and performs, composes, records and leads a university-based ensemble, as well as training PhD students in Arab music, some of whom have gone on to found ensembles of their own. A new international interchange occurred when the UCSB Middle East Ensemble, led by this writer (Racy's former student), was invited by the Egyptian government to present a two-week concert tour during the summer of 2010. The fifty-four-member ensemble performed nine concerts in four different cities in Egypt, including four concerts at the Cairo Opera House.

Throughout its long history, the eastern Arab world has been home to a dynamic and multifaceted art-music tradition, with its plethora of genres, treatises, performers, patrons, instruments and systems of melodic and rhythmic modes. Ever-changing in response to cultural, political and technological developments, this music stands as one of the world's great traditions.

Further reading

Virginia Danielson's *The Voice of Egypt*, Laura Lohman's *Umm Kulthum* and Michal Goldman's film *Umm Kulthum* offer excellent in-depth studies of the music, life and times of the twentieth-century superstar singer. Scott Marcus's *Music in Egypt* and Jonathan Shannon's *Among the Jasmine Trees* focus on music in modern-day Egypt and Syria respectively. Racy's *Making Music in the Arab World* provides a rare inside-the-music view of the various factors involved in the production of aesthetically-engaging music. The *Garland Encyclopedia of World Music* vol. 6, *The Middle East*, provides a wealth of articles on a great variety of topics including music theory, pedagogy, gender and historical issues.

Recommended listening

Umm Kulthum, *Ana fi Intizarak*, Sono Cairo 0039, 1997. 1943 recording of one of Umm Kulthum's many famous songs.

Umm Kulthum, *Inta 'Umri* [Enta Omry], Sono Cairo 94 SDCD 01B60, 1994. 1964, composed by Muhammad 'Abd al-Wahhab, an historic first product of the long-awaited collaboration between Egypt's most famous singer and composer. In all, they produced ten songs together.

Fayrouz, *Andaloussiyat*, Voix de l'Orient VDL CD 522, 1997. One of Fayrouz's most famous recordings (from 1966), including modern renditions of a number of famous muwashshah songs.

'Abd al-Halim Hafiz, *Sawwah*, EMI 310519, 1997; Zayy al-Hawa, Virgin 848363, 2004. Two of the great singer's most famous songs.

Farid al-Atrash, *al-Rabi'*, Sono Cairo 95 SDCD 01B41, 1995. One of his most famous songs; the introduction includes an extended oud improvisation (taqasim) by the singer/composer.

Simon Shaheen et al., *Turath: Masterworks of the Middle East*, Silva Screen TSQD9025, 1992. A 1991 recording with a selection of instrumental compositions and solo improvisations by these US-based master musicians.

Ali Jihad Racy and Simon Shaheen, *Taqasim: Art of Improvisation in Arabic Music*, Lyrichord, LYRCD 7374, 1993. Improvisations by the two US-based masters of eastern Arab art music.

13 Turkey

Robert Labaree

Buoyed by dinner and many glasses of spirits, the guests settle in the living room with sweets, and some open instrument cases. Laughter and the tinkle of metal spoons on tea glasses mingle with the sound of a long-necked lute being tuned. A young woman tries out her zither, while an older man blows tentative tones on his flute. Another young woman balances a short-necked fiddle on her knee: it's tear-drop shaped, and its voice is surprisingly large; a percussionist inspects his frame drum with brass jingles. Now the sound of the flute, breathy and full of overtones, cuts through the talk, its melody moving meditatively upward in free rhythm as the other players provide quiet drones; the fiddle and lute step in, and the three converse together, conclude together. Then instruments and drum begin to move as one, in a piece in a stately tempo. After the final refrain, a guest begins to sing, freely at first, then joined by instruments. Another song follows, then others, the tempo increasing as the listeners sip tea, comment or sing along; a phone rings unanswered. Suddenly the instruments are hushed, playing a steady ostinato as a singer, eyes closed and head to one side, enters high. He begins with sustained notes, then recites on a few pitches with dramatic pauses, trilling and bending the notes with occasional rapid passages. The intense feeling resolves in a final song in quick tempo, with applause at the end, interrupted by a fast postlude. More tea is poured, and the music is submerged once more in conversation.

TURKS use a term adapted from the West, *klasik Türk müziği*[1] ('classical Turkish music'), as a catch-all for the musical practices and repertoires of the Ottoman Turkish upper classes over six centuries which continue to the present day. An alternate form, *Türk sanat müziği* ('Turkish art music'), is also a Western adaptation. Like 'classical' and 'art' as used in Europe and North America, the terms are intended in part to convey a sense of high status and cultural depth. This chapter will avoid such distracting associations by substituting a different term: *Turkish makam music*. 'Makam' is a word the Turks inherited from the Arabs (*maqam*), so by using it to describe this music we are instantly linking it to its regional heritage. In Arabic and Ottoman music-theory writings since the thirteenth century, maqam/makam carries the meaning of 'melodic mode', in the same general sense in which we refer to the melodic modes of medieval Europe and the ragas of India. Thus makam also helps to place Ottoman music globally, as one of the world's melody-centred, or monophonic, traditions.

◂ Musical Gathering, Istanbul, about 1700. (Paper, opaque watercolour, gold, 38.2 × 24.8 cm.)

In 1923 the Ottoman Turkish dynasty – founded in the fourteenth century, and for much of its span the self-appointed guardian of Muslim civilisation in the Mediterranean – was replaced by a resolutely secular Turkish republic. In the eight decades since the end of Ottoman rule, Turkish makam has created a place for certain pre-twentieth-century Ottoman musical sensibilities in the ever-expanding range of repertoires in Turkey's musical life. As with Western classical music, Turkish makam enters cultural life through public concerts, radio and television, recordings and the internet, but only since 1974 has it been taught in state-supported conservatories.

To most modern Turks this music, like Western classical music to Europeans and Americans, carries with it suggestions of the past, of nostalgia for pre-modern life, and a sense that it is an elite music for the few. But it continues to evolve in the hands of new generations of musicians, bringing a special seriousness, virtuosity and invention to a Turkish niche audience.

■ A street-level survey of Turkish music

Back in the 1980s I performed an audio experiment which illustrates the niche in which this *klasik* set of practices and repertoires now fits. Late one afternoon, as I got off the ferry at Kadıköy on the Asian side of the Bosphorus, I turned on my cassette recorder and began to walk, taking in all the sounds of the street. Through the open windows of the practice rooms at the Kadıköy branch of the Istanbul conservatory came the sounds of teenage pianists practicing Bach two-part inventions and boogie woogie bass lines. Next to the quay a nineteenth-century mosque, too small to afford a full-time müezzin, broadcast a recording of the afternoon call to prayer from its single minaret. Scratches on the record punctuated the same Arabic words being heard at that moment, mostly delivered by a live muezzin, from the minarets of each of the city's more than two thousand mosques (but here no one prayed, or even stopped). The music shops and cafés on the cobbled streets going up the hill had speaker systems too: American, British and Turkish jazz and rock, Turkish pop mixing Turkish instruments, guitars and synthesisers and Turkish folk music including that of the traditional Anatolian troubadour (*aşık*) whose poetry is saturated with references to mystical Islam. A restaurant with white tablecloths added a bit of Verdi to the mix. In this short walk, my tape had captured a fair sampling of contemporary Turkish musical life. The main element missing from this array was the repertoire which is the subject of this chapter.

There are reasons for its absence, and the performance described at the opening of this chapter suggests some of them. As flies on the wall of that fictionalised middle-class living room, we could observe that this music arose naturally out of informal conversation: in this intimate setting the voice is central and the words of the older songs (mostly in a language no longer spoken, which mixes Turkish with Persian and Arabic) reflect the centuries-old association of Turkish makam with Islamic mysticism, in which the unattainable love-object is often ambiguously mortal and divine. The ensemble is small and transparent, allowing every musician to be heard. Etiquette governs the musical texture of

A Bektashi djem in Anatolia: a ritual of one of Turkey's ecstatic religious orders

the performance, as in polite society – *lütfen buyurunuz* ('please, after you'): your turn, now my turn, now together. A single melody attracts the listener's attention, yet the texture is complex, spontaneous and multi-voiced, with one instrument of each type speaking as a soloist. The result is like the conversation from which the performance emerged, where each voice can be heard and appreciated.

In certain ways we could have been flies on the wall in an aristocratic mansion or Ottoman palace in the eighteenth century. Women were then often prominent performers as well, though usually as family members, servants or members of the harem. Before the twentieth century, in a society shaped more profoundly by religion, this music was dominated by members of Sufi *tarikats*, the mystical Islamic brotherhoods outlawed by the new Republic in the 1920s; in recent decades these have been returning to public life. The instruments in this performance are versions of those in the eighteenth century, as is much of the musical terminology; even some of the repertoire is by musicians born in that time.

No wonder such a sensitive multi-century concoction is so rarely heard on the street (but then, how often is a Haydn string quartet heard on the street either?). No wonder attempts continue to be made by musicians, abetted by government arts policy since the 1920s, to fatten this intimate conversational model with mixed choruses and large orchestras, to compete with the sheer heft of the Western symphony orchestra, the concert grand piano, the *bel canto* singing style and four-part harmony. For modern Turks have a full plate: virtually any music available to listeners in the United States and Europe is available to them. Many under the age of sixty heard more Mozart and Jimi Hendrix than Hamamizade Dede Efendi (1778–1846) as children. As comparison-shoppers they, like listeners of Western classical music, hear Turkish classical music as just one voice among many.

Therefore we must ask: what special qualities does Turkish makam music have that allow it to hold its place in a field which includes Turkish folk music, Turkish pop, Turkish jazz, Turkish symphonic music and Turkish film music? Part of the answer is not musical at all, since both the practice and the meaning of music (any music, Eastern or Western) arise from history. Long before we have heard the first note of Turkish classical music, we have been prepared for what to expect from it, and even for what it means. So before taking the plunge into the terrain of *koma* and *vezin*, *peşrev* and *taksim*, it is to history we must turn.

■ History

> ... infidels are not to mount a horse, wear a sable fur, fur caps, European silk, velvet and satin. Infidel women are not to go about in the Muslim style and manner of dress and wear Paris overcoats ...
>
> From a royal decree by Sultan Murad IV in 1631[2]

> It may be confirmed for a proper truth that, if the western princes had been lords of Asia, instead of the Saracens and Turks, there would be now no remnant of the Greek church, and they would not have tolerated Mahometanism, as these Infidels have tolerated Christianity ...
>
> Entry on 'Mahomet' in the 1697 *Dictionnaire historique et critique*
> by French Protestant philosopher Pierre Bayle[3]

As is suggested by these two seventeenth-century sources, one Turkish and the other European, the history of the Ottomans is no simple matter to summarise, especially when viewed from both sides of its borders: six hundred years of dynastic rule by the house of Osman, preceded by seven hundred years of Arabic Muslim rule to which the Ottomans were heirs, and incorporating at one time or another all the peoples, religions, languages and lands from North Africa (excluding Morocco) to the border of present-day Iran, from the Persian Gulf to the Black Sea and much of the Balkans.

Two historical themes may help sharpen our understanding of Ottoman music and its twentieth-century continuation.

▶ A Euro-Ottoman symbiosis[4]

Until recent decades, European-language accounts of Ottoman-European relations have tended to emphasise conflict. But the historian Richard Goffman's term 'symbiosis' suggests something more like a mutual dependency – by no means devoid of conflict, but also more interconnected. This is a view of politics and economics which prepares us to hear Ottoman music as former generations in the West never could. For them, Turkish music was inseparable from the conflict paradigm, the embodiment of inalterable otherness – Turkish barbarity, aggression and depravity in another form. But music is also promiscuous, carried in the air and in memory over boundaries of neighbourhood and ethnicity, making the idea of interaction and mutual dependence as good a place to begin our exploration of Ottoman history and music as the idea of continual conflict.

▶ Diversity as an Ottoman policy

The Ottomans never wavered in their belief in the superiority of the Muslim message to mankind, viewing the non-Muslim peoples of their empire as second-class citizens – 'separate, unequal and protected', as one historian has put it[5] – and charging them with a special tax. General Muslim practice designated monotheistic communities which chose not to convert to Islam 'people of the book' *(ahl al-kitab)* because of the obvious textual links between the Old and New Testaments and the Qur'an. But the Ottomans saw the ethnic and religious diversity of their domain as essential to the empire's internal harmony and economic strength, and took extra steps to manage it. Greek, Armenian and Jewish communities, each an official Ottoman minority *(millet)*, lived in their own neighbourhoods and towns, spoke their own languages, and lived by their own codes under their own religious leaders who answered to the Ottoman authorities.

The participation of Jews and Christians in Ottoman society (especially in its economic life) was vigorously protected when competition among groups threatened the status quo, even leading at times to the suppression of troublesome Muslim groups. As historian Cemal Kafadar has pointed out, Ottoman tolerance was less like modern tolerance and closer to the original Latin word – *toleo*, meaning 'to bear', as in 'how much pain can you bear?'[6] And until the rise of European-style nationalism in the nineteenth century, the Ottoman region could bear considerable diversity. This picture of a pragmatic cosmopolitanism provides a useful platform for approaching Ottoman makam music: a polyglot mix of Arabic, Persian, Greek, Jewish, Armenian and Turkish cultural inheritances, developed through a long history of direct and sustained interactions among distinct and stable communities.

■ The Ottoman Empire and its Mediterranean inheritance

In the year 1299 a regional Turkmen chieftain known as Osman separated from the confederacy of the Selçuk Turks which had spread from the East and taken much of Anatolia from the Byzantine empire over the preceding century, and became the first of the *Osmanlı* or Ottoman rulers. He was renamed Osman I by later generations to mark his place in a potent and growing dynastic line. In the fourteenth century that dynasty assumed the title *sultan* (Arabic: 'supreme authority'), and eventually several other titles reflecting the empire's cultural heritage: *han* or *khan* (Turkmen) and *padişah* and *hünkar* (Persian). By the time the sultanate was abolished as an institution by the newly created Turkish National Assembly in 1922, thirty-six Ottoman sultans had come and gone, with the last of them, Mehmed VI, ushered quietly into exile in Monte Carlo.

The Ottomans succeeded to a series of Muslim empires in the Middle East and North Africa which made capital cities first in Damascus and then in Baghdad. The highly Persianised Seljuk Turks, who planted the seeds of an enduring Persian legacy within Ottoman culture, made their capital in Konya, in central Anatolia. After the Seljuks, the Ottomans made capitals farther west in Bursa (1324), Edirne (1363) and finally Constantinople (1453). The spiritual centre of each of these Muslim empires remained the so-called Hicaz, the region incorporating the holy cities of Mecca and Medina on the Arabian peninsula. The succession of Islamic capitals from the eighth to the fifteenth centuries, however, shows a gradual shift from the Middle East (the Arabic kingdoms) to Anatolia and Europe (the Turks). From 1453 to 1923 the Ottoman centre at Constantinople/Istanbul physically straddled the Bosphorus, the waterway dividing the two parts of the Eurasian subcontinent. Inhabitants of modern Istanbul still speak of the eastern and western halves of their city as *Asya* (Asia) and *Avrupa* (Europe), as casually as Parisians refer to *la rive gauche* and *la rive droite*.

Yet it is no accident that the map of the Mediterranean Muslim empire at its height under the Ottoman sultan Süleyman I in the sixteenth century should so closely resemble that of the Christian Byzantine empire at its greatest extent in the sixth century under the emperor Justinian: both Justinian and Süleyman had their eyes fixed on an earlier benchmark. Before the Byzantines, the pagan Roman empire in the second century CE had reached from Britain to Persia, and Greek Christian rulers after Constantine the Great in the fourth century had been inspired to live up to the pagan model. Beginning in the seventh century, ambitious Arabic, Berber and Turkish Muslim rulers also aspired to adapt the Roman model, now Christian, to their own purposes. 'Rome' now had a second capital city in Constantinople on the Bosphorus, which Constantine had favoured over the city of Rome as the centre of gravity for Christianity. The conqueror of Constantinople, Sultan Mehmed II, referred to himself as Caesar of Rome, *kayzer-i Rum*. Today, the word *Rum* in Turkish commonly stands for 'Greek' (by extension Christian), since that is what the model of 'Rome' had meant to Middle Eastern Islam.

The extent and rapidity of the spread of Islam from China to Spain – including the fall of Constantinople to the Ottomans in 1453 – was not lost on rulers of Europe, instilling a sense that the Christian lands were beset by hostile non-Christian forces. Yet conflict and competition for land and souls in the Mediterranean world also had the effect of creating a mutually defining sense of identity on both sides. European maps of the world in the centuries after Columbus depicted an *orbis christiani,* the Christian regions (Europe) staked with crosses, bounded on the west by the Atlantic Ocean and to the east and south by regions – mostly Ottoman – flagged with the crescent of Islam. Parallel concepts to orbis christiani, inherited by the Ottomans from earlier Muslim theologians, divided the world starkly between *dar al-Islam* and *dar al-harp*, 'the house of Islam' and the 'the house of struggle', ameliorated only by *dar al-suh*, 'the house of truce'. Moreover, internal conflicts – Muslim against Muslim and Christian against Christian – were the rule on both sides. But even though brisk commerce

A band in Ottoman Aleppo, depicted by Alexander Russell in 1794 under the title 'The Chamber Music drawn from Life'. As described by Russell, 'the first is a Turk of lower class, he beats the Diff. The person next to him is an ordinary Christian and plays the Tanboor. The middle figure is a Dervish, he is playing the naie. The fourth is a Christian of middle rank, he plays the Kamangi. The last man, he beats the Nakara with his fingers in order to soften the sound for the voice, but the drum sticks appear from under his vest.'

between the Muslim and Christian kingdoms rarely ceased, even in wartime, each side continued to pay lip service to the unity of their religious communities with concepts like *umma* (the community of Muslim believers) and *Christendom*. Each side defined the extent of its own community according to where the other community stopped, and each nurtured its own dream of a world united behind its particular revealed truth.

■ Music and the end of the Ottoman Empire

> As for oriental music, it has continued to stagnate. For, in preserving quarter tones, it has always been deprived of harmony. After it was translated into Arabic by Farabi, this unhealthy music found success at the court and was transmitted to the Persians and the Ottomans ...
>
> Ziya Gökalp, 1923[7]

These words of Ziya Gökalp (1876–1924), an influential thinker during the transition period from Ottoman empire to Turkish republic, echo the more extreme sentiments of the generation of Turkish leaders who emerged during and after the First World War. Centuries of wariness of the non-believing civilisation to the west, followed by guarded curiosity about its workings – both attitudes compatible with an enduring Euro-Ottoman symbiosis – was replaced within a few decades by the one-sided conviction that much of the 'oriental' culture of the Ottomans now stood in the way of progress. Practices of law, finance, education and industry were openly borrowed from the same nations which, as victors over the Axis Powers (Austria-Hungary plus the Ottomans), had just dictated the terms of the Treaty of Sèvres (1920) which partitioned the multicultural Ottoman empire into separate national entities. In the view of President Mustafa Kemal Atatürk (1881–1938) and his ministers, the demise of the Ottoman world was final and history appeared to have moved on, leaving the Ottoman region behind. It was time to catch up.

Post-Ottoman policies tended to treat modernisation as a package of inseparable features: secularism, stock markets, universal education and the European alphabet were considered of a piece with staff notation, pianos and symphony orchestras. Beginning in 1928, the Ottoman Sufi orders which had for so long provided many of the most influential figures of Ottoman music were suppressed, their meeting-places locked and their ceremonies forced underground. The secular concert hall was promoted as the ideal setting for Turkish music of all kinds, where a stage, applause, tuxedoed performers and ensembles with conductors created a museum-like neutrality for musical practices shorn of their historical contexts.

Perhaps the most far-reaching legacy of the post-Ottoman reform period is the historical schism set up between monophonic and polyphonic musical practices. Taking Europe's unique historical development from monophony to polyphony as the exclusive standard, Ottoman makam music had not even reached the Renaissance. The German composer Paul Hindemith, a consultant on Turkish music education, said in his final report to Atatürk in 1938 that Turkish makam music is 'unsuited to polyphonic treatment – and in all attempts to develop music an ordered combination of various voices is essential.'[8] The choice was clear: the way of melody leads back, the way forward was with harmony. It is this newly secularised and western-leaning environment in which the idea of a 'classical' Turkish music was born.

▪ Turkish makam music

As an introduction to both Ottoman music of the past and current Turkish practice, consider the notation of a nineteenth-century Ottoman song in Example 13.1, published in the early 1980s in Istanbul.

> Come, you tall beauty, tomorrow
> Let us secretly walk over to the river at Göksu
> Hidden from others' eyes
> Let us secretly walk over to Göksu
> You are a rose bud, a flirtatious blossom
> Take delight and open your eyes, smile a little
> You have not gone in two years, at least this Summer
> Let us secretly walk over to Göksu

EX. 13.1 *Gel seninle yarın ey serv-i revan*, a classical song (şarkı) by Hacı Sadullah Ağa (1760–1825)

(1) Hacı Sadullah Ağa (1760–1825), the composer of this song, was a famous Ottoman singer and court musician and a contemporary of Beethoven (1770–1827). The son of a famous religious singer, at an early age Sadullah was offered a place in the palace school in Istanbul by Sultan Abdülhamit I (r. 1774–89) to be trained in music, languages and literature. He served as a palace musician for much of his adult life. This is his traditional Ottoman name: *Hacı* tells us that he had made the pilgrimage to Mecca (*hac*) and *Ağa* means 'lord' or 'master', suggesting that he was of the landowning class. Sadullah, his given name, is Arabic, meaning 'blessed of God'. Following the Ottoman custom Sadullah had no surname. To a Turkish reader, the very name of this composer would immediately evoke a bygone era.

(2) *Ağır aksak* is the name of the song's rhythmic cycle or *usul*, a key feature of Ottoman musical form. The 9/4 metre signature and metronome marking (♩ = 60) are redundant twentieth-century adaptations: ağır aksak itself stands for a nine beat cycle in a particular pattern of weak and strong beats divided 2–2–2–3.

Ağır means 'slow', 'serious' or 'heavy' and indicates a slower tempo. Aksak means 'limping', a term assigned to some cycles combining groups of two and three beats.

(3) *Hicazkâr şarkı* refers to the song's melodic mode, *Hicazkar makam*, with a basic scale form of G–A♭–B𝄫–C–D–E♭–F♯–G, and its general form, şarkı. The flat and sharp symbols at the beginning of each new line (4) mimic the familiar western key signature which signals which accidentals to expect, but the word Hicazkâr itself actually tells a musician more about the scales, accidentals and melodic behaviour of the piece than a key signature.

The notation used here relies on western musical conventions, first introduced in the nineteenth century – including the five-line staff, fractional note values (½, ¼, ⅛) and key and metre signatures. Some of the Turkish accidentals are different from western standards, suggesting more pitch choices than on the piano: for example, 'backward' flats (𝄫) and flats with a slash (♭). Accidentals change in this piece, suggesting the presence of something like modulation in Western music. Also, the notation is monophonic: it only represents the pitches and rhythms of a melody, with no harmony implied and no special parts for instrumental accompaniment.

(5) *Poetry*. Translation aside, the poetic craft of this two-stanza poem – its rhyme scheme, uniformity of 11-syllable lines and repetition of refrains – catches the eye. In the 1980s, some fifty years after the end of Ottoman rule, and after nearly a century of language and alphabet changes, the editor of this notation added explanatory information. The patterns of nonsense syllables at (6) (*fâilâtün* [*feilâtün*] *fâilâtün fâilün*) represent the poetic metre of each line (*vezin*), a method of teaching and composing poetry inherited from the Arabs and Persians and developed further by the Ottomans. The editor's glossary (7) provides Arabic or Persianate expressions (left side) with their modern Turkish equivalents (right side), like some modern English editions of Chaucer and Shakespeare.

■ Makam: melodic system, melodic strategy, and melodic family

The place to begin any discussion of Turkish makam music is where any Turkish musician would begin, with the concept of *makam* itself. The word 'makam' cuts across too many familiar conventions to be captured in a single term from the European tradition. It is best approached from three overlapping points of view: first, from a general perspective, as an abstract term; second, from the perspective of performers and composers; and third, from the perspective of the listener.

In its most general sense, makam is a melodic system encompassing both composition and performance and the entire historic repertoire of Turkish music, as in the phrase 'Turkish makam music'. Turkish theorists today list at least sixty makams, perhaps one hundred and twenty if we include less common ones. Makam, in this sense, is a kind of a filing system for the whole repertoire. A piece or improvisation not classifiable by makam would be anomalous.

To composers and performers, a makam is a strategy for creating new melodies – part scale, part melodic template, part aesthetic rule book. In the traditional oral training of *meşk*, the student imitates the most minute details of intonation, style and gesture characteristic of each makam. Performing and composing in makam are treated as one practice: as you learn by imitation to recreate the work of past musicians, you are also learning to create for yourself.

To audiences, every melody in Turkish makam is heard as a member of a particular melodic family exhibiting common behavioural traits. Like any human family, all melodies in *Hüseyni makam*, for example, resemble each other and are different from other melodic families, even though each individual melody in the family is unique. But Hüseyni, like a human family, is also potentially infinite: the number of unique melodies creatable from the pool of Hüseyni traits is endless and the makam is always growing, as performers add new qualities to the pool. Knowledgeable listeners can hear and appreciate fresh revisions to a makam, but they will also be alert to perceived violations of its identity.

The Mediterranean culture that the Ottomans inherited through the Christian Byzantines brought with it the traditions of pre-Christian Greek music theory, which the Arabs had translated from classical Greek writings in the eighth and ninth centuries. What Ottoman and Arabic theorists called the science of music (*ilm-i musiki*) included the structure of tetrachords and scales, and mathematical theories for the systematic tuning of intervals – the same science brought into European music in the Middle Ages.

Familiar as the Turkish notation system now looks (as in Example 13.1 above), the pitches represented by the notes on the staff are actually different from those on the piano. In the West, the whole step (for example, A–B or C♯–D♯) is divided in two equal parts. In Turkey, each whole step is divided into nine equal parts, each part called a *koma*. This is what the musicians expect to hear when the notation is executed. In notation, there are just three sharps and three flats (not nine), representing the most common ways that the whole step is divided in practice, and performers treat those six accidentals flexibly, sometimes flatter and sometimes sharper depending on context.

The following diagram compares Turkish and Western flats and sharps, showing how the pitches in the two systems do not line up. (1k, 4k and 5k = 1 koma, 4 koma and 5 koma)

Western system	A ↓	B♭ ↓	B ↓	...	E ↓	F ↓	F♯ ↓
	↑	↑ ↑	↑ ↑		↑	↑ ↑	↑ ↑
Turkish system	A	B♭ B♭ 5k 4k	B♮ B 1k	...	E	F F♯ 1k	F♯ F♯ 4k 5k

Within Turkish makam music these tiny discriminations of pitch – for example, between a B♭ (5 komas) and a B♭ (4 komas) – are important traits distinguishing one makam from another.

The Arabs also passed to the Ottomans the classical Greek method of constructing scales with the tetrachord (fourth) and pentachord (fifth), four-note and five-note scale-wise sequences of pitches which in modern Turkish music are the basic building blocks of every makam. In practice, tetrachords are concise transposable pitch groupings, which signal to the listener and performer the cues to melodic families. Moreover, new makams are invented by re-combining familiar tetrachords. Not unlike modulation between different keys in Western harmonic music, modulation from one makam to another harnesses distinct makam identities to create subtle and sometimes dramatic contrasts. Often very slight alterations of a tetrachord can provide the connection to another makam.

But any Turkish makam musician will tell you that the most important aspects of makam are not its objective scales, tunings and tetrachords, even though conversation among musicians is impossible without them. Two modern concepts now embody the subjective aspects of makam: characteristic melodic gesture or *çeşni* ('flavour'), and characteristic melodic pathway or *seyir* ('journey', 'progress'). These old terms have risen to standard usage in makam pedagogy only since the mid-twentieth century.

A çeşni, also referred to as a stereotyped melodic phrase, is a small nugget of makam identity, usually incorporating only a few pitches. A well-known sequence of tones – a kind of tune fragment – can immediately trigger a listener's memory of repertoire in a particular makam. In this respect, çeşni is comparable to allusion in poetry where the poet may trigger a whole cluster of associations to a familiar phrase. Like poetic allusion, çeşni can deliver depth and richness of detail in a single condensed utterance.

Seyir, or melodic pathway, has become the single most important feature of a makam in post-Ottoman pedagogy. The term is now used in three ways:

- Seyir is a general word for the sum of all the subjective qualities of a makam – the behavioural tendencies which characterise it.

- Seyir may also stand for three standardised paradigms of melodic direction a makam may follow – 'ascending' (*inici*), 'descending' (*çıkıcı*) and 'ascending-descending' (*inici-çıkıcı*). The three typical pathways are summarised as a line connecting a melody's beginning and ending pitches. Uşşak, Hüseyni and Muhayyer makams, for example, have nearly identical scales (A–B♭–C–D–E–F[♯]–G–A), but their seyirs differ: Uşşak melodies (ascending seyir) start around A (its *karar* or final), rise, then fall to the A; Hüseyni melodies (ascending–descending seyir) start around E, rise to the upper octave, then fall to A; Muhayyer melodies (descending seyir) start around the upper octave and fall to the A. Aesthetically, the three paradigms come across as gravitational metaphors, with the karar as the force drawing all melodic movement down to a conclusion. Seyir is also a vocal metaphor: tension increases and decreases as the voice moves higher and lower in the singer's range.

- Seyir can also be a model melody, created on the spot by a teacher to illustrate the essential progression of the makam. However, existing repertoire and recorded *taksims* (improvisations) by respected musicians remain the preferred exemplars of seyir.

Usul: the rhythmic mould

> With regard to the metre the oriental music surpasses highly the European music. There are twenty-four kinds of metres (which are called *usul*) by which the pace of time is measured. [Thus], there is great difficulty in singing correctly and perfectly, as well as [in playing] exactly the songs on an instrument because every author strives to compose songs at his pleasure with the metre and rhythms he likes, and because they are so intricate, those who do not know the metre cannot play the songs at all, even though they were to hear that song a thousand times ...
>
> Prince Dimitrie Cantemir, 1734[9]

Putting Turkish makam music in the simplest possible way, once a musician or a listener is equipped with the detailed and fluid melodic paradigms of makam, then that melodic material may be poured into a particular pattern of strong and weak beats (*usul*) to construct clear and replicable musical forms with a distinctive character. A single cyclical pattern may range in length from two beats to 120 beats, a repertoire of more than a hundred different patterns from which a composer may choose. Here are a few of the most common patterns in use today, presented in a combination of western-style note values with the syllables *dum* and *tek* (inherited from Arabic music), which stand for heavy and light beats on a drum. Usul is thus an notation of an exemplary rhythmic accompaniment as well as a compositional paradigm.

Düyek (8/8)
düm tek tek düm tek
 1   2   1   2   2

Aksak Semai (10/8)
düm te kâ düm tek tek
 2   1   2   2   2   1

Raksan (15/8)
düm tek tek düm tek kâ düm tek te kâ
 1   1   1   2   2   2   1   2

Devri kebir (28/8)
dümdüm tek düm tek tekedüm tek tek düm ta hek tek kâ tek kâ
  2   2   2   1   1   1   4   4   2   2   2   1   1   1

Until the twentieth century, this system of rhythmic cycles also went by the Arabic name *iq'a* ('falling' or 'causing to fall'). The term used today is the Turkish word usul, with a non-musical meaning of 'method', 'order' or 'manner'. Limiting usul to the Western notion of metre robs it of some of its richness: usul is today written like the familiar Western time signature (4/4, 6/8, 10/8 and so on), but it also conveys a sense of tempo, quality of motion and melodic style. So-called *ağır* ('heavy') usuls (see Example 13.1) tend to move at a slower pace, leaving more room for subdivisions of the beat, while cycles that are *yürük* ('fast', 'light') tend to be quicker. A song in an ağır cycle will tend to be more melismatic, with more notes per syllable, giving it more formality than a yürük cycle, which will tend toward more syllabic settings with one note per beat.

But until the twentieth century, usul was also a way that musical forms were composed, fixed and remembered in the primarily oral tradition of Turkish makam music. The Moldavian prince Dimitrie Cantemir (1673–1723), an influential Ottoman composer and theorist in his own right, compared musical metre in Turkish makam music with the idea of preserving compositions in notation, noting that 'the composers of songs do not indicate the pitches and the time value, which are extensive yet easy usage for Europeans'. Usul, he says, provided the structure by which pieces were remembered and transmitted 'without error' in the absence of notation. Even today, musicians will rehearse a piece in the traditional manner by singing it to themselves while tapping their hands on their knees, *düm-tek-tek-düm-tek*, right–left–left–right–left, the shape of the heavy and light beats providing a mould into which the voice pours the makam.

By the eighteenth century, it seems that musicians were as engaged in inventing new rhythmic structures as they were in inventing new makams. New usuls could be created by recombining short modules of existing usuls or by creating longer compound structures, the rhythmic analogy to compound makams. For example, *Zincir usul* (120 beats), already in use in the seventeenth century, is composed of five shorter usuls strung together: 16 + 20 + 24 + 28 + 32.

■ Musical form

From usul it is an easy transition to musical form in Turkish makam music. Usuls establish the rhythmic mould of a composition – the strong and weak stresses that give melody a lasting and memorable shape. The gravitational pull of makam away from and toward a karar, or final pitch, also articulates form, comparable to the 'home and away' harmonic movement of Western music over at least five centuries. A few examples of traditional genres will illustrate the shaping power of makam and of usul, and even of the absence of usul.

The performance described at the opening of this chapter was a version of the traditional Ottoman suite of secular vocal pieces known as *fasıl* which has parallels in the *wasl*, *muwashshah* and *nuba* of North Africa and the Middle East. The following diagram shows a modern example (1990) of fasıl performance by the Kudsi Ergüner ensemble, the structure is a lighter and shorter version of the more rigidly ordered eighteenth-century fasıl, with just five songs played without pause.

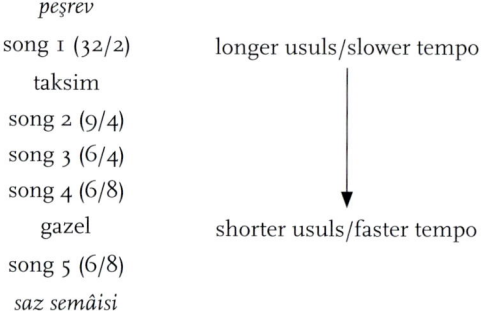

The songs are framed by an instrumental prelude called *peşrev* (from *peş*, Persian for 'head') and an instrumental postlude called *saz semâisi* ('instrumental listening piece'). Makam unifies the suite: all the songs are in either *Hicaz* makam (A–B♭–C♯–D–E–F♯–G–A) or the closely related *Hicaz-Hümâyûn* makam (A–B♭–C♯–D–E–F–G–A). Following the earlier Ottoman model, usul provides this suite's structural logic, with the songs (by a variety of composers over three centuries) arranged from longest and slowest usuls to shortest and fastest, creating a gradual build in excitement over about thirty minutes.

The *fasıl*'s peşrev and saz semâisi, composed in Hicaz-Hümâyûn makam by the eighteenth-century composer Veli Dede, have an identical rondo-like form in which three or four sections called *hane* ('house', 'place') alternate with a recurring *teslim* or refrain (see the following diagram). But for composer, performer and listener alike, it is usul which distinguishes the two otherwise identical forms in the same makam. The steady tempo and duple feel of the peşrev in Çember usul (24/4) clearly sets it apart from the saz semâisi, shaped by the limping rhythm of *aksak semai* usul (10/8) and the fast waltz time of *yürük semai* usul (6/8).

peşrev in Hicaz-Hümâyûn makam (Veli Dede, 18th century)

hane 1	A	24/4
teslim	B	
hane 2	C	
teslim	B	
hane 3	D	
teslim	B	
hane 4	E	
teslim	B	

saz semâisi in Hicaz-Hümâyûn makam (Veli Dede, 18th century)

hane 1	A	10/8
teslim	B	
hane 2	C	
teslim	B	
hane 3	D	6/8
teslim	B	10/8

The instrumental *taksim* and the vocal *gazel* are examples of makam artistry illustrating how usul is important, even when absent. Both forms have been featured in the fasıl since at least the eighteenth century, where their free rhythm melodic movement provides contrast within the usul-based logic of the suite. Turkish listeners are likely to hear the unmetred taksim and gazel (sometimes called 'vocal taksim') as akin to Qur'anic chant (*tilavet*), which by Islamic tradition is never to be metrical or pre-composed. Any singer capable

Key instruments in Turkish maqam *(clockwise from top left)*: ney, oud, kanun, tanbur, rebab, bendir. The tanbur has become an icon of Turkish makam music's refined sense of pitch, with room on its extremely long neck for forty or more adjustable frets. Only the kanun, with its ten to thirteen tuning levers per course, fully expresses in hardware the Turkish system's nine divisions of the whole step.

of the various types of free-rhythm, improvised song is probably a *hafız*, a singer (traditionally male) who has been rigorously trained in his youth in the traditional science of Qur'anic chant (*tecvid*), learning how to make makam the vehicle for the Angel Gabriel's Revelations in Arabic to the Prophet Mohammed in the seventh century. The career path of many a famous twentieth-century secular recording artist began with training as a hafız. These indirect associations of free rhythm and performer-control with Muslim spirituality are likely to lead many Turkish listeners to hear a special seriousness and emotional depth in taksim and gazel, regardless of the setting.

Despite the suppression of Turkish Sufi orders by the government throughout much of the twentieth century, their repertoire has found a place in performance and pedagogy. Students often learn Sufi devotional vocal genres such as the *ilahi* and *nefes*, less for their ritual meaning than as concise models of a makam's seyir. *Ayin*, the music of the famous whirling ceremony or *sema* of the Mevlevi brotherhood, has also become a concert staple, sung or played instrumentally. The ayin's four-movement form is a setting of the Persian poetry of Mevlana Celaluddin Rumi (1207–73), the founder of the Mevlevi order. The energy of the ayin moves fasıl-like through a metrical logic from longer, slower usuls with subdivided beats to faster usuls with one note per beat, with taksim providing a free-rhythm contrast at the beginning and end.

Instruments

Turkish musical instruments are as much the product of the aesthetic values of makam music as they are the creator of those values. Many of these instruments are shared by other peoples of the Mediterranean region who are part of the larger makam-playing family: the short-necked lute (*oud*), the zither (*kanun*), the end-blown cane flute (*ney*), the short, bowed pear-shaped fiddle (*kemençe*), the bowed spike fiddle (*rebab*), the circular frame drum (*bendir*), the goblet drum (*darbuka*) and the frame drum with brass jingles (*def*). But the small copper kettle drums (*kudum*) and the long-necked lute (*tanbur*) are today primarily limited to Turkey. The tanbur has become an icon of Turkish makam music's refined sense of pitch, with room on its extremely long neck for forty or more adjustable frets. Only the kanun, with its ten to thirteen tuning levers per course, fully expresses in hardware the Turkish system's nine divisions of the whole step.

Photographs may illustrate the basic structure, shape and size of the instruments used in Turkish makam music, but there is much that is important which is not visible. Two tendencies in Turkish instrument design are well-matched to monophonic makam performance: first, instrument-building has favoured idiosyncratic sound qualities over technical expansion; second, instruments and instrument-playing tend to be modelled on the human voice.

A theme of Western instrument evolution has been the restless experimentation with hardware and technique to enhance uniformity of tone, tuning and agility from top to bottom of the range. By contrast, consider the Turkish ney, consisting of a length of hollow reed with six finger holes and a thumb hole and a mouthpiece of buffalo horn, virtually unchanged since the thirteenth century, even as the number of makams and the tendency to modulate has grown. The Western flute's 'pure tone' allows the instrument to maintain its precise place in harmonic textures while, in its ideal solo or small group setting, the rich and fat tone-colour of the ney satisfies the ear with the complexity of each pitch. The orchestral flute can reliably execute twelve pitches per octave with great agility and accuracy, but on the slower-moving ney, any pitch can be altered nearly a whole step by subtly tilting the head, allowing the player to bend and sculpt each pitch.

The capacity of the human voice to infinitely mould pitch and to create an individualised sound is still the essential benchmark of Turkish instruments, whether plucked, blown or bowed. The natural human voice-range of about one and a half octaves is reflected in the tendency for even instrumental repertoire to stay within those limits, and contrasts sharply with the piano's eight octaves and the six octaves of nineteenth-century orchestral music.

Since the early twentieth century vibrato has become a default practice for Western vocal music and stringed instruments, even in large ensembles. In makam music, vibrato is selectively employed, one of an array of techniques for shaping melody. On a sustained note, players of kemençe, rebab or violin, for example, often execute the initial attack without vibrato, gradually adding an expressive end to the pitch. The default lack of vibrato in voice and instrument once again focuses the ear on nuances of melodic treatment and fine gradations of pitch. For Western classical musicians attempting to learn makam performance style, the selective and controlled use of instrumental and vocal vibrato is often a difficult hurdle, requiring a restructuring of technique and performance habits from the ground up.

■ The practice of Turkish makam music: a summary and supplement

> From this it may be said that French Music is simple, noble and natural; Italian Music lively, animated and attractive; and Turkish or Oriental Music soft and luxurious.
>
> Charles Henri de Blainville, 1767[10]

The impression of softness and luxury which the eighteenth-century French musician, scholar and traveller Charles Henri de Blainville heard in Turkish music was no doubt coloured by the contemporary European view of 'Oriental' culture itself as degenerate. The following general characteristics both summarise and supplement what has been said so far about Turkish makam, usul, repertoire and instruments. Just as Blainville (whose writings showed an unusual openness and empiricism) continually compared Turkish music with the music he knew best, the following concise characterisations are intended to direct attention to what may strike Western listeners as distinctive about the current practice of this music in Turkey.

It is monophonic, but its textures are often complex. No matter how many Turkish musicians are playing together at one time, they all focus on executing a single melody line, though each may interpret it differently. This monophonic

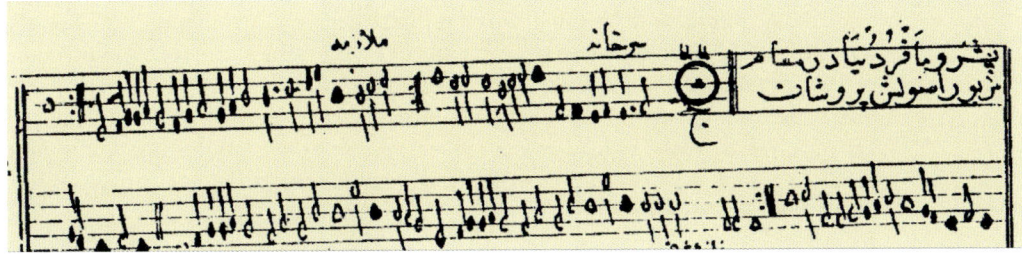

Above: Ottoman makam written in staff notation (but read right to left) by Ali Ufki (1610–75), originally a Polish church musician named Wojciech Bobowski who became a slave in Istanbul, converted to Islam and became one of the Ottoman empire's leading composers.

Left: Fifty years later the Moldavian prince Dimitrie Cantemir (1673–1723) was enslaved in a similar way, and notated makam in a way which respected the refinement of its intervals.

Below: An example of Cantemir's instrumental notation using the Arabic alphabet

Bottom: Evterpi (1830) – Byzantine notation of Ottoman makam, with Turkish song texts written in Greek letters

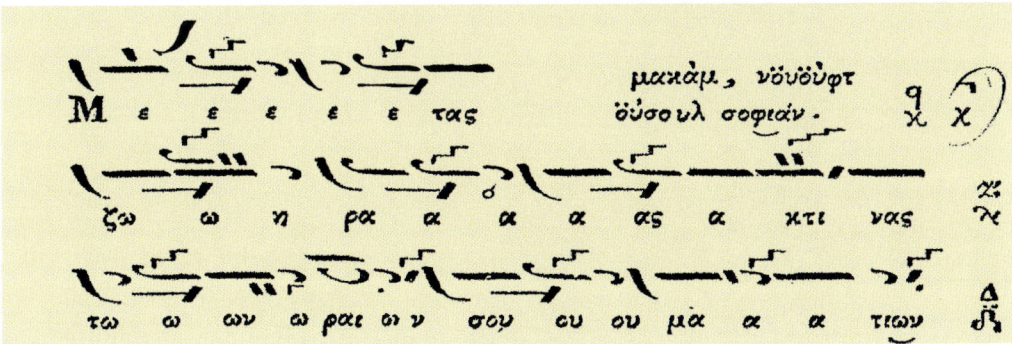

orientation has always been a problem for Western observers. The French traveller Michel Febvre observed in 1688 that the Turks 'do not know music and have only the simple unison'.[11] The absence of the familiar harmony of his own music felt to Febvre like a deficit, comparable to a human with only one eye. Febvre came by these views honestly: Western histories from the Enlightenment to the present have tended to narrate Western musical development as an inevitable ten-century progression from simple to complex, from single- to multi-voiced music. From this perspective, monophonic music would be analogous to either European medieval or peasant music, where monophony has also continued to thrive. But in Turkey, monophony as a music-making strategy – and the tendency to preserve single melodic lines in notation – has in no way ruled out complex textures, or the interaction of multiple voices in performance.

It is an oral tradition, but it has created a place for musical notation. Staff notations can be found on the music stands of many makam music sessions in Turkey today. Less obvious are the handful of Ottoman repertoire collections created in a variety of notation systems from the mid-seventeenth to early twentieth centuries. And yet, unlike in Europe, the science of notation remained marginal in Turkey until the twentieth century. Illustration 13.10 shows the work of the renowned musician and linguist Ali Ufki, born Albert Bobowski (1610–75), a Polish Protestant. Taken captive by the Ottomans as a young man, he converted to Islam and rose to a position of influence as a translator and musician in the Ottoman court, living most of his life as a slave (*kul*) in the Ottoman domains. His manuscript collection of more than a thousand instrumental and vocal pieces represents the first application of Western staff notation to Ottoman music. (Note: the notation is read from right to left, as in Arabic script.)

This and most other examples of Ottoman notation were executed either by Muslim converts like Ali Ufki, or by non-Muslims such as prince Dimitrie Cantemir, who created his own variant of earlier notations based on the Arabic alphabet, or the Armenian Hamparsum Limoncuyan (1768–1839), who adapted the notation system of Armenian church music. In the nineteenth century, lavish collections of makam music were also published in the musical writing system of the Greek Orthodox Church for the benefit of educated Greek-speaking Ottomans. All these examples may be taken as possible outcomes of an Ottoman inclination westward, and of a long-standing Ottoman policy encouraging diversity.

In 1826 the Italian bandmaster known as Donizetti Paşa (Giuseppe Donizetti, 1788–1856, brother of the opera composer Gaetano) was invited to adapt European instruments, notation and pedagogies to the palace orchestra for sultan Mahmud II. In the early twentieth century, a program of systematic conversion of Ottoman repertoire to staff notation began in earnest. Today, music students spend much of their lesson imitating what the teacher plays, but they are also expected to sing fluently from notation using solfège like their counterparts in Paris and New York.

It is performer-centred, but it reveres composers. Today, Turkish makam musicians take greater liberties with the preserved music of the past than do their counterparts in the West, where musicians have evolved into two groups of specialists – composers who create music, and performers who execute the composers' written scores. A Turkish makam musician of today – like the ideal musician in Europe until around 1825 – is one who can read notes fluently and accurately, but who is expected to personalise and elaborate on pre-composed pieces, to create preludes and interludes around them, and to make his or her own music, with or without notation. By the First World War, the only Western repertoire where the roles of performer and composer are blended in this way was the African-American art form, jazz. The term usually applied today to performer-generated composition is 'improvisation', now considered a specialty of jazz. Turkish musicians sense that these different expectations of Western audiences can lead to a misunderstanding of their music: the multi-instrumentalist İhsan Özgen's description of makam music as *ortadoğu cazı* ('Middle Eastern jazz'), attempts to bridge the gap. But there is no general Turkish equivalent to 'improvisation', making it an uncomfortable fit for makam music. In this chapter, descriptive expressions like 'performance generation' and 'performer-controlled' have been preferred.

It is an art of continuous variation, but it values fixed compositions. Because Turkish performers create individualised renditions in every performance of a composition, each of those performances can be strikingly different. When two or more performers simultaneously create different interpretations of the same melody, the result is elaborated unison or heterophony. Three players playing from an identical notation will probably find opportunities to insert their own connective passages, slides, sustained notes, delayed attacks, elisions and decorations. Each will take moments to withdraw into the background or to project into the foreground. Individually transcribed, each player's part would look quite different and the composite sound is rich and multi-voiced. Makam itself provides each player with a more comprehensive model of how a melody is to go than is simply found on the page. Musicians understand that the composer's notated melody is a variant of the makam, which is itself infinitely variable.

Its concerts are secular, but much of its repertoire has roots in the sacred. Since the end of Ottoman rule, public concerts of Turkish makam music have conformed to the secular framework of the Western concert hall. But the repertoire and practices of mystical Islamic devotional music, its ritual meanings muted but not erased, have been adapted for performance alongside secular urban love songs and Ottoman instrumental pieces. The secular free-rhythm taksim and gazel, and the art of the Qur'anic chanter, have roots which intertwine, and much of the ostensibly secular love poetry of Ottoman song is infused with the vocabulary of Islamic mysticism. Even the peşrev, the instrumental prelude to the secular Ottoman suite, has a long association with the Mevlevi whirling ritual, and the cane flute remains linked in Turkish perception with the fourteenth-century Sufi poetry of Celaluddin Rumi: 'Listen to the reed and the tale it tells / how it sings of separation: ever since they cut me from the reed bed, / my wail has caused men and women to weep ...'[12]

Turkish makam in the world

> One must beware of mistaking for genuine Turkish military music that Janissary music ... for which new pieces from German pens appear daily. The difference between both is endlessly great. Our German-Turkish military music cannot even boast the same instruments, much less the same taste.
>
> Franz Joseph Sulzer, 1781[13]

> The musical technique of the West is, among all others, the most evolved, the most precious and the most powerfully expressive ... Our national music will be born when our national melodies will be set according to this technique. Our musical future depends on it. It is truly our single hope for the future.
>
> Halil Bedii Yönetken, Director General of the Fine Arts in Turkey, 1924[14]

These observations by two influential figures in eighteenth-century Germany and twentieth-century Turkey suggest that cultural influence between the Ottoman regions and Europe has been, in the long run, a two-way street. Franz Joseph Sulzer bears witness to one phase of the early European fascination with the 'orient'. Halil Bedii Yönetken expresses the relatively late Turkish infatuation with all things European. The idea of a multi-century Euro-Ottoman symbiosis is still worth keeping in mind, helping to make sense of this perennial two-way traffic.

In the story of mutual east–west influence, the *alla turca* phenomenon is a key element. This popular faux-Turkish style lasted more than a century and found its way into opera, orchestral and chamber music scores by Rameau, Gluck, Mozart, Haydn, Beethoven, Mendelssohn and Rossini, to mention just the most famous of the 'pens' Sulzer alludes to. Ottoman ceremonial wind and percussion ensembles called *mehterhane* struck European travellers as novel, inspiring imitations called 'janissary bands' or *bando turca* which could be heard frequently on the street corners and stages of European cities. But by 1826, more than a century after the Ottomans' last unsuccessful siege of Vienna, the distinctive march-like bass drum and triangle of the *alla turca* section of Beethoven's Ninth Symphony stood less for barbarians at the gate than the populism of the European street.

The aggressive sonorities and persistent rhythm of the European variants on Ottoman mehterhane captured the popular Western view of the barbarity and violence of the East, crowding out all other models of Ottoman music. This is the quality and the instrumentation which evolved over three centuries into what is now the marching band, spawning a global array of adaptations, including jazz, all featuring the uniquely Ottoman combination of winds, cymbals and drums.

The story of this peculiarly European and militaristic 'Turkish' style took an ironic turn in the nineteenth century. When Donizetti Paşa introduced European instruments and notation to Turkey at the request of Mahmut II, his musical mission was part of a much larger westernising effort. In a parallel move, the disbanding in 1826 of the historic elite Janissary corps (*yeniçeri*) required the creation of a new European-style army with a new European sound. A Western-style marching band of European brass instruments – the heir of Europe's *alla turca* craze – replaced the mehterhane that had inspired it. What had arrived in the West in the sixteenth century as an oriental import came back to the East, three centuries later, as an occidental import.

The monophonic nature of Turkish makam music – its emphasis on conversational interaction among performers engaged in continuous variation of melody – allows it to stand out in the global array of musical practices. Perhaps the long history of European and Ottoman interaction has positioned the Ottoman musical heritage to help carve a niche for monophony in a world dominated by Europe's peculiar model of polyphony. As Turkish makam music perpetuates the blended role of composer-performer abandoned by Western classical music, it continues to emphasise oral transmission of melodies supplemented by notation. It persists in cultivating the low-tech refinement and vocalism of its instruments, lending the music a non-technological quality and a human scale. This music may have been born in a theocracy, but its intimate textures are transparent, with every voice heard, creating musical events which are responsive to both performers and audiences – qualities well-matched to rising global expectations of institutions which are participatory and transparent.

Moreover, makam music in all its Mediterranean vernaculars still possesses infinite possibilities, leaving room for endless expansion of its vocabulary through continual variation in performance, and through its long-standing invitation to invent new modal and rhythmic structures out of old ones.

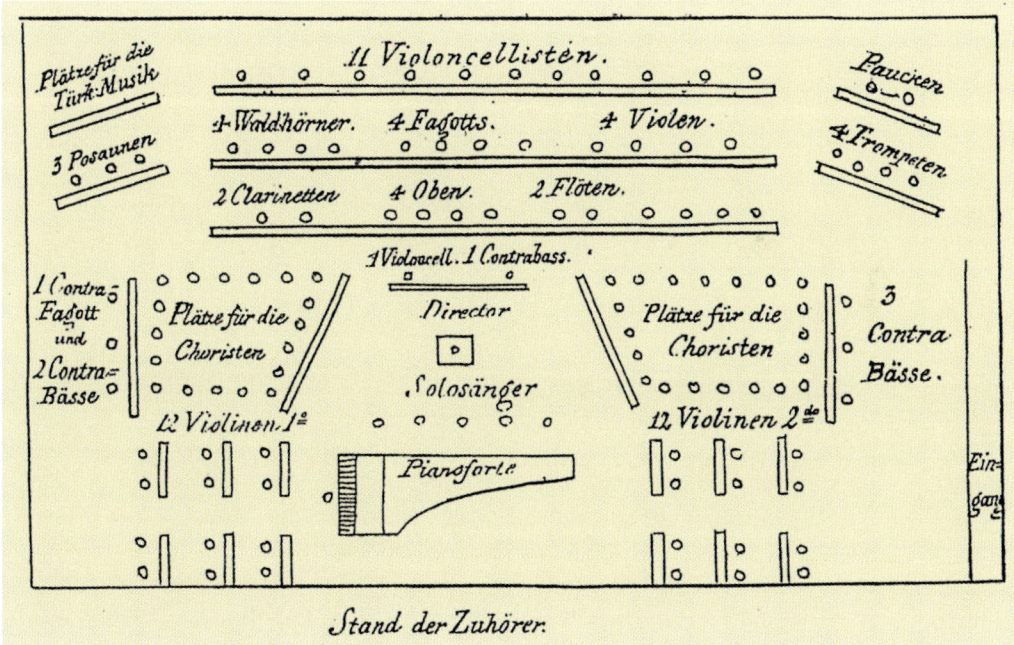

The seating arrangement for a large orchestra in Paris in 1810. In addition to places for trombones (Posaunen), timpani (Pauken) and trumpets (Trompetten), places are reserved *(upper left)* for Türk Musik (instruments unspecified).

While Turks and non-Turks continue to market makam music as a nostalgic phenomenon, avant-garde Western art-music since the mid-twentieth century has increasingly explored open-ended structures, unrepeatable events, indeterminacy, performer control and audience interaction – all qualities compatible with an Ottoman model. Unlike European listeners of the past, we can now hear Turkish makam's monophonic musical strategies not as outdated, but as sympathetic to at least some of the newest trends in Western music. This may point to the advent of a new kind of Euro-Ottoman synthesis.

Further reading

Eliot Bates's *Music in Turkey* provides a readable introduction to the contemporary Turkish music scene for a general audience, with an accompanying CD. This is a realistic and pluralistic view in which Turkish makam music, like classical music in Britain and the United States, continues to be important for a relatively small audience, but does not dominate public attention. Various shorter articles in *The Garland Encyclopedia of World Music* vol. 6, *The Middle East* are also intended for non-specialist readers, focusing on selected topics rather than general introductions; the volume also includes a CD of examples. For those desiring a more detailed source on Turkish makam practice, Murat Aydemir's *Turkish Music Makam Guide* is a concise manual of sixty makams with recorded examples, presenting the scale, general behavioural characteristics and a sample composition in notation for each makam. The most authoritative historical study in English of the Ottoman classical repertoire is Walter Z. Feldman's *Music of the Ottoman Court*, though it is not intended for a general readership and is focused primarily on instrumental music. Miriam Whaples's 'Exoticism in Dramatic Music' and Benjamin Perl's 'Mozart in Turkey' are examples of the considerable literature on Europe's fascination with the exotic, and especially the *alla turca* phenomenon of the seventeenth and eighteenth centuries. Donald Quataert's *The Ottoman Empire* is an excellent and readable example of the new Ottoman historical writing which argues for a more interconnected picture of Euro-Ottoman relations.

A profusion of internet sites created by an international mix of Turkish music enthusiasts may be accessed by simply searching for relevant keywords. These sites are motivated by interests ranging from the commercial to the nationalistic, so let the reader beware. The online catalogue of Kalan Müzik (http://www.kalan.com) is the best one-stop site for browsing and buying high quality Turkish recordings from classical to folk and pop, and in recent years Neyzen.com (http://neyzen.com) has made itself the best single source for notations of Turkish music, organised by makam. Both of these sites have options for readers of English.

Recommended listening

Re-issues of earlier 78 and 33⅓ rpm recordings which have become the benchmarks of twentieth-century musicianship include:

Tanburi Cemil Bey [1910–14], 3 vols, Traditional Crossroads 4274, 1994–5. The most revered of all late Ottoman musicians, a multi-instrumentalist virtuoso who lived from 1871–1916.

Gazeller, 3 vols [c. 1910–50s], Kalan 67, 072, 360, 1997–2006. Secular vocal improvisations on Ottoman poetry, mostly by singers trained in koranic chant.

Niyazi Sayın and Necdet Yaşar [1950s–80s] (2 CDs), Kalan 361, 362, 2006. Schooled in the recordings of Tanburi Cemil Bey, this ney and tanbur duo set the standard for later twentieth-century performance.

Recent performances of a range of repertoires and approaches by leading musicians, all of whom recognise earlier performers like those above as their standard:

Salih Bilgin and Murat Aydemir, *Nevâ*, Kaf KB 01 34 Ü 1327 022, 2001. A ney and tanbur duo in the generation after Niyazi Sayın and Necdet Yaşar.

Bezmara, Kalan 296, 2004. An example of 'historical performance' in recent Turkish music using reconstructed instruments and carefully researched repertoire from the seventeenth and eighteenth centuries.

Yahudi Bestekarlar, Golden Horn 501257 2, 2001. Recent performances of compositions by the most famous Ottoman Jewish composers from the eighteenth to twentieth centuries.

Mevlâna: Sûzidil-ârâ Ayin-i, Kent 100172 2, 1993. A typical late twentieth-century performance of music for the Mevlevi Sufi whirling ceremony. Music by Sultan Selim III (1761–1808), words by Mevlana Celalladin Rumi (1207–73).

14 Iran

Ameneh Youssefzadeh

In a garden of cypress and pine trees under the soft summer night, tiny water-canals and candlelit paths lead to a polygonal kiosk open on all sides, with an open dais in front. Six cushions in a half-moon arrangement face an audience – men and women, young and old – seated around the stage. From behind the pavilion appear six young musicians: five men with instruments, and a woman in a white evening dress with long sleeves and high neckline; her companions are in white shirts and beige trousers. To applause they take their places on the dais and the men tune their instruments: a lute, fiddle, zither, flute and drum. Each instrumentalist is highlighted during a slow introduction, which is followed by a rapid virtuoso section on zither and drum. Singing in Farsi, the vocalist delivers an evocative line: 'On my tomb, sit down with wine and a musician', and the forcefully-plucked lute gives an improvised response. The two continue their exchange while members of the audience gently nod as they sing along in a whisper. The meditative mood gives way to an energetic song from singer and ensemble, and the performance ends with a lively instrumental number.

W E are in the garden of the Hāfezieh, where the Persian poet Hāfez (1326–90) is buried. This is in Shiraz, also known as the city of *Gol o Bolbol* ('flower and nightingale'). Such gardens have been popular venues for the performance of Persian classical music for centuries, and for musicians, poets and philosophers they have been a refuge from daily life, with many – like the twelfth-century poet, mathematician and philosopher Omar Khayyām – choosing to be buried there: 'My grave will be in a spot where, every spring, the north wind will scatter blossoms on me.'[1]

The story goes that a Persian poet was discussing music with some Westerners who compared their music to an ocean, and Persian music to a miserable drop. 'Indeed,' answered the poet, 'but that ocean is only water, while this drop is a tear'.[2] Essentially intimate, Persian classical music is closely bound up with poetry and mysticism, and customarily involves the singing of verses by poets such as Hafez, Sa'di and Rumi. As the leading authority on Persian classical music Nur 'Ali Borumand (1905–77) has shown, text and music are inextricably intertwined: echoing a verse by the thirteenth-century poet Amir Khosrow Dehlavi, he once observed to the American musicologist Stephen Blum that 'verses without melodies are like a bride without jewels'.[3]

◀ A young man playing the lute: a sixteenth-century miniature in watercolour, gold and ink, adorning the poetry collection of Sultan Ibrahim Mirza. (Folio 88r from a Diwan of Sultan Ibrahim Mirza, by 'Abd-Allah Shirazi ('Abd-Allah al-Mudhahhib), Mashhad, Iran, 1582. Paper, ink, opaque watercolour, gold, silver. 23.8 × 16.5 cm.)

The Hafezieh is a traditional meeting place for musicians and poets, and in hosting the Shiraz Art Festival in the 1960s and '70s it became an important venue for Persian classical music. The last such event was held in 1977, just prior to the revolution which established Iran as an Islamic Republic and ushered in wholesale political, social and cultural changes. Many of these changes directly affected artists and women: the hijab head-covering was mandated by law, and women were prohibited from singing solo for any audience which included men. Musicians and composers found themselves subject to investigation and abuse from the authorities, and many fled the country. Some of these restrictions have been eased over time, but others still apply. These pressures are not new, however; they have affected Persian musicians for centuries.

■ Historical background

Iran forms a bridgehead between the Middle and Far East, and a crossroads for migration and trade. Its history has been punctuated by invasions: by the Greeks in the fourth century BCE, the Arab Muslims in the seventh century CE and the Mongols in the thirteenth century; in modern times it has experienced two revolutions. Yet in contrast to those ancient civilisations of the Middle East which became Arabised, Iran has preserved its cultural identity, and – most importantly – its language.

It was known to the Western world as Persia until 1935, when the reigning monarch Rezā Shāh Pahlavi (r. 1925–41) requested that the international community refer to it as Iran (from middle Persian Ērān, 'Aryan'), which was how its native population knew it. Iranians use the term 'Persian' (Farsi) only for language, while in the West 'Persian' is used to refer to Iranian culture including music, miniatures, carpets, literature and poetry. Iranian is used as a geographical term, as in 'Iranian Plateau', or as an ethno-linguistic descriptor as in 'Iranian languages'.

But the label 'Persian' is highly regarded, implying reference to the great empires of the past beginning with that of Cyrus II (Kurosh), known also as Cyrus the Great (r. 576–30 BCE). The Achaemenid Empire which he established (550–330 BCE) stretched from the Indus valley in the east across all of Western Asia into Greece in Europe, and as far as Libya in northern Africa. Thanks to this imperial expansion, followed by the reciprocal conquests of Alexander the Great (336–23 BCE) whose realm superseded the Persian domain, the Greek connection in Persian cultural history is strong. Descriptions of Persian music during these periods come primarily from Greek historians such as Herodotus (484–25 BCE), whose exposure to music was mostly confined to military contexts. Musical exchange between Persians and Greeks is suggested by similarities of performance practice such as heterophony, and the use of musical modes for improvisation. A similar musical cross-fertilisation was fostered by trade along the Silk Road: the Persian *barbat* lute was the ancestor of both the Chinese *pipa* and the Japanese *biwa*.

Iran has long been home to many ethnic groups including Turks, Kurds, Baluchis, Lors and Arabs, who live mostly on the periphery of the current political boundaries; each community has its own language and musical tradition. As there are many affinities between languages and musical styles, sung poetry has long been appreciated in Iran; musicians were often poets, and vice versa. Persian classical music as practiced today developed primarily in the political and cultural centres of Qazvin, Shiraz, Isfahan and Tehran, on the central Iranian plateau. It is thought to be one of the oldest musical systems in the world, and its origins were courtly: since antiquity it has played a key role in the royal palaces. During the Sassanid dynasty (224–651 CE) poet-singers enjoyed the same high status as scribes, physicians and astronomers. The most celebrated royal patron was King Khosrow II Parviz (r. 591–628), whose love of music is still reflected in a large cliff relief in western Iran where he is shown being escorted on a riverside hunt by a band of female harpists. Khosrow's reign represented a golden age for classical music, and, led by his court minstrel Bārbad, this music fed into what scholars now believe was a common Arabic-Persian modal system which prevailed from the mid-thirteenth century to the beginning of the sixteenth century, before dividing into separate systems.[4] Many nomenclatures in Arabic, Turkic and above all Azerbaijani music are of Persian origin.

After the Arab conquest of the Persian empire in the seventh century, Persian musicians and scholars – whose culture the Arabs greatly respected – became dispersed throughout the Islamic world. Most prominent among these were Ebrāhim Mawseli (742–803) and his son Esḥāq Mawseli (767–850), Abu Naṣr Fārābi (tenth century), Ibn Sinā, known as Avicenna in the West (eleventh century), Qoṭb-al-Din of Shirāz (fourteenth century) and Abdol Qāder Marāqi (fifteenth century). The Arabs adopted the 'Persian lute' (*'ud fāresi*), making it their principal instrument for urban and court music.[5] Moreover, the performance of Persian poetry – which lay at the heart of Persian classical music – has extended at various times beyond Iran to other areas where Persian was used as a spoken and written language, such as Afghanistan and Tajikistan, plus parts of the Indian sub-continent and Turkey where literary Persian was an important cultural language. Persian poets such as Ferdowsi (tenth century), Nezāmi (twelfth century), Rumi (thirteenth century), Sai'di (thirteenth century) and Hafez (fourteenth century) celebrated music and dance, and often used instruments as metaphors for human feelings, as in Rumi's *Masnavi*, 'Song of the Reed Flute' (see Example 14.1 below).[6]

Though no explicit prohibition of music is found in the Qur'an, Islamic attitudes towards music have been ambivalent: while writing about music has always been a respected intellectual pursuit, the legitimacy of listening to and performing it has been a subject of controversy among jurists and theologians. Although this has often been triggered by the association of music with indulgence in wine and sensuality, music and wine are the key components in the Persian tradition of *razm o bazm* ('battle and feast'). Every ruler from the Achaemenid period until the twentieth century employed two classes of musician: those who performed in military ensembles on the battlefield and at ceremonial functions (*razm*), and those who performed at court festivities and banquets (*bazm*) and in the women's quarters, the harem.

THE OTHER CLASSICAL MUSICS

The periods of decline through which Persian music has passed have been mostly due to the withdrawal of court patronage. One of the most significant of these periods occurred during the Safavid dynasty, which ruled Iran from 1501 to 1722. This was when the foundations were laid for Iran's future identity through the conversion of most of the population from Sunni to Shi'a Islam (which has since become the country's official religion), and for the creation of a strong state within borders which are approximately those of today's Iran. Art and architecture were at their height under the Safavids, but the new power of the religious authorities led to a decline in both music and musical scholarship. Yet the greatest Safavid ruler, Shah Abbās I (r. 1587–1629), was an ardent patron of visual art and music: he moved his capital from Qazvin to Isfahan, which became the centre for those arts; meanwhile music continued to be cultivated at the courts of Herat in the east and Gilan by the Caspian Sea. By the end of the Safavid period, the religious authorities' enforcement of sharia law resulted in music, wine and dance being banned from all court and social gatherings. Many musicians migrated to India and Turkey, while others took refuge in the Sufi *Khāneqāh*, religious meeting places which became a channel for the preservation and diffusion of classical music. With Muslim musicians forbidden to practice their trade, Jewish and Armenian musicians came to dominate the profession.

■ *The Qājār era (1785–1925)*

The political instability of the eighteenth century was resolved when Agā Mohammad Shah (1742–97) established the Qajar dynasty (1785–1925), choosing Tehran as his capital. The Qajar era had great significance both for Iran's modern history and for its music. Music flourished at the courts of Fateh 'Ali Shah (r. 1798–1834) and Nāser al-Din Shah (r. 1848–96), and the diminished tradition of *razm o bazm* was restored: this was when leading musicians assembled the elements of the repertoire which constitutes the canon of Persian classical music today. Its codification is attributed to the court musician Mirzā Abdollāh (1845–1918), a prominent player and teacher of the *setār* lute; he and his brother, *tār* master Aqā Hoseyn Qoli (d. 1913), organised the music they had learned from their father, Ali Akbar Farhāni, and cousin Mirza Gholām Hossein, into a *radif* (row, or order) for the instruction of their pupils. The radif is the basis of modern Persian classical music with its extensive corpus of composition and improvisation, and with its function as teaching material.

Western music was introduced into Iran during the Qajar period, initially in association with military activities, as in Turkey and Egypt. During the reign of Naser al-Din Shah experts came from France to organise a military band for ceremonial events at court, and a music division was established in Dar al-Funun (Polytechnic School, the first modern school for boys, set up in 1851) to teach Western wind instruments and music theory. By the start of the twentieth century Iranian musicians were acquainted with Western staff notation, instrumentation and harmony, and the violin had become popular among players of the *kamāncheh*

◀ A cliff relief in Western Iran reflecting King Khosrow II Parviz's love of music. This sixth-century monarch presided over a golden age of Persian classical music, and is here shown being escorted on a riverside hunt by a band of female harpists *(detail below)*.

THE OTHER CLASSICAL MUSICS

This painting by Kamal al-Molk in 1893 portrays the private ensemble of King Nasir al-Din Shah, himself a painter, poet and Westerniser, whose dictatorial style led to his assassination in 1896. The instruments being played are *(from left to right)* the zarb, tar, kamancheh and santur, and in the back row a dayereh.

spike fiddle. The piano, being cumbersome and costly, was at first reserved for the nobility, and was taught by players of the *santur* hammered zither.

The two most notable figures associated with this rising interest in Western music were Darvish Khān (1872–1926) and 'Ali Naqi Vaziri (1886–1978), both virtuoso *tār* (long-necked lute) players with training in Western music theory. Darvish made some of the earliest recordings of Persian classical music in London, and is best known for adding a sixth string to the tar. Vaziri studied music in France and Germany, and in 1923 opened the first independent music conservatory in Tehran. He tried to modernise Persian music by using Western staff notation, harmony and performance contexts.

Musicians in the Qajar era were called 'amale tarab (labourers for pleasure); classical musicians who performed for the king were called 'amale tarab khāsse (special labourers for pleasure). Outside the court and aristocratic milieux, music was performed by urban entertainers (motrebs) who constituted a well-defined trade and were often Jewish or Armenian. Their basic ensemble consisted of players on the tar, the zarb goblet hand drum and the dāyereh frame drum with jingles, plus a dancer.

In contrast to the socially marginalised motrebs, 'learned' amateur musicians enjoyed high social status: there are many accounts of members of high society, doctors and scientists, who were also fine musicians, and who performed for small circles of connoisseurs. Yusef Forutan (1891–1978), an aristocratic setar master, typically refused to be photographed with his instrument in his hand, fearing that he might be taken for a motreb.[7] It was thanks to Vaziri's efforts to revive the traditional arts, coupled with government patronage and increasing contact with the West, that the status of classical musicians was gradually raised.

The beginning of the twentieth century was marked by a weakening of Qajar rule, intensive British and Russian influence, and the Constitutional Revolution of 1905–11 which transformed Iran's polity, reducing the influence of kings and nobility as well as that of the religious authorities. Secular modernism was on the rise, inspired by Western ideologies of nationalism and liberalism. This period saw new methods of music teaching, the formation of professional orchestras with both Western and Persian instruments, and the advent of recording, which disseminated classical music more widely.

Following the Constitutional Revolution, Tehran's first public concert of classical Persian music was organised by Anjoman-e Okhuvvat, a brotherhood association whose members came from prominent Iranian families; the event was held in a garden on the outskirts of Tehran to celebrate the birthday of the first imam of the Shi'a, 'Ali ibn Abi Tāleb. Meanwhile Darvish Khan invited twenty leading musicians to form an orchestra under his direction, combining Persian and Western instruments. It became fashionable to give benefit concerts, with the education minister organising them for poor scholars and orphans, and with the war minister doing the same for starving Russians during the famine of 1921. Such concerts took place in open-air soirées, at garden parties and in Tehran's Grand Hotel, where the first concerts with ticket sales opened to the public. But the audiences were mostly male, since before the reforms of 1936 Muslim women rarely appeared in public without the veil. With the introduction of Western-style theatres, public performance of classical music became the norm.

■ The Pahlavi era (1925–79)

Both Persian and Western classical music, and hybrids of the two, continued to prosper after the Qajar era ended. In 1924 Reza Khān, commander-in-chief of the armed forces, seized power and, encouraged by the British, declared himself king the following year, thus inaugurating the Pahlavi dynasty. Inspired by his neighbouring contemporary Mustafa Kemal Atatürk (1881–1938) in the recently-established Republic of Turkey, Reza Shah imposed many political, cultural and social reforms to modernise the country. His support for women's rights was both notable and controversial: he banned the *chador* in favour of Western dress, and encouraged the integration of women into public life; the classical singer Qamar al Moluk Vaziri (1905–59) was amongst the first women to benefit from these reforms. On succeeding his father in 1941, Mohammad Rezā Shah (1919–80) continued his efforts to modernise Iranian society.

After its introduction to Iran in 1940, radio became an important source of musical patronage. One of the most prominent figures associated with Radio Iran was Ruhollāh Khāleqi (1906–65), a prolific writer and champion of Persian classical music who arranged its traditional forms for orchestra. In 1944 he founded the Society for National Music, which was the precursor for the Conservatory for National Music (Honarestān-e Musiqi-ye Melli), created in 1949 under the aegis of the education ministry. The primary objective of these institutions was to support native traditions, and to revive interest in Iranian instruments, which had become less popular than Western ones. Even so, the violin, clarinet and piano (used widely in Persian music by this time) were also taught as part of the conservatory curriculum.

During the last two decades of Mohammad Reza Shah's reign the pace of Westernization became even more rapid. The educated class was infatuated with Western music, classical as much as popular, in part because of its 'superior' associations, while those who preferred classical Persian music were regarded as behind the times and opposed to change.[8] This debate reflected the larger crisis in Iranian national identity.

In 1961, UNESCO sponsored an International Congress in Tehran, entitled 'The preservation of traditional forms of the learned and popular music of the Orient and the Occident'. At issue was the growing trend towards musical Westernisation in both Iran and neighbouring countries, and the question of how to control it; in 1962 the influential writer Jalāl Al-e Ahmad (d. 1965) compared the Iranians' obsession with the West to a disease.[9] The 'hybridisation' and 'vulgarisation' of Persian classical music became the subject of intensive debate, with the musicologist Bruno Nettl reporting that in Tehran in the late 1960s classical music in its 'serious and complex' style was only practiced by a very few musicians, while a lighter and more rhythmic style was taking over as a result of Western influence.[10]

At this point both the Iranian Ministry of Culture and State Radio and Television began actively sponsoring classical Persian music in an attempt to preserve it, and in 1965 the music department of the fine arts faculty at Tehran University began teaching a course on its theory and practice. There Nur 'Ali Borumand, one of its most influential authorities, taught the radif repertoire to leading contemporary musicians. In 1970, spurred by Borumand, the Centre for the Conservation and Diffusion of Music was created under the aegis of state television. This brought together the best musicians of the day, including the singer 'Abdollah Davāmi (1891–1980), the tar player 'Ali Akbar Shahnāzi (1897–1985), the setār player Yusef Forutan (1891–1978) and the kamancheh player 'Asqar Bahāri (1905–1995). Thus was Persian classical music transmitted and

Despite his blindness, Nur 'Ali Borumand became the twentieth century's leading teacher of Persian classical music, as well as one of its most celebrated exponents.

preserved during the 1970s. Many of today's classical masters – including the tar and setar players Dāriush Talā'i (b. 1953), Mohammad Rezā Lotfi (1947–2014) and Hossein 'Alizādeh (b. 1951), and the singers Mohammad Rezā Shajariān (b. 1940) and Parisā (b. 1950) – studied at the Centre, and became teachers themselves.

Recordings and publications by these musicians were sponsored by both broadcasters and the ministry, and festivals were held to highlight their music, most notably the Shiraz Art Festival, which also featured performances by traditional musicians from India, Vietnam, Indonesia, Japan and Egypt in concerts in the Hāfezieh. Studies of Persian classical music – by both Iranian and foreign scholars – proliferated.

▪ The revolution of 1978–9 to today

The revolution of 1978–9, which forced Mohammad Reza Shah into exile, was initially a political reaction against the authoritarianism of a regime that was perceived as subservient to Western hegemony, principally by the United States. It was a multi-party and multi-ideological revolution, and many classical musicians participated by composing and performing revolutionary songs.

The first decade of the Islamic Republic, which established a conservative theocracy, was marked by eight years of war with Iraq and by stringent new regulations on behaviour, including the segregation of the sexes in public, the introduction of new dress codes, the closing of theatres and cinemas and the banning of music in public and in the media; revolutionary songs sung by men were for a while the only music permitted to be broadcast, and women were banned from singing and dancing for audiences which included men. Many forms of music were affected; Iranian and Western popular music were deemed arousing and vulgar, and female pop singers such as Googoosh (b. 1950) were either silenced or left the country. But although musical institutions were officially closed, music continued to be performed and taught privately and the number of people willing to learn Persian classical music increased greatly, along with a growth in domestic music-making. Popular Iranian music went underground, resurfacing in diaspora communities such as the large one in Los Angeles.

The end of the Iran-Iraq War in 1988 and the death of Ayatollāh Khomeini a year later led to a relaxation of restrictions on musical performance. At the end of his life, Khomeini had issued a *fatwa* authorising the buying and selling of instruments, and permission for specific concerts was occasionally granted, with a recital by Mohammad Reza Shajarian to celebrate the end of the war being a significant event. Six performances were scheduled to take place in Tehran's most prestigious opera house, but because the unexpected demand far exceeded the space available, the hall's security department cancelled the last three concerts.[11] In 1989 Hossein Alizadeh founded 'Hamāvāyān' ('singing together'), an ensemble which included a chorus of male and female singers, and performers on Persian classical instruments: 'I wanted to reintroduce women's voices in public', he explained.[12] While solo female singing is still prohibited to male audiences, choral singing is permitted, under the rationale that individual women's voices are hard to identify.[13]

Perhaps the most important musical event at this time was the re-opening of the music department at Tehran University in 1989, after a decade of closure. In September 1992, Ayatollah Khamene'i, then Guide of the Republic, launched a campaign against 'cultural aggression from the West' which conferred a certain legitimacy on Iranian music, both classical and of different ethnic groups, this being regarded as an affirmation of national identity. A revival of interest in classical music was one by-product of the continuing ban on popular music during the 1990s, as restrictions on its performance eased and the output of classical cassettes and CDs increased dramatically.[14]

Yet public performances and recordings continued to be closely monitored by the Ministry of Culture and Islamic Guidance (known by its abbreviated title, Ershad, 'guidance'). All planned concerts had to be submitted for preliminary censorship with regard to the type of music and the content of the lyrics, which 'should not include words which might offend social and religious dignity'; this mirrored a similar censorship in literature, where a few 'un-Islamic' words could be deemed – and still are at the time of writing – sufficient to disqualify a book from publication. Classical musicians objected to this; as a result the most prominent among them were exempted from Ershad authorisation, but most chose to perform abroad because of the ever-present threat of arbitrary, last-minute cancellations. Over the past two decades, in order to display Iran's cultural heritage, both the Ministry of Culture and the Islamic Propaganda Organisation have sponsored festivals of Persian classical and Iranian regional music, the most important being the *Fajr* ('dawn') festival which marks the anniversary of the revolution. Classical masters rarely attend these events, regarding them as propaganda tools of the government.

In 1997 the landslide election of President Mohammad Khātami, who was seen as a reformer, led to cultural policies reflecting a slightly more liberal turn. Certain forms of popular music were permitted, as were public performances by women (though only for all-women audiences). However, since the election of President Mahmud Ahmadinejād in 2005 there has been a return to stricter censorship, and obtaining a permit to publish books or recordings or to give a performance has become much more difficult. Despite this, Persian classical music continues to be taught in universities, cultural centres and private institutions – of which there are more than a hundred in Tehran, supported by individual patrons – and by masters who teach and perform in private homes.

It should be remembered, however, that until the twentieth century most classical music was performed in private gatherings – for small circles of connoisseurs, at Sufi brotherhoods, for family and friends, or in festivities including poetry recitation: the public concert was essentially a Western phenomenon. Moreover, apart from military music, public musical performance took place mostly in the context of religious and ceremonial rituals which are not considered 'musical' per se: these include events in *zurkhāneh* (Iran's traditional fitness-clubs), the recitation of the Qur'an (*tajwid*), the call to prayer ('*azān*), the recitation of the national epic *Shāhnāmeh* (*naqqāli*), the Shi'a Passion play (*ta'zieh*) and the singing of laments (*rowzeh-khāni*); ta'zieh and rowzeh-khani both commemorate the martyrdom of the Shi'a Imam Hossein and his family in the battle of Karbelā in 680. Such ceremonies require singers skilled in classical music, and they have been crucial supports for classical music during its periods of decline and discrimination. And in Iran, as in many parts of the Middle East, classical singers have traditionally honed their skills in the call to prayer and the recitation of the Qur'an; many celebrated singers from the first half of the twentieth century sang in the ceremonial mourning rites mentioned above. Mohammad Reza Shajaryan was a noted *qāri* (reciter of the Qur'an) before gaining fame as a classical performer.

■ Canon

Bārbad, minstrel-poet of the Sassanian king Kosrow II Parviz, is thought to have helped establish the modal model that developed into the system forming the basis for Persian classical music today. He is said to have created seven 'royal modes' (*Khosrowani*), thirty derived modes and 360 melodies, corresponding to the number of days respectively in a week, month and year. The nature of these compositions is unknown, but some of their names survived into the Islamic period thanks to Persian poets and scholarly writing in Arabic. This was when the great theorists of the 'science' of music – led by Al-Farabi – turned music into an aspect of mathematical philosophy, attaching specific meaning to intervals, modes, scales and rhythmic cycles. While the language of scholarship was mainly Arabic, from the thirteenth century onwards important Persian

works were written on the subject by scholars such as Qoṭb-al-Din of Shirāz and Qader Maraqi. The former is said to have been the first to use the word *maqām* as a general term for mode, and to have given an important account of the modal system. Although the character and names of the modes changed, the notion of seven modes and their association with stars and nature has survived, as has the idea of the principal modes having a number of subsidiary melodic components, often associated with places and other external associations.

After a period of relative decline in musical scholarship during the Safavid dynasty, leading musicians made a deliberate attempt to conserve and codify their vanishing heritage. Thus did two celebrated musical brothers – setar-master and court musician Mirza Abdollāh and tar-master Aqa Hoseyn Qoli – come to crystallise the classical canon as it is now performed. It is based on seven primary modes called *dastgāh*, and five secondary modes called *āvāz*. Each dastgah or avaz is comprised of short units or melody-types called *gusheh* ('corner'); a series of gusheh arranged in a fixed order is called a radif. The radif provides the framework for improvisation and composition, and is the central resource for sung Persian poetry. The closest relative to this system is the Azerbaijani *muğam*. In Borumand's words, 'The radif is the principal emblem, the heart of Persian music.' There are between two and three hundred gusheh in this essentially solo repertoire.

While each musician and teacher has his own version of the radif (usually referenced by his name), the radifs have much in common. Each dastgah in the radif has its particular pitch-set, or scale, its unique configuration of intervals, and its hierarchy of scale degrees. The intervals used include the whole and half-tones common to the Western tuning system, as well as the three-quarter and five-quarter tones characteristic of much Middle Eastern music

Each dastgah provides the basis on which its associated gusheh melodies are composed; it dictates not only the pitches but also the relative importance of specific pitches. Most significant of these are the *shahed* ('witness'), which acts as the tonal centre around which the melody evolves; the *ist* ('stop'), a temporary stopping-note; the *moteghayer* ('changeable'), which is a variable pitch; the *āqāz* ('initial') and the *forud* (cadential descent). Gusheh melodies are composed in accordance with these and other guiding principles relating to rhythm, improvisation and sentiment.

Gusheh may be named after places, ethnic groups, situations, emotional states and types of poem; each has its own character in terms of modal structure and melodic or rhythmic pattern. Many gusheh have an ambitus of no more than a fourth or fifth. Some have particular importance, such as *darāmad* ('coming out', introduction), which is usually the first gusheh performed in a dastgah or avaz, and whose principal motif acts as a theme for the whole performance. Some dastgah have more than one daramad. Most gusheh are from thirty seconds to six minutes in length; they are usually strung together in gradually ascending order of pitch before returning to the opening pitch at the end; most involve singing, though some are purely instrumental. And while

◂ Poet-singers enjoyed the same high status as scribes, physicians and astronomers in the Sassanid dynasty (224–651). *Inset detail, lower left:* Court minstrel Barbad plays the lute, a barbat, for Khosrow II Parviz.

an instrumental radif may include up to three hundred gusheh, vocal ones have fewer, although as they are continually evolving, new gusheh can always be added. The choice of mode, or dastgah, is dependent on the mood of both the musician and his audience, as each mode is considered to have its own character – meditative, majestic, cheerful, tragic or melancholic. Musicians use the term *hāl* to describe the mood and ethos of an event, but the word also denotes the mystical state essential to all creation of musical beauty.

As a corpus of pedagogical material the radif is transmitted orally, and the process can take years: once 'internalised' (as the tar and setar master Dariush Tala'i puts it), the radif becomes the basis for improvisation and composition: the process 'goes beyond apprenticeship and has to become a state of mind'.[15] As most gusheh have vocal origins and are built on poetic metres, the student also learns verses appropriate to each. Notated and published versions of radif first appeared in the early twentieth century, although master musicians still prefer to teach orally. But oral transmission was not always straightforward: Mirza Abdollah and Aqa Hoseyn Qoli sometimes had to hide behind a door to overhear and learn melodies which their teacher had refused to impart to them. In the twentieth century, recordings and the radio became an additional tutelary source.

But melody is only one focus: rhythm is the other. Over time, the complex repertoire of rhythmic cycles attested to in the medieval treatises has been abandoned and reduced to shorter cycles. The rhythm of Persian classical music has often been described as free or unmetred. However, the rhythmical structure of the melody in the improvised sections (which are known as avaz, and are not to be confused with the avaz modes in the radif) is guided by the metrical structure of the verse – the *'aruz* system of Arabo-Persian versification, with its fixed arrangement of long and short syllables.

In the avaz section, the singer usually chooses a different gusheh for each line of the poem, which is usually a *ghazal* – a poetic form with rhyming couplets and a refrain in the same metre. Meanwhile a melodic instrument follows, imitates or improvises a response to the singer's phrases. These exchanges between singer and instrumentalist are called *sāz o avaz* ('instrument and singing') and are considered to be the most engaging part of the performance. A performer usually improvises within the limits of a particular dastgah, but may also modulate from one dastgah into another.[16] A solo instrumentalist can also perform avaz, sometimes accompanied by a drummer.

A singer's skill may be measured by his or her choice of the appropriate poem for the appropriate dastgah to fit the occasion and the mood of the audience; clarity of diction is considered essential. Ornamentation is another important facet of Persian classical music: Iranian singers have developed an elaborately ornamented style called *tahrir* which sounds like a fast, flexible yodelling – a passage of many notes performed on just one syllable of text which is added at the end of each half-line of verse.

The saz o avaz sections are introduced, interrupted and concluded by pre-composed pieces with a steady beat, in regular groups of two, three or four beats. There are four types of pre-composed piece: *pishdaramad*, *chaharmezrab* and *reng* (all instrumental), and *tasnif* (vocal); these are largely

EX. 14.1 The opening line of Rumi's 'Masnavi' as sung by the late Mahmud Karimi (1927–84) in Navā, which is one of the principal dastgahs in the gusheh of Shah Khatā'ī; transcribed by the Iranian ethnomusicologist Mohammad Taqi Mas'udiye (1927–98). The rhyming couplet is composed of two hemistichs of eleven syllables, each in one of the variants of ramal meter in fixed arrangement of long (L) and short (S) syllables in this scheme: LSLL/LSLL/LSL. As is evident, the vocal rhythm is a reflection of the poetic metre.

```
   L   S L L   L   S L L  L S L
   beš –no az ney çon he- kā-yat mi-ko-nad    (sung twice)
   waz ğo- dā- i -hā še- kā- yat mi-ko-nad
   Hear the reed flute, how it does complain
   And how it tells of separation's pain
```

of twentieth-century origin, with known composers. The pishdaramad (pre-introduction) is played heterophonically by an instrumental ensemble; chaharmezrab ('four beats') is a fast virtuoso piece, with a repeated rhythmic pattern usually played by a soloist. A reng is a rapid dance in 6/8 metre which usually marks the conclusion of a dastgah. A tasnif is a metric song with instrumental accompaniment, whose lyrics need not be drawn from classical poetry but can also be topical: tasnif have often addressed political and social issues such as women's rights and religious and political autocracy. Among the most eminent exponents of this genre were the poet-musicians Abol Qāsem 'Āref Qazvini (1882–1934), 'Ali Akbar Sheydā (1844–1906) and the poet Malek al-Sho'arā Bahār (d. 1951). Their tasnif remain key elements of the classical repertoire today.

A complete performance of Persian classical music is expected to include pishdaramad, chaharmezrab, avaz, tasnif and reng, all deployed with a certain flexibility. This is analogous to the compound suites found elsewhere in the Middle East, as with the Iraqi *maqām* or the *nawba* of North Africa.[17] At an informal gathering the improvised avaz can last over half an hour, followed by one or more tasnif, but in concerts and on radio these are usually limited to ten or fifteen minutes.

THE OTHER CLASSICAL MUSICS

Borumand was taught by Darvish Khan *(top left)* and himself taught tar-maestro Dariush Tala'i *(top right)*. *Below left:* the kamancheh in the hands of Kayhan Kalhor, one of its leading present-day exponents, and, below right, as played in this sixteenth-century miniature: Young musician. Qazvin, Iran, about 1580. (Paper, ink, opaque watercolour, gold. 34.4 × 23.7 cm.)

Instruments

The most typical classical performance configuration consists of a male or female singer accompanied by one or more instruments, as depicted in Persian miniature paintings from the thirteenth century onwards. The principal instruments are the two long-necked lutes, tar and setar; the trapezoidal santur hammered zither; the kamancheh spike fiddle; the ney reed flute; and the goblet-shaped zarb drum. Other instruments such as the *ud* (a short-necked lute), the *daf* and *dāyereh* (frame drums) and the *qānun* (a plucked dulcimer) are also found.

The tar and setar are the instruments most closely identified with Persian classical music. The tar is descended from the ancient *rabāb*, and was developed in Iran towards the end of the eighteenth century. Its double-bowled body is shaped like a figure eight, and its ultra-thin lambskin membrane creates a brilliant sonority. The body is of mulberry with a maple or walnut neck; the twenty-five moveable frets are of gut. The six metal strings in three courses are plucked with a metal plectrum. The setar's more refined and intimate sound is considered to be well suited for women. Smaller than the tar and with a single-bowl shape, it has the same number of frets; to its three strings ('seh') a fourth is added for resonance; it is plucked with the long nail of the forefinger.

The santur, a trapezoidal zither or dulcimer, is made of a hard wood such as walnut; the two mallets (*mezrābs*) are light and pliable, and typically padded with felt. There are two rows of nine bridges (*kharak*), each holding a course of four strings for a total of seventy-two strings, which are anchored to the left of the instrument and strung across the face to tuning pegs on the right side.

The kamancheh is a spike fiddle with a bowl-shaped resonator of gourd or wood and four melodic strings. The face of the resonator is covered with a thin lamb-skin or fish-skin membrane; the fretless neck passes through the body to create a spike at the bottom, with the instrument held on the player's knee and played with a horsehair bow. This is loosely strung, to allow variation in tension when pulled across the strings; the musician rotates the instrument as it is played, keeping the bow on a relatively stable plane.

The ney end-blown reed flute is common throughout the Middle East, and in thirteenth-century Persia it became the principal instrument for the dervish dancers' mystical gatherings. In the Persian classical style it is finely nuanced, reflecting the human voice in its lower register and delicately imitating birdsong at the top. There are five finger-holes and a thumb-hole on the back; the blowing end is wrapped in metal, with a sharply bevelled edge on its interior; the length varies depending on the pitches required, and performers come on stage with a set of instruments.

The zarb (also called the *tombak*, *tonbak* or *dombak*) is a goblet-shaped drum, and has been the primary percussion instrument since the early nineteenth century; it is larger than most such drums in the Middle East. Modern instruments may have synthetic skins, but traditional ones have a thicker skin of camel or calf. The prominent master of the zarb, Hossein Tehrani (1911–73), is celebrated for having introduced new rhythmic techniques in zarb performance, raising it to the status of a solo instrument.

Music in Iran today

Among classical musicians in contemporary Iran, the clash of authenticity versus innovation is the subject of ongoing debate. Those who innovate within the framework of tradition are called *now āvarān-e sonnati* ('bringing newness to tradition'); one of the most prominent in this group is the composer and performer Hossein Alizadeh. Like many other musicians, he believes that the radif is still most suited to Persian classical poetry, but that new melodic and rhythmic models are needed for modern poetry. Many musicians have found new modes of expression by incorporating elements of regional styles, and through collaboration with classical musicians of other cultures. Those of the kamancheh player Kayhan Kalhor (b. 1963) reflect collaboration with the traditions of North India, Turkey and – with the Kronos Quartet – Europe.

One of today's most popular singers of Persian classical music is Parisa (b. 1950), here seen performing beneath a back-projection of her own image.

Traditional ensembles are now often expanded through new polyphonic arrangements, with the addition of instruments either borrowed from other traditions (Afghan *rabāb* or Baluchi *sorud*) or newly invented, such as the *saghar*, a long-necked lute designed and made by the vocalist Mohammad Reza Shajarian. The daf frame drum, once Iran's principal rhythmic instrument and the main instrument of Kurdish dervishes, has been reintegrated into traditional ensembles. Tempos have generally become faster. The prohibition on women singing solo for male audiences persists, but all-female ensembles have become more prominent, and women have also taken on a greater role as instrumentalists, including in mixed-sex ensembles, playing all kinds of instruments – Iranian classical and regional as well as Western. Amateurs have tended to give way to professionals, and the status of classical music has been raised as a result.

All this means that musical life in contemporary Iran is thriving, whether classical or semi-classical, fusion, regional, rock, pop or jazz, whether authorised or not. Persian classical music and its associated theory is taught both in universities and privately, supported by many publications by Iranian scholars and musicians. Most of the repertoire of the great masters of the past has been published with notation and released on cassettes and CDs. Private homes remain an important venue, as when concerts are held in public they still need a permit from Ershad. The control – and prohibition – of musical performance remains a live issue.

In 2009 UNESCO honoured the Persian radif as part of the 'intangible cultural heritage of humanity', and while it is now sustained in Iran through government and private patronage, it is also passionately supported by the musical diaspora in Europe and in the United States, most notably in Los Angeles. Moreover, Persian classical music is also finding a growing international audience thanks to the 'world music' boom. Meanwhile, many Iranians feel it important to affirm this positive aspect of their culture, to counteract other facets of their country's international image. In short, Persian classical music is full of contemporary significance, and remains an enduring, living tradition.

Further Reading

An overview of the history and the practice of Persian classical music with a good section on instruments is Jean During, Zia Mirabdolbaghi and Dariush Safvat's *The Art of Persian Music*. For more technical detail on the theory of Persian music see Hormoz Farhat's *The Dastgah Concept in Persian Music* and the chapters by Margaret Caton and Dariush Tala'i in *The Garland Encyclopedia of World Music* vol. 6, *The Middle East*. In the same volume Stephen Blum gives an excellent introduction on musical practices in Iran. For a pedagogical presentation of *radif* with notation and sound recording see Tala'I's *Traditional Persian Art Music*. Good articles on instruments, musicians and musical terms are to be found in *Encyclopædia Iranica*, available online (www.iranicaonline.org). More emphasis on vocal repertoire is provided by Owen Wright's *Touraj Kiaras and Persian Classical Music* and Rob Simms and Amitr Koushkani's studies of Mohammad Reza Shajarian and the art of avaz.

Recommended listening

Faramarz Payvar Ensemble, *Iran: Persian Classical Music*, Elektra, LC 0286, 1991 (originally released in 1974).

Iman Vaziri Parissa and Ali Rahimi, *Simplicity: Persian Traditional Music*. Cologne Music, 2007.

Mohammad Reza Shajarian, Hossein Alizadeh, Kayhan Kalhor and Homayoun Shajarian, *Faryad, Masters of Persian Music* (2 CDs), World Music Institute 468023, 2003.

Hossein Alizadeh and Madjid Khaladj, *Iranian Music Improvisations*, Buda 3259119860822, 2000.

Mahmud Karimi, *Vocal Radif of Persian Classical Music*, Mahoor Institute of Culture and Art, M.CD128, 2003.

The Mahoor Institute of Cultural Art (www.mahoor.com) is an excellent source for recordings of both Persian classical music and Iranian regional traditions.

The Central Asian steppes are rich in nomad musics, but a large swathe of territory – represented by the shaded portion of this map – is home to the *shashmaqom*. Deriving from the highly-developed culture of medieval Iran, this is the region's most venerated music, traditionally supported by wealthy merchants and the nobility.

15 Uzbekistan and Tajikistan
Will Sumits

It's late afternoon, and the palace courtyard is filling with people. Musicians arrive, take out their lutes and tune until they resonate in unison. The first beat of the frame-drum signals the entrance of the other instruments, and the pulse stills conversation. The patron and his guest take their places, and the court singer begins a song in praise of a love which is at once human and divine; the instrumentalists join in singing the next song. Then the performance starts to traverse a variegated landscape of melodies and rhythms, shifting between vocal and instrumental passages, competitive sections and solos. The patron's impassive gaze goads the ensemble to ever greater virtuosity till they rise in unison to a sustained peak, after which they slip seamlessly into their final piece, gradually descending back to their starting note.

'Central Asia' today comprises not only the republics of Uzbekistan, Tajikistan, Turkmenistan, Kazakhstan and Kyrgyzstan, but also the northern parts of Iran, Afghanistan, Pakistan, Kashmir and western China extending to the southern reaches of Siberia and Mongolia. Because most of this region was absorbed into the Soviet Union at the start of the twentieth century, the West has only recently been afforded proper access to its cultures, but Central Asia has intrigued outsiders for centuries. Its situation at the centre of the world's largest continental land-mass gave rise to the trade routes which collectively came to be known as the Silk Road, and it was along this colossal network linking the Far East with Europe that merchants, emissaries and adventurers travelled to and from the furthest corners of the earth. Accounts by Marco Polo, Xuan Zang, Ibn Battuta and others provided the rest of the world with insights into its economic and political realities, but culture was seldom their primary concern. And while ornate silk brocades, precious gems and rare spices are what the Silk Road conjures up in the popular imagination, Central Asia's musical heritage contains treasures every bit as precious.

Of all the musical traditions in Central Asia which might be considered 'classical', this chapter will focus on those of the ancient urban centres of Uzbekistan and Tajikistan. The classical music played today in those countries developed primarily in the ancient cities of Bukhara, Samarqand, Khiva and Qoqand, all of which served as the political and cultural centres of the dynasties that dominated Central Asia for five centuries. In these cities the term *maqām* is used to denote the repertoires of 'classical' music. Over the course of history this word has acquired a variety of meanings in the Islamic world, but it has always indicated elevated musical forms embodying both a repertoire of refined musical

The fifteenth-century Registan square in Samarqand with its three madrassas, which were originally centres of secular science as well as of religious learning

works and a highly-developed musical theory and system of modes. While musicians in much of the Arabic- and Turkic-speaking worlds will understand a maqam as a musical mode, the term has acquired an extended meaning in Central Asia. Here a maqam (conventionally transliterated as maqom) denotes a suite comprising traditional songs and melodies performed as an ordered series of movements, following traditionally prescribed guidelines for rhythmic and melodic progression. These suites are essentially anthologies of musical works, and their structuring reflects a long period of evolution guided by the aesthetics of master musicians. They have strong ties to the system of musical theory which developed in the early centuries of the Islamic period, and which reached its pinnacle in fifteenth-century Herat in northern Afghanistan. Central Asia became heir to this heritage, in which performance gradually replaced musical theory as the guiding influence.

Today the Uzbek and Tajik maqom repertoires are found in three main local traditions: the *shashmaqom* of Bukhara and Samarqand, the *chaharmaqom* of Qoqand and the Ferghana Valley, and the *alta-yarim maqom* of Khiva. These traditions differ in the number of their suites, in the pieces contained in them, and in the poetry which is sung. There are also regional differences in performance style, but to the untrained ear these differences are outweighed by the similarities, most notably in instrumental and vocal sonorities. Geographical proximity and cultural interaction have ensured much musical cross-pollination, and there is much shared repertoire.

The term *klasik* is often used today by Central Asian musicians to describe their maqom suites: this term was adopted from Western usage at the beginning of the twentieth century. But there has long been a distinction between the music performed by professional musicians, including maqom and *mumtāz kuylar* ('great songs'), and the folk repertoires performed by non-professionals. Maqom performance requires familiarity with many rhythms and modes and the memorisation of many complex melodies. Add to this the integration of a complex system of poetic metres, plus many centuries of poetry, and one can understand why maqom is often considered an Oriental counterpart to European classical music.

■ History

Since musical traditions are continuously evolving it is seldom possible to indicate their historical starting points, and this is particularly true of Central Asia. There is evidence to suggest that suite repertoires known today as maqom may have evolved over the course of the late seventeenth and eighteenth centuries, and that by the mid-nineteenth century the corpus of suites that is the basis of today's repertoire had taken shape. But their history can be traced back further, since they derive from the accumulated body of musical knowledge known throughout the medieval Islamic world as the 'science of music'.

The classification of music as a 'science' was underpinned by the classical Greek texts which were translated in great numbers soon after the advent of Islam. The early music theorists of the Islamic world, such as al-Kindi (d. 873) and al-Farabi (d. 950), were familiar with Greek scientific works on astronomy, medicine, music, the natural sciences and philosophy. While their works on music integrate some classical models, they made new contributions as they attempted to create a musical system which could accommodate the varied musical traditions that had become a part of established Islamic culture. The intellectual atmosphere in the imperial capital Baghdad during the ninth and tenth centuries must have been dynamic and vivid: scholars from all corners of the Islamic empire found their way there, where the 'House of Wisdom' had been instituted by the Abbasid caliphs in order to translate Greek, Persian and Indian treatises in the creation of a world 'Treasury of Wisdom' (*khazina al-hikma*). Amid the flurry of translation, and powered by this influx of scholars, artists and musicians, advances were made in many fields of the sciences and humanities, contributing to the golden age of Islam which continued until the twelfth century.

The 'science' of music included the physics of sound, the division of the octave into intervals, the primary musical modes and the principles of rhythm. Since music was categorized as a science, it was made to fit into a framework which mirrored the organizational principles of other sciences such as astronomy, medicine and cosmology. The overlapping of these sciences within an overarching cosmological framework allowed theorists to discuss the therapeutic qualities of music, as well as the ties between the musical modes and the primary elements and humours which govern the delicate balance of nature and human health. While some of these topics found their way into later musical discourse, the thirteenth and fourteenth centuries witnessed the rise of prominent musical scholars such as Safi ad-Din Urmawi (d. 1294) and Qutb ad-Din Shirazi (d. 1311), who championed a new classification system for musical modes that would become the armature for this science. It is at this time that maqom becomes established as the term for 'mode', and explanations of the twelve primary maqoms and their derivative *shu'ba* and *avāz* modes becomes central to all theoretical musical discourse.

This science reached its peak of development in the fifteenth century with the writings of 'Abdulqādir Marāghi (d. 1435), who completed his seminal work in Herat. Building on the works of his predecessors Urmawi and Shirazi, Maraghi expanded the modal corpus to include not only the twelve maqoms and the six avaz, but also an expanded group of twenty-four shu'ba derivative modes. This system gained canonical status, and served as the basis of modal theory in Persian, Arabic and Turkic treatises throughout the fifteenth to seventeenth centuries.

Maraghi's career reflects the political turmoil of the period in which he lived. Born in the Azeri region of north-western Iran, he was a court musician not only in Baghdad and Herat, but also in Tabriz and Samarqand. He had already been appointed chief court musician in Baghdad when Timur – better known today as Tamerlane – captured Baghdad in 1393 and brought him back to his capital at Samarqand. He was then sent to Tabriz as a musician for one of Timur's sons, but later escaped to Baghdad until in 1401 he was captured by Timur again, and brought back a second time to Samarqand. He was later entrusted to Timur's youngest son Shahrukh in Herat, where he completed the work that helped pave the way for the musical and cultural renaissance which blossomed after his death. Maraghi's contributions to music transcend regional and linguistic boundaries, and even today he is still venerated by musicians throughout the Middle East and Central Asia.

Despite its political upheavals, the Timurid period was an era of great cultural achievement: best remembered for his military conquests, Timur was also a vigorous patron of the arts, causing mosques and madrassas to be built whose intricate mosaics and awe-inspiring domes can still be seen in Bukhara and Samarqand. He sought out and sent back to his capital the best artists, architects and musicians from the lands he conquered. But it was at the court of the last Timurid ruler of Herat, Husayn Bāyqarā (ruled 1470–1506), that music and the arts had their finest efflorescence: this 'Timurid Renaissance' was a second golden age for poetry, music, miniature-painting, calligraphy and architecture, and it provided the momentum for later musical developments as far away as the Ottoman courts of Turkey and the Mughal courts in India. Stories preserved in extant histories bear witness to this, such as the following account of a student of the Herati musician Ustad Shadi:

One of Ustad Shadi's apprentices was the Ottoman musicologist Zayn al-Abiddin Husayni. He came from his Anatolian homeland to Herat where he studied music with Ustad Shadi. He earned the respect of Bayqara and Navā'ī and eventually returned to his homeland. He played the *chang* and the *'ud* very well. One of the Ottoman kings, Sultan Qo'rqud, heard his playing and exclaimed, 'You must have been in the court of Sultan Ya'qub and Sultan Bayqara', and bestowed great gifts upon him.[1]

Bayqara's patronage served as the model for the Ottoman rulers in the fifteenth and sixteenth centuries; the Timurid ruler Babur (1483–1530), who hailed from the Ferghana valley, established a similar patronage system when he founded the Mughal empire.

Bayqara's patronage of the arts was so generous that several of the poets and musicians in his court themselves became patrons. The lands he granted them allowed them not only greater freedom in their work, but also enabled some to turn their land into educational institutions, which were then further supported by endowments to employ musicians and artisans as teachers. This system greatly raised their status, as attested by the contemporary *tazkira* dictionaries containing hundreds of biographies of artists, poets and musicians.

The musician-poets with whom Bayqara filled his court – he was himself a trained musician – included 'Alī Shīr Navā'ī, 'Abdurahmān Jāmī (d. 1492) and 'Abdullah Marvārīd, who became high-ranking ministers. With Bayqara's patronage the Herati miniature painter Kamāliddin Behzād (1450–1535) ran a workshop which had such far-reaching influence that his œuvre is still regarded as the apogee of Persian miniature-painting. The writer Wāsifī, whose *Badāyi' al-Waqāyi'* describes the cultural splendour of the time, recounts in an early sixteenth-century manuscript:

> Amir 'Alishir Nava'i had a *ghazal* in the *mustazād* meter, for which Khoja 'Abdullah Sadr Marvarad composed a *savt*. It became known as 'Sarmast va Girebān Chāk' and it gained such fame that there was not a house or a palace in all of Herat in which this song was not found. Then Hāfiz Qirāq sang this *savt* along with the *qanun*, and soon the nobility and commoners at gatherings of all sorts were playing the 'Chāk'. Lovers came side by side to request this song from the musicians.[2]

This passage testifies to the brilliance of one of Bayqara's advisors, and it also reflects the collaborative atmosphere which then prevailed. Nava'i's artistic talents seem to have been outweighed only by his generosity – he was the most prominent patron of the day. Many musicians contributed to this cultural renaissance, but Bayqara and Nava'i were its orchestrators.[3]

One of the musicians with whom Nava'i maintained a close friendship was a wrestler named Pahlivān Mohammad. Skilled in composing poetic riddles, and adept at singing his verses, Pahlivan was admired by both Nava'i and Bayqara, and became the recipient of a land grant which he turned into a charitable foundation to provide food and lodging for visiting artists, musicians and dervishes. Named *Ni'mati Abad,* this lodge became one of Herat's hotspots for artistic and musical discourse, and often hosted musical soirees; with so many musicians passing through, Pahlivan's generosity and talents became famed.

With the end of Bayqara's rule came an end to a golden age that had lasted nearly five decades in Herat. While Timur's descendant Babur was gaining a foothold in India that would give rise to the Mughal dynasty, much of Central Asia fell under the rule of the Shaybānid dynasty, which lasted throughout the sixteenth century. After the fall of Timurid rule in Herat there was an exodus of many of its artists and musicians; some went to Bukhara and Samarqand, while others moved west towards Mashad, Tabriz or the Ottoman Empire; yet others followed Babur south to India. Exacerbated by growing political instability, and by the fact that the Shaybanid rulers were not patrons in the mould of the Timurids, the musical development of the region then went into a decline, but there seems to have been enough momentum generated in Herat to keep music alive and developing. It continued to play a role in the daily life of ordinary people, as well as at court, and the repertoire went on growing.

One of the best-known musicians of sixteenth-century Bukhara was Najmiddin Kavkabi (d. 1535), who had studied in Herat during Bayqara's reign. On his return to Bukhara he became a teacher and gained the respect of the emir, who commissioned him to write a treatise, copies of which survive. It is evident from this, and from other anonymously-authored works, that this century saw a shift away from the mathematically-precise music theory of previous centuries and towards a renewed focus on practice. The joining together in performance of different melody-types became increasingly important, and musicians strove to classify the melodic devices used to move between modes. Kavkabi referred to these transitional melody-types as *murakkibat*, while other authors used the term *gushe* to refer to such intermediary modal entities. Thus did the practice of modulation become indispensable to art-music performance. This trend continued through the seventeenth century, leading to the performance of modal suites consisting of multiple melody-types requiring knowledge of many modes, as well as the ability to move between them.

The development of these suites can be seen as the practical manifestation of the system of modal theory which had prevailed in preceding centuries: suites had been performed since the early Islamic period, but their integration into melodic and rhythmic modulation was an innovation of the sixteenth and seventeenth centuries. Now the guidelines for performance became more codified. Musical treatises from the late seventeenth century indicate that a corpus of four modal suites known as the *chahar shadd* became widespread throughout the region. Its performance may have begun as an exercise through which musicians could put their knowledge of modal theory into practice, but it soon became a prerequisite for the training of professionals.

Historically, the chahar shadd can be seen as the prototype of Central Asia's maqom suites, and possibly as the forerunner of the *dastgah* suites in Iran and Azerbaijan as well. What began as the performance of a sequence of modes soon came to integrate song forms, different rhythms and a body of texts by Persian and Central Asian Sufi poets. The transition from the chahar shadd to the chaharmaqom and shashmaqom is difficult to trace, however, due to the

This seventeenth-century painting of a ghijak player is of Mughal provenance, but the Mongol dress and hat suggest Central Asia; it reflects how the instrument was played. (*The kamancheh player*, Agra, India, about 1600. Paper, opaque watercolour, 33.2 × 20.5 cm.)

absence of eighteenth-century historical accounts, and it is unclear when the term 'maqom' came to replace *shadd* as the word for 'suite'. What is known is that in the mid-nineteenth century musical literature re-emerged after more than a century of quietude, and it is here that we find the first references to the shashmaqom tradition of Bukhara. Interestingly, when shashmaqom emerges from the shadows of history, it does so as a fully developed and highly structured repertoire consisting of six suites. Nineteenth-century shashmaqom literature comes in the form of textbooks containing the sung poetry, but these books also contain the names of the modes and often the rhythms used for each composition: they are playlists and textbooks for the entire repertoire. Barring variations in the poetry, and minor differences in the sequencing of the suites, these nineteenth-century versions are largely consistent, particularly in regard to their modal and rhythmic progressions, with the shashmaqom repertoire of today.

Oral tradition tells us that as a result of the oppressive rule imposed by the emirs of Bukhara in the eighteenth century, much of the population fled Bukhara for neighbouring areas of Khorasan in northern Iran and to the Mughal Empire in India, though many may have returned to Bukhara in the late eighteenth and early nineteenth centuries. Among those who left were many musicians, both Muslim and Jewish. This eighteenth-century mass migration has not been well documented, but still persists in the collective memory of Bukharans. Abdurauf

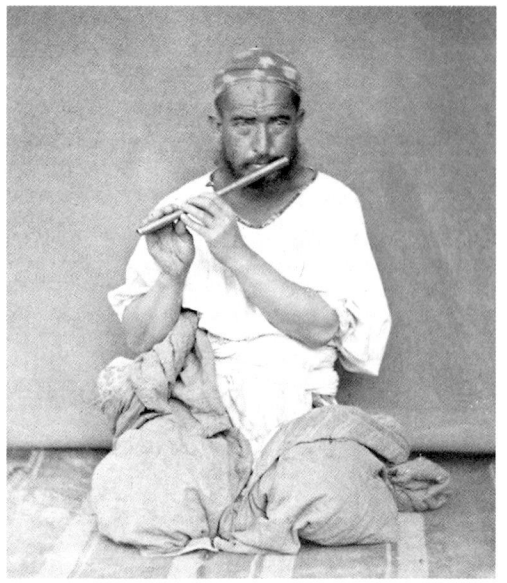

Musicians in Central Asia, c. 1870

Above: Nay and doira
Below: Ghijak and dutar

Fitrat, who served as the minister of education in Soviet Bukhara until his execution in 1936, mentions it in his *Uzbek Classical Music and Its History* (1927):

> The Manghit khāns were ignorant and dishonest rulers. The people had to adapt by trying to live a beggar's existence. Certainly these ruthless and immoral rulers did not have any appreciation of the fine arts, and people living under this dishonest and oppressive rule had no chance to work as artists or musicians. When this chaotic rule was beginning [c. 1785], migration from Uzbekistan to India also began. The Mughal Dynasty of the famous Babur Mirza in India had come to epitomise the arts, and as a result Uzbekistan's great artists, poets, musicians and scholars migrated there. This migration left the world of the arts in Uzbekistan without life.[4]

This migration may have influenced the development of maqom in Bukhara, and it is likely that a group of modal suites already formed the core of the classical repertoire in Bukhara prior to it. What is certain is that by the early nineteenth century, the shashmaqom repertoire had become the dominant musical tradition there, but it was not written down until mid-century, when musicians and singers began to compile song texts in compendiums called *bayāz*. And it is in the earliest extant bayaz, from 1848, that we find the first mention of the name shashmaqom. Meanwhile, the tradition had been established in Khorezm, and had been adopted by musicians in Khiva. The Khivan historian-musicologists Mulla Bekjon Rahmoni Og'li and Muhammad Yusuf Devonzoda tell us in their *History of the Music of Khorezm* (1925) how the shashmaqom arrived in Khiva:

> In the time of Muhammad Rahimkhān I (ruled 1805–1825), the Khivan musician Niyāzjān Khoja went to the region of Bukhara and learned the known shashmaqom repertoire on the tanbur, and then returned to Khiva. As soon as he arrived in Khiva, he attracted the attention of the instrumentalists and musicians of Khorezm; the musicians Makhdūmjān Qāzi and Ustā Muhammadjān learned the whole shashmaqom repertoire from him. They in turn began to teach what they had learned to aspiring *shāgird*s and soon they had trained many students on the tanbur. During this period there were no changes or alterations made to the music, but the influence of the shashmaqom melodies began to spread among the people, and their love for them began to grow.[5]

Gaining prestige among the nobility, the shashmaqom now entered a period of rapid development. Muhammad Rahim Khān II, who ruled Khorezm from 1864 to 1910, commissioned his court musician Pahlivān Mirzabāshi (1825–99) to develop a form of notation so that the repertoire could be used for training new musicians. The result was a tablature notation based upon the frets of the *tanbur*, which was also used to notate the repertoire of local *dutar* suites. This tablature became widespread in Khorezm during the last decades of the nineteenth century and first quarter of the twentieth, and many copies of it have survived. Khorezm's musicians contributed to the development of the suites by adding new compositions, which led to the creation of a new suite. The authors of *History of the Music of Khorezm* describe this process:

THE OTHER CLASSICAL MUSICS

The musicians of Khorezm added various songs and melodies to the known shashmaqom repertoire until an additional half maqom came to be recognised, and from the shashmaqom repertoire the *alti-yarim maqām* blossomed: *maqām rāst, maqām navā, maqām segāh, maqām dugāh, maqām buzruk* and *maqām panjigāh*. According to this division of the *maqām*s, the melodies of *panjigāh* from the *maqām-i rāst* were considered to form half of an additional suite.⁶

However, the maqom panjigah never grew into a full maqom, and today the tradition is referred to as the alti-yarim maqom, or the 'six-and-a-half' maqom. The nineteenth century saw much musical innovation in Khorezm and Bukhara, with Bukharan musicians collectively creating a secondary branch of six mini-suites. The last emirs of Bukhara were avid maqom fans, with some great musicians working in their courts. We might speculate how maqom might have evolved, had the region not been subject to the Soviet invasion.

The shashmaqom was sedulously cultivated by the latter-day rulers of Central Asia's city-states. Mohammed Alim Khan *(left)*, the last Emir of Bukhara, played the dutar; Feruz Khan, whose son Isfandiyar *(right)* was the last Khan of Khiva, instigated tanbur notation and punished his musicians for deviations from strict convention.

UZBEKISTAN AND TAJIKISTAN

■ Central Asian maqom during the Soviet era

The expanding Soviet Union occupied most of Central Asia, meeting local resistance with murderous oppression, and the integration of Central Asian societies into the Communist social framework was rapidly forced through. In the emirates of Bukhara, Qoqand and Khiva, virtually every facet of society was abruptly transformed.

From the beginning of the Soviet period the implementation of Marxist-Leninist policies in music brought changes in the way maqom was performed and taught. The Soviet education system was centralised and regimented, and the oral transmission of musical knowledge, which had been traditional, was replaced by new teaching methods in government-run music schools and

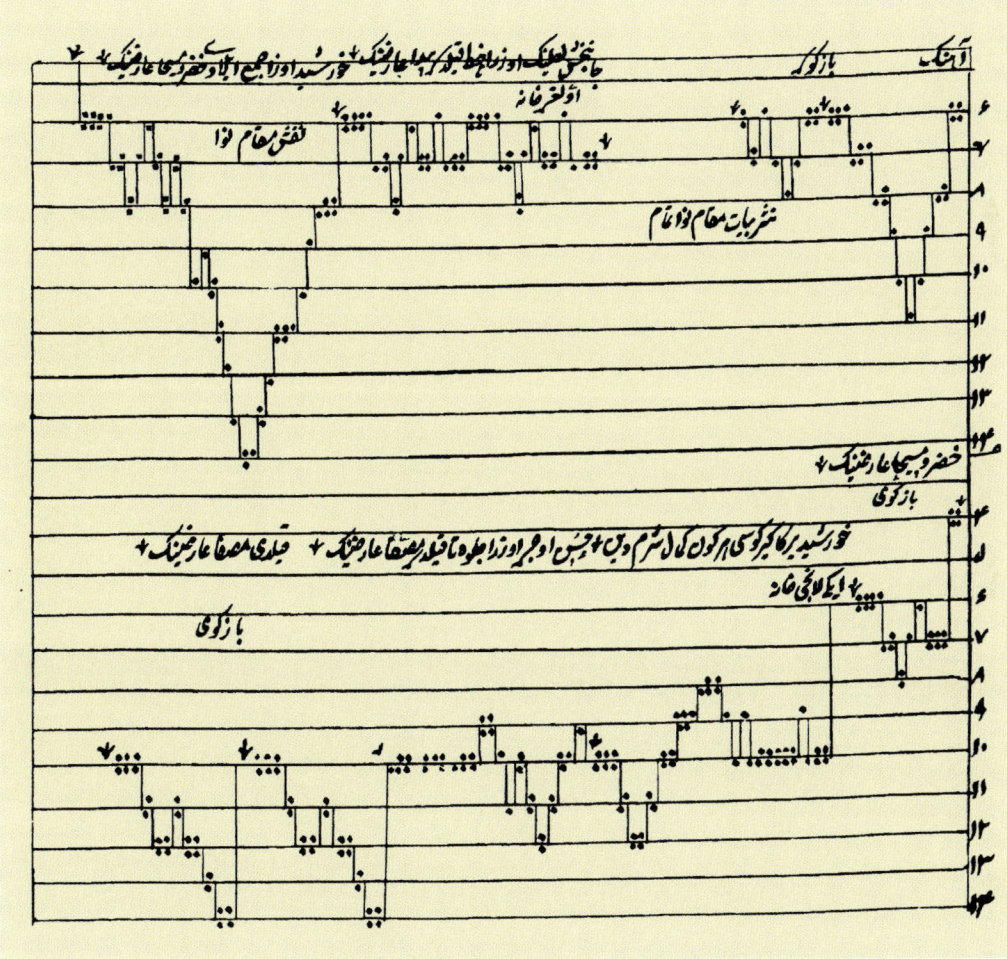

An indigenous system of tablature for the tanbur developed in the late nineteenth century for the Khorezm maqom, one of the three principal classical repertoires of Central Asia

conservatories. From a young age, musically inclined students were sent to specialised primary and secondary schools; there they were taught Western notation, were schooled in Western classical theory, and were exposed to an aesthetic based upon European classical ideals. The Soviet musical education system certainly produced positive results, as attested by several generations of Central Asian virtuosi, but the instatement of a curriculum emphasising European theory and performance had deleterious effects on maqom performance.

Yet Soviet musicologists were dispatched to the newly-created states to study musical tradition, documenting all they could: by 1925 the Soviet musicologist Victor Uspenskiy had transcribed and published the entire shashmaqom repertoire, using Western notation. But the fact that his publication did not include the Persian-Tajik lyrics of the suites is indicative of the way in which the concept of 'musical heritage' would be used as a tool of Communist propaganda to create national consciousness – and national musical identities – in accord with Marxist-Leninist cultural policy. The newly-drawn political boundaries of the Central Asian states did not reflect the cultural, linguistic or musical geography of the region, but served a divide-and-rule policy for the newly-occupied territories, whose cultural traditions were used to create new 'national' identities designed to bolster popular support for the Communist state.

One result of this was that the shashmaqom found itself at the centre of a nationalistic tug-of-war. Its homeland, the ancient city of Bukhara, was indeed a cosmopolitan centre with diverse ethnic groups. But the Bukharan shashmaqom was primarily sung in Tajik-Persian, which had been the lingua franca for Central Asian poets for more than a millennium. Now that Bukhara was located within the Soviet state of Uzbekistan, cultural policy-makers deemed it necessary to transform the shashmaqom into a musical monument to 'Uzbek' culture and to promote it as the 'national' masterwork of the new state. These efforts started early, as evidenced by Fitrat's *Uzbek Classic Music and its History*, part of whose importance lies in the fact that it is one of the first musicological works to be published in the Soviet era by a local scholar. But its insistence that the shashmaqom is an 'Uzbek' tradition reflects the nationalising efforts of the Soviets. Competing publications of the shashmaqom repertoire printed in Tajikistan and in Uzbekistan further attest to this polarisation.

Although Soviet musicologists transcribed thousands of folk songs and maqom melodies in order to preserve them, they were simultaneously striving to 'modernise' a music which they viewed as an archaic remnant of Central Asia's feudal past. It became policy to alter the way instruments were constructed, and to favour a well-tempered chromatic division of the octave, thus drastically changing the intervals and maqom's overall sonority. To the discerning ear, shashmaqom recordings from the early twentieth century reveal very different intervals from those most commonly heard today. Microtonal intervals were commonplace: this was one of the defining characteristics of Central Asian maqom. Although some musicians continued to use these intervals, the Soviets' modernisation resulted by and large in their abandonment as hindering the advance of the classical tradition. Musicians who received their primary musical

Turgun Alimatov (1922–2008) was the most influential maqom exponent of recent times. Photographed here with his son Alisher, he was master of the tanbur, dutar and sato (a bowed tanbur which he was instrumental in reviving). He regarded maqom as a spiritual matter, his precept being: 'First a musician must tune himself. Then he must tune his instrument. Only after that can he tune the listener.' After a career as a violinist in Tashkent's Muqimi Theatre of Musical Drama he joined the radio station, but his refusal to follow the official Rajabi line on 'correctness' meant that recognition of his excellence was belated. He never sang, but his instrumental sound was intensely lyrical. MC

education during the Soviet period were trained according to the new policies, with the tempered division of the octave leading to changes in the tuning of the tanbur, and with changes in the maqom suites themselves. There are still some musicians who work microtonally, but such intervals have become known as *yavvoy parda*, 'wild intervals', and are today mostly associated with the performance style of the blind musicians known as *qāri*.

Meanwhile the tempered octave served to bring maqom and the folk music of the region closer to western European models, with the aim being to let the shashmaqom take its place on the world stage as one of the classical traditions of the minority peoples of the Soviet Union. Traditional instruments had their fretting changed and were made in bass, alto and soprano sizes to permit maqom and folk music to be played in orchestral arrangements. Thus, rather than in small ensembles of five or six musicians, maqom began to be performed by orchestras with as many as sixty musicians, giving rise to hybrid genres in which traditional motifs were backed by five-part harmony and presented in Western classical forms. Operas were written by local composers who drew on traditional epic love stories such as 'Layli and Majnun' or 'Shirin and Farhad', which they set to symphonic arrangements for 'national' instruments.

Because most official performances were organised in accordance with the Soviet Ministry of Culture and its local branches, it might appear that these changes were all-pervasive. However, not all Central Asia's musicians accepted this makeover of their art. Despite state-sponsored concerts of orchestral maqom, there were many informal occasions where small ensembles continued to perform traditionally. And while Soviet musicology permitted the documentation of entire repertoires of folk and classical music, there was also an effort to determine the most 'correct' versions of the maqom suites, to create supposedly definitive standards of performance. These versions acquired canonical status in the 1950s through the publication of the complete notated shashmaqom by the Uzbek musician Yunus Rajabi, whose version came to be regarded as the repertoire in its most perfect form. This reduced that stylistic diversity which was part of the shashmaqom's richness.

■ Maqom in Central Asia today

Though some aspects of Soviet musical ideology have survived the dissolution of the Soviet Union, the maqom traditions of Uzbekistan and Tajikistan are today regarded as the region's highest form of art-music, and are promoted by the governments of Uzbekistan and Tajikistan as their 'national' music. But maqom is not widely popular: its core audience consists of musicologists, students and a small body of connoisseurs, plus the performers' friends and relatives. Most young people are more interested in pop, both Central Asian and Western, but there are enough students of traditional folk and maqom music to ensure a future generation of maqom performers. Indeed, recent years have seen a revitalisation in both its study and performance, with non-governmental organisations such as the Aga Khan Trust for Culture and UNESCO supporting schools and projects led by 'tradition bearers', reinstating traditional master-pupil tuition, and supporting international tours by ensembles of traditional master-musicians. One such institution is the Academy of Maqom in Dushanbe, Tajikistan, a specialist school for the teaching and performance of shashmaqom which was founded by its director Abduvali Abdurashidov with support from the Aga Khan Music Initiative in Central Asia and from UNESCO. Its students are rigorously trained in both theory and performance, and must master all the poetic metres, rhythms and melodies. In 2007 the first class to graduate gave a six-day concert series in which they performed all the suites in their entirety. As a result, students have now begun to create new maqom compositions, thus reverting to nineteenth-century practice. It's too early to say whether any of the new pieces will endure, but this still represents a notable achievement.

In 2000 the president of Tajikistan declared 12 May the Day of Shashmaqom, and this is now an annual event celebrated by televised concerts organised by the Ministry of Culture. In 2003, the shashmaqom tradition of Bukhara was named

Above: With his Academy of Maqom in Dushanbe, Tajikistan, Abduvali Abdurashidov (centre) plays the sato, delivering traditional maqom forms and also creating new ones. The other instruments are *(from left to right)*, dutar, doira and tanbur.

Right: For the past twenty years the reigning diva of Ferghana maqom has been Munajat Yulchieva, whose name means 'prayer' and whose career had an unlikely start. Born on a cotton farm in 1960, this Uzbek singer was rejected for singing 'out of tune' by the opera department of the Tashkent conservatory, but on the day of her rejection her talent chanced to be spotted by the rabab master Shawqat Mirzaev, who took her under his wing. Her subsequent fame, coupled with her unique timbre – which comes from deep inside – has made her a role model for younger female singers. 'The performer should sing as if addressing God with an inner voice,' she says, 'and the chest voice, or "Sufi" tone, reflects that.'

MC

Qasimjon and Baba Raykhon performing at an informal evening āsh for friends and relatives in Isfara, Tajikistan

as one of the 'Masterpieces of Oral and Intangible Heritage of Humanity' by UNESCO, and has in recent years gained a wider international recognition; this in turn has prompted new local and state support. However, the support received by musicians and music teachers at state institutions is not enough to subsist on, so most supplement their incomes by playing in pop-music wedding bands, or by non-musical work.

In some respects the nationalising tendencies championed in the Soviet era persist today, including the changes to the division of the octave, and to the tonality of the music. Soviet-style televised concerts with gaudy decor and lip-synched 'phonogram' performances of maqom are common, but these events mask the true revival occurring as musicians and scholars realise the importance of recovering aspects of performance which have become almost extinct. And although the present musical education system in Uzbekistan and Tajikistan is much as it was in Soviet times, there is now a slow return to traditional methods of teaching. A walk through the conservatories in the capitals of both countries will reveal groups of students sitting with teachers and learning maqom melodies by ear. In northern Tajikistan, a network of eleven local music schools based on traditional *ustod-shogird* (master-apprentice) training has been established by the dutar player Sultonali Khudoberdiev with support from international cultural organisations; the Ministry of Culture's support for this initiative is another positive indicator. In places often far from the capital cities, maqom performance is truly alive.

And there are still traditional settings and occasions where maqom is played. Wedding banquets often rely on local pop singers accompanied by modern ensembles with keyboards and electric guitars, bass and violins for dance renditions of folk and maqom songs. But performances with traditional acoustic instruments continue to play an important role, notably in the early-morning *āsh* gatherings of male relatives and friends on the day of a wedding. At such events a feast is prepared of *plov* or *āsh*, a Central Asian rice dish with meat, and the guests listen to maqom and congratulate the groom and his family. Maqom performances may also accompany circumcision rites for young boys.

■ Instruments

The quintessential maqom instrument in Uzbekistan and Tajikistan is the *tanbur*. This long-necked lute has a venerable history in Central Asia: descriptions of it appear in the tenth century in al-Farabi's discussion of the fretting of the Khorasani version. 'Tanbur' is a common name for a wide variety of long-necked lutes across the Middle East and Central Asia: the tanbur as it exists in Uzbekistan and Tajikistan is quite distinct from instruments bearing the same name in other regions. The Central Asian version is between 100 and 120 cm in length; at its base is a sound chamber made from a single piece of aged mulberry wood and covered with a thin mulberry face, aged and smoked in a wood fire to obtain its deep reddish-brown hue. It is strung with three or four metal strings, plucked with a metal plectrum on the tip of the index finger, and has thick frets wound from gut; it may also be played with a bow. Its length and low-tension strings create a delicate sound which is full in both low and high registers, and the playing technique and plucking methods allow subtle ornamentation; its frets stand high enough above the fingerboard to allow for glissando between notes, and for the characteristic *nāla*, or moaning sound, which seems to gently fluctuate back and forth around each note.

The shashmaqom suites are inextricably intertwined with the tanbur. Its tuning system and the arrangement of its frets define the melodic contours of the repertoire, and the performance of shashmaqom has been tied to this instrument since the early stages of its development. It is not known precisely when the tanbur emerged as the primary maqom instrument, but it is safe to say that is has been of central importance since at least the beginning of the nineteenth century, and probably well back into the eighteenth. Oral histories and musician biographies indicate that the great shashmaqom masters of the mid-nineteenth century were primarily tanbur players. Writing in 1925, Fitrat claimed that 'the tanbur is the greatest of our musical instruments'; he went on to give a detailed account of its history and construction, and of the three tunings used in performance of the suites.

Also made of mulberry, the *dutar* ('two strings') is almost as central as the tanbur to maqom performance, and is used both for solos and accompaniment. Its two silk strings create a soft and intimate sound, and it has for centuries been the preferred instrument of women players, often in the home. There are compositions which belong solely to the dutar and are rarely performed on other instruments; in Khiva there is a repertoire of maqom suites known as the *dutar maqom yollari* ('melodies of the dutar maqom'). It is believed that the Khorezmian dutar maqom suites represent the oldest stratum of maqom music in Khorazm, predating the arrival of the shashmaqom. Many copies of Khorezmian tanbur tablature notation also include notation for the dutar.

The *chang* is also a key instrument in maqom performance. Struck with small wooden mallets, this hammered dulcimer is placed on a stand or on the musician's lap, and although it's still used today, it is not as popular as it was in the sixteenth and seventeenth centuries, as attested by the number of chang players whose names were recorded in the musical literature of that time.

Borrowed from the Uyghurs in the 1920s, the *rabab* is a long-necked lute with five strings which is played with a small ebony plectrum. It is often referred to as the 'Kashgar rabab' to distinguish it from other Afghan and Pamiri instruments bearing the same name. Originally it had tied frets made from wound gut, but today it is most commonly constructed with metal frets, and its sound chamber is covered with fish skin. The rabab is commonly used in maqom performance, and some of the great exponents of Central Asian maqom made the rabab their preferred instrument. It is held close to the chest, usually resting on the forearm.

The *ghijak* is a spike-fiddle with a spherical parchment-covered sound chamber connected to a short neck without frets. It is played upright, resting on the knee, with a bow; similar spike-fiddles are found in Iran, Azerbaijan and Kurdistan, where the instrument is known as the *kemanche*. The ghijak's lack of frets makes it ideal for producing the melismatic 'moaning' ornaments so characteristic of Central Asian maqom.

The *surnay* is a conical oboe with a double reed; its piercing sound suits it to outdoor festivities, but it is also used in special repertoire of surnay maqoms which are usually performed solo, or accompanied by a pair of kettle-drums called *naqqara* which are played with mallets.

The *nay* is a transverse flute of turned wood or reed; the *doira* is the main accompanying percussion instrument: a circular frame-drum covered by hide, this usually has metal jingles attached around its inner rim.

Further reading

Until the publication of Theodore Levin's pioneering cultural odyssey *The Hundred Thousand Fools of God* in 1996, the indigenous music of Central Asia had been as closed to the English-speaking world as everything else in this region. Levin's three decades of observing, recording and interviewing in historic cities and remote mountain villages allowed him to piece together a richly evocative portrait of Muslim and Jewish musical traditions, with their social and religious underpinnings; he charts the renaissance of semi-defunct cultures as the Soviet yoke was lifted, and examines the shashmaqom diaspora in New York. Levin's *Music of Central Asia* (2015), co-edited with the Kyrgyz scholar Elmira Köchümkulova, has now comprehensively answered the need for an accessible textbook on the region's multifarious styles and traditions; it's designed not only for students in the West, but also to help young people in Central Asia to re-engage with their partially-obscured heritage. Written by leading musicians and ethnographers, illustrated by audio and video recordings, and including artistic credos from musicians, its essays cover everything from the historical development of instruments and performance to the arts of oral poetry and epic recitation. Meanwhile one of the contributors to that book has produced her own study: Razia Sultanova's delineation of woman's roles in Sufi culture (*From Shamanism to Sufism*, 2011) contains much chapter-and-verse detail on what is played and sung, and why. The UNESCO compilation *History of Civilizations of Central Asia* (2000) includes essays on the Kyrgyz Manas epic, and on the development of modal systems from the ninth to the fifteenth centuries. Svat Soucek's *A History of Inner Asia* (2000) gives the best short account of the region's political past and present; he shows how nomad rule gave way to settled societies, and how medieval religious and cultural traditions have persisted, despite Tsarist and Soviet attempts to erase them. Nicola Di Cosmo, Allen Frank and Peter Golden's *The Cambridge History of Inner Asia* (2009) includes useful essays on the links between literature, painting and music at the Timurid courts.

Michael Church

Recommended listening

Ouzbekistan: les grandes voix du passé (1940–1965), Ocora C 560142, 1999. The leading singers of the Ferghana tradition, captured during their heyday.

Turgun Alimatov, *Ouzbekistan*, Ocora C 560086, 1995. The most influential latter-day instrumentalist from that tradition, accompanied by his son Alisher.

Abduvali Abdurashidov, *Tadjikistan: Classical Music and Songs*, Ocora C 560254, 2013. Accompanied by a singer and players on the dutar and doira, Tajikistan's leading exponent of the shashmaqom gives a lovely *tour d'horizon*.

Monajat Yultchieva, *Ouzbekistan*, Ocora C 561060, 2008. The greatest living female singer of Central Asia delivers songs in the Ferghana style.

Monajat Yultchieva, *Concert at the Theatre de la Ville*, Eva DVD, 2008. In concert, and also in a film in which she takes us back to her native village.

Notes

Introduction

1. Von Hornbostel, '*Die Probleme der vergleichenden Musikwissenschaft*'.
2. Offering an account of the crisis which engulfed all forms of traditional culture in Mali in January 2012, Andy Morgan's book *Music, Culture and Conflict in Mali* – including interviews with many musicians – is the authoritative guide.
3. Boulez, *Orientations*, 421. Boulez's *Rituel In Memoriam Maderna* suggests a strong affinity with gagaku.
4. Seeger, *Why Suya Sing*.
5. Maddocks, *Harrison Birtwistle: Wild Tracks*, 42–5.
6. Powers, 'Classical Music, Cultural Roots, and Colonial Rule', 32.
7. Randle Cotgrave, *Dictionarie of the French and English Tongues* (London, 1611).
8. Daniel Heartz and Bruce Alan Brown, 'Classical', In Sadie (ed.), *The New Grove Dictionary of Music and Musicians* vol. 5, 924.
9. Harris, *The Making of a Musical Canon in Chinese Central Asia*, passim.
10. Ivan Moody, liner note to Kontakion, *Mysteries of Byzantine chant*, Philips 454-057-2, 1996.
11. The best introduction to Georgian polyphony is Joseph Jordania's chapter in *The Garland Encyclopaedia of World Music*, vol. 8, *Europe*.
12. For a fine demonstration of mugam, listen to Faik Chelebi, *The Classical Mugam of Azerbaijan* (Silk Road House, 2013). There is very little information on Azeri mugam available in English: Simon Broughton's July 2013 essay in *Songlines* is the most accessible source.
13. An illuminating account of this process can be found in the late Peter Fletcher's heroic global synthesis, *World Musics in Context* (Oxford, 2001), 202–9.
14. *The Art of the Oud*, Ocora C 583068, 2001.
15. Nettl, *The Study of Ethnomusicology*, 36.
16. Levin, *The Hundred Thousand Fools of God*, 48.
17. *Longing for the Past*, released on the Dust-to-Digital label in 2013, is the first survey to be made of the 78 rpm record era in South-East Asia, where pioneering European record companies – whose interest was commercial rather than musicological – passed the torch to local labels in the Thirties. Its scope is majestic, covering music recorded as long ago as 1906 in Vietnam, Laos, Cambodia, Thailand, Burma, Malaysia and Indonesia; its four CDs are accompanied by a hardback book containing essays, period photographs and detailed track annotations by a team of ethnomusicologists led by Terry E. Miller.
18. Fox, 'Repatriation as Reanimation through Reciprocity', in Bohlman (ed.), *The Cambridge History of Western Music*, 552.
19. See the *Kronos Explorer Series* and *A Thousand Thoughts*, Nonesuch, 2014.
20. *From Another World: A Tribute to Bob Dylan*. Buda Musique 3758744, 2014.
21. *Bali: Gamelan and Kecak*. Nonesuch Explorer Series 7559-79814-2, 1989/2003.

22 Cook, 'Western Music as World Music', in Bohlman (ed.), *The Cambridge History of Western Music*, 94.
23 *Tengir-Too: Mountain Music of Kyrgyzstan*. Smithsonian Folkways 40520, 2006.
24 The refined artistry of Kazakh folk-singing can be heard in Elmira Janabergenova's *Songs from the Aral Sea* (Silk Road House, 2013). In *The Epic Korughly* (Silk Road Housem, 2013), the Kazakh singer Bidas Rustembekov accompanies himself on the dombra in a musical retelling of the most famous Central Asian epic. The field-recordings by Michael Church on *Songs from the Steppes: Kazakh Music Today* (Topic, 2005) survey Kazakh folk music in all its forms.

1 Thailand, Laos, Cambodia, Vietnam

1 Verney, *Notes on Siamese Musical Instruments*, 5.
2 De Marini, *Histoire nouvelle et curieuse*, 363.
3 Tachard, *A Relation of the Voyage to Siam*, 186.
4 Neale, *Narrative of a Residence at the Capital of the Kingdom of Siam*, 237.
5 Swangviboonpong, *Thai Classical Singing*, 143.
6 Nguyen, 'Restructuring the Fixed Pitches of the Vietnamese Dan Nguyet Lute', 56.

2 Java

1 In *Algemeen Handelsblad*, 31 October 1937, quoted by Kunst, *Music in Java*, 249.
2 Modern Javanese and the national language Indonesian both use Roman script and the essentials of pronunciation are relatively easy to grasp. The vowel *e* is pronounced rather like its French equivalent, as it can have either a grave or acute accent, or none; if it has no accent it should be pronounced as in 'th*e*', not as in 'th*e*m' or 'th*e*e' or 'th*e*y'. Rules governing the vowel *a* in Javanese are complex; it is often pronounced more like the *o* somewhere between 'd*o*t' and 'd*o*te'. The consonant *c* is pronounced *ch*; *g* as in 'go', not 'giraffe'; *r* is rolled; *th* (also *dh*) is retroflex (the tongue slightly curled back) and is pronounced more or less like the English *t*, never as the English *th*.
3 The upper case version refers to the province of Central Java, while the lower case 'central' refers to a more general area, including zones that are not officially within Central Java. The gamelan described in this chapter is usually called Central Javanese, despite also being prevalent beyond the strict administrative limits of the province.
4 The idea of handling focuses attention on the hands, which produce the instrumental sounds (while the mouth produces the vocal ones).
5 Sumarsam, *Gamelan*, 117.
6 Gamelan music is mainly pentatonic, so few pieces have all seven pélog pitches and none has all seven with equal emphasis or frequency. A common pentatonic extraction from the seven pélog pitches uses the first, second, third or fourth, fifth and sixth notes, while another uses the second, third, fifth, sixth and seventh.

7 There are exceptions: Kunst, *Music in Java*, 482–9, reproduced a Javanese score using staff notation and the present author supplied one using the standard kepatihan system and my modified staff notation in *A Guide to the Gamelan*, 108–19. These were intended only to give an overview of what typically happens in a gamelan piece rather than mimic the prescriptive function of a Western score.

8 In Perlman, *Unplayed Melodies*, 104.

9 See ibid., 105.

10 A performance of this piece, from the Mangkunegaran palace with all instrumental and vocal parts, can be heard on the 2003 CD *Indonesia, Java – Court Gamelan* vol. 2 (Nonesuch 7559-79721-2, originally released as an LP in 1977, Nonesuch H-72074).

11 A good example of how influential theoretical writings were also produced by distinguished performers and teachers, especially since independence, is Becker and Feinstein's *Karawitan*.

12 Roy Howat has drawn some more specific connections between 'Pagodes' and gamelan techniques in his chapter 'Debussy and the Orient'.

13 To complicate matters further, the word *musik* is not normally used to refer to gamelan music (for which the Javanese term karawitan exists) but more to Western music and other non-indigenous types. Thus *musik klasik* is a good equivalent of our 'classical music' and has nothing to do with Javanese gamelan music.

3 Japan

1 Japanese personal names will be given in the traditional order: family name first.

2 The Hepburn romanisation system is used here. Pronunciation of Standard Japanese is approximately as follows. Vowels are similar to Spanish except for *u*, which nearly rhymes with English 'should'. Macrons (shown only on first use) represent a longer duration of the same vowel sound. The *r* is a 'flap' as in Spanish. Between voiceless consonants, *i* and *u* are often unvoiced (whispered); thus *shite* is pronounced sh'tay (rhyming with English 'stay').

3 Among numerous English-language sources on togaku, Steven Nelson's chapters in Tokita and Hughes (eds), *The Ashgate Research Companion to Japanese Music* provide the best scholarly introduction.

4 Several strands of evidence demonstrate this retardation and variation; see Marett, 'Tôgaku: where have the Tang melodies gone'.

5 From Zeami's *Kakyō* (1424); quoted in Yamazaki (ed.), *On the Art of the Nō Drama*, 103.

6 Malm's *Nagauta* provides a detailed analysis of two contrasting nagauta. Tokita's 'Music in *kabuki*' discusses other kabuki musics as well.

7 For details on all aspects of shakuhachi see Tsukitani, 'The *shakuhachi* and its music'.

8 Quoted from Murasaki, *The Tale of Genji* vol. 1, 142.

9 Hughes, 'No nonsense', explains the logic behind Japanese oral mnemonics and introduces similar systems from other music cultures.

10 Koizumi, 'Musical scales in Japanese music'.

11 Full-score staff transcriptions of togaku pieces are found in several of books listed under Further Reading; a good example may be found in Nelson, 'Court and religious music (2)', 56–7.

12 See for example Atkins, *Blue Nippon*, 40, 245–58.

4 China: The Guqin Zither

1. See Wu Zhao (ed.), *Zhongguo guqin zhencui*.
2. Liang, *The Chinese Ch'in*, 52, 56, 78–80.
3. See Lawergren, 'Western Influences on the Early Chinese Qin-Zither'.
4. DeWoskin, *A Song for One or Two*, 138.
5. See Egan, 'The Controversy over Music and "Sadness"'.
6. Gulik, *The Lore of the Chinese Lute* 88; Yung, 'Historical Interdependency of Music', 84–5; Yung, 'Music of *Qin*', 3.
7. Tse, 'From Chromaticism to Pentatonism', 7–22ff, 168.
8. Liang Ming-yueh, sleeve note to *Chinese masterpieces for the ch'in, ancient and modern*, Lyrichord LP LLST 7342 (1980).
9. Shen Caonong et al., *Guqin chujie*, has a full survey of tunings.
10. Lindqvist, *Qin*, 252.
11. Kouwenhoven, 'Meaning and Structure'; Dahmer, *Die große Solosuite Guanglingsan*, 128–30.
12. Liang, *The Chinese Ch'in*, 136; DeWoskin, *A Song for One or Two*, 130.
13. See Mitani, 'Some melodic features of Chinese qin music', 126–34; Yung, 'Not Notating the Notatable'; Lee, 'Reading Between the Lines'.
14. Mitani, 'Some melodic features of Chinese qin music', 127–8.
15. See Ivanoff, 'Invitation to the fifteenth-century plectrum lute' 8, 11–13; Tilney, *The Art of the Unmeasured Prelude for Harpsichord*.
16. Liang, *The Chinese Ch'in*, 120.
17. Kouwenhoven, 'Bringing to life tunes of Ancient China', 48.
18. Yung, 'Choreographic and Kinesthetic Elements in Performance', 512; See also Yung, 'Music of *Qin*'.
19. For changes in qin performance, see also Yung, 'Historical Interdependency of Music'; Wu Wenguang, 'Wu Jinglüe's Qin Music in Its Context'; Dai, 'Plum Blossom – Three Variations'; and Huang, 'The Parting of the Way'.
20. Yung, 'Music of *Qin*', 5.

6 North India

1. As a guide to pronunciation, long vowels are marked thus: ā as in 'father', ī as in 'piece', ū as in 'clue'. Unmarked vowels are short: a as in 'about', i as in 'pit', u as in 'put'. The vowels e, o and āī are similar to the English vowels in 'play', 'go' and 'high' respectively, but more like the corresponding vowels in Italian. These pronunciation marks are also included on titles of works, but they are omitted from personal and place names, and from technical terms once they have been introduced.
2. It can be heard in Bor, *The Raga Guide*, CD 1, track 16. Examples 6.1–4 were transcribed by the author.
3. Shekhar and Chenoy, *Dargah Quli Khan, Muraqqa'-e Dehli*, 122.

8 Mande jaliyaa

1. Tracey, *African Dances of the Witwatersrand Gold Mines*, 1952.
2. Anderson, 'The Miko Modal System of Kiganda Xylophone Music', 1971.
3. Perman, Personal communication, 2015.
4. Niane, *Sundiata*, 1965.
5. Battúta, *Travels in Asia and Africa 1325–1354* (1926), 326.
6. Ibid., 328.
7. Duran, Fosu-Mensa and Stapleton, 'On Music in Contemporary West Africa', 234.
8. Charry, *Mande Music*, 105–11.
9. An excellent insight into the nature of this relationship for both men and women is given by Marloes Janson in 'Praising as a Gendered Activity'.
10. Knight, 'Music out of Africa: Mande Jaliya in Paris', 69.
11. See Knight, 'Mandinka drumming'.
12. Farmer, 'A North African Folk Instrument', 27.
13. Park, *The Travels of Mungo Park*, 213.
14. See Rouget, 'Sur les Xylophones Equiheptaphoniques des Malinké'. Studies confirming Rouget's findings are Jessup, *The Mandinka Balafon*; and Knight, 'Vibrato Octaves'.
15. The principal studies of kora tunings are King, 'The Construction and Tuning of the Kora' and Knight, 'Vibrato Octaves'.
16. The principal studies of ngoni tunings are Coolen, 'The Wolof Xalam Tradition' and Lucy Duran, 'A Preliminary Study of the Wolof Xalam'. Charry's *Mande Music* covers most thoroughly the history, terminology and tuning of all the Mande instruments, including the guitar.
17. Rouget, *Musique des Malinké* (CD booklet), 16.
18. Knight, 'Mandinka Jaliya', 81.
19. Charry, *Mande Music*, 250–2.

9 North American Jazz

1. Southern, *The Music of Black Americans*, 54–7.
2. Widmer, 'The Invention of a Memory', 71.
3. Foster, *New York by Gas Light with Here and There a Streak of Sunshine* (1850), quoted in Southern (ed.), *Readings on Black American Music*, 139.
4. See Lhamon, *Raising Cain*, 1–55.
5. Schuller, *Early Jazz*, 10–21.
6. Wilson, 'Afro-American and West African Music', 20.
7. See Kubik, *Africa and the Blues*.
8. Berliner, *Thinking in Jazz*, 19.
9. Ibid., 207.
10. Shapiro and Hentoff (eds), *Hear Me Talkin' To Ya*, 50.
11. Lomax, *Mister Jelly Roll*, 86.
12. Foster, *The Autobiography of Pops Foster*, 16.
13. Zimmer, 'How Baseball Gave Us "Jazz" the Word'.
14. Goffin, 'Jazzmen's Greatest Kicks'.
15. Copland, 'From the '20s to the '40s and Beyond'.
16. Shaw, *The Trouble with Cinderella*, 106–7.
17. For a survey of jazz education, see Prouty, *Knowing Jazz*, Chapter 2, 'Jazz Education and the Education and the Tightrope of Tradition', 46–77.
18. See *Jazz Planet*, in particular E. Taylor Atkins's introductory essay, 'Toward a Global History of Jazz' (xi–xxvii).

10 Europe

1. Hayburn, *Papal Legislation on Sacred Music*, 18.
2. Luther, *Luther's Works* vol. 54, 129–30.
3. Taruskin, *The Oxford History of Western Music* vol. 1, passim.
4. Earl of Chesterfield, *Letters*, 203.
5. Kant, *Critique of Practical Reason*, 161–2.
6. Weber, *The Protestant Ethic*, 181.
7. In his 1913 article 'Taste' ('Du goût'), quoted in Lockspeiser, *Debussy: His Life and Mind* vol. 1, 115.
8. Howat, *The Art of French Piano Music*, 113.

11 North Africa and the Eastern Mediterranean: Andalusian Music

1. See reference and translation in Rubiera Mata, *Literatura Hispanoárabe*, 52. In later versions the notable of Cordoba is identified as Abū Hafs 'Umar ibn Qalhīl and the singing-girl as Masābīḥ ('lights' or 'lamps'), who had learned her art from Ziryab himself.
2. al-Maqqarī, *Analectes sur l'histoire et la littérature des Arabes d'Espagne* vol. 2, 96–7; the earlier text of Ibn Ḥayyān, *Al-Sifr al-thānī min kitāb al-muqtabas l-Ibn Ḥayyān al-qurtubī*, 306, says that she was the daughter of one of the leaders of the Basques, and cites only that she studied music, with no mention of poetry, history or literature. Al-Maqqari may have had this from another source, or may have added it to embellish her image. The Arabic word *adab* can refer to both literature or to courtly etiquette.
3. Ibn Khaldūn, *Muqaddima* vol. 2, 767.
4. It is noteworthy that the songs of the Troubadours underwent a parallel development starting with simpler forms and, over time, developing more and more elaborate rhyme schemes.
5. Alvarez (trans. and ed.), *Songs of Love and Devotion*, 58–9.
6. Aḥmad al-Shirwānī (*Ḥadīqat al-afrāh li-izālat al-atrāh*, 472–3), quoted in Khallāf, *Qurṭuba al-Islāmiyya fī l-qarn al-ḥādī 'ashar al-mīlādī – al-khāmis al-hijrī*, 323–4.
7. al-Ṭanjī, 'al-Ṭarā'iq', 103; Liu and Monroe, *Ten Hispano-Arabic Songs*, 37.
8. By Ibn Abī al-Rabī' (860–940 CE).
9. By Ibn al-Qaṭīfa (d. ?).
10. Shadow puppetry is an art form still practised in the Middle East and as far east as Indonesia. The audience sits in front of a cloth screen and the flat puppets are manipulated by the puppeteer with back-lighting so that the shadow of the puppets is projected onto the screen.
11. Al-Ṭanjī, 'al-Ṭarā'iq', 103; Liu and Monroe, 37–8; the final phrase in brackets has been crossed out in the original manuscript.
12. al-Ḥumaydī, *Jadhwat al-muqtabis*, 223.
13. See Farmer, *The Song Captions in the 'Kitāb al-aghānī al-kabīr'*, for a reconstruction of the notes and intervals in use in ninth- and tenth-century Baghdad.
14. This is commonly called the 'quarter-tone' system in English, though that term is somewhat misleading, implying that chromatic sequences of quarter tones are used. In fact they are not; the term refers instead to a nineteenth-century European music theory which used quarter-, half- and whole-tones as the basic units for measuring intervals.
15. There are small variations in the basic rhythm as the performance moves through the three different tempi of the sections.
16. al-Ṭanjī, 'al-Ṭarā'iq', 115–16; Liu and Monroe, *Ten Hispano-Arabic Songs*, 43–4.
17. See Reynolds, 'Music in Medieval Iberia'.

12 The Eastern Arab World

1 Farmer, 'The Music of Islam', 435.
2 Farmer, *A History of Arabian Music*, 86.
3 Farmer, 'The Music of Islam', 428.
4 Sawa, 'Kitāb al-Aghānī', 355–6.
5 Farmer, 'The Music of Islam', 428.
6 See Racy, 'Waṣlah Ghina'iyyah' and 'Music in Nineteenth-Century Egypt'.
7 El-Shawan, 'The Socio-Political Context of al-Mūsīka al-'Arabiyyah in Cairo', 103.
8 Laborde, *Essai sur la Musique Ancienne et Moderne* vol. 1, 436–9.
9 See Marcus, *Music in Egypt*, which focuses on maqam Rast in six different genres of music and also the call to prayer.
10 See Racy, *Making Music in the Arab World*.
11 See Habib, *The Superstar Singer Fairouz*.

13 Turkey

1 The pronunciation of Turkish musical terms since the official switch to from Arabic/Persian alphabet to Roman alphabet in 1927 is very similar to English. However, certain letters require special attention: ı ('i' with no dot), like the 'a' in 'legal'; ö, like the French 'deux'; ü, like the French 'une'; c, like 'gem'; ç, like 'church'; ş, like 'sh'; ğ, silent, elongates previous vowel.
2 Barkey, *Empire of Difference*, 120–1.
3 Peter Bayle, *The Dictionary Historical and Critical of Mr. Peter Bayle* vol. 4 (New York: Garland, 1984), 29; quoted in Kalın, 'Roots of Misconception: Euro-American Perceptions of Islam Before and After September 11'.
4 Barkey, *Empire of Difference*, 120.
5 Ibid., 120.
6 Kafadar, Personal communication, 1995.
7 Gökalp, *Türkçülüğün Esasları*, 99.
8 Hindemith, *Selected Letters*, 137.
9 Dimitrie Cantemir, *The History and the Growth Decay of the Ottoman Empire*, trans. N. Tindal (1734); quoted in Popescu-Judetz, 'Demitire Cantemir's Theory of Turkish Art Music', 103.
10 Blainville, 'A General, Critical, and Philological History of Music', 6.
11 Febvre, 'Theatre de la Turquie', 21.
12 Rumi, *Mesnevi* [opening lines], trans. Edmund Helminski.
13 Franz Josef Sulzer, *Geschichte des Transalpinischen Daciens* [1782]; Quoted in Whaples, 'Exoticism in Dramatic Music', 320.
14 Yönetken, 'Milli Musiki'.

14 Iran

1. Pope and Ackerman, 'Gardens', 1428.
2. During, 'Music, Poetry and the Visual Arts in Persia', 84.
3. Youssefzadeh, 'Une passion pour l'Iran', 237.
4. See Wright, *The Modal System of Arab and Persian Music*.
5. Neubauer, 'Music History'.
6. Schimmel, *Rumi's World*, 197.
7. During et al., *The Art of Persian Music*, 28.
8. Pakdaman, 'La situation du musicien dans la société persane', 338.
9. Jalāl Al-e Ahmad, *Gharbzadegi* (published in 1962 in Iran); English version: *Gharbzadegi ('Weststruckness')* (Lexington, KY: Mazda Publishers, 1982).
10. Nettl, 'The Role of Music in Culture', 85; 'Persian Classical Music in Tehran', 148.
11. During, 'L'oreille islamique' 142–3.
12. Personal communication with Alizādeh, Tehran, February 2002.
13. Alizādeh first used women's voices in film scores. He composed many film scores for films such as *Gabbeh* (1996), directed by Mohsen Makhmalbaf, and *Half Moon* (2006), directed by Bahman Ghobadi.
14. Youssefzadeh, 'Une passion pour l'Iran', 35–61.
15. Talā'i, *Traditional Persian Art Music*, 1–2.
16. This procedure is called *morākab-khāni* and can be vocal or instrumental.
17. See al-Faruqi, 'The Suite in Islamic History and Culture'.

15 Uzbekistan and Tajikistan

1. Fitrat, *O'zbek Klassik Musiqasi*, 44.
2. *Vāsifī, Badā'i al-Waqā'i*.
3. These musicians include Yusuf Andijānī, 'Alī Shunqār, Pahlivān Muhammad, Sāhib Balkhī, 'Alijān Ghijjakī, Zayn al-'Ābidin Husayni, Hāfiz Basir, Mir Murtaz, 'Alishāh Būka and Khoja Yusuf Burhān.
4. Fitrat, *O'zbek Klassik Musiqasi*, 48.
5. Bekjon and Devonzoda, *Xorazm Musiqiy Tarixchasi*, 9.
6. Ibid., 16.

Bibliographies

Introduction

Bohlman, Philip V. (ed.). *The Cambridge History of World Music*. New York: Cambridge University Press, 2014.

Boulez, Pierre. *Orientations: Collected Writings*, ed. Jean-Jacques Nattiez. London and Boston: Faber, 1986.

Broughton, Simon. 'Azerbaijani Mugham: A Guide to the Music of the Free Country'. *Songlines* 93 (July 2013), 36–45.

Chatwin, Bruce. *The Songlines*. London: Vintage, 1987.

Harris, Rachel. *The Making of a Musical Canon in Chinese Central Asia: The Uyghur Twelve Muqam*. Aldershot: Ashgate, 2008.

von Hornbostel, Erich M. 'Die Probleme der vergleichenden Musikwissenschaft'. *Zeitschrift der Internationalen Musikgesellschaft* 7 (1905), 85–97.

Levin, Theodore. *The Hundred Thousand Fools of God: Musical Travels in Central Asia (and Queens, New York)*. Bloomington: Indiana University Press, 1996.

Maddocks, Fiona. *Harrison Birtwistle: Wild Tracks – a Conversation Diary*. London: Faber, 2014.

Morgan, Andy. *Music, Culture and Conflict in Mali*. Freemuse: Copenhagen, 2013.

Murray, David (ed.). *Longing for the Past*. Atlanta: Dust-to-Digital DTD-28, 2013.

Nettl, Bruno. *The Study of Ethnomusicology*. Urbana: Illinois University Press, 2005 [revised edition].

Powers, Harold S. 'Classical Music, Cultural Roots, and Colonial Rule: An Indic Musicologist looks at the Muslim World'. *Asian Music* 12/1 (1980), 5–39.

Sadie, Stanley and John Tyrrell (eds). *The New Grove Dictionary of Music and Musicians*. 2nd ed. 29 vols. London: Macmillan, 2001; *Grove Music Online*, www.oxfordmusiconline.com.

Seeger, Anthony. *Why Suya Sing: A Musical Anthropology of an Amazonian People*. Cambridge: Cambridge University Press, 1987.

1 Thailand, Laos, Cambodia, Vietnam

General

Cogniat, Raymond. *Danses d'Indochine*. Paris: Chroniques du Jour, 1932.

Collaer, Paul. *Südostasien*. Musikgeschichte in Bildern, Band I: Musikethnologie, Lieferung 3. Leipzig: VEB Deutscher Verlag für Musik, 1979.

Miller, Terry E., and Sean Williams (eds). *The Garland Encyclopedia of World Music* vol. 4, *Southeast Asia*. S.v. Sam-Ang Sam, Panya Roongruang and Phong T. Nguyen, 'The Khmer People', 151–217; Terry E. Miller, 'Thailand' and 'Laos', 218–334 and 335–62; and Phong T. Nguyen, 'Vietnam', 444–517. New York: Garland, 1998.

▶ *Cambodia*

Cravath, Paul. *Earth in Flower: The Divine Mystery of the Cambodian Dance Drama*. Holmes Beach, FL.: DatASIA, 2007.

Daniélou, Alain. *Musique du Cambodge et du Laos*. Pondichéry: Institut français d'indologie, 1957.

Groslier, George. *Cambodian Dancers: Ancient and Modern* (based on *Danseuses Cambodgiennes Anciennes et Modernes*, Paris: 1913). Holmes Beach, FL.: DatASIA, 2012.

Sam, Chan Moly. *Khmer Court Dance*. Newington, CT: Khmer Studies Institute, 1987.

Sam, Sam-Ang. *Musical Instruments of Cambodia*. Osaka: National Museum of Ethnology, 2002.

——, and Patricia Shehan Campbell. *Silent Temples, Songful Hearts*. Danbury, CT: World Music Press, 1991.

▶ *Laos*

Chonpairot, Jarernchai. 'Lam Khon Sawan: A Vocal Genre of Southern Laos'. PhD diss., Kent State University, 1990.

de Marini, Giovanni-Filippo. *Histoire nouvelle et curieuse des royaumes de Tunquin et de Lao*, trans. (from Italian) P. de Marini Romain. Paris: Gervais Clouzier, 1666.

Miller, Terry E. *The Traditional Music of the Lao: Kaen Playing and Mawlum Singing in Northeast Thailand*. Contributions in Intercultural and Comparative Studies, 13. Westport, CT: Greenwood Press, 1985.

——. 'Laos'. In *The New Grove Dictionary of Music and Musicians*, 2nd ed. (see under ■ **Introduction** above).

▶ *Thailand*

Dhanit Yupho. *Thai Musical Instruments*, trans. David Morton. Bangkok: Fine Arts Department, 1960.

Miller, Terry E. 'The Theory and Practice of Thai Musical Notations'. *Ethnomusicology* 36/2 (1992), 197–222.

——, and Jarernchai Chonpairot. 'A History of Siamese Music Reconstructed from Western Documents, 1505–1932'. *Crossroads* 8/1 (1994), 1–192.

Morton, David. *The Traditional Music of Thailand: Introduction, Commentary, and Analyses*. Los Angeles: Institute of Ethnomusicology, UCLA, 1968 [with vinyl recording].

——. *The Traditional Music of Thailand*. Berkeley: University of California, 1976.

Myers-Moro, Pamela. *Thai Music and Musicians in Contemporary Bangkok*. Berkeley: Centers for South and Southeast Asia Studies, University of California, 1993.

Neale, Frederick Arthur. *Narrative of a Residence at the Capital of the Kingdom of Siam*. London: Offices of the National Illustrated Library, 1852.

Phoasavadi, Pornprapit 'Ros', and Patricia Shehan Campbell. *From Bangkok and Beyond: Thai Children's Song, Games, Customs.* Danbury, CT: World Music Press, 2003.

Roongruang, Panya. 'Thai Classical Music and its Movement from Oral to Written Transmission, 1930–1942: Historical Context, Method, and Legacy of the Thai Music Manuscript Project'. PhD diss., Kent State University, 1999.

Swangviboonpong, Dusadee. *Thai Classical Singing: Its History, Musical Characteristics and Transmission.* London: Ashgate, 2003.

Tachard, Guy. *A Relation of the Voyage to Siam Performed by Six Jesuits.* London: J. Robinson and A. Churchil, 1688.

Verney, Frederick. *Notes on Siamese Musical Instruments.* London: Clowes and Sons, 1885.

Wong, Deborah. *Sounding the Center: History and Aesthetics in Thai Buddhist Performance.* Chicago: University of Chicago, 2001.

▶ Vietnam

Le Tuan Hung. *Dan Tranh Music of Vietnam: Traditions and Innovations.* Melbourne and Tokyo: Australia Asia Foundation, 1998.

Nguyen Thuyet Phong. 'Restructuring the Fixed Pitches of the Vietnamese Dan Nguyet Lute: A Modification Necessitated by the Modal System'. *Asian Music* 18/1 (1986), 56–70.

Nguyen, Phong, and Patricia Shehan Campbell. *From Rice Paddies and Temple Yards: Traditional Music of Vietnam.* Danbury, CT: World Music Press, 1990.

Tran van Khe. *La musique vietnamienne traditionnelle.* Paris: Presses Universitaires de France, 1962.

2 Java

Becker, Judith. *Traditional Music in Modern Java.* Honolulu: The University Press of Hawaii, 1980.

Becker, Judith, and Alan Feinstein (eds). *Karawitan: Source Readings in Javanese Gamelan and Vocal Music.* 3 vols. Ann Arbor: Center for South and Southeast Asian Studies, University of Michigan, 1987.

Brinner, Benjamin. *Knowing Music, Making Music: Javanese Gamelan and the Theory of Musical Competence and Interaction.* Chicago: University of Chicago Press, 1995.

——. *Music in Central Java: Experiencing Music, Expressing Culture.* New York and Oxford: Oxford University Press, 2008.

Howat, Roy. 'Debussy and the Orient'. In C. Andrew Gerstle and Anthony Milner (eds), *Recovering the Orient: Artists, Scholars, Appropriations*, 45–81. Chur: Harwood, 1994.

Kunst, Jaap. *Music in Java: Its History, its Theory and its Technique.* 2 vols, ed. E. L. Heins. The Hague: Martinus Nijhoff, 1973.

Lindsay, Jennifer. *Javanese Gamelan*. Kuala Lumpur: Oxford University Press, 1992.
Perlman, Marc. *Unplayed Melodies: Javanese Gamelan and the Genesis of Music Theory*. Berkeley, Los Angeles and London: University of California Press, 2004.
Pickvance, Richard. *A Gamelan Manual: A Player's Guide to the Central Javanese Gamelan*. London: Jaman Mas Books, 2005.
Sorrell, Neil. *A Guide to the Gamelan*. London: Faber, 1990 (rev. 2000).
Sumarsam. *Gamelan: Cultural Interaction and Musical Development in Central Java*. Chicago: University of Chicago Press, 1995.
Van Ness, Edward C., and Shita Prawirohardjo. *Javanese Wayang Kulit: An Introduction*. Kuala Lumpur: Oxford University Press, 1980.

3 Japan

Atkins, E. Taylor. *Blue Nippon: Authenticating Jazz in Japan*. Durham, NC: Duke University Press, 2001.
Hughes, David W. 'No Nonsense: The Logic and Power of Acoustic-iconic Mnemonic Systems'. *British Journal of Ethnomusicology* 9/2 (2000), 93–120.
Kagawa Gaseikai (ed.). *Gagaku hōshōfu* [Gagaku shō notation]. Iiyama, Kagawa: Kagawa Gaseikai, 1985 (5th printing).
Koizumi, Fumio. 'Musical Scales in Japanese Music'. In Fumio et al. (eds), *Asian Musics in an Asian Perspective*, 73–9. Tokyo: Heibonsha, 1977.
Malm, William P. *Nagauta: The Heart of Kabuki Music*. Tokyo: Tuttle, 1963. Repr. Westport, CT: Greenwood, 1976.
——. *Six Hidden Views of Japanese Music*. Berkeley: University of California Press, 1986.
——. *Traditional Japanese Music and Musical Instruments*. Tokyo: Kodansha, 2000. Replaces Malm, *Japanese Music and Musical Instruments* (1959).
Marett, Allan. 'Tôgaku: Where Have the Tang Melodies Gone, and Where Have the New Melodies Come From?' *Ethnomusicology* 29/3 (1985), 409–31.
Murasaki Shikibu. *The Tale of Genji*, transl. Edward G. Seidensticker. London: Secker and Warburg, 1976.
Nelson, Steven G. 'Court and Religious Music (1): History of *Gagaku* and *Shōmyō*', and 'Court and Religious Music (2): Music of *Gagaku* and *Shōmyō*'. In Tokita and Hughes (eds), *The Ashgate Research Companion to Japanese Music*, 35–48 and 49–76.
Picken, Lawrence et al. (eds). *Music From the Tang Court, Fascicle 1*. Oxford: Oxford University Press, 1981.
Provine, Robert, Yoshihiko Tokumau and J. Lawrence Witzleben (eds). *The Garland Encyclopedia of World Music* vol. 7, *East Asia: China, Japan, and Korea*. New York: Routledge, 2002.
Sei Shōnagon. *The Pillow Book*, transl. Meredith McKinney. London: Penguin, 2006.

Tokita, Alison McQueen. 'Music in *Kabuki*: More than Meets the Eye'. In Tokita and Hughes (eds), *The Ashgate Research Companion to Japanese Music*, 229–60.

——, and David W. Hughes (eds). *The Ashgate Research Companion to Japanese Music*. Farnham, UK: Ashgate, 2008.

Tsukitani, Tsuneko. 'The *Shakuhachi* and its Music'. In Tokita and Hughes (eds), *The Ashgate Research Companion to Japanese Music*, 145–68.

Wade, Bonnie C. *Music in Japan: Experiencing Music, Expressing Culture*. Oxford: Oxford University Press, 2005.

Yamazaki, Masakazu (ed.). *On the Art of the Nō Drama: The Major Treatises of Zeami*, transl. J. Thomas Rimer. Princeton: Princeton University Press, 1984.

4 China: The Guqin Zither

Addiss, Stephen. *The Resonance of the Qin in East Asian Art*. New York: China Institute, 1999.

Dahmer, Manfred. *Die große Solosuite Guanglingsan*. Frankfurt: Peter Lang (Frankfurter China-Studien), 1988.

Dai Xiaolian. 'Plum Blossom – Three Variations: A Study of the *Guqin* Piece *Meihua san nong* (Plum Blossom – Three Variations)'. *CHIME* 12–13 (1998), 124–41.

DeWoskin, Kenneth J. *A Song for One or Two: Music and the Concept of Art in Early China*. Ann Arbor: Center for Chinese Studies, University of Michigan, 1982.

Egan, Ronald. 'The Controversy over Music and "Sadness" and Changing Conceptions of the *Qin* in Middle Period China'. *Harvard Journal of Asiatic Studies* 57/1 (1997), 5–66.

Goormaghtigh, Georges. *L'Art du Qin: deux textes d'esthétique musicale chinoise traduits et commentés par G. Goormaghtigh*. Brussels: Instut Belge des Hautes Études Chinoises, 1990

Gulik, R. H. van. *Hsi K'ang and his Poetical Essay on the Lute*. 2nd ed. Tokyo: Monumenta Nipoponica, Sophia University, 1969.

——. *The Lore of the Chinese Lute*. 2nd ed. Tokyo: Monumenta Nipoponica, Sophia University 1969.

Huang, Yi-ping. 'The Parting of the Way: Three Generations of Ch'in Performance Practice'. PhD diss., University of Maryland, 1998.

Ivanoff, Vladimir. 'Invitation to the Fifteenth-Century Plectrum Lute: The Pesaro Manuscript'. In Victor Anand Coelho (ed.), *Performance on Lute, Guitar and Vihuela: Historical Practice and Modern Interpretation*, 1–15. Cambridge: Cambridge University Press, 1997.

Kouwenhoven, Frank. 'Bringing to Life Tunes of Ancient China: An Interview with Laurence Picken'. *CHIME* 4 (1991), 40–65.

——. 'Meaning and Structure: The Case of Chinese Qin (Zither) Music.' *British Journal of Ethnomusicology* 10/1 (2001), 39–62.

Lawergren, Bo. 'Western Influences on the Early Chinese Qin-Zither.' *Bulletin of The Museum of Far Eastern Antiquities* 75 (2003), 79–109.

Lee, Shek-kam. 'Reading Between the Lines: The Rhythmic Information in Qin Handbooks'. Masters diss., University of Pittsburgh, 1995.

Liang, Ming-Yueh. *The Chinese Ch'in, Its History and Music*. San Francisco: Chinese National Music Association, 1972.

Liang, Mingyue. *Music of the Billion: An Introduction to Chinese Musical Culture*. New York: Heinrichshofen Edition, 1985.

Lieberman, Fredric. *A Chinese Zither Tutor: The Mei-an ch'in-p'u*. Seattle and Hong Kong: Hong Kong University Press / University of Washington Press, 1983.

Lin Chen. *Chumo qinshi – Jin xiandai qinshi xushi* [*A concise history of qin in modern times*]. Beijing: Wenhua yishu chubanshe, 2011.

Lindqvist, Cecili. *Qin*. Stockholm: Albert Bonniers Förlag, 2006.

Mitani, Yoko. 'Some Melodic Features of Chinese Qin Music'. In D. R. Widdess and R. F. Wolpert (eds), *Music and Tradition: Essays on Asian and Other Musics, Presented to Laurence Picken*, 123–40. Cambridge: Cambridge University Press, 1981.

Qinyu jicheng [*Anthology of qin music*]. 30 vols. Compiled by the Qin Research Institute, Shanghai, Beijing. 2009

Shen Caonong et al. *Guqin chujie* [*A basic introduction to guqin*]. Beijing: Renmin yinyue chubanshe, 1961.

Tilney, Colin. *The Art of the Unmeasured Prelude for Harpsichord*. London: Schott, 1995.

Tse, Chun Yan Victor. 'From Chromaticism to Pentatonism: A Convergence of Ideology and Practice in Qin Music of the Ming and Qing Dynasties'. PhD diss, Chinese University of Hong Kong, 2009.

Wu, Wenguang. 'Wu Jinglüe's Qin Music in Its Context'. PhD diss, Wesleyan University, 1990.

Wu Zhao (ed.). *Zhongguo guqin zhencui* [*China's valuable qins*]. Beijing: Beijing guqin yanjiuhui, 1998.

Xu Jian. *Qinshi chubian* ('Preliminary survey of the history of qin'). Beijing: Renmin yinyue chubanshe, 1982.

Yung, Bell. 'Choreographic and Kinesthetic Elements in Performance on the Chinese Seven-String Zither'. *Ethnomusicology* 28/3 (September 1984), 505–17.

——. 'Historical Interdependency of Music: A Case Study of the Chinese Seven-String Zither'. *Journal of the American Musicological Society* 40/1 (1987), 82–91.

——. 'Not Notating the Notatable: Re-evaluating the *Guqin* Notational System'. In Bell Yung and Joseph Lam (eds), *Themes and Variations: Writings on Music in Honor of Rulan Chao Pian*, 45–58. Columbus, OH: Editions Orphée, 1994.

——. 'Music of *Qin*: From the Scholar's Study to the Concert Stage'. *ACMR Reports* 11 (1998), 1–14.

Zha Fuxi. *Zha Fuxi Qinxue wencui* [*Collected Essays on Qin*]. Hangzhou: Zhejiang University Press, 1995.

5 Chinese Opera

Dolby, William. *A History of Chinese Drama*. London: Paul Elek, 1976.
——— (trans.). *Eight Chinese Plays from the 13th Century to the Present*. New York and London: Columbia University Press and Paul Elek, 1978.
Halson, Elizabeth. *Peking Opera: A Short Guide*. Hong Kong: Oxford University Press, 1966.
Mackerras, Colin (ed.). *The Rise of the Peking Opera 1770–1870: Social Aspects of the Theatre in Manchu China*. Oxford: Clarendon Press, 1972.
———. *The Chinese Theatre in Modern Times: From 1850 to the Present Day*. London: Thames and Hudson, 1975.
———. *The Performing Arts in Contemporary China*. London: Routledge & Kegan Paul, 1981.
———. *Chinese Theater: From its Origins to the Present Day*. Honolulu: University of Hawaii Press, 1983.
Pian, Rulan Chao. 'Peking Opera: *Jingju*'. In Provine et al., *The Garland Encyclopedia of World Music* vol. 7, 281–7 (See under 3 **Japan** above).
Schönfelder, Gerd. *Die Musik der Peking-Opera*. Leipzig: Deutscher Verlag für Musik, 1972; *Die Musik der Peking-Opera: Notenbeilage*. Leipzig: Deutscher Verlag für Musik, 1972.
Siu Wang-Ngai and Peter Lovrick. *Chinese Opera: Images and Stories*. Vancouver: UBC Press/Seattle: University of Washington Press, 1997.
Wichmann, Elizabeth. *Listening to Theatre: The Aural Dimension of Beijing Opera*. Honolulu: University of Hawaii Press, 1991.
Zhao Menglin and Yan Jiqing. *Peking Opera Painted Faces: With Notes on 200 Operas*. Beijing: Morning Glory Publishers, 1996.

6 North India

Arnold, Alison (ed.). *The Garland Encyclopaedia of World Music* vol. 5, *South Asia: The Indian Subcontinent*. New York and London: Routledge, 2000.
Bakhle, Janaki. *Two Men and Music: Nationalism in the Making of an Indian Classical Tradition*. Oxford: Oxford University Press, 2005.
Bor, Joep (ed.). *The Raga Guide*. Nimbus Records, 1999.
———, Philippe Bruguière et al. *Gloire des princes, louange des dieux: patrimoine musical de l'Hindoustan du XIVe au XXe siècle*. Paris: Cité de la Musique, 2003.
———, François Nalini Delvoye, Jane Harvey and Emmie te Nijenhuis (eds.). *Hindustani Music: Thirteenth to Twentieth Centuries*. New Delhi: Manohar, 2010.
Clayton, Martin. *Time in Indian Music: Rhythm, Meter, and Form in North Indian Rag Performance*. Oxford: Oxford University Press, 2000.
Farrell, Gerry. *Indian Music and the West*. Oxford: Clarendon Press, 1997.
Jairazbhoy, Nazir Ali. *The Rāgs of North Indian Music: Their Structure and Evolution*. London: Faber, 1971. 2nd ed., Bombay: Popular Prakashan, 1995.
Kippen, James R. *The Tabla of Lucknow: A Cultural Analysis of a Musical Tradition*. Cambridge: Cambridge University Press, 1989.

Manuel, Peter. *Thumri in Historical and Stylistic Perspective*. Delhi: Motilal Banarsidass, 1989.
McNeil, Adrian. *Inventing the Sarod: A Cultural History*. Calcutta: Seagull Books, 2004.
Miner, Allyn. *Sitar and Sarod in the 18th and 19th Centuries*. Wilhelmshaven: Florian Noetzel Verlag, 1993.
Neuman, Daniel M. *The Life of Music in North India: The Organization of an Artistic Tradition*. Detroit: Wayne State University Press, 1980.
Powers, Harold S. et al. 'India, subcontinent of' and 'Mode', in *The New Grove Dictionary of Music and Musicians*, 2nd ed. (see under ■ **Introduction** above).
Rowell, Lewis. *Music and Musical Thought in Early India*. Chicago: University of Chicago Press, 1992.
Ruckert, George. *Music in North India: Experiencing Music, Expressing Culture*. Oxford: Oxford University Press, 2004.
Sanyal, Ritwik, and Richard Widdess. *Dhrupad: Tradition and Performance in Indian Music*. Aldershot: Ashgate, 2004.
Shekhar, Chander, and Chenoy, Shama Mitra. *Dargah Quli Khan, Muraqqa'-e Dehli: The Mughal Capital in Muhammad Shah's Time*. Delhi: Deputy Publication, 1989.
Sorrell, Neil, and Ram Narayan. *Indian Music in Performance: A Practical Introduction*. Manchester University Press, 1980.
Wade, Bonnie. *Khyāl: Creativity Within North India's Classical Music Tradition*. Cambridge: Cambridge University Press, 1984.
Wulff, Donna Marie, 'On Practicing Music Religiously: Music as Sacred in India'. In Joyce Irwin (ed.), *Sacred Sound: Music in Religious Thought and Practice*. Chico: Scholars Press, 1983.

7 South India

Allen, Matthew Harp. 'Standardize, Classicize and Nationalize: The Scientific Work of the Music Academy of Madras, 1930–52'. In Peterson and Soneji (eds), *Performing Pasts*, 90–129.
Arnold, Alison (ed.). See under 6 **North India** above.
Catlin, Amy. 'Karnatak Vocal and Instrumental Music'. In Arnold (ed.), *The Garland Encyclopedia of World Music* vol. 5, 209–35.
Jackson, William J. *Tyāgarāja and the Renewal of Tradition: Translations and Reflections*. New Delhi: Motilal Barsidass, 1994.
Kassebaum, Gayathri Rajapur. 'Karnatak Raga'. In Arnold (ed.), *The Garland Encyclopedia of World Music* vol. 5, 89–109.
Nelson, David Paul. 'Karnatak Tala'. In Arnold (ed.), *The Garland Encyclopedia of World Music* vol. 5, 138–61.
Pesch, Ludwig. *The Oxford Illustrated Companion to South Indian Classical Music*. 2nd ed. New Delhi: Oxford University Press, 2009.

Peterson, Indira Viswanathan. 'Renewing Cultural History through the Novel: Music and Dance as Tamil Tradition in Kalaimani's *Tillana Mohanambal*'. In Peterson and Soneji (eds), *Performing Pasts*, 252–80.

——, and Davesh Soneji (eds). *Performing Pasts: Reinventing the Arts in Modern South Asia*. New Delhi: Oxford University Press, 2008.

Powers, Harold S. 'Classical Music, Cultural Roots, and Colonial Rule: An Indic Musicologist looks at the Muslim World'. *Asian Music* 12/1 (1980), 5–39.

——. 'Musical Art and Esoteric Theism: Muttuswami Dikshitar's *Ānandabhairavī kīrtanams* on Shiva and Shakti at Tiruvarur'. In Michael W. Meister (ed.), *Discourses on Siva: Proceedings of a Symposium on the Nature of Religious Imagery*, 318–40. Philadelphia: University of Pennsylvania Press, 1984.

Schofield, Katherine Butler. 'Reviving the Golden Age Again: "Classicization," Hindustani Music, and the Mughals'. *Ethnomusicology* 54/3 (2010), 484–517.

Subramanian, Lakshmi. 'Embracing the Canonical: Identity, Tradition, and Modernity in Karnatak Music'. In Peterson and Soneji (eds), *Performing Pasts*, 43–70.

Viswanathan, Tanjore, and Matthew Harp Allen. *Music in South India: The Karnatak Concert Tradition and Beyond*. New York: Oxford University Press, 2004.

Weidman, Amanda Jane. 'Listening to the Violin in South Indian Classical Music'. In Richard K. Wolf (ed.), *Theorizing the Local: Music, Practice and Experience in South Asia and Beyond*, 49–63. New York: Oxford University Press, 2009.

8 Mande Jaliyaa

Anderson, Lois. 'The Miko Modal System of Kiganda Xylophone Music'. PhD diss., University of California, 1971.

Battúta, Ibn. *Travels in Asia and Africa 1325–1354*. Translated and selected by H. A. R. Gibb. New York: Robert McBride & Co., 1929. A preferred newer edition is Nehemia Levtzion and J. F. P. Hopkins (eds), *Corpus of Early Arabic Sources for West African History*. Princeton, NJ: Markus Wiener Publishers, 2000.

Charry, Eric. *Mande Music*. Chicago: University of Chicago Press, 2000.

Coolen, Michael. 'The Wolof Xalam Tradition of the Senegambia'. *Ethnomusicology* 27/3 (1983), 477–98.

Duran, Lucy. 'A Preliminary Study of the Wolof Xalam'. *Recorded Sound* 79 (January 1981), 29–36.

——, with Kwabena Fosu-Mensa and Chris Stapleton. 'On Music in Contemporary West Africa'. *African Affairs* (London) 86/43 (April 1987), 227–40.

Farmer, Henry George. 'A North African Folk Instrument'. *Journal of the Royal Asiatic Society* 60 (1928), 25–34.

Janson, Marloes. 'Praising as a Gendered Activity: How Jalimusoolu and Jalikeolu Exercise their Profession in Eastern Gambia'. *Mande Studies* 4 (2002), 65–82.

Jessup, Lynn. *The Mandinka Balafon: An Introduction with Notation for Teaching*. La Mesa, CA: Xylo Publications, 1983.

King, Anthony. 'The Construction and Tuning of the Kora'. *African Language Studies* 13 (1972), 113–36.

Knight, Roderic. 'Mandinka Jaliya: Professional Music of West Africa'. PhD diss., University of California, 1973.

——. 'Mandinka Drumming'. *African Arts* 7/4 (1974), 24–35.

——. 'Music out of Africa: Mande Jaliya in Paris'. *The World of Music* 33/1 (1990), 52–69.

——. 'Vibrato Octaves: Tunings and Modes of the Mande Balo and Kora'. *Progress Reports in Ethnomusicology* 3/4 (1991), 1–49.

Niane, Djibril Tamsir. *Sundiata: An Epic of Old Mali*. London: Longmans, 1965.

Park, Mungo. *The Travels of Mungo Park*, ed. Ronald Miller. New York: Dutton, 1954. [Original text: *Mungo Park, 1799: Travels in the Interior Districts of Africa*. London: Nicol.]

Rouget, Gilbert. 'Sur les Xylophones Equiheptaphoniques des Malinké'. *Revue de musicologie* 55/1 (1969), 47–77.

——. *Guinée: Musique des Malinké*. CD with booklet. Paris: Le Chant du Monde, CNR 274 1112, 1999.

Tracey, Hugh. *African Dances of the Witwatersrand Gold Mines*. Johannesburg: African Music Society, 1952.

9 Jazz

Atkins, E. Taylor (ed.). *Jazz Planet*. Jackson: University Press of Mississippi, 2003.

Berliner, Paul. *Thinking in Jazz: The Infinite Art of Improvisation*. Chicago: University of Chicago Press, 1994.

Copland, Aaron. 'From the '20s to the '40s and Beyond'. *Modern Music*, Jan.–Feb. 1943, 78–82.

DeVeaux, Scott. *The Birth of Bebop: A Social and Musical History*. Berkeley: University of California Press, 1997.

Foster, Pops. *The Autobiography of Pops Foster*. Berkeley: University of California Press, 1971.

Giddins, Gary, and Scott DeVeaux. *Jazz*. New York: Norton, 2009.

Goffin, Robert. 'Jazzmen's Greatest Kicks'. *Esquire*, August 1944, 142.

Hobsbawm, Eric. *The Jazz Scene*. Rev. ed. New York: Pantheon Press, 1993.

Kubik, Gerhard. *Africa and the Blues*. Jackson: University Press of Mississippi, 1999.

Lhamon, W. T. *Raising Cain: Blackface Performance from Jim Crow to Hip Hop*. Cambridge, MA: Harvard University Press, 2000.

Lomax, Alan. *Mister Jelly Roll: The Fortunes of Jelly Roll Morton, New Orleans Creole and 'Inventor of Jazz'*. New York: Duell, Sloane and Pierce, 1950.

Prouty, Ken. *Knowing Jazz: Community, Pedagogy, and Canon in the Information Age*. Jackson: University Press of Mississippi, 2012.

Schuller, Gunther. *Early Jazz: Its Roots and Musical Development*. New York: Oxford University Press, 1968.
——. *The Swing Era*. New York: Oxford University Press, 1989.
Shapiro, Nat, and Nat Hentoff (eds). *Hear Me Talkin' to Ya: The Story of Jazz as Told by the Men who Made it*. New York: Rinehart, 1955.
Shaw, Artie. *The Trouble with Cinderella (an Outline of Identity)*. New York: Farrar, Straus and Young, 1952.
Southern, Eileen. *The Music of Black Americans: A History*. 2nd ed. New York: Norton, 1983.
—— (ed.). *Readings on Black American Music*. 2nd ed. New York: Norton, 1983.
Ward, Geoffrey C. *Jazz: A History of America's Music*. New York: Knopf, 2000.
Widmer, Ted. 'The Invention of a Memory: Congo Square and African Music in Nineteenth-Century New Orleans'. *Revue française d'études américaines*, 2003.
Wilson, Olly. 'The Significance of the Relationship between Afro-American and West African Music'. *Black Perspective in Music* 2/1 (Spring 1974), 3–22.
Zimmer, Ben. 'How Baseball Gave Us "Jazz" the Word'. *Boston Globe*, 25 March 2012.

10 Europe

Bukofzer, Manfred. *Music in the Baroque Era*. New York: Norton, 1947.
Chesterfield, Earl of. *The Letters of Philip Dormer Stanhope, Earl of Chesterfield, With the Characters*, ed. John Bradshaw. London: Allen and Unwin, 1926.
Dahlhaus, Carl. *Nineteenth Century Music*. Berkeley: University of California Press, 2005.
Goodall, Howard. *The Story of Music*. London: Chatto & Windus, 2013.
Griffiths, Paul. *Modern Music and After*. Rev. ed. Oxford: Oxford University Press, 2011.
Hayburn, Robert F. *Papal Legislation on Sacred Music 95 AD to 1977 AD*. Collegeville, MN: The Liturgical Press, 1979.
Howat, Roy. *The Art of French Piano Music: Debussy, Ravel, Fauré, Chabrier*. London and New Haven: Yale University Press, 2009.
Kant, Immanuel. *Critique of Practical Reason*, trans. and ed. Mary J. Gregor. Cambridge: Cambridge University Press, 1996.
Knighton, Tess and David Fallows (eds). *Companion to Medieval and Renaissance Music*. Berkeley, California: University of California Press, 1998.
Latham, Alison (ed.). *The Oxford Companion to Music*. Oxford: Oxford University Press, 2002.
Lockspeiser, Edward. *Debussy: His Life and Mind* vol. 1. London: Cassell, 1962.
Lockwood, Lewis. *Beethoven*. New York: Norton, 2005.
Luther, Martin. *Luther's Works* vol. 54, ed. and trans. Theodore G. Tappert. Philadelphia: Fortress Press, 1967.
Powell, John. *How Music Works*. London: Penguin, 2010.
Randel, Don Michael. *Harvard Dictionary of Music*. Cambridge, MA: Harvard University Press, 2003.

Rosen, Charles. *The Classical Style*. Rev. ed. New York: Norton, 2005.
Ross, Alex. *The Rest is Noise*. London: Fourth Estate, 2008.
Scruton, Roger. *The Aesthetics of Music*. Oxford: Oxford University Press, 1997.
Swafford, Jan. *Brahms*. New York: Vintage Books, 1999.
Taruskin, Richard. *The Oxford History of Western Music*. 5 vols. Oxford: Oxford University Press, 2005.
Tovey, Donald. *Essays in Musical Analysis*. Oxford: Oxford University Press, 1981.
Weber, Max. *The Rational and Social Foundations of Music*. Carbondale, IL: Southern Illinois University Press, 1958.
——. *The Protestant Ethic and the Spirit of Capitalism*, trans. Talcott Parsons. London: Allen and Unwin, 1976.

11 North Africa and the Eastern Mediterranean: Andalusian Music

Alvarez, Lourdes Maria (trans. and ed.). *Abū l-Ḥasan al-Shushtarī: Songs of Love and Devotion*. Mahwah, NJ: Paulist Press, 2009.
Danielson, Virginia, Scott Marcus and Dwight F. Reynolds (eds). *The Garland Encyclopedia of World Music* vol.6, *The Middle East*. New York and London: Routledge, 2002.
Davis, Ruth Frances. *Ma'lūf: Reflections on the Arab Andalusian music of Tunisia*. Lanham, MD: Scarecrow Press, 2004.
Farmer, Henry George. *A History of Arabian Music to the XIIIth Century*. London: Luzac, 1929 (repr. 1967, 1994).
——. *The Song Captions in the 'Kitāb al-aghānī al-kabīr'*. London: Baron, 1955.
Guettat, Mahmoud. *La musique arabo-andalouse* vol. 1. Paris: El-Ouns, 2000.
——. 'The Andalusian Musical Heritage'. In Danielson et al. (eds), *The Garland Encyclopedia of World Music* vol. 6, 441–54.
al-Ḥumaydī, Muḥammad. *Jadhwat al-muqtabis*. Beirut: Dār al-Kitāb al-Lubnānī, 1983.
Ibn Ḥayyān. *Al-Sifr al-thānī min kitāb al-muqtabas l-Ibn Ḥayyān al-qurtubī*, ed. Maḥmūd 'Alī Makkī. Riyāḍ: Markaz al-Malik Fayal li-l-Buḥūth wa-l-Dirāsāt al-Islāmiyya, 2003.
Ibn Khaldūn. *al-Muqaddima* vol. 2. Tunis: al-Dār al-Tūnisiyya li-l-Nashar, 1989.
Jones, L. Jaffran. 'The 'Isāwiyya of Tunis'. In Danielson et al. (eds), *The Garland Encyclopedia of World Music* vol. 6, 515–22.
Khallāf, Muḥammad. *Qurṭuba al-Islāmiyya fi l-qarn al-ḥādī 'ashar al-milādī*. al-Dār al-tūnisiyya lil-nashr, 1984.
Liu, Benjamin M., and James T. Monroe. *Ten Hispano-Arabic Songs in the Modern Oral Tradition*. Berkeley, Los Angeles and Oxford: University of California Press, 1989.
al-Maqqarī, Aḥmad ibn Muḥammad. *Analectes sur l'histoire et la littérature des Arabes d'Espagne*. 2 vols. Leiden: Brill, 1855–61. Repr. Amsterdam: Oriental Press, 1967.

Reynolds, Dwight F. 'Music'. In María Rosa Menocal, Raymond Scheindlin and Michael Sells (eds), *The Cambridge History of Arabic Literature: The Literature of Al-Andalus*, 60–82. Cambridge: Cambridge University Press, 2000.

——. 'Al-Maqqarī's Ziryāb: The Making of a Myth'. *Middle Eastern Literatures*, 11/2 (Special issue, ed. Shawkat Toorawa, 2008), 155–68.

——. 'Music in Medieval Iberia: Contact, Influence, and Hybridization'. *Medieval Encounters* 15 (2009), 236–55.

——. 'The Re-creation of Medieval Arabo-Andalusian Music in Modern Performance'. *Al-Masāq: Islam and the Medieval Mediterranean* 21/2 (August 2009), 175–89.

Rubiera Mata, María Jesús. *Literatura Hispanoárabe*. Alicante: Universidad de Alicante, 2004.

Shannon, Jonathan Holt. *Among the Jasmine Trees: Music and Modernity in Contemporary Syria*. Middletown, CT: Wesleyan University Press, 2006.

al-Ṭanjī, Muḥammad Ibn Tāwīt. 'al-Ṭarā'iq wa-l-alḥān al-mūsīqiyya fī Ifrīqiya wa-l-Andalus'. *Abḥāth* 21 (1968), 93–116.

Touma, Habib Hassan. 'Andalusian *Nūba* in Morocco'. In Danielson et al. (eds), *The Garland Encyclopedia of World Music* vol. 6, 455–64.

Wagner, Mark S. *Like Joseph in Beauty: Yemeni Vernacular Poetry and Arab-Jewish Symbiosis*. Leiden and London: Brill, 2009.

12 The Eastern Arab World

Danielson, Virginia. *The Voice of Egypt: Umm Kulthūm, Arabic Song, and Egyptian Society in the Twentieth Century*. Chicago: University of Chicago Press, 1997.

—— See also under **11 North Africa and the Eastern Mediterranean** above.

Farmer, Henry George. 'The Music of Islam'. In Egon Wellész (ed.), *The New Oxford History of Music*, 421–77. London: Oxford University Press, 1957.

——. See also under **11 North Africa and the Eastern Mediterranean** above.

Goldman, Michal (prod., dir. and writer). *Umm Kulthum: A Voice Like Egypt*. Video recording. Waltham, MA: Filmmakers Collaborative, 1996.

Habib, Kenneth. 'The Superstar Singer Fairouz and the Ingenious Rahbani Composers: Lebanon Sounding'. PhD diss., University of California, Santa Barbara, 2005.

al-Ḥifnī, Maḥmūd. *al-Mūsīqā al-Naẓariyya* [*Music Theory*]. 6th ed. Cairo: Maktabat al-Nahḍah, 1972. First published 1938.

Laborde, Jean Benjamin de. *Essai sur la Musique Ancienne et Moderne* vol. 1. Paris: Ph.-D. Pierres, 1780.

Lohman, Laura. *Umm Kulthum: Artistic Agency and the Shaping of an Arab Legend, 1967- 2007*. Middletown, CT: Wesleyan University Press, 2010.

Marcus, Scott. 'Modulation in Arab Music: Documenting Oral Concepts, Performance Rules and Strategies'. *Ethnomusicology* 36/2 (1992), 171–95.

——. 'Solo Instrumental Improvisation (*Taqāsīm*) in Arab Music'. *Middle East Studies Association Bulletin* 27 (1993), 108–11.

———. 'The Interface Between Theory and Practice: The Case of Intonation in Arab Music'. *Asian Music* 24/2 (1993), 39–58.

———. 'The Eastern Arab System of Melodic Modes in Theory and Practice: A Case Study of *maqām Bayyātī*'. In Danielson et al. (eds), *The Garland Encyclopedia of World Music* vol. 6, 33–46.

———. 'The Rhythmic Modes of Middle Eastern Music'. In Danielson et al. (eds), *The Garland Encyclopedia of World Music* vol. 6, 89–92.

———. *Music in Egypt: Experiencing Music, Expressing Culture*. New York: Oxford University Press, 2007.

Mashāqa, Mīkhā'īl. *al-Risāla al-Shihābiyya fī al-Ṣinā'a al-Mūsīqiyya* [*The Shihabi Treatise on the Musical Art*], c. 1840. Loose English translation by Eli Smith: 'A Treatise on Arab Music (chiefly from a work by Michail Meshakah, of Damascus)'. *Journal of the American Oriental Society* (Boston) 1/3 (1847), 171–217. Published with a French translation, commentary, and introductory remarks by P. L. Ronzevalle: 'Un traité de musique arabe moderne'. *Mélanges de la Faculté Orientale* vol. 6, 1–120. Beirut: Université Saint-Joseph, 1913.

Racy, Jihad Ali. Review of *Waṣlah Ghina'iyyah* et al. *Ethnomusicology* 24/3 (1980), 603–6.

———. 'Music in Nineteenth-Century Egypt: An Historical Sketch'. *Selected Reports in Ethnomusicology* 4 (1983), 157–79.

———. *Making Music in the Arab World: The Culture and Artistry of Ṭarab*. New York: Cambridge University Press, 2003.

Sawa, George. 'Kitāb al-Aghānī'. In Danielson et al. (eds), *The Garland Encyclopedia of World Music* vol. 6, 351–6.

Shannon, Jonathan. See under **11 North Africa and the Eastern Mediterranean** above.

El-Shawan, Salwa. 'The Socio-Political Context of al-Mūsīḳa al-'Arabiyyah in Cairo, Egypt: Policies, Patronage, Institutions, and Musical Change (1927–77)'. *Asian Music* 12/1 (1980), 86–128.

Wright, Owen. 'Ibn al-Munajjim and the Early Arabian Modes'. *The Galpin Society Journal* 19 (1966), 27–48.

13 Turkey

Aydemir, Murat. *Turkish Music Makam Guide*, ed. and trans. Erman Dirikcan. Istanbul: Pan Yayıncılık, 2010.

Barkey, Karen. *Empire of Difference: The Ottomans in Comparative Perspective*. New York: Cambridge University Press, 2008.

Bates, Eliot. *Music in Turkey: Experiencing Music, Expressing Culture*. Oxford: Oxford University Press, 2011.

Blainville, Charles Henri de. 'A General, Critical, and Philological History of Music' [excerpts], trans. Robert Martin. *Turkish Music Quarterly* 4/4 (Autumn 1991), 4–10.

Danielson, Virginia, et al. See under **11 North Africa and the Eastern Mediterranean** above.

Feldman, Walter Z. *Music of the Ottoman Court: Makam, Composition and the Early Ottoman Instrumental Repertoire*. Berlin: Verlag für Wissenschaft und Bildung, 1996.

Gökalp, Ziya. *Türkçülüğün Esasları* [The Fundamentals of Turkishness], trans. and ann. Robert Devereux. Leiden: E. J. Brill, 1968 (orig. 1928).

Hindemith, Paul. *The Selected Letters of Paul Hindemith*, trans. and ed. Geoffrey Skelton. New Haven: Yale University Press, 1995.

Kalın, İbrahim. 'Roots of Misconception: Euro-American Perceptions of Islam Before and After September 11'. *The World Wisdom Online Library*, 2008, http://www.worldwisdom.com/uploads/pdfs/58.pdf.

Febvre, Michel. 'Theatre de la Turquie' [excerpts], trans. Robert Martin. *Turkish Music Quarterly* 5/2–3 (Spring-Summer 1992), 21.

Mevlana Celaleddin Rumi. *Mesnevi*, trans. Edmund Helminski. Putney: Threshold Books, 1981.

Perl, Benjamin. 'Mozart in Turkey'. In John A. Rice (ed.), *Essays on Opera (1750–1800)*, 265–81. Farnham: Ashgate, 2010.

Popescu-Judetz, Eugenia. 'Demitrie Cantemir's Theory of Turkish Art Music'. *Studies in Oriental Arts*, 99–146. Pittsburg: Duquesnes University Institute of Folk Arts, 1981.

Quataert, Donald. *The Ottoman Empire, 1700–1922*. Cambridge: Cambridge University Press, 2000.

Whaples, Miriam Karpilow. 'Exoticism in Dramatic Music, 1600–1800'. PhD diss., Indiana University, 1958.

Yönetken, Halil Bedii. 'Milli Musiki'. *Darülelhan Mecmuası*. Istanbul: Evkaf-ı İslamiye Matbaası, 1924.

14 Iran

Blum, Stephen. 'Iran: An Introduction'. In Danielson et al. (eds.), *The Garland Encyclopedia of World Music* vol. 6, 823–38.

Caton, Margaret. 'The Concept of Mode in Iranian Music: Shur' and 'Performance Practice in Iran: Radif and Improvisation'. In Danielson et al. (eds), *The Garland Encyclopedia of World Music* vol. 6, 59–76 and 129–43.

During, Jean. 'Music, Poetry and the Visual Arts in Persia'. *World of Music* 24/1 (1982), 72–86.

——. 'L'Oreille islamique: dix années capitales de la vie musicale en Iran, 1980–1990'. *Asian Music* 23/2 (1992), 135–64.

——, Zia Mirabdolbaghi and Dariush Safvat. *The Art of Persian Music*. Washington, DC: Mage, 1991. With accompanying CD, *Anthology of Persian Music, 1930–1990*.

Farhat, Hormoz. *The Dastgah Concept in Persian Music*. Cambridge Studies in Ethnomusicology. Cambridge: Cambridge University Press, 1990, repr. 2004.

Al-Faruqi, Lois Ibsen. 'The Suite in Islamic History and Culture'. *The World of Music* 27/3 (1985), 46–66.

Mas'udiye, Mohammad Taqi. *The Vocal Radif of Traditional Iranian Music According to the Version of Mahmoud Karimi*. Tehran: Mahoor Institute of Culture and Art, 2003.

Nettl, Bruno. 'Nour-Ali Boroumand: A Twentieth-Century Master of Persian Music'. *Studia Instrumentorum Musicae Popularis* 3 (1975), 167–71.

——. 'Persian Classical Music in Tehran: The Processes of Change'. In Nettl (ed.), *Eight Urban Musical Cultures: Tradition and Change*, 146–85. Urbana, Chicago, London: University of Illinois Press, 1978.

——. 'The Role of Music in Culture: Iran, A Recently Developed Nation'. In Nettl, Charles Hamm and Ronald Byrnside, *Contemporary Music and Music Cultures*, 71–100. New Jersey: Prentice Hall, 1975.

Neubauer, Eckhard. 'Music History ii: CA. 650 to 1370 CE'. *Encyclopædia Iranica online*, http://www.iranicaonline.org/articles/music-history-ii.

Pakdaman, Nasser. 'La situation du musicien dans la société persane'. In J.-P. Charnay (ed.), *Normes et valeurs dans l'Islam contemporain*, 325–43. Paris: Payot, 1966.

Pope, Arthur U., and Phyllis Ackerman. 'Gardens'. In Pope and Ackerman (eds), *A Survey of Persian Art* vol. 3, 1427–45. Tehran: Sorush Press, 1977.

Schimmel, Annemarie. *Rumi's World: The Life and Work of the Great Sufi Poet*. Boston & London: Shambhala Publications, 2001.

Simms, Rob and Amitr Koushkani. *The Art of Avaz and Mohammad Reza Shajarian: Foundations and Contexts*. Lanham, MD: Lexington Books, 2012.

——. *Mohammad Reza Shajarian's Avaz in Iran and Beyond, 1979–2010*. Lanham, MD: Lexington Books, 2012.

Tala'i, Dariush. *Traditional Persian Art Music: The Radif of Mizra Abdollah*. Musical Notation, Commentary and Performance by Dariush Tala'i. Costa Mesa, CA: Mazda Publishers, 2000. Book accompanying a set of five compact discs, *Traditional Persian Art Music*.

——. 'A New Approach to the Theory of Persian Music: The Radif and the Modal System'. In Danielson et al. (eds), *The Garland Encyclopedia of World Music* vol. 6, 865–74.

Wright, Owen. *The Modal System of Arab and Persian Music AD 1250–1300*. Oxford: Oxford, University Press, 1978.

——. *Touraj Kiaras and Persian Classical Music: An Analytical Perspective*. SOAS Musicology Series. Farnham: Ashgate, 2009. With accompanying CD, *Rose without thorns*.

Youssefzadeh, Ameneh. 'The Situation of Music in Iran since the Revolution: The Role of Official Organizations'. *British Journal of Ethnomusicology* 9/2 (2000), 35–61.

——. 'Une passion pour l'Iran: entretien avec Stephen Blum'. *Cahiers de musiques traditionnelles* (Genève: Ateliers d'ethnomusicologie) 23 (2010), 231–48.

15 Uzbekistan and Tajikistan

Bekjon, Mulla and Muhammad Yusuf Devonzoda. *Xorazm Musiqiy Tarixchasi*, ed. O. Matyoqubov. Tashkent: Yozuvchi Nashriyoti, 1998. First published in 1925.

Bosworth, C. E., and M. S. Asimov (eds). *History of Civilizations of Central Asia*, vol. 4 part 2. Paris: UNESCO, 2000.

Di Cosmo, Nicola, Allen J. Frank and Peter B. Golden (eds). *The Cambridge History of Inner Asia: The Chinggisid Age*. Cambidge: Cambridge University Press, 2009.

Fitrat, Abdurauf. *O'zbek Klassik Musiqasi va Uning Tarikhi*, ed. A. Samad. Tashkent: 'Fan' Nashriyoti, 1993. First published in 1927.

Levin, Theodore. See under ■ **Introduction** above.

—— and Köchümkulova, Elmira (eds). *Music of Central Asia*. Bloomington: Indiana University Press, 2014.

Soucek, Svat. *A History of Inner Asia*. Cambridge: Cambridge University Press, 2000.

Sultanova, Razia. *From Shamanism to Sufism: Women, Islam, and Culture in Central Asia*. London: IB Tauris, 2011.

Vāsifī, Zayn ad-Dīn. *Badā'i al-Waqā'i*, ed. A. N. Boluirev. Tehran: Intishārāt-i Bunyād-i Farhang-i Irān, 1970.

▶ Index

A page reference in *italics* indicates an illustration.
A reference such as 362n6 indicates note 6 on page 362.

Abbās I, 325
'Abd al-Raḥmān, 249
'Abd al-Ṣamad, 'Abd al-Bāsiṭ, 282
'Abd al-Wahhāb, Muhammad, 277
Abdollāh, Mirzā, 325, 333, 334
Abdulhamit I, 303
Abdurashidov, Abduvali, 354, 355
Abhinavagupta, 147
Abu Khalil al-Qabbani, Ahmad, 277
Abū l-Faraj al-Iṣbahānī, 272
    Book of Songs (*Kitāb al-Aghānī*), 272
Academy of Ancient Music, 232
Academy of Maqom, Dushanbe, 354, 355
Academy of Oriental Music, Cairo, 15
accordions, 279, 289
Afghanistan, 195, 323, 341, 342
Africa
    classical-music traditions, 179–81
    map, *178*
    and the roots of jazz, 200–1
    see also Andalusian Music; *jaliyaa*, Mande
Aga Khan Trust for Culture (AKTC), 18, 354
ageng, 65, 67
Agra, 148, *149*
Ahmadinejād, Mahmud, 331
Aimard, Pierre-Laurent, 3, 5
Aka Pygmies, 3, 4–5, 18
Akbar, 148, *150*
ālāp, 142, 144, 148, 149, 153
ālāpana, 168, 169
Albania, 6, 18
Albany, New York, 200
albogon, 265
albogue, 265
alboka, 265

Al-e Ahmad, Jalāl, 328
Aleppo, 2, 257, 267, 271, 290, 301
Alexander the Great, 322
Algeria, 262, 263, 265, 266–7
'Alilo' songs, 9
Alim Khan, Mohammed, *350*
Alimatov, Alisher, *353*
Alimatov, Turgun, *353*
'Alizādeh, Hossein, 329, 330, 338
All India Radio, 151, 168
alla turca, 316–17, *318*
allelluias, 9
alta-yarim maqom, 342–3
Anatolia, 296, 297, 299, 300, 345
Andalusian music
    forms, 252–7
    history, 248–51
    instruments, 263–5
    map, *246*
    modes, rhythms and the *nūba*, 260–3
    music today, 266–8
    overview, 247–8
    performance, 257–9
Andalusiyyāt (Fayrouz), 267
Andes, 3
Angkor, 26
Angkor's Bayon, *27*
anupallavi, 169
Aoki Reibo II, *84*
Arab world, eastern
    early history, 272–4
    instruments, 289
    iqā', 285
    maqām, 281–5
    overview, 271
    recent history, 274–81
    Sabah Fakhri and Fayrouz, 290
    today, 291–2
    see also Andalusian music
Arabic Music Ensemble, 271, 278, 280, 291

arangētram, 161
Argentina, 8
Arisawa, Shino, *101*
Armstrong, Louis, 207, *208*, 211, 214
Arom, Simha, 3, 5
āsh gatherings, 356, *357*
Ashanti, 180–1
Ashkenazi Jews, 267
Asmahān, 277
al-Aṭrash, Farīd, 277, 280, 287, 291
Atatürk, Mustafa Kemal, 15, 302, 327–8
Aurangzeb, 148–9
Australian Aboriginals, 3
avant-garde jazz, 211
Avicenna (Ibn Sīnā), 272, 323
āvāz, 333
Azerbaijan, 9, 323, 333, 346, 358
Aztec Empire, 8

Ba-aka people, 180
Babur, 345, 346
Babylon, 9
Bach, Johann Sebastian, 75, 77, 102, 226, 228, 232, 239, 241, 244, 296
    'Air on a G String', 228
    chorale preludes, 3
    preludes and fugures, 10
    Sonata in G minor for solo violin, *229*
    'Wachet Auf', 228
Baghdad, 3, 249, 251, 261, 272, 273, 300, 343, 344
Bahār, Malek al-Sho'arā, 335
Bahāri, 'Asqar, 328
bala, 184, 189, 191, 192
balafon, 184, 189, 192
Bali, 19, 52, 53, 70, 71
Balkans, 23

387

Les Ballets Africains, 194
Les Ballets Russes, 190, 240
balo, 184, 185, 190
balungan, 56, 60–1, 62, 64–5, 67, 71
Bambara people, 181
ban, 132
ban gu, 132
Ban Somdet Chao Phraya, 40
Banaras, 140, 149, 153
Bangladesh, 139
bangzi, 109, 132
bānsurī, 157
barang *miring*, 60
Bārbad, 323, 331, 333
barbat, 322, 332
Bardi, Count, 224
Barenboim, Daniel, 21
Barnet, Charlie, 211
Baroque music, 3, 8, 10, 32, 33, 40, 122, 218, 226, 233–4, 238, 239, 244
Bartók, Béla, *xxii*, 15–16, 209
Bashir, Munir, 9
Battúta, Ibn, 181, 187
bayan, 14
Bāyqarā Husayn, 344–6
bebop, 209–11
Bechet, Sidney, 207
Beethoven, Ludwig van, 8, 10, 75, 109, 235–6, 238, 316
   Fidelio, 235
   Piano Sonata no. 23, 'Appassionata', 236
   Symphony no. 5, 236
   Symphony no. 9, 6, 316
Behzād, Kamāliddin, 345
Beijing opera (*jingju*), 127, 130, 131–6
Beirut, 271, 278, 290
bells
   karinya, 188
   nenge, 185
   neo, 188, 189
bendir, 311
Benny Goodman Orchestra, 207
Bergson, Henri, 240
Berlin, 18, 21, 39, 241

Berlioz, Hector, 237, 238
   Symphonie fantastique, 237, 238
bhakti, 165
Bhatkhande, Narayan, 149
Bhatt, Vishwamohan, 157
Bhumibol Adulyadej, Rama IX, 40
Bihāg, 142–4
bīn, 153
birimintingo, 190
Birtwistle, Harrison, 3
biwa, 77, 78–9, 87, 94, 97, 322
Bizet, Georges, 240
   Carmen, 240
Blainville, Charles Henri de, 312
blue notes, 202
Blum, Stephen, 321
Bobowski, Albert (Ali Ufki), 313, 314
Bohemia, 239
Bolden, Charles 'Buddy', 204
bolon, 182, 186, 187–8
Bolivia, 8
Bombay, 150
*bonang*s, 53, 56
Borodin, Alexander, 8
Borumand, Nur 'Ali, 321, 328, 333
Bosphorus, 296, 300
Boulez, Pierre, 2, 361n3
Brahms, Johannes, 239
Brazil, 2–3, 8, 213
Brecht, Bertolt, 134
Brikama, 186
Briouel Ensemble, 264
Britten, Benjamin, 2, 70–1
   Curlew River, 101
   The Prince of the Pagodas, 70
broadcasting, 151, 168
   see also radio; television
Buddhism, 17
   China, 128
   Japan, 80, 84, 89, 91
   Java, 52
   Thailand, Laos and Cambodia, 33, 42
   Zen, 17, 80, 84, 86
Buddhist chant, 80, 89, 91
bugaku, 76
Buganda, 3, 180

Bukhara, 341, 342, 344, 346, 347, 349, 350, 351
bunka-fu, 89
bunraku, 77, 84, 92
būq, 263–5
Burgundy, 224
Burkina Faso, 181
Burma, 26
Bursa, 300
Byrd, William, 224
Byzantine
   chant, 8–9
   Empire, 299, 300, 305
   notation, 313

ca hue, 45, 46
ca tru, 6, 7, 18, 46
Cage, John, 19, 21, 242
Cai Deyun (Tsar Teh-yun), 124
Cai Yong, 113, 115
Cairo, 11, 15, 267, 270, 271, 273, 274, 277, 278, 279, 285, 286, 287, 291, 292
Cairo Congress of Arab Music, 15, 15, 273, 278
Cairo Opera House, 247, 267, 292
Cairo Symphony Orchestra, 278
Calcutta (Kolkatta), 149, 150
call-and-response, 201–2
Cambodia
   creating the music, 29–31
   forms, 32–6
   history, 25–8, 39, 41–2
   map, 24
   overview, 28–9
   performance, 42
   tunings, scales and modes, 36–7
Cambridge History of World Music, 21
Cantemir, Dimitrie, xix, 307, 308, 314
   notation, 313
canti fermi, 62, 222, 224
Cantigas de Santa Maria, 254
Carnatic (Karnatak)
   classical tradition, 166–8
   history, 162–6

Carnatic (Karnatak) *continued*
   melody and *rāga*, 170–3
   rhythm and *tāla*, 173–4
   voices and instruments, 174–6
Carnegie Hall, New York, 209, 213
Castiglione, Baldassare, *Book of the Courtier*, 225
cello, 279
çeşni, 306
Central African Republic, 180
Central Asia
   history, 343–50
   influence of, 114–15, 157
   instruments, 357–9
   invasion of India, 148
   map, 340
   overview, 23, 341–3
   during the Soviet era, 351–4
   today, 354–7
Cephas, Kassian, photograph of gamelan, 54
Chabrier, Emmanuel, *España*, 240
chahar shadd, 346–7
chaharmaqom, 342–3, 346
chaharmezrab, 334–5
Cham people, 26
chamber music
   China, 114
   Europe, 316
   jazz as, 199
   Turkey, 301
   Vietnam, 44, 45, 46
chang, 358
Chang'an, 118
chant, 218–19
   Buddhist, 80, 89, 91
   Byzantine, 8–9
   Gregorian, 216, 218–19, 220, 222
   Qur'anic, 309, 311, 315
Chaplin, Charlie, 134
charanam, 169
Charlemagne, 218
Charry, Eric, 182
Châtelet theatre, Paris, 3, 4–5
Chatwin, Bruce, *The Songlines*, 2
Chaurasia, Hariprasad, 157

Chen Kaige, 134, 136
Chengdu, 120
Chennai (Madras), 166, 167
Chesterfield, Lord, 233
Chiang Ching, 135
Chicago, 205, 207
China
   autonomous regions, 7
   concepts of classical music, 108–9
   influence, 26, 32, 42, 44, 76, 87
   map, 104
Chinese opera, 127–8, *129*
   ensemble, *133*
   history, 128–30
   jingju, or Beijing opera, 131–4, 136
   kunqu, 130–1
   visual elements, 130
   yangbanxi, 135
ching, 30, 37
chirikara, 84
Chongqing Museum, 120
Chopi, 3, 180
Chopin, Fryderyk, 236, 237–8
choruses, 201, 202
Christianity
   attitudes to music, 17, 259
   and the Ottoman Empire, 299, 300–1
   sacred music, 218, 221, 222, 227
Chūshingura, 74
ciblon, 51
cinema, *see* film and cinema
Cixi, Empress Dowager, 131
clarinets
   Andalusian music, *al-būq*, 263–5
   Europe, 238
   North American jazz, 207
   Iran, 328
Classical style, Europe, 233–4
Clayton, Buck, 213
clempung, 53
Coleman, Ornette, 211, *212*
Coltrane, John, 211
Common Practice, 225, 228, 241

composition
   and the definition of classical music, 6
   eastern Arab music, 280
   Europe, 220
   Iran, 334
   North American jazz, 209
   North India, 142–7
   South India, 165
   Thailand, Laos, Cambodia, 32–6
   Turkey, 304–5, 314–15
Conakry, 178, 185
concertato principle, 226, 227
Confucius, 105, 113, 118
Congo, 3
Congress of Arab Music, 15, *15*, 273, 278
conservatories
   Andalusian, 266
   Central Asia, 352
   China, 108
   eastern Arab world, 278
   Middle East, 16
   Turkey, 296
   Vietnam, 46
Constantine the Great, 300
Constantinople, 300; *see also* Istanbul
Cook, Captain James, xix
Cook, Nicholas, 21
cool jazz, 211
Copland, Aaron, 209, 242
cor anglais, 238
Cordoba, 249–51, 257–9, 261, 265
   Musicians' Capital, *266*
Corelli, Arcangelo, 227, 228
cornets, 225–6
court music
   definitions, 3
   Andalusian, 250–1, 257
   Buganda, 180
   Cambodia, 27–8
   China, 107, 109, 113
   eastern Arab, 272
   Europe, 221, 227
   Japan, 76–7
   Java, 54–5, 60

court music *continued*
  Laos, 28
  North India, 148
  South India, 164, 165, 166
Cowell, Henry, *The Universal Flute*, 101
Creole Jazz Band, 207
Creoles, 204
Cu Long, 46
Cuba, 23
cymbals
  China, *naobo*, 132
  Chinese opera, 131
  Laos, *sing*, 30
  South India, *tālam*, 176
  Thailand, Laos and Cambodia, 27, 30, 31, 37
Cyrus II (Kurosh) (Cyrus the Great), 322

da Ponte, Lorenzo, 234
dadaiko, 78–9
daf, 337, 338
daff, see *riqq*
La Dafne, 225
Dāghir, 'Abduh, 291–2
Damascus, 249, 271, 272, 278, 300
dan bao, 44
dàn dáy, 7, 46
dan nguyet, 44, 45
dan nhi/dan co, 46
dan tranh, 44, 45
dance
  Africa, 180
  Europe, 221–2, 227, 240
  Japan, 76, 78, 84, 99
  Java, 52–5, 58
  North American jazz, 202, 207
  South India, 163
  Thailand, Laos and Cambodia, 33, 42
danmono, 88
darbuka, 311
darbukka, 289
Dariush Tala'i, *336*
Darvish Khān, 326, 327, *336*
Dasgupta, Buddhadev, 144, 145, 146, 149, 157

dastgāh, 333–5
Davis, Miles, *212*, 214
Davāmi, 'Abdollah, 328
dawr, 275
Day of Shashmaqom, 354
dāyereh, 326, 327, 337
de Marini, Giovanni-Filippo, 29
Debussy, Claude, 2, 70, 239, 240
  Estampes, 240
  'Pagodes', 70, 240
Dede, Veli, 309
Dede Efendi, Hamamizade, 297
def, 311
Degung, 52
Delacroix, Eugène, 237
Delhi, 148, 149, 153
Delta of the Nine Dragons, 46
demung, 53
Devonzoda, Muhammad Yusuf, and Mulla Bekjon Rahmoni, and Muhammad Yusuf Devonzoda Og'li, *History of the Music of Khorezm*, 349–50
dhrupad, 148–9, 152, 153
Diabate, Mamadou, 195
Diabate, Toumani, 191, *196*
diaspora communities, 17–18
dieu, 44
diff, 301
Dikshitar, Balusvami, 174–5
Dīkshitar, Muttusvāmi, 164, 165
al-Dīn al-Urmawī, Ṣafī, 272
dissonance, 225
Dixieland jazz, 207
dizi, 131, 132
doira, 355, 359
dombak, 337
dombra, 22, 23
Dominguez, Paul, 204
Donizetti, Gaetano, 314
Donizetti, Giuseppe (Donizetti Paşa), 314, 316
donkilo, 190
donso konni, 188
drama, *see* dance; theatre and drama

drums
  parallels, 3
  Africa
    drum ensembles, 180
    drum troupes, 184
    entenga, 180
    kunang, 185
  Andalusian music, 263
  Central Asia
    doira, 355, 359
    naqqara, 359
  China
    ban gu, 132
    gu, 132
    tanggu, 132
  Chinese opera, 131
  eastern Arab music
    darbukka, 289
    ṭabla, 279, 289
  Iran
    daf, 337, 338
    dayareh, 326, 327, 337
    dombak, 337
    tombak, 337
    tonbak, 337
    zarb, 326, 327, 337
  Japan
    kakko, 77, 78–9
    kotsuzumi, 80
    ōtsuzumi, 80
    taiko, 77, 78–9, 80, 84
  Java
    ciblon, 51
    kendhang, 53, 56, 67
  North India
    pakhāvaj, 148, 153
    ṭabla, 149, 153, 154, 157
  South India
    kanjira, 163, 172
    mrdangam, 162, 163, 164, 169–70, 172, 173, 176
    tala, 163
    tavil, 176
  Thailand, Laos and Cambodia, 27
    khawng khaek, 38
    klawng tat, 31, 43
    kong taphone, 30
    sampho, 30, 31

drums *continued*
 Thailand, Laos and Cambodia *continued*
  skor thom, 31
  taphon, 30, 43
 Turkey
  bendir, 311
  darbuka, 311
  def, 311
  diff, 301
  kudum, 311
  nakara, 301
 Vietnam, 7
Dufay, Guillaume, 224
Dugha, 181
Dunstable, John, 224
Duran, Lucy, 182
Dushanbe, 354, *355*
dutar, *348*, *355*, *358*
Dvořák, Antonín, 239
Dylan, Bob, 19
Dyula people, 181

eastern Arab world
 early history, 272–4
 instruments, 289
 iqā', 285
 maqām, 281–5
 overview, 271
 recent history, 274–81
 Sabah Fakhri and Fayrouz, 290
 today, 291–2
Eastern Mediterranean, *see* Andalusian music
Edirne, 300
Edo, *77*, *83*, *88*
Edo Period, 77, 81, 88, 89, 91
education
 teaching in schools, 17
 Central Asia, 357
 Chinese universities, 108
 Egypt, 278, 280
 Europe, 232
 Iran, 328
 North American jazz, 211, 213
 North India, 150–1
 see also training
Egypt, 15, 263, 267, 277

Elgar, Edward, 241
Ellington, Edward 'Duke', 207, 209
 with his band, *198*, *208*
 Black, Brown and Beige, 209
Ellis, A. J., 36
England, 226–7, 232
English Gamelan Orchestra, 71
entenga, 180
Ergüner, Kudsi, 308
erhu, 108
Ershad (Ministry of Culture and Islamic Guidance), 330, 338
Eskimo (Inupiat) song recordings, 18
'Etenraku', 98
Europe
 Baroque, 226–32
 Classical style, 232–4
 influence of, 15, 108, 278, 281, 325–6, 327, 328, 352
 medieval, 218–22
 and the Ottoman Empire, 298–9
 overview, 2, 217–18
 Renaissance, 222–5
 Romantic era, 235–9
 twentieth century fragmentation, 239–42
Europe, James Reese, 241
Evterpii (notation), *313*

Fajr ('dawn') festival, 331
Fakhri (Fakhry), Sabah, 267, 290, 291
fantasia, 3
al-Fārābī (Abu Naṣr Fārābī), 272, 274, 323, 331, 343, 357
Farewell, My Concubine (1993 film), 136
Farhāni, Ali Akbar, 325
Farmer, Henry George, 15, 187, 272, 273
fasıl, 308–9
Fayrouz, 267, 271, 290, 291
Febvre, Michel, 314
Ferdowsi, 323
Ferghana Valley, 342, 345, 355
festivals, 21
Fez, 257, 264

Fez Festival of Sacred Music, 21
fiddles and violins
 Afganistan, spike-fiddlers of the spirit world, *16*
 Andalusian music, 264
  rabāb, *263*, 264
  violin, 264
 Central Asia
  ghijak, *347*, *348*, *358*
  qyl qobyz, 22, *23*
 China
  erhu, 108
  jing erhu, 132
  jinghu, 132, *133*
 eastern Arab music
  kamān, 289
  kamānja, *274*, 289
  violin, *279*, 289
 Europe, 226, 235
  violin family, 227
 Iran, 325–6
  kamāncheh, 325, *326*, 328, 336, 337, 338, 347
 Japan, *kokyū*, *93*, 95
 Java
  rebab, 56, 65, 67
 North India, violin, 157
 South India, *163*, *172*, *174*
 Thailand
  saw duang, 30
  saw sam sai, 30
  saw u, 30, *32*
 Turkey
  kemençe, *301*, 310, 311, 312
  rebab, 311, *312*
 Vietnam, *dan nhi/dan co*, 46
film and cinema, 37, 241, 267, 272, 277, 278, 287, 291, 329
 music, 151, 158, 277, 298, 369n13
Finland, 239
Fitrat, Abdurauf, 347–9, 352, 358
 Uzbek Classical Music and Its History, 349, 352
Flanders, 224
Florence, 224

flutes
  Andalusian music, reed flute, 263
  Central Asia, *nay, 348, 359*
  China
    dizi, 131, 132
    xiao, 119
  eastern Arab music, *nāy, 274, 279, 286, 289*
  Europe
    orchestral flute, 92, 312
    piccolo, 238
  Iran, *ney, 337*
  Japan
    hitoyogiri, 85
    nōkan, 80, 83
    ryūteki, 77, 78–9, 94
    shakuhachi, 84–7, 85, 95, 101
    shinobue, 83
  Java, *suling, 56*
  North India, *155*
    bānsurī, 157
  South India
    Karnatak flute, 162
    transverse wooden flute, 175
    venu, 163
  Thailand, *khlui, 30, 32*
  Turkey, *ney, 301, 310, 311–12*
  Vietnam, 44, 45
    sao, 46
folk music
  definitions, 6
  Central Asia, 353–4
  India, 162
  Japan, 92, 95–6, 100
Forbidden City Museum, Beijing, 107, 110
Forever Enthralled (2009 film), 134
Forutan, Yusef, 327, 328
Fox, Aaron A., 18
France, 226–8, 232
free jazz, 211
French Indochina, 27
Frescobaldi, Girolamo, 226
front line, 202, 207
Fu'ad, King, 15
Fuke sect, 86
Funa-Benkei, 98

fusion, 19
  jazz, 211

Gabrieli, Giovanni, 226
gadhon, 65
gagaku, 2, 19, 76–7, 78–9, 80, 91, 92
gakudaiko, 78–9
gakunin, 76–7
Galli-Curci, Amelita, 134
gambang, 56, 57, 65, 67
gambang kayu, 53
Gambia, 178, 181, 182, 185, 186, 188, 189, 191, 193, 195
gamelan, 10, 53, 54, 362n6
  canon, 60–1
  cultural history, 51–5
  form, shape, function, 55–7
  influence of, 3, 70–2, 240
  music theory, 67–8
  notation, 62–7
  performance, 57–9
  today, 68–70
  tuning systems, 59–60
Gamīl, Alfred, 292
garapan, 61, 67, 71
gat, 144, 145
'Gathutkaca Winisuda', *69*
gāyakī, 152
Gayan Samaj, 167
gazel, 309, 315
Gel seninle yarın ey serv-i revan, 302–3
gendèr barung, 53, 56, 57, 65, 67
gendèr panerus, 53, 56, 57
gendered performance
  Africa, 184, 188, 193
  Andalusian music, 250, 258
  Central Asia, 358
  Chinese opera, 130, 132
  eastern Arab music, 272, 277
  Iran, 322, 330, 331, 338
  Japan, 80, 81, 82
  Java, 56–7, 57, 61, 67
  Malta, 1
  North India, 152–3, 155, 157
  Ottoman Turkey, 297
  South India, 168
  Turkey, 311

gendhing, 60–1
Georgia, 9, 18
Germany, 3, 226–7, 228, 232, 239, 241
gerongan, 67
Ghana, 195
ghana competitions, 1
ghatam, 164, 175, 176
ghijak, 347, 348, 358
Ghosh, Pannalal, 157
gidayū music, 84
Gillan, Matt, *101*
Gillespie, Dizzy, *212*
Girija, 175
Glass, Philip, 242
Gluck, Christoph Willibald, 316
Goffman, Richard, 298
Gökalp, Ziya, 301
gongs
  China, *xiao luo, 132*
  Chinese opera, 131
  Japan, *shōko, 77, 78–9*
  Java, 51–2, 53, 55, 57
    ageng, 65, 67
    bonangs, 56
    gong ageng, 67
    kempul, 53, 65, 67
    kenong, 53, 65, 67
    kethuk-kempyang, 53, 65, 67
  Thailand, Laos and Cambodia, 9, 27, 38
    khawng mong, 31
    khawng wong lek, 30, 31, 37
    khawng wong yai, 30, 31, 32, 35, 43
    khong vong noi, 30
    khong vong nyai, 30
    kong tauch, 30
    kong vong thom, 30, 31
    song lang, 46
Goodman, Benny, 207, 211, 213
Googoosh, 330
Gosh, Nikhil, 14
gottuvādyam, 174
Greece
  Byzantine Greek chant, 8–9
  influence on Europe, 220, 226
  music theory, 17, 305–6
  and Persia, 322

Greer, Sonny, 208
Gregorian chant, 216, 218
Gregory, Pope, 218
griot, 182, 194–5, 196
gu, 132
Guan Pinghu, 107, 115, 124
gudian yinyue, 108, 109
Guido of Arezzo, 12, 220
Guidonian hand, 219, 220
Guillaume, Seventh Count of Poitiers and Ninth Duke of Aquitaine, 221
guimbri, 187
Guinea, 178, 181, 184, 185, 191, 194
Guinea-Bissau, 178, 181
guitars
    eastern Arab world, 289
    Vietnam, 44
        luc huyen cam, 46
guqin zither, 17, 106, 110, 117, 120
    early history, 113–15
    instrument itself, 109–13
    modern playing, 122–4
    music and nature, 115–17
    overview, 105–7
    qin music, 118–21
    rhythm and metre, 121–2
gusheh, 333–4, 346
Guttila Jātaka, 140
Gwalior, 148, 149, 151

Hāfez, 321, 323
Ḥāfiẓ, 'Abd al-Ḥalīm, 280, 291
Hancock, Herbie, 195
Handel, George Frideric, 132, 227, 228, 232
Hanoi, 46
Hardin, Lil, 208
Hardwicke, Otto, 208
Haridas, Swami, 150
harmonium, 157
harps
    Africa
        bolon, 182, 186, 187–8
        donso konni, 188
        innanga, 180
        kora, 182, 186, 187, 189–90, 191, 192

harps *continued*
    Burma, *saung-gauk*, 140
    Central Asia, *jaw*, 23
    Europe, chromatic harp, 238
    North India, *vīnā*, 140
Harris, Rachel, 7
Harrison, Lou, 71
Hawkins, Coleman, 207
Haydn, Joseph, 109, 233–4, 234–5, 236, 297, 316
    'Nelson' Mass, 217
    String Quartet, op. 33 no. 1, 233
    Symphony no. 94, 'Surprise', 233–4
He Luting, 108
Henderson, Fletcher, 207
Herat, 16, 325, 342, 344, 345–6
Herodotus, 322
Hersch, Fred, 203
heterophony, 33, 67, 77, 83, 86, 95, 263, 315, 322, 335
Hicaz, 300
hichiriki, 77, 78–9, 94
Hindemith, Paul, 15, 15, 302
Hinduism, 52–3, 152
Hindustani music
    history, 147–51
    and Karnatak, 162, 164, 169, 170, 172, 173, 175
    overview, 139–42
    rāga and *tāla*, 142–7
    voices and instruments, 152–7
hitoyogiri, 85
Ho Chi Minh City, 46
hocketing, 3
Hodges, Johnny, 209
Homrong (The Overture) (2004 film), 37, 40
homrong chao, 33
homrong yen, 33
Hong Kong, 122, 124, 136
honkyoku, 86–7, 99
Hood, Mantle, 68
Hossein, Mirza Gholām, 325
Hot Five, 207, 208
House, Ginevra, 101
The House of Oud (*Bayt al-'Ūd*), 291

Howat, Roy, 240
Hu Guangjing, 124
Hue, 43, 46
Huizinga, Leonhard, 51
Huizong, Emperor, 107
Hun Sen, 41
Husayni, Zayn al-Abiddin, 345

Iberian Peninsula, 248–9
Ibiza, 1
Ibn 'Abd Rabbihi, 249–50
ibn al-Mahdī, Ibrāhīm, 272
Ibn Khaldūn, 252
ibn Kulayb, Ahmad, 258
ibn Nāfi, Alī (Ziryāb), 249–50, 251
Ibn Sīnā (Avicenna), 272, 323
Ikuta school, 88
Ikuyama Kengyo, *Hagi no Tsuyu*, 96
ilm-i musiki, 9, 305
improvisation
    concept of, 12
    Andalusian music, 263
    Chinese opera, 130
    eastern Arab music, 275, 280, 284–5
    Iran, 333–4
    Mande *jaliyaa*, 195
    North American jazz, 203, 207, 209–11
    North India, 140, 142–7
    South India, 168–9, 174
    Thailand, Laos and Cambodia, 33, 36
    Turkey, 306, 314–15, 315
    Vietnam, 44
    see also garapan
India
    influence of, 29, 44
    map, 138
    notation, 12, 14
    North India
        history, 147–51
        overview, 139–42
        rāga and *tāla*, 142–7
        voices and instruments, 152–7

India *continued*
  South India
    arangētram, 161
    classical tradition, 166–8
    concerts and programmes, 168–70
    history, 162–6
    melody and *rāga*, 170–3
    rhythm and *tāla*, 173–4
    voices and instruments, 174–6
  Indonesia
    gamelans, 52
    Hindu-Javanese legacy, 53–4
    jingju, or Beijing opera, 136
    see also Bali; Java
  innanga, 180
  intervals, *see* scales and intervals
  Inupiat (Eskimo) song recordings, 18
iqā', 285
irama, 23, 60–1, 67
Iran
  canon, 331–5
  historical background, 322–5
  instruments, 337
  music today, 338–9
  Pahlavi era, 327–9
  Persian culture and influence, 272, 274, 300, 322
  poetry, 10, 321–2
  Qājār era, 325–7
  post revolution, 329–31
Iraq, 9, 256
'Irawan's Wedding', *69*
Irbil, 21
Irvis, Charlie, *208*
Isfahan, 323, 325
Isḥāq al-Mawṣilī, 272
Ishikawa Toyonobu, woodblock print of kabuki actors, *93*
Islam
  Andalusian music, 248–9
  attitudes to music, 17, 259, 272–3, 323, 325
  call to prayer, 10, 282–3
  Mali, 195
  North India, 148, 152
  and Ottoman policy, 298

Islam *continued*
  Qur'anic chant, 309, 311, 315
  and the 'science of music', xix, 9, 343–4
  spread of, 300
  see also Sufism
Islamic Empire, 248–9
Ismail, Khedive, 278
ison, 9
Israel, 267
Issyk-Kul, Lake, *20*
Istanbul, 274, 294, 296, 300, 302, 303, 313
Italy, 18, 224, 225–7, 232

Jaipur, 149
jakhe, 32
jali muso, 188, 189, 191, 193
jali ndingo, 193
jaliyaa, 8, 178–97
  aesthetics of, 191–2
  instruments, 184, 187–8
  learning, 193
  metre and rhythm, 192
  music and its history, 181–2
  structure, 190–1
  today, 194–5
  tonal material, 188–9
Jāmī, 'Abdurahmān, 345
Janissary music, 316
Japan
  classical musics today, 100–2
  gagaku, *noh* and *kabuki*, 76–84, *78–9*, *81*, *82–3*, *93*
  musical aspects of classical genres, 87–97
  musical forms, 98–9
  notation, *12*, *14*
  overview, 75–6
  the *shakuhachi*, 84–7
Java
  canon, 60–1
  cultural history, 51–5
  form, shape, function, 55–7
  gamelan, 53, 54, 362n6
  gamelan today, 68, 70
  influence of, 70–2, 240
  music theory, 67–8
  notation, 62–7

Java *continued*
  performance, 57–9
  tuning systems, 59–60
jaw harp, 23
jazz
  America's indigenous classical form, 8
  forms, 200–3
  history, 204–13
  influence of, 241
  origins, 199
  roots of, 191
Jebateh, Nyulo, 191–2
Jewish people, 247, 252, 259, 267, 268, 299, 325, 327, 347, 359
  music, 9, 21, 268
  poetry, 253–6, 259
  see also Judaism
Ji Kang, 111, 115, 116, 118
Jinan, 129
jing, 130
jing erhu, 132
jinghu, 132, *133*
jingju (*jingxi*), or Beijing opera, 127, 130, 131–6
Jinyu Qin Society, 124
Jiu kuang (*Drunken madness*), 122
  notation, *110*
Jiu xiao huanpei ('Heavenly jade jewel'), *110*
Jobarteh, Sonah, 193
Jogja (Yogyakarta), 54–5
John of Salisbury, 221
Johnson, Frank, 200
Josquin des Prez, 223, 224
Judaism, 259
Justinian, Emperor, 300

kabuki, 77, 81–4, *82–3*, *93*, 100
Kadıköy, 296
Kafadar, Cemal, 299
kakko, 77, *78–9*
Kalhor, Kayhan, 336, 338
Kamal al-Molk, painting, *326*
Kamal Bai, 149
kamān, 289
kamāncheh, 325, *326*, 328, 336, 337, 338, 347
kamānja, 274, 289

kangen, 76
kanjira, 163, 172
Kante, Facelli, 194
kanun, 310, 311
Kanuteh, Jabele, 186
karawitan, 59
    see also gamelan
karinya, 188
Karnatak (Carnatic)
    classical tradition, 166–8
    history, 162–6
    melody and *rāga*, 170–3
    rhythm and *tāla*, 173–4
    voices and instruments, 174–6
Karthick, 175
Kashmir, 341
Katz, Jonathan, 6
Kavkabi, Najmiddin, 346
Kazakhstan, 22, 23, 341, 362n24
kecak, 19
Kedār, 143–4
Keita, Fodeba, 194
Keita, Modibo, 195
Keita, Salif, 194, *196*
kemençe, 301, 310, 311, 312
kempul, 53, 65, 67
kendhang, 53, 56, 67
kenong, 53, 65, 67
kepatihan notation, 62–5
Ketawang Puspawarna, 53, 61, 64, 65, 66
kethuk-kempyang, 53, 65, 67
kettledrums
    Central Asia, *naqqara*, 359
    Europe, *timpani*, 217, 317
    Guinea, *kunang*, 185
    Turkey, *kudum*, 311
keyboards, 289
khaen, 44
'Khamen sai yok', 33–4
Khan, Ali Akbar, 149, 157
Khan, Amanissa, 7
Khan, Amir, 151
Khan, Amjad Ali, *156*
Khan, Asad Ali, *156*
Khan, Bade Ghulam Ali, 151
Khan, Bismillah, 157
Khan, Isfandiyar, *350*
Khan, Sultan Rashid, 7

Khan, Vilayat, 151, 154
Khātami, Mohammad, 331
khawng mong, 31
khawng wong lek, 30, 31, 37
khawng wong yai, 30, 31, 32, 35, 43
khayāl, 148, 148–9, 153–4
Khayyām, Omar, 321
khim, 32
Khiva, 341, 342, 349, 351, 358
klawng khaek, 38
klawng tat, 31, 43
Khāleqi, Ruhollāh, 328
khlui, 30, 32
Khmer classical music, 26, 27, 29–32, 34, 42
    see also Cambodia
Khmer Empire, 26
    see also Cambodia; Laos; Thailand
Khmer Rouge, 28, 41
Khomeini, Ayatollāh, 330
khong vong noi, 30
khong vong nyai, 30
Khorezm (Khorazm), 349–50, 351, 358
Khosrow Dehlavi, Amir (Amir Khusrau), 148, 321
Khosrow (Kosrow) II Parviz, 323, 325, 331, *333*
khrueang sai ensembles, 32, 35
Khudoberdiev, Sultonali, 357
Khusrau, Amir (Amir Khosrow Dehlavi), 148, 321
Kiganda sound, 180
al-Kindī, *272*, *273*, 343
Kinko school, 86
Kiran, Pramath, *164*
kīrtanam, 165, 169, 173
Kochkor-Ata, 20
Koita, Ami, 193
Koizumi Fumio, modal types, 91, 92
kokyū, 93, 95
Kolkatta (Calcutta), 149, 150
koma, 305
komusō, 85, 86
komuz, 22, 23
kong taphone, 30
kong tauch, 30

kong vong thom, 30, *31*
konni, 187
konting, 187
kontingo, 186
Konya, 300
kora, 182, 186, 187, 189–90, *191*, *192*
Korea, 89, 96
Kosrow (Khosrow) II Parviz, 323, 325, 331, *333*
koto, 14, 77, 78–9, 87–9, 93, 94, 95, 97
kotsuzumi, 80
Koukouzeles, Ioannes, 9
Kouyate, Bala Faseke, 183
Kouyate, Bassekou, 194, *195*
Kouyate, Kandia, 193
Kouyate, Madu, *194*
Kouyate, Moustapha, 194
*kraton*s (courts), 54–5
Krishna, 142, 154, *155*
kriti, 165, 168–9, 170, 171, 173, 174
Kronos Quartet, 19, 195, 338
Ksetrayya, 164
kudum, 311
Kumar, Arjun, *164*
Kumaresh, Jayanthi, *164*
kumbengo, 190, 192, *192*, 193
kunang, 185
kunqu, 127
Kunqu opera, 128, 130–1
Kunst, Jaap, 68
    Music in Java, 68, 72
Kurosawa Kinko, 86
Kurosh (Cyrus II, the Great), 322
Kuyateh, Sona, 189
Kyai Telaga Rukmi, 53
Kyoto, 76, 77, 79
Kyrgyzstan, 20, 22, 23, 341

La Loubere, Simon de, 39
    Du Royaume de Siam, 39
Labaree, Robert, 10
Laberia, 6
lai, 44
LaMothe, Ferdinand (Jelly Roll Morton), 205–7, *206*
Lan Xang, 26

lanat ek mai, 30
lanat thum mai, 30
lao sheng, 129
Laos
    creating the music, 29–31
    forms, 32–6
    history, 25–8, 39, 40–1, 41–2
    map, 24
    overview, 28–9
    performance, 42
    tunings, scales and modes, 36–7
laras pélog, 59–60
laras sléndro, 59–60
Lassus, Orlande de, 224
Lawergren, Bo, 115
Lebanon, 267, 278, 280, 290
Léonin, 220
Léry, Jean de, xix
Levin, Theodore, 12, 359
Liezi yu feng, 'Liezi riding on the wind', 115
Ligeti, György, 3, 5
Limoncuyan, Hamparsum, 314
Lin Youren, 117
Lincoln Center, New York, 199
Lincoln Center Jazz Orchestra, 211
Lisbon, 18
Liszt, Franz, 236, 237, 238
    Mephisto Waltzes, 238
Liu Changqing, 115
Lobban, Bill, 41
Lokananta, 51–2
Lomax, Alan, 17, 18
London, 18, 21, 28, 101, 102, 195, 199, 232, 235, 326
Longing for the Past (anthology of recordings), 36n17
Lotfi, Mohammad Rezā, 329
Louk, Haim, 264
Louis XIV, 227
Luang Phabang, 40–1
Luang Phradit Phairoh, 40
luc huyen cam, 46
Lucknow, 149, 153
Ludwig of Bavaria, King, 237
luk khawng, 32

Lully, Jean-Baptiste, 227
lutes
    Afghanistan
        rabāb (*rabob*), 155, 338
    Africa
        konni, 187
        konting, 187
        kontingo, 186
        ngoni, 186, 187, 190
        xalam, 187
    Andalusian music, 249
        'ūd, 263
    Central Asia
        dombra, 22, 23
        dutar, 348, 355, 358
        komuz, 22, 23
        rabab ('Kashgar rabab'), 358
        sato, 355
        tanbur, 353, 355, 357–8
    China
        pipa, 87, 107, 114–5, 119, 123, 322
        sanxian, 83, 132
        yueqin, 115, 132, 133
    eastern Arab music, *oud*, 272, 274, 279, 286, 287
    Europe, 225–6
    Iran
        barbat, 322
        saghar, 338
        setār, 154, 337
        tār, 326, 326, 327, 337
        ud, 337
        'ud fāresi, 323
    Japan
        biwa, 77, 78–9, 87, 94, 97, 322
        sanshin, 83
        shamisen, 82–3, 87–8, 93, 95, 97, 101
    North India
        bīn, 153
        rudra vīnā, 153
        sārangī, 155, 153, 157
        sarod, 155, 156
        sitar, 149, 154, 156
        surbahār, 154
        tambūrā (*tānpurā*), 154–5, 156

lutes *continued*
    South India
        gottuvādyam, 174
        Southern vina (*sarasvatī-vīnā*), 174
        tambūrā (*tānpurā*), 170
        vīnā, 160, 162, 164
    Turkey
        oud, 310, 311
        tanbur, 301, 310, 311
    Vietnam, 45
        dàn dáy, 7, 46
        dan nguyet, 44, 45
Luther, Martin, 224

ma, 23, 95–6
Ma, Yo-Yo, 19
Machaut, Guillaume de, 221
    Mass, 222
machine music, 240–1
Madras (Chennai), 166, 167
madrigal, 226
Mahler, Gustav, 238
Mahmud (Mahmut) II, 314, 316
maholi ensembles, 32
mahori ensembles, 30, 35
mai khaeng, 30
makam music, 10, 15, 23, 295, 302–6, 312–18
Malaysia, 52, 136
Mali, 1, 23, 178, 181, 187, 193, 194, 195, 361n2
    Old Mali, 180–2
Malinke people, 181
Malta, 1
Mande culture, 181–4
    map, 178
    see also *jaliyaa*
Mandingo Griots Society, 195
Mandinka people, 181
Mangkunegara IV, 61, 64
Maninka people, 181
Mantua, 224, 225
Mao Zedong, 124, 135
maqām, 9–10, 6, 18, 275, 278, 281–5, 333, 341–2
maqom, 9, 341–4, 346–7, 349–54, 357
    instruments, 357–9

Maratha court, 164, 165
Marāqi, Abdol Qāder ('Abdulqādir Marāghi), 323, 333, 344
Marcus, Scott, 12
Marsalis, Wynton, 8, 211
Martini, Padre, 227
Martopangrawit, R. L., 62
Marvārīd, 'Abdullah, 345
The Mascot (New Orleans), cover, 205
Mashāqa, Mīkhā'īl, 281–2
Masnavi (Rumi), 323
Mataram kingdom, 54
Mawseli, Ebrāhim, 323
Mawseli, Eshāq (Ishaq al-Mawsili), 273, 274, 323
mbira, 180
McPhee, Colin, 71
Medina, 250, 300
Meera (1945 film), 167
Mehmed II, 300
Mehmed VI, 299
mehterhane, 316
Mei Lan (Mei Lan-Fang), 134, 135, 136
Meihua san nong (*Plum blossom melody*), 122
Meiji Period, 77, 88, 89, 100
Meiji sentei-fu, 77
Mekong Delta, 46
Mendelssohn, Felix, 233, 316
Menuhin, Yehudi, 235
meri, 87, 99
Merriam, Alan, 2
Messiaen, Olivier, 70
  Turangalîla-Symphonie, 70
metallophones
  Cambodia, *roneat dek*, 31
  Java, 55, 56, 58
    gendèr barung, 53, 56, 57, 65, 67
    gendèr panerus, 53, 56, 57
metre, *see* rhythm and metre
Meyerhold, Vsevolod, 134
Miki Minoru, 100
Milan, 224
Miley, Bubber, 208
Milhaud, Darius, 241

minimalism, 2, 242
minzu yuetuan, 109
Mirza, Ibrahim, poetry collection, 321
Mirzabāshi, Pahlivān, 349
Miyagi Michio, 88–9
  'Eihei no kōtai' ('Changing of the guards'), 88–9
  'Haru no umi' ('Spring sea'), 88
Miyagi Michio Museum, Tokyo, 89
miyako-bushi, 92, 95
Mizrachi Jews, 267
Mochizuki Tasaku III, 98
modal organisation
  overview, 9–10
  āvāz, 333
  dastgāh, 333–5
  dieu, 44
  Europe, 220, 221
  Japan, 91–2, 94–5
    Koizumi's modal types, 92
  lai, 44
  makam, 10, 295, 302–6
  maqām, 275, 278, 281–5, 333, 341–2
  maqom, 341–4, 346–7, 349–54, 357
  muğam, 9, 12, 333
  nūba, 260–3
  pihuang, 133–4
  rāga, 140, 142–7, 154, 168, 169, 170, 172–3
  and the 'science of music', 343–4
Mohammed Shah Rangile, 148, 149
mohori ensemble, 32
Monk, Thelonious, 212
monochords, Vietnam, 45
  dan bao, 44
monophony, 10, 309, 312–14
Monteverdi, Claudio, 6, 223, 225, 226, 227
  The Coronation of Poppea, 227
  Orfeo, 225
Morgan, Andy, *Music, Culture and Conflict in Mali*, 361n2
Morgenland Festival, 21

Morocco, 9, 247, 248, 249, 256, 258, 262, 263, 265, 266, 267, 268, 278, 298
morsing, 164, 176
Morton, David, 47
Morton, Jelly Roll (Ferdinand LaMothe), 205–7, *206*
mouth organs
  China, *sheng*, 119, 131, 132
  Japan, *shō*, 77, 78–9, 90, 94, 96–7
  Thailand and Laos, *khaen*, 44
mouth-harps, 164, 176
Moving Pictures (jazz ensemble), 195
Mozambique, 3, 180
Mozart, Wolfgang Amadeus, 6, 10, 227, 230–1, 232, 233, 234, 235, 236, 297, 316, 318
  Così fan tutte, 234
  Symphony no. 39 in E♭, 233
mrdangam, 162, 163, 164, 169–70, 172, 173, 176
muezzin, 10, 296
muğam, 9, 12, 333
Mughal Empire, 148
Muhammad 'Abd al-Wahhab, 278, 280
Muhammad of the Black Pen, drawing of spike-fiddlers of the spirit world, 16
Mullova, Viktoria, 235
Mumbai (Bombay), 150
al-Munajjim, Ibn, 273
murakkibat, 346
Murali, A. S., 164
Murasaki Shikibu, *The Tale of Genji*, 87, 94
Musée Cernuschi, Paris, 123
music theory
  Andalusian music, 262
  Central Asia, 342
  eastern Arab world, 273–4, 278
  Greek, 305, 343–4
  Iran, 333
  Islamic world, 343–4
  Java, 67–8
  Ottoman, 295
  South India, 163

music theory *continued*
  Thailand, Laos, Cambodia, 36–7
musicians
  Africa, 181, 183–4
  Central Asia, 345, 353
  China, 109, 114, 122–3
  Europe, 221
  Iran, 323, 327
  Japan, 76–7, 85, *85*, 86, 101
  North American jazz, 200, 204, 211, 213
  North India, 151, 153
  South India, 168
  Southeast Asia, 41
  Turkey, 314–15
al-mūsīqā al-andalusiyya, *see* Andalusian music
Musorgsky, Modest, 8, 239
muwashshaḥ, 2, 252–8, 263, 267, 269, 275, 285, 290, 308
  map, *246*
Mysore, 166

Nadir Shah, 149
nāgasvaram, 175
nagauta, 95, 96, 99
Nahāwand *maqām*, 283–5
Nakao Tozan, 86
nakara, 301
nang yai, 43
nanxi, 128
Nanyadeva, 147
naobo, 132
naphat, 33, 36
naqqara, 359
Nara, 76
Narayan, Aruna, 157
Narayan, Ram, 157
nashīd, 257–8
Navā'ī, 'Alī Shīr, 345
nay (Central Asia), *348*, 359
nāy (eastern Arab flute), 274, 279, 286, *289*
nayashi, 99
Neale, Frederick Arthur, 29
Near Eastern Music Ensemble, 292
nenge, 185

neo, 188, *189*
Nepal, 139
Neptune, John Kaizan, 101
Nettl, Bruno, 12, 328
New Japanese Music (*shin nihon ongaku*) movement, 88
New Orleans, 199, 200, 202, 203, 204, 205, 207, 208
New York, 18, 21, 131, 151, 194, 195, 196, 200, 201, 207–8, 209, 240, 292, 314, 359
ney (Iran), 337
ney (Turkey), *301*, 310, 311–12
Nezāmi, 323
ngoni, 186, 187, 190
Ngoni Ba, 195
Nguyen dynasty, 43
Nguyen Manh Tien, 7
Nguyen Thuy Hoa, 7
Nguyen Thuyet Phong, 44
Nguyen Van Mui, 7
nihon buyō, 84
noh (nō), 77–82, *81*, 83–4, 89, 91, 92
  musical forms, 98–9
  rhythm and metre, 97
  training, 100
  vocals, 94–5
nōkan, 80, 83
Norodom Sihamoni, 41
Norodom Silhanouk, 41
North American jazz, *see* jazz
North India
  history, 147–51
  overview, 139–42
  rāga and *tāla*, 142–7
  voices and instruments, 152–7
notation
  overview, 10–14
  Central Asia, 349–50
    tablature for the *tanbur*, *351*
  China, 13, 107, 112, 118, 120
    tablature notation, *110*
  eastern Arab music, 280
  Europe, 10, 216, 218, 220, 221, 229, 243
  Iran, 334
  Japan, 14, 76, 77, 89–91, *90*
  Java, 62–7, *64*, *66*

notation *continued*
  sléndro pitches on a stave, *65*
  North American jazz, *193*
  North India, 12, *14*
  South India, 12, 162, 163, 163–4, 167, *170*
  Thailand, Laos and Cambodia, 13
  Turkey, 302, 304, 305, 307, *313*, 314
Notoprojo, K. P. H., *63*
Notre Dame, Paris, 220
nūba, 260–3
Nyman, Michael, 71
  Time's Up, 71

Oberlin College, 195
oboes
  Central Asia, *surnay*, 359
  Khmer, *sralai*, 30
  Laos, *pi*, 30
  North India, *shahnāī*, 157
  Thailand, *pi*, 30, *31*, 43
  Vietnam, 44
Og'li, Mulla Bekjon Rahmoni, and Muhammad Yusuf Devonzoda, *History of the Music of Khorezm*, 349–50
Ohno Tadaaki, 91
Oliver, Joe 'King', 207
opera
  Central Asia, 354
  Chinese, 127–8, *129*
    ensemble, *133*
    history, 128–30
    jingju, or Beijing opera, 131–4, *136*
    kunqu, 130–1
    visual elements, 130
    yangbanxi, 135
  European, 225–6, 227, 232, 234, 238–9
orchestras
  African, 3, 180, 194
  Andalusian, 247, 257, 263, 267
  Central Asian, 15, 353–4
  Chinese, 109, 113, 114
  dance, 200, 204
  jazz, 207, 209, 211

orchestras *continued*
   European, 37, 52, 109, 207, 225–6, 227, 230–1, 237, 238, 240, 241, 297, 302, 317
   Iranian, 327, 328
   Middle Eastern, 271, 281, 289, 290
   Turkish, 297, 314
   see also gagaku, gamelan
organum, 86, 220
Original Dixieland Jazz Band, 205, *206*, 241
Osman, House of, 298, 299
Osman I, 299
ōtsuzumi, 80
Ottoman Empire, 274, 275, 295, 296, 298–302
oud, 9, 274, 279, 286, 287, *310*, 311
Ozawa Seiji, 75

Paganini, Niccolò, *235*
Pahlivān Mohammad, 345–6
pakhāvaj, 148, 153
Pakistan, 139, 341
Palestrina, Giovanni Perluigi, *223*, 224, 240
pallavi, 169
Paluskar, Digambar, 149
panerusan, 56
panpipes, 3, 113, 114
Paris, 3, 194, 195, 220, 232, 236, 240, 241, 298, 314, 317
   Exhibition Universelle, 70, 240
   University, 221
Parisā, 329, *336*
Parisius, Ludolf, 1
Park, Mungo, 8, 187
Parker, Charlie, *210*
   'Now's the TIme', 210
Partch, Harry, 10
pathet, 10, 44, 59–61, 62, 67, 71
Pathet Lao regime, 28, 40
Patiala, 149
Pattammal, D. K., *167*, 168
peking, 53
pélog, 59, 60, 64, 362n6
The Peony Pavilion (Chinese opera), 131

performance
   and the definition of classical music, 6
   Andalusian, 257
   Central Asia during the Soviet era, 354
   China, 107, 123–4
   Europe, 232
   Iran, 331
   Java, 57–9
   North American jazz, 213–14
   North India, 151
   South India, 168–70
   Turkey, 304–5
periya mēlam, 176
Pérotin, 220
   Sederunt principes, 220
   Viderunt omnes, 220
Persia, *see* Iran
Persian culture and influence, 272, 274, 300, 322
Peru, 8
peşrev, 308, 309, 315
phách, 7, 46
Phibun-Songkhram, Plaek, 40
Philadelphia, 200
Philippines, 136
phleng naphat, 33, 36, 37
phleng thao, 35, *35*
pi, 30, 31, 43
piano
   China, 108
   Europe, 237
   Iran, 326, 328
   Japan, 88
   prepared, 19
   Turkey, 302
piccolo, 238
Picken, Laurence, 123
Pickford, Mary, 134
pihuang, 133–4
Pillai, Vadivelu, 175
pinpeat, 29–30
pinpeat ensemble, *31*, *38*, 43
pipa, 13, 87, 107, 114–15, *119*, 123, 322
piphat, 3, 29–30
piphat mai nuam, 30

Pippin III, King of the Franks, 218
pishdaramad, 334–5
Plato, 17, 221, 233
poetry
   Arabic, 248, 252–3
   Europe, 221
   Iran, 334–5, 338
   Java, 61
   Jewish, 253–6, 259
   North India, 152
   Persia, 321–2, 323
   South India, 164–5, 169
   Sufi, 7, 148, 255–6, *256*, 315
   Tang China, 118
   Turkey, 304
   Uzbekistan and Tajikistan, 344–5
   Vietnam, 46
polyphony, 10–12
   Europe, 220–1, 222, 224, 228
   Japan, 95
   Java, 56, 67
   Turkey, 302
Portugal, 248–9
Poulenc, Francis, 70, 71
   Concerto in D minor for two pianos and orchestra, 70
Powers, Harold S., 6, 171
prepared piano, 19
primitivism, 240–1
Pritchard, Alwynne, *Nostos ou Topos II*, *243*
Pu Xuezhai, 115, 124
Puradaradāsa, 164, 173, 174
Puspawarna, 53, 61, 64, 65
Pygmies, 3, 4–5, 18

Qabbānī, Nizār, 292
Qalam, 250
qānūn, 274, 279, 286–9, *288*, 337
al-Qass, Sallāma, 272
Qazvin, 323, 325, 336
Qazvini, Abol Qāsem 'Āref, 335
qin, *see guqin* zither
Qincao (Cai Yong), 113
Qinqu jicheng, 124
Qiu Ming, 118
Qoli, Aqā Hoseyn, 325, 333, 334

Qoqand, 341, 342, 351
Qoṭb-al-Din, 323, 333
qudūd songs, 290
qupai system, 128
qyl qobyz, 22, 23

rabāb (*rabob*) (Afghan), 17, 338
rabāb (Andalusian), 263, 264, 265, *268*
rabab ('Kashgar rabab'), 358
rabel, 263
Racy, Ali Jihad, 292
radif, 10, 12, 17, 325, 333–4
radio, 21, 51, 55, 68, 70, 151, 157, 168, 191, 193, 195, 207, 267, 277–8 291, 296, 328, 334, 335, 353
rāga
　North India, 140, 142–7, 154
　South India, 168, 169, 170, 172–3
Ragamala, 141
rāgam-tānam-pallavi, 169, 173
ragtime, 205, 207
　influence of, 241
Raḥbānī, ʿAṣṣī, 290
Raḥbānī, Manṣūr, 290
Rahim Khān, Muhammad, II, 349
Rajabi, Yunus, 354
Rāma (Ram), 142, 165
Rama III, 27
Rama IV (Mongkut), 39
Rama V, 39
Rama VI, 39–40
Rama VII, 40
Rama VIII, 40
Rama IX, Bhumibol, 40
Ramakrishna, Kumbakonam, *172*
Ramamurthy, Vittal, *175*
Ramani, N., *163*
Rameau, Jean-Philippe, 227, 316
Ramprasadh, T. V., *172*
Rampur, 149
ranat ek, 29–30, *31*, *37*, *43*
ranat thum, 30, *31*, *37*
Rao, Raja, *163*
Ravel, Maurice, 240
razm o bazm, 325

rebab (Java), 56, 65, 67
rebab (Turkey), 311, 312
rebec, 263
recorders, 225–6
recording, 1, 17, 18, 151, 168, 277
Reich, Steve, 242
　Music for mallet instruments, voices, and organ, 3
religion, 17
　see also Buddhism; Christianity; Hinduism; Islam; Judaism; shamanism; Sufism
reng, 334–5
Renzong, Emperor, 131
Reynolds, Dwight, 21
Reza Shāh Pahlavi, 322, 327–8
rhythm and metre
　Africa, 201
　　Mande *jaliyaa*, 192
　　speech rhythm, 188
　Andalusian music, 260–3
　China, *guqin*, 121–2
　Chinese opera, 134
　Europe, medieval, 220–1
　eastern Arab world *iqāʿ*, 285
　Iran, 334–5
　Japan, 95–7
　North American jazz, 201–3
　North India, *tāla*, 140, 142–7, 154
　parallels, 3
　and the 'science of music', 343–4
　South India, *tāla*, 168–9, 173–4
　Thailand, Laos, Cambodia, 37
　Turkey
　　usul, 303, 307–8
Rimsky-Korsakov, Nikolai, 8
riqq, 274, 279, 288, 289
Roach, Max, 203
'Rokudan' ('Six sections'), 88
roneat dek, 31
roneat ek, 30, 31
roneat thom, 30
Rossini, Gioachino, 316
Rouget, Gilbert, 191
Rudolf, Adam, 195
rudra vīṇā 153, *156*

Rumi, Celaluddin (Jalaluddin), 17, 311, 321, 323
　'Masnavi', *335*
Russell, Alexander, 'The Chamber Music drawn from Life', *301*
Russia, 8, 240
Rysbek Jumabaev, *20*
ryūteki, 77, 78–9, *94*

Sacko, Amy, *194*
Saʿdi (Saiʾdi), 321, 323
Sadullah Ağa, Hacı, 303
Safi al-Din al-Urmawī, 274
saghar, 338
al-Sāḥir, Kāẓim, 292
Said, Edward, 21
St Mark's Cathedral, Venice, 226
Sairam, Aruna, *175*
Sallama (1945 film), 272
Salvador-Daniel, Francesco, xix
samāʿī, 275–6, *276*
samāʿī Bayyātī al-Thaqīl, 273
Samarqand, 341, 342, *342*, 344, 346
sampho, 30, 31
Sangare, Oumou, *193*
Sangītaratnākara ('Mine of Jewels of Music'), 165
sankyoku, 86, 88, 89, 95, *96*, 101
sanshin, 83
santūr (Iran), 326, *326*, 337
santūr (North India), 157–8
sanxian, 83, 132
sao, 46
sāranghī, 153, *155*, 157
sarasvatī-vīṇā, 174
Saraswati, 161
sarod, 155, *156*
saron, 53
sataro, 190
sato, 355
saung-gauk, 140
saw duang, 30
saw sam sai, 30
saw u, 30, 32
Sawai Tadao, *100*
saxophones, 207, 289

scales and intervals
  overview, 9–10, 15
  Andalusian music, 262
  Central Asia, 352–3
  China, 118–21
  classical Greek, 305–6
  eastern Arab music, 273–4, 278, 281–5
  Europe, 220, 228, 232
  Guidonian hand, *219*
  Iran, 333
  Japan, 88, 91–2
  Mande *jaliyaa*, 188–90
  North India, 142–3
  South India, 170–3
  Thailand, Laos, Cambodia, 36–7
  Turkey, 305–6
  Vietnam, 44
Schiff, András, 10
Schoenberg, Arnold, 10, 241, 242
  Erwartung, 241
School of Oriental and African Studies, London, *101*
Schubert, Franz, 236
Schuller, Gunther, 201
Schumann, Robert, 236, 237
  Frauenliebe und -leben, 237
Schütz, Heinrich, 226, 228
se, 113, 115, *119*
Seeger, Anthony, 2
Sei Shōnagon, 100
Sekaten festival, *54*
Seljuk Turks, 300
Sellars, Peter, 131
Senegal, 23, 178, 181
sep noi ensemble, 32
sep nyai, 29–30
Sephardic music, 21, 247, 267, 268
Serekunda, 189
setār, 154, 337
Seville, 265
seyir, 306
Shadi, Ustad, 344–5
Shah, Agā Mohammad, 325
Shah, Fateh 'Ali, 325
Shah, Mohammad Rezā, 328, 329

Shah, Nāser al-Din, 325
Shaheen, Simon, 292
Shahjahan, 148
shahnāī 157
Shahnāzi, 'Ali Akbar, 328
Shahrukh, 344
Shajariān, Mohammad Rezā, 329, 330, 331, 338
shakuhachi, 84–7, *85*, 92, 95, *101*
shamanism, 20, 22, 23, 240
shamisen, 82–3, 87–8, *93*, 97, *101*
Shamma, Naseer, 291
Shandong Opera School, *129*
Shanghai, 130, 213
  Conservatory, 108
Shanghai Kunqu Company, 131
Shankar, Anoushka, *156*
Shankar, Ravi, 151, 154, *156*
Shantaram, Tirukakkara S., *172*
Sharma, Shivkumar, 158
Sharqi, Hussein Shah, 148
shashmaqom, 1, 12, 18, 23, 342–3, 346–7, 349–50, 352–8, 359
  map, *340*
Shāstrī Syāma, 164, 165
Shaw, Artie, 213
shawms, 109, 114, 172, 175
Shelley, Percy Bysshe, 17
sheng, 119, 131, 132
shengqiang, 130
Shenqi mipu (Handbook of Spiritual and Marvellous Mysteries), 118
Sheydā, 'Ali Akbar, 335
Shiba Sukeyasu, 91
Shibaraku, *82–3*
Shijing (Book of Odes), 113
shin nihon ongaku (New Japanese Music) movement, 88
shinobue, 83
Shiraz, 321–2, 323
Shiraz Art Festival, 322, 329
Shirazi, Qutb ad-Din, 344
Shiva, 142
shō, 77, 78–9, 90, 94, 96–7
shōko, 77, 78–9
Shona music, 180
Shori, Miyan, 149
Shreesundarkumar, B., *163*

shu'ba, 344
Shujing (Book of History), 113
al-Shushtarī, 256
Siam, *see* Thailand
Sibelius, Jean, 239
Sichuan, 113, 114, 120, 123
Silhanouk, King, 28
Silk Road, 19, 114, 322, 341
sing, 30
Singapore, 136
singing styles
  Africa, 180
  Andalusia, 250–1, 252–8, 260–3
  Brazil, Suya people, 2–3
  Central Asia, 342–3, 346
  China, 122, 130–1
  Chinese opera, 128, 132, 133–4
  eastern Arab music, 275, 285, 290
  Europe, 218, 220, 221, 222, 225–6, 227
  Georgia, 9
  Iran, 334
  Japan, 80, 88, 94–5
  Java, 56–7, 61
  Mande *jaliyaa*, 188–92
  North India, 148–9, 152–3
  South India, 165–6, 174
  Thailand, Laos, Cambodia, 34
  Turkey, 309, 311
  Vietnam, 46
sinh tien, 46
Sisavang Vong, King, 28
sitar, 149, 154, *156*
skor thom drum pair, *31*
Slavonic culture, 8
slèndro tuning, 59–60, 64, 65
slenthem, 53, 65
smooth jazz, 211
Snowden, Elmer, *208*
Solo (Surakarta), 54–5, 62
sonata, 3, 222, 236
sonata form, 234
song lang, 46
Sorrell, Neil, 10
sorud, 338
South America, 8

South India
   arangētram, 161
   classical tradition, 166–8
   concerts and programmes, 168–70
   history, 162–6
   melody and *rāga*, 170–3
   rhythm and *tāla*, 173–4
   voices and instruments, 174–6
Southern vina (*sarasvatī-vīnā*), 174
Soviet Union, in Central Asia, 351–4
Spain, 21, 259, 267, 300
   Andalusian music, 247–51, 257, 265, 267–8, 275
   Western classical music, 240
spike-fiddles, *see* fiddles and violins
sralai, 30
Sri Lanka, 162
Sriramkumar, R. K., *163*
Stanislavsky, Konstantin, 134
Stephen II, Pope, 218
Stern, Samuel Miklos, 252
Sterne, Laurence, *Sentimental Journey*, 234
stile fantastico, 122
Stockhausen, Karlheinz, 2, 101
   Jahreslauf, 101
Strauss, Richard, 238, 241
   Alpensinfonie, 120
   Metamorphosen, 241
Stravinsky, Igor, 8, 209, 239, 240, 241
   The Rite of Spring, 240
Strayhorn, Billy, 209
Subbulakshmi, M. S., 167, 168
Sudharsono, Ki Manteb, 69
Sufism, 3, 17, 18, 142, 152, 359
   Andalusian Music, 247, 259, 260
   Central Asia, 355
   Iran, 325, 331
   poetry, 7, 148, 255–6, 315, 346
   Turkey, 297, 302, 311
suite, 3
Sukarna, Ono, 63
Sukri, Uking, 63
Süleyman I, 300

suling, 56
Sulzer, Franz Joseph, 316
Sumanguru, Susu, 181, 183
Sumanguru Kante, 194
Sumidagawa (play), 101
Sun Yuqin, 124
Sunda, 52
Sundiata (Sunjata; Son-jara), 181, 183
Sunjata Keita, 194
Suntharawathin, 34–5
suona, 132
Surakarta (Solo), 54–5, 62
surbahār, 154
surnay, 359
Suso, Foday Musa, 195
Suso, Jali Nyama, 188, 194
Suso, Mawdo, 185
Susu people, 184
Suya people, 2–3
swing, 203, 207, 209
Syllah, Modulai, 185
symphonic jazz, 207
symphony, 60, 135, 222, 241, 244
symphony orchestra, 37, 52, 109, 207, 297, 302
Syria, 2, 9, 256, 263, 267, 277, 280

ṭabla, 14, 149, 153, 154, 157, 279, 289
tahrir, 334
Taigu yiyin, 116
taiko, 77, 78–9, 80, 84
Taiwan, 124, 136
Tajikistan
   history of Central Asia, 343–50
   instruments, 357–9
   overview, 341–3
   shashmaqom, 18
   during the Soviet era, 351–4
   today, 354–7
Takemitsu Tōru, 21, 75, 100
takht, 9, 274–5, 286, 289
taksim, 309, 315
Taksin, king, 26
tāla, 14, 140, 142–7, 154, 168–9, 173–4
tala drum, 163

Talā'i, Dāriush, 329, 334
tālam, 176
Tāleb, 'Ali ibn Abi, 327
Tallis, Thomas, 222, *223*
Tambasansang, 186
tambourines
   Andalusian music, 263, *264*
   eastern Arab music, *riqq*, 274, 279, *288*, 289
tambūrā (*tānpūrā*), 154–5, *156*, 170
Tamerlane (Timur), 344
Tamils, 162
Tan Dun, 107
   Gaoshan liushui ('High Mountains and Flowing Streams'), 107
tanbur, 301, 310, 311, 353, 355, 357–8
tanggu, 132
Tanjore (Tanjavur), 164, 165, 166, 172
Tansen, 148, *150*
   descendants, 149, 152, 153, 155, 157
taphon, 30, 43
tappā, 149
taqāsīm, 275, 280, 284
ṭaqṭūqa, 277
tār, 326, *326*, 327, 337
Taruskin, Richard, 225, 244
tasnif, 334–5
tavil, 176
Taylor, Billy, 214
Taylor, Cecil, 211
Tchaikovsky, Pyotr Ilyich, 75
Tehran, 6, 323, 325, 326, 327, 328, 330, 331
Tehran Symphony Orchestra, 6
Tehran University, 328, 330
Tehrani, Hossein, 337
Telemann, Georg, 228, 232
television, 29, 107, 151, 191, 193, 195, 215, 267, 278, 290, 291, 296, 328
Tengir-Too, 20
tetrachordal structure, 273, 281, 283, 284–5, 287, 305
al-Tīfāshī, Aḥmad, 257–8, 263

402

Thailand
    creating the music, 29–31
    forms, 32–6
    history, 25–8, 39–40, 41–2
    jingju, or Beijing opera, 136
    map, 24
    overview, 28–9
    performance, 42
    tunings, scales and modes, 36–7
thang, 32
thao, 35
theatre and drama
    eastern Arab music, 277
    Japanese music theatre, 74, 77–84, *81*, *82–3*, *93*, 98–9
    South India, 163
    Thailand, Laos and Cambodia, 42, *43*
    Vietnam, 44
    wayang shadow plays, 52–4, *58*, *61*, *69*
    see also opera
Thompson, John, 119, 124
thumrī, 149, 152–3, 153–4
timbila, 180
timpani, 317
Timur (Tamerlane), 344
Timurid dynasty, 344–5, 346
Tirunal, Svāti, 166, 175
tōgaku, 76, 77, 84, 87, 89, 94, 95, 98
Tōgi Hideki, 100, 102
Tokyo, 2, 77, 78, 89, 91, 100
Tokyo University of the Arts, 91, 100
Tomar, Man Singh, 148
tombak (*tonbak*), 337
Toure, Ali Farka, 193, *194*, *196*
Tozan school, 86
training
    Andalusian music, 250, 258
    eastern Arab music, 272
    Europe, 221
    Japan, 100–1
    Mande *jaliyaa*, 193
    North American jazz, 211–13
    North India, 140–2, 152

training *continued*
    South India, 163, 166
    see also education
Traore, Rokia, 193
Travancore, 166, 175
trio sonata, 227
trombone, 202, 207, 225–6, 238, 317
Troubadours, 255, 367n4
Tsar Teh-yun (Cai Deyun), 124
Tsukushi school, 87–8
tuba, 238
tuning and temperament
    Central Asia, 353
    Europe, 237
    Japan, 88
    Java, 59–60
    Mande *jaliyaa*, 189–91
    Thailand, Laos and Cambodia, 36–7
Tunisia, 249, 258, 262
Turkey
    conquest of parts of India, 148
    history, 298–9
    instruments, 311–12
    makam music, 10, 302–4, 312–15
        influence, 316–18
        melodic system, 304–6
    modernisation, 15
    musical form, 308–11
    overview, 295–8
    usul, 307–8
    see also Ottoman Empire
Twelve Muqam, 7
Tyāgarāja, 164, *164*, 165, 168, 169
    Endu dāginādo, 169, *170*, *171*

Uchida Mitsuko, 75
'*ūd* (Andalusian), 263
ud (Iran), 337
'*ud fāresi* (Persian lute), 323
Udaipur, 149, 155
Ufki, Ali (Albert Bobowski), *313*, 314
Uganda, 180
Umm Kulthūm, 272, 277–8, 279, 280, 291

UNESCO
    Central Asia, 354, 357
    China, 7
    Intangible Cultural Heritage policy, 18, 101
    Iran, 328, 339
    Japan, 77
    Vietnam, 43
upaj, 140
al-Urmawi, Safi ad-Din, 281, 344
Uspenskiy, Victor, 352
usul, 303, 307–8
Utagawa Toyokuni III, woodblock print of kabuki theatre, *82–3*
'Uthman, Muhammad, 275
Uyghur music, 7
Uzbekistan
    history of Central Asia, 343–50
    instruments, 357–9
    overview, 341–3
    shashmaqom, 18
    during the Soviet era, 351–4
    today, 354–7

vāggeyakāra, 165
Vaidyanathan, J., *175*
van Gulik, Robert, 123
Varanasi (Banaras), 140, 149, 153
Varèse, Edgard, 240–1
    Intégrales, 240–1
variation form, 3
varnam, 168
Vaziri, 'Ali Naqi, 326
Vaziri, Qamar al Moluk, 328
A Venerable Old Man, *81*
Venice, 224, 226, 227, 232
venu, 163
Verdi, Giuseppe, 6, 238, 239, 278, 298
    Aïda, 278
    Rigoletto, 278
Verney, Frederick, 28
vibrato, 23, 35, 95, 118, 119, 121, 188, 312
Vichailak, Ittisoontorn, 37, 40
Victoria, Tomás Luis de, 224
Vienna, 75, 234, 235, 316
Vietnam, 24, 25–6, 42–6

Villoteau, Guillaume-André, xix
Vinu, Avanbeeshwaram S. R., 172
violins, see fiddles and violins
Vivaldi, Antonio, 227, 228
vīnā (harp), 140
vīnā (lute), 160, 162, 164
vocal styles, see singing styles
von Hornbostel, Erich, 1, 15
von Swieten, Baron, 232

Wagner, Richard, 6, 227, 236–7, 238–9
   Die Meistersinger von Nurnberg, 238–9
   Tristan und Isolde, 238–9
wagon, 87
waḥda, 283–5
Wang Di, 124
Wāsifī, 345
   Badāyi' al-Waqāyi', 345
waṣla, 263, 275–7
Wat Phra Kheo (Temple of the Emerald Buddha), 31, 43
wayang, 52–4, 58, 61, 69
Weber, Carl Maria von, 236, 238
Weber, Max, 237
Wei Zhongle, 124
Weimar, Duke of, 236–7
Wenger, Gert-Matthias, 14
West-East Divan Orchestra, 21
Western classical music
   Baroque, 226–32
   Classical style, 232–4
   influence of, 15, 108, 278, 281, 325–6, 327, 328, 352
   medieval, 218–22
   overview, 2, 217–18
   Renaissance, 222–5
   Romantic era, 235–9
   twentieth century fragmentation, 239–42
Whiteman, Paul, 207
Widdess, Richard, 6
Williams, Cootie, 209
Williams, Mary Lou, 212
Wilson, Olly, 201
Wilson, Teddy, 211
'world music', 1, 19, 21, 242, 339

Wu, Emperor, 115
Wu Jinglüe, 124
Wu Man, 123
Wu Zhonghai, 124

xalam, 187, 195
xiao, 119
xiao luo, 132
xiao sheng, 129, 130
Xiao Xiang shui yun (Mist and Clouds over Xiao and Xiang Rivers), 120, *121*, 122
Xiao Youmei, 108
Xinjiang, 7
Xu Jian, 124
Xu Yuanbai, 123
xylophones
   Africa, 181
      bala, 184, 189, 191, 192
      balafon, 184, 189, 192
      balo, 184, 185, 190
      Bambara xylophone, 188–9
   Java
      gambang, 56, 57, 65, 67
      gambang kayu, 53
   Mozambique
      Chopi xylophone orchestras, 3, 180
      timbila, 180
   Thailand, Laos and Cambodia, 38
      lanat ek mai, 30
      lanat thum mai, 30
      ranat ek, 29–30, 31, 37, 43
      ranat thum, 30, 31, 37
      roneat ek, 30, 31
      roneat thom, 30

Yamada school, 88
Yamamoto Hōzan, 100
yangbanxi, 135
Yatsuhashi Kengyō, 88
Yazīd I, 273
Yemen, 256
Yogyakarta (Jogja), 54–5
Yönetken, Halil Bedii, 316
Youlan ('Solitary Orchid'), 118
Young, Lester, 212

Yu Shaozhe, 120
Yuefu, 115
yueqin, 115, 132, 133
Yulchieva, Munajat, 355

zajal, 252–3, 257–8
zaju, 128
Zalzal, Manṣūr, 274
zarb, 326, 327, 337
Zeami, 79–80, 98
Zemtsovsky, Izaly, 12
Zen Buddhism, 17, 80, 84, 86
Zeng of Yi, tomb of, 114
Zha Fuxi, 124
Zhang Ziqian, 116
Zhao Ji, 'Listening to the qin', 106
zheng, 87, 113
Zheng Chengwei, 117
Zhou Enlai, 124
Zimbabwe, 180
Ziryāb (Alī ibn Nāfi), 249–50, 251
zithers and hammered dulcimers
   Central Asia, chang, 358
   China
      guqin, 105–7, *106*, 109–24, *110*, *117*, *120*
      se, 113, 115, 119
      yueqin, 115, 132, 133
      zheng, 87, 113
   eastern Arab music, qānūn, 274, 279, 286–9, *288*
   Iran
      qānun, 337
      santūr (Iran), *326*, 326, 337
   Japan
      koto, 77, 78–9, 87–9, 93, 94, 95, 97
      wagon, 87
   North India, santūr, 157–8
   Thailand
      jakhe, 32
      khim, 32
   Turkey, kanun, 310, *311*
   Vietnam, 45
      dan tranh, 44, 45
Ziyangxian, 120
zokusō, 88